WARNING! Using this text's Web site can make this course more enjoyable.

Here's how. The Web site features:

- *Links* to Featured Companies' online annual reports and Web sites.

- *An Online Tutor*, with responses to your questions within 48 hours.

- *An Online Learning Center*, including full access to study aids, graphics, PowerPoint slides, and exercises with the purchase of a password.

- *A Free (!) Practice Set for Accounting Cycle Review*, an opportunity to review the accounting cycle by downloading this practice set.

- *Technology for You*, a link to McGraw-Hill's Online SuperCenter for Accounting Resources (OSCAR), featuring quick demos of additional technology available to help you understand and use accounting.

- *New Of Interest boxes*, additional Of Interest information to provide insights into what is happening in the business world today.

- *New Pause and Reflect Questions*, additional chapter-by-chapter questions to get you thinking about the concepts covered in the text.

- *Key Terms*, a comprehensive list of all the key terms featured in the text, including definitions and chapter references.

- *A Spanish/English Glossary*, a unique study tool that will bridge the translation for introductory accounting terms.

- *Communication Skills*, featuring links to other Web sites and information about how to attain additional resources to help develop your communication skills.

VISIT THE *INTRODUCTION TO ACCOUNTING: AN INTEGRATED APPROACH*, 2/E WEB SITE AT:

http://www.mhhe.com/ainsworth

Introduction to Accounting

An Integrated Approach

VOLUME II
CHAPTERS 14 TO 16
SECOND EDITION

Penne Ainsworth
University of Wyoming

Dan Deines
Kansas State University

R. David Plumlee
University of Utah

Cathy Xanthaky Larson
Middlesex Community College

Boston   Burr Ridge, IL   Dubuque, IA   Madison, WI   New York   San Francisco   St. Louis
Bangkok   Bogotá   Caracas   Lisbon   London   Madrid
Mexico City   Milan   New Delhi   Seoul   Singapore   Sydney   Taipei   Toronto

McGraw-Hill Higher Education

*A Division of The **McGraw-Hill** Companies*

INTRODUCTION TO ACCOUNTING: AN INTEGRATED APPROACH

Copyright © 2000, 1997 by The McGraw-Hill Companies, Inc. All rights reserved. Printed in the United States of America. Except as permitted under the United States Copyright Act of 1976, no part of this publication may be reproduced or distributed in any form or by any means, or stored in a database or retrieval system, without the prior written permission of the publisher.

This book is printed on acid-free paper.

1 2 3 4 5 6 7 8 9 0 VNH/VNH 9 0 9 8 7 6 5 4 3 2 1 0 9

ISBN 0-07-030676-1 (combined volume)
ISBN 0-256-26902-5 (volume 1)
ISBN 0-07-303316-2 (volume 2)

Vice president/Editor-in-Chief: *Michael W. Junior*
Publisher: *Jeffrey J. Shelstad*
Developmental editor: *Kelly Lee*
Marketing manager: *Rich Kolasa*
Senior project manager: *Denise Santor-Mitzit*
Production supervisor: *Michael R. McCormick*
Designer: *Jennifer McQueen Hollingsworth*
Cover photo: *Jean Y. Rusniewski/Tony Stone Images*
Senior photo research coordinator: *Keri Johnson*
Photo research: *Feldman & Associates Inc.*
Supplement coordinator: *Becky Szura*
Compositor: *Shepherd Incorporated*
Typeface: *10/12 Times*
Printer: *Von Hoffmann Press, Inc.*

Library of Congress Cataloging-in-Publication Data

Introduction to accounting : an integrated approach / Penne Ainsworth
    . . . [et al.].—2nd ed.
      p.   cm.
    Includes index.
    ISBN 0-07-030676-1 (set)
    1. Accounting   I. Ainsworth, Penne.
  HF5635.I655   2000
  657—dc21   99-34638

INTERNATIONAL EDITION   ISBN 0-07-116931-8
Copyright © 2000. Exclusive rights by The McGraw-Hill Companies, Inc. for manufacture and export.
This book cannot be re-exported from the country to which it is consigned by McGraw-Hill.
The International Edition is not available in North America.
http://www.mhhe.com

First, and foremost, we dedicate this text to our families without whose love and support we never could have completed this project. To our spouses, Scott Ainsworth, Linda Deines, Marlene Plumlee, and Doug Larson, and to our children, Heather, Dusty, Jennifer, Jeff, Matt, Sarah, Ashley, J. D., and Robyn, we love you and we thank you for your patience. Finally, we would like to thank our development editor, Kelly Lee, our publisher, Jeff Shelstad, and the production and marketing departments at Irwin/ McGraw-Hill.

Penne Ainsworth
Dan Deines
R. David Plumlee
Cathy Xanthaky Larson

About the Authors

Penne Ainsworth
University of Wyoming

Penne Ainsworth, Ph.D., CMA, CIA, and CPA (inactive). Penne received her Ph.D. from the University of Nebraska. She is an associate professor in the accounting department at the University of Wyoming. Penne co-authored the original application for the grant Kansas State University received from the Accounting Education Change Commission (AECC). She won the Kansas State Bank Outstanding Teacher Award in 1993 and the Senior Teaching Award in the College of Business at the University of Wyoming in 1999. Penne's research focuses on managerial accounting and accounting education. Her work has been published in *Issues in Accounting Education* and other journals. She is a member of the AAA, the IMA, and the IIA.

Dan Deines
Kansas State University

Dan Deines received his undergraduate degree in history from Fort Hays State University, a Masters in Business from Emporia State University, and his Ph.D. in Accounting from the University of Nebraska. He has been at Kansas State University since 1982 and currently holds the Ralph Crouch, KPMG Peat Marwick Chair. Dan received the College of Business's Outstanding Educator Award in 1987 and in 1994 received the College of Business Outstanding Advising Award. He was the co-coordinator for Kansas State University's accounting curriculum revision sponsored by the Accounting Education Change Commission. He is a member of the AAA, the Kansas Society of CPAs, and the AICPA. Dan was the chairman of the AICPA's Accounting Careers Subcommittee and was a member of the Accounting Education Executive Committee.

R. David Plumlee
University of Utah

R. David Plumlee earned both his Bachelors and Masters degrees from the University of Oklahoma, and is a CPA. After receiving his Ph.D. at the University of Florida, David taught at the University of North Carolina and Kansas State University and was the Baird, Kurtz and Dobson Faculty Fellow at the University of Kansas. He also taught at the University of Michigan, before moving to the University of Utah. He has published research in a number of scholarly journals including *Journal of Accounting Research* and *The Accounting Review*. David has earned teaching awards at the Universities of Kansas and Utah.

Cathy Xanthaky Larson
Middlesex Community College

Cathy Xanthaky Larson, CPA, received her BS in Business Administration from Salem State College and her MBA from Bentley College. Cathy is a tenured professor at Middlesex Community College and an adjunct professor at Salem State College. She is a member of the AICPA, AAA, Massachusetts Association of Accounting Professors, and Teachers of Accounting at Two Year Colleges (TACTYC). She served as vice president of TACTYC for 5 years and was elected as Union Treasurer of the Massachusetts Community College Council in 1998. Cathy received Middlesex's Faculty Member of the Year Award in 1985 and 1990 and was recently listed in the Who's Who among America's Teachers. Cathy also is the recipient of the 1999 Northeast Regional Faculty Member Award given by the Association of Community College trustees (ACCT) and has been nominated for the William H. Meardy Faculty Member Award.

WHY INTEGRATE?

We feel the primary reason "to integrate" financial and managerial accounting is due to the student population most of us serve. Having as many as 85% non-accounting majors in the first-year accounting course is not unusual, with business majors usually making up the majority of students. We need to motivate and better serve these non-accounting students.

Introduction to Accounting: An Integrated Approach recognizes that financial and managerial accounting are subsystems of the same accounting information system. While these subsystems serve different user groups, we do not feel one is more important than the other. We instead **emphasize the business event** and analyze it from both an external (financial reporting) and an internal (managerial reporting) perspective. Our students respond positively to this business event focus.

Understanding the Integrated Approach

Introduction to Accounting: An Integrated Approach revolves around three major themes. The overriding theme of the text is that **accounting is an information system which serves two diverse sets of users.** Traditionally, accounting has been taught as two separate and distinct segments—financial accounting and managerial accounting. Consequently, many of our students never gain an understanding of accounting as a process of providing information about business to both internal (managerial) and external (financial) users. An understanding of how and why accounting information is used by internal and external stakeholders is vital, regardless of a student's major.

The second theme is organizational in nature—**operating events followed by financing and investing events.** In order to divide the content of an introductory accounting text into two segments, we have chosen the sequence of information in the cash flow statement as a model. The first half of the textbook examines accounting for operating events while the second half of the book examines accounting for financing and investing events. Operating events are examined first because, in general, these events are easier to understand and require less prerequisite information. This supports the notion of organizing elements from simple to complex. Financing and investing events, which require an understanding of the time value of money, are more complex and require a broader depth of understanding. Our classroom experience has shown that financing and investing activities are more easily understood after learning about business operating activities.

The final theme of the textbook is the business cycle. Businesses operate by **planning activities, then performing (recording) those activities, and finally evaluating/controlling those activities.** Therefore, in this text accounting information is presented in the order in which it is used by businesses. This theme is used to present information in a logical, coherent manner. Information in the first half of the text is organized as follows.

Introduction to business and accounting

Planning for operating activities (events)

Performing (recording) operating events

Evaluating and controlling operating events

A similar format is adopted for the second half of the text.

Introduction to financing and investing activities

Planning for investing and financing activities (events)

Performing (recording) financing and investing events

Evaluating and controlling business—financing, investing, and operating activities

By concentrating on these three themes, students will learn how and why events are planned, performed (recorded), and evaluated by different user groups. Students will understand why different reporting mechanisms are necessary for different user groups and how these reports are presented and analyzed. And perhaps most importantly, students will gain a greater understanding of business, which will certainly help them whether they choose accounting, business, or something else as their field of study.

WHAT ARE THE MAIN OBJECTIVES OF THIS UNIQUE TEXT?

Introduction to Accounting: An Integrated Approach is designed to benefit everyone, again regardless of their chosen major. In designing the text, we incorporated these six objectives.

1. To Focus on the Use of Accounting Information by Internal and External Stakeholders

We maintain a consistent focus throughout this text on the use of accounting information, rather than the preparation of accounting information. As mentioned earlier, the process of recording, adjusting, and closing events and their impact on financial statements is covered, but it is not the primary focus. This more balanced approach will benefit all students. Non-accounting majors will gain an appreciation for the use of accounting information, and accounting majors will better understand what various accounting information users need, while at the same time gaining a complete preparation for future courses in accounting.

2. To Integrate Financial and Managerial Accounting

Introduction to Accounting: An Integrated Approach consistently emphasizes the business event and analyzes the event from both an external (financial reporting) and an internal (managerial decision making) perspective. Our approach allows business majors, accounting majors, and all other students to walk away from this first accounting course with an understanding of business and the role of accounting.

3. To Stimulate Interest in the Field of Accounting

Classroom experience has shown that the approach of *Introduction to Accounting: An Integrated Approach* will serve as the greatest way to motivate interest in the discipline of accounting. As students gain an understanding and appreciation of the broader role of accounting in the business world, they are more likely to express interest in accounting as a field of study. Dropout rates in the first accounting course at Kansas State declined from approximately 50% to under 20% during the first two years of implementing this new approach. Similarly, accounting student enrollments increased by approximately 15%. Penne Ainsworth is now seeing similar results at the University of Wyoming.

4. To Order Content Elements in a Logical Manner

Learning is obviously enhanced by presenting topics in a logical and coherent sequence. While we realize all text authors attempt to do this, we follow three simple tenets in this text: Simple topics are presented before more complex topics; business events are presented before transactions; and accounting is presented within a business cycle context.

5. To Promote Active Learning

Various pedagogical devices are used to stimulate active learning experiences for the student. Most obvious are the Pause and Reflect questions posed at various times throughout each chapter. These questions serve as a checkpoint for the student's understanding of the material, as well as a critical thinking stimulus. Additionally, the Cases, Computer Applications, Critical Thinking, and Ethical Challenge sections at the end of all chapters give the student the opportunity to apply their accounting knowledge to a broader business setting, and virtually always require learning and exploring outside of the text. Active learning promotes retention, and these features will aid student retention.

6. To Promote Effective Communication

Again, many of the end of chapter materials can and should be used to help exercise students' written and oral communication skills. Additional classroom activities are provided in the Instructor's Resource Manual, described below. These skills will be necessary tools in a career in accounting or any other field.

WE WILL HELP YOU IMPLEMENT THE INTEGRATED APPROACH

We provide the following supplements for you in order to ease your transition to *Introduction to Accounting: An Integrated Approach.*

INSTRUCTOR'S RESOURCE MANUAL: A GUIDE FOR IMPLEMENTING THE INTEGRATED APPROACH W/ CD-ROM, VOLUMES 1 (0-07-030694-X) & 2 (0-07-235670-7)

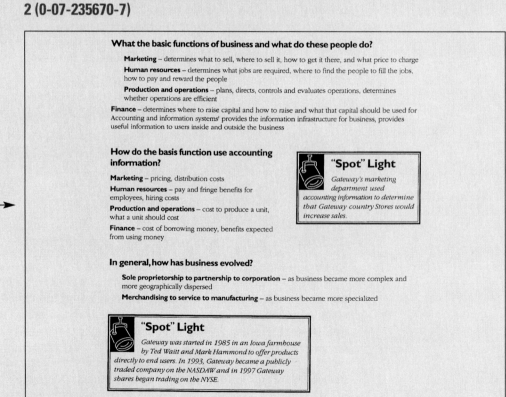

Based on many user comments, and interviews conducted by Penne Ainsworth as she worked with users on their classroom issues, this completely revised manual contains:

- Very detailed teaching notes for each chapter.

- Discussion outlines.

- Penne's own PowerPoint® illustrations.
- Two test/retest quizzes.
- Two in-class cases.
- A unique continuing cooperative learning case following the organization of the text.

Team Activities

We suggest using team activities in, rather than outside, the classroom. We have found that students today are more likely to commute and have jobs, families, etc. that make meeting outside the class time difficult if not impossible. We have found that team building can occur with in-class activities. The following four activities are offered as possibilities for in-class.

Test/Retest (T/R)

A test/retest quiz is a short, 5-point, typically multiple choice, closed-book quiz given at the beginning of class when a new chapter is started. The student takes the quiz individually and hands it in. Then, the same quiz is retaken in the student learning team. The average of the individual and team score is recorded. This avoids the "slacker" problem because of the individual earns a 0 and the team earns a 5, the individual receives only a 2.5 as a recorded score. Test/retest quizzes are excellent motivation devices to encourage students to read the assigned materials BEFORE coming to class. Although test/retest quizzes consume class time to administer (typically 5 - 10 minutes), overall, they save class time because the instructor can focus on the issues in the chapter rather than the definitions of key terms. The instructor's materials contain 2 test/retest quizzes for each chapter.

Homework Review (HR)

We believe that homework is an integral part of the learning experience. Recall, the old proverb that states:

I hear, I forget
I see, I remember
I do, I understand

This manual, consisting largely of handouts, is provided loose-leaf with three-hole drills to allow you to easily store materials in a binder and duplicate them as needed. You are also provided with a CD-ROM of these same materials to allow you the opportunity to alter the materials as needed.

ADDITIONAL INSTRUCTOR SUPPLEMENTS

You may order *Introduction to Accounting: An Integrated Approach* to come to you and your students in a variety of ways. The following text options can be packaged with any of the student supplements listed in the 'To the Student' at a considerable cost savings for your students.

- Volume Options
- The complete text, Chapters 1–26, (0-07-030676-1)
- Volume 1, Chapters 1–13, (0-256-26902-5)
- Volume 2, Chapters 14–26, (0-07-303316-2)

Solutions Manual w/ CD-ROM, Volumes 1 (0-07-303321-9) & 2 (0-07-235786-X)   Prepared by the authors and verified for accuracy by Cathy Xanthaky Larson, this manual contains detailed solutions to all end-of-chapter material. The Solutions Manual is also provided to you on CD-ROM to assist you in your classroom presentations.

Solutions Transparencies Volumes 1 (0-07-030674-5) & 2 (0-07-030675-3)   Exercises and problems from the Solutions Manual are reproduced in acetate format for maximum instructor efficiency.

Ready Shows (PowerPoint® Presentations), Volumes 1 (0-07-561560-6) & 2 (0-07-561559-2) Prepared by Jayne Maas of Towson University, these electronic slides consist of approximately 45 slides per chapter. Accompanied by an Instructor's Manual demonstrating how to use them, these initial slides give you great freedom to build a more lively and modern classroom presentation.

Ready Slides (Teaching Transparencies), Volumes 1 (0-07-303322-7) & 2 (0-07-303323-5) These color acetates taken from the Ready Shows will help you in your classroom presentation. There are roughly ten color-ready slides per chapter chosen to help you demonstrate the most important concepts covered in each chapter.

Presentation Manager CD-ROM (0-07-235141-1) This is your all-in-one resource. It contains the Instructor's Manual, Test Bank, and PowerPoint presentations organized by chapter. Thanks to the Presentation Manager, you can create a multimedia presentation that incorporates video, PowerPoint and Lecture Outlines into one presentation.

Online Learning Center, Volumes 1 (0-07-236485-8) & 2 (0-07-236486-6) Within the book's Web site, there is a password-protected Online Learning Center. As an adopter of this text, you and your students will have full access to graphics, PowerPoint slides, exercises, as well as online testing and grading. This McGraw-Hill content is so comprehensive that you needn't change a thing. But you can still customize if you wish. You can delete content, add a personal course syllabus, provide Internet links, or integrate your own material.

Test Bank, Volumes 1 (0-07-030693-1) & 2 (0-07-235673-1) Prepared by Lola Dudley of Eastern Illinois University, this manual consists of approximately 1,100 questions, exercises, and problems.

Computerized Test Bank (0-07-561562-2) Available in Windows and developed using Diploma—a new and easy to use software—this option provides you more flexibility in designing assessment tools.

Financial and Managerial Accounting Video Series Developed by Dallas County Community College District, these short, action-oriented videos provide the impetus for lively classroom discussion. The focus is on the use of accounting information for decision making in contemporary business environments. Video segments emphasize the impact of transactions on financial statements.

WE HAVE LISTENED TO YOU

The market research and developmental process employed to ensure the quality of *Introduction to Accounting: An Integrated Approach* was extensive. The Second Edition has been tremendously aided by the comments of the following people, who provided insightful comments/criticisms/enhancements along the way.

Chapter-by-Chapter Surveys
Lauren Tien (TA) *Kansas State University*
Jason Ryan (TA) *Kansas State University*
Casey Carlson (TA) *Kansas State University*
Lynn Griffin *North Carolina A&T State University*
Lola Dudley *Eastern Illinois University*
Leila Kennedy *Greenbrier Community College Center*
Debbie Luna *El Paso Community College*
Mary Greenawalt *The Citadel*
Stan Lindquist *Grand Valley State University*
Debra McKilskey *Central Michigan University*
Dave Durkey *Weaver State University*

Joe Colgan *Ft. Lewis College*
Christine Cring *SUNY—Morrisville*
Roby Sawyers *North Carolina State University*
Patricia Williams *Friends University*
David Collins *Bellarmine College*
Elizabeth Ammann *Lindenwood College*
User Diaries
Sherrie Koechling-Andrae *Lincoln University*
David Rozelle *Western Michigan University*
Francis Sakiey *Mercer County Community College*
Melanie Middlemist *Colorado State University*
Mark Kaiser *SUNY—Plattsburg*
John Perrier *Towson University*

Jayne Maas, *Towson University*

Suzanne Roe *University of Wyoming*

Glenn Owen *Alan Hancock College*

Craig Sasse *Rockhurst College*

Charles Zlatkovick *University of Texas—El Paso*

Maureen Conroy *University of Toledo*

Susan Haugen *University of Wisconsin—Eau Claire*

Judy Hinman *Spokane Community College*

Hossein Nouri *College of New Jersey*

Bob Rosaker *University of South Dakota*

Karen Walton *John Carroll University*

Ken Abramowicz *University of Alaska—Fairbanks*

Charles Smith *Millikin University*

Fred Smith *Kansas State University*

Ken Mark *Kansas City, Kansas Community College*

Joyce Griffin *Kansas City, Kansas Community College*

Doug Brown *Montana State University—Billings*

Abdus Shahid *College of New Jersey*

Alexander Sannella *Rutgers University—Newark*

Jayne Fuglister *Cleveland State University*

Douglas Frazier *Millersville University*

Gil Zuckerman *North Carolina State University*

Cindy Seipel *New Mexico State University*

Alan McNamee *Lyon College*

Renee Rigoni *Monroe Community College*

Dave Hancock *Northwest Missouri State University*

Leonard Stokes *Siena College*

Russell Hardin *Pittsburgh State University*

William Tignanelli *Towson University*

Scottie Barty *Northern Kentucky University*

Carol Buchl *Northern Michigan University*

Rebecca Phillips *University of Louisville*

We would also like to thank Suzanne Roe for accuracy-checking the IRM. In addition, we thank all the students who used previous versions of these materials and gave us valuable suggestions for improvement. We would also like to thank the students of Kansas State University who used previous drafts of this textbook and gave us valuable suggestions for improvement.

HOW HAVE WE RESPONDED WITH THE SECOND EDITION?

GENERAL REVISIONS

* New chapter opening vignettes in every chapter to get students interested in concepts discussed throughout the chapter. We asked reviewers to consider what companies would interest students the most and based on reviewer response, we have chosen the following exciting organizations: Intel, Burger King, The GAP, Microsoft, Ben & Jerry's, PepsiCo, Reebok, and Dell Computers.

- Three to five Pause & Reflect boxes get students thinking about concepts in the chapter. Suggested solutions are referenced in each box and are found in the end-of-chapter material for each chapter.

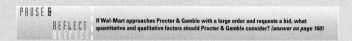

PAUSE & REFLECT | If Wal-Mart approaches Procter & Gamble with a large order and requests a bid, what quantitative and qualitative factors should Procter & Gamble consider? *(answer on page 160)*

- Of Interest features, which were well received in the First Edition, have been completely revised and selected Of Interests feature technology applications! Professors can use these to get students talking about current issues in Accounting. Additional, up-to-date Of Interests will be added to the text's web site regularly to help keep class discussions current.

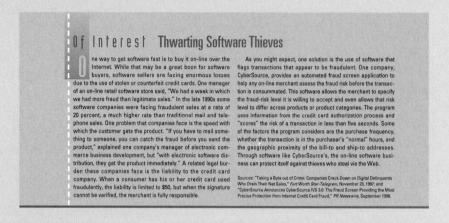

Of Interest — Thwarting Software Thieves

One way to get software fast is to buy it on-line over the Internet. While that may be a great boon for software buyers, software sellers are facing enormous losses due to the use of stolen or counterfeit credit cards. One manager of an on-line retail software store said, "We had a week in which we had more fraud than legitimate sales." In the late 1990s some software companies were facing fraudulent sales at a rate of 20 percent, a much higher rate than traditional mail and telephone sales. One problem that companies face is the speed with which the customer gets the product. "If you have to mail something to someone, you can catch the fraud before you send the product," explained one company's manager of electronic commerce business development, but "with electronic software distribution, they get the product immediately." A related legal burden these companies face is the liability to the credit card company. When a consumer has his or her credit card used fraudulently, the liability is limited to $50, but when the signature cannot be verified, the merchant is fully responsible.

As you might expect, one solution is the use of software that flags transactions that appear to be fraudulent. One company, CyberSource, provides an automated fraud screen application to help any on-line merchant assess the fraud risk before the transaction is consummated. This software allows the merchant to specify the fraud-risk level it is willing to accept and even allows that risk level to differ across products or product categories. The program uses information from the credit card authorization process and "scores" the risk of a transaction in less than five seconds. Some of the factors the program considers are the purchase frequency, whether the transaction is in the purchaser's "normal" hours, and the geographic proximity of the bill-to and ship-to addresses. Through software like CyberSource's, the on-line software business can protect itself against thieves who steal via the Web.

Sources: "Taking a Byte out of Crime: Companies Crack Down on Digital Delinquents Who Drain Their Net Sales," *Fort Worth Star-Telegram*, November 23, 1997; and "CyberSource Announces CyberSource IVS 3.0: The Fraud Screen Providing the Most Precise Protection from Internet Credit Card Fraud," *PR Newswire*, September 1998.

- To help students learn how to use the Internet and make them aware of the kind of information the Internet can provide, we have created Internet exercises for each chapter. Internet Exercises have been added to the Computer Applications section in the End-of-Chapter Material for every chapter. Internet addresses for vignette companies are also included with each vignette to encourage students to visit each company's Web site.

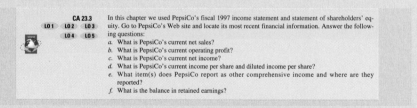

CA 23.3
LO 1 LO 2 LO 3
LO 4 LO 5

In this chapter we used PepsiCo's fiscal 1997 income statement and statement of shareholders' equity. Go to PepsiCo's Web site and locate its most recent financial information. Answer the following questions:
a. What is PepsiCo's current net sales?
b. What is PepsiCo's current operating profit?
c. What is PepsiCo's current net income?
d. What is PepsiCo's current income per share and diluted income per share?
e. What item(s) does PepsiCo report as other comprehensive income and where are they reported?
f. What is the balance in retained earnings?

- The Annual Report Booklet has been eliminated. Students are encouraged to seek out financial information for each company directly from the companies' Web sites. Students can link directly to this information through the Ainsworth home page. This keeps the annual report information current and allows students to respond to new questions posted to the Web site each semester. Suggested solutions will be posted in a password protected section on the Web site for instructors.

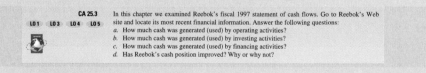

CA 25.3
LO 1 LO 3 LO 4 LO 5

In this chapter we examined Reebok's fiscal 1997 statement of cash flows. Go to Reebok's Web site and locate its most recent financial information. Answer the following questions:
a. How much cash was generated (used) by operating activities?
b. How much cash was generated (used) by investing activities?
c. How much cash was generated (used) by financing activities?
d. Has Reebok's cash position improved? Why or why not?

SPECIFIC CHAPTER REVISIONS:

PART 1: INTRODUCTION

Chapter 1: Accounting Information and Business

- Discussion of cash versus accrual accounting has been added.

- FASB Concepts Statements are discussed in greater detail.

- This chapter now contains a more formal introduction to the basic accounting elements: assets, liabilities, owners' equity, revenue, and expenses.

Chapter 2: Operating Cycles and Internal Control

- Expanded coverage of internal controls. This coverage was formerly in Chapter 3 of the first edition.

- A discussion of business cycles is helpful before discussing the financial statements; therefore, the content of Chapters 2 and 3 has been switched from the first edition.

- In addition, since the discussion of internal control is a central theme, this chapter discusses the cash controls formerly found in Chapter 11 in the first edition.

Chapter 3: Accounting and Its Role in Business

- This chapter introduces event analysis and focuses on the identification of assets, liabilities, owners' equity, revenues, and expenses.

- The impact of accounting events on financial statements is stressed.

- Based on reviewers' comments, detailed event analysis is postponed until Chapter 7. This chapter merely introduces event analysis and shows how the results of events are linked to the financial statements.

PART 2: PLANNING

Chapter 4: Revenue, Costs, and Profit Planning

- The majority of content from the first edition has been retained.

- Based on reviewers' comments, the discussion of regression analysis has been simplified.

Chapter 5: Short-Term Operating Decisions

- Chapter 5 now focuses on relevant variable analyses for decision making.

- Using an activity-based costing approach, this chapter shows how short-term operating decisions are analyzed.

- This chapter contains much of the information from Chapter 6 in the first edition. It has been moved to Chapter 5 to provide a better link between cost behavior and estimation in Chapter 4 to decision making in Chapter 5.

Chapter 6: Planning and Budgeting

- Retains coverage from Chapter 5 in the previous edition with greater emphasis on pro forma financial statements including the statement of cash flows.

- This chapter has been moved from Chapter 5 to Chapter 6 to provide a stronger link between pro forma financial statements and actual financial statements.

- A primary focus of this chapter is sales versus cash receipts versus accounts receivable and purchases versus cash disbursements versus accounts payable.

- This chapter provides a link to accrual-based accounting in Chapters 7–11.

- This chapter includes the cash management issues from Chapter 11 in the first edition.

PART 3: RECORDING

Chapter 7: Accounting: Event Analysis

- Chapter 7 from the previous edition has been divided into two chapters (Chapters 7 and 8).

- The new Chapter 7 focuses on transaction analysis in an increase/decrease format.

- Based on reviewers' comments, this new chapter has been added to focus on event analysis in detail, before debits and credits are introduced.

Chapter 8: Recording and Communicating in the Accounting Cycle

- This new Chapter 8 focuses on the accounting cycle, including adjusting and closing entries.

- This chapter adds debits and credits to the discussion in Chapter 7 and examines adjusting and closing entries.

Chapter 9: Recording and Communicating in the Expenditure Cycle

- A new vignette featuring Unitog Company has been added to this chapter. Unitog provides uniforms for companies, such as Anheuser-Busch, Priority Mail, and CITGO. This vignette helps students understand how to account for the events that occur in the expenditure cycle, including the acquisition and use of goods and services involved in a firm's operations.

Chapter 10: Recording and Communicating in the Revenue Cycle

- Boeing Company is featured in this chapter's opening vignette. This vignette helps students understand how the successful employment of goods and services yields corresponding benefits that increase the income and net worth of a company.

- The new Of Interest feature for this chapter discusses companies that have been caught manipulating their books to make operations look more profitable.

Chapter 11: Recording and Communicating in the Conversion Cycle

- This chapter uses Anheuser-Busch Companies to explain how a company analyzes events that occur during the conversion cycle. Anheuser-Busch offers a good example of a diversified company with significant activities devoted to its manufacturing processes (conversion activities).

- The new Of Interest feature for this chapter discusses backflush costing.

PART 4: EVALUATION

Chapter 12: Revenue and Expenditure Cycles: Analysis and Control

- The GAP is used in this chapter's opening vignette which will help students understand how companies evaluate how well they are performing their operating activities (how much inventory to buy, how to price products, etc.).

Chapter 13: Conversion Cycle: Analysis and Control

- This chapter has been revised to feature quality and time-management issues up front and contains an overview of overhead variance analysis.

- This chapter discusses nonfinancial as well as financial measures of performance and provides a link that can be traced back to Chapter 1.

PART 5: PLANNING AND DECISION MAKING IN THE INVESTING AND FINANCING CYCLES

Chapter 14: The Time Value of Money: A Tool for Decision Making

- This chapter uses Paine Webber in the opening vignette to help students understand how internal and external stockholders use the concept of the time value of money.

Chapter 15: Planning for Investing Activities

- This coverage, formally in Chapter 17, has been moved to Chapter 15 to provide a more realistic flow of thought. First, assets must be needed, then capital must be raised to purchase the assets.

Chapter 16: Managing Human Resources and Other Noncapitalized Assets

- This chapter has been revised to have a stronger focus on managing noncapitalized assets and includes a discussion of the Balance Scorecard Approach to provide a more contemporary approach to employee evaluation and motivation.

Chapter 17: Planning for Equity Financing

- Chapter 17 contains expanded coverage of planning for equity financing.

Chapter 18: Planning for Debt Financing

- As with Chapter 17, Chapter 18 has been developed out of Chapter 15 in the previous edition and contains expanded coverage of planning for debt financing.

PART 6: RECORDING

Chapter 19: Recording and Communicating Equity Financing Activities

- Stone Container Corporation, an industry leader in packaging products, is used in this chapter's opening vignette to help students understand how and why equity financing is unique to different forms of organizations.

- The Of Interest feature for this chapter discusses the merger Stone Container made with Jefferson Smurfit Corporation and how this merger will increase profitability and generate greater operating cash flows.

Chapter 20: Recording and Communicating Long-Term Debt Financing Activities

- This chapter uses Wal-Mart in the opening vignette to help students understand how long-term debt can be used to finance a company's operational infrastructure and generate higher returns for its stockholders.

- The Of Interest feature for this chapter discusses how to use Spreadsheets for Bond Payments.

Chapter 21: Recording and Communicating Operational Investment Activities

- This chapter uses American Skiing Company to help students understand how companies use long-term investments to acquire facilities necessary to conduct basic business activities.

- The Of Interest feature for this chapter discusses how to use Excel® for Depreciation.

Chapter 22: Recording and Communicating Nonoperational Investment Activities

- This chapter now begins with coverage of equity investments and discusses investments in debt securities at the end of the chapter.

- How these investments are communicated on financial statements is stressed.

- The authors separate equity securities from debt securities to help students understand the difference since the financial press often blurs the distinction.

PART 7: EVALUATION

Chapter 23: Firm Performance: Profitability

- Based on reviewers' comments, coverage of financial versus physical capital has been eliminated from this chapter and discussion of absorption versus variable versus throughput has been added to create more of a managerial flavor.

Chapter 24: Firm Performance: Financial Position

- This chapter uses the firm of Quaker Oats to help students understand how the balance sheet is used, along with its related disclosures, to show the resources a company has and where it might use operating profits. Students will also learn how to use accounting information to predict how profitable a company might be, how easily a company can pay debts, and how likely stockholders are to receive dividends.

Chapter 25: Firm Performance: Cash Flows

- Expanded examples on how to calculate cash flows have been added to this chapter.

- The direct method is illustrated to aid students' understanding of the indirect method. Internal users need the details provided by the direct method.

Chapter 26: Firm Performance: A Comprehensive Evaluation

- Expanded discussion of inter-firm comparisons have been added to this chapter so that students understand how financial statements can be analyzed to make investment decisions.

Over the last decade, accounting education has been evolving quite considerably. Prior to this evolution, many leading educators and employers were becoming increasingly critical of accounting student graduates, and classroom and instructional resources. The *Accounting Education Change Commission* was formed, and the challenge was presented to accounting faculty to improve classroom approaches, instructional resources, and ultimately student graduates.

Kansas State University was one of the initial universities to accept this challenge and redesign their accounting curriculum. Their basic goal was to provide all students, regardless of chosen major, a better understanding of business and accounting's role within the business world. In addition, Kansas State was committed to improving their students' critical thinking skills, communication skills, problem solving abilities, and ability to work in teams.

This text, *Introduction to Accounting: An Integrated Approach,* is an outgrowth of this challenge. Penne, Dan, and David, the three lead authors, all were involved in redesigning the Kansas State accounting curriculum and particularly, the first course. Their efforts and those of the fourth author, Cathy, produced this book, which is now a successful second edition adopted at over 100 schools. We hope you enjoy this text and your course.

ORGANIZATION OF THIS TEXT

The Road Ahead

Beginning each chapter, you will see a beacon feature used to help you understand where you are within the business cycles. Each time you begin a new part of the business cycle, you are given a brief review entitled The Road Traveled, You Are Here, and the Road Ahead. When convering a chapter that falls within a business cycle, you are given a You are Here beacon to remind you that you are within the same cycle.

SUPPLEMENTS DESIGNED TO HELP YOU EXCEL

We provide the following supplements for you as you study and learn from *Introduction to Accounting: An Integrated Approach.*

Study Guide, Volumes 1 (0-07-030684-2) & 2 (0-07-030685-0) Prepared by Debra Kerby and Scott Fouch of Truman State University, this manual will reinforce the concepts found in the text through chapter by chapter review, additional Pause and Reflect questions, and short essay assignments.

PowerPoint Ready Notes, Volumes 1 (0-07-030689-3) & 2 (0-07-030690-7) Prepared by Jayne Maas of Towson University, this useful tool will allow for a more efficient classroom setting by giving you a master template for note taking. Mirroring the PowerPoint slides available to the instructor, you will have a beginning point so you can concentrate on the classroom presentation instead of furiously taking notes.

Windows Tutorial (0-07-235138-1) Explanations of correct and incorrect answers are provided and scores are tallied. Instructors may request either a free master template for you to use/copy or shrinkwrapped version which is available to you for a nominal fee. This Tutorial is available in a convenient Windows® platform, includes new questions (not taken from the Study Guide), allows you to review your answers supported by detailed explanations, and includes text page number references when correcting you.

Student Software CD-ROM (0-07-235144-6)   This new CD contains four valuable pieces of software, including our popular General Ledger Applications Software, Spreadsheet Applications Template Software, the above-mentioned Tutorial Software, and Essentials of Accounting, a multimedia accounting cycle review. This new CD can be purchased for a nominal price either separately or shrinkwrapped with the text.

Web site, *http://www.mhhe.com/ainsworth*   This comprehensive Web site designed especially to accompany the text offers you: links to annual reports and featured companies, an Online Tutor, an Online Learning Center (with the purchase of a password), a free practice set for accounting cycle review, quick demos of additional technology available to help you understand and use accounting, new Of Interests, new Pause and Reflect Questions, a Key Terms quick reference, access to a Spanish/English glossary, and links to other Web sites containing information on how to attain additional resources to help develop your communication skills.

Online Learning Center, Volumes 1 (0-07-236591-9) & 2 (0-07-236612-5)   Within the book's Website, there is a password-protected Online Learning Center. As a user of this text, you will have full access to graphics, PowerPoint slides, additional, as well as online testing. This McGraw-Hill content is so comprehensive that it will reinforce concepts covered in classroom and allow you the additional study tools you need to get ahead in your course. Based on your instructor, you may be able to access the course syllabus, visit important Internet links selected by your instructor, and review additional course materials.

General Ledger Applications Software (GLAS) (0-07-030688-5)   This general ledger program will solve selected end-of-chapter material from the recording chapters (7–11 and 18–21). It also will allow for any problem requiring journal entries (in the recording chapters) to be solved via its custom features.

Spreadsheet Template Application Software (SPATS) Volumes 1 (0-07-561567-3) & 2 (0-07-029308-2)   This spreadsheet-based software uses Excel to solve selected problems and cases in the text. These selected problems and cases are identified in the text margins of the end-of-chapter material in the text with an appropriate icon.

Ultimate Interiors Practice Set (0-07-030683-4)   This manual practice set, prepared by Cathy Larson will allow additional reinforcement of the accounting cycle presentation in Chapter 7. It is available free to users of this text.

TO THE STUDENT

Brief Road Map

Road Map

CHAPTER 20

Recording and Communicating Long-Term Debt Financing Activities

CHAPTER 21

Recording and Communicating Operational Investment Activities

CHAPTER 22

Recording and Communicating Nonoperational Investment Activities

---

CHAPTER 26

Firm Performance: A Comprehensive Evaluation

PART FIVE

THE ROAD TRAVELED

Chapters 1–3 explored the evolution of accounting and the role of accounting in today's business environment. Chapters 4–6 investigated the planning process for operating activities and how accounting information is used in this process. Chapters 7 and 8 introduced the accounting cycle and the process of recording and communicating accounting events. Chapters 9–11 built on these ideas as we examined recording expenditure, revenue, and conversion cycle events. Chapters 12 and 13 discussed the role of accounting in the process of evaluating operating activities.

YOU ARE HERE

The second half of this text follows the format developed in the first half—planning, performing, and evaluating. Now we explore business investing and financing activities. Chapter 14 discusses the risk-reward relationship, the concept of compound interest, and uses these ideas to examine the time value of money. Chapter 14 provides the tools to make capital budgeting, human resources, and financing decisions.

THE ROAD AHEAD

Chapter 15 uses the time value of money concepts discussed in Chapter 14 to examine the capital budgeting process. We explore how companies determine whether certain long-term projects should be accepted or rejected. Chapter 16 explores the business considerations involving investments in human capital. Chapter 17 is the first of two chapters that explore the process of raising the capital necessary to run the business and enable it to invest in long-term projects and human capital. Chapter 17 investigates equity (owner) financing and Chapter 18 considers debt (creditor) financing.

LEARNING OBJECTIVES

LO 1 Explain the cyclical relationship of financing, investing, and operating decisions.

LO 2 Describe the distinction between return of and return on investment and the difference between rate of return and expected rate of return.

LO 3 Explain the risk-return relationship.

LO 4 Describe the difference between simple and compound interest and how interest relates to the time value of money.

LO 5 Demonstrate how to use the future value of the amount of $1 and the present value of the amount of $1 to solve problems that involve lump-sum cash flows at different points in time.

LO 6 Demonstrate how to use the future value of an annuity and the present value of an annuity to solve problems that involve annuity cash flows.

The Time Value of Money:
A Tool for Decision Making

PAINE WEBBER
www.painewebber.com

Founded in 1879, Paine Webber Group Inc. is today one of the world's largest full-service securities and commodities firms with 299 offices worldwide and approximately 16,600 employees, and in 1997 Paine Webber had a record year. As a participant in a record-setting bull market, Paine Webber exceeded its previous record income by 14 percent. Paine Webber's current and future success is based on its ability to assess the risks and returns of investments in the capital markets and use the time value of money to meet the needs of its individual and business clients. Individual investors invest to achieve financial goals such as buying a dream home and having enough money for a comfortable retirement. Businesses invest in the securities market in an effort to improve the firm's liquidity, increase its profitability, and reduce its risk.

Paine Webber meets its clients' needs by providing financial expertise and then providing the investment products necessary to achieve their goals. For example, suppose you are planning your retirement and have decided that you want to have $1,000,000 when you retire at age 65. You will need answers to questions such as: How much do I need to invest each year to achieve my goal? What

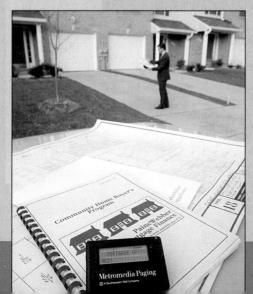

are the risks and rewards associated with the various investment alternatives available? How will my choice of investments affect the amount I need to invest each year? How do I acquire these investments? While the material in this chapter will show you the answer to the first question, a Paine Webber representative can provide answers to the last three questions.[1]

[1]Paine Webber is the registered trademark of PaineWebber Incorporated, the operating company of Paine Webber Group Inc.

n earlier chapters, we focused on examining how businesses operate, how decision makers use accounting information for planning business operations, how the accounting system captures the operating information surrounding business events, and how internal and external stakeholders use accounting information to evaluate a firm's operations. The remaining chapters of the text examine the investing and financing activities of a business enterprise. We will learn how management uses accounting information to plan for these types of activities, how the accounting system captures these events, and how internal and external stakeholders use accounting information to evaluate the firm's financing and investing decisions.

THE MANAGEMENT CYCLE

LO 1

The cyclical nature of the planning, performing, and evaluating phases of a business and the relationship of operating, investing, and financing activities to these phases were first described in Chapter 3 and are again illustrated in Exhibit 14.1. At the strategic level, firms conduct long-term planning for operating, investing, and financing activities, which in turn impacts the short-term planning at the operating level. At the operating level, the

EXHIBIT 14.1

The Management Cycle

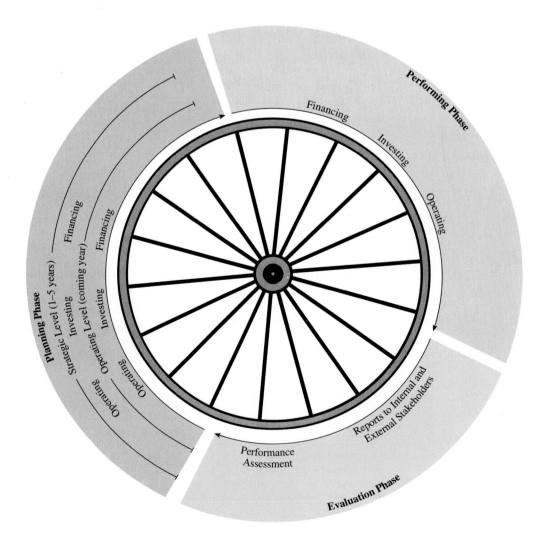

company first plans the firm's operating activities based on expected consumer demand for the company's goods and services. These planning activities were discussed in Chapters 4–6. In the next step, decision makers ascertain the investments in long-term assets necessary to support the operating activities planned for the firm. For example, suppose Paine Webber anticipates a significant increase in customer demand for its brokerage services. The operating budget would trigger the planning process to expand the computer system so the increased demand could be met. The third step involves determining how to finance these investments. Once the amount of funds needed to acquire the assets are determined, planners must decide on the source of the financing—debt financing (creditors) or equity financing (owners' contributions). Once the planners have decided on the hardware needed to expand the computer system, Paine Webber's planners must decide whether to borrow the funds or use equity financing and, they must evaluate the impact of their decision on the firm's risk and return. (We discuss the impact of the debt versus equity financing decision in Chapter 18.)

While the planning phase starts with operating activities and ends with financing activities, the performance phase reverses the sequence. In a start-up company, financing events are the first captured by the accounting system as the company raises the necessary capital. The accounting system is used to record these events and makes a distinction between debt and equity financing. Next companies invest in the operating infrastructure necessary for the firm's operations. The accounting system is used to record these events and notes the difference in the type of assets acquired. Finally, the firm begins operating and the accounting system captures the operating events as described in Chapters 7–11. Management's goal is to utilize the company's resources effectively and efficiently so the operating activities generate an operating profit. Operating profits generated are used for three primary purposes: (1) to pay the interest on borrowed funds, (2) to reward the owners in the form of dividends (or in the form of withdrawals in proprietorships and partnerships), and (3) to reinvest funds in the firm to maintain the existing operational capacity and to finance additional long-term investments in the firm. Paine Webber's 1997 financial statements reveal that $2,544,550,000 of operating profits *were* used to meet the interest on its debt, $82,918,000 *were* distributed to owners in the form of dividends, and $332,531,000 *were* reinvested in the firm.

The evaluation phase provides information about a firm's performance to internal and external stakeholders. Recall that Chapter 3 described how the financial accounting subsystem communicates information to external stakeholders while the management accounting subsystem generates information to internal stakeholders. The financial accounting subsystem describes the firm's operating results on the income statement and in the operating section of the cash flow statement. The investing activities captured by the financial accounting subsystem are summarized in the long-term asset sections of the balance sheet and the investment section of the cash flow statement. The financing activities are reported to external stakeholders using the statement of stockholders' equity, the liability and stockholders' equity sections of the balance sheet, and the financing section of the cash flow statement.

The cycle starts again when the management team begins planning for the operating, investing, and financing activities of the next time period. The amount and sources of funds needed for new investments depend on management's operating plans and the long-term assets needed to successfully implement the plans. If additional investments are needed to support

Both personal and business investments require adequate planning.

planned operating activity, will the firm borrow from creditors, solicit contributions from new or existing owners, or use the funds generated by last year's operations?

Before going any further, however, it is imperative that you understand the fundamental concepts underlying financing and investing decisions. In this chapter we expand the definitions of return and risk and introduce the concept of the time value of money. These essential tools for making financing and investing decisions are as important as hammers, saws, and tape measures are to a carpenter building a house. With these tools, you can make informed financing and investing decisions for a business enterprise. In addition, these tools are also useful for making personal financial decisions, such as determining how much to save for a comfortable retirement or your children's college education and the best way to finance the purchase of a car, a house, or a business after graduation.

RETURN OF AND RETURN ON INVESTMENT: WHAT IS THE DIFFERENCE?

LO 2

The concept of *return* is associated with investing decisions involving the acquisition of assets, such as certificates of deposit, government bonds, and new equipment. There are two types of return: return *of* investment and return *on* investment. When assessing investment alternatives, investors expect to receive a **return of investment**—that is, the return of the amount initially invested. For example, if you invest $1,000 in a savings account for one year, you expect, at a minimum, to receive $1,000 at the end of the year. The $1,000 you receive at the end of the year is your return of investment.

Return on investment is money received in excess of the initial investment. If the $1,000 in the savings account generates $1,050 at the end of one year, there is a *return of* the initial $1,000 investment and a *return on* the investment of interest of $50.

The Importance of Time

Return on investment is not adequate to differentiate among investments because it does not consider the length of time that investments are held or the amount of the initial investment. For example, investments X and Y, shown in Exhibit 14.2, generate a return on investment of $300 and $400, respectively. How would you choose between the two investments based on the dollar amount of the return? You might select investment Y because its return is $100 greater than investment X. However, this does not consider the length of time investments X and Y were held. If the $1,300 accumulated by investment X on January 1, 1999, is reinvested and held as long as investment Y (until July 1, 2000), it could generate an additional return that equals or exceeds the $100 difference between the two investments.

EXHIBIT	14.2	Return on Investment			

Investment X			**Investment Y**		
January 1, 1999 Invest		$(1,000)	January 1, 1999 Invest		$(1,000)
January 1, 2000 Receive		1,300	July 1, 2000 Receive		1,400
Return on investment on January 1, 2000		$ 300	Return on investment on July 1, 2000		$ 400

The Importance of the Amount of the Initial Investment

Even when investments are held for the same period of time, the amounts of the initial investment can distort comparisons. Consider investments X, Y, and Z in Exhibit 14.3. One might choose to make investment Z because it has the largest dollar amount of return on investment of the three investments. However, this choice does not take into account the differences in the size of the initial investments—$1,000, $2,000, and $3,000, respectively.

What we need to analyze the investments realistically is a common-size measure of performance, that is, a measure that allows us to compare and rank the performance of investments regardless of the size of the initial investment.

EXHIBIT 14.3 Rate of Return

	Investments		
	X	Y	Z
January 1, 1999 Invest	$(1,000)	$(2,000)	$(3,000)
January 1, 2000 Receive	1,100	2,160	3,180
Return on investment	$ 100	$ 160	$ 180
Rate of return calculation	$ 100	$ 160	$ 180
	$1,000	$2,000	$3,000
Annual rate of return	10%	8%	6%

Rate of Return

The **rate of return** (a percentage) measures the performance of investments on a common-size basis and eliminates any distortion caused by the size of the initial investment. Exhibit 14.3 uses the rate of return formula, shown below, to determine the rate of return for investments X, Y, and Z. We calculate rate of return as follows:

$$\text{Rate of return} = \frac{\text{Dollar amount of return on investment}}{\text{Dollar amount of initial investment}}$$

In these cases, the 10 percent rate of return on investment X is greater than those on investments Y (8 percent) and Z (6 percent).

The rate of return on investments is usually expressed as an annual (one-year) rate even if the life of the investment is greater or less than one year. The return percentage in Exhibit 14.3 is based on a one-year time period and is called the *annual rate of return.*

Investments can have a negative rate of return when they do not recover the initial investment; that is, when there is a failure to get a return of investment. For example, if an investment returns only $800 of the $1,000 initially invested, the $200 difference is described as a 20 percent negative rate of return [($800–$1,000)/$1,000].

In the example in Exhibit 14.3, we measured the performance of the investments by calculating the rates of return on investment *after* the returns were generated by the investments. However, most investments are made before investors know what their actual rates of return will be. How can potential investors measure the performance of investments before knowing the actual rate of return the investments will generate?

Expected Rate of Return

Unfortunately, individuals make investment decisions without the benefit of clairvoyance and, as a result, they must predict rates of return on investments they are considering. The predicted return rate is known as the **expected rate of return,** a summary measure of an investment's performance, stated as a percentage, based on the possible rates of return and the likelihood of those rates of return occurring. The expected rate of return is a useful measure for choosing among investment alternatives.

To ascertain an investment's expected rate of return, it is necessary to (1) forecast the investment's possible rates of return, (2) establish a probability that each forecasted rate of return will occur, and (3) multiply each forecasted return by its respective probability and sum the resulting products.

To illustrate, assume that an investor has the opportunity to buy a gold mine for $100,000. Exhibit 14.4 lists the four possible outcomes to expect in terms of dollars and rates of return on the investment. The exhibit also shows the probability of the four outcomes occurring. The investor believes that there is 1 chance in 100 (0.01), or a 1 percent chance, of the miners hitting the "mother lode" and getting a 1,000 percent rate of return ($1,000,000/$100,000). At the other extreme, there are 39 chances in 100 (0.39), or a 39 percent chance, of finding "no lode" and a negative 100 percent rate of return (–$100,000/$100,000). The expected rate of return for this gold mining investment is 21 percent, as calculated in Exhibit 14.4.

EXHIBIT 14.4   Expected Outcomes and Probabilities

Possible Outcomes	Possible Returns	Rate of Return If Event Occurs	Probability of Outcome
Mother lode	$1,000,000	1,000%	0.01
Full lode	150,000	150	0.20
Baby lode	50,000	50	0.40
No lode	(100,000)	(100)	0.39

Expected rate of return (ERR) = $(0.01 \times 1,000\%) + (0.2 \times 150\%) + (0.4 \times 50\%) + (0.39 \times -100\%) = 21\%$

The gold mine's 21 percent expected rate of return does not mean that the gold mine will earn a 21 percent rate of return. Instead, it summarizes the gold mine's possible rates of return.

Do not confuse the expected rate of return with the actual rate of return on an investment. An investor estimates the expected rate of return before making the investment, while the actual rate of return on an investment is calculated after the outcome of the investment is revealed at some future date. For example, if the miners do hit the "full lode," the actual return of the investment is 150 percent rather than the 21 percent expected rate of return.

The concepts of return of investment, return on investment, rate of return, and expected rate of return are fundamental when making any investment decision. However, investors do not automatically select the investment alternative that generates the highest expected rate of return. Before selecting an investment, it is necessary to appraise not only the expected return but also the risk of the investments under consideration.

WHAT IS THE RISK OF INVESTMENT?

LO 3

Risk is the exposure to the chance that an unfavorable outcome will occur at some future point in time. Typically, people take risks because some monetary or psychic reward is possible. For example, people go to Las Vegas and gamble even though they know that casinos are profitable because most people lose money. However, there are many people who are willing to put their money at risk in the hope of beating the odds and winning. The likelihood of losing money is offset by the belief that it is possible to beat the odds and by the enjoyment of actually taking the risk itself.

Attitudes toward Risk

The amount of risk people are willing to assume depends on their attitudes toward risk and the decision under consideration. People who enjoy risky situations are called risk seekers, whereas those who avoid risk are called risk avoiders. However, the decision under consideration may change the decision maker's normal attitude toward risk. For example, in terms of taking physical risks, a mountain climber is a risk seeker; however, the climber might be a risk avoider when making investment decisions that affect his or her ability to finance the next climbing expedition.

Risk is associated with the uncertainty of an unfavorable outcome actually occurring. To illustrate, assume that an alternative to the previous gold mine investment is buying a $100,000 one-year U.S. government security that yields a 5 percent rate of return. Because the U.S. government has never defaulted on its debt, there is little doubt that the government will return the initial investment of $100,000 and pay an actual return on investment of $5,000 ($100,000 × 0.05). This investment, therefore, has very little risk because there is very little chance of an unfavorable outcome occurring.

Investing in the gold mine could generate an actual rate of return that is much greater than the government security. However, the gold mine investment is risky because there is a significant chance of losing the entire investment. In this case, the choice the investor makes depends on how willing he or she is to risk the $100,000 investment for a possible return.

Measuring Risk

The risk of any investment is related to the possibility of earning less than the expected rate of return and is impounded in the expected rate of return figure. Impounding means that the expected rate of return captures the effects of both the positive and the less desirable outcomes of an investment in one summary measure of return. For example, the gold mine investment's 21 percent expected rate of return is based on possible returns that range from a 1,000 percent rate of return and a negative 100 percent rate of return.

There are several ways to measure the risk of an investment. The **relative risk ratio** is a rather simple common-size risk measure that reflects the risk of an investment as a percentage of the expected return lost if the worst-case outcome occurs.[2] The amount of risk depends on the difference between the worst possible outcome and the expected rate of return. Because the relative risk ratio is a common-size measure, it is possible to rank respective risks of two or more investments from high to low.

$$\text{Relative risk ratio} = \frac{\text{Expected rate of return} - \text{Lowest possible rate of return}}{\text{Expected rate of return}}$$

To illustrate how to use the relative risk ratio, assume that an investor is considering investment alternatives A and B, presented in Exhibit 14.5. Both investment A and investment B cost $100,000 and have two possible outcomes. The two outcomes of each investment have the same 0.5 probability, or a 50 percent chance of occurring.

EXHIBIT 14.5	Expected Rate of Return and Relative Risk Ratio	
	Investment A	**Investment B**
Amount invested	$100,000	$100,000
Possible outcomes	10,000 (0.5)	20,000 (0.5)
and (probabilities)	11,000 (0.5)	1,000 (0.5)

Expected Rates of Return

Panel A: Calculated Using Rates of Return

Investment A:

$$\frac{\$10,000}{\$100,000}(0.5) + \frac{\$11,000}{\$100,000}(0.5) = 10\%(0.5) + 11\%(0.5) = 10.5\%$$

Investment B:

$$\frac{\$20,000}{\$100,000}(0.5) + \frac{\$1,000}{\$100,000}(0.5) = 20\%(0.5) + 1\%(0.5) = 10.5\%$$

Panel B: Calculated Using Expected Returns

$$\text{Expected rate of return} = \frac{\text{Expected return on investment*}}{\text{Amount of initial investment}}$$

Investment A: $10,500 / $100,000 = 10.5%

Investment B: $10,500 / $100,000 = 10.5%

Relative Risk Ratios

Panel C: Calculated Using Rates of Return

Investment A: $\dfrac{10.5\% - 10\%}{10.5\%} = 4.76\%$

Investment B: $\dfrac{10.5\% - 1\%}{10.5\%} = 90.48\%$

Panel D: Calculated Using Expected Returns

Investment A: $\dfrac{\$10,500 - \$10,000}{\$10,500} = 4.76\%$

Investment B: $\dfrac{\$10,500 - \$1,000}{\$10,500} = 90.48\%$

*Expected returns:

Investment A: $10,000 (0.5) + $11,000 (0.5) = $10,500

Investment B: $20,000 (0.5) + $1,000 (0.50) = $10,500

---

[2]This measure assumes that there is a normal distribution of possible returns. Therefore, the expected rate of return is the midpoint of the range of returns, and the relative risk ratio measures the difference between this midpoint and the worst possible outcome in the range of outcomes. When the outcomes are not distributed normally around the mean, the relative risk ratio is not an appropriate measure of risk. Other measures of risk, in such cases, would require the use of statistics.

Panels A and B of Exhibit 14.5 show two methods for calculating the expected rates of return for investments A and B. The first method uses rates of return, described earlier. Panel B calculates the expected rate of return using an investment's expected return. An **expected return** is a summary measure of an investment's performance stated in dollars that is based on the dollar amount of the possible returns on investment and the probability of those returns occurring. Both methods indicate that investments A and B have the same 10.5 percent expected rate of return. However, the investments do not have the same risk.

Panel C of Exhibit 14.5 calculates the relative risk ratios using expected rates of return, while Panel D shows how to calculate the ratios using expected returns. The relative risk ratios provide a means of quantifying a difference in the risk of the two investments.

To determine the relative risk ratio using rates of return, subtract the worst possible rate of return from the expected rate of return. This yields the amount of the expected rate of return lost if the worst outcome occurs. For example, for investment A, the amount of the expected rate of return lost is 0.5 percent, which is the difference between investment A's expected rate of return, 10.5 percent, and the worst possible rate of return, 10 percent ($10,000/$100,000). Dividing this difference (0.5%) by the expected rate of return (10.5%) yields the percentage of the expected return that is lost if the worst outcome occurs. For investment A this percentage, or relative risk ratio, is 4.76 percent.

Determining the relative risk ratio using expected returns follows similar procedures, but dollar values rather than percentages are used. For example, the expected return for investment A is $10,500 and its worst return expected is $10,000. When the $500 difference between these two returns is divided by the expected return ($10,500), the relative risk ratio is 4.76 percent. In either case, the common-size measure provides a basis for comparing the risk of the investment alternatives. The larger the relative risk ratio, the higher an investment's risk.

Investment A loses only 4.76 percent of the expected return if the worst outcome occurs. Investment B, however, is riskier because if the worst outcome actually occurs, 90.48 percent of the expected return is lost.

The relative risk ratio quantifies the risk of an investment and helps investors determine if the risk of the investment is justified given its potential return.

THE RISK-RETURN RELATIONSHIP

Risk and return are directly related; that is, the greater the risk, the greater the return the investor expects. When choosing among investment alternatives, investors want the investment with the highest return, but they must also consider the riskiness of the investment. Typically, investors select investments with the highest expected return for a given level of risk. For example, Paine Webber would consider investment A in Exhibit 14.5 to be more desirable than investment B because it has the same expected rate of return as investment B (10.5 percent), with lower risk (4.76 percent versus 90.48 percent).

To consider investment B as a legitimate alternative, Paine Webber would need a greater expected return before assuming the greater investment risk. This increase in the expected rate of return is called a **risk premium.**

Assume that Paine Webber would want investment B to yield an expected rate of return of 16.5 percent in order to make up for the higher risk. The additional 6 percent desired (16.5 percent versus 10.5 percent) is the risk premium placed on this investment and compensates Paine Webber for assuming the additional potential risk of the investment. The expected rate of return including the risk premium is called the **risk-adjusted expected rate of return.**

Changes in an investor's risk-adjusted rate of return (assuming the outcomes and their probabilities remain the same) affect the amount the investor will pay for an investment. Also, the amount of the investment varies inversely with the change in risk-adjusted rate of return. That is, when the risk-adjusted expected rate of return increases, an investor pays less for the investment in order to achieve the revised expected (risk-adjusted) rate of return.

To illustrate why this occurs, assume that Paine Webber revises its assessment of an investment's risk but not the outcomes or probabilities of those outcomes occurring.

For example, in order to get a 16.5 percent risk-adjusted expected rate of return on investment B, Paine Webber will revise the price it is willing to pay for investment B from $100,000 to $63,636 (calculated below) using the expected rate of return formula. If the seller of investment B accepts $63,636 rather than $100,000, then Paine Webber's initial investment of $63,636 will have a risk-adjusted expected rate of return of 16.5 percent.

$$\text{Expected rate of return} = \frac{\begin{array}{c}(\text{Probability})(\text{Outcome}) + (\text{Probability})(\text{Outcome}) \\ + \ldots + (\text{Probability})(\text{Outcome})\end{array}}{\text{Amount invested in B}}$$

$$0.165 = \frac{(0.5)(\$20,000) + (0.5)(\$1,000)}{\text{Amount invested in B}}$$

$$0.165 \times \text{Amount invested in B} = \$10,500$$

$$\text{Amount invested in B} = \$63,636$$

Now, both investment A and investment B are equally desirable to Paine Webber because the price of investment B reflects the 6 percent risk premium it demanded. That is, Paine Webber is compensated for the additional risk by the reduction in the price of investment B from $100,000 to $63,636, which increases the expected return on investment B from 10.5 to 16.5 percent.

PAUSE & REFLECT

If you were a risk seeker, would you have demanded a risk premium for investment B? *(answer on page 508)*

This example illustrates the direct relationship between risk and return. Investors who are risk avoiders and assume greater risk want a greater expected rate of return on their investments. Keep in mind that the notions of risk and return are based on investors' beliefs about the likelihood of future events. *Therefore, the assessment of risk and return and the resulting valuation of investments are the result of subjective assessments and the ability of the buyer and seller of the investment to agree on a price.*

Risk Factors Considered in Determining Expected Return

All investors expect some return on their investment, even if an investment has no risk. The determination of the expected return on any investment begins with an assumption called the **risk-free rate of return,** or the rate of return that a virtually riskless investment produces. Risk premiums for risk factors associated with particular investments are added to the risk-free rate to determine the risk-adjusted expected rate of return of an investment. There are three primary risk factors to consider that generate risk premiums: inflation risk, business risk, and liquidity risk.

Inflation Risk Inflation causes the purchasing power of the monetary unit to decline. For example, suppose $2.00 buys a loaf of bread on January 1, 1999, but at the end of the year the same loaf of bread costs $2.10. The purchasing power of the dollar declined by 5 percent ($0.10/$2.10 = 0.05, or 5%) during 1999 because it now takes $2.10 instead of $2.00 to buy the same loaf of bread at the end of the period. **Inflation risk,** then, is the chance of a decline in the purchasing power of the monetary units during the time money is invested. It is factored into every investment decision to allow for the chance of inflation during the investment period. If an investor expects inflation to continue at the same rate into the foreseeable future, he or she must add a constant percentage as the inflation risk premium to the expected return for any investment being considered.

Business Risk   **Business risk** is the risk associated with the ability of a particular company to continue in business. A business fails when its revenues do not cover its operating expenses or when cash flows are insufficient to pay the interest or principal on the business's debt. The business risk factor reflects the likelihood of a company ceasing normal operations. For example, a company in financial difficulty has to pay a higher rate of interest on its debt than a financially sound company because its financial difficulty increases the chance that the business may not be able to continue its operations.

A bank's prime interest rate is the interest rate charged to the bank's most financially sound customers. The rate of interest on borrowed funds increases as the chance of business failure increases. For example, an airline company such as America West, which filed for bankruptcy protection in 1993, has a higher business risk than Southwest Airlines, which has never faced similar financial difficulties.

Liquidity Risk   Investments that are quickly converted into cash are considered to be liquid. **Liquidity risk** is the chance that an investment cannot be readily converted into cash and generates a risk premium to compensate investors for the inability to convert their investment into cash quickly. For example, a holder of 100 shares of Nike stock could quickly sell the shares on the New York Stock Exchange; therefore, such an investment is considered to be liquid. On the other hand, if an investor purchased 100 shares of Utica State Bank stock, which is not traded on any organized stock exchange, a quick conversion of the stock to cash would be difficult. If the investor needs cash immediately, she might have to reduce the price of the stock substantially in order to attract a buyer. On the other hand, she could borrow money until she finds a buyer who would be willing to pay the higher price. Then the investor would repay the principal and interest on the loan from the proceeds of the sale of the stock. In either case, to compensate for liquidity risk, an investor would have a higher expected rate of return for investing in Utica State Bank stock than in a company with more readily marketable stock.

To illustrate how risk factors work, assume that an investor is considering the purchase of Utica State Bank stock. Assume that the investor expects a 4 percent inflation rate and that estimates for the business risk and liquidity risk premiums for Utica State's stock are 3 percent and 1 percent, respectively. If the risk-free rate of return is 3 percent, the risk-adjusted expected rate of return for Utica State's stock is 11 percent, as shown below:

Risk-free rate of return	3%
Inflation risk premium	4
Business risk premium	3
Liquidity risk premium	1
Risk-adjusted expected rate of return	11%

Thus, to compensate for the respective risks anticipated, the investor needs an 11 percent risk-adjusted expected rate of return to make the Utica State Bank investment worthwhile.

PAUSE & REFLECT   For many years, rates charged by banks for long-term loans such as home mortgages were lower than rates charged for short-term loans, such as car loans. In the mid-1970s this relationship reversed, and long-term loans were charged a higher interest rate than short-term loans. Why did this relationship change? *(answer on page 508)*

Investors' Perception of Return and Risk

We are now aware that, in order to earn a higher rate of return, investors must assume more risk. All investors want to obtain the greatest return possible on their invested funds but must temper their investment decision by the amount of risk they are willing to assume. On an individual basis, investment decisions are subject to the investor's willingness to accept risk.

A company's management team makes similar return-risk assessments as it invests the resources of the firm. However, its investment decisions cannot be based exclusively on the team members' personal attitudes toward risk. The risk that management assumes must be consistent with the risk preferences of the firm's owners because managers act on the owners' behalf.

Perception of Return and Risk on Borrowed Funds

Businesses use borrowed funds in the expectation of earning a greater return on the funds they invest than the cost of borrowing the funds (interest). Therefore, businesses want to minimize the interest on the borrowed funds. To do so, these businesses must convince their creditors (lenders) that the investments made with the borrowed funds will generate a return sufficient to pay the interest and principal on the loan. The lower the probability that a firm will default on the payment of interest or principal on a loan, the lower the rate of interest creditors will charge for borrowed funds. A lower interest rate improves the chance of increasing the rate of return on the business owners' investment. The business, in such situations, would earn more on its borrowed funds, with the excess return going to the owners.

Borrowing money, soliciting contributions from owners, and investing these funds all involve evaluating dollar amounts at different points in time. Understanding the relationship of money and time is critical to all investing and financing decisions.

TIME VALUE OF MONEY

LO 4

The expectation that investments generate returns over time implies that a dollar today, given that it can generate a return on investment over time, is worth more than a dollar one year from today. This concept is known as the *time value of money.*

The **time value of money** is the tool used to solve problems involving the comparison of cash flows that occur at different points in time. While you may not be directly responsible for calculating the impact of the time value of money on a business decision, it is important to understand what such calculations mean, as well as when specialists might be required to provide you or your firm with such information.

The time value of money allows individuals and businesses to determine the cash equivalent today of cash flows that will occur at some point in time in the future. The interest rates assumed determine the size of the cash equivalent given for a particular period of time.

For example, if an investor could receive 10 percent interest on his investments, $100 on January 1, 1999, is the cash equivalent of $110 on January 1, 2000. Thus any amount less than $110 on January 1, 2000, is not as valuable as $100 on January 1, 1999. It follows that any amount greater than $110 on January 1, 2000, is more valuable than the $100 on January 1, 1999, because the most the $100, 10 percent investment could generate on January 1, 2000, is $110. Thus, assuming a 10 percent return, the following relationships hold:

1/1/99		1/1/00
$100	is cash equivalent of	$110
100	is worth more than	108
100	is worth less than	112

Our illustration describes the concept of cash equivalents and the role that interest rates play in determining cash equivalents. However, before going any further, it is necessary to understand the two alternative methods for calculating interest on an investment.

Simple and Compound Interest

As you know, interest is the cost of borrowing money and can be calculated on either a simple or compound basis. **Simple interest** is interest calculated only on the amount borrowed. The amount of interest depends on the amount loaned or borrowed (principal), the annual interest rate, and the amount of time the principal is used. Recall that the formula for calculating interest is:

$$\text{Principal} \times \text{Rate} \times \text{Time} = \text{Interest}$$

For example, assume that you borrow $1,000 for two years at 10 percent simple interest. The amount of each year's interest is computed using the original $1,000. The calculation of simple interest below for the two-year period is:

Year 1	$1,000 × 0.10 × 1 = $ 100
Year 2	$1,000 × 0.10 × 1 = 100
Total simple interest	$ 200
Add: Principal	1,000
Total amount due on note	$1,200

The total amount you owe on the note on its maturity date is $1,200, or $1,000 of principal plus $200 of interest.

Compound interest is interest that is based on a principal amount that includes interest from previous time periods. Like simple interest, compound interest is interest calculated on the principal in the first interest period. However, at the start of the second interest period, the interest from the first period is added to the principal and becomes part of the principal on which interest is calculated for the second period. The process of adding interest to the principal is called **compounding** and is repeated at the start of each subsequent interest period. In other words, compound interest includes *interest paid on interest.*

To illustrate, assume that you borrow $1,000 for two years at a 10 percent interest rate that is compounded annually. The total amount of interest due at the end of two years is $210, as shown below.

Year 1	$1,000 × 0.10 × 1 = $100
Year 2	$1,100* × 0.10 × 1 = 110
Total compound interest	$210

*$1000 principal + $100 interest from year 1 = $1,100.

The difference between the amount of compound and simple interest is the $10 interest charged on Year 1's interest of $100. Note that the first year's interest of $100 becomes part of the principal on which the second year's interest of $110 is calculated [($1,000 + $100 interest) × 0.10 × 1 = $110]. The computation of the total amount you would owe on the note on its maturity date, $1,210, is:

Total interest	$ 210
Add: Principal	1,000
Total amount due on note	$1,210

This illustration shows how to compound interest annually; however, it is possible to compound interest more frequently. By increasing the frequency of the compounding, more interest accumulates on the note.

To illustrate, suppose the 10 percent interest on the $1,000 note is compounded semiannually. Thus the interest on the note is added to the principal every six months. Consequently, the total amount of interest on the note for two years is $215.51, as shown below.

Year 1:		
First six months	$1,000 × 0.10 × 1/2 = $	50.00
Second six months	$1,050 × 0.10 × 1/2 =	52.50
Year 2:		
Third six months	$1,102.50 × 0.10 × 1/2 =	55.13
Fourth six months	$1,157.63 × 0.10 × 1/2 =	57.88
Total compound interest		$ 215.51
Add: Principal		1,000.00
Total amount due on note		$1,215.51

The $215.51 of interest for two years is $5.51 more than the interest incurred when the interest was compounded annually. After six months, $50 of interest is added to principal and, as a result, interest for the first year is $2.50 higher than the $100 interest incurred when compounding the 10 percent rate annually. Therefore, as the frequency of compounding increases, the total amount of interest increases. Interest can be compounded quarterly, monthly, daily, hourly, or even continuously.

Based on the concept of compounding, there are four basic tools used to determine cash equivalents of cash flows that occur at different points in time. These four tools are (1) the future value of the amount of $1, (2) the present value of the amount of $1, (3) the future value of an annuity, and (4) the present value of an annuity.

We have shown how to calculate the total amount due on a note at some point in the future. The combination of principal and interest on the principal at some specified date in the future (due date) is the note's **future value.** By using the formula for the *future value of the amount of $1* (shown and defined below) it is possible to quickly calculate future values. *Appendix Table 1 at the end of the text is based on the output of this formula.*

The future value of the amount of $1, or, in notation, a_{ni}, is

$$a_{ni} = (\$1 + r/c)^n$$

Where

r = Annual rate of interest

c = Number of compoundings in one year

n = Number of compoundings over the entire time period

i = Interest of each compounding period (r/c)

The **future value of the amount of $1** is the amount that $1 becomes at a future date, if invested at a specified annual interest rate (r) and compounded a certain number of times per year (c) over the investment period. The future value factor for the amount of $1 invested at 10 percent for two years, compounded annually, is $a_{2,10\%} = (\$1 + 0.10/1)^2 = \$1.21$. We find the future value factor, 1.21, in Table 1 (Appendix) by locating the intersection of the $n = 2$ row and the 10 percent interest column.[3] Therefore, the future value of a two-year, $1,000 loan at 10 percent interest compounded annually is $1,210 ($1,000 × 1.21).

If interest is compounded semiannually, what is the future value factor of the amount of $1 at 10 percent? Using the formula $a_{4,5\%} = (\$1 + 0.10/2)^4$, the future value factor is 1.2155. The 4 in $a_{4,5\%}$ indicates the number of semiannual compoundings in the two-year period and 5 percent represents the interest (r/c) during each semiannual compounding period. In Appendix Table 1, locate the intersection of the $n = 4$ row and the 5 percent interest column to find the 1.2155 factor. Therefore, the future value of a two-year, $1,000 note at 10 percent interest compounded semiannually is $1,215.50 ($1,000 × 1.2155).

The future value of the amount of $1 is a means of determining the amount of money in the future that is equivalent to an amount today. For example, assume that a customer owes a company $1,000 and wants to delay the payment for two years. How much will the company accept two years from today in lieu of collecting $1,000 today from the customer?

If the company earns a 10 percent rate of interest compounded semiannually on its investments, the customer must pay $1,215.50 two years from today, which is the cash equivalent of $1,000 today, as shown below.

Present value	×	$a_{4,5\%}$	=	Future value
$1,000	×	1.2155	=	Future value
		$1,215.50	=	Future value

Investment companies like Paine Webber use the future value of the amount of $1 to determine retirement amounts. For example, suppose an individual wants to invest $5,000 in a Paine Webber retirement plan for her daughter on the child's fifth birthday. The investor would want to know how much her daughter will have in her retirement account on her 55th birthday. If the representative of Paine Webber assumes a 10 percent rate of return, compounded annually, the daughter's account will have a balance of $586,954.50 upon her retirement, as shown below.

Present value	×	$a_{50,10\%}$	=	Future value
$5,000	×	117.3909	=	Future value
		$586,954.50	=	Future value

---

[3]All the table values are in dollars even though they are not labeled.

The cash equivalent today of some specified amount of cash at a specified date in the future is called the **present value** of that future amount. It is equivalent to the future amount less the interest that has accumulated over the intervening time period. For example, the present value of $110 one year from today is $100 if the interest rate is 10 percent compounded annually [$110 – ($100 × 0.10 × 1)].

Present value problems can be solved using the future value of the amount of $1. For example, what amount must be invested today to accumulate $1,215.50 two years from today if the money can be invested at a 10 percent interest rate that is compounded semiannually? The answer to this question is presented below.

Present value	×	$a_{4,5\%}$		=	$1,215.50
Present value	=	$1,215.50	×		$\dfrac{1}{a_{4,5\%}}$
	=	$1,215.50	×		$\dfrac{1}{1.2155}$
	=	$1,215.50	×		0.8227
	=	$1,000			

A more direct way to determine the dollar equivalent today of some amount in the future is to use the **present value of the amount of $1** formula presented below. The present value of the amount of $1 represents the amount of money that, if invested today at some compounded interest rate for a specified time period, will equal $1 at the end of that time period. *Appendix Table 2 at the end of this book is based on the output of this formula.*

The present value of the amount of $1, or, in notation, $p_{n,i}$, is

$$p_{n,i} = \frac{1}{a_{n,i}}$$

or

$$p_{n,i} = \frac{1}{(\$1 + r/c)^n}$$

Where

r = Annual rate of interest

c = Number of compoundings in one year

n = Number of compoundings over the entire time period

i = Interest of each compounding period (r/c)

The present value of the amount of $1 is the reciprocal of the future value of the amount of $1. The present value of $1 two years from today is $0.8227. That is, $0.8227 invested today at 10 percent interest compounded semiannually will become $1 in two years. The factor, 0.8227, is found by looking in Appendix Table 2 and locating the intersection of the n = 4 row and the 5 percent interest column. If $0.8227 is the present value of $1, then the present value of $10,000 is $8,227 ($10,000 × 0.8227). Likewise, by using the formula for the present value of the amount of $1, we can determine that the present value of $10,000 is $8,227.

Like future values, the number of compoundings affects the size of the present value. However, present values decrease as the number of compoundings increase. For example, what is the present value of $10,000 at 10 percent for two years compounded quarterly?

We determine the present value factor, 0.8207, by looking in Table 2 and finding the intersection of the n = 8 row and the 2.5 percent interest column (or by using the formula). If the present value of $1 is 0.8207, then the present value of $10,000 is $8,207, as shown below.

Future value	×	$p_{8,2.5\%}$	=	Present value
$10,000	×	0.8207	=	Present value
		$8,207	=	Present value

To develop a plan to finance her college education requires an understanding of the time value of money.

Note that increasing the number of compoundings each year decreases the dollars needed today to achieve the same future value.

Investment companies use the present value of the amount of $1 to resolve problems similar to the earlier example involving the $5,000 investment on the daughter's fifth birthday. Now, however, assume that the investor wants to know how much she has to invest on her daughter's fifth birthday so that her daughter will have $50,000 for college on her 18th birthday. If the Paine Webber representative assumes that the investment will earn 10 percent interest compounded annually, he will tell the investor to invest $14,485, as shown below.

Future value	$\times$	$p_{13,10\%}$	=	Present value
$50,000	$\times$	0.2897	=	Present value
		$14,485	=	Present value

Finding Unknown Rates or Time Periods

All present or future value problems involve four elements: (1) the interest rate for each compounding period, r/c; (2) the number of compounding periods, n; (3) the present value amount; and (4) the future value amount. When examining the relationship of present and future values, it is necessary to use these four elements to determine either unknown future or present values. These four elements are also useful when calculating unknown interest rates or the length of time periods for investments. Solving for these unknowns is important when we discuss capital budgeting in Chapter 15.

To illustrate, assume that $1,000 is invested today for two years and the interest is compounded semiannually. What annual interest rate is necessary to accumulate $1,215.50? To answer this question, we must determine the factor for the present value of the amount of $1 as illustrated below.

Future value	$\times$	$p_{4,i}$	=	Present value
$1,215.50	$\times$	$p_{4,i}$	=	$1,000
		$p_{4,i}$	=	$1,000/$1,215.50
		$p_{4,i}$	=	0.8227

The factor 0.8227 is the present value of $1 for four periods at some unknown interest rate. Determining the interest for each compounding period (r/c) involves performing three steps:

1. Using the present value of the amount of $1 table (Appendix Table 2), locate four compounding periods on the left side of the table.

2. Starting at row 4, move right along the row until the present value factor of 0.8227 is located.

3. At the table value 0.8227, move up the column to the interest rate at the top of the column, 5 percent.

The 5 percent interest rate, however, is not the annual interest rate. Rather, 5 percent is the interest rate for each compounding period. Because interest is compounded semiannually, we multiply 5 percent, the interest rate for the compounding period (i), by 2, the number of compoundings during one year (c), to find the annual interest rate of 10 percent. Similarly, we can solve this problem using the future value of $1 as follows:

Present value	×	$a_{4,i}$	=	Future value
$1,000	×	$a_{4,i}$	=	$1,215.50
		$a_{4,i}$	=	$1,215.50/$1,000
		$a_{4,i}$	=	1.2155

The factor 1.2155 is the future value of $1 for four periods at some unknown interest rate. To determine the interest rate, use Appendix Table 1 and locate the four compounding periods. Then move right across this row to locate the future value factor of 1.2155. Move up the column to the interest rate, 5 percent. Remember to multiply the 5 percent semiannual rate by 2 compounding periods per year to determine the annual interest rate of 10 percent.

We follow similar procedures if the number of compounding periods (n) is unknown. For example, assume that $1,000 is invested today at 10 percent interest compounded semiannually. How long will it take for this investment to result in $1,215.50? To answer this question, we determine the present value of the amount of $1 as illustrated below.

Future value	×	$p_{n,5\%}$	=	Present value
$1,215.50	×	$p_{n,5\%}$	=	$1,000
		$p_{n,5\%}$	=	$1,000/$1,215.50
		$p_{n,5\%}$	=	0.8227

After we determine the table value, we use a similar three-step approach to determine the number of compounding periods:

1. Using the present value of $1 table (Table 2), locate the 5 percent interest rate (10%/2 compoundings) at the top of the table.

2. Moving down the 5 percent column, locate the present value factor of 0.8227.

3. At the 0.8227 present value factor, move to the left to find the number of compounding periods, four.

We have arrived at the number of compounding periods, but not the length of time of the investment period. To determine the time period in years, divide n, the number of compoundings in the life of the investment, by c, the number of compoundings in one year. In this case, there are four semiannual compounding periods, so it would take two years ($n/c = 4/2 = 2$ years) to achieve this goal. Similarly, this problem can be solved using the future value of $1 as illustrated previously.

ANNUITIES

LO 6

An **annuity** is a series of equal cash payments made at equal intervals. Car or house payments are examples of annuities.

Understanding the future or present value of annuities is very helpful in making financing and investment decisions. For example, suppose a consultant completed a project for a client and sent a bill for $15,000. The client offers to pay the bill by making payments of $5,000 a year for the next three years. Because the consultant understands the time value of money, she rejects this offer. However, if she extends this client credit, how does the consultant determine the amount of the yearly payments that would be the equivalent of $15,000 cash today? We will examine the future and present values of annuities in order to answer this type of question.

Future Value of an Annuity

The **future value of an annuity** is the amount of money that accumulates at some future date as a result of making equal payments over equal intervals of time and earning a specified interest rate over that time period. The amount of money that accumulates is a function of (1) the size of the payments, (2) the frequency of the payments, and (3) the interest rate used over the life of the annuity. Businesses and individuals use the future value of annuities to determine the amount to save on a regular basis to buy new assets or retire debt at some future date.

EXHIBIT 14.6

Future Value of an
Ordinary Annuity

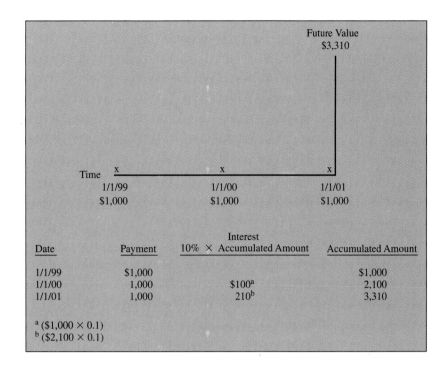

Date	Payment	Interest 10% × Accumulated Amount	Accumulated Amount
1/1/99	$1,000		$1,000
1/1/00	1,000	$100[a]	2,100
1/1/01	1,000	210[b]	3,310

[a] ($1,000 × 0.1)
[b] ($2,100 × 0.1)

Exhibit 14.6 illustrates the future value of an annuity. Notice that the three $1,000 payments plus the compound interest accumulate to a future value of $3,310. An annuity assumes that the final payment is made on the future value date; consequently, *there is one less interest period than the number of payments.*

$A_{n,i}$ is the symbol for the future value of an annuity, and the annuity factor represents the future value of a $1 annuity, given some annual interest rate and a specified number of payments.[4] The values in Appendix Table 3 are the factors produced by the formula for the future value of an annuity. The left side represents the total number of annuity payments (n). The interest rates across the top represent the interest rates earned during the time period between each annuity payment. This interest rate (i) is determined by dividing the annual interest rate (r) by the number of compoundings during the year (c), that is, $i = r/c$. *The formula assumes that interest is compounded every time a payment is made; therefore, the number of compoundings in a year is equal to the number of payments made in one year.* The intersection of the row and column represents the factor produced by the formula for the future value of an annuity.

To illustrate, let's find the future value of a three-payment, $1,000, annual annuity that earns 10 percent interest. First, it is necessary to find the appropriate factor by locating the number of payments ($n = 3$) on the left side of Appendix Table 3 and the interest rate ($i = r/c = 10\%/1$) at the top of the column. At the intersection of the appropriate row (3) and column (10%) is the factor 3.3100. The 3.3100 factor represents the amount that three annual payments of $1 would accumulate to when the third payment is made. Thus

---

[4]Future value of an annuity, or, in notation, $A_{n,i}$:

$$A_{n,i} = \frac{(\$1 + r/c)^n - \$1}{r/c}$$

Where

    r = Annual rate of interest

    c = Number of compoundings in one year

    n = Number of payments

    i = Interest rate for annuity period (r/c)

solving for the unknown in the equation below gives the future value of a three-payment, $1,000, annual annuity.

Annuity	×	$A_{3,10\%}$	=	Future value
$1,000	×	3.310	=	Future value
		$3,310	=	Future value

Performing this calculation results in the same solution as the year-by-year calculations of the future value used in Exhibit 14.6, but it is much faster.

Present Value of an Annuity

The **present value of an annuity** is the amount of money that, if invested at some interest rate today, will generate a set number of equal periodic payments that are made over equal time intervals. Exhibit 14.7 shows the cash flows and interest of the present value of an annuity.

Note that the first $1,000 payment occurs one period after the present value date and that the number of payments (three) equals the number of interest periods (three). If the present value of $2,486.90 earns 10 percent interest compounded annually, then the present value amount can generate three $1,000 payments. Each $1,000 payment consists of 10 percent interest earned on the present value amount at the beginning of the period and the return of a portion of the present value (principal). Every payment reduces the present value amount until the last payment brings the present value balance to zero.

The data presented in Exhibit 14.7 describe a personal application of the present value of an annuity. Suppose that after graduating you want to borrow some money to furnish your new apartment. After setting up a budget, you conclude that you can afford annual payments of $1,000 for the next three years. If the interest rate available for the loan is 10 percent, the maximum amount you can borrow is $2,486.90, which you will repay in three annual payments of $1,000. Each payment you make pays the interest on the loan and part of the loan's principal (see Exhibit 14.7).

Your first payment of $1,000 covers the 10 percent interest of $248.69 incurred on the $2,486.90 borrowed at the start of the previous year. The remaining $751.31 reduces the

EXHIBIT   14.7

Present Value of an Ordinary Annuity

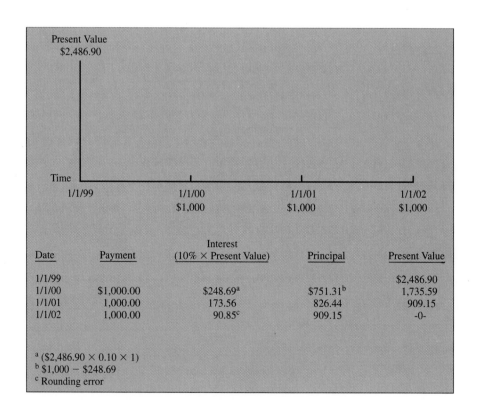

Date	Payment	Interest (10% × Present Value)	Principal	Present Value
1/1/99				$2,486.90
1/1/00	$1,000.00	$248.69[a]	$751.31[b]	1,735.59
1/1/01	1,000.00	173.56	826.44	909.15
1/1/02	1,000.00	90.85[c]	909.15	-0-

[a] ($2,486.90 × 0.10 × 1)
[b] $1,000 − $248.69
[c] Rounding error

principal of the loan. The amount due after the first payment is $1,735.59. Each subsequent $1,000 payment follows the same pattern until the loan is repaid on January 1, 2001.

The formula for the present value of an annuity, like the future value of an annuity, uses a $1 annuity and a specified interest rate to calculate a present value factor for an annuity, $P_{n,i}$.[5] The values in Appendix Table 4 at the end of the book are the factors generated by the formula. As in Appendix Table 3, the left side of Table 4 represents the total number of payments (n), while the interest rates at the top of the columns are the rates earned during each annuity period (i). Like the future value of an annuity, we assume that the interest is compounded every time a payment occurs. Therefore, the interest rate for the period (i) is determined by dividing the annual interest rate (r) by the number of payments during one year (c), or $i = r/c$.

Using Table 4 to determine the annuity factor in the example described in Exhibit 14.7, locate the intersection of the $n = 3$ row (the number of payments) and the $i = 10$ percent interest column ($i = r/c = 10\%/1$). Using the equation presented below and the factor from Table 4, it is possible to calculate the present value of the $1,000, three-payment, annual annuity.

Annuity	×	$P_{3,10\%}$	=	Present value
$1,000	×	2.4869	=	Present value
		$2,486.90	=	Present value

The $2,486.90 is the cash equivalent today of three $1,000 payments made one year apart, starting one year from today and assuming a 10 percent interest rate.

Annuities and Compound Interest

The annuity problems illustrated to this point assumed that the number of payments per year corresponds to the number of times the interest is compounded. However, in order to determine the appropriate interest rate to use to calculate annuities, it is necessary to divide the annual interest rate (r) by the number of payments during one year (c). To illustrate an annuity with more than one compounding in a year, let's use the future value of an annuity problem we discussed earlier.

Suppose that instead of investing $1,000 in each of the next three years, you decide to invest $500 every six months. Find the future value of an annuity factor for a six-payment, 10 percent annuity in Table 3. The factor is located at the intersection of the $n = 6$ row and the 5 percent column (10%/2). See the solution to this annuity problem in Exhibit 14.8. Note that the process for determining the future value of this semiannual annuity is the same as that for determining an annual annuity, except the payments are more frequent and the interest compounds with each payment.

Solving Annuity Problems

Annuity problems may seem rather straightforward at this point, but they can become confusing rather quickly. Take, for instance, the problem presented at the start of the annuity section about payment of $15,000 of consulting fees over three years. It is clear that the consultant, in this case, should reject the first offer of three annual payments of $5,000 in lieu of the $15,000 fee. However, how is it possible to determine the amount of three future payments that would be acceptable in lieu of $15,000 today?

We will look at a four-step process for solving such annuity problems and then apply this process to a variety of business situations.

---

[5]Present value of an annuity, or, in notation, $P_{n,i}$:

$$P_{n,i} = \frac{\$1 - \$1/(\$1 + r/c)^n}{r/c}$$

Where

r = Annual rate of interest

c = Number of compoundings in one year

n = Number of payments

i = Interest rate for annuity period (r/c)

EXHIBIT 14.8 Future Value of Three-Year, Semiannual, $500 Ordinary Annuity

Annuity	×	$A_{6,5\%}$	= Future Value
$500	×	6.8019	= Future Value
		$3,400.95	= Future Value

Interest Date	Payment	Interest (10% × Accumulated Amount)	Accumulated Amount
1/1/99	$500.00		$ 500.00
7/1/99	500.00	$ 25.00[a]	1,025.00
1/1/00	500.00	51.25	1,576.25
7/1/00	500.00	78.81	2,155.06
1/1/01	500.00	107.75	2,762.81
7/1/01	500.00	138.14	3,400.95

*($500 × 0.05) = $25

Step 1. Determine Whether the Problem Is an Annuity Does the problem involve payments of the same amount made over equal periods of time using a constant interest rate? If the answer is yes, it is an annuity problem. In this case, you want to know the size of the three equal payments made one year apart. Also, one interest rate is assumed, although it is not stated at this point, so it is an annuity problem. If it is not an annuity problem, it is either a future or present value of the amount of $1 problem like those discussed earlier.

Step 2. Determine Whether the Annuity Is Present or Future Value Deciding whether the problem involves the future or present value of an annuity is essential, but often difficult. For example, you might conclude that, because the unknown annuity payments occur in the future, this is a future value problem. However, the problem of determining the size of the payments for the $15,000 fee is a present value problem, as we demonstrate in Exhibit 14.9.

Determining whether we are dealing with the future or present value of an annuity depends on the relationship of the annuity payments to the *lump sum*. Every annuity, whether present or future value, has a large sum of money or an asset with a specified monetary value as one of its features. With the future value of an annuity, the lump sum or future value occurs after the annuity payments are made. However, in the case of the present value of an annuity, the lump sum or present value precedes the annuity payments.

EXHIBIT 14.9

Lump Sums and Payment Periods

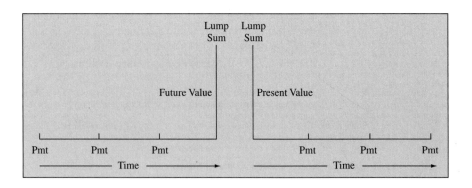

Exhibit 14.9 illustrates the relationship between the timing of the annuity payments and the lump sums for both future and present value problems. By identifying the relationship of the timing of the annuity payments to the annuity's lump sum, we can determine the type of annuity. The $15,000 service fee charged is the lump sum, and the payments come after the lump sum; therefore, this is a present value of an annuity problem.

Step 3. Identify the Missing Annuity Element All annuities involve four fundamental elements: (1) a specified number of payments, n; (2) equal cash payments; (3) an interest rate for each annuity period, i (r/c); and (4) a lump sum of money (either a present or future value). If three of the four elements are known, it is possible to determine the remaining element.

In the case of the $15,000 fee, only two of the four elements are known—the present value ($15,000) and the number of payments (3). To find the amount of the annuity, an interest rate, i, is necessary. Assume that the consultant wants a 9 percent return on her money.

Step 4. Solve for the Missing Element At this point, it is necessary to calculate the value of the missing element. If, in Step 2, we determined that the annuity is a future value of an annuity, then we use Equation (14.1) below and Appendix Table 3 to solve the problem. On the other hand, if the annuity is a present value of an annuity, then we use Equation (14.2) below and Appendix Table 4.

$$\text{Annuity} \times A_{n,i} = \text{Future value of annuity} \qquad (14.1)$$
$$\text{Annuity} \times P_{n,i} = \text{Present value of annuity} \qquad (14.2)$$

The answer is now at hand—the interest rate is 9 percent, the number of payments is 3, and the amount of the present value is $15,000. Because this is a present value of an annuity problem, the amount of the annuity is found by using Equation (14.2):

$$\text{Annuity} \times P_{3,9\%} = \text{Present value of annuity}$$
$$\text{Annuity} \times 2.5313 = \$15,000$$
$$\text{Annuity} = \$\ 5,925.81$$

This analysis indicates that the consultant would accept three, $5,925.81 annual payments because they are the equivalent of $15,000 today, assuming a 9 percent interest rate. Another way to think of this is that the consultant is lending her client the value of her service for three years. If the client makes three $5,925.81 payments, this will ensure the recovery of the $15,000 fee and also generate a 9 percent rate of return on the "loan."

Time Value Flowchart The flowchart in Exhibit 14.10 summarizes the process of solving both amount of $1 problems and annuity problems. The first decision is to determine whether the problem is an amount of $1 problem or an annuity problem. If the problem is an annuity, the flowchart describes the same steps just discussed. However, if the problem is an amount of $1 problem, the first step is to determine whether we want to use the present or future value of the amount of $1. For example, suppose we wanted to know how much we had to invest today in order to have $10,000 in five years if we could earn 8 percent interest compounded semiannually. This is not an annuity problem; the flowchart identifies the problem as a present value problem because we need to know an amount today. We solve the problem by using the present value formula:

$$\text{Future value} \times p_{10,4\%} = \text{Present value}$$
$$\$5,000 \times 0.6756 = \text{Present value}$$
$$\$3,378 = \text{Present value}$$

Of Interest

Using Excel and Financial Calculators to Solve Time Value of Money Problems

Using Financial Calculators

There are a variety of financial calculators on the market today. Two of the most popular and affordable models are the Hewlett-Packard 10B and the Texas Instruments BA-35. We discuss the functions of each of these calculators below.

Hewlett Packard 10B uses the following inputs:

P/YR   Number of periods per year **(c)**

N   Total number of payments **(n)**

I/YR   Annual interest rate entered as a whole number **(r)**

PV   Present value

FV   Future value

PMT   Amount of each periodic payment

Texas Instruments BA-35 uses the following inputs:

N   Total number of payments **(n)**

%i   Interest rate per period entered as a whole number **(r/c)**

PMT   Amount of each periodic payment

PV   Present value

FV   Future value

CPT   Compute answer

Let's solve the following problems using these two calculators. If you invest $100 every month for 10 years and earn 12 percent annually, how much money will you have in 10 years?

Hewlett Packard 10B		Texas Instruments BA-35	
Enter	**Key**	**Enter**	**Key**
12	P/YR	12x10=	N
12x10	N	12/12=	%i
12	I/YR	0	PV
		100	PMT
0	PV	CPT	FV
100	PMT		
	FV		

Returns:	Returns:
-23,003.869 (negative since cash outflows)	23,003.869

EXHIBIT   14.10   Time Value of Money Flowchart

Is this an annuity problem?
(Equal payments at equal time intervals at a constant rate of interest)

— No ——————— Yes —

Is the amount unknown in the future or today?

Future ——————— Today

$PV \times a_{ni} = FV?$ $FV \times p_{ni} = PV?$

Where:

FV = Future value amount
a_{ni} = Future value of amount of $1 for n compounding periods at i interest rate
$i = (r/c)$
r = Annual interest rate
c = Number of compoundings in one year
PV = Present value amount

PV = Present value amount
p_{ni} = Present value of amount of $1 for n compounding periods at i interest rate
$i = (r/c)$
r = Annual interest rate
c = Number of compoundings in one year
FV = Future value amount

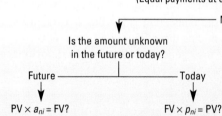

Are the payments before or after the lump sum amount?

Before ——————— After

Future Value
$A \times A_{ni} = FV$

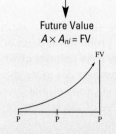

A = Annuity amount
A_{ni} = Future value of annuity factor
Where:
n = Number of payments
i = Interest rate for each annuity period
FV = Future value amount
Must know three of following four to solve: $A, n, i,$ and FV

Present Value
$A \times P_{ni} = PV$

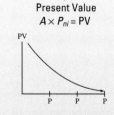

A = Annuity amount
P_{ni} = Present value of annuity factor
Where:
n = Number of payments
i = Interest rate for each annuity period
PV = Present value amount
Must know three of following four to solve: $A, n, i,$ and PV

You want to buy a car for $25,000. The dealer will get you financing at 10 percent annually for 5 years. What is your monthly payment?

Hewlett Packard 10B

Enter	Key
12	P/YR
12x5	N
10	I/YR
25,000	PV
0	FV
	PMT

Returns:
−531.176 (negative since cash outflows)

Texas Instruments BA-35

Enter	Key
12x5=	N
10/12=	%i
25,000	PV
0	FV
CPT	PMT

Returns:
531.176

Using Excel

Excel and other spreadsheet programs can be used to solve present and future value problems quickly and easily if you understand a few basic commands. For Excel you need three main functions: future value, present value, and payment. Excel uses the following inputs:

Rate   Interest rate per period entered as a decimal **(r/c)**

Nper   Total number of periods **(n)**

Pmt   Amount of each periodic payment

PV   Present value

FV   Future value

Type   Omit for our purposes

Let's solve the same problems described above using Excel. Save $100 per month for 10 years at 12 percent interest:

Go to: Insert/Function/Financial/FV/Okay

Line	Enter
Rate	.12/12
Nper	12*12
Pmt	100
PV	0
	Okay

Returns: −23,003.87 (Negative due to cash outflow)

Buy $25,000 car by making monthly payments for 5 years at 10 percent interest:

Line	Enter
Rate	.10/12
Nper	12/5
PV	25,000
FV	0
	Okay

Returns: −531.176 (Negative due to cash outflow)

BUSINESS APPLICATIONS OF THE TIME VALUE OF MONEY

It is important to be able to apply the time value of money to business in a variety of ways. Using the time value of money is an important tool that captures the economic substance of business events so that information provided to decision makers does not mislead them. The following examples illustrate how accountants use the time value of money to facilitate business decisions.

Asset Valuation

Suppose that Paine Webber purchases a plot of land on July 1, 1999, for a new office in Santa Monica, California. It agrees to pay for the land with four semiannual payments of $100,000 each beginning January 1, 2000. If Paine Webber typically borrows money at a 12 percent annual rate, what is the cost of the land?

Some people might argue that the cost of the land is $400,000, or the sum of the four $100,000 payments. However, this clearly disregards the time value of money and overstates the cost of the land. Given the facts of the problem and following the flowchart, we can determine the land's cost.

Step 1: Is the problem an annuity? Yes, because there are four equal payments over four semiannual periods.

Step 2: Is the annuity a present or future value? The cost of acquiring the land today is the lump sum in this case. Because the payments occur *after* the acquisition date, it is a present value problem.

Step 3: What is the missing annuity element? There are four payments (n=4). The interest rate is 6 percent (i=6%) because the semiannual payments create semiannual compounding (r/c, or 12%/2). The annuity payments are $100,000 each; therefore, the missing element is the present value.

Step 4: Solve for the missing element.

Annuity	×	$P_{4,6\%}$	=	Present value
$100,000	×	3.4651	=	Present value
		$346,510	=	Present value

Therefore, the actual cost of the land is $346,510. The difference between this amount and the sum of the payments ($400,000) is the amount of interest paid on the loan over the life of the loan ($400,000 – $346,510 = $53,490).

What is the effect on the cost of the land if the annual interest rate were 8 percent instead of 12 percent? Table 4 shows that the value for $P_{4,4\%}$ is 3.6299. Therefore, the cost of the land would increase to $362,990 if the interest rate were 8 percent rather than 12 percent. Note that the lower the interest rate, the higher the cost of the asset because *a lower interest rate causes present values to increase.*

Financial Planning

An understanding of the time value of money helps individuals or businesses meet financial goals. Suppose that you approached a Paine Webber representative about establishing a retirement plan that would generate $1 million when you retire at age 65. You want to make 40 yearly payments into the retirement plan starting on your 26th birthday. The Paine Webber representative believes that her retirement account can earn a 10 percent rate of return on your investment. How much do you have to pay each year to achieve this goal? We will use the flowchart to solve this problem.

Step 1. This is an annuity because the payments are the same size and are made yearly.

Step 2. This is a future value of an annuity problem because the lump sum, $1 million, occurs after the annuity payments.

Step 3. The future value is $1 million, the interest rate is 10 percent, and there are 40 payments. The amount of the annuity is the missing element.

Step 4.

Annuity	×	$A_{40,10\%}$	=	Future value
Annuity	×	442.5926	=	$1,000,000
		Annuity	=	$2,259.41

Based on the available information, if you make 40 payments of $2,259.41 starting on your 26th birthday and the retirement fund earns 10 percent interest, you will have $1 million when you retire at age 65.

Early and systematic savings can create a financially secure retirement.

PAUSE & REFLECT

Many lotteries advertise that you can win $20 million when in fact you win $1 million a year for 20 years. Given your new knowledge of the time value of money, what is the cash equivalent today of the $20 million prize if the going interest rate is 8 percent? *(answer on page 508)*

The management cycle reflects the interrelationship of a firm's planning, performing, and evaluating activities. Planning the firm's operating, investing, and financing activities and then executing these plans are based on the belief that the firm will generate a return *of* and a satisfactory return *on* the investments made by the creditors and owners of the firm.

Risk is impounded in the expected return of an investment. Investments are exposed to three types of risk: inflation risk, business risk, and liquidity risk. Each type of risk is factored into the risk assessment of any investment. Management must consider the relationship of return and risk, both when trying to invest funds at its disposal and when trying to acquire funds from owners and creditors.

Considering the time value of money is essential for long-term investing and financing decisions. The future value of a dollar is the amount that a dollar will become if invested today for a specific period of time at a specific rate of interest. The present value of a dollar is the amount today that is equivalent to a dollar at some specified future time when invested at a specified rate of interest. Present and future values also can be calculated for annuities.

- The rate of return is a common-size measure of the return on an investment and presumes the return of and a return on the investment. The expected rate of return of an investment is a summary measure of possible rates of return the investment might generate that investors use to evaluate alternative investments.

- The risk of an investment is the chance it will result in an unfavorable outcome. The relative risk ratio is a common-size measure used to evaluate the risk of prospective investments.

- A person's willingness to make risky investments depends on whether he or she is a risk seeker or a risk avoider. Risk avoiders want an additional return called a risk premium for accepting any additional risk.

- A firm's management invests the firm's resources in an attempt to maximize the return of the firm at a level of risk that is acceptable to the firm's owners. However, when borrowing funds, management tries to minimize the risk of the firm in order to lower the cost of using borrowed funds.

- The time value of money is a tool that uses compound interest to determine the cash equivalents for single or multiple cash flows that occur at different points in time.

KEY TERMS

annuity A series of equal cash payments made at equal intervals

business risk The risk associated with the ability of a particular company to continue in business

compound interest Interest that is based on a principal amount that includes interest from previous time periods

compounding The process of adding interest to principal for purposes of interest calculation

expected rate of return A summary measure of an investment's performance, stated as a percentage, based on the possible rates of return and on the likelihood of those rates of return occurring

expected return A summary measure of an investment's performance stated in dollars that is based on the dollar amount of the possible returns on investment and the probability of those returns occurring

future value The combination of principal and the interest on the principal at some specified date in the future

future value of an annuity The amount of money that accumulates at some future date as a result of making equal payments over equal intervals of time and earning a specified rate of interest over that time period

future value of the amount of $1 The amount that $1 becomes at a future date, if invested at a specified annual interest rate and compounded a certain number of times per year over the investment period

inflation risk The chance of a decline in the purchasing power of the monetary units during the time money is invested

liquidity risk The chance that an investment cannot be readily converted to cash

present value The cash equivalent today of some specified amount of cash at a specified date in the future

present value of an annuity The amount of money that, if invested at some rate of interest today, will generate a set number of equal periodic payments that are made over equal time intervals

present value of the amount of $1 The amount that, if invested today at some compound interest rate for a specified period of time, will equal $1 at the end of that time period

rate of return A percentage measurement of the performance of investments on a common-size basis

relative risk ratio A common-size measure of an investment's risk based on the percentage of expected return lost if the worst-case outcome occurs

return of investment The return of the amount initially invested

return on investment The money received in excess of the initial investment

risk-adjusted expected rate of return An expected rate of return including the risk premium

risk-free rate of return The rate of return that a virtually riskless investment produces

risk premium An increase in the rate of return expected by an investor for assuming greater investment risk

simple interest Interest calculated only on the amount borrowed

time value of money A tool used to solve problems involving the comparison of cash flows that occur at different points in time

ANSWERS TO THE PAUSE & REFLECTS

p. 491, Risk-seeking investors would be willing to pay $100,000 for Investment B only if it was the only investment and all other investors were also risk-seekers. However, because the market consists of numerous investment alternatives and investors with a variety of risk preferences, risk-seekers would not be willing to pay $100,000 when they could find an investment with similar risk that would compensate them for the risk associated with the cash flows. Therefore, risk-seekers would demand the risk they are taking be impounded in the price of the investment ($63,636).

p. 492, Short-term interest rates became lower than long-term interest rate because lenders considered long-term lending riskier than short-term lending. Long-term loans were considered riskier because inflation during this time period was very volatile and the inflation rate at some time during the life of a long-term loan might exceed the interest earned on the loan. Therefore, to compensate for inflation risk the interest rate for long-term loans was increased. Short-term loans had less risk then long-term loans because if inflation increased the loan would come due in a short period of time and the money could be loaned again but at a higher rate.

p. 506, Assuming that the lottery pay $1,000,000 per year every year for 20 years starting today the present value of the lottery would be $1,000,000 plus the present value of nineteen $1,000,000 payments in the future or:

$$
\begin{array}{ccccc}
A & \times & P_{19,8\%} & = & PV \\
\$1,000,000 & \times & 9.6036 & = & PV \\
& & \$9,603,600 & = & PV
\end{array}
$$

Therefore $10,603,600 ($1,000,000 + $9,603,600) is the value today winning a $20 million lottery if the interest rate is 8 percent.

QUESTIONS

1. What is the sequence in the planning phase of the management cycle and how does it differ from the sequence in the performance phase?

2. What are a business's three sources of funds?

3. What is the distinction between return *of* investment and return *on* investment?

4. How does *rate* of return on an investment differ from return on investment? What are the advantages of using a rate of return on investment when choosing among alternative investments?

5. Explain in your own words the concept of annualized rate of return.

6. Under what conditions does a negative rate of return occur?

7. Define *risk*. How does a person's attitude toward risk affect his or her decision-making process?

8. Contrast expected rate of return on an investment with the actual rate of return on investment.

9. What is the purpose of the relative risk ratio?

10. Describe the relationship between risk and return and give an example of the relationship.

11. What is a risk premium? Describe the three factors that generate risk premiums and give an example of each.

12. How is the price of an investment related to its risk-adjusted rate of return?

13. Contrast the perspective of return and risk of a firm borrowing funds with that of a firm lending funds.

14. Explain what is meant by the time value of money.

15. How does simple interest differ from compound interest?

16. Describe the four elements of the future value of the amount of $1.

17. How does the future value of an amount of $1 differ from the present value of an amount of $1? How are they similar?

18. What are the characteristics of an annuity?

19. What is the difference between the future value and present value of an annuity?

20. Describe the four-step process for solving annuity problems.

End-of-chapter activities that require a financial calculator have an asterisk (*) after the number.

EXERCISES

E 14.1
LO 2

Each of the three investments below cost $400,000. Calculate the expected rate of return on these investments. Each outcome described below will occur at the end of one year.

	Possible Outcome	Probability
Investment A	$40,000	0.3
	30,000	0.4
	20,000	0.3
Investment B	$50,000	0.1
	35,000	0.4
	25,000	0.3
	20,000	0.2
Investment C	$60,000	0.4
	40,000	0.3
	10,000	0.3

E 14.2
LO 3

Calculate the relative risk ratio for each of the investments in E14.1. Which of the investments would you prefer? Why?

E 14.3
LO 3

Valarie Boyde wants a risk-adjusted expected rate of return of 15 percent on her investments. What price would Valarie be willing to pay for investment P if she predicts the following outcomes and probabilities of those outcomes occurring one year from today?

	Possible Outcome	Probability
Investment P	$15,500	0.5
	21,200	0.2
	13,500	0.3

E 14.4
LO 4   LO 5

How much will an investment of $8,000 be worth at the end of five years if it earns:
a. 10 percent simple interest?
b. 10 percent interest compounded annually?
c. 10 percent interest compounded semiannually?
d. 10 percent interest compounded quarterly?

E 14.5
LO 5

What is the present value of $8,000 five years from today if interest is:
a. 10 percent compounded annually?
b. 10 percent compounded semiannually?
c. 10 percent compounded quarterly?

E 14.6
LO 5

What will be the maturity value of $20,000 deposited in a three-year certificate of deposit that earns 8 percent interest compounded semiannually?

E 14.7
LO 5

Heather Ross just graduated with a Masters of Accountancy degree and has accepted a staff accounting position with a firm and will receive a salary of $42,000. The firm guarantees that Heather will receive a 5 to 9 percent raise each year for the next five years depending on her performance. What will Heather's salary be in five years if she gets a 5 percent raise each year? What would her salary be in five years if the annual raise is 9 percent?

E 14.8*
LO 5

Lori Rock is 30 years old today and wants to return to school by the time she is 35 to pursue her Ph.D. in taxation. She wants to have $28,000 set aside by the time she is 35 to help defray the cost of the program. How much must she invest today, her 30th birthday, to achieve her goal if she can generate a 9 percent return compounded quarterly on the invested funds?

E 14.9
LO 5

Shirley and Max Logston are going to put $3,000 in a savings account that pays 8 percent interest that is compounded semiannually to fund their new daughter's college education. How much will be in the education fund 18 years from today when their daughter starts college?

E 14.10
LO 5

If $7,500 was invested five years ago and has accumulated to $11,019.75, what rate of interest was earned if the interest was compounded annually?

E 14.11
LO 5

If $60,000 was invested at 8 percent and has grown to $85,692, how many years has the money been invested if interest was compounded quarterly?

E 14.12
LO 5

Answer each of the following independent questions:
a. If $30,000 is invested today at 6 percent compounded quarterly, how long will it take to accumulate $40,407?
b. If $8,000 is invested today and will accumulate to $30,957.60 in 10 years, what annual interest rate compounded semiannually will generate this amount?

E 14.13
LO 5

How long will it take to double an investment of $4,300 if the investment can generate an 8 percent return that is compounded semiannually?

E 14.14
LO 6

Determine the future value of the following annuities, assume each annuity can earn 10 percent interest and the first payment is made on January 1, 1999:
a. Six annual payments of $15,000 each
b. 12 semiannual payments of $7,500 each
c. 24 quarterly payments of $3,750 each

E 14.15
LO 6

Determine the present value of the following annuities as of today, January 1, 1999, if the annuity earns an 8 percent interest rate:
a. Five annual payments of $10,000 starting January 1, 2000
b. 20 quarterly payments of $2,500 starting April 1, 1999
c. 10 semiannual payments of $5,000 starting July 1, 1999

E 14.16
LO 6

The Dukas Diner has just purchased a new convection oven for $45,000. Dukas paid $7,000 down and is going to borrow the remaining $38,000. The Manhattan National Bank will loan money at 10 percent interest.
a. What will the payments be if the payments are made quarterly over the next three years?
b. What will the payments be if the payments are made semiannually over the next three years?
c. What will the payments be if the payments are made annually over the next three years?
d. Set up an annuity table for your solution (c) to prove it.

E 14.17
LO 6

Roger Hatfield is going to make three annual payments of $3,500 each into a savings account starting today, March 1, 2000.
a. How much will Roger have in his savings account on March 1, 2002, if he can get 9 percent interest?
b. Set up an annuity table to prove your answer.

E 14.18
LO 6

The BRHC Corporation has just borrowed $30,000 to purchase lodge furniture for its guest suites and is going to make 10 yearly payments of $5,309.55 beginning one year from today. What is the annual interest rate BRHC Corporation is paying?

E 14.19
LO 6

Pappy Khouri is going to make semiannual payments of $8,592.54 until he has accumulated $200,000. If he can earn 12 percent interest on his investment, how long will it take him to accumulate $200,000?

E 14.20*
LO 6

Trego County wants to raise $4,000,000 to finance the construction of a new high school. The school board wants to make semiannual payments to repay the loan over the next 15 years. What will be the amount of the payments assuming the interest rates presented below?
a. 10 percent
b. 9 percent
c. 8 percent

PROBLEMS

P 14.1
LO 2 LO 3

Two investment alternatives are described below.

Investment A: $300,000		Investment B: $320,000	
Probability	Return	Probability	Return
0.2	$25,000	0.3	$(10,000)
0.3	28,000	0.3	30,000
0.3	32,000	0.2	70,000
0.2	35,000	0.2	110,000

Required
a. Which investment has the greatest expected rate of return?
b. Calculate the relative risk ratio for each investment.
c. Which investment would you choose?
d. What is the basis of your choice?
e. Is there any circumstance that would change your choice?

P 14.2
LO 2 LO 3

An investment analysis has determined the returns and the probabilities of the return for investments A and B shown below.

Investment A		Investment B	
Probability	Return	Probability	Return
0.3	$15,000	0.2	$10,000
0.4	20,000	0.3	30,000
0.2	40,000	0.3	25,000
0.1	(10,000)	0.2	20,000

Required
a. Determine the price of investment A if its expected rate of return is 12 percent.
b. Determine the price of investment B if its expected rate of return is 8 percent.
c. Given the prices determined for the investments, calculate the relative risk ratio for each investment.
d. Explain the relationship between expected return and price.

P 14.3
LO 4 LO 5

Santa Fe Corporation just sold inventory with a cost of $180,000. In exchange for the inventory, Santa Fe received $20,000 cash and a note promising to pay $300,000 in five years (there is no interest rate specified on the note).

Required
a. How much did Santa Fe make on this sale if it usually loans money at 10 percent interest compounded annually?
b. How much did Santa Fe make on this sale if it usually loans money at 12 percent interest compounded annually?
c. How much did Santa Fe make on this sale if it usually loans money at 8 percent interest compounded annually?
d. Explain how the interest rate assumed on a note like this affects the income of the company.

P 14.4*
LO 4 LO 5

Zack Kohlrus just received $100,000 from winning the lottery. He has decided to spend $20,000 immediately and to invest the remaining $80,000 for five years.

Required
a. If he can get an 8 percent rate of return that is compounded quarterly, how much will he have at the end of five years?
b. If he can get a 10 percent rate of return that is compounded quarterly, how much will he have at the end of five years?
c. If he can get an 11 percent rate of return that is compounded quarterly, how much will he have at the end of five years?

P 14.5
LO 6

Richard Ott and Lanny Chastine are huge Elvis Presley fans and are planning to travel to Memphis to tour "Graceland" and enroll in an Elvis impersonation course while there. They are planning to make the pilgrimage in three years on June 1, 2002. They are each going to put $1,500 in a savings account every six months starting today, June 1, 1999. They can earn a 6 percent annual interest rate.

Required

a. If their last payment is three years from today, how much will each have for the trip?
b. If they can earn 8 percent annually, how will this affect the amount each of these fans will accumulate?

P 14.6*
LO 6

Lesley Givarz can afford $350 per month car payments for three years. The interest rate on car loans is 12 percent.

Required

a. How much can she spend for a car?
b. How much can she spend for a car if she could make payments of $350 per month for three years but the interest rate is 9 percent?
c. How would your answer to "a" change if Lesley could make a $2,200 down payment?
d. How would your answer to "b" change if Lesley could make a $2,200 down payment?

P 14.7
LO 6

Wayne Purinton has signed a contract to buy a tract of land for the Banner Road Hunt Club on March 1, 2000. The contract calls for Wayne to make three annual payments of $36,500 starting March 1, 2001, with a final payment of $45,000 on March 1, 2004. Wayne can borrow money at 9 percent interest.

Required

a. What price did Wayne pay for the land?
b. What is the price of the land if the interest rate is 7 percent?
c. Explain why the land's cost calculated in (a) and (b) above differs when the cash flows are the same.

P 14.8
LO 6

Steffens Company just acquired office furniture that had a list price of $400,000. The furniture store said that it would finance the entire price at 0 percent interest by letting the company make eight quarterly payments of $50,000 starting three months from the date of purchase.

Required

a. If Steffens Company can borrow money at 8 percent, what is the cost of the office furniture?
b. What is the cost of the office furniture if Steffens Company usually borrows money at 6 percent?
c. What is the cost of the office furniture if Steffens Company agrees to make four semiannual payments of $100,000 each if it usually borrows money at 8 percent?

P 14.9
LO 6

Randy Lemon, the CFO of Polara Corporation, has identified two buildings that are suitable for its new office. For building A, Polara will have to pay $245,000 a year for 10 years, while building B will cost $175,000 a year for 15 years. The interest rate on both loans is 9 percent.

Required

a. Which building is less expensive?
b. Which building is less expensive if building A has payments of $150,000 for 20 years and the interest rate is 9 percent?

P 14.10
LO 6

BDO Siedman has acquired a new computer system at a price of $240,000 and is considering two financing alternatives. If National Bank makes the loan, BDO Siedman will make 10 annual payments of $35,766.98 to repay the debt. If First State Bank makes the loan, the payments will be $24,110.91 every six months for the next six years.

Required

a. What is the interest rate charged by National Bank?
b. What is the interest rate charged by First State Bank?
c. What other factors should BDO Siedman take into consideration when deciding which bank to use?

P 14.11*
LO 6

Agnes Anderson, a CPA has just billed a customer $19,000 for services rendered. The customer wants to pay for this bill by making quarterly payments over the next three years.

Required

a. Determine the amount of the customer's quarterly payments if Agnes wants an 8 percent annual return on the loan.
b. Determine the amount of the customer's quarterly payments if Agnes wants a 9 percent annual return on the loan.

c. Assume Agnes wants an 8 percent return, but the customer wants to make semiannual payments over the next three years. Determine the amount of the payment that Agnes would find acceptable in this situation.

P 14.12
LO 6

Brooke Beyer wants to have $1,000,000 in his retirement account when he retires on his 60th birthday. He is 26 today and will make annual payments once he starts paying into the retirement fund.

Required

a. How much will Brooke have to pay annually to achieve his goal if he can get an 8 percent annual rate of interest and he starts payments at:
1. Age 26
2. Age 36
3. Age 46
b. How would your answer to "a" change if Brooke could get a 10% return?

P 14.13
LO 6

Brooke Beyer is confident he can achieve his goal of accumulating $1,000,000 by his 60th birthday as described in P 14.12. He wants to know how much cash the $1,000,000 will provide after he retires at age 60.

Required

a. How much cash will Brooke receive if he can earn 10 percent interest and if he wants to receive 30 semiannual payments starting six months after his 60th birthday?
b. How much cash will Brooke receive if he can earn 10 percent interest and if he wants to receive 20 annual payments starting at age 61?
c. How much cash will Brooke receive if he can earn 10 percent interest and if he wants to receive only interest on the $1,000,000 annually starting at age 61?
d. How much of Brooke's $1,000,000 will remain at the end of plans (*a*) and (*b*)?
e. How much of Brooke's $1,000,000 will remain after 20 years of plan (*c*)?

P 14.14
LO 6

Fred Neuman is 30 years old today and wants to retire at age 65. On his 65th birthday he wants to start receiving $85,000 a year for 30 years. Fred will start making payments today and will make his last payment on his 64th birthday.

Required

How much must he make in annual payments from age 30 to 64 to achieve his retirement goal if he can earn the following interest rates over the entire time period?
a. 7 percent
b. 9 percent

P 14.15
LO 6

Holly Elliott was given the assignment of finding suitable office space for her company. She found a great office in an upscale office park that requires a three-year lease. There are two options to pay for this lease. The first is to pay $160,000 on the first day of the lease, and the second is to make quarterly payments of $15,800 for three years starting three months from today. She must decide which of the two payment methods is the most economical for her company. Holly knows the firm usually borrows money at 12 percent interest.

Required

Which payment plan should Holly select? Why?

CASES
LO 1 **LO 4** **LO 6**

C 14.1

Banner Corporation, a small manufacturing firm, wants to establish a pension fund for its 10 employees who range from 28 to 51 years of age. Banner wants each employee who retires with the firm at age 65 to receive an annual pension on the retirement date that is 70 percent of the employee's annual wages at retirement. What factors must Banner Corporation take into consideration in order to determine how much the firm must contribute to the pension fund each year in order to meet the terms of its retirement plan?

C 14.2
LO 4 **LO 6**

Cole Eberle is trying to buy a new Dodge Quad Cab pickup and has been negotiating with two dealerships on identical trucks with sticker prices of $32,200. The first dealer is offering to finance the truck at 0 percent interest for the next 36 months, or $894.44 ($32,200/36 months) per month. The second dealer has offered to sell Cole the truck for $26,000 and Cole will finance the price with a bank loan over the next 36 months at a 12 percent annual rate of interest. How much will Cole pay the bank each month? Which of the two deals is better for Cole if 12 percent is the going truck loan interest rate? Why would Chrysler Corporation be willing to loan money at 0 percent interest? Under what circumstances would Cole choose to take the 0 percent interest over bank financing over a similar period?

CRITICAL THINKING

CT 14.1

LO 4 LO 5 LO 6

Chad Parker, your boss at Parker's Waterbed & Futons, has seen the "no interest" advertising of other furniture stores and wants to use this promotion to attract new customers. Currently, his cost to buy a futon is $200 and he is selling them for $550. He is also charging 18 percent interest for customers who buy on credit. Chad wants to offer 24 months' interest-free financing. What price must he charge if he wants to maintain his current profit margin and still make 18 percent interest?

CT 14.2

LO 4 LO 5 LO 6

On September 1, 1999, the Little Broadway Players signed a note to raise cash to buy a theater. The terms of the note call for seven annual payments of $5,000 and an interest rate of 9 percent. However, because the Players are just starting this enterprise, the bank has agreed to defer the first of the seven payments until September 1, 2002. How much cash will the bank loan the Little Broadway Players given the terms of this note?

ETHICAL CHALLENGES

EC 14.1

LO 4 LO 5 LO 6

Many furniture stores advertise that they will finance purchases made during a particular time period at 0 percent interest. Is this type of promotion deceptive and unethical? Justify your position.

EC 14.2

LO 3

Lincoln Savings and Loan of California, while under the direction of Charles Keating, sold investments to its customers, promised them very high rates of return, and assured them these were safe investments. When these investments failed, the investors lost their entire investment. Keating defended the sale of these investments saying he did not intend to harm anyone and that reasonable investors should have realized that investments with high rates of return are risky. What responsibility does a bank or savings and loan have to monitor the investment decisions of its customers?

COMPUTER APPLICATIONS

S

CA 14.1

LO 6

Organza Florist needs to buy a new delivery van. The automobile dealership has a van it will sell for $25,800. Organza has obtained bank financing for five years at 10 percent interest.

Required

Use a computer spreadsheet package.
a. What is the amount of each monthly payment?
b. Prepare a monthly payment schedule that indicates the amount of interest and principal paid each month over the term of the loan.

CA 14.2

LO 6

Zerfelt Company plans to buy a new computer in five years. It can save $100 each month toward the computer purchase.

Required

Use a financial calculator to calculate the following. Assume independent situations.
a. How much will Zerfelt have available at the end of five years if it can earn 6 percent?
b. How much will Zerfelt have available at the end of five years if it can earn 8 percent?
c. How much will Zerfelt have available at the end of five years if it can earn 6 percent and it increases its monthly payment to $150?
d. If Zerfelt delays its computer purchase for an additional two years, how much will Zerfelt have available at the end of seven years if it can earn 8 percent and invests $100 per month?

CA 14.3

LO 1

Go to Paine Webber's Internet address and do the following:
a. Write a brief description of Paine Webber and identify four of the firm's products and/or services.
b. Using the "News & Quotes" section, find the ticker symbol and current stock price for three companies of your choice.

PART FIVE

YOU ARE HERE

Chapter 15 investigates the steps involved in the capital budgeting process and how time value of money concepts and accounting information are used to make capital budgeting decisions. We explore how companies determine whether certain long-term projects should be accepted or rejected. The chapter focuses on the net present value method but other capital budgeting processes are considered.

The relevant variable analysis learned in Chapter 5 applies, but capital budgeting focuses on the determination of the present value of future cash flows. Therefore, Chapter 15 relies heavily on the concepts learned in Chapter 14. Once you understand how companies decide what to invest in, we will look at how they raise the capital needed to make the investments (Chapters 17 and 18).

LEARNING OBJECTIVES

LO 1 Describe the capital budgeting process.

LO 2 Explain and apply the net present value method of discounted cash flow analysis.

LO 3 Describe the time-adjusted rate of return method of discounted cash flow analysis.

LO 4 Explain the impact of taxes on the net present value method.

LO 5 Describe how judgment and uncertainty impact the capital budgeting process.

Planning for Investing Activities

The Goodyear Tire & Rubber Company was incorporated in 1898 in Ohio and today is one of the world's largest manufacturers of tires and rubber products. With its international headquarters located in Akron, Ohio, the company employs over 95,000 people worldwide. Goodyear's principal business is the development, manufacture, distribution, and sale of tires that range in size from golf cart tires to tires for giant earth-moving equipment. Goodyear promotes its passenger tire line with racing endorsements, with effective television advertising, and by covering sporting events with its fleet of Goodyear Blimps. Goodyear's latest product is a passenger tire that will run for 50 miles at 55 miles per hour after being punctured. The company expects that this technology will ultimately make spare tires obsolete. Goodyear also produces rubber-related chemicals, makes rubber products such as belts and hoses, runs retail outlets that sell a variety of automotive products and services, and even owns and operates an oil pipeline.

www.goodyear.com

Given the products it produces, it is not surprising that the largest item on Goodyear's December 31, 1997, balance sheet was its $4,149.7 million investment in properties and plants. Goodyear has an ongoing program to increase its

production capacity by building or acquiring new plants and improving the efficiency of existing plants by modernizing them. In its 1998 10K, Goodyear described expenditures made to acquire new facilities and modernize existing facilities and the expenditures it plans to make in the near future. For example, Goodyear purchased Consol Limited, a tire company in South Africa, and modernized plants in Freeport, Illinois; Valleyfield, Quebec; Napanee, Ontario; Fayetteville, North Carolina; Debica, Poland; and Beaumont, Texas. The company also said it was planning to build a new $60 million passenger tire manufacturing plant in Brazil.

Goodyear's plans to acquire these assets, which make up the firm's infrastructure, must be consistent with its long-term strategic objectives. Goodyear's management wants to make only those long-term investments that will increase the wealth of the corporation and its shareholders. The question for Goodyear and, in fact, for all companies is how to determine whether an investment in plant and equipment will generate a return sufficient to merit its acquisition.

THE CAPITAL BUDGETING PROCESS

LO 1

Capital budgeting is the process managers use for analysis and selection of the long-term investments of a business. Because the amounts spent on long-term investments, such as buildings, equipment, and even other businesses, are usually quite large and, therefore, affect the long-term profitability of the firm, they require systematic and careful consideration.

The capital budgeting process requires cooperative input from functional departments throughout the organization. For example, without the marketing department's forecast of demand for the firm's services or products in the operating stage of the planning phase, it would be difficult for a firm to assess its potential need for plant expansion. Without the production department's recommendations for the timely acquisition of machines to cut costs and improve product quality, it might be difficult to maintain efficiency. The finance department fulfills an important capital budgeting function by monitoring the cost and sources of funds needed to pay for selected projects. Finally, the accounting department collects, organizes, analyzes, and distributes the information necessary to facilitate capital budgeting decisions.

While the capital budgeting process itself is unique to each firm or enterprise, its four basic processes apply in all situations. Notice that the capital budgeting process is involved in the planning, performance, and evaluation phases of the management cycle:

1. Identifying long-term investment opportunities

2. Selecting appropriate investments

3. Financing the selected investments

4. Evaluating the investments

We address each of these in turn.

Identifying Long-Term Investment Opportunities

The capital budgeting process usually involves the acquisition of operational investments. These assets provide the infrastructure of the business enterprise—that is, the facilities and equipment necessary for a firm to conduct its basic business activities. For example, a new car dealership needs a showroom and a car lot in order to sell cars. Goodyear needs equipment to produce its tires and patents to protect the company from duplication of its products by other firms. Physicians need offices and medical equipment to provide quality healthcare services to their patients.

To identify investment opportunities, managers must recognize what is included in the cost of a firm's long-term investments. In addition, they must understand both their motives for making these investments and the organizational and other mechanisms that identify the need for operational investments.

What Expenditures Are Included in the Cost of a Firm's Long-Term Operational Investments? There are many expenditures that you might not normally think of as being part of an investment that are included in its cost. In addition to the purchase price of an asset, the related sales tax, freight charges, brokerage fees, and installation costs all become part of an investment's (asset's) cost when they are reasonable and necessary to get the asset ready for its intended use. For example, if Goodyear pays $200,000 for a scanner that detects flaws in tires, $500 for freight charges, and $10,000 for installation, the cost of the scanner would be $210,500 because all of these expenditures are reasonable and necessary to get the equipment ready for its intended use. Identifying this cost establishes the basis for determining whether future cash flows are generating both a return of and a return on investment.

Why Make the Investment?   There are three significant reasons that companies make capital investments. The first is the need to replace worn-out or unproductive operating assets, such as buildings, machinery, and equipment. The critical factor in deciding to replace assets is knowing what constitutes a worn-out or unproductive asset. This decision must come from operating personnel who are familiar with the capabilities of the old assets and their proposed replacements.

Another reason to make a capital expenditure is to expand the business's operating capacity. This decision is stimulated by increased demand for existing products and services or the demand for new products or services. Usually, the marketing department identifies these opportunities in the planning phase of the management cycle. Once the marketing department quantifies the production necessary to meet the increased demand, it informs the firm's production managers. The production managers use the marketing department's projections to determine the specifications of the asset(s) that can meet the increased demand.

Finally, capital expenditures are made to comply with mandates of the government. To comply with environmental or safety regulations, companies are often required to make capital expenditures that alter their normal operating activities. For example, power companies that use coal-fired generating plants are required to install costly scrubbers to reduce the pollutants emitted from their power plants that cause acid rain, smog, and other environmental hazards.

What Mechanisms Identify the Need for Capital Expenditures?   An organization's strategic planning document, which covers a 5- to 10-year time period, is one means of identifying long-term investment opportunities. Such documents reflect top management's vision of how the organization will grow and change during the period of the plan. Long-term plans identify and include the required capital expenditures associated with changes anticipated by management—for example, replacement of existing equipment or plant expansions.

Suppose Goodyear created a five-year plan in 1999 that called for the construction of a new manufacturing plant in 2004. The plan would outline management's assumptions about both the demand for Goodyear's tires and the profitability of the company for the specified period. While the goals in the five-year plan are subject to change as each year passes, the document helps management focus its efforts on the basic company goals. The planning document is rolled forward each year when management reassesses its long-term commitments in relation to the company's yearly performance.

Long-term planning documents are not the only means of identifying investment opportunities. Because businesses exist in a dynamic environment, management must be able to identify and evaluate business opportunities whenever they occur, even if they are unexpected. For example, suppose Goodyear becomes aware of a new type of tire mold that could reduce the number of defective tires by 20 percent. Goodyear would begin the capital budgeting process to determine if it should replace its existing tire molds, even though replacement might not have been planned until some time in the future.

Selecting Appropriate Investments

Once management identifies a potential capital expenditure, it evaluates the investment to assess whether it is capable of generating a satisfactory rate of return for the firm. Any return that is greater than or equal to the firm's cost of capital is considered a satisfactory return.

Cost of Capital   A firm's **cost of capital** is often calculated as the weighted-average cost of a firm's debt and equity financing. It represents the amount of return that the assets of the firm must generate in order to satisfy *both* creditors and owners. Recall that the cost of debt financing is the rate of interest the creditors receive for the use of their money, and the cost of equity financing is the rate of return the owners receive for the use of their money. Owners expect the firm to provide a return on their investment, and, if they are not satisfied, they can dispose of their holdings in the firm or vote to replace the management of the firm. Calculating the amount of return that owners expect is unique to each firm.

Calculating a firm's cost of capital is complicated, and the following example simplifies the process in order to illustrate the concept. Assume that Benchmark Corporation is financed by using $1,000,000 of debt and $3,000,000 of stockholders' equity. If the debt has an interest rate of 12 percent, and the stockholders demand a 16 percent rate of return, what is the cost of capital? Exhibit 15.1 shows that Benchmark's cost of capital is 15 percent. This amount is the weighted average of the returns demanded by the creditors and owners and represents the minimum rate of return that the firm's assets must generate to keep both creditors and stockholders satisfied.

EXHIBIT	15.1	Benchmark Corporation's Cost of Capital

Capital Structure

Assets	=	Liabilities	+	Stockholders' Equity
$4,000,000	=	$1,000,000	+	$3,000,000

Source of Financing	Amount Financed	Cost of Financing
Liabilities	$1,000,000	12%
Stockholders' equity	3,000,000	16
Total amount financed	$4,000,000	

$$\text{Ratio of debt to total financing} = \frac{\$1,000,000}{\$4,000,000} = 0.25$$

$$\text{Ratio of stockholders' equity (SE) to total financing} = \frac{\$3,000,000}{\$4,000,000} = 0.75$$

Cost of Capital (CC)

$$CC = (\text{Cost of debt})(\text{Debt ratio}) + (\text{Cost of SE})(\text{SE ratio})$$
$$CC = (12\%)(0.25) + (16\%)(0.75)$$
$$CC = 15\%$$

Ignoring the complicating factor of income taxes, assume that Benchmark's earnings before interest for the year are $560,000, or a 14 percent rate of return on the $4,000,000 of the firm's assets. Exhibit 15.2 shows that, while the creditors of the firm would receive their required amount of interest (12%), the remaining income ($440,000) is not sufficient to generate the 16 percent rate of return demanded by the stockholders. Instead, it generates only a 14.67 percent rate of return.

EXHIBIT	15.2	Return on Assets Less than Cost of Capital

Income before interest	$560,000
Less: Interest to creditors	(120,000)
Residual distribution available for stockholders	$440,000

$$\text{Return for creditors} = \frac{\text{Interest}}{\text{Debt}} = \frac{\$120,000}{\$1,000,000} = 12\%$$

$$\text{Return for stockholders} = \frac{\text{Residual}}{\text{Stockholders' equity}} = \frac{\$440,000}{\$3,000,000} = 14.67\%$$

However, when the rate of return on assets (Earnings before interest and taxes/Total assets), meets or exceeds the cost of capital, both creditors and stockholders are satisfied. Exhibit 15.3 illustrates how a 16 percent return on Benchmark's assets ($640,000/ $4,000,000) would satisfy both creditors and stockholders.

EXHIBIT	15.3	Return on Assets Greater than Cost of Capital

Income before interest	$640,000
Less: Interest to creditors	(120,000)
Residual distribution available for stockholders	$520,000

$$\text{Return for creditors} = \frac{\text{Interest}}{\text{Debt}} = \frac{\$120,000}{\$1,000,000} = 12\%$$

$$\text{Return for stockholders} = \frac{\text{Residual}}{\text{Stockholders' equity}} = \frac{\$520,000}{\$3,000,000} = 17.33\%$$

Because the assets produced a 16 percent rate of return, which is greater than the 15 percent cost of capital (Exhibit 15.1), the creditors' interest demands (12%) were met, and the stockholders' demands for a 16 percent return were exceeded (17.33%).

This illustrates the importance of a firm's cost of capital in management's decisions regarding acceptable investments in the capital budgeting process. The cost of capital is also called a *hurdle rate*. Unless management's analysis indicates that the expected rate of return on a long-term asset meets or exceeds the hurdle rate, the investment in the asset would not be able to satisfy both the creditors' and owners' desire for a satisfactory return.

Cash Flow Analysis   In order to estimate the rate of return of a potential investment, decision makers must be able to estimate the future cash inflows and outflows attributable to the investment if it is acquired. These cash flows represent the future costs and benefits of acquiring the asset. Management must be able to estimate cash flows with as much care and precision as possible because the accuracy of the estimates directly affects the quality of the investment decision.

Financing the Selected Investments

The decision about how to finance capital expenditures comes only after management has made a decision to acquire them. The firm has a choice of using debt or equity financing, and the firm's finance department must consider how the financing decision will affect the financial leverage of the firm.

Buying copiers is a capital budgeting decision.

Once financial management makes the financing decision, the implications of this decision are introduced into the capital expenditure and financing budgets. The **capital expenditure budget** presents information regarding the amount and timing of the capital expenditures planned for the designated time period. The **financing budget** outlines the amounts and sources of funds needed to finance the firm's investments for the designated time period.

The components of an organizational budget illustrated in Exhibit 15.4 show how the capital expenditure and financing budgets interface with the overall budgeting process. The investing and financing budgets at the end of a fiscal period are compared to the financing and investing events that actually occurred during the year. This examination may impact the operating budget for the coming year. For example, suppose Goodyear budgeted for the addition of a new production line that was never acquired. The failure to make this budgeted expenditure will impact the amount of production Goodyear could budget for in the coming year. Once the operating budgets are developed, specific decisions about what long-term assets to acquire and how to finance these acquisitions are built into the investing and financing budgets. Finally, all of these budget data appear in the pro forma financial statements of the firm.

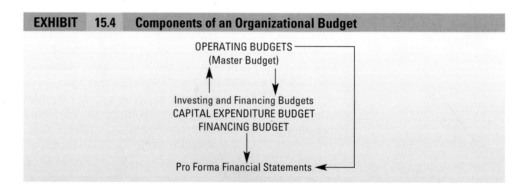

EXHIBIT 15.4 Components of an Organizational Budget

Evaluating the Investments

Evaluating capital expenditures occurs in two phases. In the **acquisition phase,** the first phase of evaluation, the management accountant is responsible for monitoring costs incurred in conjunction with the asset's acquisition. The purpose of this phase is to control the cost of the project by identifying how the actual acquisition expenditures deviate from budgeted acquisition expenditures in a timely manner and to hold accountable those responsible for the deviations.

The second evaluation phase, called the **postaudit,** involves comparing the cash flow projections made in preacquisition analysis with actual cash flows generated by the asset. The postaudit evaluates the accuracy of the original cash flow projections and methods and assumptions used. It is a starting point for finding ways of improving future cash flow estimates.

Accountants play a vital role in the entire capital budgeting process. They are responsible for gathering the estimated projections and actual data, preparing timely reports on their findings, and distributing these findings to those involved in planning for, acquiring, and operating the capital assets. The accountants' reports assist decision makers in the capital acquisition process and are useful for gaining insights into how to improve the capital budgeting process itself.

DISCOUNTED CASH FLOW ANALYSIS

Discounted cash flow analysis is a method of evaluating investments that uses the time value of money to assess whether the investment's expected rate of return is greater than the firm's cost of capital. If the expected rate of return is greater than the firm's cost of capital, the firm should acquire the asset.

Discounting cash flows refers to the practice of finding the present value of expected future cash flows. The rate of return used to determine present values is called the *discount rate.*

Net Present Value Method

LO 2

The **net present value method** of discounted cash flow analysis requires that decision makers find the present value of an investment's estimated future cash flows by using the firm's cost of capital as the discount rate. If the cost of the asset is less than the present value of the estimated future cash flows, the investment's return is greater than the firm's cost of capital, making it a favorable investment.

The net present value (NPV) method includes the following four steps:

1. Identify (estimate) the timing and amount of all cash inflows and outflows associated with the potential investment over its anticipated life.

2. Calculate the present value of the expected future cash flows using the firm's cost of capital as the discount rate.

3. Compute the net present value by subtracting the initial cash outflows necessary to acquire the asset from the present value of the future cash flows.

4. Decide to make or reject the investment in the capital asset. If the net present value is zero or positive, the proposed investment is acceptable. If the NPV is negative, the company should reject the project.

The following example illustrates the net present value method. Assume that Goodyear is considering the acquisition of a new tire mold that costs $759,325 and has a useful life of four years. Management estimates that the tire mold will save Goodyear $250,000 per year over its life. If Goodyear's cost of capital is 10 percent, should it acquire the tire mold?

Exhibit 15.5 illustrates the four steps in the NPV method of analysis used to resolve this capital budgeting decision. Step 1 identifies the initial cash outflow of $759,325 necessary to acquire the tire mold and the $250,000 estimated cash inflows Goodyear expects in each of the next four years. Step 2 calculates the present value of the expected future cash flows using the 10 percent cost of capital, $792,475. Step 3 calculates the net present value by subtracting the initial cash outflow from the present value of the future cash flows, $33,150. In Step 4 Goodyear will decide to make the investment if it expects the investment to generate a return greater than the cost of capital. In this case the NPV is positive which means that *if the cash inflows occur as expected,* the tire mold will generate a return greater than the cost of capital and Goodyear should acquire the machine.

EXHIBIT 15.5 Net Present Value Method—Goodyear Tire Mold

Step 1: Identify the cash flows.

Calculator:
r = 10
c = 1
n = 4
PMT = 250,000
FV = 0
PV = 792,466

	Time (years)				
	0	1	2	3	4
Cash to acquire	$(759,325)				
Cash inflows		$250,000	$250,000	$250,000	$250,000

Step 2: Find the present value of future cash flows.

$$\text{Present value of annuity} = \text{Annuity} \times P_{4,10\%}$$
$$= \$250,000 \times 3.1699$$
$$= \$792,475$$

Step 3: Compute the NPV.

Present value of cash flows (see Step 2)	$792,475
Initial cost of tire mold	(759,325)
Net present value	$ 33,150

Step 4: Accept or reject the asset acquisition.

Accept because the NPV is positive; therefore, if the cash flows occur as projected, the rate of return on the tire mold will be greater than the firm's cost of capital.

The decision, in this case, is to acquire the new tire mold because its NPV is positive, $33,150 (Step 3). If the cash flows occur as projected, the new tire mold will have a greater return than Goodyear's 10 percent cost of capital, or the firm's hurdle rate of return. While the net present value method reveals that the rate of return on the tire mold is greater than the cost of capital, it does not reveal the expected rate of return. The uncertainty involved in estimating the projected cash flows impacts all capital budgeting decisions. Dealing with this uncertainty is discussed later in the chapter.

What NPV Tells Us   Why does a positive NPV indicate that the rate of return is greater than the cost of capital? The answer lies in understanding Step 2 of the analysis illustrated in Exhibit 15.5. The present value of the future cash flows represents the *maximum price* that Goodyear would pay for the tire mold because it is based on the minimum rate of return, 10 percent, that Goodyear would accept. Stated another way, if Goodyear invested $792,475 in an asset and received $250,000 each year for four years, it would recover its original investment and receive a 10 percent return on its investment. Exhibit 15.6 illustrates how the cash flows expected (column 2) would provide both a 10 percent return on a $792,475 investment (column 3) and the return of the $792,475 initial investment (column 4).

EXHIBIT	15.6	Proof of 10 Percent Return		
(1)	(2)	(3)	(4)	(5)
	Expected	10 Percent	Return of	
Time (years)	Cash Inflow	Return on Investment	Investment	Investment
0				$792,475.00
1	$250,000.00	$79,247.50	$170,752.50	621,722.50
2	250,000.00	62,172.25	187,827.75	433,894.75
3	250,000.00	43,289.48	206,610.52	227,284.23
4	250,000.00	22,715.77*	227,284.23	–0–

*Difference due to rounding.

The maximum price that Goodyear would pay for the tire mold is $792,475 given the projected cash flows and Goodyear's desired minimum rate of return of 10 percent (Goodyear's cost of capital). If Goodyear pays an amount greater than $792,475, and the $250,000 cash flows occur as projected, the investment in the new equipment would yield a rate of return that is less than the required 10 percent.

If Goodyear pays any amount less than $792,475, and the $250,000 cash flows occur as expected, the new equipment will yield a rate of return greater than 10 percent. The positive NPV of $33,150 means that Goodyear is paying less than the amount required to generate a 10 percent return and, therefore, will receive a rate of return higher than 10 percent. Thus, if an investment of $792,475 that produces $250,000 cash at the end of each year for the next four years yields a 10 percent return, then Goodyear's investment of $759,325 that generates the same cash flows must earn more than a 10 percent return on the investment. How much more than 10 percent is determined by using the time-adjusted rate of return, discussed in the next section.

What NPV Does *Not* Represent   A project's NPV does *not* represent the amount of profit or loss that the asset will realize. For example, if the estimated cash flows for Goodyear's tire mold were $230,000 per year, the present value of the cash flows would be $729,077 ($230,000 × 3.1699), and the project would have a negative net present value of $(30,248) ($729,077 – $759,325 price of the tire mold). This does not mean that Goodyear would lose $30,248. Rather, it means that the maximum price Goodyear should pay for a tire mold to produce four annual $230,000 cash flows yielding a 10 percent return would be $729,077. Before Goodyear could earn a 10 percent rate of return, the seller would have to lower the price of the tire mold by $30,248. If the seller is unwilling to lower the price by at least $30,248, then Goodyear should not buy the equipment.

Time-Adjusted Rate of Return Method

LO 3

The **time-adjusted rate of return (TARR)**, also known as *the internal rate of return*, is another discounted cash flow method used to determine whether a firm should acquire a long-term asset. It requires using the cost of the potential investment as the present value of the projected cash flows in order to determine the rate of return of the proposed investment. (In contrast, the NPV method discounts the future cash flows by using the cost of capital to determine the present value of the projected cash flows.) However, the time-adjusted rate of return calculates the rate of return on the investment given the future cash flows and then compares the TARR to the cost of capital to see if it is higher or lower than the hurdle rate. The TARR method has three steps:

1. Identify (estimate) the timing and amount of all cash inflows and outflows associated with the investment over its life.

2. Determine the time-adjusted rate of return.

3. Decide to make or reject the investment in the asset under consideration. Make the investment if its time-adjusted rate of return is greater than the cost of capital; otherwise, reject the investment.

Exhibit 15.7 shows the time-adjusted rate of return for Goodyear's new tire mold. In this illustration, the cash flows in Step 1 are the same as those featured in the net present value method shown in Exhibit 15.5. We use the present value of an ordinary annuity to calculate the time-adjusted rate of return. The cost of the new machine, $759,325, is the present value of the four-payment, $250,000 annuity. That is, the machine is expected to generate four $250,000 payments, but the rate of return that generates this cash flow is still unknown.

EXHIBIT 15.7 Time-Adjusted Rate of Return

Step 1: Identify the cash flows.

		Time (years)			
	0	1	2	3	4
Cash outflows	$(759,325)				
Cash inflows		$ 250,000	$250,000	$250,000	$250,000

Step 2: Calculate the time-adjusted rate of return.

$$\text{Annuity} \times P_{4,?\%} = \text{Cost of the investment}$$
$$\$250,000 \times P_{4,?\%} = \$759,325$$
$$P_{4,?\%} = \$759,325/\$250,000$$
$$P_{4,?\%} = 3.0373$$
$$?\% = 12\%$$

Step 3: Accept or reject the acquisition.
Acquire the tire mold because, if the cash flows occur as projected, the time-adjusted rate of return is greater than the cost of capital.

$$\text{TARR } 12\% > \text{CC } 10\%$$

Calculator:
PV = (759,250)
PMT = 250,000
c = 1
n = 4
FV = 0
r = 12

Calculating the rate of return is possible because it is the only unknown element in the present value of an ordinary annuity formula. Dividing the annuity ($250,000) into the price of the mold ($759,325) produces the present value factor of an ordinary annuity, 3.0373. The rate is found in Appendix Table 4 at the end of the book by locating four payments on the left side of the table and then moving across the row until finding the 3.0373 factor under the 12 percent column. Thus the machine's time-adjusted rate of return is 12 percent.

The decision to acquire the new machine is very straightforward. Goodyear should acquire the new machine because it is expected to generate a 12 percent rate of return, which is greater than its 10 percent cost of capital.

The Effect of Uneven Cash Flows on Net Present Value

The discounted cash flow methods just illustrated used equal cash flows each period. In reality, cash flows generated by operating assets are seldom constant over time. We now illustrate how to use the net present value method when estimated cash flows are uneven. Exhibit 15.8 shows, in Step 1, a new set of cash flows that the tire mold is expected to generate if it is acquired. As you can see, there are now both cash inflows and cash outflows. The difference between the inflows and outflows in each year is called the net estimated cash flows. In this case, the *net estimated cash flows* decrease in each year of the asset's four-year life.

EXHIBIT 15.8 Uneven Cash Flows and Net Present Value

Step 1: Identify the cash flows.

		Time (years)			
	0	1	2	3	4
Cash to acquire	$(759,325)				
Operating cash flows:					
Cash inflows		$ 450,000	$490,000	$470,000	$460,000
Cash outflows		(150,000)	(230,000)	(230,000)	(260,000)
Net cash flows	$(759,325)	$ 300,000	$260,000	$240,000	$200,000

To calculate the net present value of the cash flows, it is necessary to find the present value of each of the estimated future cash flows using the present value of the amount of $1. Exhibit 15.9 shows Step 2, discounting each year's estimated cash flows using the 10 percent cost of capital. The sum of each of these discounted cash flows is the present value of all the future cash flows and represents the maximum price the firm should pay for the new tire mold given the cash flows expected. The remaining steps of the net present value method show that the net present value of $45,181 is positive and that the initial cost of the asset is less than the maximum price of $804,506 Goodyear should pay. Therefore, Goodyear should buy the tire mold.

Calculator:
r = 10
PMT = 0
c = 1
n = 1 FV = 300,000
       PV = 272,727
n = 2 FV = 260,000
       PV = 214,876
n = 3 FV = 240,000
       PV = 180,316
n = 4 FV = 200,000
       PV = 136,603

EXHIBIT 15.9 Net Present Value of Uneven Cash Flows

Step 2: Find the present value of future cash flows.

Time (years)	Net Cash Flows (from Exhibit 15.8)	×	10 Percent PV Factor	=	Present Value
1	$300,000	×	0.9091	=	$272,730
2	260,000	×	0.8264	=	214,864
3	240,000	×	0.7513	=	180,312
4	200,000	×	0.6830	=	136,600
Present value of future cash flows				=	$804,506

Step 3: Compute the NPV.

Present value of future cash flows	$804,506
Initial cost of the asset	759,325
Net present value	$ 45,181

Step 4. Accept or reject the asset acquisition.
Acquire the tire mold because the NPV is positive; therefore, if the cash flows occur as projected, the return earned on the asset is greater than the cost of capital.

PAUSE & REFLECT

In both the even and uneven cash flow scenarios, the estimated cash flows for the four-year period totaled $1,000,000. Why is the present value of the future cash flows in Step 2 larger for the uneven cash flows example, $804,506, than for the even cash flow example, $792,475? *(answer on page 542)*

Advantages and Disadvantages of the Discounted Cash Flow Methods

The major advantage of the time-adjusted rate of return method is that once it is calculated the decision about whether to make a capital expenditure is rather straightforward. If the cost of capital is lower than the time-adjusted rate of return on the project, the project should be accepted. If the cost of capital is greater than the TARR, the project should be rejected.

The disadvantage of TARR is the time-consuming, trial-and-error process required when dealing with uneven cash flows. In contrast, the net present value method is easier to compute because its requirements include only the firm's cost of capital, the projected cash flows, and the initial cost of the project.

The major advantage of the net present value method is that it can be adjusted for risk, while the time-adjusted rate of return cannot. The further into the future cash flows are projected, the riskier they become because the cash flows are more uncertain. The net present value method adjusts for this risk by incorporating higher discount rates for later cash flows. The TARR cannot adjust for this risk because it is based on the assumption that the asset produces only one rate of return over its entire life.

For example, assume Goodyear is considering the acquisition of a building that costs $152,000 and that it expects to use seven years. Exhibit 15.10 lists the estimated cash flows along with the discount rates that Goodyear is going to use to assess the acquisition. Note that in years 4 and 5, the rate is 13 percent and in years 6 and 7 the rate is 15 percent. These higher rates reflect Goodyear's desire to adjust the discount rate (cost of capital) for the risk associated with the greater uncertainty in projecting cash flows for these later periods. If Goodyear does not adjust for the increased risk and uses 12 percent for all seven years, the analysis would have generated a positive NPV of $5,451 and a recommendation to acquire the building. However, when the rates are adjusted for the risk associated with the uncertainty surrounding the estimates of the future cash flows, the NPV is a negative $2,563 and Goodyear would not acquire the building. The TARR cannot be adjusted for the change in risk during the discount period.

Assumptions Underlying Discounted Cash Flow Analysis

Three common assumptions underlie discounted cash flow analysis:

1. **All cash flows are known with certainty.** Although cash flow projections are really estimates and, therefore, are subject to uncertainty, we are willing to accept this assumption. The net present value method can adjust for the risk of uncertainty without increasing the complexity of the model.

2. **Cash flows are assumed to occur at the end of the time period.** Although cash flows occur throughout the year, any distortion caused by this assumption is not sufficient to significantly affect the decision.

3. **Cash inflows are immediately reinvested in another project that earns a return for the company.** This assumption does not take into consideration the fact that cash flows might be distributed to stockholders or creditors. The NPV method assumes that the cash flows are reinvested at a rate equal to the cost of capital. The time-adjusted rate of return model assumes that the return is reinvested at the project's rate of return.

These assumptions, while not always realistic, provide the structure that makes net present value and time-adjusted rate of return effective capital budgeting tools, if the decision maker considers these limitations.

EXHIBIT 15.10   Risk-Adjusted Cash Flows

Time (years)	Net Cash Inflows	Discount Rate
1	$20,000	12%
2	30,000	12
3	35,000	12
4	43,000	13
5	45,000	13
6	40,000	15
7	39,000	15

Risk-Adjusted Net Present Value

Time	Net Cash Flows	×	PV Factor	=	Present Value
			12%		
1	$20,000	×	0.8929	=	$ 17,858
2	30,000	×	0.7972	=	23,916
3	35,000	×	0.7118	=	24,913
			13%		
4	43,000	×	0.6133	=	26,372
5	45,000	×	0.5428	=	24,426
			15%		
6	40,000	×	0.4323	=	17,292
7	39,000	×	0.3759	=	14,660
Present value of risk-adjusted future cash flows				=	$149,437
Less: Price of building					(152,000)
Negative net present value					$ (2,563)

Net Present Value without Risk Adjustment

Time	Net Cash Flows	×	12% PV Factor	=	Present Value
1	$20,000	×	0.8929	=	$ 17,858
2	30,000	×	0.7972	=	23,916
3	35,000	×	0.7118	=	24,913
4	43,000	×	0.6355	=	27,327
5	45,000	×	0.5674	=	25,533
6	40,000	×	0.5066	=	20,264
7	39,000	×	0.4523	=	17,640
Present value of risk-adjusted future cash flows				=	$157,451
Less: Price of building					(152,000)
Positive net present value					$ 5,451

The Source of Cash Flows

The discounted cash flow methods incorporate cash flows into the models because the acquisition and operation of capital assets produce cash flows. What is not always obvious about this process is the source of these cash flows. The following description reviews the typical cash inflows and outflows used in capital budgeting projects.

The initial cash outflows are the expenditures made to acquire the asset in addition to other acquisition costs such as freight charges, sales tax, and installation costs. Another possible related cash outflow that could occur is an increase in working capital. Working capital, or the excess of current assets over current liabilities, increases when a project requires more cash on hand, supplies, and inventories. When acquiring a new manufacturing facility, for example, a company might need additional cash and inventory to operate the facility on a day-to-day basis.

Cash inflows occur during the investment's life because the investment generates revenues, decreases operating expenses, or both. For capital budgeting purposes, a decrease in operating expenses is considered to be a cash inflow because it increases the cash flows of the firm. At the end of the investment's life, cash inflows occur when the amount of working capital necessary to operate the facility is reduced and the investment is sold for salvage.

In discounted cash flow analysis, the cash flows can be either certain and precise or quite uncertain and imprecise. For example, there is little uncertainty about the amount of cash outflows necessary to acquire the asset. However, the amount of cash inflows from the sale of the asset at the end of its useful life is much more uncertain.

Managers should make their cash flow projections with the best information possible, including information obtained from postaudit evaluations that help evaluate cash flow projections and find ways to improve the process of projecting cash flows.

Income Taxes and Cash Flows

LO 4

Income taxes can significantly affect capital budgeting decisions because they change both the amount of cash inflows and cash outflows used in the capital budgeting process. Understanding how income taxes affect discounted cash flow techniques is essential to the proper use of these methods.

Because income taxes are paid based on the amount of income a business generates, they typically represent cash outflows. Proposed capital expenditures will affect the firm's income and, therefore, the tax liability of the firm. Because Goodyear's financial statements and tax structure are too complex to create a realistic illustration of the impact of taxes on the capital budgeting process, we will use the Benchmark Corporation to describe the impact of taxes on capital budgeting decisions.

After-Tax Cash Flows   **After-tax cash flows** are the estimated cash flows associated with a potential investment *after* considering the impact of income taxes. Determining the after-tax cash flows is the first step in the discounted cash flow analysis used by for-profit businesses.

Exhibit 15.11 presents the Benchmark Corporation's accrual basis and cash basis income statements in sections A and B, respectively. These statements show how capital expenditures impact the income statements, the company's taxes, and the firm's cash flows.

Assume that the tax rate for Benchmark is 40 percent, that it collects all revenues, and that all expenses, except depreciation, are paid with cash. Benchmark's accrual basis accounting income (net income) is $36,000 (section A) and includes depreciation expense of $10,000. The company's cash basis income is $46,000 (section B) because depreciation expense is not included as it is a noncash expense.

EXHIBIT	15.11	Benchmark Corporation Income Statements: Accrual and Cash Basis

Benchmark Corporation
Income Statement

A. Accrual Basis

Sales	$100,000
Operating expenses	(30,000)
Depreciation expense	(10,000)
Income before taxes	$ 60,000
Tax expense*	(24,000)
Net income	$ 36,000

B. Cash Basis

Sales	$100,000
Operating expenses	(30,000)
Depreciation expense	–0–
Cash before taxes	$ 70,000
Tax paid*	(24,000)
Cash from operations	$ 46,000

*40% × Accrual basis income.

After-Tax Cash Inflows Capital expenditures can generate taxable cash inflows and, consequently, an increase in the amount of income taxes due. An after-tax cash inflow is the difference between the taxable cash inflow and the amount of tax paid on it.

Exhibit 15.12 shows how Benchmark's accrual basis (section A) and cash basis (section B) income statements are affected by two independent situations: (1) when cash sales increase [column 2] and (2) when cash operating expenses decrease [column 3]. Note that the $10,000 increase in income before taxes (section A), created by both situations 2 and 3, increases the income tax paid by $4,000 (from $24,000 [$60,000 × 0.4] in column 1 to $28,000 [$70,000 × 0.4]) in the scenarios described in columns 2 and 3. Therefore, when cash inflows increase by $10,000 in columns 2 and 3 of section B, cash outflows will increase by $4,000 due to the increase in taxes paid, and the after-tax cash inflows are $6,000 ($10,000 – $4,000). This is reflected in the $6,000 increase in the cash basis income from operations shown in columns 2 and 3 in section B.

EXHIBIT 15.12	Tax Effects on Increased Cash Flows		

Benchmark Corporation
Income Statement

		Increases in Cash Due to	
	(1) Exhibit 15.11	(2) Increase in Cash Sales	(3) Decrease in Cash Operating Expenses
A. Accrual Basis			
Sales	$100,000	$110,000	$100,000
Operating expenses	(30,000)	(30,000)	(20,000)
Depreciation expense	(10,000)	(10,000)	(10,000)
Income before taxes	$ 60,000	$ 70,000	$ 70,000
Tax expense*	(24,000)	(28,000)	(28,000)
Net income	$ 36,000	$ 42,000	$ 42,000
B. Cash Basis			
Sales	$100,000	$110,000	$100,000
Operating expenses	(30,000)	(30,000)	(20,000)
Depreciation expense	–0–	–0–	–0–
Cash before taxes	$ 70,000	$ 80,000	$ 80,000
Tax paid	(24,000)	(28,000)	(28,000)
Cash from operations	$ 46,000	$ 52,000	$ 52,000

*40% × Accrual basis income ($60,000 × 0.4) in column 1 and ($70,000 × 0.4) in columns 2 and 3.

Use the formula below as a shorter method to determine the after-tax cash inflows:

$$\text{After-tax cash inflows} = \text{Taxable cash inflows} \times (1 - \text{Tax rate})$$
$$= \$10,000 \times (1 - 0.40)$$
$$= \$6,000$$

The (1 – Tax rate) portion of the formula represents the portion of $1 of pretax cash inflows, or $0.60, that would remain after paying the 40 percent tax due on $1. Therefore, if this relationship is true for $1, then 60 percent of any dollar amount of taxable cash inflows will yield the after-tax cash flows.

After-Tax Cash Outflows Cash outflows associated with capital expenditures after acquisition normally include cash expenditures made to operate or maintain the asset. After-tax cash payments are smaller than pretax cash payments because pretax cash payments reduce the income subject to tax and, therefore, the firm's tax liability.

To illustrate the impact of deductible cash outflows on taxes, assume that Benchmark Corporation's cash operating expenses increased by $10,000 from $30,000 to $40,000 as illustrated in Exhibit 15.13. As a result, the income before taxes decreases by $10,000, and taxes decrease by $4,000, from $24,000 to $20,000 (shown in section A). Note in section B of Exhibit 15.13 that while the cash before taxes decreased $10,000, from $70,000 to $60,000, the cash from operations decreased by only $6,000, from $46,000 to $40,000. The decrease in cash is only $6,000 because the $10,000 increase in cash operating expenses reduced taxable income and, therefore, created a tax savings of $4,000.

EXHIBIT	15.13	Tax Effects on Decreased Cash Flows

Benchmark Corporation
Income Statement

	(1) Exhibit 15.11	(2) Increase in Cash Operating Expenses
A. Accrual Basis		
Sales	$100,000	$100,000
Operating expenses	(30,000)	(40,000)
Depreciation expense	(10,000)	(10,000)
Income before taxes	$ 60,000	$ 50,000
Tax expense*	(24,000)	(20,000)
Net income	$ 36,000	$ 30,000
B. Cash Basis		
Sales	$100,000	$100,000
Operating expenses	(30,000)	(40,000)
Depreciation expense	–0–	–0–
Cash before taxes	$ 70,000	$ 60,000
Tax paid	(24,000)	(20,000)
Cash from operations	$ 46,000	$ 40,000

*40% × Accrual basis income ($60,000 × 0.4) in column 1 and ($50,000 × 0.4) in column 2.

As indicated previously for cash inflows, the use of a formula is a shorter way to determine the after-tax cash outflows of a deductible cash expenditure:

$$\text{After-tax cash outflows} = \text{Deductible cash outflows} \times (1 - \text{Tax rate})$$
$$= \$10,000 \times (1 - 0.40)$$
$$= \$6,000$$

Here the (1 – Tax rate) represents the after-tax cost of spending $1. When multiplied by the deductible cash outflows, it yields the after-tax cash outflows.

Noncash Expenses

Depreciation, like all noncash expenses, does not directly decrease cash, but it reduces income subject to tax and, therefore, the related amount of income taxes due on income. Therefore, depreciation provides a **tax shield** because it reduces the potential amount of a firm's tax liability by reducing its taxable income without affecting its pretax cash flows. Tax shields keep firms from being taxed on the recovery of the cost of their investments.

To illustrate, assume that a company invests $5,000 in an asset that will last only one year and, at the end of the year, the use of the asset will have contributed $6,000 to the company's revenue. The $6,000 is a combination of a $5,000 return *of* investment and a $1,000 return *on* the investment. Only $1,000 of the $6,000 cash inflow is subject to tax because it is the amount of income generated by the $5,000 investment.

Now assume that the $5,000 asset has a five-year life and, by its use, creates cash inflows of $1,200 in each of these five years. If the company depreciates the cost of the asset equally over five years, the return on investment each year would be as follows:

| | Years | | | | | |
	1	2	3	4	5	Total
Cash flows	$1,200	$1,200	$1,200	$1,200	$1,200	$6,000
Depreciation	(1,000)	(1,000)	(1,000)	(1,000)	(1,000)	(5,000)
Return on investment	$ 200	$ 200	$ 200	$ 200	$ 200	$1,000

Just as in the case of the one-year investment, the firm is not taxed each period on the return *of* the investment ($1,000), only on the return *on* the investment ($200). Thus the amount of yearly depreciation effectively shields $1,000 of the yearly cash inflows of $1,200 from taxes because it represents the return of the initial investment. Note that the total amount of cash inflows, $6,000, less the sum of the depreciation, $5,000, yields the same $1,000 return on investment as the one-year investment in the previous example.

PAUSE &
REFLECT

Why are the cash inflows generated from the use of land not shielded from taxation?
(answer on page 542)

Depreciation's tax shield creates a tax savings and, therefore, indirectly increases the amount of net cash flows for firms. In Exhibit 15.14, section A, column 2, we illustrate depreciation's tax shield by eliminating the $10,000 of depreciation from Benchmark's income statement. With no depreciation, income before taxes increases by $10,000 from $60,000 to $70,000 and the related amount of taxes increases by $4,000 from $24,000 to $28,000, because more income is subject to tax. As a result, even though Benchmark's net income increases by $6,000 (section A) by eliminating depreciation, its cash from operations actually decreases by $4,000, from $46,000 to $42,000, as shown in section B. Therefore, while depreciation reduces accounting income, it shields Benchmark from $4,000 in taxes.

EXHIBIT 15.14   Tax Effect of Depreciation

Benchmark Corporation
Income Statement

	(1) With Depreciation	(2) No Depreciation
A. Accrual Basis		
Sales	$100,000	$100,000
Operating expenses	(30,000)	(30,000)
Depreciation expense	(10,000)	–0–
Income before taxes	$ 60,000	$ 70,000
Tax expense*	(24,000)	(28,000)
Net income	$ 36,000	$ 42,000
B. Cash Basis		
Sales	$100,000	$100,000
Operating expenses	(30,000)	(30,000)
Depreciation expense	–0–	–0–
Cash before taxes	$ 70,000	$ 70,000
Tax paid	(24,000)	(28,000)
Cash from operations	$ 46,000	$ 42,000

*40% of Accrual basis income ($60,000 × 0.40) in column 1 and ($70,000 × 0.4) in column 2.

Use the following formula to determine the amount of cash saved as a result of non-cash expenses. Note that the tax rate is applied directly to the amount of depreciation.

$$\text{Cash saved as a result of noncash expense} = \text{Depreciation (or any deductible noncash expense)} \times \text{Tax rate}$$
$$= \$10,000 \times 0.40$$
$$= \$4,000$$

When projecting the amount of cash flows for a project, the tax savings generated by depreciation are a critical part of the process. The only uncertainty involved in projecting these cash savings is whether the tax rates will remain the same over the life of the asset.

In Chapter 21, we describe various depreciation methods used to allocate the cost of the asset over its useful life. For financial reporting purposes, companies select the method that best matches depreciation expense with the benefits the asset generates over the asset's life. However, when determining taxable income, companies use accelerated depreciation methods approved by the Internal Revenue Service. These tax depreciation methods allow more (accelerated) depreciation in the first years of an asset's life and, therefore, create larger tax shields earlier in the asset's life and smaller tax shields later in the asset's life. These accelerated tax shields allow firms to take advantage of the time value of money. That is, the firm would prefer to get more of the tax savings from depreciation earlier rather than later in the asset's life.

Gains and Losses on Disposal

In capital budgeting decisions, the disposal of assets occurs when organizations either re-place old assets or sell the assets for salvage at the end of their useful life. When a firm disposes of such assets, there are usually two sources of cash flows: (1) the proceeds of the sale and (2) the change in the amount of taxes due when the asset is sold for a gain or a loss.

In Chapter 8 we referred to book value as the original cost of an asset less the accumu-lated depreciation taken to a particular point in time. The book value represents the unde-preciated portion of the asset's original cost rather than the market value of the asset, or the amount for which the company could sell the asset on the market.

A gain on disposal occurs if the proceeds from the sale of an asset exceed its book value at the date of disposal. A loss on disposal occurs if the proceeds from the sale of an asset are less than its book value at the date of the sale.

To illustrate the cash flows surrounding the disposal of an asset, we will describe both a gain and a loss on disposal. Assume that Benchmark Corporation has a piece of equip-ment that originally cost $10,000 and that at the point of sale the equipment has a book value of $2,000. Recall that Benchmark's tax is 40 percent.

Gain and Its Tax Effects If the equipment is sold for $3,000 cash, there would be a gain on disposal of $1,000:

Cash proceeds from the sale	$3,000
Less: Book value of equipment	2,000
Gain on disposal	$1,000

Although $3,000 cash is received from the sale, the actual cash flows from the dis-posal are $2,600 due to the effect of Benchmark's 40 percent tax rate:

Cash proceeds from the sale	$3,000
Less: Taxes paid on gain ($1,000 × 0.40)	400
Net cash proceeds from disposal	$2,600

The gain from the transaction increases income by $1,000 and, therefore, increases taxes by $400. As a result, the $400 in taxes paid on the gain ($1,000 × 0.40) reduces the $3,000 proceeds of the sale, leaving $2,600 as the net cash proceeds (inflow to Benchmark).

The formula to determine the cash inflows from the disposal of an asset with a gain is as follows:

$$\text{Net-of-tax cash flows from asset sold with a gain} =$$
$$\text{Proceeds from disposal} - (\text{Gain on disposal} \times \text{Tax rate})$$

Loss and Its Tax Effects   If the equipment is sold for $1,500 cash, there would be a loss on disposal of $500:

Cash proceeds from the sale	$1,500
Less: Book value of equipment	2,000
Loss on disposal	$(500)

Although only $1,500 is received from the sale, the cash inflows from the transaction actually are $1,700. The sale of the equipment generates $1,500 in cash, while the loss reduces Benchmark's income by $500 and, therefore, reduces its taxes by $200 ($500 × 0.40):

Cash proceeds from the sale	$1,500
Add: Taxes saved on loss ($500 × 0.4)	200
Net cash proceeds from disposal	$1,700

The following formula describes how the cash flows from the disposal of assets with a loss are determined:

$$\text{Net-of-tax cash flows from asset sold with a loss} =$$
$$\text{Proceeds from disposal} + (\text{Loss on disposal} \times \text{Tax rate})$$

The following list summarizes the formulas utilized to determine the after-tax cash flows that are in turn used in discounted cash flow analysis:

After-Tax Cash Inflows

Taxable cash inflows $\times$ (1 – Tax rate)

After-Tax Cash Outflows

Deductible cash outflows $\times$ (1 – Tax rate)

Cash Savings from Deductible Noncash Expenses

Depreciation (any deductible noncash expense) $\times$ Tax rate

Net-of-Tax Cash Flows from Assets Sold at a Gain

Proceeds from disposal – (Gain on disposal $\times$ Tax rate)

Net-of-Tax Cash Flows from Assets Sold at a Loss

Proceeds from disposal + (Loss on disposal $\times$ Tax rate)

CAPITAL BUDGETING: A COMPREHENSIVE EXAMPLE

This comprehensive illustration is designed to review most of the capital budgeting topics covered to this point. In the illustration assume that Goodyear is considering the acquisition of a new $900,000 computer system on January 1, 1999, for its Fayetteville, North Carolina plant and will use the net present value method to assess the potential investment. The following facts are related to this capital budgeting decision:

- The computer system will increase the speed and accuracy of Goodyear's delivery system and has a useful life of seven years.

- The greater efficiency in filling orders will increase revenues by $160,000 each year of the computer's life, but it requires a one-time $100,000 increase in the amount of inventory in order to avoid running out of stock.

- The computer system will reduce labor costs by $30,000 each year but cause utility costs to increase $20,000 each year.

- The computer system will be depreciated equally over the next five years resulting in annual depreciation expense of $180,000.

- The book value of the old computer system is $120,000; its market value is $80,000.
- The new computer system can be sold at the end of year 7 (1/1/2006) for $160,000.
- Goodyear has a 12 percent cost of capital.

Exhibit 15.15 provides the after-tax cash flows anticipated as a result of the acquisition. Determining the cash flows net of their tax effects is the first step in net present value analysis.

EXHIBIT 15.15   Identification of After-Tax Cash Flows

1/1/99
Cash outflows:

Cost of computer system (no tax effect)		$(900,000)
Investment in working capital (no tax effect)		(100,000)

Cash inflows:

Proceeds from sale of old equipment	$ 80,000	
Add: Tax savings from loss (see below)	16,000	
Net cash inflows from sale of old computer system		96,000

1/1/00–1/1/06
Net operating cash inflows:

Increase in sales	$160,000
Decrease in labor costs	30,000
Increase in utility costs	(20,000)
Net cash inflows from operations—Pretax	$170,000

After-tax cash inflows = $170,000 × (1 − 0.40) = $102,000

1/1/00–1/1/04
Annual depreciation $900,000/5 = $180,000
Tax savings on depreciation tax shield = Depreciation × Tax rate
= $180,000 × 0.4
= $72,000

1/1/06
Cash inflows:

Release of working capital (no tax effect)		$ 100,000
Proceeds from sale of the computer system	$160,000	
Less: Tax on gain (see below)	(64,000)	
Net cash inflows from sale of new conveyer		96,000

Tax effects of gain/loss

Proceeds from sale of old computer system, 1/1/99	$80,000
Less: Book value of old computer system	(120,000)
Loss on disposal	$(40,000)

Tax savings on loss ($40,000 × 0.4) = $16,000

Proceeds from sale of new computer system, 1/1/06 =	$160,000
Less: Book value of new computer system	–0–
Gain on disposal	$160,000
Tax on gain ($160,000 × 0.40)	= $ 64,000

- The initial cash outflows on 1/1/99 consist of the cost of the computer system ($900,000) and the additional inventory required to operate the system efficiently ($100,000).
- If the computer system is purchased, Goodyear can sell the six computers used currently. The computers have a total book value of $120,000, and they can be immediately sold for a total of $80,000. The $40,000 loss creates a tax savings of $16,000 (see cash inflows, 1/1/99).
- The proceeds of the sale plus the tax savings from the loss will reduce the initial cash outflows of the computer system by $96,000.

- The net operating cash inflows that result from the acquisition of the computer amount to $102,000 after taxes (see after-tax cash inflows, 1/1/00–1/1/06).

- The depreciation creates a tax shield that produces a tax savings of $72,000 per year (see 1/1/00–1/1/04).

- At the end of the computer's useful life, Goodyear will reduce its amount of inventory and sell the computer. Because the computer is fully depreciated in 2004, its book value is zero and, as a result, the gain on the sale of the computer will equal the $160,000 in proceeds from the sale. The gain on the sale is subject to $64,000 tax, which reduces the cash proceeds to $96,000 ($160,000 proceeds from sale – $64,000 tax on gain) (see 1/1/06).

Exhibit 15.16 shows the cash flows for each year of the useful life of the computer and, using a 12 percent cost of capital as the discount rate, calculates the net present value of the computer. Take a moment to be sure you understand these calculations.

Calculator:
r = 12
c = 1
FV = 0
n = 7
PMT = 102,000
PV = 465,503

n = 5
PMT = 72,000
PV = 259,544

FV = 196,000
n = 7
PMT = 0
PV = 88,660

| **EXHIBIT** | **15.16** | **Net Present Value Computation** |

Step 1: Identify the cash flows (see Exhibit 15.15).

		Time (years)						
	1/1/99	1/1/00	1/1/01	1/1/02	1/1/03	1/1/04	1/1/05	1/1/06
a	$(900,000)							
b	(100,000)							
c	96,000							
d		$102,000	$102,000	$102,000	$102,000	$102,000	$102,000	$102,000
e		72,000	72,000	72,000	72,000	72,000		
f								100,000
g								96,000
Total	($904,000)	$174,000	$174,000	$174,000	$174,000	$174,000	$102,000	$298,000

Where:
  a = Cost of computer system
  b = Investment in working capital—inventory
  c = After-tax proceeds from sale of old computers
  d = After-tax operating cash inflows
  e = Tax savings on depreciation tax shield
  f = Release of working capital
  g = Net cash inflows from sale of the computer system

Step 2: Calculate the present value of future cash flows.

Time	Cash Flows (Step 1)	×	$P_{n,12\%}$	=	Present Value
1/1/00	$174,000	×	0.8929	=	$155,365
1/1/01	174,000	×	0.7972	=	138,713
1/1/02	174,000	×	0.7118	=	123,853
1/1/03	174,000	×	0.6355	=	110,577
1/1/04	174,000	×	0.5674	=	98,728
1/1/05	102,000	×	0.5066	=	51,673
1/1/06	298,000	×	0.4523	=	134,785
Present value of future cash flows				=	$813,694

Step 3: Compute the net present value.

Present value of future cash flows	$813,694
Less: Initial cost of acquisition (Step 1)	(904,000)
Net present value	$(90,306)

Step 4: Make decision about acquisition of capital investment.
Investment decision: Reject proposal to acquire the computer system because NPV is negative.

The computer produces a negative net present value of $(90,306), as shown in Step 3. If Goodyear acquires the computer and the cash flows remain as projected, the rate of return on the computer system will be less than Goodyear's cost of capital or minimum acceptable rate of return. Therefore, Goodyear should not purchase the computer system.

Calculating the net present value of the computer system yielded a measure that helps management decide whether to acquire this capital asset. However, the apparent mathematical precision of this process should not obscure the fact that it is based on human judgment. The impact and importance of good judgment in the capital budgeting process is the focus of the rest of this chapter.

CONFLICTING SIGNALS: A PERFORMANCE EVALUATION PROBLEM

LO 5

Discounted cash flow analysis and accrual accounting are based on different assumptions. Discounted cash flow analysis considers only the amount and timing of cash flows, whereas accrual accounting measures the economic consequences of business transactions, whether or not cash was a part of the transaction. When a decision maker does not understand the differences in these two systems, the potential for suboptimal capital budgeting decisions exists.

For example, Beth Engler, the eastern division manager of Benchmark Corporation, is opposed to the acquisition of a new plant for which she will be responsible, even though it has a positive net present value. She bases her opposition on the fact that the projected accounting income of the plant during its four-year life shows that the plant would have a net loss in each of its first two years. The negative income in these first two years will have a significant impact on the division's income, and Beth's performance is evaluated based on the division's accounting earnings. Her yearly bonus is 5 percent of the division's accounting income. (We discuss bonuses in more detail in Chapter 16.)

Exhibit 15.17 depicts the effects of the apparent conflict between NPV and accrual basis accounting income. Assume that the cost of capital for Benchmark Corporation is 12 percent. You can see that the NPV of the new plant is a positive $35,794, which indicates that the plant would be a favorable investment for Benchmark Corporation. The projected accrual income for the plant indicates that, for the first two years of its life, the plant will generate losses of $40,000 and $10,000, respectively.

EXHIBIT	15.17	Conflict between NPV and Accrual Basis Accounting Income: Benchmark Corporation

				Time (years)		
		0	**1**	**2**	**3**	**4**
Cash flows:						
Plant cost		$(200,000)				
Cash revenues			$10,000	$40,000	$140,000	$150,000

Cash flows	×	$p_{n,12\%}$	=	Present value
$10,000	×	.8929	=	$ 8,929
$40,000	×	.7972	=	31,888
$140,000	×	.7118	=	99,652
$150,000	×	.6355	=	95,325
Present value of future cash flows			=	$235,794
Less: Plant cost				(200,000)
Net present value				$ 35,794

		Time (years)		
	1	**2**	**3**	**4**
Accrual income				
Revenues	$ 10,000	$ 40,000	$140,000	$150,000
Depreciation	(50,000)	(50,000)	(50,000)	(50,000)
Net income (loss)	$(40,000)	$(10,000)	$ 90,000	$100,000

The evaluation system encourages Ms. Engler to oppose the acquisition of this plant, despite the fact it is a good decision for the company. If the Benchmark Corporation acquires the plant, Ms. Engler will be penalized by losing a potential bonus in years 1 and 2.

Management accounting systems need evaluation mechanisms that reward managers for decisions that increase the wealth of the firm. For Benchmark Corporation, the evaluation system clearly allows for conflicts based on its bonus reward structure. This, of course, can lead to decisions that are not in the company's best interest. We discuss this issue in more detail in Chapter 16.

CAPITAL BUDGETING AND THE NEED FOR INFORMED SPECULATION

Capital budgeting relies upon the use of many technical tools to facilitate the decision-making process. What is often lost in the process of applying these tools is the realization that informed speculation is a necessary component of the capital budgeting process. What do we mean by *informed speculation*? Because making capital budgeting decisions requires the personal judgment of decision makers, forecasting can be affected by personal perceptions of the decision maker.

PAUSE & REFLECT

Suppose the person responsible for forecasting cash flows took a very conservative approach and the resulting net present value on a $500,000 project was a negative $110. Should the project be rejected? Would your answer be the same if the cash flows were based on very optimistic assumptions? *(answer on page 542)*

Managers should keep the subjective aspects of the capital budgeting process in mind when evaluating the output of their computations. People who review the input and output of accounting systems should recognize the subjective nature of the capital budgeting process and provide the support necessary to facilitate this dynamic process. Sensitivity analysis is one way to deal with the uncertainty inherent in the capital budgeting process.

Sensitivity Analysis

Sensitivity analysis, which we described in Chapter 4, reflects the results of changing a key assumption in a decision model. Capital budgeting uses sensitivity analysis to evaluate how a change in estimated cash flows or discount rates might affect the capital budgeting decision.

To illustrate, assume that Benchmark has a 10 percent cost of capital and is considering two $100,000 investments, A and B, shown in Exhibit 15.18. Benchmark's accountants have suggested that the cash flow estimates may vary downward by as much as 10 percent. The exhibit illustrates how a 10 percent fluctuation might affect the investment decision.

For investment A, the possible fluctuation in cash flows from $32,000 per year (line 2) to $28,800 (line 3) would not affect the decision to acquire the investment because both possible cash flows have positive net present values of $21,306 and $9,175, respectively.

Investment B, on the other hand, has a small NPV, $2,352, and a 10 percent drop in the projected cash flows from $27,000 to $24,300 would result in a negative NPV of ($7,884), leading to the suggestion that Benchmark should reject the investment. The closer the NPV is to zero and the greater the uncertainty about the cash flows, the greater the chance of making an incorrect investment decision. Sensitivity analysis helps clarify this type of risk.

Qualitative Factors

In addition to the uncertainty about future cash flows, managers must also consider qualitative factors that affect capital expenditure decisions. For example, suppose a firm is considering the construction of a new parking garage, and discounted cash flow analysis indicates that the parking garage will yield a return well above the firm's cost of capital. However, the construction of the parking garage would require the destruction of an important historic landmark. The decision to build the garage must take into consideration this qualitative factor as well as the financial considerations.

EXHIBIT 15.18 Sensitivity Analysis

Investment A

Price	$100,000
Estimated annual cash inflows for five years	32,000
Estimated cash flows reduced 10% ($32,000 × 0.90)	28,800

$$\text{Present value of future cash flows} = \text{Annuity} \times P_{5,10\%}$$
$$= \$32,000 \times 3.7908$$
$$= \$121,306$$

$$\text{Present value of future of reduced cash flows} = \text{Annuity} \times P_{5,10\%}$$
$$= \$28,800 \times 3.7908$$
$$= \$109,175$$

	Forecasted Cash Flows	
	$32,000	**$28,800**
Present value of future cash flows	$121,306	$109,175
Initial cost of investment A	(100,000)	(100,000)
Net present value	$ 21,306	$ 9,175

Investment B

Price	$100,000
Estimated annual cash inflows for five years	27,000
Estimated cash flows reduced 10% ($27,000 × 0.90)	24,300

$$\text{Present value of future cash flows} = \text{Annuity} \times P_{5,10\%}$$
$$= \$27,000 \times 3.7908$$
$$= \$102,352$$

$$\text{Present value of future of reduced cash flows} = \text{Annuity} \times P_{5,10\%}$$
$$= \$24,300 \times 3.7908$$
$$= \$92,116$$

	Forecasted Cash Flows	
	$27,000	**$24,300**
Present value of future cash flows	$102,352	$ 92,116
Initial cost of investment B	(100,000)	(100,000)
Net present value	$ 2,352	$ (7,884)

Destroying an historic structure to put up a needed parking garage is an ethical dilemma.

In some cases, the nature of the investment may deter its acquisition despite a positive net present value. For example, a chemical company might reject the acquisition of a commercial fishing operation even though the computations of net present value indicate that it would exceed the firm's cost of capital. Management might reject this investment opportunity because it has no expertise in the fishing business.

Of Interest Using Spreadsheets for Capital Budgeting

preadsheets are an ideal way to quickly and easily calculate net present values and to use sensitivity analysis in capital budgeting. To calculate net present value in Excel, the function =NPV(rate, value1, value2, . . .) is used. The rate is the discount rate over the length of one period. The range is a series of future payments (negative values) and income (positive values). However, Excel assumes that the initial payment is made at the end of the first period.

For example, to use Excel for the comprehensive example illustrated in the chapter, simply enter the cash flow amounts in a column, enter the interest rate, and enter the net present value function. Assuming cash flows are entered in column A, rows 1–5, and the required interest rate is entered in column A, row 6, then the output appears in column A, row 7 with

the following command: =NPV(A6, A1:A5). The resulting amount, $(30,196.69), is returned in column A, row 7. Notice that this in not the same answer shown in Exhibit 15.5 due to the assumption that the first cash flow occurs at the end of the first period.

To use the NPV function assuming that the initial cash outflow is at the beginning of the period, simply eliminate it from the cash flows entered and subtract it from the resulting value. For example, enter the following in column A, row 7: =NPV(A6, A2:A5)+A1. The result, $(33,216.36), is returned in column A, row 7 (the difference is due to rounding). Sensitivity analysis is completed by simply changing the cash flows and/or the interest rate. The result will change automatically.

X Microsoft Excel - NPV end

File Edit View Insert Format Tools Data Window Help

A7 =NPV(A6, A1:A5)

	A	B	C	D	E	F	G	H	I	J	K
1	-759250										
2	250000										
3	250000										
4	250000										
5	250000										
6	10%										
7	$30,196.69										
8											
9											

X Microsoft Excel - NPV beginning

File Edit View Insert Format Tools Data Window Help

A7 =NPV(A6, A2:A5)+A1

	A	B	C	D	E	F	G	H	I	J	K
1	-759250										
2	250000										
3	250000										
4	250000										
5	250000										
6	10%										
7	$33,216.36										
8											
9											

Capital budgeting is an important process used for analysis and selection of a firm's long-term investments. It requires input from many functional areas in the firm in order to be effective.

- Capital budgeting is the process used to select the long-term investment of a business and involves identifying the firm's long-term investment needs, determining the investment alternatives that can satisfy its needs, deciding which investments to acquire, and evaluating the performance of the investments after acquisition.

- Investments are made to replace worn or obsolete assets, expand the firm's operating capacity, or comply with government mandates.

- The cost of capital is the minimum acceptable return for a firm's assets and serves as a hurdle rate for screening potential investments.

- Firms use discounted cash flow analysis as a tool to evaluate whether potential investments meet the firm's cost of capital. Decision makers who use discounted cash flow analysis should consider the uncertainty about future cash flows and the qualitative aspects of the capital expenditure decision under consideration.

- Decision makers use net present value (NPV) and time-adjusted rate of return (TARR) cash flow analysis methods to assess whether an investment will generate a return that is greater than a firm's cost of capital.

- NPV uses the cost of capital to discount the projected cash flows of an investment and to determine the maximum price a firm should pay for an asset and still generate a satisfactory return. If the cost of the investment exceeds this price, the investment should be rejected.

- TARR uses the cost of the potential investment as the present value of the projected cash flows and derives the rate of return on the project given the projected cash flows. The investment is accepted or rejected based on whether the rate of return exceeds the firm's cost of capital.

- The two phases of evaluating capital expenditures are (1) determination of whether the actual cost to acquire the assets was consistent with cost projections, which occurs during the process of acquiring the asset; and (2) the postaudit phase, which takes place after acquisition to determine if the initial projections were reasonable and to review the methods and assumptions used.

- Discounted cash flow analysis is based on assumptions that (1) all cash flows are known with certainty, (2) cash flows occur at the end of the time period, and (3) cash inflows are immediately reinvested in another project that earns a return at the same rate for the company.

- Income taxes reduce cash revenues and expenses, and depreciation provides tax shields from taxes. The tax effect of gains and losses reduces and increases, respectively, the proceeds from the disposal of assets.

- Capital budgeting and management incentives based on accrual accounting can result in suboptimal decisions.

- Sensitivity analysis is a means of evaluating how capital budgeting decisions would change if the assumptions about estimated cash flows change.

KEY TERMS

acquisition phase The first capital expenditure evaluation phase in which the management accountant monitors costs incurred in conjunction with the asset's acquisition

after-tax cash flows The estimated cash flows associated with a potential investment after considering the impact of income taxes

capital budgeting The process used for analysis and selection of the long-term investments of a business

capital expenditure budget A budget that describes the amount and timing of the capital expenditures planned for the designated time period

cost of capital The weighted-average cost of a firm's debt and equity financing

discounted cash flow analysis A method to evaluate investments that uses the time value of money to assess whether the investment's expected rate of return is greater than a firm's cost of capital

financing budget A budget that outlines the amounts and sources of funds needed to finance the firm's investments for the designated time period

net present value method A discounted cash flow analysis that requires decision makers to find the present value of an investment's estimated future cash flows by using the firm's cost of capital as the discount rate

postaudit The second evaluation phase of the capital budgeting process, which involves comparing cash flow projections made in the preacquisition analysis with actual cash flows generated by the asset

tax shield A noncash expense that reduces the potential amount of a firm's tax liability by reducing its taxable income without affecting its pretax cash flows

time-adjusted rate of return (TARR) A discounted cash flow method that requires using the cost of a potential investment as the present value of the projected cash flows in order to determine the rate of return on the proposed investment

ANSWERS TO THE PAUSE & REFLECTS

p. 527, Although the total cash flows are the same, the present value of the uneven cash flows is greater because more cash was received closer to the present value date than the even cash flows.

p. 532, Cash flows from land are not shielded from taxation because land is not depreciated. Land is not depreciated because we assume that land is not used up over time.

p. 538, If the negative NPV is based on very conservative numbers, it is reasonably possible that more realistic numbers would yield a positive NPV. Unless the decision maker is a very risk-averse person it would be reasonable to accept this project. The situation is just the opposite with very optimistic projections. Unless the decision maker was a risk seeker the project would probably be rejected.

QUESTIONS

1. What is the purpose of capital budgeting and why is it important?
2. How are long-term investments identified in a business?
3. List and briefly describe the four basic processes of the capital budgeting process.
4. What is a firm's cost of capital and what role does it play in the capital budgeting process?
5. What does a positive net present value tell the person making a capital budgeting decision?
6. Describe the four steps used in the net present value method.
7. What is the decision rule used to accept or reject a potential investment when using the net present value method? Why does it work?
8. What does the time-adjusted rate of return tell the person making the capital budgeting decision?
9. There are three steps used in the time-adjusted rate of return method. Why is each important?
10. Compare and contrast the time-adjusted rate of return method and the net present value method.
11. What are the advantages and disadvantages of both the net present value method and the time-adjusted rate of return method?
12. Why can't the TARR be adjusted for changing levels of risk?
13. Identify and explain the three key assumptions underlying discounted cash flow analysis.
14. Why do we continue to use capital budgeting techniques that are based on assumptions that do not always reflect business reality?
15. How do income taxes impact the cash flows of capital budgeting decisions?
16. How does a noncash expense create a tax shield?

17. What causes gains and losses from the disposal of assets?

18. Describe how taxes impact the cash flows generated by the disposal of assets.

19. Why is sensitivity analysis useful in capital budgeting?

20. What constitutes a qualitative factor in a capital budgeting problem?

EXERCISES

E 15.1
LO 1

Greenwood Corporation's capital structure consists of $2,690,000 of assets and $1,600,000 of liabilities. Ross Greenwood, the corporation's CEO and largest shareholder, says that the debt has an average interest rate of 9 percent and that stockholders want a 14 percent return. What is Greenwood Corporation's cost of capital?

E 15.2
LO 2

Fargo Company is considering purchasing a new machine with a cost of $9,000, no salvage value, and a useful life of five years. The machine is expected to generate $2,850 in cash inflows during each year of the machine's five-year life. Fargo Company's cost of capital is 14 percent. Disregarding taxes, what is the maximum price Fargo should pay for this machine? Why? Compute the net present value of the machine. Should Fargo Company acquire the machine? Why or why not?

E 15.3
LO 3

McGuire, Inc., is considering the acquisition of a baseball winder that costs $46,200. The baseball winder has an expected life of 10 years and is expected to reduce production costs by $8,857 a year. McGuire's cost of capital is 12 percent. Disregarding the impact of taxes, compute the time-adjusted rate of return of the baseball winder. Should McGuire acquire the baseball? Why?

E 15.4
LO 3

Eric Burke is the chief financial officer of 56th Street Enterprises. He is considering the acquisition of a pasta processor with a cost of $936,000 and an installation cost of $22,000. His analysis suggests that the pasta processor will produce $192,850 a year for the next eight years. Disregarding the impact of taxes, what is the pasta processor's time-adjusted rate of return? Should Eric buy the pasta processor if the firm's cost of capital is 14 percent?

E 15.5
LO 2

The Sheridan Company is considering replacing its manual accounting system with a computerized accounting system. As of January 1, 2000, the software package and related equipment will cost the company $300,000 and are expected to have a useful life of five years. Sheridan's analyst has forecast that efficiencies created by the new system will reduce the cost of operating the accounting system by the following amounts:

2000	$ 60,000
2001	90,000
2002	150,000
2003	75,000
2004	75,000

Disregarding taxes and assuming that Sheridan's cost of capital is 12 percent, what is the maximum price Sheridan should pay for this accounting system? What is the net present value of the software package and related equipment? Should Sheridan Company buy the accounting system? Why or why not?

E 15.6
LO 2

Nemazi Company is contemplating the acquisition of a new copier on December 15, 1999. The copier costs $42,600, has an estimated life of six years, and is expected to save paper and time, as well as reduce repair cost. The cash Nemazi expects to save as a result of buying the copier over the next six years is as follows:

2000	$14,000
2001	12,000
2002	10,000
2003	8,000
2004	6,000
2005	4,000

Disregarding taxes, what is the maximum price Nemazi should pay for the copier if its cost of capital is 15 percent? Calculate the net present value of the new copier. Should Nemazi Company buy the copier? Why or why not?

E 15.7
LO 4

Lewis and Clark Corporation's sales for the year were $1,500,000 and operating expenses were $600,000. Included in the operating expenses was $100,000 of depreciation expense. If Lewis and Clark's tax rate is 30 percent, calculate the after-tax cash flows of sales, operating expenses, and depreciation. Given the information above, what are Lewis and Clark's after-tax cash flows?

E 15.8

LO 4

In January 1999, Rock Company bought a new delivery van for $20,000 that it expects to use for four years. The new van will increase delivery revenue each year by $10,700. The projected gas and repair expense and accelerated depreciation expense for each of the next four years are as follows:

	Gas and Repair Expense	Accelerated Tax Depreciation
1999	$2,700	$7,000
2000	3,250	6,000
2001	4,000	4,000
2002	4,500	3,000

If Rock's tax rate is 30 percent, what is the tax shield created by the depreciation for each year? What are the after-tax cash flows for each year?

E 15.9

LO 4

Bublitz Construction Company purchased a new steamroller on July 1, 1995, for $155,000. On April 22, 1999, Bublitz sold the steamroller. On the date of the sale, the accumulated depreciation on the steamroller was $50,700. Bublitz's tax rate on the date of the sale was 30 percent. What is the book value of the steamroller on April 22, 1999? If the steamroller sold for $116,000 cash, what is the after-tax cash inflow from the sale of the steamroller? If the steamroller sold for $94,000 cash, what is the after-tax cash inflow from the sale of the steamroller?

E 15.10

LO 4

On November 12, 1999, Pointer Corporation sold a pickup truck for $6,000 and gave a copier to a local boys and girls club. The truck originally cost $12,000 and had accumulated depreciation of $8,455 when it was sold. The copier originally cost $1,500 and had accumulated depreciation of $975 when it was donated to the local boys and girls club. If Pointer's tax rate is 30 percent, what are the cash flows generated by these two transactions?

E 15.11

LO 2 LO 4

As of January 1, 2000, Nance Company wants to acquire a new machine costing $182,000. The machine has an estimated useful life of seven years and no salvage value. Nance's tax rate is 30 percent and the annual depreciation on the machine is $26,000. The expected pretax cash flows are as follows:

	Pretax Cash Revenues	Pretax Cash Expenses
2000	$64,000	$22,000
2001	72,000	24,000
2002	80,000	30,000
2003	66,000	20,000
2004	60,000	28,000
2005	69,000	18,000
2006	50,000	16,000

If Nance Company has a 12 percent cost of capital, what is the maximum price Nance should pay for the machine? Why? Calculate the net present value of this project. Should Nance buy the machine? Why or why not?

E 15.12

LO 2 LO 4

In 1999, Sprong Corporation is considering investing in a new five-year project that will require an initial cash outlay of $630,000. When the project is undertaken, Sprong will sell old equipment with an initial cost of $400,000 and accumulated depreciation of $275,000 for $50,000 cash. Sprong's management anticipates that the new project will generate $280,000 of cash revenue and require $88,000 of cash expenses in each of the five years. Depreciation associated with the project is $80,000 each year. Sprong has a 11 percent cost of capital and a 30 percent tax rate. Calculate the project's net present value. Should Sprong undertake the project? Why or why not?

E 15.13

LO 2 LO 4

Leland Corporation is trying to decide whether or not to make the following two investments. The first is a piece of equipment that costs $40,000 but will save the company $9,000 after taxes in each year of its 10-year life. The second is a patent that costs $60,000 but will generate $9,400 in after-tax cash flows over its 17-year life. Leland Corporation's cost of capital is 14 percent. Calculate the net present value of each investment. Should the company acquire one, both, or neither investment?

E 15.14

LO 2 LO 4

In January 2000, LaClair Imports generated the data below about investments A and B which the company is considering. LaClair's cost of capital is 12 percent, and its tax rate is 30 percent.

	Investment A	Investment B
Initial Cost	$104,000	$150,000
Annual depreciation	26,000	25,000
Net pretax cash inflows:		
2000	38,000	48,000
2001	42,000	46,000
2002	34,000	60,000
2003	36,000	51,000
2004		53,000
2005		52,000

What is the net present value of each investment? Would you recommend that LaClair purchase one, both, or neither investment? Why?

E 15.15
LO 2   LO 4

Late in 1999, the Hailie Klocke Corporation has projected the pretax cash flows shown below for a wongdogotter that cost $470,000. If Klocke's tax rate is 40 percent and its cost of capital is 14 percent, calculate the net present value for this piece of equipment. Should Klocke invest in the wongdogotter? Why or why not?

	Pretax Cash Inflows	Pretax Cash Outflows	Accelerated Tax Depreciation
2000	$220,000	$350,000	$180,000
2001	400,000	320,000	160,000
2002	600,000	280,000	130,000
2003	620,000	240,000	
2004	520,000	230,000	

Would your answer be the same if the depreciation was $94,000 each year for five years and the pretax cash flows remained the same? Why?

E 15.16
LO 2   LO 4

In 1999, Murphy Corporation is considering the acquisition of a new $1,040,000 diagnostic machine and has projected the after-tax cash flows related to the machine. Chris Kohlrus, Murphy's manager, has decided to use multiple cost of capital figures to calculate the net present value of this potential investment. The cash flows and cost of capital figures are presented below. Calculate the net present value of the investment. Should Murphy buy the diagnostic machine? Why or why not?

	Cost of Capital	Years	After-Tax Cash Flows
1999–2001	12%	1999	$240,000
2002–2004	14	2000	260,000
2005–2006	15	2001	253,000
		2002	290,000
		2003	310,000
		2004	222,000
		2005	240,000
		2006	220,000

E 15.17
LO 2   LO 4

Jeff Suttle, a manager for the Salina Company, has projected the after-tax cash flows shown below for a $131,000 machine he wants to buy in December 2000. The cash flows represent a worst-case scenario for the machine.

	After-Tax Cash Flows
2001	$31,650
2002	34,050
2003	34,500
2004	33,750
2005	34,500
2006	34,600

Kathy Saxton, another Salina Company manager, feels that the projected cash flows are much too conservative and that they should be higher by as much as 5 percent each year. Salina's cost of capital is 14 percent. Calculate the net present value of the machine based on the given projections. Should Salina buy the machine?

E 15.18

LO 2 **LO 4**

The Liberal Corporation is trying to decide whether to acquire a new manufacturing facility. Three after-tax cash flows have been projected for the $580,000 facility's 15-year life. Liberal has a 15 percent cost of capital.

	Projections 1	Projection 2	Projection 3
After-tax cash flows	$97,500/year	$99,625/year	$102,500/year

Calculate the net present value of each cash flow projection. Should Liberal buy the manufacturing facility? Under what circumstances and why?

E 15.19

LO 2 **LO 4**

In 1999, the Fairbanks Company is considering whether to replace its old de-icer with a more efficient de-icer that costs $50,000. The old de-icer has a book value of $8,000 and can be sold for $10,000. The new de-icer will save $14,000 of operating cash flows before taxes in each of the next five years. Fairbanks will take $10,000 of depreciation in each of the next five years, it has a 40 percent tax rate and a 16 percent cost of capital. Calculate the NPV of this potential investment. Should Fairbanks buy the new de-icer?

E 15.20

LO 2 **LO 4** **LO 5**

Bucklin Company is a small company that employs 15 people in a town with a population of about 9,000. Ryan Sloan, Bucklin's plant manager, is considering the acquisition of a new machine that will cost $474,500. The machine will replace five long-time employees and is expected to generate savings of $105,600 in after-tax cash flows for the next 10 years. Bucklin's cost of capital is 18 percent. Based on the net present value of the machine, should Bucklin buy the machine? Are there qualitative factors that Sloan should consider in his decision? Why?

PROBLEMS

P 15.1

LO 2

The following cash savings are expected to occur if the city of Boone, Iowa, buys a trash truck at the start of 1999 that costs $93,000. The city of Boone pays no taxes and has a cost of capital of 10 percent.

1999	$28,000
2000	26,000
2001	27,000
2002	29,000
2003	28,500
2004	25,400

Required

a. What is the maximum price Boone should pay for the trash truck?
b. Calculate the net present value of the trash truck.
c. Should the city of Boone acquire the trash truck? Explain your answer.

P 15.2

LO 2 **LO 4** **LO 5**

Arbor Doctors, Inc., is considering replacing an existing cherry picker with a new cherry picker. The existing cherry picker originally cost $45,000 and has a book value of $22,000 today. The old cherry picker costs $37,000 per year to operate and can be sold today for $20,000.

The model HL250 cherry picker costs $40,000 and is expected to have a four-year life and no salvage value. The HL 250 will be depreciated at $10,000 per year and costs $26,000 to operate.

Arbor Doctors' cost of capital is 15 percent and its tax rate is 30 percent.

Required

a. Calculate the net present value of the HL250 cherry picker.
b. Should Arbor Doctors replace its existing cherry picker? Explain your answer.

P 15.3

LO 2 **LO 4** **LO 5**

Millennium Corp. manufactures lenses for telescopes. Millennium is considering replacing a machine that grinds lenses and has received a proposal from a vendor for the new lens grinder. Millennium Corp. has a 16 percent cost of capital and a 30 percent tax rate.

The vendor will sell the company a new machine for $310,000 and buy the old machine, which has a $20,000 book value, for $30,000. The new machine is expected to generate $95,000 of pretax cash inflows, and the company can recognize $62,000 of depreciation expense each year of its five-year life.

Required

a. Calculate the net present value of the new machine.
b. Should Millennium buy the new machine? Explain your answer.

P 15.4

LO 2　LO 4　LO 5

At the end of 1999, Bezdek Corporation is planning to buy a new machine for $80,000. The new machine has a useful life of seven years and is expected to have no salvage value. The pretax cash flows and the depreciation for tax purposes are described below. Bezdek's tax rate is 30 percent and its cost of capital is 15 percent.

	Pretax Cash Flows	Tax Depreciation
2000	$21,500	$20,000
2001	25,000	16,000
2002	22,000	14,000
2003	20,000	8,000
2004	19,000	6,000
2005	17,500	4,000
2006	16,000	2,000

Required

a. Calculate the net present value for the new machine.

b. Should Bezdek buy the new machine? Why?

P 15.5

LO 2　LO 4　LO 5

As of April 2000, Robinson Guide Service is considering the acquisition of a new fishing boat that costs $120,000. If the new boat is purchased, an old boat with a book value of $45,000 will be sold for $32,000. The new boat is expected to have a useful life of six years and to have no salvage value. The pretax cash flows and depreciation are shown below. Robinson Guide Service has a cost of capital of 15 percent and a tax rate of 30 percent.

	Pretax Cash Inflows	Pretax Cash Outflows	Depreciation
2000	$67,500	$30,000	$36,000
2001	84,000	45,000	32,000
2002	73,500	37,500	23,000
2003	67,500	34,500	12,000
2004	62,000	30,000	11,000
2005	59,000	32,000	6,000

Required

a. Calculate the net present value for the new boat.

b. Should Robinson Guide Service buy the new boat? Explain your answer.

P 15.6

LO 2　LO 4　LO 5

Gooch Company wants to replace a machine that has a zero book value and a market value of $6,400 in January 1999. The new machine Gooch is considering has a cost of $25,000 and an estimated useful life of five years. The new machine will create cost savings of $7,250 per year. The machine will require an additional investment in working capital of $2,000, which would be recovered at the end of the machine's life. Depreciation on the new machine would be $5,000 per year. Gooch has a 30 percent tax rate and a 14 percent cost of capital.

Required

a. Calculate the net present value of the new machine.

b. Should Gooch Company buy the machine? Explain your answer.

P 15.7

LO 2　LO 4　LO 5

Atwood Company is examining a proposal to acquire a new production facility in December 1999. If the new facility is acquired, Atwood will sell one of its plants. The new facility would cost $5,400,000 and would have an expected life of 15 years. The old plant has a book value of $700,000 and can be sold for $1,050,000. The tax law will permit the new plant to be depreciated over 10 years at $540,000 a year. At the end of the facility's life, the projected cost of dismantling and disposing of the facility is $130,000.

Due to the length of the new facility's life, Atwood wants to use 12 percent as the cost of capital for the first 10 years and 15 percent for the last 5 years. Atwood's tax rate is 30 percent. The estimated pretax cash flows for the new facility are listed below.

	Estimated Pretax Cash Flows
2000–2002	$(100,000)
2003–2007	580,000
2008–2009	430,000
2010–2014	490,000

Required

a. Develop a schedule of projected after-tax cash flows for the new facility.

b. Calculate the net present value of the new facility.

c. Should Atwood buy the new facility? Why or why not?

P 15.8

LO 2   LO 4   LO 5

Ellis Cake Company is considering a new, more efficient machine to replace its existing snack cake machine. While the new machine won't produce more snack cakes, it will reduce the cost of producing the snack cakes. The snack cakes are sold in a twin pack at $1 per pack, and management expects to sell 400,000 packs in each of the next six years.

The old machine originally cost $80,000 and currently has a book value of $48,000 and a remaining useful life of six years. The new machine will cost $220,000 and would have a useful life of six years. The following information is available to help resolve this capital budgeting question:

	Old Machine	New Machine
Expected Annual Cash		
Operating expenses:		
Variable cost per pack	$0.48	$0.29
Fixed operating expenses	$14,000	$13,000
Noncash Expenses		
Annual depreciation	8,000	35,000
Market value of machine:		
Today	32,000	220,000
In six years	–0–	20,000

Ellis's tax rate is 30 percent and its cost of capital is 12 percent.

Required

a. Calculate the net present value for the new machine.

b. Should Ellis buy the new machine? Why or why not?

P 15.9

LO 2   LO 4   LO 6

In December 1999, Utah Company is trying to decide whether to buy one, both, or neither of the investments shown below. Utah's cost of capital is 16 percent and its tax rate is 30 percent. Neither investment has a salvage value.

	Investment A	Investment B
Price	$860,000	$860,000
Annual depreciation	172,000	172,000
Projected pretax cash flows:		
2000	296,200	254,000
2001	326,200	283,400
2002	383,400	312,000
2003	440,800	340,400
2004	496,000	368,600

Required

a. Compute the net present value for both investments.

b. Assume that the cash flows could vary up and down by as much as 10 percent. How would fluctuation affect the investment decision?

c. Given the potential fluctuations, which investment would you consider acceptable? Explain your decision.

P 15.10

LO 2   LO 4   LO 5

Devore Specialties manufactures promotional gifts. In January 1999, Devore developed a promotional gift for hardware stores, and its sales force has generated orders for this product for the next three years. To produce this product, Devore had to buy two new machines and lease more building space. Each new machine cost $100,000 and installation costs were $35,000 each. To test-run both machines costs a total of $15,000. The additional space was leased for $12,000 per year for three years starting in January 1999.

The entire cost of the equipment will be depreciated over the next three years for tax purposes. Despite the zero book value at the end of the third year, the equipment can be sold for $24,000. The company expects to increase its inventory by $32,000 in the first year; this excess inventory will be disposed of in the last year of the equipment's life.

The company projects the following estimates of the revenue and cash expenses for this product:

	1999	2000	2001
Sales revenues	$250,000	$400,000	$200,000
Variable operating expenses	87,500	175,000	77,500
Depreciation	95,000	95,000	95,000
Rent expense	12,000	12,000	12,000

Required

a. Prepare a schedule showing the after-tax cash flows for this project if Devore's tax rate is 30 percent.

b. Calculate the net present value for this project if Devore's cost of capital is 20 percent.

c. Comment on whether Devore should have taken the orders for this new promotional product.

CASES

C 15.1
LO 2 LO 4 LO 5

As of January 10, 1999, you have just completed a discounted cash flow analysis on a $250,000 investment. You calculated that the net present value of the after-tax cash flows shown below is $63,570 using the company's cost of capital of 15 percent. You reported your findings to your supervisor and recommended that the company make the investment.

To your surprise, the supervisor rejected the acquisition. He said that it is company policy not to invest in any project in which the cash flows do not recover the initial investment in three years. He points out that of the $250,000 expended, only $190,000 would be recovered in three years.

	After-Tax Cash Flows
1999	$ 20,000
2000	50,000
2001	120,000
2002	100,000
2003	100,000
2004	90,000
2005	80,000
Present value of cash flows at 15% cost of capital	$313,570
Cost of investment	250,000
Net present value	$ 63,570

Write a memo explaining why the company should make this investment and why the company should scrap its three-year payback rule.

C 15.2
LO 2 LO 4 LO 5

Rooks Products, Inc., manufactures a product it sells for $25. Rooks sells all of the 24,000 units it is capable of producing at the current time, and a marketing study indicates that it could sell 14,000 more units. To increase its capacity, Rooks must buy a machine that has the capacity to produce 50,000 units of its product.

The existing equipment can produce the product at a variable cost of $16 per unit. Today it has a book value of $80,000 and a market value of $60,000. It has a remaining life of five years but no salvage value. The depreciation on the old equipment is $16,000 per year.

The new equipment could produce 50,000 units at a variable cost of $12 per unit. The new equipment would cost $500,000 and has a five-year life, which would be depreciated at a rate of $100,000 per year. If the new machine is purchased, fixed operating costs will decrease by $20,000 per year.

If Rooks' cost of capital is 18 percent and its tax rate is 30 percent, should Rooks buy the new machine? Why or why not?

CRITICAL THINKING

CT 15.1
LO 2 LO 4

Tuttle Corporation is going to buy one of the two machines described below. Each machine meets the specifications for a particular task in the company. Tuttle's tax rate is 30 percent, and its cost of capital is 15 percent. Which machine should Tuttle buy and why?

Machine A: Costs $90,000 to acquire and $12,000 cash a year to operate in each year of its 10-year life. Annual depreciation is $9,000, and the machine has no salvage value.

Machine B: Costs $50,000 to acquire and $24,600 a year to operate in each year of its 10-year life. Annual depreciation is $5,000, and the machine has no salvage value.

CT 15.2
LO 6

Your supervisor has just completed a discounted cash flow analysis on a 15-year, $3,000,000 project. She is very excited that the net present value was positive and is getting ready to report her findings to senior management and to strongly recommend that the company undertake the project.

Upon reviewing the computations, you discover that the net present value on this $3,000,000 project was a positive $351. What factors about the analysis would you suggest that your supervisor consider before she makes her report strongly recommending this project?

ETHICAL CHALLENGES

EC 15.1
LO 1 LO 5

Wal-Mart has run into opposition when it has tried to open Wal-Mart stores in certain New England and Pennsylvania towns. Wal-Mart's capital budgeting process has determined that these locations would be profitable for the corporation. However, these communities have successfully fought to keep Wal-Mart from opening new stores. The communities argue that a Wal-Mart store will destroy the downtown business of the community and hurt the town's quality of life. Despite being rebuffed by the citizens of these towns, Wal-Mart has continued its efforts to locate stores in these communities. Should Wal-Mart continue or stop its efforts to open stores in these communities? Why or why not?

EC 15.2
LO 1 **LO 5**

The Short Corporation has the opportunity to manufacture a new chemical but will have to buy a new machine that costs $350,000 to produce the chemical. The net present value of the new machine is $2,500. However, you have learned that in calculating the net present value, the cost of disposing of the waste product that the EPA has labeled mildly hazardous was excluded. Short disputes the EPA's claim that the waste product is toxic. Therefore, Short's management decided it could avoid the disposal cost by dumping the waste with other trash. Should Short buy the new machine? Why or why not?

COMPUTER APPLICATIONS

CA 15.1
LO 2 **LO4** **LO 5**

Rutherford Company wants to determine whether it should invest in a piece of equipment that costs $1 million and is expected to last 10 years. At the end of the 10-year period, the equipment will be scrapped and have no salvage value. Rutherford has a 12 percent cost of capital. The expected after-tax net cash flows of the equipment (including the tax shield) are shown below:

Year	After-Tax Cash Flows
1	$ 225,000
2	200,000
3	250,000
4	250,000
5	(300,000)
6	250,000
7	250,000
8	225,000
9	125,000
10	50,000

Required

Use a computer spreadsheet package.
a. What is the net present value of this equipment assuming the cash flows begin one year from today?
b. What is the net present value of this equipment assuming cash flows begin today?
c. Should Rutherford invest in the equipment? Why or why not?

CA 15.2
LO 2 **LO4** **LO 5**

Barnes & Son, Inc., wants to buy a new printing press. The cost of the press is $300,000 and it is expected to last for 10 years, after which it will be scrapped with no salvage value. Barnes & Son has an 8 percent cost of capital. The pretax net cash inflows are shown below. Barnes & Son is subject to a 40 percent tax rate.

Year	Pretax Cash Flow
1	$ 80,000
2	90,000
3	100,000
4	110,000
5	100,000
6	90,000
7	75,000
8	60,000
9	50,000
10	25,000

Required

Use a computer spreadsheet package.
a. What is the net present value of the printing press assuming the cash flows begin one year from today?
b. What is the net present value of this equipment assuming cash flows are 5 percent smaller each year?
c. Should Barnes & Son invest in the new printing press? Why or why not?
d. What would your answer be if the cost of capital was 18%?

CA 15.3
LO 1

Select a company of your choice and then locate its home page on the Internet. Using the company's financial statements taken from its home page, identify two investing events that occurred in the past year that could have used capital budgeting in planning for their acquisition. Identify two investing events the company is currently planning. Print out the evidence that supports your findings.

PART FIVE

LEARNING OBJECTIVES

LO 1 Explain what a company's human resources decisions are and how they are linked to its strategy.

LO 2 Describe the costs incurred in and the benefits derived from employee recruitment, selection, training, and development processes.

LO 3 Describe the type and cost of benefits provided to employees during and after employment.

LO 4 Explain how a company uses the balanced scorecard approach to manage its noncapitalized assets.

APPENDIX

LO 5 Compare and contrast motivation and leadership theories and their implications for employee evaluation and reward systems.

Planning Investments in Human Resources and Other Noncapitalized Assets

MICROSOFT
www.microsoft.com

Microsoft Corporation, founded in 1975 by Bill Gates (then 20 years old), has become the world's largest manufacturer of personal computer software. Its products include operating systems, server applications, productivity applications, interactive media, and Internet tools. Microsoft products are available in more than 30 languages in more than 50 countries.

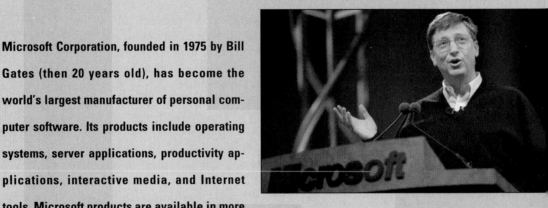

In 1998, the company employed over 25,000 people, of which over 8,000 were employed outside the United States. In 1998, 71.5 percent of the workforce were male and 28.5 percent were female, 29.2 percent were between 20 and 29 years of age, and 51.1 percent were between 30 and 39 years of age.

Microsoft is heavily engaged in research and development to support its ability to grow into the future. In addition, Microsoft employees are actively engaged in sales-support activities to ensure customer satisfaction. Microsoft is known for its outstanding employee benefits program that enables it to attract and retain qualified employees who are committed to growth. Clearly, Microsoft is a company that values its human capital.

I n Chapter 1, you learned that assets are probable future benefits obtained and controlled by the entity. However, companies manage many other items that have value but do not fit the accounting definition of an asset. For example, a company's reputation is valuable, but it is not an accounting asset because it cannot be measured objectively. Likewise a company's research and development activities are not assets. We call these items that have future value but do not qualify as assets as **noncapitalized assets.** One of the most important noncapitalized assets is human capital—that is, an investment in people. Human capital is not considered an asset because it is not controlled by the company. In Chapter 9, we discussed employee pay and payroll taxes. In this chapter, we take another look at employees as we explore human resources management. Then we look at how companies use the balanced scorecard approach to manage their human and other noncapitalized assets.

PAUSE & REFLECT

When sports teams sign players to long-term contracts, are the contracts considered assets?
(answer on page 569)

HUMAN RESOURCES MANAGEMENT

LO 1

Human resources (HR) management is the set of policies and procedures companies use to ensure effective and efficient use of their human capital. As we have seen, successful companies manage their resources to achieve the best results, and HR must be managed just like the financial, technological, and other resources of the company. HR management does not exist in a vacuum. It is shaped by the company's external environment and organizational strategy. We explore these issues next.

External Environment and Organizational Structure

The external environment can be considered a continuum with certainty at one end and uncertainty at the other end. A certain environment is characterized as one where the products and customers are established, the competition is known, and cost control is a primary concern. Companies operating in a certain environment tend to focus inward. That is, they tend to treat the external environment as given and concentrate on ways to improve operating efficiency. These companies usually have a **mechanistic organizational structure** in which activities and employees are arranged by functions—that is, production, research and development, marketing, accounting, and finance. Control is maintained at the top of the hierarchy, and the organization is characterized as following rules and procedures.

An uncertain environment is characterized as having rapidly changing products and/or customer bases, incoming and outgoing competitors, and creativity as a primary concern. Companies operating in this environment tend to focus outward. That is, they concentrate on customer satisfaction and new product development. These companies often have an **organic organizational structure** in which activities and people are arranged by cross-functional teams—that is, team members from production, research and development, marketing, accounting, and finance. Thus decision making is decentralized and the organization has few formalized rules and regulations.

Organizational Strategy

Organizational strategy is a company's long-term plan for using its resources including its human capital. An organization's strategy is a function of its external environment and its organizational structure. We can think of strategy as a continuum with efficiency at one end and flexibility at the other. That is, a company adopts a strategy that focuses more on efficiency of operations or more on flexibility of operations.

Companies adopting an **efficiency strategy** focus primarily on the reduction or containment of costs, improvements in productivity, and penetration of their products and services in the market by having the lowest cost. For example, Lincoln Electric, Inc., a manufacturer of nuts and bolts for electrical applications, follows an efficiency strategy because it is in a more certain environment and has a mechanistic organizational structure. It actively engages in activities designed to reduce production costs and focuses its marketing efforts on cost-conscious buyers. In companies using an efficiency strategy, human resources management focuses on building skills in the current workforce, specializing in production and control, promoting from within, and job-specific training. The performance evaluation and reward systems in these companies usually focus on meeting or improving budgeted amounts.

Companies adopting a **flexibility strategy** strive to adapt to changing market conditions by expanding (or contracting) product lines, customer bases, and markets. For example, Microsoft follows a flexibility strategy in part due to its uncertain environment and organic structure. It strives to provide the latest in technology to its customers all over the world. In companies using a flexibility strategy, human resources management focuses on hiring needed skills in the global marketplace, maintaining flexibility in the workforce, and training for a broad set of skills. The performance and reward systems in these companies usually focus on product development ideas and creativity.

Exhibit 16.1 illustrates how the company's environment, focus, structure, and strategy are related to its human resources management. Thus we would expect companies in rapidly changing industries such as computer technology to focus outward (market-based focus), to have organic organizational structures, and to adopt flexibility strategies. These companies are likely to use the latest in technology and need employees who are creative and adaptable. On the other hand, we would expect companies in stable industries such as steel manufacturing to focus inward (cost-based focus), to have mechanistic organizational structures, and to adopt strategies of efficiency. These companies tend to use more established technologies and have less need for creativity in the workforce. We examine the costs and benefits of human capital management next.

EXHIBIT 16.1	**Relationship of Human Resources Management and Strategy**	
	Flexibility Strategy	**Efficiency Strategy**
Environment	Uncertainty	Certainty
Focus	External	Internal
Structure	Organic	Mechanistic
Human Resources Management	1. Hire skills needed 2. Staff externally 3. Maintain broad skill base 4. Maintain flexibility	1. Build skills needed 2. Promote from within 3. Use narrow skill base 4. Use job-specific training

RECRUITMENT AND SELECTION, TRAINING AND DEVELOPMENT, AND THE COSTS OF HUMAN CAPITAL

LO 2

Human resources management begins with planning. The company must understand its future needs for human capital and plan for ways to meet those needs. In a broad sense, human resources planning consists of four steps:

1. Determine job skills needed in the future.

2. Assess the skills of the current workforce.

3. Determine the future supply of human capital.

4. Prepare a strategic plan for obtaining human capital.

First, management must determine the job skills needed in the future. This requires a careful consideration of future technology changes, new domestic and foreign markets, and new products and services the company has planned. Managers must answer questions such as:

• What technology will be used in the future?

• What countries will be trading partners?

• What specialized products and services will be provided?

The answers to these questions help managers determine the demand for certain job skills.

The second step the company takes is to assess the skills of its current workforce. To do this, it must analyze its current workforce by answering questions such as:

- What is the average age of the workforce?

- What is the educational level of the workforce?

- What is the technical sophistication of the workforce?

- What are the language capabilities of the workforce?

The answers to these questions compared to the answers to the questions in the first step help managers determine where voids exist.

In the third step, the company must assess the future supply of human capital. Managers must analyze the market of human capital. To do this requires a demographic analysis of where labor is located, what the future cost of labor might be, and what skills the future labor force is likely to possess. Managers must know:

- Will human capital be available locally, regionally, domestically, and/or from other countries?

- What is the expected future cost of labor in each of the above areas?

- How well will labor be trained and educated in the future? Who will do the training?

The answers to these questions help managers understand the supply side of the labor market.

Finally, the company should prepare a strategic plan for obtaining human capital. This strategic plan is based on the analysis of the demand for (Step 1 and Step 2) and supply of (Step 3) labor. In addition, the company must consider the environment (certain or uncertain) and organizational structure (mechanistic or organic) expected in the future. The strategic plan should include processes for recruitment, selection, training, and development of human capital. We look at recruitment and selection as well as training and development issues next. Then we examine the types of compensation plans used by companies.

Recruitment and Selection: Costs and Benefits

Once a company knows what skills it needs, it must know where to find people who have these skills. Organizations use a variety of methods to recruit and select employees. Some companies run print advertisements of job openings, some use the Internet, some recruit on college campuses, and many employ professional headhunters to locate prime job candidates. Regardless of the means used to locate people, the company must be aware of legal restrictions, such as the Civil Rights Act of 1965, which prohibits discrimination. In addition, because recruitment and selection of employees can be a time-consuming and expensive process, the company must ensure that its practices result in the best people being hired for a specific job.

The costs of recruitment and selection are many and varied. For example, a company may have a human resources or personnel department to handle human resources issues. The costs of this department include the following:

- Salaries paid to HR employees

- Costs of advertising for positions

- Travel costs incurred to interview potential employees

- Costs incurred for recordkeeping within the HR department to indicate compliance with regulations

- Costs incurred for recordkeeping within the HR department to maintain past, present, and future employee files

- Costs incurred to conduct employment tests and/or background investigations of potential employees

What are the benefits of a recruitment and selection strategy? First, a good recruitment and selection strategy minimizes the chance of hiring incompetent and unproductive employees. Second, because the costs incurred to recruit and select as well as the costs incurred to train and develop (discussed next) are high, a process that helps ensure a good fit between the employee and the company saves the company money in the long run. Finally, a well-developed recruitment and selection process indicates compliance with labor regulations, thereby reducing the chances of labor-related litigation.

Training and Development: Costs and Benefits

Once employees have been hired, they must be trained and developed for the specific requirements of the company. Many companies offer employee orientation activities to acquaint employees with company policies. Some of the items discussed in such sessions include (1) company history, (2) product and service requirements, (3) employee benefits, (4) employee evaluations, and (5) company chain-of-command. The purpose of orientation sessions is twofold. First, new employees must be educated about company policy. Second, orientation sessions are designed to make employees less apprehensive about their new positions. Information dissemination is a key tool in reducing anxiety.

Following, or in conjunction with, orientation, companies often conduct formal or informal training sessions. Training sessions are designed to provide employees with skills needed to conduct their jobs. Some companies send new hires to formal training sessions conducted by professional educators within the organization. For example, Arthur Andersen, LLP, provides its new employees with several weeks of training at its St. Charles training facility outside of Chicago. Other companies provide on-the-job training. In either case, significant costs are incurred. The costs of formal off-the-job training are obvious. The company must maintain a training center, training staff, and materials, and it must provide compensation to the new recruits during training. The costs of informal or on-the-job training may be more subtle. For example, the employee may make mistakes while learning his or her job. If these mistakes are noticed, they must be corrected; therefore, a cost is incurred. If these mistakes are not noticed, a more significant cost may be incurred in the future. For example, a mistake made by an assembly-line worker, if uncorrected, could result in a defective product. As you learned in Chapter 13, defective products lead to customer ill will, which is an important cost.

The benefits of training programs are twofold. First, employees who are trained are less likely to make costly mistakes. Thus costs associated with defects and customer ill will are avoided. Second, employees who are trained are more likely to continue their employment with the company than are employees who are merely "thrown to the wolves." A trained employee is more comfortable in his or her new job and typically feels a greater sense of loyalty to the company. This, in turn, saves the company the cost of recruiting, selecting, and training replacements. Some companies strive to make new employees feel that they are part of the team, not merely workers. For example, Wal-Mart and Saturn refer to their employees as "associates" to create a sense of community and increase employee satisfaction.

Are Employees Assets?

The focus on employee's skills and morale should not end after initial orientation and training. Successful companies continually monitor their employees and provide development for them throughout their tenure with the company. Employee development is the process of continuing education for employees. The costs and benefits of employee development are similar to employee training, but development occurs throughout the employee's time with the company. For example, some companies cross-train employees. This means that employees are trained to do more than one job. Other companies train employees for future activities. An added benefit of the latter type of employee development is flexibility. That is, a company that develops its employees for tomorrow is better able to adapt as conditions require.

In most organizations, orientation, training, and development are necessary but not sufficient activities to keep employees happy and productive. In addition, companies must motivate employees to work in the organization's best interests (see the appendix at the end of this chapter). Employees must also receive a benefits package that encourages them to continue employment.

EMPLOYEE BENEFITS

LO 3

As discussed in Chapter 9, when companies pay their employees, they also withhold voluntary and mandatory amounts for such items as union dues, retirement savings, and taxes. In addition to the regular wages and salaries paid to employees, many companies also provide additional benefits such as health and life insurance, paid leave, and bonuses for employees. Whether employees are accountants, production workers, or upper-level managers, the wages and other benefits paid them are part of the cost of obtaining and maintaining the company's human capital. Therefore, employee benefits must be carefully planned as part of the overall investment in human resources. We first look at compensation plans that define how a company pays its current employees. Then we examine other benefits "paid" to current employees such as insurance, paid leave, and cash bonuses based on performance.

Compensation Plans

Companies pay their employees using a variety of plans. Some companies pay employees **piece-rate pay.** That is, the employee receives compensation based on the number of items completed. For example, in the clothing manufacturing industry, it is common for employees to be paid based on the number of articles of clothing manufactured. A variation of piece-rate pay is **commission pay.** A commission, typically used for sales personnel, is a percentage of revenue generated. Commissions are usually based on net sales or contribution margin. Companies use piece-rate pay to encourage productivity, therefore, the company expects compensation costs to increase as productivity increases.

The most common form of compensation is **hourly pay.** The employee is paid a certain amount per hour with, perhaps, more per hour for overtime. In this situation, the amount of pay is not based on the amount of work completed.

Employees have many demands on their time.

Calvin and Hobbes

by Bill Watterson

Finally, some employees are paid **salary pay,** compensation based on a fixed amount per period, typically one month. In this situation, the amount of pay is independent of the number of hours worked or the amount of work done.

An individual company may use any one or a combination of these compensation plans. For example, sales personnel are often paid a fixed salary plus a commission to encourage productivity. Companies often use hourly pay and salaries to encourage time-on-task. Therefore, the company expects compensation costs of hourly employees to increase only if more time is required to accomplish the objectives of the company.

Health and Life Insurance

In general, when a business buys an insurance policy, it is buying protection for its assets. For example, a flood insurance policy protects the company from substantial loss of property due to floods because the company receives insurance proceeds to replace the assets lost. A fire insurance policy protects the company from substantial loss of property due to fire because the company receives insurance proceeds in the event of loss. A life insurance policy on a key executive protects the company from substantial loss in the event of the executive's untimely death because the company receives insurance proceeds in the event of such a loss. However, in most cases when a company provides health and life insurance for its employees, it is not the beneficiary of the policy. In these cases, is the company receiving any benefit from the insurance? Let's explore the issues.

Why do companies pay for health and life insurance for their employees and subsidize insurance payments for the employees' families? The best answer is that by offering these forms of compensation in addition to wages and salaries, companies can recruit and retain better employees at a lower overall cost to the company. If a company offered its employees a wage rate high enough to allow them to buy their own insurance, it would cost the company more than it does to offer lower wages to employees and to buy health and life insurance policies directly. It is less expensive for companies to buy health and life insurance because they can do so at group insurance rates that are lower than individual rates. Therefore, the cost of paying lower wages plus insurance is lower than the cost of paying higher wages. In addition, employees may be reluctant to leave positions where health and life insurance benefits are provided; a company thereby saves recruitment, selection, and training costs. Based on these facts, it seems that companies do, in fact, receive benefits from insuring employees and their families.

Paid Leave

Most businesses pay employees during certain times when the employee is not working. For example, companies pay sick leave, family leave, and vacation leave. Sick leave and vacations are typically paid leave. That is, employees receive wages and salaries as if they had been working. Family leave—that is, leave for family reasons such as the birth or adoption of a child, the care of elderly parents, or the illness of a spouse—may be paid or unpaid. Some companies pay employees for a certain amount of family leave; others simply ensure the employee a job when the family leave expires. In both cases, however, there is a cost to the company. When an employee is on leave, his or her work must be completed by someone else. This person may be another employee of the company, or as is increasingly common, a temporary worker may be hired.

As with insurance benefits, companies offer paid or unpaid leave based on the belief that these benefits help attract and retain better employees. Thus the company benefits by reducing recruiting, selecting, training, and development costs.

Bonuses

A bonus is a fringe benefit, or a part of the company's compensation plan, that is contingent on the occurrence of some future event. For example, sales employees may be given bonuses if their individual or group sales exceed some targeted amount. Production employees may be given a bonus if production quotas are met. In these cases, the individual or group performance is fairly easy to measure (the dollar amount of sales or the number of units produced), so the link between performance and reward is clear.

However, the link between effort and performance of upper-level managers is more difficult to measure. An upper-level manager spends time supervising, making decisions, thinking, networking, and planning. The output of these activities is typically not measurable in quantitative terms. Thus upper-level managers' bonuses are often based on broader organizational measures such as net income. In this way, the manager is encouraged to increase the profitability of the company. When the company's profits increase, the bonus payment increases. From the company's perspective, there is an additional consideration, however. The bonus payment is an expense to the company. Thus the bonus, itself, affects net income and, therefore, income taxes as shown in the following condensed income statement:

Sales
Less cost of goods sold
Gross margin
Less operating expenses other than bonuses
Income before bonus and income taxes
Less bonus
Income before income taxes
Less income taxes
Net income

It is important that companies consider the effect of the bonus on income and income taxes when they set the bonus rate and bonus base. The **bonus rate** is the percentage the bonus will pay; for example, 5 percent or 10 percent. The **bonus base** is the form of income the bonus rate is applied to; for example, income before bonus and income taxes, income before income taxes, or net income.

To illustrate the calculation of a bonus, we use the following information:

Income before bonus or income taxes	$1,000,000
Income tax rate	30%
Bonus rate	10%

This information is used to illustrate the impact various bonus bases have on the company's net income and cash outflows. For this illustration, we assume that all bonuses and income taxes are paid in cash in the period incurred.

Bonus Based on Income before Bonus or Income Taxes   If the bonus is based on income before bonus or income taxes, the bonus base is $1 million. The resulting bonus is $100,000 ($1,000,000 × 10%). The company's net income and cash outflows associated with the bonus and income taxes are shown below.

Income before bonus and income taxes	$1,000,000
Less bonus (0.10 × $1,000,000)	100,000
Income before income taxes	$ 900,000
Less income taxes (0.30 × $900,000)	270,000
Net income	$ 630,000
Cash paid for bonuses	$ 100,000
Cash paid for income taxes	270,000
Total cash outflows	$ 370,000

This situation is fairly straightforward and the calculations are not difficult. But when the bonus is based on income after the bonus, the computations are more complex.

Bonus Based on Income before Income Taxes   Let's return to the original information. If the bonus is 10 percent of income before income taxes (i.e., after the bonus), the bonus formula is:

$$\text{Bonus} = (\text{Income before bonus} - \text{Bonus}) \times \text{Bonus rate}$$

Therefore, the bonus amount is $90,909, as follows:

$$\text{Bonus} = (\$1,000,000 - \text{Bonus}) \times 0.10$$
$$\text{Bonus} = \$100,000 - 0.10\,(\text{Bonus})$$
$$1.1\,(\text{Bonus}) = \$100,000$$
$$\text{Bonus} = \$90,909$$

The resulting net income and cash outflows associated with the bonus and income taxes are calculated as follows (all amounts are rounded to the nearest dollar):

Income before bonus and income taxes	$1,000,000
Less bonus	90,909
Income before income taxes	$ 909,091
Less income taxes (0.30 × $909,091)	272,727
Net income	$ 636,364
Cash paid for bonuses	$ 90,909
Cash paid for income taxes	272,727
Total cash outflows	$ 363,636

Notice that by basing the bonus on income after the bonus, the company is able to increase its net income and decrease its total cash outflows.

Bonus Based on Net Income   What happens if the bonus is based on net income (i.e., after bonus and after taxes)? In this case, we have two formulas to work with: one to calculate the bonus and another to calculate the income taxes as shown below.

[1]   Bonus = (Income before bonus and income taxes – Bonus
                    – Income taxes) × Bonus rate

[2]   Income taxes = (Income before bonus and income taxes – Bonus)
                    × Tax rate

Using the information given above, we know the following:

[1]   Bonus = ($1,000,000 – Bonus – Income taxes) × 0.10
[2]   Income taxes = ($1,000,000 – Bonus) × 0.30

Now we simplify the income tax equation [2] and insert it into the bonus equation [1] for the "Income taxes" variable as follows:

[2]   Income taxes = ($1,000,000 – Bonus) × 0.30
                    Income taxes = $300,000 – 0.30 (Bonus)

[1]   Bonus = ($1,000,000 – Bonus – **[$300,000 – 0.30 {Bonus}]**) × 0.10
                    Bonus = ($1,000,000 – Bonus – $300,000 + 0.30[Bonus]) × 0.10
                    Bonus = $100,000 – 0.10(Bonus) – $30,000 + 0.03(Bonus)
                    Bonus = $70,000 – 0.07(Bonus)
                    1.07(Bonus) = $70,000
                    Bonus = $65,421

The resulting net income and cash outflows associated with the bonus and income taxes are calculated as follows:

Income before bonus and income taxes	$1,000,000
Less bonus	65,421
Income before income taxes	$ 934,579
Less income taxes (0.30 × $934,579)	280,374
Net income	$ 654,205
Cash paid for bonuses	$ 65,421
Cash paid for income taxes	280,374
Total cash outflows	$ 345,795

DEFERRED COMPENSATION

Deferred compensation is an employee benefit that is earned in one period and "paid" out in a future period. We discuss next two types of deferred compensation: cash compensation and stock options.

Deferred Cash Compensation

Often both companies and employees benefit from deferred cash compensation. The company benefits because it is able to invest the compensation amount and, therefore, the present value concepts you learned in Chapter 14 apply. For example, assume a company offered a key employee $1,000,000 in deferred compensation payable in five years. Assuming the company can invest at 10 percent annual interest, what is the present value of this deferred compensation?

$$\$1,000,000 \times P_{5,10\%}[1] = \text{Present value}$$
$$\$1,000,000 \times 0.6209 = \$620,900$$

Thus the cost of this $1,000,000 deferred compensation to the company is only $620,900. The company receives the benefits associated with recruiting and retaining high-quality human capital at a reduced cost.

How is this a benefit to the employee? Wouldn't the employee rather have the cash now? The answer is, it depends. If the employee cannot invest at 10 percent, he or she is better off receiving the $1,000,000 later. But even if the employee can earn the same rate as the company, another issue exists—the employee's present and future tax rate. As you know, the tax system in the United States is progressive; that is, at lower-levels of income, the tax rate is lower. Therefore, if the employee expects a lower tax rate in the future, he or she might be better off deferring the compensation and, therefore, paying less tax. Thus, the employee also benefits from this deferred compensation arrangement.

Stock Options

Some companies offer employees the option of purchasing capital stock rather than receiving cash as deferred compensation.[2] An employee stock option plan offers employees the option of purchasing the company's capital stock (from the company) at some specified price within some specified period of time. The benefits to the company are threefold. First, the company has no current cash outflow. Second, because the employee must continue working for the company in order to exercise the option, the company has saved recruiting, selecting, training, and development costs. Third, the options generally do not result in any expense to the company. However, there is one potential drawback. The options, when exercised, may result in the employee being able to retire. Consider Microsoft, for example. Many of its early employees exercised their options and retired as very wealthy people. While this is good for the employee, it may not be good for Microsoft because it loses talented, trained employees.

The value of the stock option plan to the employee depends on what happens to the market value (selling price of the stock in the market) of the stock in the future. For example, assume Employee A is offered an option on December 31, 1999, to buy 100 shares of the company's stock at $50 per share on December 31, 2001. If the market value of the stock on December 31, 2001, is $60 per share, Employee A will exercise the option. Employee A pays the company $5,000 (100 shares × $50 per share) and then can sell those shares in the market for $6,000 (100 shares × $60 per share). The employee gains $1,000. On the other hand, if the market value of the stock on December 31, 2001, is only $45 per share, Employee A will not exercise the option. Does the employee have to pay the difference between the option price of $50 per share and the current market value of the stock, $45? No; the employee simply forgoes the opportunity to exercise the option.

As with deferred cash compensation, an added benefit accrues to employees whose tax rate decreases before the option is exercised. Another benefit is that, sometimes, employees can sell their stock options rather than waiting until the option date to exercise them. From the company's perspective, another significant benefit of stock options is the sense of ownership instilled among employees. Because the employee benefits more if the market price of the stock increases, the employee is motivated to ensure that the company is successful. Thus the stock option serves to entice employees to act like owners.

POST-RETIREMENT BENEFITS

Employers and employees regard benefits received after retirement as an important part of the current benefit package. Post-retirement benefits include all the benefits employees

---

[1]See Table 2 at the end of the book.

[2]Capital stock can also be offered as current compensation. In this case, the transaction is taxable at the time the stock is received at the market value (current selling price) of the stock.

Of Interest Microsoft's Employee Benefits

Microsoft offers its employees three basic deferred compensation plans. It has a stock purchase plan where employees can purchase stock at six-month intervals for 85 percent of the current market value. It has a 401(k) savings plan where employees can defer up to 15 percent of their salary on a pre-tax basis. Finally, Microsoft offers a stock option plan, which vests in approximately 4.5 years from the date the option is granted. The following is a description of Microsoft's deferred compensation plans:

Employee Stock and Savings Plans

Employee stock purchase plan
The Company has an employee stock purchase plan for all eligible employees. Under the plan, shares of the Company's common stock may be purchased at six-month intervals at 85% of the lower of the fair market value on the first or the last day of each six-month period. Employees may purchase shares having a value not exceeding 10% of their gross compensation during an offering period. During 1996, 1997, and 1998, employees purchased 3.6 million, 2.8 million, and 2.2 million shares at average prices of $18.86, $29.82, and $54.42 per share. At June 30, 1998, 36.8 million shares were reserved for future issuance.

Savings plan
The Company has a savings plan, which qualifies under Section 401(k) of the Internal Revenue Code. Participating employees may defer up to 15% of pretax salary, but not more than statutory limits. The Company contributes fifty cents for each dollar a participant contributes, with a maximum contribution of 3% of a participant's earnings. Matching contributions were $15 million, $28 million, and $39 million in 1996, 1997, and 1998.

Stock option plans
The Company has stock option plans for directors, officers, and employees, which provide for nonqualified and incentive stock options. The option exercise price is the fair market value at the date of grant. Options granted prior to 1995 generally vest over four and one-half years and expire 10 years from the date of grant. Options granted during and after 1995 generally vest over four and one-half years and expire seven years from the date of grant, while certain options vest over seven and one-half years and expire after 10 years. At June 30, 1998, options for 222 million shares were vested and 523 million shares were available for future grants under the plans.

Sources: Microsoft Corporation, *1998 Annual Report;* <www.microsoft.com/msft/ar98/financial/notes>.

---

receive after retirement such as pensions, continued health insurance coverage, and other perks such as office or parking space. We focus on pensions and health coverage because these costs are significant.

Types of Post-Retirement Benefit Plans

There are two basic types of post-retirement benefit plans: defined contribution plans and defined benefit plans. In a **defined contribution plan,** the employer promises to make specific contributions to the plan, but the post-retirement benefits received by retirees are not specified. For example, assume that Microsoft has a defined contribution plan whereby it contributes $500 per month for each employee. When the employee retires, he or she can receive benefits from the plan, but the amount of benefit received is a function of (1) the total amount contributed on the employee's behalf and (2) the interest and dividends earned by the plan. Defined contribution plans are often matching plans. That is, the employee can contribute a certain amount to the plan and the company will match this amount. Therefore, the defined contribution plan is contributory (discussed later).

In a **defined benefit plan,** the employer promises to pay the employee a specified amount at retirement, but the contributions made to the plan are not specified. For example, assume that Microsoft has a defined benefit plan whereby each employee can receive $500 per month when he or she retires. The amount that the employer must contribute to the plan is a function of (1) the expected return on the plan resources and (2) the time remaining until the employee retires.

In both the defined contribution and defined benefit plans, the time value of money techniques learned in Chapter 14 are applicable. As a simple example, assume that an employer has a defined contribution plan whereby $1,000 is contributed each year for Employee B. Further assume that Employee B will be covered by the plan for 30 years and will retire at age 65, at which time the employee will receive all benefits.[3] Finally, assume that the benefit plan is expected to earn 10 percent annually. We need to determine two items: the amount contributed to the plan by the employer and the amount received by Employee B.

Because this is a defined contribution plan, the amount contributed by the employer is simply $1,000 per year. To determine the amount Employee B receives, we calculate the future value of this $1,000 annual annuity for 30 periods earning 10 percent:

$$\$1,000 \times F_{30,10\%}{}^4 = \text{Future value}$$
$$\$1,000 \times 164.4940 = \$164,494$$

Therefore, the employer invests $1,000 annually for 30 years, and Employee B receives a lump-sum payment of $164,494 upon retirement.

Now consider a simple example of a defined benefit plan. Assume that an employer promises to pay Employee C a lump-sum payment of $200,000 upon retirement. Further assume that Employee C plans to retire in 25 years. Finally, assume that the employer believes it can earn 12 percent interest on annual payments made to the benefit plan. Again, we need to determine two things: the amount contributed to the plan by the employer and the amount received by Employee C.

In this case, the amount received by Employee C is known—$200,000. To determine the annual contribution required by the employer, we must determine the annual annuity needed for 25 periods at 12 percent interest:

$$\text{Annuity} \times F_{25,12\%}{}^5 = \text{Future value}$$
$$\text{Annuity} \times 133.3339 = \$200,000$$
$$\text{Annuity} = \$1,500$$

Therefore, the employer invests $1,500 annually for 25 years, and Employee C receives a lump-sum distribution of $200,000 upon retirement.

Other Characteristics of Post-Retirement Benefit Plans

There are three other characteristics of benefit plans that are important to employees and employers. The first concerns whether the employee has a right to the benefits if employment ceases. The second concerns whether the employee contributes personal funds to the benefit plan. The third concerns how the benefit plan is funded.

When an employee has rights to the benefit plan even if the employee is not employed at the time, the benefit plan is a **vested plan.** If the employee has no rights to the benefit plan when employment ceases, the benefit plan is an **unvested plan.** Employees should exercise caution in this area because many employers require a certain length of employment before benefits vest. If an employee and his or her employer contribute to the benefit plan, the plan is a **contributory plan.** If only the employer contributes to the benefit plan, the plan is a **noncontributory plan.** If only the employee contributes to the plan, the plan is independent from the employer and, therefore, is not a company benefit plan. Finally, if the employer makes periodic payments to an independent funding agent, the benefit plan is a **funded plan.** If the employer retains control of the benefit plan funds, the plan is an **unfunded plan.** Healthcare plans are typically unfunded, while most pension plans are funded. Exhibit 16.2 illustrates the relationship among the employer, employee, and funding agent in a funded benefit plan. Notice that the employer (or employer and employee) makes cash payments to the agent. The agent, in turn, invests the funds. The employee receives payment(s) from the agent upon retirement.

THE BALANCED SCORECARD

LO 4

Since the mid-1990s many companies have adopted a management strategy known as the *balance scorecard approach.* Companies that adopt the balanced scorecard approach recognize that noncapitalized assets enable the company to do the following:

---

[3]We have simplified this example by having the employee receive a lump-sum payment upon retirement. Typically, employees choose to receive periodic payments from their benefit plans.

[4]See Table 3 at the end of the book.

[5]Ibid.

EXHIBIT   16.2

Funded Benefit Plans

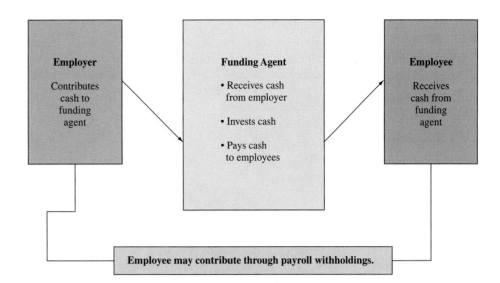

Employer	Funding Agent	Employee
Contributes cash to funding agent	• Receives cash from employer • Invests cash • Pays cash to employees	Receives cash from funding agent

Employee may contribute through payroll withholdings.

- Develop customer relations and loyalty.
- Introduce innovative products and services.
- Enhance employee skills and knowledge.
- Use technology and information effectively.

The **balance scorecard approach** is used to translate a company's strategy into objectives and plans organized into four perspectives: (1) financial, (2) internal process, (3) customer, and (4) learning and growth. The balanced scorecard approach is useful both for directing activities and for evaluating results. Companies use the four perspectives to ensure that both financial and nonfinancial performance measures are utilized and to acknowledge the linkages between the perspectives. For example, if a company improves customer relations, profitability is enhanced. If the company enhances employee skills, customer relations may improve. We examine each of these perspectives below.

Financial Perspective

Financial measures of performance are critical to the survival of any company. A company must create profits in order to remain attractive to investors and creditors, so companies use a variety of financial measures to control activities and measure results. In Chapters 12 and 13 we examined several measures used by companies to monitor operating performance. For example, ratio analysis is used to evaluate the revenue and expenditure cycles while variance analysis is used to evaluate the conversion cycle. In Chapters 23–26 we will examine the role of financial statements and financial statement analysis in performance evaluation. In addition to these types of measures, companies assess the growth in stock prices and market share as indicators of financial performance. Internally, the most widely used financial measure of performance is *return on investment (ROI)*. Recall from Chapter 14 that return on investment is the return generated by an investment divided by the amount of the investment. Companies, likewise, measure the return generated by the business divided by the investment made in the business. Thus return on investment (discussed in greater detail in Chapter 26) is measured as net income divided by total assets. It is important that the company consider both the net income generated and the assets used. For example, assume Company A has a net income of $100,000 and assets of $1,000,000. Company B also has a net income of $100,000 but its assets are only $500,000. Which company is better? If we use ROI as the financial measure of performance, Company B (ROI = 20%) is better than Company A (ROI = $10%).

PAUSE &
REFLECT

How could a company use the ratios discussed in Chapter 12 to analyze the financial perspective? *(answer on page 569)*

Surveys are often used to determine customer satisfaction.

Internal Process Perspective

The internal process perspective looks at the processes and people used by the company. It seeks to find measures of improvement in both the way work is done and the manner in which people are utilized in the company. In Chapter 13 we also looked at measures used by companies to monitor product quality and customer response time. These measures are part of the internal process perspective. If a company can reduce its nonvalue-added time, it can improve its internal processes. In addition, as part of the internal process perspective, companies often monitor quality costs. As you know, a company that increases its voluntary quality costs can decrease its involuntary quality costs and, therefore, reduce the total cost of quality.

Another part of the internal process perspective is the company's relationship with its suppliers. As companies move closer to a JIT environment, supplier relationships become increasingly important. Companies monitor these relationships by rating their suppliers on items such as number of on-time deliveries, cost, and innovation. Innovation concerns the willingness of the supplier to work with the company to improve quality and simplify design.

The last component of the internal process perspective concerns employees. Companies like Microsoft often monitor employee satisfaction, employee retention, and employee productivity. Some common measures used include employee satisfaction surveys, exit interviews for departing employees, and revenue generated per employee. These measures seek to determine how well the current workforce is operating.

PAUSE &
REFLECT How could a company use the ratios discussed in Chapter 12 to evaluate the internal process perspective? *(answer on page 569)*

Customer Perspective

The customer perspective relates to managing the company's largest noncapitalized asset—its customer base. Companies develop strategies to increase the value of their customer assets by increasing market share (the percentage of business in a given market that a particular business sells), by acquiring more or larger customers, and by increasing customer satisfaction and, thereby, retaining more or larger customers.

To increase market share, the company must add value by providing products and services demanded by customers. To increase customer satisfaction, the company must add value by providing quality and reliability. The relationship of the customer perspective to the internal process perspective is clear here.

Employee training is an important part of the learning and growth perspective.

Companies monitor the customer perspective by tracking the number of new customers acquired, the amount of profit generated by new customers, and the growth in market share. Customer satisfaction is measured through customer surveys, by monitoring the number of customer complaints, and by monitoring the time it takes to resolve a customer complaint. In addition, companies often monitor telephone conversations between customers and customer-service representatives to ensure prompt, courteous service to customers. Finally, because it is usually less expensive to keep a current customer than it is to obtain a new customer, companies measure customer retention. Common measurements used include number of customers lost, customer loyalty (determined through surveys), customer response time, and changes in customer buying habits.

PAUSE &

REFLECT   How is the customer perspective related to the financial perspective? *(answer on page 570)*

Learning and Growth Perspective

The learning and growth perspective involves managing the company's future, a noncapitalized asset. The company's future relates, in part, to its research and development activities. For many companies, expenditures for research and development are sizable and, therefore, must be carefully planned and managed. However, even though these expenditures may provide a future benefit, they, like other noncapitalized assets, do not meet the definition of an asset and, therefore, are expensed as incurred. Microsoft, for example, expends large amounts each year on research and development. These amounts are expensed as incurred even though Microsoft believes they have future benefit.

The learning and growth perspective is closely related to the internal process perspective. In order to succeed in the future, the company must educate and cross-train its employees. It must invest in its infrastructure, and it must be able to adapt to changes in technology.

Companies monitor the learning and growth perspective by measuring investments in technology, employee education programs, and business process improvements—that is, changes in the way a company operates. In addition, the information needs of the company now and in the future must be considered. Investments in information technology are monitored to ensure that the company's information systems (including its accounting system) are compatible with suppliers' and customers' systems now and in the future. Companies also monitor the number of new products introduced and the time it takes to get new products to market. For example, Microsoft is very concerned about how quickly its products are introduced, so it monitors new product development closely. Finally, companies must provide incentive systems to ensure that employees are working in the best interests of the company. We discuss this issue next.

The Balanced Scorecard and Reward Systems

As the above discussion illustrates, expenditures for noncapitalized assets are important—a company must invest in its future. Because these expenditures are not capitalized, they result in expenses on the income statement. Therefore, when rewards (bonuses) are based on net income, a manager may be reluctant to invest the resources if it means his or her bonus will be smaller. **Goal incongruence** occurs when an employee's goals (higher bonuses) and the company's goals (investments in the future) are not aligned. For example, assume that Microsoft wants to commit $500,000 to the customer or learning and growth perspective, but it rewards managers a 10 percent bonus based on net income. In this situation, the manager may not be motivated to expend resources on customer relations or research and development because these expenditures will reduce net income by $500,000 and, therefore, reduce the manager's bonus by $50,000 ($500,000 × 0.10). Proponents of the balanced scorecard approach consequently advocate basing bonuses on measurable outcomes *from all four perspectives.*

Exhibit 16.3 indicates some measurable outcomes that can be used to reward employees. Notice that the balanced scorecard approach does not suggest that financial measures of performance, such as net income or return on investment, be abandoned. Rather, it states that *other measures of performance should be used in addition to financial measures.* This approach requires planning because the information system of the company must be set up to capture nonfinancial information.

EXHIBIT 16.3	Balanced Scorecard Measures
Perspective	**Measures**
Financial	Net income
	Return on equity
	Return on investment
Internal process	Employee satisfaction
	Employee turnover
	Throughput time
	Quality costs
	On-time deliveries by suppliers
Customer	Market share
	Customer response time
	Number of new customers
	Number of customers retained
Learning and growth	Number of new products introduced
	Time to market
	Number of employees trained
	New technology adapted
	Investments in information technology

SUMMARY

Human resources management is the way companies ensure efficient and effective use of their human capital. A company's human resources management is a function of its environment and structure as well as its strategy. Companies must understand the costs and benefits regarding employee recruitment and selection as well as training and development. In addition, employee compensation and benefits must be considered. Current compensation and benefits consist of pay, insurance, leave, and bonuses.

- Deferred compensation and benefits include deferred payments, stock options, and post-retirement benefits.

- The balanced scorecard approach is used to monitor company activities and reward employees for achieving desired outcomes.

- The four perspectives of the balanced scorecard approach are financial, internal process, customer, and learning and growth.

KEY TERMS

balanced scorecard approach A management approach used to translate a company's strategy into objectives and plans organized into financial, internal process, customer, and learning and growth perspectives

bonus base The form of income the bonus rate is applied to

bonus rate The percentage the bonus will pay

coercive power (Appendix) Power resulting from the manager's ability to punish employees

commission pay Compensation based on the percentage of revenue generated

contributory plan A post-retirement benefit plan where both the employee and employer contribute

defined benefit plan A post-retirement benefit plan where the employer promises to pay the employee a specified amount at retirement, but the contributions made to the plan are not specified

defined contribution plan A post-retirement benefit plan where the employer promises to make specific contributions to the plan, but the post-retirement benefits received by retirees are not specified

efficiency strategy A strategy focused primarily on the reduction or containment of costs, improvements in productivity, and penetration of products and services having low cost

expert power (Appendix) Power resulting from the perception that the manager is the most competent person or has the best knowledge base in the situation

flexibility strategy A strategy focused primarily on adapting to changing conditions by expanding (or contracting) product lines, customer bases, and markets

funded plan A post-retirement benefit plan where the employer makes periodic payments to an independent funding agent

goal incongruence A situation in which an employee's goals and the company's goals are not aligned

hourly pay Compensation based on a certain amount per hour worked

human resources (HR) management The set of policies and procedures companies use to ensure effective and efficient use of their human capital

legitimate power (Appendix) Power resulting from the manager's position in the company hierarchy

mechanistic organizational structure A structure in which activities and employees are arranged by function

noncapitalized assets Items that have future value but not do qualify as assets

noncontributory plan A post-retirement benefit plan where only the employer contributes to the plan

organic organizational structure A structure in which activities and employees are arranged by cross-functional teams

organizational strategy A company's long-term plan for using its resources

piece-rate pay Compensation based on the number of items completed

reward power (Appendix) Power resulting from the manager's ability to grant rewards to employees

salary pay Compensation based on a fixed amount per period

unfunded plan A post-retirement benefit plan where the employer retains control of the benefit plan funds

unvested plan A post-retirement benefit plan where the employee has no rights to the benefit plan when employment ceases

vested plan A post-retirement benefit plan where the employee has rights to the benefits even if the employee is not employed at the time

ANSWERS TO THE PAUSE & REFLECTS

p. 554, Often these contracts are considered assets because they invoke certain legal rights to the company holding them.

p. 565, The return on sales and gross margin ratios could be used to analyze the profitability of operations. The current and quick ratios could be used to analyze the cash position of the company.

p. 566, The accounts receivable turnover and days in the collection period could be used to analyze revenue cycle activities. The inventory turnover, days in the selling period, payables turnover, and days in the payment period could be used to analyze expenditure cycle activities.

p. 567, Ultimately, if the customers are not happy, the company's profits will suffer. Customer perspective measures tend to be leading indicators of trouble. Therefore, these measures can be monitored to ensure that the company continues to be successful.

p. 572, If a student is in a course that they feel they cannot earn an A no matter how hard they study, the student is not motivated. Likewise, if a student is in a course that they feel they can earn an A with little or no effort, the student is not motivated.

p. 573, Typically, Theory Y managers are more successful in organic structures because these managers encourage innovation and achievement which is crucial to a flexible organization.

APPENDIX 16

LO 5

MOTIVATION AND LEADERSHIP

An important part of human resources management is motivating and leading employees. Many motivation and leadership theories have been advocated at various times in history. We look at four such motivation theories and two theories of leadership next. We also examine how performance and reward systems are influenced by these theories.

MOTIVATION THEORIES

Motivation theories concern the attributes of work and the work environment that encourage employees to work in the best interests of the employer. These theories can be grouped into two types: need theories and perception theories. Need theories focus on employees' requirements (food, clothing, responsibility, opportunities for advancement, etc.), while perception theories focus on how employees see the efforts they put forth and the rewards received for those efforts.

Need Theories

Abraham Maslow[6] proposed one of the earliest need theories. According to Maslow, people are motivated to fulfill a hierarchy of needs, illustrated in Exhibit 16.4. When needs at the lower levels of the hierarchy are met, they are no longer motivational. The needs at the upper levels of the hierarchy then become motivational. The lower-level needs consist of physical factors such as food, clothing, shelter, and safety. Accordingly, a person who is hungry or needs clothing to survive is motivated to meet these needs and not to bother with higher-level needs such as self-esteem. Once the lower-level needs are met—that is, the person is no longer hungry or in need of clothing—they no longer act as motivators. The person then must be motivated by higher-level needs. The higher-level needs are belongingness, the need to feel wanted by others; esteem, the need to be recognized by others; and self-actualization, the need to achieve one's personal best.

EXHIBIT 16.4

Maslow's Hierarchy of Needs

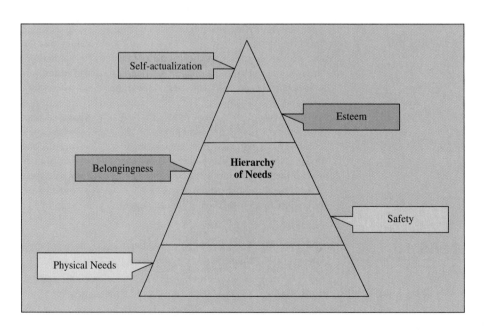

------

[6]Abraham Maslow, *Motivation and Personality* (New York: Harper & Row), 1954.

How does Maslow's theory relate to employee compensation and rewards? Does it imply that different employees are motivated by different rewards? Absolutely. If an employee is one paycheck away from poverty, that employee may be more motivated by money than another employee who has a relatively comfortable physical existence. On the other hand, an employee who does not really *need* more money may be more motivated by recognition. This is not to say that this employee would decline a raise if it were offered, but rather, that the employee might be more motivated by recognition. For example, compare a recent college graduate to Bill Gates. Which person is more likely to be motivated by money? Which person has higher-order needs such as esteem or self-actualization? Chances are that the recent college graduate needs money more than Bill Gates and, therefore, is motivated by lower-level needs. In contrast, Bill Gates is probably motivated more by esteem and self-actualization because his lower-level needs have been met.

Fredrick Herzberg's[7] theory on motivation focuses on two distinct sets of needs that he referred to as *hygiene factors* and *motivator factors.* According to Herzberg, hygiene factors, also known as *dissatisfiers,* do not motivate; but if they are absent or poorly delivered, decreased motivation occurs. On the other hand, motivator factors, also known as *satisfiers,* when increased do lead to increased motivation. Some hygiene and motivator factors are listed below.

Hygiene Factors—Dissatisfiers	Motivator Factors—Satisfiers
Supervision	Achievement
Interpersonal relations	Recognition
Working conditions	Responsibility
Salary and benefits	Advancement
Job security	Type of work performed

According to Herzberg, if a person has poor supervision, poor interpersonal relations with his or her coworkers, or poor working conditions, that person's motivation is decreased. Likewise, an inadequate salary, benefit package, or job security will lessen motivation, but improving these factors will not motivate. In other words, improving these hygiene factors can only lessen dissatisfaction; it cannot increase satisfaction. To increase motivation, the company must increase the opportunities for the employee to achieve and be recognized for that achievement. The company can also enhance the type of work performed to increase motivation. One way to enhance the work is to allow employees the flexibility to determine how the work is performed.

Herzberg's theory, like Maslow's, has implications for employee evaluation and reward systems. It suggests that an adequate salary, benefit package, and working conditions are expected (needed) by employees and, therefore, little long-term motivation is provided by improving these factors. On the other hand, increasing a person's ability to achieve tasks and improving the nature of the tasks performed are motivational. Likewise, recognizing employee achievements and rewarding those achievements with advancement and increasing responsibility also serve to motivate performance.

Perception Theories

V. H. Vroom's[8] model of motivation, referred to as *expectancy theory,* relates a person's motivation to the importance he or she places on, or the desire to achieve, certain outcomes *and* the person's expectation that a given level of effort will result in the achievement of the outcome. Thus motivation is a function of both outcome and effort and can be written as follows:

$$M = f(O,E)$$

Where

M = Motivation

O = Attractiveness of the outcome

E = Expected effort needed to achieve the outcome

In other words, motivation increases when a person desires the outcome *and* when that person thinks that his or her efforts will lead to the desired outcome.

---

[7]F. Herzberg, B. Mausner, and B. Snyderman, *The Motivation to Work* (New York: John Wiley & Sons), 1959.

[8]V. H. Vroom, *Work and Motivation* (New York: John Wiley & Sons), 1964.

For example, assume a person highly desires recognition on the job, but this person believes that his efforts will not result in praise from his boss. Will this person be motivated? According to this theory, no, because while he desires the outcome, he does not believe the outcome is achievable. Likewise, assume that another person believes it very likely that she will get promoted, but she does not want the promotion because it requires relocation to another city. Will this person be motivated? Again, the answer is no, because although the outcome is likely, the outcome is not desired. On the other hand, assume a person very much wants a raise and is convinced that if he works hard in the next year, the raise will be granted. Is this person motivated? Yes, because he wants the outcome *and* he believes his effort will result in the outcome.

As the above examples illustrate, one important implication of Vroom's theory concerning evaluation and reward systems is that performance must be clearly linked to rewards. It is important that employees understand how they can achieve outcomes, and it is important that management understands what outcomes employees desire.

PAUSE & REFLECT Many students find they can apply Vroom's theory to their experiences in different courses taken in college. Can you? *(answer on page 570)*

J. S. Adams[9] developed another perception-type theory known as *equity theory.* Adams postulated that people compare their efforts and resulting rewards with those of relevant others. If inequity exists, motivation decreases. What is interesting about this theory is that the inequity works in both directions. The employee who feels slighted is not motivated, but neither is the employee who feels patronized.

As an extreme example, assume Employee A works 50 hours a week and receives a salary of $750 per week. Employee A is happy because she believes that $750 a week is an appropriate salary for a 50-hour workweek. Now assume a new person, Employee B, is hired. Employee B also receives a salary of $750 per week, but he works only 40 hours per week. Is Employee A motivated? Is Employee B motivated? According to Adams's theory, neither employee is motivated because both perceive inequity in the reward structure. It is fairly easy to understand why Employee A is not motivated. Employee A perceives that her rewards are equivalent to Employee B, but her efforts exceed Employee B's. Therefore, Employee A believes that inequity exists, her motivation decreases, and she will likely exert less effort in the future. On the other hand, Employee B perceives that his effort is less than Employee A's but that his rewards are equivalent. Employee B also believes that inequity exists, his motivation decreases, and he will likely do one of two things:

- Convince himself that his effort is equivalent to Employee A's (i.e., "I may work fewer hours, but I work harder")

- Compare himself to someone else (i.e., "I should compare myself to Employee C because she also works 40 hours per week")

According to equity theory, when people are faced with an inequitable situation, they do one of the following:

- Change their effort

- Change their perceptions of self

- Change their perceptions of others

- Change reference persons

- Quit

Again, the above example illustrates the importance of linking rewards with performance. It is also important that employees understand the relationship between rewards and performance, that managers understand the importance placed on various rewards by employees, and that the performance leading to a particular reward is clearly communicated.

---

[9]J. S. Adams, "Inequity in Social Changes," in *Advances in Experimental Social Psychology,* edited by L. Berkowitz (New York: Academic Press), 1965.

Both need and perception theories tell us something very important about employee motivation and company reward systems. All these theories indicate that money may not motivate employees in the long run, while other rewards such as recognition and advancement may have a more lasting effect. In fact, psychological research has shown that the motivational effect of money is short-lived. In addition, it is important that company rewards are desired by and communicated to employees to avoid feelings of inequity in the work environment.

LEADERSHIP THEORIES

The discussion of motivation theories clearly illustrates the important role played by management in motivation. How a manager approaches this role depends, in part, on his or her attitude and power base.

Attitude

Douglas McGregor[10] theorized that managers have two different attitudes about employees that lead to two completely different leadership styles. A manager with a Theory X attitude believes that employees are lazy, must be coerced to work, and strive to avoid responsibility. A manager with this attitude tends to closely oversee employees. This manager often uses threats to motivate (i.e., "increase your output or you'll be fired"). Employees working for a Theory X manager typically are not given authority, responsibility, or flexibility.

On the other hand, a Theory Y manager believes that people like work, will work toward goals laid out for them, and will commit to goals that are rewarded. A manager with a Theory Y attitude thinks that employees will accept, and often desire, responsibility, the opportunity to exhibit creativity, and personal growth. Managers with this attitude tend to adopt an easy-going management style where employees are loosely supervised, allowed to set their own goals (within company guidelines, of course), and rewarded for achievement and creativity.

PAUSE & REFLECT Which manager, Theory X or Theory Y, will be more successful in a company with an organic structure? Why? *(answer on page 570)*

Power

Another aspect of leadership concerns the source of the manager's power. We discuss four types of power: expert, legitimate, reward, and coercive.

Expert power results from the perception that the manager is the most competent person or has the best knowledge base in the situation. A manager leading from this power base typically must maintain credibility, keep informed of issues, and avoid making subordinates feel inferior. **Legitimate power** results from the manager's position in the company hierarchy. A manager leading from this power base must follow proper channels, exercise authority, and explain the reasoning behind decisions. **Reward power** results from the ability of the manager to grant rewards to employees. A manager using this power base to lead must ensure that rewards are clearly linked to performance, that performance is achievable, and that rewards are desired. Finally, **coercive power** results from the manager's ability to punish employees. A manager using this power base to lead must ensure that punishments are clearly understood by employees, that sufficient warning is given before punishments are invoked, and that punishments are appropriate for the situation.

What are the implications of these leadership theories on compensation and reward systems? First, Theory X managers tend to use reward or coercive power bases. Theory Y managers tend to use expert or legitimate power bases. Therefore, Theory X managers are more likely to base rewards on achieving certain measurable goals, such as meeting the budget, and may fire or demote employees who do not achieve the goals. On the other hand, Theory Y managers are more likely to base rewards on employee creativity and assumption of responsibility and may further reward employees with recognition and advancement.

---

[10]Douglas McGregor, *The Human Side of Enterprise* (New York: McGraw-Hill), 1960.

QUESTIONS

1. What is a noncapitalized asset?
2. What is human resources management?
3. How is a company's organizational strategy related to its external environment?
4. How is a company's organizational strategy related to its focus?
5. How is a company's organizational structure related to its external environment?
6. Explain the steps in the human resources planning process.
7. Describe the costs and benefits of the recruitment and selection process.
8. Describe the costs and benefits of the training and development process.
9. Explain the various types of compensation plans used by employers.
10. Why do companies provide health and life insurance for employees?
11. Why do companies provide paid and unpaid leave for employees?
12. Why are bonuses often based on income?
13. Why do companies provide deferred compensation?
14. What is the difference between a defined contribution plan and a defined benefit plan for post-retirement benefits?
15. What is the difference between a vested and an unvested benefit plan?
16. Explain the difference between a contributory and a noncontributory benefit plan.
17. Explain the difference between a funded and an unfunded benefit plan.
18. Describe the four perspectives of a balanced scorecard approach.
19. Explain the types of measures used to evaluate the financial perspective.
20. Describe the measures used for evaluating the internal process perspective.
21. Explain the measures used to evaluate the customer perspective.
22. Explain the measures used for evaluating the learning and growth perspective.
23. What is goal incongruence?

Appendix

24. Describe Maslow's need theory.
25. Describe Herzberg's need theory.
26. Describe Vroom's expectancy theory.
27 Describe Adam's equity theory.
28. Describe the differences between Theory X and Theory Y managers.
29. Describe the differences in power bases used by managers.

EXERCISES

E 16.1
LO 1

Classify each of the following as a capitalized or noncapitalized asset. Use **C** for capitalized and **NC** for noncapitalized.

_____ a. Accounts receivable
_____ b. Buildings
_____ c. Customers
_____ d. Employees
_____ e. Inventory

E 16.2
LO 1

Classify each of the following as a capitalized or noncapitalized asset. Use **C** for capitalized and **NC** for noncapitalized.

_____ a. Land
_____ b. Learning
_____ c. Patents
_____ d. Research and development
_____ e. Technology developments

E 16.3
LO 1

Refer to Anheuser-Busch, introduced in Chapter 11. Based on your knowledge of this company, determine its environment, focus, organizational structure, and strategy.

Environment:	Certain versus Uncertain
Focus:	External versus Internal
Organizational structure:	Mechanistic versus Organic
Strategy:	Efficiency versus Flexibility

E 16.4
LO 1

Refer to Walt Disney Company, introduced in Chapter 7. Based on your knowledge of this company, determine its environment, focus, organizational structure, and strategy.

Environment:	Certain versus Uncertain
Focus:	External versus Internal
Organizational structure:	Mechanistic versus Organic
Strategy:	Efficiency versus Flexibility

E 16.5
LO 1

Refer to Burger King, introduced in Chapter 4. Based on your knowledge of this company, determine its environment, focus, organizational structure, and strategy.

Environment:	Certain versus Uncertain
Focus:	External versus Internal
Organizational structure:	Mechanistic versus Organic
Strategy:	Efficiency versus Flexibility

E 16.6
LO 1

Refer to Intel, introduced in Chapter 1. Based on your knowledge of this company, determine its environment, focus, organizational structure, and strategy.

Environment:	Certain versus Uncertain
Focus:	External versus Internal
Organizational structure:	Mechanistic versus Organic
Strategy:	Efficiency versus Flexibility

E 16.7
LO 3

Gurley Company pays its production employees on a piece-rate basis at the rate of $1.50 per item. It pays each member of its sales force a salary of $500 per period plus a commission of 5 percent of net sales. Last period, Gurley produced 250,000 items, employed 10 sales personnel, and sold 200,000 items at $8 each. What is Gurley's total payroll cost (ignore payroll taxes) for the period?

E 16.8
LO 3

Elmendorf Company has the following compensation plan:

Managers	Salary $2,500 per month
Sales personnel	Salary $500 per month
	Commission 8 percent of net sales
Production personnel	$2 per item produced
Other personnel	$6 per hour worked

Elmendorf employs 3 managers, 15 sales personnel, 100 production employees, and 50 other employees. This month, Elmendorf produced 60,000 units and sold 50,000 units at $10 each. Other personnel worked an average of 160 hours during the month. What is Elmendorf's total payroll cost (ignore payroll taxes)?

E 16.9
LO 3

Roe, Inc., pays its managers a bonus based on income before bonus and income taxes. Its bonus rate is 12 percent. Its marginal income tax rate is 28 percent. Roe's income before bonus and income taxes is $800,000. What is the total bonus paid to managers?

E 16.10
LO 3

Refer to E 16.9. If Roe bases its bonus on income before income taxes (after bonus), what is its total bonus payment?

E 16.11
LO 3

Refer to E 16.9. If Roe bases its bonus on net income (after bonus and after income taxes), what is its total bonus payment?

E 16.12
LO 3

Refer to E 16.9. What are Roe's total cash outflows, assuming that both the bonus and income taxes are paid in cash? What is Roe's net income?

E 16.13
LO 3

Refer to E 16.10. What are Roe's total cash outflows, assuming that both the bonus and income taxes are paid in cash? What is Roe's net income?

E 16.14
LO 3

Refer to E 16.11. What are Roe's total cash outflows, assuming that both the bonus and income taxes are paid in cash? What is Roe's net income?

E 16.15
LO 3
Walker Company offers a deferred compensation package to its employees. Walker will contribute $2,000 per year for each employee and believes it can earn 12 percent annually on its benefit plan. Assuming Jane Stelton works for Walker Company for 35 years before retiring, how much will she receive (lump-sum) upon retirement?

E 16.16
LO 3
Richtermeyer Enterprises offers its employees a defined benefit plan whereby each employee will receive a lump-sum distribution of $150,000 upon retirement. Dick Washington will retire in 20 years. If the plan earns 10 percent annually, what is the annual contribution required for Dick?

E 16.17
LO 3
Johnson Company offers a deferred compensation package to its employees. Johnson will contribute $5,000 per year for each employee and believes it can earn 8 percent annually on its benefit plan. Assuming Sally Ellison works for Johnson Company for 15 years before retiring, how much will she receive (lump-sum) upon retirement?

E 16.18
LO 3
Brown Enterprises offers its employees a defined benefit plan whereby each employee will receive a lump-sum distribution of $200,000 upon retirement. Dave Bayberry will retire in 30 years. If the plan earns 9 percent annually, what is the annual contribution required for Dave?

E 16.19
LO 3
Carrie Hillcrest, an employee at Lane Company, has an employee benefit plan whereby the Lane Company invests $500 per month in a funded pension plan. If the plan earns 7 percent annually during the 30 years Carrie works for Lane Company, how much money will she receive at retirement?

E 16.20
LO 3
Duncan Company offers its employees a defined benefit plan whereby each employee will receive a $300,000 lump-sum payment upon retirement. Karen Fairweather will retire in 40 years. If the plan earns 8.5 percent annually, what is the monthly payment required for Karen's pension fund?

E 16.21
LO 4
Determine balanced scorecard financial measures for Anheuser-Busch (introduced in Chapter 11).

E 16.22
LO 4
Determine balance scorecard customer measures for Walt Disney (introduced in Chapter 7).

E 16.23
LO 4
List balanced scorecard internal process measures for Eddie Bauer (introduced in Chapter 2).

E 16.24
LO 4
List balanced scorecard learning and growth measures for Intel (introduced in Chapter 1).

PROBLEMS

P 16.1
LO 3
Webster Company has provided the following income statement information for you to determine its annual bonus payments:

Sales	$5,000,000
Less cost of goods sold	3,000,000
Gross margin	$2,000,000
Less selling and administrative expenses	1,500,000
Income before bonus or income taxes	$ 500,000

Webster is subject to a 30 percent annual income tax rate. Its bonus rate is 15 percent.

Required
a. If Webster's bonus base is income before bonus or income taxes, what is the total bonus payment?
b. If Webster's bonus base is income before income taxes (after bonus), what is the total bonus payment?
c. If Webster's bonus base is net income (after bonus and income taxes), what is the total bonus payment?

P 16.2
LO 3
Refer to P 16.1. Assume that Webster pays its bonuses and income taxes in cash. Determine the total cash payment and net income resulting from each of the alternative bonus bases.

P 16.3
LO 3
Banasiewicz Enterprises has a defined contribution post-retirement plan. It contributes $6,000 each year to this plan for each of its ten managers and earns an average of 8 percent on its investments.

Required
a. Bob Smith retires in 10 years. What is his expected lump-sum payment upon retirement?
b. Shelly Redstone retires in 15 years. What is her expected lump-sum payment upon retirement?
c. Steven Hencks retires in 20 years. What is his expected lump-sum payment upon retirement?

P 16.4
LO 3

Grant, Inc., has a defined benefit plan for each of its managers. The plan states that each employee will receive a lump-sum distribution of $625,000 upon retirement. Grant believes it can earn an average of 10 percent on its investments.

Required

a. Mary Joseph retires in 10 years. What is the annual contribution required to her retirement fund?

b. José Ellington retires in 15 years. What is the annual contribution required to his retirement fund?

c. Jan Hinga retires in 20 years. What is the annual contribution required to her retirement fund?

P 16.5
LO 3

Refer to P 16.3. Assume the Banasiewicz Enterprises contributes $500 monthly, rather than $6,000 yearly.

Required

a. What is Bob Smith's lump-sum retirement payment?

b. What is Shelly Redstone's lump-sum retirement payment?

c. What is Steven Henck's lump-sum retirement payment?

d. Why does the monthly payment result in a different retirement amount than determined in P 16.3 even though the same annual contribution is made?

P 16.6
LO 3

Refer to P 16.4. Assume that Grant, Inc., makes monthly, rather than annual, contributions to its retirement fund.

Required

a. What is the monthly contribution required for Mary Joseph?

b. What is the monthly contribution required for José Ellington?

c. What is the monthly contribution required for Jan Hinga?

d. Why is the monthly payment multiplied by 12 less than the annual payment calculated in P 16.4?

P 16.7
LO 3

(This problem requires prior study of Chapter 4.) Grossman Enterprises sells its product for $30 per unit. Its unit-related costs are $20 and its facility-sustaining costs are $600,000 per period. Grossman has no batch-related or product-sustaining costs. Grossman is subject to a marginal tax rate of 20 percent. Its bonus rate is 10 percent. Its targeted after-tax income is $200,000 per period.

Required

a. How many units must Grossman sell to achieve its targeted income if its bonus base is net income (after bonus and after income taxes)?

b. How many units must Grossman sell to achieve its targeted income if its bonus base is income before income taxes (after bonus)?

P 16.8
LO 3

Wells, Inc., provides its employees with a defined contribution post-retirement plan. It contributes $600 each month to this plan for each of its managers. Wells believes it can earn an annual average of 15 percent on investments. If Dell Stocker retires after 30 years, how much can he receive per month if he expects to live another 20 years and earn 8 percent?

P 16.9
LO 3

Varca Company provides its employees with a defined benefit pension plan. It contributes $450 each month per employee. Varca earns an average of 13 percent on its investments. If Phil Leder retires after 25 years, expects to live another 30 years after retirement, and can earn 6 percent on his investments, how much can he receive monthly from his retirement account?

P 16.10
LO 4

Design a balanced scorecard approach for Mattel (introduced in Chapter 3).

P 16.11
LO 4

Design a balanced scorecard approach for Procter & Gamble (introduced in Chapter 5).

P 16.12
LO 4

Design a balanced scorecard approach for The Gap (introduced in Chapter 12).

CASES

C 16.1
LO 1   LO 3

Refer to the annual report of the company you chose in Chapter 1. Prepare responses to each of the following:

a. Does the company refer to its employees as assets? If so, what specifically does it say?

b. Does the company discuss other noncapitalized assets? If so, what specifically does it say?

c. Does the company report pension liabilities? If so, how large is this liability compared to the company's other liabilities?

d. Does the company report other post-retirement benefits? If so, what does it disclose?

e. Are the company's post-retirement benefits a defined benefit or a defined contribution plan?

f. Does the company report stock options? If so, what does the company disclose?

C 16.2
LO 1 **LO 3**

Refer to the annual report of Anheuser-Busch, introduced in Chapter 11. Answer the following questions:

a. Does the company refer to its employees as assets? If so, what specifically does it say?

b. Does the company discuss other noncapitalized assets? If so, what specifically does it say?

c. Does the company report pension liabilities? If so, how large is this liability compared to the company's other liabilities?

d. Does the company report other post-retirement benefits? If so, what does it disclose?

e. Are the company's post-retirement benefits a defined benefit or a defined contribution plan?

f. Does the company report stock options? If so, what does the company disclose?

CRITICAL THINKING

CT 16.1
LO 2 **LO 3**

Allen Company is considering two different post-retirement plans. Plan A calls for monthly contributions of $100. Plan B calls for annual contributions of $1,500. Each plan is expected to earn 10 percent annually. If an employee plans to work for Allen Company for 25 years, which plan will the employee prefer?

CT 16.2

Refer to CT 16.1. Which plan will Allen Company prefer?

Appendix

CT 16.3
LO 5

Think of a person whom you consider to be a good leader. This person could be a teacher, a political figure, a boss, a member of the clergy, a member of your family, and so on. List the characteristics this person possesses that make her or him a good leader. Now think of a person in a leadership position that you consider a poor leader. List the characteristics this person possesses that make him or her a poor leader. Compare your two lists. Are these characteristics polar opposites? Why or why not?

ETHICAL CHALLENGES

EC 16.1
LO 1 **LO 2**

The FASB defines assets as follows:

> Probable future economic benefits obtained or controlled by a particular entity as the result of past transactions or events.

Based on your reading of this chapter, write a brief essay describing why human and other noncapitalized assets should, or should not, be reported to external users. In your analysis, be sure to consider this issue from the following points of view:

a. The company and upper management

b. Stockholders and creditors

c. Employees

EC 16.2
LO 1 **LO 2**

Companies are often accused of overcompensating their key executives while at the same time cutting lower-level positions and laying off employees. The companies argue that this is good practice. Write a point-counterpoint essay about this issue.

COMPUTER APPLICATIONS

CA 16.1
LO 3

Refer to P 16.8. Using a spreadsheet package, prepare a table that shows how the company's $600 monthly contribution grows during Dell Stocker's 30 years of employment.

CA 16.2

Refer to P 16.8. Using a spreadsheet package, prepare a table that shows how Dell Stocker's retirement account is reduced over his 20-year, post-retirement period.

CA 16.3

Find Microsoft on the Internet. What type of employment opportunities are available? What fringe benefits does Microsoft offer its employees?

PART FIVE

YOU ARE HERE

Chapter 17 is the first of two chapters that explores the process of raising the capital necessary to run the business and enable it to invest in long-term projects and human capital. In Chapters 15 and 16 we planned investing activities that would require significant financing. This chapter (and Chapter 18) completes the planning phase by examining the ways companies can finance their long-term investments. Chapter 17 discusses owner financing issues for partnerships and corporations. We explore the planning process of obtaining contributions from owners and making distributions to them. In addition, for corporations, we study the differences between common and preferred stock.

LEARNING OBJECTIVES

LO 1 Explain the risks and rewards of equity financing.

LO 2 Describe the characteristics of partnerships.

LO 3 Describe the characteristics of corporate equity instruments.

Planning for Equity Financing

Ben & Jerry's ice cream is one of America's better known entrepreneurial success stories. The flavors of its premium ice cream—Chunky Monkey, Cherry Garcia, Chubby Hubby, Phish Food, and Wavy Gravy—have captured our imagination and taste buds. However, behind

BEN & JERRY'S
www.benjerry.com

the tasty ice cream is a company which believes that business should be a force for progressive social change. The unique corporate mission created by its founders, Ben Cohen and Jerry Greenfield, consists of the following three interrelated parts:

Product: To make, distribute and sell the finest quality all natural ice cream and related products in a wide variety of innovative flavors made from Vermont dairy products.

Social: To operate the company in a way that actively recognizes the central role that business plays in the structure of society by initiating innovative ways to improve the quality of life of a broad community: local, national and international.

Economic: To operate the company on a sound financial basis of profitable growth, increasing value for our shareholders and creating career opportunities and financial rewards for our employees.[1]

[1] Ben & Jerry's, *1997 Annual Report,* p. 1.

While Ben & Jerry's stockholders' equity provides a means of financing the firm's operations, its ownership structure serves to keep the company an "independent, Vermont-based business focused on its three-part corporate mission."[2] The company has accomplished its goal by establishing two classes of common stock: Class A common stock and Class B common stock. Class A common stock has one vote per share, whereas Class B common stock has 10 votes per share. Ben Cohen, Jerry Greenfield, and Jeffrey Furman hold shares representing 45 percent of the firm's voting power. This ownership structure minimizes the chance that an outside interest could buy enough shares and, therefore, votes to gain control of the company. By blocking hostile takeovers with their ownership structure, the company founders and principal stockholders can manage the firm's operations independent of any unwanted outside influence.

[2]Ben & Jerry's, 1997 Form 10K.

Chapter 15 described how capital budgeting helped plan for the acquisition of the long-term investments that will profitably support the firm's operations. In Chapter 16 we learned how to plan for the investment in the human capital necessary for the planned operations. The final stage in the planning phase is planning how to finance these investments, which we examine in this chapter (equity financing) and in Chapter 18 (debt financing).

Firms acquire funds from three sources: (1) owners' contributions, (2) earnings generated by the firm's operating activities, and (3) debt. We classify the three sources of funds into two financing categories: equity and debt. **Equity financing** is a means for firms to obtain funds in exchange for an ownership interest in the firm. Firms raise equity funds when owners acquire a financial interest in the firm and when management elects to reinvest the firm's earnings in the firm. **Debt financing** arises when a company obtains funds (cash) in exchange for a liability to repay the borrowed funds.

USING THE OWNERS' MONEY

LO 1

Regardless of the legal form of business entity, owner financing comes from people or other entities acquiring an ownership interest in the firm or the company reinvesting the firm's earnings. The first source includes the investors' contribution of assets to the firm in exchange for an ownership interest in the business entity. Initial contributions provide the funds necessary to begin the firm's operations, while subsequent contributions are used for expansion. The second source of owner financing is reinvested earnings. The net income of a firm represents the increase in the net assets of the firm as a result of its operations. The net income, or earnings, belongs to the owners and is either distributed to them or reinvested in the firm. When the earnings are reinvested in the business entity, the owners are keeping the funds in the entity and, thereby, increasing their interest in the firm.

Rewards and Risks of Equity Financing

Before a business can begin, the owners of the firm commit their resources to the enterprise in the expectation that the business will produce a satisfactory return on their initial investment. Ownership is attractive because the return the business generates on owners' investment is limited only by the performance of the firm. In addition to realizing financial rewards, many owners enjoy the psychological reward of knowing they own a business enterprise.

Owners of a business entity face the risk of not receiving a satisfactory return on their invested funds or of losing some or all of their investment if the business fails. The owners' risk is directly related to the firm's ability to sell goods and services, cover operating expenses, and generate sufficient net income to provide a satisfactory return on their investment. Obviously, firms that consistently provide a satisfactory return on the owners' investment have less risk than those whose earnings and returns are more erratic.

How Is Equity Financing Used?

Contributions by owners are usually used to acquire long-term assets such as buildings, equipment, land, patents, and franchises that provide the infrastructure for the firm's operations. Owner contributions also are used to retire long-term notes and, therefore, reduce the firm's risk of defaulting on its long-term debt. The earnings reinvested in the firm are used to support the daily operations, acquire long-term assets, or retire long-term debt, based on recommendations by management.

WHAT TO CONSIDER WHEN PLANNING THE FORM OF THE BUSINESS ENTITY

Selecting a business ownership structure is one of the first and most important planning activities. As you know, the three basic forms of business entities are the sole proprietorship, partnership, and corporation and each has its advantages and disadvantages. Sole proprietorships and partnerships have three important advantages. The first is their ease of formation. Because they are not separate legal entities, they do not have the costly and time-consuming registration requirements of corporations. The second advantage is that the income generated by sole proprietorships and partnerships is taxed only once. That is, the income generated by a sole proprietorship or partnership is reported as taxable income on each owner's Form 1040. (Partnerships must complete an informational partnership return, but their income is reported as taxable income on each partner's Form 1040.) In contrast, income generated by a corporation, as we discuss shortly, is taxed twice. Finally, sole proprietors and partners are more likely to manage the business and be involved in its operations; they choose these forms of organization because they enjoy the psychological and financial rewards they offer.

Sole proprietorships and partnerships share two disadvantages. The first is the risk associated with unlimited liability; that is, owners can lose not only what they have invested in the firm, but also their personal assets when the assets of the firm do not satisfy the creditors' claims. The second disadvantage is the inability to raise large amounts of equity capital. The equity capital raised by sole proprietorships and partnerships is limited to the personal resources of the owners. While partnerships can generate more capital by increasing the number of partners, the risk posed by mutual agency probably limits the amount of capital the firm can raise from its owners' contributions. Recall from Chapter 1 that mutual agency creates a risk that is unique to partnerships because it allows any partner to bind all partners to a contract whether or not they approve of the contract. For example, when one partner signs a contract and the deal goes bad, the loss puts the assets of the business and the personal assets of all partners at risk. Mutual agency also applies to the performance of each partner. For example, a partner in a CPA firm who loses a malpractice suit puts the personal assets of the other partners at risk if the firm's malpractice insurance and the proceeds from the sale of the partnership assets are not sufficient to cover the claims of the lawsuit.

PAUSE & REFLECT

If the personal assets of a partner are at risk from activities in the firm, can the business assets be at risk from the nonbusiness or personal activities of a partner? *(answer on page 602)*

Corporations have three major advantages that are all tied to the fact that a corporation is a separate legal entity. The first advantage is limited liability, which means that owners of a corporation can lose only the amounts invested in the firm. The second advantage is the corporation's ability to raise large amounts of capital by selling its stock (one unit of ownership). Unlike partnerships, individual stockholders cannot bind the corporation because the corporation is a separate legal entity; only those authorized by the corporation can bind the corporation to a contract. The third advantage is unlimited life. Unlike sole proprietorships and partnerships, which are limited to the life of the owner(s), a corporation's life is limited only by its ability to remain a going business concern.

Corporations have two disadvantages. The first is the time and money it takes to become incorporated and then satisfy the regulatory requirements necessary to maintain the corporate status. For example, Ben & Jerry's must file reports with Vermont's secretary of state, get and maintain permission to operate in other states, and report annually (10K) and quarterly (10Q) to the Securities and Exchange Commission. The second disadvantage of incorporating is double taxation. Due to its status as a legal entity, the corporation's profits

Four alternative ownership structures are used to resolve the taxation and liability problems of traditional partnership and corporate structures: the limited partnership, the limited liability partnership (LLP), the Subchapter S corporation (S Corporation), and the limited liability company (LLC).[1]

Limited Partnership

A limited partnership has one or more general partners and one or more limited partners. While the general partners are personally responsible for the debts of the firm (unlimited liability), the limited partners are liable only for their investment in the partnership. However, limited partners do not have the same rights as a general partner; that is, the limited partner cannot manage the firm or enter into contracts on behalf of the firm. Limited partners who take such action lose their limited liability status. Like any partnership, the income of the partnership is taxed only once. In most states, the limited partnership must be registered with the secretary of state in accordance with the Revised Uniform Limited Partnership Act. The registration must disclose the following:

a. the name of the limited partnership;

b. the general character of the business;

c. the address of the office and the name and address of the agent;

d. the name and the business address of each partner, listing general and limited partners separately;

e. the amount of cash and a description and statement of the value of the other property or services contributed by each partner;

f. the times at which, or events on the happening of which, additional contributions are to be made by each partner;

g. any power of a limited partner to make an assignee of that partner's partnership interest to another limited partner;

h. the events permitting a partner to withdraw from the partnership;

i. the rights of the partners to receive distributions of the limited partnership property;

j. the rights of partners to receive a return of their capital contribution; and

k. the time or events up to which the limited partnership is to be dissolved.[2]

Limited Liability Partnership (LLP)

A limited liability partnership (LLP) follows the same basic structure as a general partnership but allows partners to benefit from partial limited liability. Partners in an LLP are personally liable for their own wrongful acts and the acts of those they directly supervise, but they are not personally responsible for the wrongful acts of another partner. Creditors and others with claims against the partnership still have recourse against the partnership assets and the individual partner's personal assets. As in the case of the limited partnership, the income of the firm is taxed only once. If an existing general partnership decides to become an LLP, it should be aware that some states will not release the partnership from obligations that existed under the general partnership.

---

are taxed first at the corporate level and then again when they are distributed to the owners in the form of dividends.

PLANNING FOR PARTNERSHIP EQUITY

LO 2

Due to the limited number of owners, sole proprietorships and partnerships measure the dollar amount of each individual owner's interest in the firm. The value of each owner's interest consists of the owner's contribution and his or her share of the firm's undistributed earnings; however, only the total of the two is disclosed on the balance sheet. In the following section, we discuss how a partner's capital can change. Tracking the changes in each partner's capital is important because it ultimately is the basis for distributing the firm's assets. For example, when a partner leaves the firm, the amount of cash the partner receives is based on the amount of equity the partner has accumulated to the date of withdrawal.

Planning the Division of Income for Partnerships

Because determining the equity of each partner is critical, planning for the distribution of the firm's income is most important. In the absence of an agreement to the contrary, the Uniform Partnership Act provides that partners share profits and losses equally. However, partners typically do not do this because each partner's involvement in the firm varies. For example, a partner who contributes $10,000 to a firm and is not involved with its operations would not receive the same share of the profits as a person who contributes $50,000 and manages the firm's activities on a daily basis. Therefore, the division of the partnership's earnings and losses usually reflects the nature of each partner's involvement.

Subchapter S Corporation (S Corporation)

Subchapter S of the Internal Revenue Code allows corporations that meet certain criteria to pass their earnings through to stockholders and, therefore, have the earnings of the enterprise taxed only once. S corporation stockholders, like other corporations, have limited liability and, therefore, have only their investment in the corporation at risk. To obtain S corporation status, the corporation must meet several criteria that may offset the tax advantages. For example, S corporations are limited to no more than 75 shareholders, none of the stockholders can be a nonresident alien, and they can issue only one class of stock. These restrictions may limit the firm's ability to raise equity capital. A disadvantage of the S corporation occurs when it generates earnings but does not pay dividends. The earnings are passed through to the shareholders who must pay the tax on their share of the earnings out of their personal assets.

Limited Liability Company (LLC)

Limited liability companies have several advantages. The first advantage is that, unlike limited partnerships that require at least one general partner, all of an LLC's owners have limited liability and, therefore, their personal assets are not at risk. The second advantage is that the LLC's earnings are taxed only once. That is, like partnerships, the LLC's net income passes through to the owners before it is subject to tax. An advantage of the LLC over the S Corporation is that the number of owners in an LLC is not limited to 75. Finally, all owners of an LLC are free to participate in the operation of the firm. Recall that in a limited partnership, limited partners can lose their limited liability status if their actions regarding the operation of the firm are construed to be those of a general partner.

An LLC has two disadvantages. The first is that it does not have continuity of life. The second is that LLC owners, unlike corporate stockholders, cannot easily transfer their ownership interest to another person or entity. However, for members of CPA firms, law firms, or any group of professionals, the ability to obtain limited liability without increasing the tax burden on the firm's earnings through double taxation far outweighs these disadvantages.

In creating an LLC, articles of organization must be filed with the secretary of state in the state in which the LLC will operate. The LLC must have at least two members at the time of organization. Most states require a written operating agreement that specifies the business the LLC is going to conduct and how the LLC will be managed. Management can be delegated to all owners or to a specified management group. When a specified management group is designated, those owners not designated are limited in their participation in the management of the firm. Typically, a member is designated to represent the company before the IRS.

[1]Information in the following section is taken from "Choice of Entity," William P. Streng, Esq., Tax Management, 1993 TAX MANAGEMENT, INC., 1231 25th Street, N.W., Washington, DC 20037.

[2]"Choice of Entity," William P. Streng, Esq., Tax Management, p. A-5, 1993 TAX MANAGEMENT, INC., 1231 25th Street, N.W., Washington, DC 20037.

A firm's partnership agreement should describe in detail how the partners agree to divide the profits and losses of the firm, which can change whenever the partners deem it appropriate. The following are commonly used methods for the division of earnings:

- Fixed ratio
- Ratio of capital account balances
- Salary allowances and some determination of distribution of any remainder
- Interest allowance on capital balances and some determination of distribution of any remainder
- Combination of salary and interest allowance and some determination of distribution of any remainder

It is important to note that partnership losses, unless otherwise specified, are divided using the same method by which profits are allocated. When using the salary allowance, interest allowance, or combination method to allocate a partnership's net loss, it is possible for some partners' capital accounts to increase. We illustrate this paradox later.

To illustrate the possible ways to divide income, we will use a partnership called Doane Company that offers accounting services. The partners are Margie and Greg Klocke and Ellie and Pat Beans. In planning for the division of partnership income, they want to examine each of the methods described above.

A fair method of dividing partnership income is essential for maintaining good partner relationships.

Fixed Ratio The partners agree to distribute income or loss in a fixed ratio of 4:2:1:1. Since 4 + 2 + 1 + 1 = 8, Margie will get 4/8, or 1/2, of the total; Greg 2/8, or 1/4; and Ellie and Pat 1/8 each. If Doane is expected to generate $48,000 of net income, using the fixed ratio method of dividing profits would increase Margie's capital account by $24,000, Greg's capital account by $12,000, and Ellie's and Pat's capital accounts by $6,000 each.

Margie	1/2	×	$48,000	=	$24,000
Greg	1/4	×	$48,000	=	12,000
Ellie	1/8	×	$48,000	=	6,000
Pat	1/8	×	$48,000	=	6,000
Total income					$48,000

Ratio of Capital Account Balances Sometimes the amount of net income is closely related to the amount invested by the individual partner in the partnership entity. Consequently, a method of allocating earnings based on the relationship of the amounts of the partners' investments offers a fair approach to distribute the firm's income. However, because of withdrawals and additional investments made during the accounting period, the capital balances may change. In such circumstances, partners must agree on which capital balances to use as a basis for earnings allocation—beginning, ending, or some average for the period.

Assume that the partners agree to divide income based on the beginning capital balances and that each of them had the capital balances shown below at the beginning of the current period:

Margie Klocke, Capital	$ 15,000
Greg Klocke, Capital	10,000
Ellie Beans, Capital	45,000
Pat Beans, Capital	30,000
Total capital	$100,000

The distribution is computed by developing a ratio of each capital balance to the total of the capital balances and then multiplying the amount of the profits by that ratio.

The ratio of Margie's capital to total capital is $15,000/$100,000, or 15 percent of the total capital balances. Greg's ratio ($10,000/$100,000) converts to 10 percent, Ellie's to 45 percent, and Pat's to 30 percent. If the partnership expects $48,000 of income for the period, the division of earnings would be as follows:

Margie	0.15	×	$48,000	=	$ 7,200
Greg	0.10	×	$48,000	=	4,800
Ellie	0.45	×	$48,000	=	21,600
Pat	0.30	×	$48,000	=	14,400
Total income					$48,000

Salary Allowances If a partner spends all or part of his or her time on partnership business while others are not as involved in operations, the partners may agree to recognize the value of these services. A salary allowance is a method of allocating partnership earnings based on the amount of time respective partners spend operating the business enterprise. Note that the salary allowance is a means of dividing income. It is *not* an expense of the business, it is *not* shown as an expense on the income statement, and it is *not* tax deductible.

Suppose Margie and Greg run the accounting service on a full-time basis, while Ellie and Pat provide tax expertise only for selected clients. In these circumstances, they agree that Margie and Greg are to receive salary allowances, with any additional amounts of profit or loss divided equally. For example, assume that Margie gets a salary allowance of $15,000 and Greg receives one of $10,000, with any remainder divided equally among the four partners.

Assume again that Doane Company expected to generate net income of $48,000. After allocating the salary allowances of $25,000, the $23,000 remainder is divided by four and allocated to each partner. Margie's capital would increase by $20,750, Greg's capital would increase by $15,750, and Ellie and Pat's capital would increase by $5,750 each. See Exhibit 17.1 for the computations showing the allocation of net income with these salary allowances.

When Margie's salary allowance is $15,000 and Greg's is $10,000, any amount of net income less than $25,000 will result in a negative remainder. The amount of the remain-

EXHIBIT 17.1	Distribution of Net Income with Salary Allowances					
Item	Margie	Greg	Ellie	Pat	Amount Distributed	Amount Remaining
Net income						$48,000
Salary allowance	$15,000	$10,000	$ –0–	$ –0–	$25,000	23,000
Remainder	5,750	5,750	5,750	5,750	23,000	–0–
Total	$20,750	$15,750	$5,750	$5,750	$48,000	$ –0–

der, whether positive or negative, is always distributed according to the terms of the partnership agreement. For example, if the expected net income is only $21,000, the negative remainder of $4,000 would be divided among all four partners. As Exhibit 17.2 shows, after the $25,000 salary allowance is awarded, each partner distribution is reduced by $1,000, or their equal shares of the negative residual. Notice that the $14,000 increase in Margie's capital is the result of a $15,000 salary allowance minus her $1,000 share of the negative remainder. Greg's capital increased $9,000 because he was allocated $10,000 for the salary allowance minus his $1,000 share of the negative remainder. Since neither Ellie nor Pat has a salary allowance, they would receive only their share of the negative remainder and, therefore, their capital is reduced by $1,000. It may seem unusual to decrease a partner's capital when the firm made a profit, but the practice follows the terms of the partnership agreement.

EXHIBIT 17.2	Distribution of Net Income with a Negative Remainder					
Item	Margie	Greg	Ellie	Pat	Amount Distributed	Amount Remaining
Net income						$21,000
Salary allowance	$15,000	$10,000	$ –0–	$ –0–	$25,000	(4,000)
Remainder	(1,000)	(1,000)	(1,000)	(1,000)	(4,000)	–0–
Total	$14,000	$ 9,000	$(1,000)	$(1,000)	$21,000	$ –0–

PAUSE & REFLECT

Why would partners knowingly construct a partnership agreement that would result in a decrease in their capital accounts when the firm generated a profit? If a partnership suffers a loss, is it possible for one or more of the partner's capital to increase after the loss is allocated? *(answer on page 602)*

Interest Allowance on Capital Balances The interest allowance method uses an interest rate multiplied by each partner's capital balance to allocate partnership earnings. This method of allocating income is an incentive designed to reward partners who invest and maintain capital in the business. Just as in the case of the salary allowance, the interest on capital balances is merely one step in the method of computing the distribution of earnings; it is *not* an expense of the firm and it is *not* tax deductible.

The partnership agreement must specify the interest rate, the capital balance (beginning, ending, or average) that the rate applied to, and the basis for allocating any residual income or losses. Assume that the partners have agreed to apply a 10 percent rate to the average capital balances for the period and that the average capital balances are as follows:

Margie Klocke, Capital	$13,000
Greg Klocke, Capital	9,000
Ellie Beans, Capital	40,000
Pat Beans, Capital	28,000
Total capital	$90,000

The interest allowance of $9,000 (10% of $90,000) is distributed as follows:

Margie	$13,000	×	0.10	=	$1,300
Greg	$9,000	×	0.10	=	900
Ellie	$40,000	×	0.10	=	4,000
Pat	$28,000	×	0.10	=	2,800
Total allocation					$9,000

Further assume that Margie, Greg, Ellie, and Pat agree to divide any remainder after interest allowances in a ratio of 4:2:1:1. Exhibit 17.3 shows the distribution among the partners, again assuming an expected net income of $48,000.

EXHIBIT	17.3	Distribution of Net Income with Interest Allowances					

	4 :	2 :	1 :	1	Amount	Amount
Item	Margie	Greg	Ellie	Pat	Distributed	Remaining
Net income						$48,000
Interest allowance	$ 1,300	$ 900	$ 4,000	$2,800	$ 9,000	39,000
Remainder	19,500	9,750	4,875	4,875	39,000	–0–
Total	$20,800	$10,650	$ 8,875	$7,675	$48,000	$ –0–

Once the initial $9,000 allowance for interest is allocated, Margie would receive an additional $19,500 (4/8 of $39,000), Greg would receive $9,750 (2/8 of $39,000), while Ellie and Pat each would receive $4,875 (1/8 of $39,000). Each partner's capital would increase by the amounts shown in the total line in Exhibit 17.3.

Given the capital balances and the 10 percent rate in this example, any loss or an income figure less than the $9,000 amount of interest allowance would result in a negative remainder that must be allocated among the partners. The process is similar to that shown in Exhibit 17.2.

Combination of Salary and Interest Allowance   Some partnership agreements provide both salary and interest allowances as well as an agreement for dividing the remainder. For example, assume that Margie receives a salary allowance of $10,000, Greg receives a salary allowance of $5,000, and that all the partners are allowed 10 percent on their average capital balances. Exhibit 17.4 shows the resulting distribution if expected profits are $48,000 and any remainder after salary and interest allowance is to be divided equally. Margie's, Greg's, Ellie's, and Pat's capital accounts will increase by $17,300, $11,900, $10,000, and $8,800, respectively, as a result of this partnership agreement.

EXHIBIT	17.4	Distribution of Net Income with Salary and Interest Allowances					

					Amount	Amount
Item	Margie	Greg	Ellie	Pat	Distributed	Remaining
Net income						$48,000
Salary allowance	$10,000	$ 5,000			$15,000	33,000
Interest allowance	1,300	900	$ 4,000	$ 2,800	9,000	24,000
Remainder	6,000	6,000	6,000	6,000	24,000	–0–
Total	$17,300	$11,900	$10,000	$8,800	$48,000	$ –0–

Admitting a new partner dissolves the old partnership and creates a new partnership. Because partnerships have unlimited liability and mutual agency, the admission of a new partner requires the approval of the existing partners. When this occurs, the partners may also rewrite certain aspects of the partnership agreement, such as the basis for distribution of earnings. This is done to clarify the rights and responsibilities of the new and existing partners after the formation of the new partnership.

A new partner is admitted in one of two ways: by purchasing all or part of the interest of an existing partner by payment to the existing partner, or by investing directly in the partnership organization.

Purchase of an Existing Interest   An existing partner can sell all or a portion of his or her interest in the firm directly to a new partner, subject to the approval of the other partners. Because the payment goes to the existing partner, the new partner would receive either all or only a portion of the selling partner's capital. Total partnership equity would remain the same.

To illustrate, assume that the partners in the Doane Company have the capital balances described below:

Margie Klocke, Capital	$13,000
Greg Klocke, Capital	9,000
Ellie Beans, Capital	40,000
Pat Beans, Capital	28,000

If Ellie Beans agrees to sell one-half of her interest, $20,000, to Tom Wenke for $30,000, and the rest of the partners agree to admit Wenke, the new capital balances would be as follows:

Margie Klocke, Capital	$13,000
Greg Klocke, Capital	9,000
Ellie Beans, Capital	20,000
Pat Beans, Capital	28,000
Tom Wenke	20,000

While Ellie Beans and Tom Wenke have agreed on a price, $30,000, the price does not correspond to the $20,000 amount in Wenke's capital account. This transaction does not change the amount of assets of the firm because Ellie Beans, not the partnership, receives the $30,000 cash. As a result, the capital of the other partners remains the same. Only Ellie Beans's capital reflects a reduction of $20,000, the same amount by which Tom Wenke's capital account is increased upon his admission.

Direct Investment in the Firm   When the new partner's admission to the partnership involves the investment of money or other assets in the firm, the payment increases the amount of the firm's total assets as well as its total owners' equity. The new partner's interest in the firm is either the same, smaller, or larger than the amount of the assets contributed.

For example, assume that the partners agree to admit Tom Wenke to a one-fourth interest if he invests $30,000 cash in the partnership. The total capital after admission of Wenke is $120,000 ($13,000 + $9,000 + $40,000 + $28,000 + $30,000). Wenke's one-fourth interest ($120,000/4) is $30,000.

Such an arrangement presumes that the existing partners are content to allow Wenke to have a capital balance equal to the amount of his investment. However, if the partnership has enjoyed above-average earnings, the existing partners may require that a new partner pay a price greater than the amount credited to his or her capital account. The excess of the cash payment over the amount of the new partner's capital account is viewed as a bonus to the existing partners.

Bonus to Existing Partners   To illustrate a bonus to existing partners, assume that the Doane partners agree to admit Wenke if he agrees to pay $40,000 in exchange for a one-fourth interest in the partnership. To compute the dollar amount of Wenke's one-fourth interest, add the amount of the original owners' equity of $90,000 to the $40,000 contributed by Wenke for a total equity of the new partnership of $130,000. Wenke's one-fourth interest in the $130,000 is $32,500 ($130,000/4). The difference of $7,500 between Wenke's contribution of $40,000 and the $32,500 of capital he receives represents a bonus to Margie, Greg, Ellie, and Pat. The $7,500 bonus would be divided among them in accordance with their original agreement on division of earnings. Assuming that the existing partners agreed to divide profits and losses equally, each partner's capital would increase $1,875 ($7,500/4).

Bonus to a New Partner   If the incoming partner has a needed skill or has an established business with above-average earnings, existing partners may offer the new partner a bonus to enter into the partnership. Assume that the existing partners decide to admit Wenke to a one-fourth interest for only $25,000 in cash because he has unique technical abilities that can improve the efficiency of their accounting services. With the $25,000 contribution, owners' equity would be $115,000—the original equity of $90,000 of Doane Company plus the $25,000 contribution from Wenke. Wenke's one-fourth equity in the new firm would be $28,750, or one-fourth of the total capital of $115,000. The difference between his $25,000 payment and the $28,750 of his capital comes from a reduction in the amounts of the original partners' capital. This $3,750 is not a loss for the partnership. Rather, it represents a bonus that Margie, Greg, Ellie, and Pat are willing to give Wenke to convince him to join the partnership. The partners would expect to make up the bonus amount via the earnings that Wenke is expected to generate. Because the existing partners share profits equally, each reduces his or her capital by $937.50 ($3,750/4) in order to increase Wenke's capital account to $28,750 to reflect Wenke's one-fourth interest in the company.

After allocating the bonus, the capital of the partners should total $115,000, $12,062.50 for Margie, $8,062.50 for Greg, $39,062.50 for Ellie, $27,062.50 for Pat, and $28,750 for Tom Wenke.

Revaluation of Assets before Admission of a New Partner

It is not unusual for a firm to revalue its assets before admitting a new partner. This usually occurs when the partnership structure has not changed for an extended period of time or when the values of the partnership's assets have changed substantially since the last change in the partnership structure. If the existing partnership assets have a fair market value in excess of their recorded book values, the increase in value represents a gain and is allocated to the original partners' capital accounts based on the terms of their profit and loss agreement. By allocating the gain before the new partner is admitted, the old partners benefit from the appreciation of the assets. If the market value of the assets is less than the book value of the assets, it is necessary to reduce the assets to their market values and allocate the loss to the original partners' capital accounts in accordance with their partnership agreement. Revaluing the assets down protects the new partner from the losses attributable to the old partners.

Withdrawal of a Partner

When a partner withdraws from a partnership, his or her interest is purchased directly by one or more of the remaining partners, by an outsider seeking admission to the partnership, or by the partnership itself. As in the case with the admission of a partner, the assets of the firm are often revalued prior to the withdrawal of a partner. The sale of a withdrawing partner's interest to existing partners or to an incoming partner requires only the transfer of the retiring partner's capital to an existing or new partner's capital.

When the partnership plans to use its assets to pay for a withdrawing partner's interest, the amount may equal, exceed, or be less than the amount of the withdrawing partner's capital. When the partner receives the same amount as his or her capital, the amount of the other partners' capital would not be affected.

When a withdrawing partner receives more than the amount of his or her capital, the difference between the withdrawing partner's capital and the amount received would reduce the remaining partners' capital in accordance with the terms of the partnership agreement. When a withdrawing partner receives less than the amount of his or her capital, the difference would increase the remaining partners' capital in accordance with the terms of the partnership agreement.

Changing the ownership in a partnership, as we have just described, is an involved process. In stark contrast is the corporate entity where stockholders can buy and sell an ownership interest in the corporation without changing the owners' equity of the firm. We examine the stockholders' equity of corporations next.

CORPORATE EQUITY INSTRUMENTS

LO 3

Corporations that have a large number of owners must issue shares of capital stock to indicate an owner's interest in the corporation and to allow the owners to increase or decrease their interest in the organization without the consent of the other owners. This section discusses the characteristics of the financial instruments used by corporations for equity financing. Understanding the characteristics of the financial instruments is essential when planning to use the corporate structure for financing a business.

In general, corporations issue two classes of stock: common and preferred, although they may have different types of each. For example, Ben & Jerry's has Class A common stock and Class B common stock.

Common Stock

If a corporation has only one class of stock, it is called common stock. **Common stock** represents the basic ownership unit of the corporation, and, unless specifically noted in the corporation's charter and bylaws, it confers all the rights of ownership.

Common stockholders have the right to vote on significant events that affect the corporation and they elect members of the board of directors who, in turn, hire the corporation's professional managers. Common stockholders normally have other rights that include the right to dividends, the right to the residual assets upon liquidation of the corporation, the right to dispose of the shares by sale or gift, and the preemptive right.

The **preemptive right** gives common stockholders the right to maintain their percentage interest in the corporation when it issues new shares of common stock. For example, suppose that Finley Graves, a common stockholder, owns 10 percent of the shares of Ben & Jerry's and that Ben & Jerry's is going to issue 200,000 new shares of common stock. The preemptive right requires that the corporation offer Finley Graves the right to buy 20,000 (200,000 × 0.10) shares of the new issue in order to maintain his 10 percent interest in the company. The trend today is for most large corporations to eliminate the preemptive right, but it is common in smaller corporations.

Common stock represents the *residual* ownership interest in the corporation because the common stockholders, upon liquidation of the corporation, receive benefits only after the corporation satisfies all creditors' and other owners' claims. Thus the common stockholders receive the remainder, or residual, interest in the corporation.

Some corporations, like Ben & Jerry's, have more than one class of common stock (Class A common stock and Class B common stock). The difference between the classes of stock usually involves the voting rights associated with each class of stock and is described in the corporation's charter and bylaws. Exhibit 17.5 shows Ben & Jerry's stockholders' equity and a note describing how the Class B common stock and preferred stock are used to keep the company in the hands of the founders.

Preferred Stock

Preferred stock represents an ownership interest in a corporation with special privileges or preferences as to liquidation and dividends. Upon liquidation of the corporation, the preferred stockholders are paid before the common stockholders. In addition, preferred stockholders are entitled to receive dividends before common stockholders receive dividends. Thus the preference conferred on preferred stockholders is in reference to common stockholders, not creditors.

In exchange for these preferences, preferred stockholders usually give up the right to vote, and the dividends they receive are usually limited to a set amount per share of stock. Preferred stock dividends are stated in either predetermined dollar amounts or as a percentage of par value (defined and discussed later in the chapter). For example, stock that is termed *$5.50 preferred* would receive a dividend of $5.50 per share before common

EXHIBIT 17.5 Ben & Jerry's Stockholders' Equity

Stockholders' equity:		
$1.20 noncumulative Class A preferred stock—$1.00 par value, redeemable at the Company's option at $12.00 per share; 900 shares authorized, issued and outstanding, aggregate preference on voluntary or involuntary liquidation—$9,000	$ 1	$ 1
Class A common stock - $.033 par value; authorized 20,000,000 shares; issued: 6,494,835 shares at December 27, 1997 and 6,364,733 shares at December 28, 1996	214	210
Class B common stock - $.033 par value; authorized 3,000,000 shares; issued: 866,235 shares at December 27, 1997, and 897,664 shares at December 28, 1996	29	29
Additional paid-in capital	49,681	48,753
Retained earnings	39,086	35,190
Cumulative translation adjustment	(129)	(118)
Treasury stock, at cost: 124,532 Class A and 1,092 Class B shares at December 27, 1997 and 67,032 Class A and 1,092 Class B shares at December 28, 1996	(1,963)	(1,380)
Total stockholders' equity	$86,919	$82,685

Control of Votes

Ben & Jerry's Class B Common Stock was created in 1987, in a two-for-one stock split. The Class B Common Stock is a non-tradable, generally non-transferable stock with ten votes per share. The Class B Common Stock is freely convertible into Class A Common stock on a share-for-share basis, and transferable thereafter. The purpose of the Class B Common Stock was to concentrate voting control of the Company in the hands of the founders and early shareholders of the company. While Directors and Officers hold significantly less than a majority of the actual shares in the Company, control of a majority of the Class B Common Stock gives the founders and directors effective control over all votes submitted to shareholders. The Company also has 900 shares of Preferred Stock outstanding, held entirely by the Ben & Jerry's Foundation. This Preferred Stock is non-tradable, but has special voting rights on certain matters, particularly possible business combinations, takeovers, or mergers. Control of these votes by the Ben & Jerry's Foundation may be regarded as an anti-takeover device.

---

stockholders would receive any dividends. If a preferred stock has a $100 par value and a 10 percent dividend rate, each preferred stockholder would receive a $10 dividend ($100 par × 0.10) for every share held.

Companies often issue preferred stock with one or more of the following five features: (1) cumulative, (2) participation, (3) call, (4) redeemable, and (5) convertible. Each feature is designed to make the preferred stock more attractive to investors and can be used individually or in combination.

Cumulative preferred stock accumulates unpaid dividends over time. When cumulative preferred stock dividends are not paid when stipulated they are called **dividends in arrears.** If a corporation does not pay dividends in a given year, the next time dividends are paid, all the preferred dividends skipped in prior years plus the preferred dividend due for the current year must be paid before the common stockholders can receive any dividends. This provides preferred stockholders some assurance that preferred dividends, if missed in one year, will be paid in a subsequent year.

To illustrate, assume that Barton Corporation has preferred stock but does not pay its normal stated amount of preferred stock dividend of $100,000 in 1998. In 1999, if the Barton Corporation pays dividends of $250,000, the preferred stockholders will receive $200,000 ($100,000 for 1998 and $100,000 for 1999), and the common stockholders will receive the residual $50,000.

Participating preferred stock allows preferred stockholders the right to receive an amount in excess of the stated dividend rate or amount. *After* common stockholders have received a dividend comparable to that paid to preferred stockholders, any dividend remaining is shared between preferred and common stockholders. The amount of the residual dividends that each class of stockholders receives depends on the terms of the participation outlined in the corporation's charter. For example, assume the Barton Corporation has participating preferred stock and declares a $500,000 dividend. If the normal preferred stock dividend is $100,000, and the common stockholders' equivalent share of the dividends is $200,000, then the residual dividend of $200,000 [$500,000 – ($100,000 – $200,000)] is divided between the preferred and common stockholders. The amount of the residual that each class of stockholder receives depends on the terms of participation outlined in the corporate charter. In many cases the division is based on the ratio of the preferred to common stock par values of the shares issued (discussed later in the chapter).

Callable preferred stock gives the corporation the right to repurchase its preferred stock at a stipulated price. If the corporation decides it wants to reduce the number of shares of preferred stock or eliminate all preferred stockholders, it can "call" or buy back some or all of the preferred stock. When the corporation "calls" the preferred stock, the preferred stockholders must relinquish their shares. The corporation must compensate the preferred stockholders for the shares relinquished. Normally, call prices are listed on the preferred stock at a certain dollar amount. Ben & Jerry's preferred stock is callable (redeemable at the option of the corporation) at $12.

Corporations call their preferred stock and liquidate the preferred stockholders' interest in the corporation when this action will benefit the common stockholders of the corporation. By eliminating preferred stockholders, the common stockholders will receive the dividends normally given to preferred stockholders.

In some cases, the preferred stock is called in order to use another less expensive source of financing. For example, if a company had issued preferred stock with a 10 percent dividend and can now issue long-term debt at 7 percent, it might be to its advantage to call the preferred stock and replace the equity financing with cheaper debt financing.

Redeemable preferred stock is similar to callable preferred stock except it gives the stockholder the option to turn in (redeem) the stock for cash at the stockholder's option. If the stockholder no longer wishes to hold preferred stock, he or she can "redeem" or sell the stock to the corporation for a predetermined price per share. Of course, preferred stockholders also could sell the stock in the secondary market at any time. The redemption price assures the preferred stockholder of a guaranteed minimum price for the stock.

For example, suppose Barton Corporation issues 5,000 shares of redeemable preferred stock with a redemption price of $50. If shareholders present 1,000 of the shares for redemption, Barton must give each shareholder $50, or a total of $50,000.

PAUSE & REFLECT

If preferred stock has a predetermined redemption price, is this security a debt instrument? In what ways is it like debt? How does it differ from debt? *(answer on page 602)*

Convertible preferred stock gives stockholders the right to convert (exchange) preferred shares for other forms of capital, as stated in the corporate charter, at the option of the preferred stockholder. Preferred stock is normally convertible into common stock, although occasionally it is convertible into debt instruments. When preferred stock is convertible into common stock, the conversion is normally stated as a number of shares, such as "convertible into four shares of common stock." This feature is attractive to both the prospective investor and the company. The prospective investor sees the option as a way to increase the return on his or her investment and is willing to pay a higher price for the security. Companies find convertible preferred stock attractive because it sells at a higher price and is more marketable.

To illustrate, assume Barton Corporation issues 5,000 shares of $20 par, 5 percent convertible preferred stock that is convertible into two shares of common stock. If later the preferred stock has a market price of $30 per share and common stock is selling for $20 per share, many preferred stockholders will convert their preferred stock for two shares of common stock worth $40. When the preferred stock is converted, it is retired and the common stock issued.

We have discussed common and preferred stock and the possible features of preferred stock. Next we describe how to identify the number of shares a corporation can sell and the number it has sold to generate equity financing.

HOW MANY SHARES ARE THERE?

When referring to the number of shares of stock associated with a corporation, we refer to the number of shares the corporation has *authorized, issued,* and *outstanding.* These three terms give financial planners and external investors some idea about the equity financing potential of the corporation. The terms also help describe the current status of equity financing.

Shares Authorized

When a company files its articles of incorporation with the secretary of state of the incorporating state, it specifies the number of shares it wants to be able to sell. The number of **authorized shares** is the total number of shares the state has approved for a corporation to sell. The corporation can issue more than the number of authorized shares only by obtaining permission from the incorporating state. The number of shares authorized is usually set high enough so additional authorization from the state is unnecessary. Ben & Jerry's has 20,000,000 shares of its Class A common stock authorized and 3,000,000 shares of its Class B common stock authorized.

Shares Issued

A corporation raises money to fund its investments by selling its stock to individuals, groups, or businesses that want to have an ownership interest in the corporation. When the corporation sells its stock initially, it has "issued" its shares. The number of **issued shares** refers to the number of authorized shares a corporation has sold to stockholders. After the corporation issues stock, shareholders are free to buy and sell the issued shares. Secondary markets such as the New York Stock Exchange and NASDAQ exist to facilitate the stockholders' desire to trade these securities. The number of shares issued is unaffected when the corporation's stock is traded in secondary markets because investors are merely trading existing shares of stock. *The number of shares issued changes only when the corporation sells more of its authorized shares or buys back and retires some of its issued shares.* As of December 27, 1997, Ben & Jerry's had 6,494,835 shares of Class A common stock issued and 866,235 shares of Class B common stock issued.

Shares Outstanding

The number of **outstanding shares** is the number of shares issued and currently held outside the corporation. Because a corporation is a legal entity, it can buy its own stock in the secondary market. Typically, a corporation buys its own shares in anticipation of reissuing the stock at a higher price and, therefore, raising additional capital. In addition, corporations purchase their stock to give to their executives as deferred compensation (as described in Chapter 16) and to protect against hostile takeovers. **Treasury stock** is the shares of a corporation's issued stock that the corporation has repurchased and intends to reissue at a later date. When a corporation buys treasury stock, it is liquidating the stockholders' interest in the corporation by giving them the corporation's cash in exchange for their ownership interest. *When a corporation buys treasury stock, it is not buying an asset; rather, it is reducing its stockholders' equity by eliminating one or more of its stockholders.* During fiscal year 1997, Ben & Jerry's purchased 57,500 shares of its Class A common stock and increased the treasury shares of this class of stock to 124,532, while the number of Class B treasury stock, 1,092, remained unchanged.

The number of shares outstanding is the number of shares issued less the number of shares of treasury stock held by the corporation. Ben & Jerry's has 6,370,303 (6,494,835 issued shares – 124,532 treasury shares) shares

Wall Street is the home of the New York Stock Exchange, the most famous secondary stock market in the world.

of Class A common stock outstanding and 865,143 (866,235 issued shares – 1,092 treasury shares) shares of Class B common stock outstanding. If the corporation has no treasury shares, the number of shares outstanding and the number issued are the same.

A corporation can buy its issued shares and then retire the shares. **Retired shares** are repurchased issued shares that the corporation will never reissue. *When shares are retired, both the number of shares issued and outstanding are decreased.*

In most states, the number of shares a company is allowed to repurchase is limited to 20 percent of the number of shares issued in order to protect corporate creditors. Because corporations have limited liability, creditors of a corporation have claim only to the assets of the corporation. If the corporation could buy all of its stock back, the stockholders would receive their interest in the corporation (cash payment for the repurchased stock) before the creditors, and the assets remaining might not be sufficient to satisfy the claims of the creditors upon liquidation.

While the number of shares authorized, issued, and outstanding provides some insight into the capital structure of the firm, monetary values must be attached to these shares to gain a complete picture of a corporation's ownership structure.

PAUSE &
REFLECT

If a corporation could buy back all its issued stock, who would own the corporation?
(answer on page 603)

CAPITAL STOCK VALUES

Capital stock has two important "values" depending on the context in which it appears. The first is par value, which is established to comply with the legal requirements of issuing stock. The second is a stock's market value, which represents the economic value of capital stock.

Par Value

Par value is an arbitrary value assigned to shares of capital stock that is approved by the state in which the business is incorporated. The par value is specified in the corporation's charter and is printed on the stock certificates. In most states, the par value is the minimum price the stock can sell for when it is sold initially. The par value for Ben & Jerry's Class A and B common stock is $0.033, while its preferred stock has a par value of $1.

Because the par value of common stock is a purely arbitrary amount, and because a high par value might impair the firm's ability to sell its shares, most par values of common stock are quite low. Ben & Jerry's par value on its common stock is a good illustration of this practice.

The **legal capital** of the corporation is the portion of stockholders' equity required by state law to be retained for the protection of the corporation's creditors. In many states it is calculated by multiplying the par value times the number of shares of stock issued. The corporation cannot pay dividends that cause its total assets to drop below the sum of its legal capital and the total liabilities of the corporation, thus providing some protection for the creditors of the corporation. For example, suppose Barton Corporation has total assets of $1,200,000, total liabilities of $800,000, legal capital of $100,000, and retained earnings of $300,000. Barton can pay dividends of only $300,000 because any dividends in excess of $300,000 would mean the corporation is providing a *return of* the stockholders' equity ahead of the creditors' claim on the assets. Because corporate creditors can be paid only from the corporation's assets, paying dividends that reduce Barton's legal capital may impair the creditors' ability to recover their investment.

The amount of proceeds received from stock issuance in excess of the par value of the stock when it is issued is called **paid-in capital in excess of par** or **contributed capital in excess of par.** This classification makes the distinction between monies received that satisfy legal capital requirements (par values) and the amounts that are in excess of the legal minimum.

No-Par Value

No-par stock does not have a minimum price assigned to each share of stock. Its initial purpose was to overcome two problems associated with par value shares: the possible need to issue stock below par value, and the confusion that existed about par values and any relationship they might have to the market values of the stocks. The legal capital of corporations that issue no-par stock is often specified by the state. Exhibit 17.6 illustrates a no-par stock certificate. Notice that there is no mention of a par value on the certificate itself.

EXHIBIT 17.6

No-Par Stock Certificate

No-par, stated value stock is stock that has a minimum price or stated value established by the corporation's board of directors but no par value specified in the charter. In effect, a stated value stock makes a no-par stock function the same way as par value stock. This type of stock allows creditors to have the assurance that a minimum amount of capital is available in the corporation to protect their interest. The advantage of stated value stock is that the board of directors decides whether to establish a stated value on the no-par stock. This creates more flexibility for the corporation than when a stock has its par value established in its articles of incorporation.

Market Value

The market value of a share of stock is the price agreed to by an unrelated willing buyer and seller. For stocks traded in organized secondary markets, the market values of stock are readily available from listings in financial news sources such as the *Wall Street Journal* and *Barron's*. For stocks that are not traded on organized exchanges, individuals who are making trades determine market values. Unlike par values, which are determined prior to the issuance of the stock and cannot be changed without approval of the incorporating state, the market value of stock is constantly changing based on willing buyers' and sellers' estimates of the value of the corporation.

The market price a corporation receives in the initial issue market determines the amount of cash the corporation receives from investors to finance its operations. Corporations continue to monitor the market value of their stock in the secondary market after the initial sale of the stock. Increasing or decreasing market values reflect the investors' perceptions of the corporation's financial condition and future profit potential. Rising stock prices reflect increasing investor confidence in future profitability, while declining prices indicate erosion of their confidence in the firm's future profitability. The market price of stock in the secondary market gives the corporation's management an idea of the amount of cash it could raise if additional stock issues are planned.

A corporation's stock price changes as investors' expectations about its future profitability change. One item that has a significant impact on investors' perception of future profitability is the amount and timing of the firm's dividends.

Traders on the floor of a
stock exchange act as agents
for the stockholders.

DIVIDENDS

Dividends are a distribution of the assets of the corporation to the owners of the corporation. Typically, these distributions are made from the earnings of the firm, providing stockholders with a *return on* their investment. However, if the dividends exceed the accumulated earnings of the firm, they are called *liquidating dividends* because they are a *return of* the stockholders' investments.

Dividends usually are distributed in the form of cash; however, corporations routinely issue stock dividends, and they can issue property dividends. A **cash dividend** is a cash distribution paid by sending checks to stockholders as of a certain date. The advantage of cash dividends is that most investors prefer this type of distribution. The disadvantage of cash dividends is that they reduce a source of equity financing. Many corporations offer what are referred to as *DRIP accounts* to encourage the reinvestment of the firm's dividends. A **dividend reinvestment program (DRIP)** is a program that allows current stockholders to use their cash dividends to buy more shares of the company's stock. Stockholders like the program because they can acquire more shares of stock without paying brokerage fees. Firms like the program because it keeps their stockholders happy while reinvesting the cash that would otherwise be paid out as dividends.

When a corporation issues a **stock dividend,** it distributes additional shares of the corporation's stock to existing stockholders. Stock dividends have no effect on the assets of the firm because each stockholder receives more shares of stock rather than corporate assets. Although each investor has more shares as a result of a stock dividend, his or her percentage interest in the corporation does not change. When planning a stock dividend, management must be aware that as the size of the stock dividend increases, the market price of the outstanding shares will decrease.

For example, if Ben & Jerry's issues a 10 percent stock dividend on the number of shares issued, a stockholder who owns 100 shares of stock will receive 10 new shares (100 shares × 0.10). However, because the number of shares that every Ben & Jerry's stockholder owns will increase by 10 percent, no single stockholder will have a greater interest in the firm than he or she did before the stock dividend. As a result, the price of the stock should decrease about 10 percent to reflect the increase in the number of shares. The advantage of a stock dividend is that in many cases the stock price drops less than the dividend percentage and, therefore, increases the stockholders' wealth. This keeps the stockholders satisfied without having to distribute the assets of the firm.

PAUSE & REFLECT

What is the benefit to the stockholder of receiving a stock dividend? Why would a corporation issue a stock dividend? *(answer on page 603)*

A **property dividend** typically involves the distribution of specific noncash assets, such as inventory or investments in other corporation's securities, to stockholders. Property dividends usually are given in corporations with just a few stockholders. They are not as popular with stockholders as cash dividends due to the difficulty of receiving and disposing of the corporation's property.

Four dates related to dividends are important to remember: (1) the date of declaration, (2) the date of record, (3) the ex-dividend date, and (4) the date of payment. Exhibit 17.7 shows the sequence of these dates, which we next describe in detail.

EXHIBIT 17.7

Dividend Dates

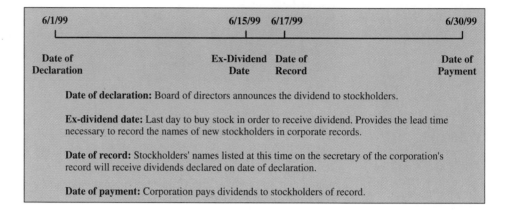

Date of declaration: Board of directors announces the dividend to stockholders.

Ex-dividend date: Last day to buy stock in order to receive dividend. Provides the lead time necessary to record the names of new stockholders in corporate records.

Date of record: Stockholders' names listed at this time on the secretary of the corporation's record will receive dividends declared on date of declaration.

Date of payment: Corporation pays dividends to stockholders of record.

Date of Declaration

The **date of declaration** is the date on which the board of directors announces its decision to pay a dividend. The board of directors usually declares dividends after the company has generated sufficient earnings and has cash on hand to provide stockholders with a return on their investment. On the date of declaration, the board of directors sets the amount of the dividend and the date to distribute it. For cash and property dividends, once the board declares the dividend, the corporation incurs the obligation to pay the dividend on the date of payment, which gives rise to a related liability. However, because stock dividends involve the distribution of shares of stock rather than the firm's assets, no liability is incurred on the date of declaration for stock dividends.

Date of Record

The **date of record** is the date on which the secretary of the corporation examines the stock ownership transfer book to determine who is officially registered as a stockholder of the corporation and, therefore, eligible to receive the corporation's dividends. Those persons listed in the ownership book on this date will receive the dividend. *Stockholders can sell their stock after this date but before the date of payment and still receive the declared dividend.* The date of record is announced at the time the board of directors declares the dividend.

Ex-Dividend Date

The **ex-dividend date** occurs two or three days prior to the date of record and is the last date when an individual can buy the stock of the corporation and still receive the corporation's declared dividend. Setting the ex-dividend date depends on how long it will take for the corporate secretary to record a change in the ownership of the stock.

Date of Payment

The **date of payment** is the date that the company pays the dividends to stockholders of record. Normally, no more than 90 days elapse from the date of declaration until the date of payment. Once the corporation has distributed the dividend, it has met its dividend obligation created on the date of declaration.

STOCK SPLITS

A **stock split** occurs when a corporation calls in its old shares of stock and issues a larger number of new shares of stock in their place. However, each stockholder retains the same percentage interest in the company after the stock split because the par or stated value of the stock also changes to reflect the number of new shares on the market.

Assume that Barton Corporation has 400,000 shares of common stock issued and outstanding with a par value of $3 per share. With its total par value at $1,200,000 (400,000 issued shares × $3 par value), the board of directors approves a three-for-one stock split. To implement the split, the company will call in all the old $3 par value common stock and replace it with 1,200,000 (400,000 × 3) shares of $1 ($3/3) par value common stock. Notice that the stock split increases (triples) the number of shares issued and decreases the par value to one-third of its original amount. However, the total par value of the shares issued remains the same, $1,200,000 (1,200,000 issued shares × $1 par value).

When a stock splits, the market price of the stock is reduced by the size of the split. For example, if Barton Corporation's stock was selling for $60 per share before the split, its price after the split would be about $20 per share. This occurs because while each stockholder owns a greater number of shares, each shareholder's ownership of the company remains unchanged.

Companies enter into stock splits for a variety of reasons. The most common reason is to lower the market price of the company's stock to make the price more affordable to a wider group of potential investors. Because stockbrokers prefer to sell stocks in **round lots,** that is, 100 shares of stock sold together, as a company becomes successful and its stock price increases, it becomes more difficult for small investors to afford round lots. Therefore, to make purchasing its shares more affordable, a corporation splits its stock to reduce the market price per share of stock. Berkshire Hathaway's common stock, which sold for over $74,000 a share in 1998, is an extreme example of what can happen when a company's management chooses not to split its stock.

While investors own the same amount of the company in terms of the percentage of shares after the split as before the split, their personal financial condition may improve as a result of the stock split. For example, in 1998 Disney had a 3-for-1 stock split. The number of shares issued tripled and the market price of the stock went from $115 per share before the split to $39 per share after the split. Therefore, a stockholder with 100 shares of Disney stock before the split, which was worth $11,500, owned 300 shares worth $11,700 (300 shares × $39) after the split. This increase in the total market value of the stock occurs because investors consider the split a positive signal from the company. That is, the investors believe that the company split the stock anticipating an increase in the firm's future profitability and, therefore, an increase in stock prices.

WHERE DO CORPORATIONS FIND EQUITY FINANCING?

LO 4

When planning to use equity financing, two sources are available. For established companies, the primary source of equity financing is the cash generated from operations. Although much of these funds are reinvested in operating activities, cash from operations can be a substantial source of equity financing. The drawback of this type of financing is that planning on a certain level of operation in order to finance a major capital expenditure can be risky.

The other source of equity financing involves the sale of stock. We know that, regardless of their size, corporations raise equity capital by issuing common and preferred stock. Smaller corporations usually raise equity capital (cash) by selling stock directly to those persons who have an interest in the business.

For business entities that are changing from a sole proprietorship or partnership to a corporation, the owners exchange their interest in the sole proprietorship or partnership for common stock of the corporation. While this exchange process raises no cash, the owners are, in effect, providing equity financing for the new business entity by contributing their interest in the old entity.

For large businesses, investment bankers, who act as an agent for the corporation and charge a fee for their service, usually sell the initial issue of capital stock. Corporations hire investment bankers to sell their securities because of the investment banker's knowledge of the securities market and ability to find buyers for the stock. The New York Stock Exchange, the American Stock Exchange, NASDAQ, and the regional stock exchanges are markets for the initial issues of capital stock.

Exhibit 17.8 illustrates the first page of the prospectus for NovaStar Financial, Inc. A prospectus is the document that describes the company and the stock being offered for sale to the public. The prospectus describes such items as the type of business the

EXHIBIT   17.8   NovaStar Prospectus

PROSPECTUS

3,750,000 Shares
NovaStar Financial, Inc.
Common Stock

NovaStar Financial, Inc. ("NovaStar" or "the Company"), organized in 1996, is a self-advised and self-managed specialty finance company which: (i) acquires single family residential subprime mortgage loans; (ii) leverages its assets using warehouse facilities, including repurchase agreements; (iii) issues collateralized debt obligations to finance its subprime mortgage loans in the long-term; (iv) purchases mortgage securities in the secondary mortgage market; and (v) manages the resulting combined portfolio of mortgage assets (the "Mortgage Assets") in a tax-advantaged real estate investment trust ("REIT") structure. The Company expects that a primary source of wholesale mortgage loans will be loans originated by NovaStar Mortgage, Inc. ("NovaStar Mortgage"), a taxable affiliate of the Company. Certain directors and officers of the Company also serve as directors and officers of NovaStar Mortgage. Under a separate agreement, NovaStar Mortgage also services mortgage loans owned by the Company.

Prior to this Offering, there has been no market for the Common Stock of the Company. See "Underwriting" for a discussion of the factors considered in determining the public offering price. The Company has been approved for listing on the New York Stock Exchange, subject to official notice of issuance, under the symbol "NFI".

The Company began operations in December 1996 following the closing of a private placement of Units (the "Private Placement"). In the Private Placement, the Company's two founders each acquired Units paid for by delivering to the Company promissory notes, each in the amount of $1,624,995, bearing interest at eight percent per annum and secured by the Units acquired. The principal amount of the notes was divided into three equal tranches. Principal due on each tranche will be forgiven by the Company if the return to Private Placement investors meets certain benchmarks and the Company will then recognize a non-cash charge against earnings. Such charges against earnings could have a material adverse effect on the Company's results of operations and dividends paid to stockholders for the affected period. See "Risk Factors" and "Management-Executive Compensation."

See "Risk Factors" beginning on page 15 for a discussion of certain factors that should be considered by prospective purchasers of the Common Stock offered hereby. These risk factors include:

- The Company's limited operating history and net losses incurred.
- The possible forgiveness of incentive notes receivable from the Company's founders, which may materially adversely affect results of operations and dividends paid for the affected period.
- Dependence on key personnel.
- The possibility of failure to maintain REIT status, which would subject the Company to tax as a regular corporation.
- The potential effects of unexpected or rapid changes in interest rates, which would negatively impact the results of operations from the subprime mortgage lending business.
- The generally higher risk of delinquency and foreclosure on subprime mortgage loans which may result in higher levels of realized losses.

- The lack of loan performance data on the Company's loan portfolio and the expectation of increasing delinquency, foreclosure and loss rates as the portfolio becomes more seasoned.
- The Company's inability to hedge against potential interest rate changes.
- The potential inability of the Company to acquire Mortgage Assets in the secondary market at favorable yields.
- The immediate dilution of $3.56 per share in net tangible book value to investors purchasing in this Offering.
- Restrictions on ownership of capital stock in the Company's charter, which may inhibit market activity in the Common Stock and discourage takeover attempts.

THESE SECURITIES HAVE NOT BEEN APPROVED OR DISAPPROVED BY THE SECURITIES AND EXCHANGE COMMISSION NOR HAS THE SECURITIES AND EXCHANGE COMMISSION PASSED UPON THE ACCURACY OR ADEQUACY OF THIS PROSPECTUS. ANY REPRESENTATION TO THE CONTRARY IS A CRIMINAL OFFENSE.

	Price to Public	Underwriting Discount(1)	Proceeds to Company(2)
Per Share	$18.00	$1.26	$16.74
Total(3)	$67,500,000	$4,725,000	$62,775,000

(1) The Company has agreed to indemnify the Underwriters against certain liabilities including liabilities under the Securities Act of 1933, as amended. See "Underwriting."
(2) Before deducting expenses payable by the Company, estimated to be $500,000.
(3) The Company has granted the Underwriters an option exercisable within 30 days after the date of this Prospectus to purchase up to 562,500 additional shares of Common Stock on the same terms and conditions set forth above to cover over-allotments, if any. If all such shares are purchased, the total Price to Public, Underwriting Discount and Proceeds to Company will be $77,625,000, $5,433,750 and $72,191,250, respectively. See "Underwriting".

The Securities are offered by the Underwriters subject to receipt and acceptance by them, prior sale and the Underwriters' right to reject any order in whole or in part and to withdraw, cancel or modify the offer without notice. It is expected that delivery for the shares of Common Stock will be made through The Depository Trust Company on or about November 4, 1997.

Stifel, Nicolaus & Company
Incorporated

NationsBanc Montgomery Securities, Inc.

October 30, 1997

corporation is engaged in, the risks of the business, how it intends to use the proceeds, and the company's audited financial statements. The cover page for NovaStar's prospectus reveals that it wants to sell 3,750,000 shares of common stock for $18 per share and raise $67,500,000. Note that the underwriters, Stifel, Nicolaus & Company and NationsBanc Montgomery Securities, Inc., are going to charge $4,725,000 to sell NovaStar's securities.

Cash raised from the issuance of common and preferred stock provides the equity financing necessary to start a business enterprise or for subsequent expansion. However, many firms that can raise sufficient cash through equity financing choose to use debt to finance operations. We examine debt financing in Chapter 18.

SUMMARY

Equity financing is provided by owners who accept the risks of ownership in exchange for its financial and psychological rewards. There are two sources of equity financing. The first source consists of the contributions owners make in exchange for an ownership interest. The second is the cash generated by the firm's operations that the owners choose to reinvest in the company.

Sole proprietorships and partnerships are easily formed but have unlimited liability. While partnerships can generate more capital, mutual agency and unlimited liability create additional risks for the members of the partnership.

The amount of a partner's capital depends on the interest granted to him or her when he or she is admitted to the partnership and how the partnership divides its income.

- Common stock represents the residual ownership in the corporation, while preferred stock represents an ownership interest with special privileges as to dividends and liquidation.

- Treasury stock is the corporation's stock that the corporation repurchases for the purpose of either reissuing it to key employees as compensation or selling at a higher price in the market at a later date.

- The market price of stock is the cash price investors are willing to pay for an ownership interest in a corporation.

- Corporations reward their stockholders by distributing to them cash, property, and stock dividends. The board of directors declares dividends on the date of declaration; dividends are distributed on the date of payment to the stockholders who are registered owners on the date of record.

- A stock split occurs when a corporation calls in all its old shares of stock and issues a larger number of new shares. The purpose of a stock split is to reduce the price per share to make the round lots of shares more affordable in the secondary market.

KEY TERMS

authorized shares The total number of shares the state has approved for a corporation to sell

callable preferred stock Preferred stock that gives the issuing corporation the right to repurchase the preferred stock at a stipulated price

cash dividend A cash distribution in the form of a check drawn on the corporation's bank account that is sent to each stockholder as of a certain date

common stock The basic ownership unit of a corporation

convertible preferred stock Preferred stock that gives the stockholder the right to convert (exchange) the preferred shares for other forms of capital, as stated in the corporate charter, at the option of the preferred stockholder

cumulative preferred stock Preferred stock that accumulates unpaid dividends over time

date of declaration The date on which the board of directors announces its decision to pay a dividend

date of payment The date on which the corporation formally pays dividends to stockholders of record

date of record The date on which the secretary of the corporation examines the stock ownership transfer book to determine who is officially registered as a stockholder of the corporation and, therefore, eligible to receive the corporation's dividends

debt financing When a company obtains funds (cash) in exchange for a liability to repay the borrowed funds

dividend reinvestment program (DRIP) A program that allows current stockholders to use their cash dividends to buy more shares of the company's stock

dividends in arrears The amount of cumulative preferred stock dividends not paid in full when stipulated

equity financing A means for a firm to obtain funds in exchange for an ownership interest in the firm

ex-dividend date The last date when an individual can buy the stock of the corporation and still receive the corporation's declared dividend

issued shares The number of authorized shares a corporation has sold to stockholders

legal capital The portion of stockholders' equity required by state law to be retained for the protection of the corporation's creditors

no-par, stated value stock Stock with a minimum issue price or stated value established by the corporation's board of directors but no par value specified in the charter

no-par stock Stock that does not have a minimum price assigned to each share of stock

outstanding shares The number of shares issued and held outside the corporation

paid-in, or contributed, capital in excess of par The amount of proceeds received from stock issuance in excess of the par value of the stock when it is issued

par value An arbitrary value assigned to shares of capital stock that is approved by the state in which the business is incorporated

participating preferred stock Preferred stock that allows preferred stockholders the right to receive an amount in excess of the stated dividend rate or amount

preemptive right A right of common stockholders that allows them to maintain their percentage interest in the corporation when it issues new shares of common stock

preferred stock An ownership interest in a corporation with special privileges or preferences as to liquidation and dividends

property dividend The distribution of specific noncash assets to the stockholders of a corporation

redeemable preferred stock Preferred stock that allows a stockholder to turn in (redeem) the preferred stock for cash at the stockholder's option

retired shares Repurchased issued shares that the corporation will never reissue

round lots 100 shares of stock sold together

stock dividend The distribution of additional shares of the corporation's stock to existing stockholders

stock split The corporation's recall of its old shares of stock and issuance of a larger number of new shares in their place

treasury stock The shares of a corporation's issued stock that the corporation has repurchased and intends to reissue at a later date

ANSWERS TO THE PAUSE & REFLECTS

p. 583, Yes the business assets of a partner are at risk from his or her personal obligations. For example suppose a partner loses a lawsuit that arose from an auto accident that occurred during his family vacation. The plaintiffs can lay claim to the partner's equity if his personal assets are insufficient to meet the claims of the lawsuit.

p. 587, Profit and loss agreements are designed to equitably distribute the profits and losses of the partnership and are based on what the partners contribute to the partnership. In some limited cases this distribution will result in what appears to be an inequitable distribution. However, if all partners are aware of these potential outcomes and they feel the profit and loss agreement is fair they will accept these paradoxical outcomes. It is when a partner is unaware of the implications of a profit and loss agreement that problems arise. Yes it is possible to have a partner(s) capital account increase when the business suffers a loss. For example, if Doane Company expects a $3,000 loss, both Margie and Greg would receive their salary allowance and the residual loss of $28,000 would be divided equally. Therefore, Margie's capital would increase by $8,000, Greg's capital would increase by $3,000 while both Ellie and Pat would experience a $7,000 decrease in capital.

p. 593, Redeemable preferred stock is legally an equity instrument but in economic substance it is a liability because it obligates the corporation to make a cash payment, the redemption price, to the preferred stockholder at some point in the future. It is like equity in that the corporation is not legally required to pay preferred stockholders dividends and preferred stockholders are paid after all creditors are paid in the event the corporation is liquidated. It is interesting to note that the SEC requires corporations who issue redeemable preferred stock to report it on the "Mezzanine" of the balance sheet, that is, between liabilities and owners' equity because it shares characteristics of both debt and equity.

p. 595, When a corporation purchases its own stock it liquidates the ownership interest of a stockholder. Therefore, if the corporation buys all its stock back it would have no stockholders and, therefore, the creditors would own the corporation.

p. 597, When a corporation issues a stock dividend, stockholders have more shares but no greater interest in the corporation. However, in many cases the total market value of the shares held increases. For example, if a stockholder held 100 shares of a corporation with a market price of $20 per share and the corporation declared a 10% stock dividend the stock price should drop to $18.18 per share and the total market value of all 110 shares should remain at $2,000 ($18.18 × 110) after the dividend. There should be no change because the assets, liabilities, and stockholders' equity have not changed as a result of the stock dividend. However, in many cases the price per share does not decrease and, therefore, the total market value of the shares held increases. For example, if the price per share did not change after the stock dividend, the stockholder described above would have stock worth $2,200 ($20 × 110 shares).

The corporation issues stock dividends when it wants to reward stockholders without distributing cash to the stockholders. This only works when the stock market views the stock dividend as a positive event. That is, the market believes the corporation is doing well and wants to reinvest earnings to generate more profits rather than distribute it to stockholders.

QUESTIONS

1. Describe the two sources of financing available to a firm.
2. What are the rewards and risks of equity financing?
3. How is equity financing used?
4. What are the advantages of a sole proprietorship and a partnership?
5. What is mutual agency and why is it risky?
6. What is unlimited liability and why is it considered a disadvantage for a partnership?
7. What are the advantages and disadvantages of a corporate ownership structure?
8. Why is a salary allowance used in the division of income?
9. Why is it possible for a partner's equity to decrease when the partnership generates a profit?
10. Under what circumstances would a new partner receive a greater interest in a partnership than the dollar amount contributed to the firm?
11. Why should partnership assets be revalued before the admission of a new partner and before the withdrawal of an existing partner?
12. Compare and contrast the following:
    a. Common stock versus preferred stock
    b. Cumulative versus participating preferred stock
    c. Callable versus redeemable preferred stock
13. What is treasury stock and why is it acquired?
14. Distinguish among authorized shares, issued shares, and outstanding shares of stock.
15. What is the distinction between the par value and market value of a stock?
16. What is Paid-in Capital in Excess of Par?
17. What are the four key dividend dates? Why is each important?
18. How does a cash dividend differ from a stock dividend?
19. What is the distinction between stock splits and stock dividends?
20. What is a prospectus?

EXERCISES

E 17.1
LO 2

Smith, Kline, and Arnold are in a partnership and have agreed to share profits and losses in a ratio of 4:5:3, respectively. Determine how much their capital will increase or decrease if the partnership has (a) net income of $56,000 and (b) a net loss of $26,000.

E 17.2
LO 2

In their partnership agreement, Crick, Cissna, and Horgan agreed that Crick should receive a salary allowance of $30,000 per year and that Horgan should receive a salary allowance of $12,000. Any remainder is divided equally among the three partners. How much should each partner's capital change if the partnership generates (a) net income of $72,000, (b) net income of $28,000, and (c) a net loss of $48,000?

E 17.3
LO 2

Glass, Frigon, and Sedlock have agreed to divide profits and losses as follows: 9 percent interest on beginning capital and the remainder divided equally. The beginning capital amounts are Glass, $120,000; Frigon, $60,000; and Sedlock, $80,000. Determine the increase or decrease in each partner's capital if the partnership generated (a) net income of $72,000, (b) net income of $20,000, and (c) a net loss of $11,600.

E 17.4
LO 2

When Panther and Bregenzer formed their partnership, it was agreed that Panther would operate the business, although Bregenzer supplied most of the financing. In view of these facts, Panther is to receive a salary allowance of $50,000 per year, each partner is to receive a 5 percent interest allowance on his beginning capital balance, and any remainder is to be divided equally.

At the beginning of the year, Panther's capital balance was $280,000 and Bregenzer's was $600,000. Determine the amount of profit or loss allocated to each partner given the following income figures: (a) net income is $150,000, (b) net income is $46,000, and (c) net loss is $80,000.

E 17.5
LO 2

Tess Seeberger, who is a partner in Wamego Company, has decided to sell her ownership interest in the firm. The balance in her capital account is $120,000. With the consent of the other partners, she sells two-thirds of her interest to Janet Taphorn, an incoming partner, for $85,000 and the remaining one-third to an existing partner, Cathy Clark, for $42,000. Cathy Clark had a capital balance of $56,000 before the change. If no partnership assets were used to buy Seeberger out, what will Taphorn's and Clark's capital balances be after Seeberger's withdrawal from the partnership?

E 17.6
LO 2

Richey and Azuara, each of whom has a partnership capital of $130,000, admit Beals to a one-third interest in the firm upon Beals' payment of $150,000 to the partnership. If Richey and Azuara share profits and losses equally, how much will each partner's capital be after Beals is admitted to the partnership?

E 17.7
LO 2

The firm of Davis and McLeod decided to admit Wilson to the partnership. Wilson paid $120,000 cash for a one-third interest in the firm. At the time, Davis had capital of $110,000, and McLeod had capital of $100,000. They share profits and losses equally. What will be the capital of each partner after the admission of Wilson?

E 17.8
LO 2

Dan Hynek was invited to join an existing partnership. He paid $260,000 to the firm for a one-fourth interest. At the time, the other two existing partners had the following capital balance: Gomez, $336,000; and Chen, $388,000. Gomez and Chen shared profits and losses on a 3:2 basis, respectively. What will be the capital of each partner after the admission of Hynek?

E 17.9
LO 2

Daran Lemon and Rob Thummel decided to accept Jeff Placek into their partnership because he has an established reputation as an excellent salesperson in the community. Placek was admitted with a one-third interest for $84,000 cash. Lemon and Thummel have capital of $94,000 and $92,000, respectively, and share profits equally. What will each partner's capital be after the admission of Placek?

E 17.10
LO 2

The partnership of Steffens and Begley needs additional financial resources. Steffens and Begley have asked Brenneman to join their partnership. Immediately prior to Brenneman's admission, they reviewed their accounting records, and all parties agreed to the following changes: revalue inventory, which was maintained on a LIFO basis, upward by $36,000 and increase the allowance for doubtful accounts by $1,500. Steffens and Begley share profits and losses on a 2:1 basis, respectively. How will the revaluation impact Steffens' and Begley's capital? Why is the revaluation necessary before Brenneman is admitted?

E 17.11
LO 2

Randy Pohlman has a capital balance of $174,000 in a partnership. The other two partners in the business have capital as follows: Ali Fatimi, $196,000; and Bob Hollinger, $162,000. Profits and losses are shared equally. What will Fatimi's and Hollinger's capital be after Pohlman withdraws under the following circumstances?

a. Pohlman sells one-half of his interest to each of the other partners for $88,000 each (not the firm's cash).
b. Pohlman was paid $190,000 cash from the partnership assets.
c. Pohlman was paid $155,000 cash from the partnership assets.

E 17.12
LO 3

Russell Inc. is authorized to issue 1,500,000 shares of its $1 par value common stock and 400,000 shares of $50 par value preferred stock. Russell sold 10,000 shares of common stock at $38.50 and 900 shares of its preferred stock at $55 per share. How much capital did Russell generate by this sale? What is Russell's legal capital?

E 17.13
LO 3

Waugh Corporation issued 6,400 shares of its $1 par value common stock for $34 per share and 700 shares of its $30 par value preferred stock for $33 per share. What is Waugh's legal capital? What is the amount of capital received in excess of the par value of common and preferred stock? Why is a distinction made between legal capital and total capital?

E 17.14
LO 3

Lebo, Inc., is authorized to issue 1,500,000 shares of no-par common stock and 800,000 shares of $40 par value preferred stock. During its first year of operation, the company issued 200,000 shares of common stock for $6,400,000 and 30,000 shares of its preferred stock for $1,350,000. The firm had net income of $425,000 for the year and paid dividends of $150,000 during the year. What is the total amount of the firm's stockholders' equity? How much of the firm is financed by contributions by its owners and how much by its operations?

E 17.15
LO 3

The board of directors of Ness Company is going to pay a dividend of $56,000 to its common stockholders. Describe what will happen on each of the dates below in relation to this $56,000 dividend.
 a. Date of declaration
 b. Ex-dividend date
 c. Date of record
 d. Date of payment

E 17.16
LO 3

Hong Products has 20,000 shares of 8 percent, $30 par value cumulative preferred stock issued and outstanding. Hong has 150,000 shares of $1 par value common stock issued and outstanding.
 a. If Hong declares an $86,000 dividend, how much of the dividend will the preferred and common stockholders receive if the preferred stock is not in arrears?
 b. If Hong declares a $120,000 dividend and the preferred stock is two years in arrears, how much of the dividends will the preferred and common stockholders receive?
 c. If Hong declares a $190,000 dividend and is two years in arrears, how much of the dividend will the preferred and common stockholders receive?

E 17.17
LO 3

When the board of directors of Hoxie Industries declared a dividend of $500,000, the corporation had 60,000 shares of 10 percent, $40 par value cumulative preferred stock outstanding. There were 400,000 shares of $1 par value common stock outstanding at the time Hoxie declared dividends. Determine the dividends the preferred and common stockholders will receive if the preferred stock is one year in arrears.

E 17.18
LO 3

The board of directors of Newark Manufacturing, Inc., declared a dividend in 1999 but did not declare dividends in 1998 or 1997. The corporation has 800,000 shares of $1 par common stock authorized and 160,000 shares issued and outstanding. It also has 300,000 shares of 5 percent, $10 par preferred stock authorized, of which 55,000 shares are issued and 50,000 shares are outstanding. The preferred stock is cumulative.
 a. Compute the amount of dividends for common and preferred stockholders if the dividend declared is $120,000.
 b. How much will preferred and common stockholders receive if the company declares dividends of $220,000?

E 17.19
LO 3

Calculate the distribution of dividends in E 17.18 assuming that the preferred stock is noncumulative.

E 17.20
LO 3

Larson Corporation has 2,000,000 shares of $0.01 par value common stock authorized, of which 750,000 shares were issued for $3,550,000 and are currently selling for $80 in the stock market. Larson Corporation is considering a two-for-one stock split. What will be the impact of the stock split on Larson Corporation?

E 17.21
LO 3

Squires Sales Inc. has 250,000 shares of $1 stated value common stock issued and outstanding. The stock had a fair market value of $32 per share on October 14 when the board of directors declared a 15 percent stock dividend to holders of record on October 20. The new shares are to be issued on November 1. Explain the impact of the stock dividend on Squires' stockholders' equity.

PROBLEMS

P 17.1
LO 2

Jerry Mai, Tom Mohr, and Gwen Ziegler all are partners in the Riga Company and have the following amounts of capital: Mai, $120,000; Mohr, $80,000; and Ziegler, $100,000. The partners currently share all profits and losses equally but are considering dividing profits and losses in a ratio of beginning capital balances.

Required

Show how income of $80,000 and a loss of $40,000 would be distributed under the current plan and the proposed plan.

P 17.2
LO 2

Assume the partners in P 17.1 want to consider the following methods of distributing Riga Company's profits and losses:
1. Salary allowances of $20,000 to Mai and $40,000 to Mohr, with any residual divided equally
2. Interest of 10 percent on beginning capital balances, with any residual divided equally
3. Interest of 10 percent on beginning capital balances; salary allowances of $20,000 to Mai, $40,000 to Mohr, with any residual divided on a 5:2:3 basis

Required

For each of the three alternatives described above, show how the following amounts would be distributed to the partners:
a. Net income of $120,000
b. Net income of $52,000
c. Net loss of $20,000

P 17.3
LO 2

Price, Young, and Odle are forming a dental partnership and are concerned about how to divide the partnership's income. Once the partnership is formed, Price will have $200,000 of capital, while Young and Odle will have capital of $100,000 and $50,000, respectively. The partnership is considering the following two methods of dividing the firm's income:

Method 1   Salaries: Price, $30,000; Young, $15,000; and Odle, $10,000
   Interest of 10 percent on beginning capital balances of all partners
   Residual divided on a 3:2:1 basis
Method 2   Salaries: Price, $15,000; and Young, $10,000
   Interest on beginning capital balances: Price, 20 percent; Young, 10 percent; and Odle, 5 percent
   Residual divided equally

Required

Show how the following income and loss amounts would be divided under each of the two methods. Discuss some reasons the partners might have used to justify each of these income distribution methods.
a. Net income of $250,000
b. Net income of $65,000
c. Net loss of $32,000

P 17.4
LO 2

Fowler and Olson are partners in a law firm and want to expand their practice by adding a partner who can specialize in real estate law. They have interviewed candidates and have narrowed the list to two attorneys. Trina Higgins has four years' experience in real estate law and would contribute $40,000 to the partnership for a one-fifth interest in the firm. Fred Neuman has 10 years' experience in real estate law and would contribute $15,000 for a one-third interest in the firm. Fowler's capital and Olson's capital in the law firm are $65,000 and $55,000, respectively, and the partners divide profits on a 3:2 basis

Required

If the partnership's assets are increased $10,000 to reflect their market value before the new partner is admitted, identify how much capital each partner will have if:
a. Trina Higgins is admitted.
b. Fred Neuman is admitted.

P 17.5
LO 2

Phil Cottel, a member of the accounting firm of Cottel, Corman, and Kline, is planning his withdrawal from the firm. Cottel has $67,000 of capital in the firm, while Corman and Kline have capital of $78,000 and $90,000, respectively. The partners share the income and losses of the firm on a 2:3:4 basis. The partners agree that before Cottel withdraws, the assets of the firm need to be reduced $9,000 to reflect their market value. The following are the alternatives proposed for Cottel's withdrawal:

1. Each partner pays Cottel $35,000 from his or her personal checking account.
2. The partnership pays Cottel $65,000 in cash and gives him equipment worth $5,000.
3. The partnership pays Cottel $60,000 in cash.

Required How much capital will Corman and Kline have after the withdrawal of Cottel under each of the proposals described above?

P 17.6
LO 3

Match the following terms with the appropriate description.

a. Authorized shares	*h.* Outstanding shares
b. Common stock	*i.* Treasury stock
c. Preemptive right	*j.* Par value
d. Preferred stock	*k.* Ex-dividend date
e. Stock split	*l.* Date of record
f. Stock dividend	
g. Dividends in arrears	

_____ 1. When a corporation buys its own shares in the secondary market
_____ 2. Minimum price a share of stock can be sold for in the initial issue market
_____ 3. Basic unit of ownership in a corporation
_____ 4. Stock that gets paid dividends first but does not have the right to vote
_____ 5. Last chance to buy stock and still get the dividend
_____ 6. Maximum number of shares a corporation can sell
_____ 7. Number of shares owned by those outside the corporation
_____ 8. When a corporation fails to pay cumulative preferred dividends
_____ 9. Changes the par value of the stock
_____ 10. Assures common stockholders they can maintain their percentage of ownership when new shares are issued

P 17.7
LO 3

For each of the following, identify the impact of the event on the assets, liabilities, and stockholders' equity by using **+** for increases, **–** for decreases, and **0** for no effect.

Event	Assets	Liabilities	Stockholders' Equity
1. Purchase of treasury stock			
2. Declared cash dividend			
3. Stock split			
4. Common stock issued			
5. Stock dividend issued			
6. Failed to pay cumulative preferred stock dividend			
7. Paid cash dividend previously declared			
8. Preferred stock issued			
9. Sale of treasury stock			
10. Board of Directors determines par value			

P 17.8
LO 3

D.C. Mercantile Corporation had the following stocks issued and outstanding when the board of directors declared a $250,000 dividend:

Preferred stock: 40,000 shares issued and 36,000 shares outstanding, 8 percent, $30 par value
Common stock: 100,000 shares issued and 90,000 outstanding, $1 par value

Required
a. Determine the amount of dividends each class of stock will receive given the following assumptions:
   1. Preferred stock is noncumulative.
   2. Preferred stock is cumulative (two years in arrears).
   3. Preferred stock is cumulative (one year in arrears).

b. What is the dividend per share for preferred and common stock in each of the scenarios described in part (**a**)?

P 17.9
LO 3

Described below is information about Husky Corporation's stockholders' equity. For each of the following events, show the impact on the items described and keep a running balance of the changes.

Event	Par Value	Common Stock Authorized	Common Stock Issued	Common Stock Outstanding	Total Par Value
	$1	2,000,000	600,000	600,000	$600,000

1. Issued 10,000 shares
   of common stock
2. Purchased 3,000 shares
   of Husky common stock
3. Declared a 10 percent
   stock dividend
4. Sold 1,000 shares of
   treasury stock
5. Declared a 2-for-1
   stock split

CASES

C 17.1
LO 1 LO 2

Stephanie Spilker has operated her own business as a sole proprietorship for several years. Although the business is quite profitable, she believes profits would increase significantly if she expanded her operations by increasing the quantity of inventory, hiring an additional employee, and doing some remodeling in the production area. This would require a minimum investment of $40,000.

The company uses FIFO inventory costing and, with the exception of the equipment that the firm owns, the assets' values on the books are reasonably close to their fair market values. The equipment has a net book value of $18,500 and a fair market value of $22,000. Spilker's capital balance is $90,000.

Preston Barton is willing to contribute $45,000 for a one-third interest in the firm providing he is allowed a 10 percent allowance on his beginning capital balance and the remaining profits are split on a 2:1, Spilker-to-Barton, basis. Since he is not very knowledgeable about Spilker's business, he wants her to continue to manage the business.

Spilker was offered a job by a larger firm at $40,000 per year, but she has a strong preference to continue her own business if she can acquire the additional capital necessary for the expansion.

Required
Prepare a brief report to Stephanie Spilker outlining your assessment of Barton's proposal. You should discuss the following:
a. What impact would the admission of Barton as a partner have on her capital account?
b. What sort of income must the firm generate to reach Spilker's goal of $40,000?
c. Do you recommend Barton's proposal? If not, what counterproposal should Spilker make?

C 17.2
LO 1 LO 2

Suzie Wong, your long-time friend, owns 1,000 shares of $1 par value common stock in Electronics, Inc. There are 1,000,000 shares of common stock authorized, and 100,000 shares are issued and outstanding.

Recently, the company was authorized to issue 20,000 shares of $50 par value preferred stock. These shares have a dividend rate of 6 percent based on par, and they are cumulative. The company expects to sell 5,000 shares of the preferred stock in the near future to finance the acquisition of more production facilities.

Suzie has studied the firm's annual reports in an effort to determine the effects the new stock issue will have on her dividends. She is confused because her $1 par value common stock has a market value of $32 per share. She has received a $4 dividend per share in recent years. The company has consistently maintained a policy of paying out 60 percent of its after-tax net income as dividends, a policy management expects to continue into the foreseeable future. Aside from being confused about the difference between par value and market value, Suzie is concerned that the company will not make enough net income to maintain her $4 per share dividend.

Required
a. Explain to Suzie in memo form the difference between par value and market value.
b. Show Suzie how to compute the minimum amount of after-tax net income the company must earn in order for her to receive a $4 per share dividend if the 5,000 shares of preferred stock are sold.
c. Would you recommend that Suzie keep the stock?

CRITICAL THINKING

CT 17.1
LO 2

Mitch Holtus and Stan Weber are partners in a company called Sports Voice. Greg Sharp has approached the partners about joining the firm, and he wants to buy a 20 percent interest in the firm. Sports Voice has $80,000 in liabilities, and its assets are undervalued by $12,000.

Holtus has a capital balance of $108,000; Weber's capital balance is $92,000. They share profits and losses equally. How much money will Sharp have to contribute to the firm to obtain a 20 percent interest if the existing partnership revalues the assets?

CT 17.2
LO 3

The Melano Corporation was authorized to issue 1,000,000 shares of $1 par common stock and 100,000 shares of $100 par, 10 percent cumulative preferred stock. To date, Melano has issued 300,000 shares of common stock and no preferred stock.

Melano is contemplating the acquisition of a new plant and wants to issue stock to raise the $1,000,000 cash to finance its acquisition. The company is trying to decide whether to issue 25,000 shares of common stock or 10,000 shares of preferred stock.

Required

Describe the advantages and disadvantages of issuing each type of stock.

ETHICAL CHALLENGES

EC 17.1
LO 1   **LO 3**

In 1999, the president of High Tech Corporation expects that the firm will generate a severe loss in 2000. He has told the members of the board of directors and other key stockholders that the corporation will buy their shares of common stock before the stock takes a dramatic drop. He says that he believes the earnings will improve in 2001 and that he will offer these treasury shares to these key stockholders before the stock price goes up again. He says he views this as compensation for their loyal service to the corporation. What is your opinion of this offer?

EC 17.2
LO 1   **LO 3**

Bob Pool is the president of Pooling Company, a sole proprietorship. Bob wants to incorporate because he recognizes the advantages of limited liability and the ability to raise additional funds by issuing stock. He proposes to issue a special class of preferred stock (to a select group of people) that has the same voting rights as common stock, is fully participating, and is convertible into long-term debt. This select group of preferred stockholders could convert their stock into a debt instrument that would have precedence over any other debt in the event of the company's liquidation. Comment on the propriety of Pool's convertible preferred stock.

COMPUTER APPLICATIONS

CA 17.1
LO 2

L&E Consulting has four partners: Leroy, Ellis, Whitney, and Jamie. During the last accounting period, its net income was $50,000. The partners are currently debating how the firm's net income should be divided among the partners. The partners are considering the following four alternatives:
1. Divide net income in the ratios of the partners' average capital balances during the year.
2. Give a $10,000 salary allowance to Leroy and a $5,000 salary allowance to Ellis and divide the remainder in the ratios of their average capital balances.
3. Give each partner an interest allowance equal to 5 percent of his or her average capital balance during the year and divide the remainder equally among the partners.
4. Divide the net income among Leroy, Ellis, Whitney, and Jamie—25 percent, 10 percent, 35 percent, and 30 percent, respectively.

The average capital balances for Leroy, Ellis, Whitney, and Jamie during the past year were $20,000, $10,000, $30,000, and $40,000, respectively.

Required

Use a computer spreadsheet package.
a. Determine each partner's share of net income using alternative 1.
b. Determine each partner's share of net income using alternative 2.
c. Determine each partner's share of net income using alternative 3.
d. Determine each partner's share of net income using alternative 4.
e. Repeat requirements (a) through (d) assuming that net income was only $10,000 for the past year.

CA 17.2
LO 3

Using the SEC's EDGAR database (<http://www.sec.gov/edgarhp.htm>), find the following for five corporations:
a. Common and preferred stock the corporation is authorized to issue
b. The par value of each class of stock
c. The number of shares authorized, issued, and outstanding of each class of stock
d. The amount of contributed capital
e. The amount of reinvested earnings
f. The number and dollar value of treasury shares held by the corporation

PART FIVE

YOU ARE HERE

Chapter 18 is the second of two chapters that explores the process of raising the capital necessary to run the business and enable it to invest in long-term projects and human capital. In Chapters 15 and 16 we planned investing activities and in Chapter 17 we looked at equity financing. This chapter completes the planning phase by investigating the ways companies can finance their long-term investments using debt. Chapter 18 examines the three basic types of notes, the cash flow implications of the various types of notes and the impact on the pro forma financial statements of issuing each of these notes.

LEARNING OBJECTIVES

LO 1 Explain the risks and rewards of long-term debt financing.

LO 2 Describe the characteristics of the three basic types of long-term debt instruments.

LO 3 Identify sources of debt financing.

LO 4 Understand how firms plan their financial structure.

Planning for Debt Financing

From its humble beginning as a local telephone company in Abilene, Kansas, Sprint has become the third largest long-distance telecommunications company in the United States. This success is due in part to a marketing department that is considered by many to be the best in the industry. While stars like Candice Bergen have promoted Sprint's most recognizable service, long-distance telecommunications, the company also offers a variety of other national and multinational communication services. Sprint offers paging services, Internet access, and Sprint PCS is a leader in static-free digital wireless communications. In 1998 it introduced a system that will give consumers Internet access, fax, television, and phone service all from one line.

www.sprint.com

In order to acquire the infrastructure necessary to support these services, Sprint uses long-term debt. According to its 1997 balance sheet, Sprint had $9,148.1 million of total debt, of which 41 percent, or $3,748.6 million, was classified as long-term debt. This means that long-term debt financed 26 percent of Sprint's $14,412.2 million of long-term assets.

As part of the capital budgeting process, once Sprint decides to make an investment in its operational infrastructure, it must plan how it will finance the acquisition. Sprint must decide whether to use stockholders' equity (discussed in Chapter 17), debt financing, or some combination of the two. When considering debt financing, Sprint must plan for the impact of debt financing on the firm and must answer questions such as: How will the cost of using borrowed funds impact the stockholders' return? What impact will debt financing have on the firm's risk and its ability to borrow funds in the future?

n Chapter 17 we learned how the ownership structures of sole proprietorships, partnerships, and corporations impact a firm's ability to raise money for the business entity. This chapter examines long-term debt financing and how firms plan for the impact of these long-term financing decisions. To begin, we will answer the fundamental question about why firms borrow. Next we will examine the characteristics of financial instruments used to borrow funds, how market interest rates affect the cash inflows generated by these notes, and the sources of debt financing. Finally, we will examine how the risks and rewards of both debt and equity financing impact a firm's plans to finance its long-term investments.

WHY BORROW?

LO 1

At first glance, the answer to the question "Why borrow?" may seem quite simple due to our personal experiences with debt. Individually, we borrow when we want to purchase a product or service but do not have enough money on hand to buy it. The desire to acquire goods or services immediately, rather than waiting until there is enough money saved to make the purchase, justifies the cost of using the borrowed funds. In business, however, the decision to borrow is centered around the risks and rewards of debt financing.

How Is Debt Financing Used?

Debt finances a firm's day-to-day operations and is used to acquire the assets that provide the infrastructure that supports operations. In general, short-term, or current, liabilities, such as accounts payable, salaries payable, and trade notes payable, finance the daily operations of the firm.

Firms use long-term liabilities to finance the acquisition of long-term assets such as buildings, equipment, land, and patents that support their operations. The cash flows these assets generate over their useful lives make it possible to meet the obligations of the long-term debt used to finance their acquisition.

Debt financing is a means for a firm to obtain funds (cash), goods, and/or services in exchange for a liability to repay the borrowed funds. Typically, liabilities require the repayment of an amount of cash that is greater than the amount of the original obligation. From the borrower's point of view, this excess amount is interest expense and represents the cost of using borrowed funds. From the lender's point of view, this additional amount is interest revenue and is the return on the investment necessary to justify lending the money to the firm.

What Is the Risk of Using Debt?

The risk of debt financing called **financial risk,** is the chance that a firm will fail because it defaults on its debt. A firm defaults if it is unable to meet (make) either the interest or principal payments that come due on the debt. When this occurs, the lender has the legal right to require the debtor to liquidate (sell) its assets to raise the cash necessary to pay the debt. Liquidating the firm's assets may drive the enterprise out of business.

For example, assume that in 1999 Jury Corporation borrowed $900,000 from the bank and signed a note agreeing to repay the money in five years and to pay 8 percent interest on the $900,000 each year over the life of the note. Suppose that the company made the yearly interest payments of $72,000 for 2000 and 2001 but, in 2002, cannot pay the annual interest. At this point, Jury Corporation has failed to comply with the terms of the note and is in default on the debt. Jury's default means the bank can, by law, demand payment of the entire note before its due date. If the company does not have sufficient cash, the bank can force the sale of enough of its assets to collect the original amount of the note plus the interest due. The sale of Jury Corporation's assets might impair its ability to continue its normal operations and could result in the demise of the firm.

Consider, however, the reward for using debt financing. When companies generate a return on their borrowed funds that is greater than the cost to them of using the borrowed funds, the owners of the companies benefit. Any excess return on the borrowed funds belongs to the owners and, therefore, increases their return on investment. When this occurs, we say that the owners used financial leverage to increase the rate of return on their investment.

Financial Leverage: The Risk and Reward of Borrowing

Financial leverage is a financing strategy designed to increase the rate of return on owners' investment by generating a greater return on borrowed funds than the cost of using the funds. To illustrate the concept, suppose that two firms, Hank Corporation and Young Company, each have $1,000,000 in assets and receive a 20 percent return on these assets before deducting interest and taxes. The only difference between these firms is how the assets of Hank Corporation and Young Company are financed. As shown below, Hank Corporation finances 100 percent of its $1,000,000 in assets by using only its owners' money. Young Company, on the other hand, borrows $700,000 at 8 percent annual interest, creating a $700,000 liability, and uses $300,000 of its owners' money.

Firm	Assets	=	Liabilities	+	Owners' Equity
Hank Corporation	$1,000,000	=	$ –0–	+	$1,000,000
Young Company	1,000,000	=	700,000	+	300,000

We show the effects of the different financing arrangements in Exhibit 18.1. Note that both companies generate $200,000 earnings before interest and taxes as a result of the 20 percent return on the $1,000,000 of assets (Rate of return on assets = Earnings before interest and taxes/Total assets). Young Company's net income, however, is further reduced by the $56,000 of interest expense ($700,000 × 0.08) charged for the use of the borrowed funds. Both firms are subject to a tax rate of 40 percent, but Young Company will pay $22,400 less in taxes than Hank Corporation because the $56,000 of interest expense is tax deductible. This means that the after-tax cost to Young Company of borrowing the funds is $33,600 ($56,000 – $22,400), or 4.8 percent [($56,000 – $22,400)/$700,000]. While Hank Corporation's net income, $120,000, is greater than Young Company's net income of $86,400, Young Company's owners have less money invested in the company than Hank Corporation's owners.

EXHIBIT 18.1 Financial Leverage

	Hank Corporation	Young Company
Income before interest and taxes ($1,000,000 × 20%)	$ 200,000	$200,000
Interest expense	–0–	56,000
Income before taxes	$ 200,000	$144,000
Tax expense (40%)	80,000	57,600
Net income	$ 120,000	$ 86,400
Rate of return on owners' equity	$\frac{\$120,000}{\$1,000,000} = 12\%$	$\frac{\$86,400}{\$300,000} = 28.8\%$

After-Tax Cost of Debt:

Interest on $700,000 debt at 8%		$ 56,000
Tax without interest	$ 80,000	
Tax with interest	57,600	22,400
Tax saving from interest		$ 33,600
After-tax cost of debt		$\frac{\$33,600}{\$700,000} = 4.8\%$
After-tax rate of interest		

The rate of return on owners' equity (ROE), discussed in greater detail in Chapter 26, measures the performance of the firm in terms of the owners' investment, as shown below:

$$ROE = \frac{\text{Net income}}{\text{Owners' equity}}$$

It might appear that because Hank Corporation's net income is higher ($120,000) than Young Company's ($86,400), Hank Corporation has the more desirable financing structure. However, as we discussed in Chapter 14, common size measures such as rate of return on owners' equity are the preferred way to compare performance. Young Company's rate of return on owners' equity, 28.8 percent ($86,400/$300,000), is greater than Hank Corporation's ROE of 12 percent ($120,000/$1,000,000).

PAUSE &
REFLECT

Suppose that you had a choice of investing $1,000 in Hank Corporation or $1,000 in Young Company. Which would you choose? Why? *(answer on page 640)*

Young Company's return on its assets, $200,000 ($1,000,000 × 0.20), is the same dollar amount as Hank Corporation's return. However, by financing $700,000 of the assets with borrowed funds, Young Company has leveraged its ROE from 12 percent to 28.8 percent.

Exhibit 18.2 shows that the 28.8 percent return is possible because Young Company is using the lender's funds to generate enough money ($140,000) to meet the interest obligation on the debt ($56,000) and to increase the owner's return on investment with the $50,400 remaining after subtracting taxes of $33,600. The additional $50,400 Young Company is making on the borrowed funds is added to the return of $36,000 generated by the owners' investment to arrive at Young Company's net income of $86,400.

EXHIBIT 18.2	Young Company's Return		
	Owners' Funds	**Borrowed Funds**	**Total**
Assets	$300,000	$700,000	$1,000,000
Rate of return (20%)	0.20	0.20	0.20
Return on assets	$ 60,000	$140,000	$ 200,000
Interest on debt	–0–	56,000	56,000
Income before taxes	$ 60,000	$ 84,000	$ 144,000
Taxes (40% of income)	24,000	33,600	57,600
Income after taxes	$ 36,000	$ 50,400	$ 86,400

$$\text{Rate of return on owners' equity} = \frac{\$36,000 + \$50,400}{\$300,000} = 28.8\%$$

Debt to Equity: A Risk Measure of Financial Leverage

Debt financing can reward business owners with high rates of return, but it also increases their exposure to the risks of default. The **debt-to-equity ratio** measures the relationship between the amount of debt and the amount of owners' equity used to finance the firm. A debt-to-equity ratio of 1 means that equal amounts of debt and owners' equity finance the firm. The larger the debt-to-equity ratio, the greater the amount of debt used to finance the firm and, therefore, the greater the financial risk. As a firm's debt increases, it needs more earnings to cover the interest incurred on its debt and, as a result, the financial risk of the firm increases. The formula for the debt-to-equity ratio presented below reflects Sprint's financial structure as of December 31, 1997:

$$\text{Debt-to-equity ratio} = \frac{\text{Total debt}}{\text{Stockholders' equity}} = \frac{\$9,159,600,000}{\$9,025,200,000} = 1.015$$

When companies plan to use debt financing, the debt-to-equity ratio is an excellent tool to assess the impact of the new debt on the firm's risk. In general, a ratio of 1 or less is considered a safe level of financial risk. However, a company can get a better assessment of its current and potential financial risk in two ways. The first is to compare the size of its planned debt-to-equity ratio with those of peer companies. (We discuss the sources of industry information in Chapter 26.) For example, if the average debt-to-equity ratio for telecommunications companies is 2, Sprint would appear to have low financial

risk. The second way to assess a firm's financial risk is to measure the firm's
the obligations of its debt. One measure of this ability is the times interest ea.

PAUSE &

REFLECT

In Chapter 17 we explained the features of redeemable preferred stock. Why did Sprint
not include its redeemable preferred stock as part of its stockholders' equity?
(answer on page 640)

Times Interest Earned: Can a Company Meet Its Obligations to Creditors?

One of the concerns a firm has when considering debt financing is whether the firm can
meet its interest obligations. The **times interest earned ratio** measures a firm's ability to
service its debt by comparing earnings before deducting interest and taxes to the amount
of interest expense for the period. Planners use the times interest earned ratio to determine whether the interest on new debt will put the firm at risk of not meeting its interest
obligations. The formula for the times interest earned ratio is presented using information
from Sprint's 1997 income statement and shows Sprint could pay its interest cost 13.1
times with its operating income. A 13.1 times interest earned ratio is an excellent ratio
because it reveals that Sprint's income would have to drop dramatically before Sprint
would be at risk of defaulting on its interest obligations. While Sprint could easily service
the interest on its debt in 1997, planners must determine whether this strong position will
continue in the future.

$$\text{Times interest earned ratio} = \frac{\text{Earnings before interest and taxes}}{\text{Interest expense}} = \frac{\$2,451,400,000}{\$187,200,000} = 13.1$$

The financial risk of a firm depends not only on the size of its debt-to-equity ratio, but
also on the volatility of its sales—that is, the tendency of its sales to increase and decrease dramatically from one time period to the next. In general, when a firm has a high
debt-to-equity ratio and a low times interest earned ratio and its sales are volatile, it has
greater financial risk. The financial risk increases because a decline in sales would substantially reduce the firm's ROE or might cause the firm to default on its debt obligations.
However, some firms, such as electric utility companies, have, and can operate with, high
debt-to-equity ratios because their sales are stable and there is little risk that they will
default.

LONG-TERM DEBT INSTRUMENTS

LO 2

When long-term debt is issued, both the borrower and lender must be careful to formalize
the terms of the debt. In corporations, the board of directors must approve the issuance of
long-term debt. Lenders may place certain restrictions on the borrowing company called
covenants, which they document in the debt agreement to protect the lenders' interest.
For example, a lender may limit the amount of additional long-term debt the company
can issue in order to provide the lender some assurance that the company's debt will not
become too large and impair the firm's ability to service its present debt commitments. *In
addition, understanding the cash flow obligations of these debt instruments allows planners to match the debt instrument with the cash flows expected from the assets being
acquired.*

As you know, notes are the written promises of firms that borrow funds. Each note describes the cash flows the borrower, or maker, of the note is willing to pay in return for
the use of the lender's, or holder of the note's, funds.

The face value of the note indicates the amount that the note's maker will ultimately
pay the note's holder. The face rate on the note determines the amount of cash interest the
maker will periodically pay the holder of the note. The amount of cash raised from the issuance of the debt is called the **proceeds** of the note. The *actual* interest rate charged for
the use of the proceeds of the note is called the **market, or effective, interest rate.** *The
market (effective) rate may or may not be the face rate of interest printed on the note. The*

market (effective) interest rate is negotiated by the borrower and the lender. The borrower wants the use of the funds at the lowest possible cost, while the lender wants the highest possible return for the risk assumed.

For example, suppose Sprint wants to borrow $500,000 for a long-term project and is willing to pay 7 percent interest. Citibank is interested in making the loan but wants an 8 percent rate on the loan. If Citibank agrees to Sprint's terms, the market rate of interest would be 7 percent, but if Sprint agrees to Citibank's terms, the market rate of interest would be 8 percent. If both parties compromise and agree to 7.5 percent, then 7.5 percent would be the market rate of interest.

When companies plan to use long-term debt financing, they typically select one of three basic types of notes. These notes are classified based on their promised cash flows and are described below.

Periodic Payment Notes

A **periodic payment note** is a debt instrument that contains a promise to make a series of equal payments consisting of both interest and principal at equal time intervals over a specified time period. For example, assume Sprint plans to borrow $500,000 on July 1, 1999, by signing a note with a $500,000 face value and agrees to repay the money quarterly over the next two years at an annual face rate of 8 percent. The amount of the quarterly payments, $68,254.73, is determined by using the present value of an annuity formula as shown below:

Annuity	×	$P_{8,2\%}$	=	Present value
Annuity	×	7.3255	=	$500,000
Annuity			=	$68,254.73

Calculator:
PV = 500,000
c = 4
n = 8
r = 8
FV = 0
PMT = 68,254.90

Periodic payment notes are typically called *installment notes.* This means that Sprint would make 8 payments of $68,254.73 each for a total of $546,037.84 over the life of the note. The difference between the total amount repaid and the face amount of the note is the *interest expense for the two-year period.* Because each payment that is made includes the interest for the last installment period; the remainder is repayment of the principal. A monthly car payment is an example of an installment note. Exhibit 18.3 illustrates Sprint's periodic note schedule for the life of the $500,000 loan period. The initial carrying value represents the $500,000 cash inflow to Sprint and the payment column describes the quarterly outflows of cash Sprint will make to pay the interest on the loan and repay the note.

The first payment of $68,254.73 would pay the $10,000 interest expense that has accumulated on the $500,000 debt for the first installment period of three months ($500,000 × 0.08 × 1/4). The remainder of the payment would reduce the amount of the principal by $58,254.73. The second payment repeats the process, except the amount of interest ex-

Automobiles that are purchased or leased are financed with installment notes.

Excel and other spreadsheet packages are very useful for setting up amortization tables for notes. All it takes is a little advanced planning and your work can be done quickly and easily using the copy function. Let's assume that your company wants to buy a $25,000 delivery truck. The dealer will finance the truck for five years at a 10 percent interest rate with monthly payments of $531.18. The question now is: How much of each monthly payment pays the interest and how much pays the principal of the note?

What columns will be needed? First, we need a monthly payment column. Then, to answer the question, we need an interest payment column and a principal payment column. Finally, we need to know the remaining balance after each payment. Set up your columns as follows:

Payment #	Payment	Interest	Principal	Loan Balance

Now go to Row 2 and enter $25,000 in the Loan Balance column. Next, fill in the Payment # column for 1 through 60 payments (5 years × 12 months per year) beginning in Row 3. Staying in Row 3, go to the Payment column and enter the monthly payment amount of $531.18. Go to Cell C3 and enter the formula to calculate monthly interest (Principal × Rate × Time): E2 × 0.1 × 1/12. Now go to Cell D3 and enter the formula to calculate the monthly principal payment (payment – interest): B3–C3. Finally, go to Cell E3 and enter the formula to determine the remaining balance (previous balance – principal payment): E2–D3. As the last step, block and copy Row 3 and paste to the remaining rows. Your spreadsheet (rows 1–4) should look similar to the following:

Payment #	Payment	Interest	Principal	Loan Balance
				25,000.00
1	531.18	208.33	322.85	24,677.15
2	531.18	205.64	325.54	24,351.61
3	531.18	202.93	328.25	24,023.36

pense, $8,834.91 ($441,745.27 × 0.08 × 1/4), is less because a portion of the principal was paid in the first quarter's payment. Notice that the quarterly payments are the same for each of the eight quarters, but, for each month, the amount of interest expense will get smaller because the principal on which the borrower pays interest is reduced with each consecutive payment.

EXHIBIT   18.3   Periodic Payment (Installment) Note Schedule

	(1)	(2) Interest Expense	(3)	(4)
Date	Payment	(0.02 × Loan Balance)	Principal	Loan Balance
7/1/99				$500,000.00
10/1/99	$68,254.73	$10,000.00[a]	$58,254.73[b]	441,745.27[c]
1/1/00	68,254.73	8,834.91[d]	59,419.82	382,325.45
4/1/00	68,254.73	7,646.51	60,608.22	321,717.23
7/1/00	68,254.73	6,434.34	61,820.39	259,896.84
10/1/00	68,254.73	5,197.94	63,056.79	196,840.05
1/1/01	68,254.73	3,936.80	64,317.93	132,522.12
4/1/01	68,254.73	2,650.44	65,604.29	66,917.83
7/1/01	68,254.73	1,336.90[e]	66,917.83	–0–

[a]$500,000 × 0.08 × 1/4 = $10,000, or $500,000 × 0.02 = $10,000.

[b]$68,254.73 – $10,000 = $58,254.73.

[c]$500,000 – $58,254.73.

[d]$441,745.27 × 0.08 × 1/4 = $8,834.91.

[e]Rounding error.

Lump-Sum Payment Notes

A **lump-sum payment note** is a debt instrument that contains a promise to pay a specific amount of money at the end of a specific period of time. Lump-sum payment notes are often called *noninterest-bearing notes* because the note specifies only a face value and a due date. Thus the note does not have a face interest rate; it specifies only the amount the borrower promises to pay back at a future date.

The amount of the face value of a noninterest-bearing note depends on the amount of money the borrower wants to use and the market interest rate the borrower and lender agree upon. Once the borrower and lender agree upon the market interest rate, the face value of the note is calculated using the present value of the amount of $1 (see Appendix Table 2 at the end of the book).

Assume Sprint wants to borrow $500,000 on July 1, 1999, for two years from the Bank of America by issuing a noninterest-bearing note. To determine the face value (the future value) of the note, assume that the bank and Sprint agree to an 8 percent market rate that is compounded semiannually. The face value of the note is calculated as follows:

$$
\begin{array}{lclcl}
\text{Future value} & \times & p_{4,4\%} & = & \text{Present value} \\
\text{Future value} & \times & 0.8548 & = & \$500,000 \\
\text{Future value} & & & = & \$584,932.15
\end{array}
$$

Consequently, Bank of America will loan Sprint, the maker of the note, $500,000 if Sprint promises to pay the Bank of America, the holder of the note, $584,932.15 in two years on July 1, 2001. If Sprint complies with the terms of the note, Bank of America will earn an 8 percent return, while Sprint will incur 8 percent interest expense.

The excess of the face value of a note over its cash proceeds is called the **discount on a note.** The discount itself represents the difference, in dollars, between the *face rate of interest,* which is zero because it is a noninterest-bearing note, and the *market rate of interest* (8%) over the life of the note. In this case, the discount is $84,932.15 ($584,932.15 − $500,000) and is the amount of *interest expense on the note for two years.* Exhibit 18.4 shows how the allocation of the discount (amortization) determines the interest expense that would be incurred in each year of the life of the note and also describes the cash flows associated with the note. This schedule is important to planners because it helps them see the difference between the interest expense that will be incurred in each time period and how this differs from the cash flows in that period. The initial **carrying value of a note** is the face value minus the discount ($584,932.15 − $84,932.15 on 7/1/99), or $500,000 in this case, and is the cash inflow Sprint will receive as a result of signing the note. The only cash outflow for Sprint will occur when it pays the face value, $584,932.15, of the note in two years.

EXHIBIT	18.4	Lump-Sum (Noninterest-Bearing) Note Schedule		
	(1)	(2)	(3)	(4)
Date	Cash Payment	Interest Expense (0.04 × Carrying Value)	Remaining Discount	Carrying Value
7/1/99			$84,932.15	$500,000.00
1/1/00	$ −0−	$20,000.00[a]	64,932.15[b]	520,000.00[c]
7/1/00	−0−	20,800.00	44,132.15	540,800.00
1/1/01	−0−	21,632.00	22,500.15	562,432.00
7/1/01	−0−	22,500.15[d]	−0−	584,932.15
7/1/01	584,932.15			−0−

[a]$500,000 × 0.08 × 1/2 = $20,000.

[b]$84,932.15 − $20,000.00 = $64,932.15.

[c]$584,932.15 − $64,932.15 = $520,000.

[d]Difference due to rounding.

Exhibit 18.4 indicates that in the first year of the note's life (7/1/99 to 7/1/00) the interest expense that Sprint will incur is $40,800.00 ($20,000.00 + $20,800.00). Notice that although interest expense will be incurred, Sprint will not pay cash to the lender, Bank of America. Sprint pays the interest expense on the note, represented by the discount of $84,932.15, when it pays the $584,932.15 face value on 7/1/01. Thus Sprint has had the use of $500,000 for two years and, by paying $584,932.15 at the end of two years, is returning the $500,000 borrowed from the Bank of America plus $84,932.15 of interest expense. This type of note can be confusing because the borrower does not receive the $584,932.15 face value when the note is issued. *Care must be taken not to confuse the face value with the proceeds of the note.* Remember, the note merely specifies the cash flows promised by the note's maker. The cash proceeds of the note depend on the market rate of interest used to find the present value of the promised cash flows. In this case, the $500,000 of proceeds are the present value of the $584,932.15 promised in two years by the maker of the note assuming an 8 percent annual market rate that is compounded semiannually.

Periodic Payment and Lump-Sum Notes

A **periodic payment and lump-sum note** is a debt instrument that combines periodic cash payments and a final lump-sum cash payment. It has a face rate of interest and a face value that indicates that the maker promises to make periodic cash interest payments *and* a lump-sum payment on the date the note matures. Because an interest rate (face rate) is printed on the note, this type of note is often referred to as an *interest-bearing note*. To determine the periodic cash payments, multiply *the face rate of interest by the face value of the note*. For example, suppose that on July 1, 1999, Sprint issues a $500,000, two-year note that has a face interest rate of 8 percent that is paid semiannually. The note is the maker's (Sprint) written promise to pay $20,000 ($500,000 × 0.08 × 1/2) every six months for two years, in addition to $500,000 at the end of the two years.

The face rate and face values are used to determine the cash flows promised by Sprint. But the amount of proceeds that Sprint receives for the note depends on the market rate of interest at the time the note is issued. When notes are prepared, the market rate and the face rate may be the same; but before the note is issued to the lender, the market rate may change. If the market rate increases, the lender would want the higher market rate; if the market rate decreases, the borrower would want the lower market rate. We will examine how the proceeds of a note are affected when (1) the market rate is greater than the face rate, (2) the market rate is less than the face rate, and (3) the market rate is equal to the face rate.

Market Rate Greater than Face Rate When the market rate of interest is *greater* than the face rate of interest, the proceeds of the note will be *less* than the face value of the note. Under these circumstances, the note will be issued at a *discount* to make the note yield the market interest rate. To illustrate, assume that Sprint takes the $500,000 note described above to the Bank of America. The banker thinks that, due to Sprint's level of risk, it needs a 10 percent interest rate before it can lend money. To make the 8 percent face rate note yield the desired 10 percent market rate, the bank determines the proceeds of the note by finding the present value of the cash flows specified on the note using the 10 percent market rate.

Because the note promises to make two types of future cash payments, two present value calculations are necessary to determine the proceeds of the note when it is issued. The first present value calculation is the present value of a $20,000 ($500,000 × 0.08 × 1/2) annuity and the second is the present value of a $500,000 lump-sum payment. The $482,270 sum of these two present values, calculated in Exhibit 18.5, is the amount Bank of America will loan Sprint and is $17,730 less than the $500,000 face value of the note. The $17,730 discount represents the additional interest expense that Sprint will incur

Calculator:
PMT = 20,000
FV = 500,000
r = 10
c = 2
n = 4
PV = 482,270.25

EXHIBIT	18.5	Market Rate Greater Than Face Rate

Cash Flows Promised by the Note
Cash flow 1   Four, $20,000 semiannual payments
Cash flow 2 $500,000 lump-sum payment, two years from today

Present Value of Promised Cash Flows

Cash flow 1	Present value of annuity	=	Annuity	×	$P_{4,5\%}$
		=	$20,000	×	3.5460
		=	$70,920		
Cash flow 2	Present value of lump sum	=	Future value	×	$p_{4,5\%}$*
		=	$500,000	×	0.8227
		=	$411,350		
Present value of cash flow 1		$ 70,920			
Present value of cash flow 2		411,350			
Present value of note (proceeds)		$482,270			

*Because the annuity is semiannual and the interest is compounded semiannually, the present value of the amount of $1 is also compounded semiannually.

over the life of the note because the market rate of interest, 10 percent, is greater than the face rate of interest, 8 percent. Sprint receives $482,270 instead of $500,000, but will have to pay $500,000 at the end of the note's life.

Since the amount of the discount is actually additional interest expense that Sprint will incur over the life of the note, the 8 percent note has effectively become a 10 percent note. Exhibit 18.6 illustrates how to determine the amount of interest expense for each period and also describes the cash flows associated with the note. In this case the initial carrying value of $482,270 is the cash inflow Sprint would receive from the note, while the cash outflows would consist of $20,000 payments every six months for two years and $500,000 at the end of the two-year note.

Notice that the cash interest (column 1) is not the same as the amount of interest expense (column 2). Remember that the cash interest is based on the face interest rate applied to the face value, while the interest expense is the market rate of interest of the note times the carrying value of the note (column 5). Sprint can use $482,270 of the Bank of America's money for six months at a cost of $24,113.50, calculated as follows:

$$\text{Effective interest} \quad = \quad \text{Principal} \quad \times \quad \text{Market Rate} \times \quad \text{Time}$$
$$\$24,113.50 \quad = \quad \$482,270 \quad \times \quad 0.10 \quad \times \quad 1/2$$

The amount that the interest expense exceeds the cash interest for the time period ($4,113.50) is the **amortized discount** (column 3). Why is there a difference? Remember that Sprint gets to use the proceeds of $482,270 but must repay the $500,000 face value at the maturity date. The discount represents $17,730 of additional interest Sprint will pay because the market interest rate is 10 percent and not the 8 percent face rate. Note that the sum of the cash interest paid, $80,000, over the life of the note (column 1) and the $17,730 discount is equal to the total amount of interest expense incurred over the life of the note, $97,730 (sum of the interest expense in column 2). The amortization process merely explains why the cash flows are not the same as the interest expense incurred in each period. As the discount is reduced each interest period, the carrying value of the note increases until the discount becomes zero and the note reaches its $500,000 face value and final cash payment. Exhibit 18.6 is a planning tool because it forecasts the note's impact on Sprint's cash flow statement, income statement, and balance sheet over the life of the note.

EXHIBIT 18.6 Discount Amortization Schedule

Date	(1) Cash Interest (0.04 × Face Value)	(2) Interest Expense (0.05 × Carrying Value)	(3) Amortized Discount	(4) Remaining Discount	(5) Carrying Value
7/1/99				$17,730.00	$482,270.00
1/1/00	$ 20,000[a]	$24,113.50[b]	$4,113.50[c]	13,616.50[d]	486,383.50[e]
7/1/00	20,000	24,319.18	4,319.18	9,297.32	490,702.68
1/1/01	20,000	24,535.13	4,535.13	4,762.19	495,237.81
7/1/01	20,000	24,762.19[f]	4,762.19	–0–	500,000.00
7/1/01	$500,000 payment of face value				–0–
Cash interest for four years			$80,000		
Plus discount on note			17,730		
Total effective interest expense (sum of column 2)			$97,730		

[a]$500,000 face value × 0.08 face rate × 1/2 = $20,000.

[b]$482,270 carrying value × 0.10 market rate × 1/2 = $24,113.50

[c]$24,113.50 – $20,000 = $4,113.50.

[d]$17,730.00 – $4,113.50 = $13,616.50.

[e]$500,000 – $13,616.50 = $486,383.50, or $482,270 + $4,113.50 = $486,383.50.

[f]Rounding error.

Market Rate Less than Face Rate   When the market rate of interest is *less* than the face rate of interest on the note, the proceeds of the note will be *greater* than the face value of the note. This means that the note is issued at a premium in order to make the note yield the market rate of interest, which is less than the face rate of interest. A **premium on a**

note, then, is the amount that the cash proceeds of a note exceed its face value because the market rate of interest is less than the face rate of interest.

To illustrate, assume that Sprint takes the same $500,000 note to the Bank of America when the market rate of interest is 6 percent. In this case, Sprint will not pay 8 percent when the 6 percent rate is available. To determine the proceeds of this note, the lender finds *the present value of the two promised cash flows using the 6 percent market rate,* illustrated in Exhibit 18.7. In this case, the Bank of America will loan Sprint $518,592, which is $18,592 greater than the face value of the note.

EXHIBIT 18.7 Market Rate Less than Face Rate

Cash Flows Promised by the Note

Cash flow 1	Four, $20,000 semiannual payments
Cash flow 2	$500,000 lump-sum payment, two years from today

Present Value of Promised Cash Flows

Cash flow 1	Present value of annuity	= Annuity	×	$P_{4,3\%}$
		= $20,000	×	3.7171
		= $74,342		
Cash flow 2	Present value of lump sum	= Future value	×	$p_{4,3\%}$*
		= $500,000	×	0.8885
		= $444,250		

Present value of cash flow 1	$ 74,342
Present value of cash flow 2	444,250
Present value of note (proceeds)	$518,592

*Because the annuity is semiannual and the interest is compounded semiannually, the present value of the amount of $1 is also compounded semiannually.

The premium of $18,592 will reduce the amount of Sprint's face interest rate to the lower market interest rate over the life of the note. Sprint will get the use of $518,592 instead of $500,000, but will only pay the $500,000 face value at maturity. Because the premium of $18,592 is not repaid, it, in effect, reduces the interest cost from the 8 percent face rate to the 6 percent market rate over the life of the note. Exhibit 18.8 illustrates how to determine the amount of interest expense for each period and describes the cash flows to and from Sprint. In this case, Sprint would have a $518,592 cash inflow from the loan but its cash outflows would be the same as when the note was issued at a discount.

EXHIBIT 18.8 Premium Amortization Schedule

Date	(1) Cash Interest (0.04 × Face Value)	(2) Interest Expense (0.03 × Carrying Value)	(3) Amortized Premium	(4) Remaining Premium	(5) Carrying Value
7/1/99				$18,592.00	$518,592.00
1/1/00	$20,000[a]	$15,557.76[b]	$4,442.24[c]	14,149.76[d]	514,149.76[e]
7/1/00	20,000	15,424.49	4,575.51	9,574.25	509,574.25
1/1/01	20,000	15,287.23	4,712.77	4,861.48	504,861.48
7/1/01	20,000	15,138.52[f]	4,861.48	–0–	500,000.00
7/1/01	$500,000 payment of face value				–0–
Cash interest for four years			$80,000		
Less premium on note			18,592		
Total effective interest expense (sum of column 2)			$61,408		

[a]$500,000 face value × 0.08 face rate × 1/2 = $20,000.

[b]$518,592 carrying value × 0.06 market rate × 1/2 = $15,557.76.

[c]$20,000.00 – $15,557.76 = $4,442.24.

[d]$18,592.00 – $4,442.24 = $14,149.76.

[e]$500,000 + $14,149.76 = $514,149.76, or $518,592 – $4,442.24 = $514,149.76.

[f]Rounding error.

As in the case of the discount, the amount of cash interest actually paid differs from the interest expense. The cash interest, or cash flow, promised by Sprint to the Bank of America is calculated by multiplying the face rate by the face value (column 1). The interest expense, $15,557.76 (column 2), is the actual cost of using the lender's money for the first six months of the note's life, as shown below:

$$\begin{array}{llllllll} \text{Interest} & = & \text{Principal} & \times & \text{Market Rate} & \times & \text{Time} \\ \$15,557.76 & = & \$518,592 & \times & 0.06 & \times & 1/2 \end{array}$$

While the cost of using the Bank of America's money for the first six months will be $15,557.76, the cash interest paid is $20,000. The difference between the cash interest and the lower interest expense for the time period is the **amortized premium, $4,442.24.** As in the case of the discount, the amount of premium amortized reflects the difference between the face rate of interest (8%) and the market rate of interest (6%). The total interest expense incurred on the funds borrowed from Bank of America is the $80,000 of cash interest Sprint will pay over the life of the note less the $18,592 premium, or $61,408 (sum of column 2). The premium is allocated over the life of the note; as it decreases each interest period, the carrying value of the note decreases. At maturity the premium will become zero and the carrying value will be the face value and final cash flow ($500,000) promised by the note.

Market Rate Equal to Face Rate   When the market rate of interest is the *same* as the face rate, the proceeds of the note will be the *same* as the face value of the note. To illustrate, assume that Sprint took the same $500,000 note to the Bank of America when the market rate is 8 percent. Exhibit 18.9 shows that the Bank of America will loan Sprint $500,000, the same amount as the face value of the note.

Calculator:
PMT = 20,000
FV = 500,000
r = 8
c = 2
n = 4
PV = 500,000

EXHIBIT   18.9   Market Rate Same as Face Rate

Cash Flows Promised by the Note

Cash flow 1	Four, $20,000 semiannual payments
Cash flow 2	$500,000 lump-sum payment, two years from today

Present Value of Promised Cash Flows

Cash flow 1	Present value of annuity	= Annuity	×	$P_{4,4\%}$
		= $20,000	×	3.6299
		= $72,598		
Cash flow 2	Present value of lump sum	= Future value	×	$p_{4,4\%}$*
		= $500,000	×	0.8548
		= $427,400		

Present value of cash flow 1	$ 72,600**
Present value of cash flow 2	427,400
Present value of note (proceeds)	$500,000

*Because the annuity is semiannual and the interest is compounded semiannually, the present value of the amount of $1 is also compounded semiannually.

**Rounded to account for rounding error in tables.

No premium or discount exists because the face rate and the market rate of interest are the same and, therefore, the *present value of the note's promised cash flows is equal to the note's face value.* Exhibit 18.10 shows that the amount of cash interest would be the same as the interest expense. Note that the carrying value of $500,000 would be the cash inflow Sprint receives for signing the note, while the cash outflows would be the same as when the note was issued at a premium or discount.

To this point we have discussed the characteristics of debt financing. Now we will examine the sources of debt financing available to companies.

EXHIBIT 18.10 Payment Schedule

Date	(1) Cash Interest (0.04 × Face Value)	(2) Interest Expense (0.04 × Carrying Value)	(3) No Amortization	(4) No Discount or Premium	(5) Carrying Value
7/1/99					$500,000
1/1/00	$20,000*	$20,000**			500,000
7/1/00	20,000	20,000			500,000
1/1/01	20,000	20,000			500,000
7/1/01	20,000	20,000			500,000
7/1/01	$500,000 payment of face value				–0–

Cash interest for four years, $80,000 = Total effective interest expense (sum of column 2), $80,000

*$500,000 face value × 0.08 face rate × 1/2 = $20,000.

**$500,000 carrying value × 0.08 market rate × 1/2 = $20,000.

SOURCES OF LONG-TERM DEBT FINANCING

LO 3

Long-term debt financing is available from a variety of sources that are classified as nonpublic and public. The nonpublic sources include individuals and institutions, such as banks and other financial institutions, other companies, and insurance companies. The public source of debt financing is the bond market.

Nonpublic Sources of Debt Financing

Nonpublic debt financing occurs when a firm enters into an agreement with a person or institution to borrow funds. For most businesses, nonpublic debt financing is the most common source of long-term debt. While firms sometimes approach individuals to borrow funds, banks and other financial institutions are the most common nonpublic sources of debt financing because they are in business specifically to lend money and want to make loans to qualified companies and individuals. Insurance companies are also a source of long-term debt financing because they need to generate a return on the premiums they receive from their policyholders.

Firms may use any of the three types of notes described earlier—periodic payment notes, lump-sum payment notes, and periodic payment and lump-sum notes—to acquire financing. The form of the note the firm plans to use depends on the cash inflows generated after the borrowed funds are invested and the impact of the note on the pro forma financial statements. We will describe how the planning process takes these factors into consideration later in the chapter. In addition to describing the face value of the note, the face rate of interest, if any, and its repayment period, the note may include covenants that protect the claims of the holder of the note.

Banks are a source of nonpublic debt financing.

Collateral   A typical means of protecting creditors' claims is to require the borrower to use some asset(s) as **collateral** for the note. Collateral is an asset or group of assets specifically named in a debt agreement to which the creditor has claim if the borrower fails to comply with the terms of the note. For example, for most car loans, the car that is acquired is collateral for the note. If the car buyer fails to make the installment payments, the lending institution can repossess the car and sell it to satisfy the debt. In most cases, the firm borrowing the money cannot dispose of the collateral unless it reaches an agreement with the lending institution about paying off the loan or providing another asset as collateral. A **mortgage** is a long-term note that is secured with real estate, such as land or buildings, as collateral.

Leases   In recent years, extensive use has been made of leasing as another way for a firm to secure the use of an asset. A **lease** is an agreement to convey the use of a tangible asset from one party to another in return for rental payments. The agreement usually covers a specified period of time. It is, in effect, a contract whereby the owner (the lessor) agrees to rent an asset to another party (the lessee) in return for rental payments. There are a wide variety of lease agreements but, in general, they fall into two classifications: operating leases and capital leases.

Typically, an **operating lease** is a rental agreement for a period of time that is substantially shorter than the economic life of the leased asset. Exhibit 18.11 shows the note to Sprint's 1997 financial statement that describes the impact of its operating leases. Notice that the note describes both the amount of gross rental expense ($410 million) in 1997 and the minimum operating lease payments the company is required to make each year until 2002.

EXHIBIT   18.11

Operating Lease Disclosure for Sprint

9. Commitments and Contingencies

Operating Leases

Minimum rental commitments at year-end 1997 for all noncancelable operating leases, consisting mainly of leases for data processing equipment and real estate, are as follows:

(in millions)	
1998	$324.1
1999	276.4
2000	174.2
2001	119.1
2002	97.1
Thereafter	243.7

Gross rental expense totaled $410 million in 1997, $401 million in 1996 and $402 million in 1995. Rental commitments for subleases, contingent rentals and executory costs were not significant.

When a lessee (user) company acquires such a substantial interest in the leased property that the lessee company, for all practical purposes, owns the asset, there is recognition of the acquisition of an asset and a related liability by the lessee. This type of lease is called a **capital lease.** A lease classified as a capital lease recognizes the substance of the economic event over the legal form of the transaction. The economic substance of the lease transaction, the lessee's control of the asset for its useful life, takes precedence over legal requirements (the formal transfer of the title from the seller to the buyer) used to determine when the transfer of ownership occurs.

When a firm enters into a capital lease, it recognizes the leased property as an asset and reflects the related liability incurred. The value of the asset is the present value of the lease payments, using the firm's market rate of interest. While Sprint reported only operating leases, Wal-Mart's January 31, 1998, balance sheet reports capital lease obligations of $2,585,000,000 (Exhibit 18.12).

EXHIBIT 18.12   **Capital Lease Disclosure for Wal-Mart**

8 Long-term Lease Obligations

The Company and certain of its subsidiaries have long-term leases for stores and equipment. Rentals (including, for certain leases, amounts applicable to taxes, insurance, maintenance, other operating expenses and contingent rentals) under all operating leases were $596 million, $561 million and $531 million in 1998, 1997 and 1996, respectively. Aggregate minimum annual rentals at January 31, 1998, under non-cancelable leases are as follows (in millions):

Fiscal year	Operating leases	Capital leases
1999	$ 404	$ 347
2000	384	345
2001	347	344
2002	332	343
2002	315	340
Thereafter	2,642	3,404
Total minimum rentals	$ 4,424	5,123
Less estimated executory costs		73
Net minimum lease payments		5,050
Less imputed interest at rates ranging from 6.1% to 14.0%		2,465
Present value of minimum lease payments		$ 2,585

Certain of the leases provide for contingent additional rentals based on percentage of sales. Such additional rentals amounted to $46 million, $51 million and $41 million in 1998, 1997 and 1996, respectively. Substantially all of the store leases have renewal options for additional terms from five to 25 years at comparable rentals.

The Company has entered into lease commitments for land and buildings for 38 future locations. These lease commitments with real estate developers provide for minimum rentals for 20 to 25 years, excluding renewal options, which if consummated based on current cost estimates, will approximate $38 million annually over the lease terms.

Calculator:
PMT = 55,481.60
c = 1
n = 5
r = 12
FV = 0
PV = 199,998.75

To illustrate a capital lease, let's assume that Sprint signs a five-year lease on equipment that has an estimated useful life of five years. Sprint agrees to pay $50,000 today and $55,481.60 per year, for five years, starting one year from today. Sprint has entered into a capital lease, because, in economic substance, it has purchased the equipment, since the lease term is the same as the life of the equipment. On the date it signs the lease, Sprint will have a long-term liability of $200,000, which is the present value of the $55,481.60, five-payment annuity at Sprint's market rate of interest, 12 percent. Sprint also would recognize a leased asset in the amount of $250,000, which is the present value of the lease payments, $200,000, plus the initial $50,000 payment. This liability is a periodic payment note, described earlier in the chapter:

$$\text{Present value of note} = \text{Annuity} \times P_{5,12\%}$$
$$= \$55{,}481.60 \times 3.6048$$
$$= \$200{,}000$$

Present value of lease payments	$200,000
Down payment	50,000
Cost of the leased asset	$250,000

Public Sources of Debt Financing: Bonds

Bonds are long-term debt instruments issued by corporations to raise money from the public. Bonds usually take the form of periodic payment and lump-sum notes. However, rather than being in the form of one note, a bond issue typically consists of a group of $1,000 face value notes (bonds) with a specified face interest rate, often paid semiannually, that mature in 10 or more years.

For example, a $5,000,000, 10-year bond issue with a 10 percent face interest rate that is paid semiannually consists of 5,000 bonds, each with a $1,000 face value. Each $1,000 bond has a 10-year life and a 10 percent face interest rate paid semiannually. These terms would be printed on a note called a **bond certificate.**

As with any note, the 5,000 bond certificates are the corporation's promise to pay the bondholders the cash flows indicated on the bond certificate. In this example, a person holding one bond would receive $50 ($1,000 × 0.1 × 1/2) every six months for 10 years and $1,000 at the end of 10 years. In total, the corporation promises to pay $250,000 ($5,000,000 × 0.1 × 1/2) cash interest every six months and $5,000,000 at the end of 10 years. The amount of cash the corporation can borrow by issuing bonds, like any other note payable, is based on the present value of the promised cash flows using the market interest rate.

Corporations issue bonds because individual financial institutions are unwilling or unable to accept the risk of making very large long-term loans to one corporation. However, because individual bonds are relatively small investing units, many investors can lend funds to the corporation. This enhances the company's ability to borrow large amounts of funds. Individual investors, banks, insurance companies, and other corporations can lend the corporation money by acquiring as many bonds as they deem prudent.

The bond contract is called a **bond indenture.** This contract specifies the amount of the bond issue, the life of the bond, the face value of each bond, and the face interest rate of the bond issue. The bond indenture also may have covenants that place restrictions on the issuing corporation. Many covenants limit the amount of long-term debt a corporation can have.

Normally, the corporation's board of directors must give formal approval before the company can issue bonds. In cases where the bonds are publicly traded on organized bond exchanges, the Securities and Exchange Commission also must approve the bond issue. Once the corporation obtains all of the necessary approvals, it can offer the bonds to the public.

The sale of a bond issue is usually handled by an underwriter at an investment banking firm. The investment banking firm can buy the entire bond issue from the corporation and then resell the bonds to the public. However, if the investment banking firm does not want to underwrite (buy) the entire bond issue, it can sell the bonds and take a percentage of the proceeds of the bond issue as a commission before remitting the cash to the corporation. In some cases, the company issuing bonds sells them directly to specific financial institutions or individuals without using an underwriter. This is called a *private (direct) placement of a bond issue.*

Regardless of whether a bond issue is underwritten, sold on a commission basis, or privately placed, the corporation obtains the use of money from a bond sale just as if it borrowed money from a bank in a traditional lending process. However, because the lender is the public, and because investment bankers must convince a variety of potential lenders to loan the corporation money, the process of borrowing the money by issuing bonds takes on the form of a sale. The buyers are acquiring, and the corporation is selling, the right to a set of future cash flows promised in each bond.

Selling the bond issue and transferring the proceeds of the sale to the corporation take place in an initial issue market. After the bonds are sold in the initial issue market, they are bought either from another individual, through bond brokers, or in a bond market like the New York Bond Exchange, called the *secondary bond market.* This secondary market

Of Interest   Bond Ratings

Moody's Investors Service, Inc., provides bond ratings for investors that describe the relative investment qualities (risk) of both initial issue bonds and bonds in the secondary market.

Moody's rates the investment quality of bonds using the nine symbols shown below. Each symbol represents a group in which the quality characteristics are broadly the same. The symbols indicated the rank of the bonds from the highest investment quality, Aaa, to the lowest investment quality, C.

Aaa   Aa   A   Baa   Ba   B   Caa   Ca   C

Aaa   Bonds that are rated Aaa are judged to be of the best quality. They carry the smallest degree of investment risk and are generally referred to as "gilt edged." Interest payments are protected by a large or by an expectionally stable margin and the principal is secure.

Baa   Bonds that are rated Baa are considered as medium-grade obligations (i.e., they are neither highly protected nor poorly secured). Interest payments and principal security appear adequate for the present but certain protective elements may be lacking or may be characteristically unreliable over any great length of time.

Caa   Bonds that are rated Caa are of poor standing. Such issues may be in default or there may be present elements of danger with respect to principal or interest.

C   Bonds that are rated C are the lowest rated class of bonds, and issues so rated can be regarded as having extremely poor prospects of ever attaining any real investment standing.

Source: *Moody's Bond Record*, Moody's Investors Service.

Sprint Debt Ratings

December 31.	1997			
	Duff & Phelps	Fitch	Moody's	Standard & Poor's
Senior Debt				
Corporate	A	A-	A3	A-
Local Telephone Companies				
Carolina Telephone & Telegraph	AA+	–	Aa3	A+
Sprint-Florida Inc.	AA-	–	A1	A
United Telephone of Ohio	AA	–	A1	A+
United Telephone of Pennsylvania	–	–	A2	–
Central Telephone Company	–	–	A1	A+
Commercial Paper				
Corporate	D1	F2	P2	A2

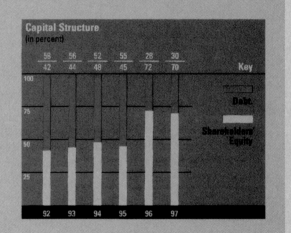

allows bondholders to sell their bonds and receive cash from their investment without waiting for the bonds to mature.

Bond prices in the secondary market are quoted as a percentage of the face value of the bond. For example, a $1,000 bond with a price of 98½ is selling for 98.5 percent of its $1,000 face value, or $985. A bond quoted at a price of 101¾ is selling for $1,017.50, or 101.75 percent of its $1,000 face value.

PAUSE & REFLECT

Many companies issue zero coupon (noninterest-bearing) bonds. What are the cash flows promised by the bond issue? Why would a company plan to issue such bonds? Why would investors buy these bonds? *(answer on page 640)*

Bond Provisions Although the contractual arrangements of bonds vary greatly, we describe bond issues in terms of how their provisions relate to ownership, repayment, and security. Each bond may have several of the following provisions. These provisions are important when planning to issue bonds because the provisions of the bond impact investors' assessment of the risk of the bond issue, which in turn impacts the market interest rate of the bond issue.

Ownership Provisions **Registered bonds** are numbered and made payable in the name of the bondholder. The issuing company or its appointed agent maintains a list, called the *bond register,* of the individuals or institutions who own the bonds. If a bond changes ownership, it is endorsed on the back and sent to the registrar for recording and reissue, and the issuing company is notified of that change. Interest on these bonds is generally paid by a check made payable to the registered owner on the interest date.

Bearer bonds are made payable to the bearer or person who has physical possession of the bond. Interest is paid by means of coupons attached to the bond. Each coupon is dated and has a dollar value shown on it. The number of coupons and the amount on each coupon depends on the face rate of interest on the bond and the frequency of interest payments during the year. For example, a 10-year, $1,000 bearer bond with a 10 percent face rate that is paid semiannually has 20, $50 coupons attached to it ($1,000 × 0.1 × 1/2). On the date printed on the coupon, the coupon is detached from the bond and deposited in a bank in the same way as a check is deposited. Bearer bonds are sometimes referred to as *coupon bonds* due to their interest payment procedures.

While bearer bonds still exist in the secondary market, the 1984 Tax Reform Act prohibited any further issuance of bearer bonds due to the difficulty the IRS had in identifying the interest income received by the bearers. These bonds were also susceptible to theft because possession is proof of ownership.

Repayment Provisions **Callable bonds** give the firm issuing the bonds the right to buy them back before the maturity date at a specified price. Corporations use the call feature when they want to ensure the retirement of all or part of their bond issue. The call feature specifies the dates on which the debtor company may call, or buy back, a bond. If a bond has a call feature, the bond indenture must also state the price, usually expressed as a percentage of the face value, that the firm will pay for the bonds on those dates. For example, if a $1,000 bond has a call price of 105, the issuing company can buy the bond back at $1,050, or 105 percent of the bond's face value ($1,000 × 1.05). Calling the bonds in for redemption is *at the option of the debtor company,* and the bond owner must surrender the securities for the call price; therefore, the call price is always greater than the face value of the bond. When planning for the repayment of the bond issue, the call price gives the issuing company more flexibility by creating another option to retire the bond issue.

Convertible bonds allow bondholders to exchange their bonds for common or preferred stock. The bond indenture describes both the time at which the conversion may take place and the number of shares of stock that the bondholder can obtain. The privilege of converting the bonds into other specific securities rests with the bondholder. Once the bonds are converted to common or preferred stock, the bonds no longer exist, and the company is no longer responsible for the cash flows promised by the bond. Convertible bonds generally have lower market interest rates because conversion gives the investors a second option that could generate higher cash flows than those promised by the bond. However, when planning to use the conversion feature, the issuing company must consider whether the additional shares issued upon conversion will dilute the existing stockholders' interest in the firm.

Bondholders only convert bonds into common stock if the stock has the potential of generating a greater return than the bond. For example, suppose a $1,000, 12 percent bond has a 50-to-1 conversion ratio; that is, when the bond is converted, the bondholder will receive 50 shares of common stock for each bond converted. If the price of the common stock is $10, the bondholder is unlikely to convert the bond, because the value of the stock received upon conversion will be only $500 ($10 × 50). However, if the common stock price rises to $40 per share, the bondholder probably would convert the bond because the value of the converted stock, $2,000, is far greater than the value of the bond.

A **serial bond** is a bond issue that has specified portions of the bond issue coming due periodically over the life of the bond issue. For example, a $20 million, 20-year bond that has $5 million of its face value maturing every 5 years over its 20-year life is a serial bond. This type of bond is useful when planned cash flows from the bond-financed project are sufficient to repay the principal earlier in the life of the bond issue.

Security Provisions **Secured bonds** have some part of the issuing corporation's assets serving as security for the loan. Quite often these bonds are secured by a mortgage on the corporation's real estate (buildings or land), in which case they may properly be called **mortgage bonds.** The object of the security feature is to assure bondholders that there are specific assets to which they have first claim in the event that the bond indenture is violated.

Unsecured bonds do not have any specific assets pledged as security against their repayment. Rather, their security rests on the general creditworthiness of the issuing company. Bondholders of unsecured bonds are general creditors of the firm just like the accounts payable creditors. Unsecured bonds are usually called **debenture bonds.** Most bond issues are of this type.

PAUSE & REFLECT

If risk and interest rates are directly related, which bond would have a lower interest rate—a debenture bond or a secured bond? *(answer on page 640)*

Subordinated bonds are unsecured bonds whose rights to repayment are ranked after, or subordinated to, some other person or group of creditors. Subordinated bonds are unsecured debts that are usually the last obligation the firm pays in the event the firm is liquidated. Their claims do, however, continue to rank ahead of the owners' claims. Exhibit 18.13 shows the liability section of Sprint's December 31, 1997, balance sheet and a portion of the note to the financial statements that describes the long-term debt of the company. Note that Sprint has used debentures and mortgage bonds in addition to a variety of other long-term debt instruments to finance its long-term investments.

PAUSE & REFLECT

What type of long-term debt instruments does Sprint use? Is Sprint's long-term debt publicly or privately financed? *(answer on page 640)*

EXHIBIT   **18.13**   **Description of Sprint's Long-Term Debt**

5. Borrowings

Long-term Debt

Long-term debt at year-end was as follows:

(in millions)	Maturing	1997	1996
Corporate			
Senior notes			
8.1% to 9.8%	1998 to 2002	$ 475.3	$ 475.3
9.5%	2003 to 2007	200.0	200.0
Debentures			
9.0% to 9.3%	2019 to 2022	350.0	350.0
Notes payable and			
commercial paper	—	866.5	—
Other			
5.4% to 8.9% [1]	1998 to 2006	237.5	194.9
Long Distance			
Division			
Vendor financing			
agreements			
7.4% to 8.9%	1997 to 1999	23.8	44.8
Other			
6.2% to 8.4%	1997 to 2007	16.5	23.1
Local Division			
First mortgage bonds			
2.0% to 7.8%	1997 to 2002	452.3	487.0
4.0% to 7.8%	2003 to 2007	346.0	346.8
6.9% to 9.8%	2008 to 2012	116.7	116.7
6.9% to 8.8%	2013 to 2017	169.6	169.8
8.8% to 9.9%	2018 to 2022	244.9	245.7
7.1% to 8.4%	2023 to 2027	145.0	145.0
Debentures and notes			
5.8% to 9.6%	1998 to 2020	237.0	275.3
Other			
2.0% to 9.8%	1998 to 2006	4.6	6.2
Unamortized debt			
discount		(6.1)	(6.7)
		3,879.6	3,073.9
Less current maturities		131.0	99.1
Long-term debt		**$3,748.6**	$2,974.8

[1] *Notes may be exchanged at maturity for Southern New England Telecommunications Corporation (SNET) common shares owned by Sprint, or for cash. Based on SNET's closing market price, had the notes matured at year-end 1997, they could have been exchanged for 3.8 million SNET shares. At year-end 1997, Sprint held 4.2 million SNET shares, which have been included in "Investments in equity securities" on the Consolidated Balance Sheets.*

Long-term debt maturities, excluding reclassified short-term borrowings, during each of the next five years are as follows:

(in millions)	
1998	$ 131.0
1999	33.4
2000	693.3
2001	40.8
2002	354.5

Property, plant and equipment with a total cost of $12.9 billion is either pledged as security for first mortgage bonds and certain notes or is restricted for use as mortgaged property.

During 1996, Sprint redeemed, prior to scheduled maturities, $190 million of debt with interest rates ranging from 6.0% to 9.5%. This resulted in a $5 million after-tax extraordinary loss.

HOW TO PLAN FOR EQUITY AND DEBT FINANCING

LO 4

In Chapter 15 we described how the capital expenditure budget identifies the long-term assets needed to support the firm's future operations and when it expects to acquire the assets. Recall that long-term assets on the capital expenditure budget were selected because management expected the investment to generate a return greater than the firm's cost of capital. Once the decision to acquire the long-term asset is made, the planning process focuses on how to finance these investments. The firm can choose between equity and debt financing. Once the decision to use debt financing is made, the firm selects the debt instrument that optimizes the firm's cash flows while minimizing its negative impact on the pro forma financial statements. After selecting the instrument, the financing budget is updated. The financing budget identifies the project being financed, when the funds are needed, whether debt or equity will be used, the source of the funds, and the type of instruments used to finance the project.

Choosing Between Debt and Equity

Firms often examine the impact of financing alternatives by using pro forma financial statements. To illustrate, let's assume that Sanders Corporation's capital expenditure budget calls for the acquisition of a new machine that costs $900,000. The new machine will produce a product that will increase sales 30 percent. The new product will have the same gross profit percentage as the firm's other products but will require an additional $10,000 of advertising each year to achieve this goal. Joe Ryan, the corporation's chief financial officer, has suggested two financing alternatives. The first is to issue $900,000 of the firm's no-par common stock; the second alternative is to issue a $900,000, 10-year, 5 percent note.

Sanders Corporation's financial statements for December 31, 1999, and selected ratios are presented in Exhibit 18.14. At this time, the company has no long-term debt and a very low debt-to-equity ratio of 0.143. Because the debt consists only of accounts payable, which incurs no interest, the company's times interest earned ratio is zero.

EXHIBIT 18.14 Sanders Corporation Financial Statements

Sanders Corporation
Income Statement
For the Year Ended December 31, 1999

Sales		$1,200,000
Cost of goods sold		700,000
Gross margin		$ 500,000
Operating expenses:		
Selling and administrative	$200,000	
Depreciation expense—building	60,000	
Depreciation expense—equipment	75,000	
Total operating expenses		335,000
Operating income		$ 165,000
Income tax expense		33,000
Net income		$ 132,000

Sanders Corporation
Retained Earnings Statement
For the Year Ended December 31, 1999

Beginning retained earnings, 1/1/99	$ 508,000
Add net income	132,000
Less dividends	(40,000)
Ending retained earnings, 12/31/99	$ 600,000

Sanders Corporation
1999 Ratios

$$\text{Debt-to-equity ratio} = \frac{\$200,000}{\$1,400,000} = 0.143$$

$$\text{Times interest earned ratio} = \frac{\$165,000}{-0-} = -0-$$

$$\text{Return on assets} = \frac{\$165,000}{\$1,600,000} = 0.103, \text{ or } 10.3\%$$

$$\text{Return on equity} = \frac{\$132,000}{\$1,400,000} = 0.094, \text{ or } 9.4\%$$

(Continued)

EXHIBIT 18.14 *Continued*

Sanders Corporation
Cash Flow Statement
For the Year Ended December 31, 1999

Cash flows from operations:	
Cash received from customers	$1,150,000
Cash paid for merchandise inventory	(650,000)
Cash paid for operating expenses	(200,000)
Cash paid for taxes	(33,000)
Net cash flows from operations	$ 267,000
Investing activities:	
Cash paid for equipment	(150,000)
Financing activities:	
Cash paid for dividend	(40,000)
Increase (decrease) in cash	$ 77,000

Sanders Corporation
Balance Sheet
December 31, 1999

Assets

Current assets:			
Cash		$100,000	
Accounts receivable		125,000	
Inventory		225,000	
Total current assets			$ 450,000
Property, plant, and equipment:			
Building	$1,200,000		
Less accumulated depreciation	300,000	$900,000	
Equipment	$ 600,000		
Less accumulated depreciation	350,000	250,000	
Total property, plant, and equipment			1,150,000
Total assets			$1,600,000

Liabilities

Current liabilities:	
Accounts payable	$ 200,000
Total liabilities	$ 200,000

Stockholders' Equity

Common stock—no par, 1,000,000 shares authorized,		
100,000 shares issued and outstanding	$800,000	
Retained earnings	600,000	1,400,000
Total liabilities and stockholders' equity		$1,600,000

Given this financial structure, the company is generating a 10.3 percent return on assets ($165,000/$1,600,000) and a 9.4 percent return on equity ($132,000/$1,400,000).

What If Equity Financing Is Used? Exhibit 18.15 shows the pro forma financial statements and selected financial ratios for the 2000 fiscal year based on the assumption that Sanders Corporation acquires the new machine using equity financing. Note that while net income is expected to increase by $64,000 ($196,000 – $132,000) to $196,000 and the debt-to-equity ratio decreases from 0.143 ($200,000/$1,400,000) to 0.082 ($200,000/$2,426,000), the return on assets, 9.3 percent ($245,000/$2,626,000) and return on equity, 8.1 percent ($196,000/$2,426,000), both decrease from current levels. The times interest earned ratio remains at zero because no interest is incurred with equity financing.

Sanders Corporation
Pro Forma Income Statement
For the Year Ended December 31, 2000

Sales (30% increase)		$1,560,000
Cost of goods sold		910,000
Gross margin		$ 650,000
Operating expenses:		
Selling and administrative	$ 210,000	
Depreciation expense—building	60,000	
Depreciation expense—equipment	75,000	
Depreciation expense—machine	60,000	
Total operating expenses		405,000
Operating income		$ 245,000
Income tax expense		49,000
Net income		**$ 196,000**

Sanders Corporation
Pro Forma Retained Earnings Statement
For the Year Ended December 31, 2000

Beginning retained earnings, 1/1/99	$ 600,000
Add net income	196,000
Less dividends	(70,000)
Ending retained earnings, 12/31/99	$ 726,000

Sanders Corporation
Pro Forma 2000 Ratios

$$\text{Debt-to-equity ratio} = \frac{\$200,000}{\$2,426,000} = 0.082$$

$$\text{Times interest earned ratio} = \frac{\$245,000}{-0-} = -0-$$

$$\text{Return on assets} = \frac{\$245,000}{\$2,626,000} = 0.093, \text{ or } 9.3\%$$

$$\text{Return on equity} = \frac{\$196,000}{\$2,426,000} = 0.081, \text{ or } 8.1\%$$

Sanders Corporation
Pro Forma Cash Flow Statement
For the Year Ended December 31, 2000

Cash flows from operations:	
Cash received from customers	$1,435,000
Cash paid for merchandise inventory	(960,000)
Cash paid for operating expenses	(210,000)
Cash paid for taxes	(49,000)
Net cash flows from operations	**$ 216,000**
Investing activities:	
Cash paid for machine	(900,000)
Financing activities:	
Cash from issue of 100,000 shares of stock	900,000
Cash paid for dividend	(70,000)
Increase (decrease) in cash	$ 146,000

(Continued)

EXHIBIT 18.15 *Continued*

Sanders Corporation
Pro Forma Balance Sheet
December 31, 2000

Assets

Current assets:			
Cash		$ 246,000	
Accounts receivable		250,000	
Inventory		275,000	
Total current assets			$ 771,000
Property, plant, and equipment:			
Building	$1,200,000		
Less accumulated depreciation	360,000	$ 840,000	
Equipment	$ 600,000		
Less accumulated depreciation	425,000	175,000	
Machine	$ 900,000		
Less accumulated depreciation	60,000	840,000	
Total property, plant, and equipment			1,855,000
Total assets			$2,626,000

Liabilities

Current liabilities:		
Accounts payable		$ 200,000
Total liabilities		$ 200,000

Stockholders' Equity

Common stock—no par, 1,000,000 shares authorized,		
200,000 shares issued and outstanding	**$1,700,000**	
Retained earnings	726,000	2,426,000
Total liabilities and stockholders' equity		$2,626,000

What If Debt Financing Is Used? Exhibit 18.16 describes the pro forma financial statements and selected financial ratios assuming Sanders Corporation borrows the $900,000 to acquire the new machine by issuing a 10-year, 5 percent note payable. Although net income is $36,000 less than the equity financing alternative due to the interest incurred, the return on equity of 10.7 percent ($160,000/$1,490,000) is higher than the 8.1 percent return expected from the equity financing alternative. While financial leverage creates a higher return on equity, the substantially higher debt-to-equity ratio, 0.74 ($1,100,000/$1,490,000), reveals the increase in the firm's risk. However, while the debt-to-equity ratio may have increased substantially, the times interest earned ratio of 5.4 ($245,000/$45,000) indicates that the corporation could withstand a substantial decrease in earnings before it would be at risk of defaulting on the note.

EXHIBIT 18.16 Sanders' Corporation Pro Forma Financial Statements If Debt Financing Used

Sanders Corporation
Pro Forma Income Statement
For the Year Ended December 31, 2000

Sales (30% increase)		$1,560,000
Cost of goods sold		910,000
Gross margin		$ 650,000
Operating expenses:		
Selling and administrative	$ 210,000	
Depreciation expense—building	60,000	
Depreciation expense—equipment	75,000	
Depreciation expense—machine	60,000	
Total operating expenses		405,000
Operating income		$ 245,000
Interest expense		**45,000**
Income before taxes		$ 200,000
Income tax expense		40,000
Net income		**$ 160,000**

EXHIBIT 18.16 *Continued*

Sanders Corporation
Pro Forma Retained Earnings Statement
For the Year Ended December 31, 2000

Beginning retained earnings, 1/1/99	$ 600,000
Add net income	160,000
Less dividends	(70,000)
Ending retained earnings, 12/31/99	$ 690,000

Sanders Corporation
Pro Forma 2000 Ratios

Debt-to-equity ratio $= \dfrac{\$1,100,000}{\$1,490,000} = 0.74$

Times interest earned ratio $= \dfrac{\$245,000}{\$45,000} = 5.4$

Return on assets $= \dfrac{\$245,000}{\$2,590,000} = 0.095$, or 9.5%

Return on equity $= \dfrac{\$160,000}{\$1,490,000} = 0.107$, or 10.7%

Sanders Corporation
Pro Forma Cash Flow Statement
For the Year Ended December 31, 2000

Cash flows from operations:	
Cash received from customers	$1,435,000
Cash paid for merchandise inventory	(960,000)
Cash paid for operating expenses	(210,000)
Cash paid for interest	**(45,000)**
Cash paid for taxes	(40,000)
Net cash flows from operations	**$ 180,000**
Investing activities:	
Cash paid for machine	(900,000)
Financing activities:	
Cash from issue of note	900,000
Cash paid for dividend	(70,000)
Increase (decrease) in cash	$ 110,000

Sanders Corporation
Pro Forma Balance Sheet
December 31, 2000

Assets

Current assets:			
Cash		$ 210,000	
Accounts receivable		250,000	
Inventory		275,000	
Total current assets			$ 735,000
Property, plant, and equipment:			
Building	$1,200,000		
Less accumulated depreciation	360,000	$ 840,000	
Equipment	$ 600,000		
Less accumulated depreciation	425,000	175,000	
Machine	$ 900,000		
Less accumulated depreciation	60,000	840,000	
Total property, plant, and equipment			1,855,000
Total assets			$2,590,000

Liabilities

Current liabilities:		
Accounts payable	$ 200,000	
Long-term liabilities:		
Note payable (5%)	**$ 900,000**	
Total liabilities		**$1,100,000**

Stockholders' Equity

Common stock—no par, 1,000,000 shares authorized,		
100,000 shares issued and outstanding	$ 800,000	
Retained earnings	690,000	1,490,000
Total liabilities and stockholders' equity		$2,590,000

The Choice The financing decision must also consider the financing decision's impact on cash flows. The pro forma cash flow statements in Exhibits 18.15 and 18.16 reveal that cash from operating activities is $36,000 smaller if debt financing is used. This $36,000 difference is due to the after-tax cost of the $45,000 interest on the note [$45,000 $\times (1 - 0.2$ tax rate)]. While debt financing will generate less cash flow than equity financing, the difference would not pose a threat to the solvency of the corporation.

While only one year of pro forma statements were prepared, if Joe Ryan is confident that projected sales of the new product can be maintained over the life of the note, it seems reasonable to choose debt financing. The rate of return for the firm's stockholders is enhanced at little risk to the firm. Jodi Ryan, however, may want to consider the use of other debt instruments.

Selecting the Appropriate Debt Instrument

Selecting the appropriate debt instrument is an important part of the planning process. When selecting the debt instrument, the planner must forecast the cash inflows expected from the project being financed and then match them with the appropriate debt instrument. For example, if Sanders Corporation is planning to invest in a project that will take several years to generate a positive cash flow, it may want to use a noninterest-bearing note to finance the project. The planner must also consider the impact of the debt instrument on the firm's income statement and balance sheet.

The repayment schedules of the debt instruments described earlier are excellent planning tools. These tables describe the impact of the debt instruments on the income statement (interest expense), balance sheet (carrying value of the note), and cash flow statement (cash paid for interest and principal) over the life of the note. These schedules let planners compare and contrast the various debt instruments at their disposal. For example, Exhibit 18.17 describes the repayment schedules of an interest-bearing note, an installment note, and noninterest-bearing note. Each of these notes could be used to finance the $900,000 machine for Sanders Corporation. These schedules provide the information necessary to help planners model the impact of their financing decision and, therefore, optimize the financing decision.

EXHIBIT 18.17 Repayment Schedules

10-Year, $900,000, 5% Installment Note

Date	(1) Payment	(2) Interest Expense (0.05 × Loan Balance)	(3) Principal	(4) Loan Balance
1/1/99				$900,000.00
12/31/99	$116,554	$45,000.00[a]	$71,554.00	828,446.00
12/31/00	116,554	41,422.30[b]	75,131.70	753,314.30
12/31/01	116,554	37,665.72	78,888.28	674,426.02

[a]$900,000 × 0.05 × 1 = $45,000.

[b]$828,446 × 0.05 × 1 = $41,422.30

10-Year, $1,466,037, Noninterest-Bearing Note

Date	(1) Cash Payment	(2) Interest Expense (0.05 × Carrying Value)	(3) Remaining Discount	(4) Carrying Value
1/1/99			$566,037.00	$900,000.00
12/31/99	0	$ 45,000.00[a]	521,037.00[b]	945,000.00[c]
12/31/00	0	47,250.00	473,787.00	992,250.00
12/31/01	0	49,612.50	424,174.50	1,041,862.50

[a]$900,000 × 0.05 × 1 = $45,000.

[b]$566,037 − $45,000 = $521,037.

[c]$1,466,037 − $521,037 = $945,000, or $900,000 + $45,000 = $945,000.

EXHIBIT 18.17 *Continued*

10-Year, $900,000, 5% Interest-Bearing Note

Date	(1) Cash Interest (0.05 × Face Value)	(2) Effective Interest Expense (0.05 × Carrying Value)	(3) No Amortization	(4) No Discount or Premium	(5) Carrying Value
1/1/99					$900,000
12/31/99	$45,000[a]	$45,000[b]			900,000
12/31/00	45,000	45,000			900,000
12/31/01	45,000	45,000			900,000

[a]$900,000 face value × 0.05 face rate × 1 = $45,000.

[b]$900,000 carrying value × 0.05 market rate × 1 = $45,000.

Exhibit 18.18 shows how each note would impact the income statement, balance sheet, and cash flow statement for its first three years. Note that except for the first year, the interest expense on each note is different. The installment note's interest decreases over the life of the note, while the interest expense on the noninterest-bearing note increases each year. In our example, the interest expense on the interest-bearing note would remain constant because the note was issued at its face value. However, if the interest-bearing note was issued at a discount, the interest expense would increase over the life of the note, but it would decrease over the life of the note if issued at a premium.

EXHIBIT 18.18 Comparison of the Impact of Three Types of Notes on the Financial Statements for Three Years

Income Statement

	12/31/00	12/31/01	12/31/02
Interest expense			
Installment note	$ 45,000.00	$ 41,422.30	$ 37,665.72
Noninterest-bearing note	45,000.00	47,250.00	49,612.50
Interest-bearing note	45,000.00	45,000.00	45,000.00

Balance Sheet

	12/31/00	12/31/01	12/31/02
Long-term debt			
Installment note	$828,446.00	$753,314.30	$ 674,426.02
Noninterest-bearing note	945,000.00	992,250.00	1,041,862.50
Interest-bearing note	900,000.00	900,000.00	900,000.00

Cash Flow Statement

	12/31/00	12/31/01	12/31/02
Cash outflows			
Installment note	$116,554.00	$116,554.00	$ 116,554.00
Noninterest-bearing note	–0–	–0–	–0–
Interest-bearing note	45,000.00	45,000.00	45,000.00

The amount of the debt that would be reported on the balance sheet varies with the type of note used. For example, the carrying value of the installment note decreases as each payment reduces the principal. The carrying value of the noninterest-bearing note increases each year as the discount is amortized. The carrying value of the interest-bearing note used in the example would remain constant. However, the carrying value of interest-bearing notes issued at a discount would increase over the life of the note, while those issued at a premium would decrease over the life of the note.

The differences in the cash flows of each note are probably the most dramatic distinction among the notes. The installment note has the greatest annual cash outflows because it is repaying both principal and interest with each payment. The annual cash payments of the interest-bearing note pays only the amount dictated by the face interest rate on the note but requires a substantial payment at the end of the note. The noninterest-bearing note has no annual cash outflows but will pay the entire note at its maturity date.

PAUSE & REFLECT

How would a company's cash outflow for income taxes be affected by its choice of debt instruments? *(answer on page 640)*

When selecting a debt instrument, planners should consider the instrument's impact on the income statement, balance sheet, and cash flow statement. Pro forma statements could be prepared to highlight the differences between the debt instruments. However, the most important of the three factors is the cash flow analysis. The firm must have confidence that it will be able to meet the cash flow requirements of the note. Failure to do so will result in the default of the note and potential liquidation of the firm's assets. To illustrate, assume that a firm's management, whose bonuses are based on net income, does not consider cash flows and decides to use installment notes on all its debt financing. The managers realize that the installment note has less interest expense over time and will, therefore, increase their bonuses. They also argue that the carrying value will decrease each year and reduce the firm's risk by reducing its debt-to-equity ratio. However, if the cash flows from the capital projects being financed do not generate sufficient cash to meet the installment payments, the firm will face a solvency crisis. Therefore, the managers would be being rewarded (with higher bonuses) for poor financing decisions.

The Financing Budget

As we discussed in Chapter 15, the financing budget is tied to the capital expenditure budget. Projects in the capital expenditure budget were selected in the capital budgeting process because they were expected to support the future operations of the firm. The financing budget identifies how the firm has decided to finance these long-term projects. While there is no standard format, the financing budget will identify when the financing is needed, whether debt or equity financing or some combination of the two will be used, the source of the financing, and finally the financial instruments it plans to use. When a new project is being considered, the financing budget is an important source of information for preparing pro forma statements for the new project. That is, the new project must fit into the current financial structure and the financial structure that has been budgeted.

Managers must consider projected cash inflows when selecting debt instruments.

Debt financing is provided by creditors and creates the risk that the firm's inability to meet interest and principal obligations will result in foreclosure on the firm's assets. Financial leverage created by debt financing creates the potential for boosting the owners' return on investment. Accounting provides vital information to internal and external decision makers about prior financing decisions and the financing alternatives available to the firm in the future.

* Financial leverage provides a reward for debt financing. It increases the rate of return on owners' equity by generating a greater return on borrowed funds than the cost of using the borrowed funds. One measure of a firm's financial leverage is its debt-to-equity ratio.

* The three basic notes used as debt instruments are the periodic payment note, the lump-sum note, and the periodic payment and lump-sum note. Each of these notes is the creditor's promise to make a particular set of payments. The present value of the cash flows using the market rate of interest determines the cash proceeds or cash equivalent of these notes.

* Debt financing is acquired from nonpublic and public sources. Nonpublic sources are banks, insurance companies, leasing companies, and individuals. Bonds are the debt instruments used to acquire debt financing from the public.

* The capital expenditure budget drives a firm's long-term financing plans. Firms choose between debt and equity financing or a combination of the two. The planning process involves examining the impact of the proposed financing alternatives on the firm's cash flow, its income, and its financial structure. Pro forma financial statements help planners identify the impact of the financing alternatives under consideration. Once the plan is finalized, it is placed in the firm's financing budget.

KEY TERMS

amortized discount The amount that interest expense exceeds cash interest for the time period

amortized premium The difference between the cash interest and the lower interest expense for the time period

bearer bond A bond that is payable to the bearer or person who has physical possession of the bond

bond A long-term debt instrument issued by corporations to raise money from the public

bond certificate The note given to bondholders

bond indenture The bond contract

callable bond A bond that gives the firm issuing the bond the right to buy it back before the maturity date at a specified price

capital lease A lease in which a company acquires such a substantial interest in the leased property that, the lessee company, for all practical purposes, owns the asset

carrying value of a note The face value of a note plus its remaining premium or minus its remaining discount

collateral An asset or group of assets specifically named in a debt agreement to which the creditor has claim if the borrower fails to comply with the terms of the note

convertible bond A bond feature that allows bondholders to exchange the bonds for common or preferred stock

covenants Restrictions that lenders place on the borrowing company to protect the lender's interest

debenture bonds Unsecured bonds; bonds with no specific assets pledged as collateral

debt financing A means for a firm to obtain funds (cash), goods, and/or services in exchange for a liability to repay the borrowed funds

debt-to-equity ratio A measure of the relationship between the amount of debt and the amount of owners' equity used to finance the firm

discount on a note The excess of the face value of a note over its cash proceeds

financial leverage A financing strategy designed to increase the rate of return on owners' investment by generating a greater return on borrowed funds than the cost of using the funds

financial risk The chance that a firm will default on its debt

lease An agreement to convey the use of a tangible asset from one party to another in return for rental payments

lump-sum payment note A debt instrument that contains a promise to pay a specific amount of money at the end of a specified period of time

market, or effective, interest rate The actual interest rate charged on a note's proceeds

mortgage A long-term note secured with real estate, such as land or buildings, as collateral

mortgage bond A bond that is secured with real estate

operating lease A rental agreement for a period of time substantially shorter than the economic life of the leased asset

periodic payment and lump-sum note A debt instrument that combines periodic payments and a final lump-sum payment

periodic payment note A debt instrument that contains a promise to make a series of equal payments consisting of both interest and principal at equal time intervals over a specified time period

premium on a note The amount that the cash proceeds of a note exceed its face value

proceeds The amount of cash raised from issuance of a note

registered bonds Bonds that are numbered and made payable in the name of the bondholder

secured bond A bond that has some part of the issuing corporation's assets serving as security for the loan

serial bond A bond issue that has specified portions of the bond issue coming due periodically over the life of the bond issue

subordinated bonds Unsecured bonds whose rights to repayment are ranked after, or subordinated to, some other person or group of creditors

times interest earned ratio A ratio that measures a firm's ability to service its debt by comparing earnings before deducting interest and taxes to the amount of interest expense for the period

unsecured bond A bond that does not have any specific assets pledged as security against its repayment

ANSWERS TO THE PAUSE & REFLECTS

p. 614, Most people would want to invest in Young because it generates a 28.8% return versus the 12% return generated by Hank. However, Young investors assume greater risk than Hank investors because the interest on the debt must be paid even if the return generated by the assets is not sufficient to pay the interest on the debt. In this situation, Hank investors would have to use their equity to pay the interest on the debt.

p. 615, Sprint's redeemable preferred stock is reported on the "Mezzanine" of the balance sheet (between the debt and equity classifications) as mandated by SEC reporting requirements. It is not included in stockholders' equity because it requires cash payments if demanded by its holders (a characteristic of debt). However, it is not included in debt because it has the legal form of an equity instrument. Some refer to the classification of redeemable preferred stock as "dequity".

p. 627, In exchange for cash received from bondholders when the bond is issued, the company issuing the zero coupon bond promises to pay the bond holders the face value of the bond on the maturity date. Companies use the proceeds of bond issues to make long-term investments they expect to generate sufficient cash flow to repay the bond and its interest. Companies issue zero coupon bonds when they are uncertain about the timing of the cash inflows from the investments funded by the bond. Investors like these bonds because the market interest rate on the bond when it is issued is locked in for the life of the bond. Investors who acquire interest bearing bonds can only achieve the bond's market rate of interest over the life of the bond if they can reinvest the cash interest at the market interest rate.

p. 629, Most students will say that a secured bond issue will have a lower interest rate because it specifies assets that will be sold to pay bondholders if the corporation defaults on the debt and, therefore, lower risk than a bond that is merely a promise to repay the bond. In general, however, debentures typically have lower interest rates because they usually have lower risk. Corporations that issue secured bonds do so because they are already at risk and bondholders need more than the corporation's promise to repay the debt before creditors are willing to loan the money. On the other hand, a corporation that issues debentures is able to do so because it has a history of stable operating performance and good credit history and, therefore, creditors believe there is little risk that the corporation will fail to meet its financial obligations. An exception to this is the issuance of junk bonds, which are debentures that have high interest rates that reflect the high risk associated with them.

p. 629, Note 5 of Sprint's annual report describes its long-term debt. The note reveals that Sprint uses Senior Notes, Debentures and First Mortgage Bonds. Sprint uses both public and private debt. Debentures and First Mortgage Bonds represent the public debt while the notes and commercial paper represent the private financing arrangements.

p. 638, The tax expense and, therefore, the cash payment will increase over time with an installment note. The tax expense and, thus, the cash paid for taxes decreases over time with a noninterest-bearing note. With an interest-bearing note issued when the market rate and face rate are the same, the tax expense and cash payment will remain constant.

QUESTIONS

1. What is financial leverage?
2. Describe the risk and rewards of financial leverage.
3. What does a firm's debt-to-equity ratio reflect?
4. What does a firm's times interest earned ratio reflect?
5. Distinguish between the market rate of interest and the face rate of interest on a note.
6. Describe the difference in the cash flows of a periodic payment (installment) note, a lump-sum (noninterest-bearing) note, and a periodic payment and lump-sum (interest-bearing) note.
7. Describe the difference in the interest expense of a periodic payment (installment) note, a lump-sum (noninterest-bearing) note, and a periodic payment and lump-sum (interest-bearing) note.
8. Describe the difference in how the carrying value of a periodic payment (installment) note, a lump-sum (noninterest-bearing) note, and a periodic payment and lump-sum (interest-bearing) note changes over the life of the note.
9. Why does a discount on a note arise?
10. Why does a premium on a note arise?
11. Compare and contrast the important features of an operating and a capital lease.
12. What distinguishes a bond from other types of debt instrument?
13. Describe how a corporation raises money by issuing bonds.
14. Describe the difference between a debenture and a mortgage bond.
15. When planning to issue a bond, why would a company use a call feature?
16. When planning to issue a bond, why would a company use a conversion feature?
17. What is the distinction between a bearer bond and a registered bond?
18. How are pro forma financial statements used for planning the financing for a project?
19. What factors should be considered when choosing a debt instrument?
20. What is the purpose of a financing budget?

End of chapter activities that require a financial calculator have an asterisk (*) after the number.

EXERCISES

E 18.1
LO 1

Koeppen Co. has $2,000,000 in assets and no liabilities, while Lacey, Inc., has $2,000,000 in assets and a $1,200,000 note payable at 8 percent annual interest. Assume that both companies are subject to a tax rate of 30 percent. What is the return on owners' equity for each company if each firm can generate a 20 percent return on its assets? Which company would be a more desirable investment? Why?

E 18.2
LO 1

The BRHC Corporation has $3,500,000 in assets and has current liabilities of $200,000 and long-term debt of $1,500,000 with a 10% interest rate. The company is subject to a 30 percent tax rate and currently makes a 20 percent return on its assets. Royce Purinton, the company president, wants to get out of long-term debt and proposes to issue $1,500,000 of stock and pay off all the long-term debt. What would be the impact of his plan on BRHC's return on equity?

E 18.3
LO 1

The Bott Corporation had its controller, Laura Wyndam, prepare the income statement below:

BOTT CORPORATION
Income Statement

Sales	$12,800,000
Cost of goods sold	5,000,000
Gross margin	$ 7,800,000
Operating expenses	6,400,000
Income before interest and taxes	$ 1,400,000
Interest expense	640,000
Income before taxes	$ 760,000
Income tax expense (30%)	228,000
Net income	$ 532,000

Bott Corporation has assets of $15,000,000 and debt of $8,000,000 that carries an 8 percent interest rate. From Laura's information, calculate the rate of return on assets, rate of return on stockholders' equity, debt-to-equity ratio, and the times interest earned ratio for Bott Corporation. What is your assessment of Bott's financial risk? Justify your position.

E 18.4
LO 1

The Garwood Corporation has assets of $13,500,000, debt of $4,600,000, earnings before interest and income taxes of $1,100,000, and a tax rate of 30 percent. Interest on the corporation's debt is $414,000 for the current year. Calculate Garwood's rate of return on assets, debt-to-equity ratio, times interest earned ratio, and rate of return on stockholders' equity. What is your assessment of Garwood's financial risk? Justify your position.

E 18.5
LO 2

On April 1, 1999, Hunnicutt Products borrowed $150,000 at 8 percent on a four-year installment loan. Annual payments starting on April 1, 2000, are $45,288. How much of the first $45,288 is principal and how much is interest? How much of the second $45,288 payment is principal and how much is interest? Describe the cash inflows and outflows associated with the note.

E 18.6*
LO 2

On November 1, 1999, Bob Hickman loaned Sam Vitkoski $23,000. Sam signed a three-year installment note that calls for 12 quarterly payments and a 9 percent interest rate. How much cash will Sam send Bob each quarter? How much of the first payment will be interest expense and how much will be principal?

E 18.7
LO 2

On June 1, 2000, Sal Sota agreed to loan his brother Juan $10,000 for three years. He wants to use a noninterest-bearing note and needs to know the face value of the note. Assume that the market rate of interest is 8 percent on the date the note is made. If the interest is compounded annually, what face value should Sal use? Prepare a schedule describing the interest expense for the life of the note. How much interest will Juan incur in each of the first two years? Describe the cash inflows and outflows Juan must plan for with this note.

E 18.8*
LO 2

Tom Balke Corporation wants to borrow $70,000 and use a noninterest-bearing note with a five-year life. If the market interest rate is 7 percent and the interest is compounded semiannually, what will be the face value of the note? How much interest expense will Tom Balke Corporation incur during the first year of the note's life? Describe the cash inflows and outflows Tom Balke must plan for with this note.

E 18.9
LO 2

The chief financial officer of Thornton Corporation, Mary Horras, is planning to issue a $300,000, three-year interest-bearing note with a face interest rate of 6 percent that is paid annually. Create an amortization schedule for the life of this note if the market interest rate is 7 percent. What will be the cash inflows associated with the note? What will be the total cash outflows over the life of the note? What is the dollar difference between the cash inflows and cash outflows? What is the total amount of interest expense Thornton will incur over the life of this note? Describe why the answers to the last two questions are related.

E 18.10*
LO 2

Mai Locker Company issued an $800,000, five-year, 8 percent interest-bearing note on July 1, 1999, when the market interest rate was 7 percent. The face rate of interest is paid semiannually. Determine the amount of cash the company will receive from the note. Describe the cash outflows Mai Locker will pay on the note over its life. Prepare an amortization table for the first year of the note's life.

E 18.11
LO 2

West Coast Delivery Corporation is planning to issue $15,000,000 in 10-year, 8 percent bonds. The bonds are dated May 1, 1999, and interest is payable annually on May 1.

If the bonds are sold on May 1, 1999, to yield the 10 percent market rate of interest, how much cash will West Coast Delivery raise by issuing the bonds? How much cash will one bond raise? How much interest expense will West Coast Delivery incur during the first year of the bond's life? How much cash will the corporation pay out during the first year of the bond's life? Describe the cash outflows of the bond for the life of the bond issue.

E 18.12
LO 2

Using the information in E 18.11, how much cash will West Coast Delivery Corporation receive if the bonds are issued to yield a 6 percent market rate of interest? How much cash will one bond raise? How much interest expense will West Coast Delivery incur during the first year of the bond's life? How much cash will the corporation pay out during the first year of the bond's life? Describe the bond's cash outflows for the life of the bond issue.

E 18.13

LO 2

Determine the cash received from a $2,000,000 bond issue if the bonds were issued at each of the following prices:

a. 97 1/2
b. 101 7/8
c. 103 1/4
d. 89 3/8

E 18.14

LO 2

On December 1, 2000, the Yunker Corporation issued bonds with a face value of $12,000,000. The bonds mature in 10 years and have a face rate of 8 percent interest that is paid semiannually. The market rate of interest when the bonds were issued was 10 percent. Prepare an amortization schedule for the first year of the bonds' life. How much interest expense is incurred in the first year of the bonds' life? How much cash is paid out in the first year of the bonds' life?

E 18.15

LO 3

The Malsom Corporation has issued bonds with a face value of $4,000,000 that are convertible on a 50:1 basis (50 shares of common stock for one bond) and have a call price of 104. Describe the cash flows if the bonds are called when their carrying (book) value is $3,900,000. Describe the cash flows if the bonds are instead converted to common stock.

E 18.16

LO 3

Chen Corporation's bonds have a face value of $11,000,000 and a call price of 103. On February 1, 2000, the bonds have a carrying value of $11,200,000 on Chen's books and a market price of 98 3/4 in the secondary market. If Chen wants to retire the entire bond issue, how much will it have to pay if it calls the bonds? How much will it pay if it buys the bonds in the secondary bond market?

E 18.17

LO 3

On October 1, 1999, Semiconductor Technologies signed a capital lease for machinery with a fair market value of $152,865 for a six-year period. The company made the first of seven $27,865 annual payments on the day it signed the lease. The interest rate is 9 percent. What is the amount of the liability generated by this capital lease? Prepare a schedule showing the first two years' lease payments. How much interest expense will Semiconductor incur in the first year of the lease?

E 18.18*

LO 3

Grimsley Company is planning to lease a piece of equipment valued at $60,000. The lease agreement calls for Grimsley to pay $6,000 on the date the lease is signed and then six semiannual lease payments. If Grimsley's interest rate is 9 percent and the lease payments are based on the $54,000, how big will the lease payment be? If the lease is considered an operating lease, how much of the first lease payment will be considered interest?

E 18.19

LO 4

Jack Yeager is the CEO of Team Stir Corporation which is going to acquire a plant that will cost $2,000,000. Yeager is considering whether to raise the cash necessary to acquire the plant by issuing stock or signing a five-year, 8 percent interest-bearing note. The market rate of interest is 8 percent. Given Team Stir's balance sheet, presented below, what impact will each of these financing decisions have on the firm's debt-to-equity ratio and the firm's financial risk? What other information would you want to assess the desirability of these financing alternatives?

TEAM STIR CORPORATION
Abbreviated Balance Sheet

Current assets	$ 1,000,000	Current liabilities	$ 600,000
Long-term assets	10,000,000	Long-term liabilities	5,000,000
Total assets	$11,000,000	Total liabilities	$ 5,600,000
		Stockholders' equity	5,400,000
		Total liabilities and stockholders' equity	$11,000,000

E 18.20

LO 4

John Rich Company's capital expenditure budget calls for a $500,000 addition to an existing plant. The company plans to issue a three-year note and is debating whether to use a three-payment, 8 percent installment note; a three-year, 8 percent, $500,000 interest-bearing note; or a noninterest-bearing note. If John Rich Company's market interest rate is 8 percent, describe the cash inflows and outflows for each year of each note's life.

PROBLEMS

P 18.1
LO 1

José Gonzalez is the chief financial officer of LB Corporation and has given you the income statement below:

LB CORPORATION
Income Statement

Sales	$12,400,000
Cost of goods sold	6,700,000
Gross margin	$ 5,700,000
Operating expenses	3,000,000
Income before interest and taxes	$ 2,700,000
Interest expense	520,000
Income before taxes	$ 2,180,000
Income tax expense (40%)	872,000
Net income	$ 1,308,000

Additional information: Total assets, $10,552,000; total liabilities, $6,500,000.

Required
 a. Calculate the rate of return on assets.
 b. Calculate the rate of return on equity.
 c. Calculate the debt-to-equity ratio.
 d. Calculate the times interest earned ratio.
 e. Explain the risks of LB Corporation using financial leverage.

P 18.2
LO 2

On November 1, 1999, Michigan Iron Works arranged to purchase a $150,000 piece of equipment by making a 20 percent down payment and signing a three-year installment loan contract with interest at 8 percent per year for the balance. The loan is to be repaid in semiannual installments starting on May 1, 2000.

Required
Prepare a repayment schedule for the first two payments of the loan and then answer the following questions:
 a. How much cash will the company pay out in the first year?
 b. How much cash will the company pay over the life of the note?
 c. How much interest expense will the note generate in the first year of the note?
 d. How much of the initial debt will be reduced in the first year of the note?

P 18.3
LO 2

Fry Construction Company acquired a trenching machine on July 1, 1999, with a list price of $42,000, by paying $12,000 down and signing a two-year, $30,000 noninterest-bearing note. The market rate of interest on the date the company acquired the machine was 9 percent.

Required
 a. What price did Fry pay for the machine?
 b. How much interest will Fry pay over the life of the note?
 c. Set up an interest schedule for the life of the note.
 d. Describe the cash flows Fry will make over the note's life.

P 18.4
LO 2

Brooke Beyer, the controller of Nanook Software, is planning to finance several projects and wants you to determine the cash inflows and outflows of the following notes. The market interest rate for Nanook Software is 8 percent.

 1. $100,000, 8 percent note, interest payable annually, due in eight years.
 2. $500,000, 10 percent note, interest payable semiannually, due in 10 years.
 3. $250,000, 7 percent note, interest payable semiannually, due in six years.

Required
 a. What is the cash Nanook will receive from each note?
 b. What are the annual cash outflows for each note?
 c. What are the total cash outflows for each note?

P 18.5
LO 2

Bullard Printing Company is going to expand its print shop and plans to borrow some of the funds necessary for the expansion. Bullard wants to issue a four-year, 9 percent, $850,000 note that pays interest annually but is concerned about the impact of the note.

Required   If Bullard's market interest rate is 10 percent, set up a repayment table for the life of the note and answer the following questions:

    a. What are the cash inflows from the note?
    b. What is the annual interest expense the note will generate?
    c. What are the cash outflows associated with the note each year?
    d. How does the carrying value of the note change over the life of the note? Why?

P 18.6*
LO 2

Mary Lou Meile is the controller for a construction company and is responsible for buying a new service truck that has a sticker price of $28,800. The dealer has offered to finance the truck at 0 percent interest for 48 months, requiring payments of $600 per month ($28,800/48 months) for 48 months. The construction company usually borrows funds at 8 percent.

Required   *a.* What cost will Mary Lou assign to the truck and the note if she accepts this offer?
    b. If the price of the truck is negotiable, at what price would Mary Lou elect to borrow the money at a bank at the market rate of 8 percent?

P 18.7
LO 3

Pfeifer Leasing Service recently purchased drilling equipment for $218,705 and wants to lease it to Gopher Excavation Company. If Gopher accepts, it will sign the lease agreement on May 1, 2000. The equipment has an estimated useful life of five years, and the lease term is for five years. During the period of the lease, Gopher will be responsible for all repairs and maintenance of the leased property. The lease agreement calls for Gopher to make five annual lease payments of $43,705 starting May 1, 2000. The interest rate is 9 percent. Gopher has asked you to help it plan for the impact of this lease.

Required   *a.* What makes this lease qualify as a capital lease?
    b. What is the value of the equipment and the amount of the liability generated by this transaction?
    c. Prepare a lease payment schedule for Gopher Excavation for the first three lease payments and answer the following questions:
        1. What are the cash flows associated with each year of the lease?
        2. What is the interest cost incurred in each of the first two years of the lease?
        3. How does the lease liability change over the first two years of the lease?
    d. What would be the advantage to Gopher if it could sign an operating lease?

P 18.8
LO 3

Sprint is planning to issue debentures with a face value of $10,000,000 on September 1, 2001. The debentures mature in 10 years and have a face interest rate of 8 percent that is paid semiannually on March 1 and September 1 of each year. Sprint is uncertain about what the market interest rate will be on those dates and has projected the following possibilities:

September 1, 2001

    Situation 1: The market rate of interest is 6 percent.
    Situation 2: The market rate of interest is 10 percent.
    Situation 3: The market rate of interest is 8 percent.

Required   For each potential market rate, calculate the price of the bond, set up an amortization table for the first year of the debenture's life, and then answer the following questions:

    a. How much cash will Sprint receive (cash inflow) from the debentures for each interest rate?
    b. What is the interest expense for the first year for each of the market interest rates?
    c. What annual cash outflows will occur for each of the market interest rates?
    d. How did the carrying value change each year under each scenario?

P 18.9
LO 4

Pallett Corporation has a $12,000,000 bond issue that has a carrying value of $11,232,125 as of September 1, 1999. For each of the assumptions below, describe cash flows that occur and the impact each scenario would have on Pallett's financial structure. Consider each scenario an independent event.

    a. Pallett Corporation's bonds have a call price of 102 and on September 1, 1999, the corporation exercised the call feature on the entire bond issue.
    b. Pallett Corporation's bonds have a 50-to-1 common stock conversion feature; that is, one bond is convertible into 50 shares of Pallett Corporation's common stock. On September 1, 1999, the bondholders converted 25 percent of the bonds into common stock.

P 18.10
LO 4

Busta Corporation's capital expenditure budget calls for the construction of a new addition to the plant and the corporation's controller plans to borrow $3,000,000 to finance a portion of the construction. While the controller has decided to issue a three-year note, she is undecided on which debt instrument to use. She wants you to show the impact of a noninterest-bearing note, a 9 percent installment note, and a 9 percent interest-bearing note on the company's cash flow statement, income statement, and balance sheet over the life of the note. The market interest rate for Busta is 9 percent.

Required

Using the format in Exhibit 18.18, show each note's impact on Busta's cash flows, income, and financial structure.

CASES

C 18.1
LO 1   LO 4

In the summer of 1992, the airline industry entered into a price war and airline ticket sales jumped dramatically as the price of tickets dropped. Despite the increase in the sale of tickets, most airlines claimed this pricing strategy hurt their short-term financial position. Keeping pace with these price cuts forced Braniff into bankruptcy. How could increasing sales cause financial hardships in the airline industry? What role did the firm's leverage play in this scenario? (Resource material can be found in the Disclosure database located in your college library or EDGAR on the internet. Examine the financial statements of several airlines for the 1991 fiscal year.)

C 18.2
LO 2   LO 3

Golden Shores Resort needs to acquire a new tour boat that costs $80,000 and is expected to be useful for approximately five years. There are three alternatives for financing the acquisition of the boat:

Alternative 1: Lease the boat for five years as a capital lease. There would be five lease payments of $20,128 each, the first of which would be paid on the date the boat was acquired.

Alternative 2: Purchase the boat outright for $80,000 from the proceeds of a $80,000, five-year, 8 percent note payable. The loan would require annual interest payments of $6,400 and repayment of the principal at the end of five years.

Alternative 3: Sign a one-year lease for $20,128 with the option to renew the lease each year for the next five years. While the lease may be renewed, the amount of the lease may increase or decrease up to 10 percent.

What are the advantages and disadvantages of each of these financing alternatives?

CRITICAL THINKING

CT 18.1
LO 1   LO 4

The chief financial officer of Nafta Company wants to finance the acquisition of a new $14,000,000 manufacturing facility in Mexico. Nafta already has $10,000,000 of debt, a debt-to-equity ratio of 2.2, and a times interest earned ratio of 1.5. What will Nafta's debt-to-equity ratio be if it incurs this debt? Write a memo to Nafta's CFO outlining the factors he should consider before taking this action.

CT 18.2
LO 1

Each of the following $5,000,000 debt instruments is subject to a 10 percent market rate of interest. When measured on a common size basis, which of the following is the most expensive debt to use?
a. $5,000,000 noninterest-bearing, 10-year note
b. $5,000,000 bond with an 8 percent face rate that is paid annually; the bond is due in 10 years
c. $5,000,000 note payable, with a 10-year life and a 12 percent face rate of interest that is paid annually

ETHICAL CHALLENGES

EC 18.1
LO 1   LO 4

Bob Posta, an accountant for Shady Manufacturing, has just learned that the company bought a new machine with a list price of $43,000 and financed the acquisition with a noninterest-bearing note. Bob decided to use a 4 percent rate to determine the value of the note rather than the market interest rate of 9 percent. What is the impact of this action on the financial statements? Is this practice considered unethical? Why or why not?

EC 18.2
LO 1   LO 4

Jury Corporation has just acquired a building by issuing a $5,000,000, 10-year, 3 percent note to the former owner of the building. Jury's top management receives bonuses based on a percentage of net income Jury values the building and the note at $5,000,000. Jury's market interest rate is 10 percent. What impact did this decision have on Jury's income in the first year of the note? Who is harmed by this practice? Who benefits from this practice?

COMPUTER APPLICATIONS

CA 18.1
LO 2

Small Company needs to borrow $10,000 to finance an addition to its manufacturing facilities. It has obtained an installment note at 8 percent interest for five years. Payments will be made quarterly beginning three months from today.

Required

Use a computer spreadsheet package.
a. What is the amount of each yearly payment?
b. Prepare a payment schedule that indicates the amount of each payment, how much of each payment is interest, how much of each payment is principal, and the remaining balance on the loan.

CA 18.2
LO 2

Greenwood Corporation needs to buy a new computer system. Dwell Computers has agreed to sell Greenwood a computer system and accept a 10-year, noninterest-bearing note payable. The market rate of interest is currently 10 percent and the value of the computer system is $53,000.

Required

Use a computer spreadsheet package.
a. What is the face value of the noninterest-bearing note?
b. Prepare a schedule that indicates the interest cost associated with the loan each year.

CA 18.3*
LO 2

Unitog Corporation issued a $1,000,000 note with a five-year life and a face interest rate of 6 percent that is paid semiannually. The market interest rate is 11 percent. Using a financial calculator, determine the cash proceeds of this note.

CA 18.4
LO 1

Find Moody's Investors Service, Inc.'s Web site and answer the following questions:
a. How did Moody's get its start?
b. What services does Moody's offer?
c. In addition to bonds, what other financial instruments does Moody's rate?

PART SIX

THE ROAD TRAVELED

Chapters 14–18 examined the role of accounting information in planning business investing and financing activities. Chapter 14 introduced the time value of money concept and showed how it is used to make financial decisions, while Chapter 15 used the same concept to determine if business investment activities should be undertaken. Chapter 16 explored the business considerations involved in investing in human capital. Chapters 17 and 18 explored the issues surrounding business financing decisions.

YOU ARE HERE

Now that we understand the process of planning, we explore the role of the accounting system during the performing phase of business—the company must begin to operate. It must raise capital and then invest it. Chapters 19–22 examine the process of recording financing and investing activities. Chapter 19 explores the recording and reporting of equity financing activities. In Chapter 17 we learned how businesses plan their equity financing activities. In Chapter 19 we learn how companies record equity financing activities in the accounting system and report them on the financial statements.

THE ROAD AHEAD

Chapters 20–22 continue to examine the process of recording financing and investing activities. Chapter 20 considers the formal process of recording and communicating debt financing activities. Chapter 21 looks at recording and reporting operational investment activities (those involving operating assets) and Chapter 22 explores the recording and communication process for nonoperational investment activities.

LEARNING OBJECTIVES

LO 1 Describe how to record and communicate equity financing activities for sole proprietorships and partnerships.

LO 2 Explain how and why corporations record contributed capital.

LO 3 Demonstrate how corporate earnings and losses are determined and how a firm's earnings are distributed to its owners.

LO 4 Explain why corporations buy treasury stock, why corporations split their stock, and how to account for these events.

LO 5 Describe the format of a corporation's stockholders' equity reporting and explain why the format is used.

Recording and Communicating Equity Financing Activities

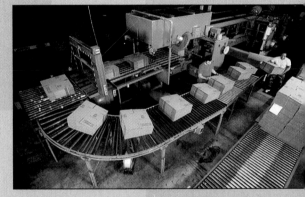

The name, Stone Container Corporation, produces images of a corporation making sturdy but impractical products rather than the one named after the founder of the company, Joseph Stone. In fact, Stone Container Corporation makes a wide variety of very practical packaging products. The company is an industry leader in the production of industrial and consumer bags; corrugated containers; and paper for magazines; newspapers, and tissues. Its products are everywhere you are: boxes for pizza, paper for the school newspaper, sacks for dog food, and those funny-looking computer boxes from South Dakota. While its headquarters are in Chicago, its products are manufactured and sold around the world.

STONE CONTAINER
www.smurfit-stone.net

In the years from 1990 to 1997, Stone Container generated a profit in only 1990 and 1995.

As a result of the losses generated during this time period, Stone Container's stockholders' equity decreased from $1,460,500,000 in 1990 to $276,900,000 in 1997.[1] This trend had its origin in 1989 when Stone Container made major acquisitions using debt financing. Stone Container's long-term debt increased from $765.1 million in 1988 to $3,536.9 million in 1989, and its interest expense jumped from $108.3 million

[1]Stone Container Corporation and Subsidiaries, *1997 Annual Report,* p. 24

to $344.7 million during this one-year period. By 1997 Stone Container financed 89 percent of its assets with debt.

In its 1997 annual report, Stone Container announced a new strategic plan to improve profitability and reduce its debt from 89 percent to 40 percent of total assets. A significant portion of this debt reduction would be paid for with the proceeds from the sale of its market pulp and publication paper operations. If successful, these strategies should improve Stone Container's ability to use equity financing in two ways. First, higher profits will increase the funds available for reinvestment and will eliminate the current deficit in retained earnings. Once Stone Container generates income, investors' expectations about the firm's future profitability will improve and its stock prices should improve. Higher stock prices will improve the firm's ability to generate cash from the sale of its common and preferred stock.

Stone Container's management faces a serious challenge in the coming years as it works to restore its profitability and reduce its financial leverage. The strategies outlined in Stone Container's 1997 annual report appear to be the first steps toward recovery. What equity instruments could Stone Container use to raise equity capital and improve its stockholders' equity? How will Stone Container's dividend policy impact stockholders' equity? If the firm distributed stock rather than cash dividends, what impact would this have on the firm's existing stockholders, cash flow, and stockholders' equity?

C hapter 17 pointed out that each form of business ownership, whether sole proprietorship, partnership, or corporation, has advantages and disadvantage due to its unique features. The accounting system records and communicates what is unique about a business's equity financing; therefore, it is important to understand the differences related to equity for each type of organization.

It is also important to look beyond the recording process to understand the nature of changes in a business's owners' equity and what events the accounting entries represent. Understanding both how and why companies make these entries and communicate resulting information is essential for owners as well as other financial statement users.

The first section of this chapter describes how to account for equity financing events pertaining to sole proprietorships and partnerships—the types of organizations that are not separate legal entities. Accounting for these two types of ownership structures is quite similar because the organizations are easy to form and have unlimited liability.

We follow the discussion of sole proprietorships and partnerships by examining the equity events of corporations. Accounting for corporate ownership reflects the complicating factor that corporations are separate legal entities that provide limited liability for their owners.

NONCORPORATE FORMS OF BUSINESS

LO 1

For sole proprietorships and partnerships, the amount of each owner's contribution and personal share of the firm's undistributed earnings are combined in one account. Use of one account reflects the fact that these organizations have economic rather than legal distinctions between the business and the owners. Combining contributed capital and retained earnings in each owner's capital account is done because, unlike corporations, the creditors of sole proprietorships and partnerships can lay claim to the personal assets of each owner if the business's assets are insufficient to meet its creditors' claims.

SOLE PROPRIETORSHIPS

Accounting for a sole proprietorship requires only one permanent balance sheet equity account, called the *owner's capital account.* The account title includes the owner's name and the designation *capital.* For example, when Joseph Stone founded Stone Container in 1926, he could have used the owner's equity account Joseph Stone, Capital.

To illustrate, assume that Joseph Stone started Stone Container by depositing $30,000 cash in the bank in the name of his new company and by contributing a building he owned on the Chicago River with a fair market value of $105,000. The entry to record the establishment of the business would be:

Cash	30,000	
Building	105,000	
Joseph Stone, Capital		135,000

Observe that the entry reflects the impact of the event on the business entity's assets and equity rather than on the owner's personal financial condition. If, during the course of the accounting period, Mr. Stone made additional contributions to the business, each contribution would be recorded in the same way as the initial contribution.

The amount in the owner's capital account changes at the end of an accounting period as revenue and expense accounts are closed to Income Summary, which, in turn, is closed to the owner's capital account. The closing entries illustrated below assume that Stone made a profit of $24,300 (Revenues, $329,000 – Expenses, $304,700) during its first year of operation:

Revenues[2]	329,000	
Income Summary		329,000
Income Summary	304,700	
Expenses		304,700
Income Summary	24,300	
Joseph Stone, Capital		24,300

The closing entries represent the magnitude of the change in the owner's interest in the business due to the firm's operating performance. The capital account, after closing, includes the original investment plus net income ($135,000 + $24,300 = $159,300). In this case, the net income generated by the firm provided a $24,300 return for the year on Mr. Stone's initial investment and increased his financial interest in the business.

Drawing Account for a Sole Proprietorship

The proprietor controls the withdrawal of assets from the business for personal use and could record the withdrawal by reducing the capital account directly. However, by using a separate owner's equity account reserved exclusively for withdrawals, the proprietor can quickly identify the amount and timing of each withdrawal from the business.

Traditionally, a contra equity account called the **drawing account** is used in proprietorships and partnerships to summarize the dollar amount of assets withdrawn from the business entity for personal use. The drawing account title includes the owner's name, such as Joseph Stone, and the label *Drawings* or *Withdrawals*. When the proprietor takes assets, most commonly cash, from the business for personal use, the drawing account is debited. If Mr. Stone withdrew $1,000 cash for his own use, the following entry would have been made:

Joseph Stone, Drawings	1,000	
Cash		1,000

The owner's decision to withdraw assets is at her or his discretion and can occur at any time. The drawing account balance reflects the running total of the amount the owner has withdrawn over a specific time period, usually one year. If Mr. Stone made withdrawals totaling $20,600 during the period, at the end of the period, the balance in the drawing account would be closed to Mr. Stone's capital account. The balance in the capital account after the closing process represents the original investment, plus net income, less the amount withdrawn ($135,000 + $24,300 – $20,600 = $138,700).

---

[2]Recall that each separate revenue and expense account is individually closed to Income Summary. We are summarizing the process here.

Joseph Stone, Capital	20,600	
Joseph Stone, Drawings		20,600

Withdrawals by the proprietor are not an expense of the business. Even though an owner who also manages the business may make regular withdrawals that resemble payment of a salary, these withdrawals are a distribution of the return on the owner's investment. However, if the withdrawal exceeds the amount of income generated by the firm, the distribution constitutes a return *of* the owner's investment.

Statement of Owner's Equity for a Sole Proprietorship

The statement of owner's equity reflects the changes in the owner's capital account from one accounting period to the next. Exhibit 19.1 illustrates how today's statement of owner's equity would reflect Mr. Stone's equity transactions in 1926.

The statement first states the owner's capital balance at the beginning of the period; it then shows any additional investments made and the increase (decrease) due to the period's net income (net loss). Finally, the statement presents the amount of drawings deducted in determining the ending balance in the capital account, which becomes the owner's equity section of the current period's balance sheet.

EXHIBIT	19.1	Statement of Owner's Equity

STONE CONTAINER COMPANY
Statement of Owner's Equity
For the Year Ended December 31, 1926

Joseph Stone, capital, 1/1/1926		$ –0–
Add owner investments	$135,000	
Net income	24,300	159,300
Subtotal		$159,300
Less drawings		(20,600)
Joseph Stone, capital, 12/31/1926		$138,700

PARTNERSHIPS

Accounting for partnership equity is similar to accounting for the equity of sole proprietorships. However, a partnership requires a separate capital and drawing account for each partner in order to determine each owner's interest in the firm. The respective capital accounts summarize the increases and decreases for each individual partner's ownership interest in the business. For example, if Laura Wyndam and Eric Burke form a partnership called Boone Enterprises, and Wyndam contributes $90,000 in cash while Burke contributes $48,000, the entry to record the transaction would be:

Cash	138,000	
Wyndam, Capital		90,000
Burke, Capital		48,000

When partners contribute assets other than cash, the noncash assets are recorded at their *fair market value at the time of contribution.* All the partners must agree upon the valuation of these noncash assets.

Occasionally, a partnership may take over an entire established business and assume its liabilities. For example, assume that Boone Enterprises wants to move to a new location and that Laura and Eric discover that Margaret Kohlrus, a sole proprietor, owns a building that is ideal for their operations. On January 1, 1999, Laura, Eric, and Margaret form a partnership called Banner Company. At this time, Boone Enterprises has assets with fair market values as follows: cash, $25,000; accounts receivable, $28,000; inventory, $42,000; and equipment, $61,000. Boone Enterprises also has accounts payable of $18,000, which the new partnership will assume. Kohlrus originally paid $75,000 for her building and $22,000 for the land, but today the fair market values of the building and land are $127,000 and $37,000, respectively. There is a $50,000 mortgage on the build-

Dream Works is a partnership of Jeffrey Katzenberg, Stephen Spielberg, and David Geffen.

ing, which the partnership will assume. We illustrate the entries to record the formation of the partnership below:

Cash	25,000	
Accounts Receivable	28,000	
Inventory	42,000	
Equipment	61,000	
Accounts Payable		18,000
Wyndam, Capital		90,000
Burke, Capital		48,000
Building	127,000	
Land	37,000	
Mortgage Payable		50,000
Kohlrus, Capital		114,000

In each instance, the incoming partner was credited with the difference between the amount of assets contributed and the liabilities assumed by the partnership. The original cost of the assets to the individuals is of no consequence to the partnership because the market value of the noncash assets represents the economic substance of the contribution event. For example, the $127,000 fair market value of the building became part of the partnership organization rather than its original cost of $75,000.

Closing Entries for Partnerships

When the revenue and expense accounts are closed to Income Summary, the income or loss generated by the partnership during the period is allocated to the partners, resulting in an increase or decrease to the capital accounts accordingly. We discussed the various ways to divide income and losses among partners in Chapter 17. For example, if Laura Wyndam, Eric Burke, and Margaret Kohlrus agreed to divide income and loss equally and the partnership generated $48,000 of income, the allocation of the income between the three partners is recorded with the following entry:

Income Summary	48,000	
Wyndam, Capital		16,000
Burke, Capital		16,000
Kohlrus, Capital		16,000

The partnership also closes its drawing accounts at this time:

Wyndam, Capital	8,000	
Burke, Capital	7,000	
Kohlrus, Capital	5,000	
Wyndam, Drawings		8,000
Burke, Drawings		7,000
Kohlrus, Drawings		5,000

Statement of Partners' Capital

The **statement of partners' capital** presents the changes in the individual partners' capital balances that result from additional contributions, the firm's income or loss, and the partners' withdrawals from the firm over a specific period of time. The balance sheet reflects ending balances in the capital accounts.

A statement of partners' capital, as illustrated in Exhibit 19.2, reflects the results of the capital events we discussed earlier. Additional investments made to the partnership by any partner during the time period appear as additions to the partner's capital account. We have assumed that Wyndam made an additional contribution during the year of $6,000.

EXHIBIT 19.2	Statement of Partners' Capital			

BANNER COMPANY
Statement of Partners' Capital
For the Year Ended December 31, 1999

	Wyndam	Burke	Kohlrus	Total
Capital balances, 1/1/99	$ 90,000	$48,000	$114,000	$252,000
Add net income	16,000	16,000	16,000	48,000
Investments	6,000	–0–		6,000
Subtotal	$112,000	$64,000	$130,000	$306,000
Less drawings	(8,000)	(7,000)	(5,000)	(20,000)
Capital balances, 12/31/99	$104,000	$57,000	$125,000	$286,000

Changing Partners: Admission of a New Partner and Withdrawal of Existing Partners

In Chapter 17 we discussed why partners are admitted to and withdraw from partnerships and how these events impact the partners' equity. In this chapter we show how these events are recorded in the accounting system.

Recall that a new partner is admitted in one of two ways: (1) by purchasing all or part of the interest of an existing partnership interest by payment to the existing partner or (2) by investing directly in the partnership organization. For our illustrations, we will use Banner Company and its capital balances as reflected in Exhibit 19.2.

Purchase of an Existing Interest   An existing partner can sell all or a portion of his or her interest in the firm directly to a new partner, subject to the approval of the other partners. Because the payment goes to the existing partner, the new partner would receive either all or only a portion of the selling partner's capital. Total partnership equity would remain the same. To illustrate, assume that on January 1, 2000, Laura Wyndam gets the permission of her partners and agrees to sell one-half of her $104,000 interest (Exhibit 19.2), $52,000, in Banner Company directly to Bradley Logsdon for $60,000. The entry to reflect this event is:

Wyndam, Capital	52,000	
Logsdon, Capital		52,000

Direct Investment in the Firm   When the new partner's admission to the partnership involves the investment of money or other assets in the firm, the payment increases the amount of the firm's total assets as well as its total owners' equity. The new partner's interest in the firm is either the same, smaller, or larger than the amount of the assets contributed. For this example, let's assume that on January 1, 2000, the partners of Banner Company agree to admit Bradley Logsdon to a one-fourth interest if he invests $95,333 cash in the partnership. The entry to record Logsdon's admission to the partnership is described below:

Cash	95,333	
Logsdon, Capital		95,333
($381,333 × 1/4 = $95,333)		

With the contribution by Logsdon, Banner Company's capital balances will increase from $286,000 to $381,333, and the $95,333 balance in Logsdon's account will be one-fourth of the firm's total capital.

Bonus to Existing Partners Let's now assume that Logsdon will contribute $114,000 for a one-fourth interest in the firm. The total capital after Logsdon's contribution will be $400,000 ($286,000 + $114,000) and his interest will be $100,000 ($400,000/4). The remaining $4,000 will be divided equally by the other partners according to their profit and loss agreement:

Cash	114,000	
Logsdon, Capital		100,000
Wyndam, Capital		1,333
Burke, Capital		1,333
Kohlrus, Capital		1,334

Bonus to a New Partner Now let's assume that the existing partners, Wyndam, Burke, and Kohlrus, decide to admit Logsdon to a one-third interest for the $114,000 in cash because he has unique technical abilities that can improve the quality and sales of their product. Logsdon's one-third equity in the new firm is $133,333 [($286,000 + 114,000)/3] and the $19,333 difference between his $114,000 contribution and the $133,333 credited to his capital account comes from a reduction in the amounts of the original partners' capital accounts. Since Wyndam, Burke, and Kohlrus share profits and losses equally, each reduces his or her capital accounts by $6,444 in order to increase Logsdon's capital account to $133,333:

Cash	114,000	
Wyndam, Capital	6,444	
Burke, Capital	6,444	
Kohlrus, Capital	6,445	
Logsdon, Capital		133,333

Withdrawal of a Partner

Recall that when the partnership uses its assets to pay for a withdrawing partner's interest, the amount may equal, exceed, or be less than the balance in the partner's capital account. When the partner receives the same amount as the balance in his or her capital account, the other partners' capital accounts are not affected. Let's assume that it is now January 1, 2001, and Eric Burke wants to withdraw from the partnership when the balances in the partnership accounts are as follows: Wyndam, Capital, $150,000; Burke, Capital, $82,000; Kohlrus, Capital, $165,000; and Logsdon, Capital, $188,000. Since Burke's capital account balance is $82,000 and the partnership is paying him $82,000, the following journal entry is needed:

Burke, Capital	82,000	
Cash		82,000

When a partner receives more than the amount reflected in his or her capital account, the difference reduces the remaining partners' capital accounts in accordance with the terms of the partnership agreement. On the other hand, if the partner receives less than the amount in his or her partnership account, the remaining partners' capital accounts are increased in accordance with the terms of their partnership agreement. In this case, we assume that Burke leaves the firm with $76,000 and, therefore, each remaining partner's account is increased by $2,000:

Burke, Capital	82,000	
Wyndam, Capital		2,000
Kohlrus, Capital		2,000
Logsdon, Capital		2,000
Cash		76,000

Revaluation of Assets before the Admission or Withdrawal of a Partner

In Chapter 17 we discussed why partnerships should revalue the firm's assets before a new partner is admitted or an existing partner withdraws. The entry below describes how assets are revalued. Let's assume that Banner Company has an accounts receivable balance of $6,000 and inventory carried at $8,000. The market values of these accounts are $5,000 and $15,000, respectively. The changes in the assets (increase in inventory of $7,000 and decrease in accounts receivable of $1,000) are shared by the partners in accordance with the profit and loss agreement of the partnership. In this case, Banner's partners share the profits and losses equally and, therefore, each partner's capital account increases $1,500 ($6,000 reduction in assets/4 partners) as shown below:

Inventory	7,000	
Accounts Receivable		1,000
Wyndam, Capital		1,500
Burke, Capital		1,500
Kohlrus, Capital		1,500
Logsdon, Capital		1,500

CORPORATIONS

Now we turn to the corporate ownership structure and its related ownership accounts. For corporations, unlike sole proprietorships and partnerships, the accounting system makes a distinction between the two principal sources of ownership funds: the contributions made by the stockholders in exchange for an ownership interest and the reinvested earnings of the firm. The capital contributed by the stockholders (owners) is recorded in the appropriate capital stock and related accounts, while the net income, net losses, and dividends are summarized in the Retained Earnings account.

Why does corporate accounting segregate the contributions made by stockholders from the undistributed earnings of the firm? Because corporations are separate legal entities and corporate stockholders have limited liability; creditors can satisfy their claims only with the corporation's assets. As a result, creditors need to know whether a distribution of corporate assets to stockholders is a *return on investment* or a *return of investment*. A return of investment for stockholders may impair creditors' claims to the corporation's assets. The distinction between contributions and reinvested earnings allows creditors to determine if distributions to the stockholders are made from the corporation's earnings (a return on investment) or whether they are a return of the stockholders' investment.

HOW TO ACCOUNT FOR CAPITAL CONTRIBUTED TO THE CORPORATION

LO 2

Recall that one of the strengths of the corporate form of business is its ability to raise large sums of money. It has such ability because its ownership structure allows a large number of people to acquire an ownership interest in the corporation for a relatively small amount of money. Investment in corporations is possible without putting the investor's personal assets (other than the amount invested) at risk if the corporation fails. Cash and other resources given by stockholders and others to the corporation are classified as contributed capital. We will now describe how to record the issuance of stock by a corporation by using Stone Container Corporation as an example.

Howard Schultz, President and CEO of Starbucks Coffee.

Accounting for Par Value Stock

As discussed in Chapter 17, the par value of stock represents the minimum issue price of the stock. When accounting for par value stock, the amount of the par value is credited to the capital stock account *regardless* of the amount paid for the shares. The total par value of the stock issued provides financial statement users with information about the amount of the corporation's legal capital.

Stock Issued above Par   Stone Container is authorized by its charter to issue 200 million shares of $0.01 par value common stock. Therefore, if an investor pays Stone Container $12 per share for 1,000 shares of its common stock, the Common Stock account is credited for $10 (1,000 shares × 0.01 par value per share). The remaining $11,990 ($12,000 – $10) is credited to an account called *Paid-in Capital in Excess of Par,* which represents the amount by which the market price of the stock exceeds the legal minimum price. The entry for this equity financing event is:

Cash	12,000	
Common Stock		10
Paid-in Capital in Excess of Par—Common Stock		11,990

Accounting for No-Par Stock

Since no-par stock does not have a minimum legal issue price for each share, the amount credited to the capital stock account is the amount received for the shares. To illustrate the difference in accounting for no-par-value stock and par value stock, we will account for the issuance of 1,000 shares of Stone Container's no-par-value common stock for $12 each. The entry below reflects this event:

Cash	12,000	
Common Stock		12,000

Notice that in both the par value and no-par cases, the $12,000 received by the corporation is credited to capital stock accounts. In the case of no-par stock, however, there is no Paid-in Capital in Excess of Par account because the shares do not have par values.

Accounting for No-Par Stated Value Stock

When a corporation is authorized to issue no-par stated value stock, the amount credited to the capital stock account is the amount of the stated value, regardless of the amount of money received at the time of the sale of stock. Entries for the issuance of no-par stated value stock are the same as par value stock, except that the Paid-in Capital in Excess of Stated Value account is used instead of the Paid-in Capital in Excess of Par account.

Noncash Stock Issue

Often corporations issue shares of stock, either in exchange for assets other than cash or in payment for services rendered. This raises the question of how to determine the dollar value of such a transaction.

When the transaction does not involve cash, the fair market value of the stock issued or of the goods or services received, whichever is more readily determinable, provides the cash equivalent amount. To illustrate, suppose that Stone Container issued 20,000 shares of its $0.01 par value common stock in exchange for equipment having a fair market value of $240,000. The entry to reflect this event is:

Equipment	240,000	
Common Stock (20,000 × $0.01)		200
Paid-in Capital in Excess of Par—Common Stock		239,800

If Stone Container could not determine the fair market value of the equipment, it would record the transaction using the fair market value of the shares of stock issued. Occasionally, the fair market value of the asset or stock is not determinable. When this occurs, the corporation records the transaction using either an appraised value of the asset or an amount set by the board of directors.

PAUSE &

REFLECT

What is a company's incentive to overvalue a noncash stock transaction? Is there an incentive to undervalue a noncash stock transaction? *(answer on page 668)*

Donated Capital

Corporations sometimes receive assets from government units without issuing common or preferred stock. For example, in 1995 Cessna Corporation received a $21 million financial package that included cash, land, buildings, and tax abatements from the city of Independence, Kansas, in exchange for locating a large manufacturing plant there that would employ 1,000 people. As a result of this situation, Cessna would record only the tangible assets it received as donated capital, as follows:

Cash	5,000,000	
Land	500,000	
Building	6,000,000	
Donated Capital		11,500,000

The **Donated Capital** account reflects the dollar value of the assets given by governmental units to a corporation that increases the contributed capital of the corporation's stockholders' equity but does not change the number of shares or shareholders.

PAUSE & REFLECT

Tax abatements certainly have economic value to Cessna. Why aren't they included in Donated Capital? *(answer on page 668)*

ACCOUNTING FOR CORPORATE EARNINGS

LO 3

The cash and assets a corporation accumulates by the issuance of stock and receipt of donations are invested in the corporation with the expectation of generating a return. The net income from corporate operations represents the return for the corporation's stockholders. The accumulation and disposition of these corporate earnings is accounted for independently from the contributions of its owners. Corporate management can elect to distribute the corporate earnings to the owners in the form of dividends, to reinvest the earnings, or to provide some combination of the two events. The following section describes how corporations account for their earnings.

Retained Earnings

Retained earnings, or the amount of a corporation's earnings since its inception less all dividends distributed, appears on the balance sheet as part of the corporation's stockholders' equity. The account normally has a credit balance because the amount of net income usually exceeds the combined amount of net losses and dividends that would reduce the balance in the account. A credit balance in the Retained Earnings account represents the amount of earnings reinvested in the corporation rather than distributed to the stockholders as dividends.

When the cumulative total of net losses plus dividends declared exceeds the cumulative total of net income, the Retained Earnings account will have a debit balance, which is referred to as a **deficit in retained earnings.** A deficit balance indicates that some portion of the stockholders' contributed capital was lost in the firm's attempt to generate income. Exhibit 19.3 shows the accumulated deficit in the stockholders' equity section of the balance sheet of Stone Container Corporation.

EXHIBIT 19.3	Stone Container's Deficit in Retained Earnings

Stockholders' equity:		
Series E preferred stock	115.0	115.0
Common stock (99.3 shares outstanding)	966.3	954.8
Accumulated deficit	(510.8)	(94.2)
Foreign currency translation adjustment	(293.3)	(178.8)
Unamortized expense of restricted stock plan	(.3)	(1.6)
Total stockholders' equity	276.9	795.2
Total liabilities and stockholders' equity	$ 5,824.1	$ 6,353.8

The accompanying notes are an integral part of these statements.

How Does Net Income and Net Loss Change Retained Earnings? When a company generates net income, the firm has increased its net assets and the stockholders' interest in the firm as a result of its ongoing operations. To illustrate this and the other equity events that impact the Retained Earnings account, we will use the Cavanaugh Cardboard Corporation. We show closing entries for Cavanaugh Cardboard Corporation as of December 31, 1999, below:

a. Sales	975,000	
Income Summary		975,000
b. Income Summary	625,000	
Cost of Goods Sold		300,000
Operating Expenses		325,000
c. Income Summary	350,000	
Retained Earnings		350,000[3]

Income Summary		Retained Earnings	
	(a) 975,000		500,000
(b) 625,000			(c) 350,000
	Bal. 350,000		Bal. 850,000
(c) 350,000			
	Bal. –0–		

How Do Dividends Change Retained Earnings? Chapter 17 described the four important dates associated with the payment of corporate dividends:

• Date of declaration

• Ex-dividend date

• Date of record

• Date of payment

Accounting entries are made only on the date of declaration and the date of payment.

Recall that on the *date of declaration,* the board of directors announces (1) the amount of the dividend, (2) the date on which investors must officially own the stock [the *date of record*] in order to receive the declared dividend, and (3) the date when the dividend will be paid [the *date of payment*]. Stockholders must acquire the stock two or three days before the date of record on the *ex-dividend date* to ensure that their ownership is duly recorded by the corporation on the date of record.

A typical dividend announcement might read as follows: "At the regular meeting of the board of directors of Cavanaugh Cardboard Corporation, on June 1, 1999, a quarterly dividend of $0.50 per share was declared payable on June 25, 1999, to the stockholders of record on June 15, 1999." Notice that the announcement specified the important dates as well as the amount of the dividend per share. If more than one class of stock is outstanding, the announcement would specify the dividend per share for each class of stock.

---

[3]When the expenses and losses exceed the amount of revenues and gains, the Income Summary account will have a debit balance, which, when transferred to the Retained Earnings account, represents a decrease in the shareholders' interest in the firm's assets resulting from the firm's ongoing operations.

For example, assume that Cavanaugh Cardboard Corporation had 150,000 shares of $1 par common stock outstanding and its board of directors declared a $0.50 per share dividend on June 1 to stockholders of record on June 15, payable on June 25. Cavanaugh would record the following entries for the declaration and payment of this $75,000 dividend (150,000 shares of common stock × $0.50 per share):

Date of Declaration

June 1	Retained Earnings	75,000	
	Dividends Payable		75,000

Ex-Dividend Date

June 12	No entry necessary. If stock is purchased after this date, the investor buying the stock will not receive the dividend.

Date of Record

June 15	No entry necessary. Those stockholders whose names appear in the stock transfer records on this date will receive the dividend.

Date of Payment

June 25	Dividends Payable	75,000	
	Cash		75,000

Once the declaration is made, the corporation incurs and records a liability in the amount of the dividends declared. Since the earnings of the corporation for each accounting period are accumulated in the Retained Earnings account through the closing entries, the distribution of those earnings reduces Retained Earnings:

Retained Earnings			
		500,000	Beginning bal.
Dividend, 6/1	75,000		
		350,000	Net income, 12/31
		775,000	Ending bal.

A corporation with preferred and common stock must determine the amount of dividends that owners of each class of stock will receive when it declares the dividends. Keep in mind that the amount of dividends that each class of stockholders receives does not necessitate changing the entries to record the events.

Stock Dividends

If a company's board of directors declares a dividend that is settled by issuing the corporation's own stock rather than cash, it has declared a stock dividend. Recall from Chapter 17 that stock dividends are issued to satisfy stockholders without distributing cash that may be needed in the business.

"Small" Stock Dividends   If the additional number of shares to be issued in settlement of the stock dividend is small, usually 20 to 25 percent or less of the shares issued, the amount debited to Retained Earnings as a dividend is the fair market value of the stock multiplied by the number of new shares issued. The fair market value is used because it approximates the value of the transaction to the stockholders. If Cavanaugh Cardboard Corporation, with 150,000 shares of $1 par value common stock issued, declared a 10 percent stock dividend, it would issue an additional 15,000 shares of stock. The amount of the debit to Retained Earnings would depend on the fair market value of the stock on the date of declaration. The amount credited to the **Stock Dividends Distributable** account on the date of declaration is the par value of the shares the corporation will issue on the date of payment. Any excess of the market price over par value is credited to Paid-in Capital in Excess of Par. If the fair market value of the stock on the date of declaration is $32 per share, the company would make the following entry:

Retained Earnings ($32 × 15,000 shares)	480,000	
Stock Dividends Distributable ($1 par × 15,000)		15,000
Paid-in Capital in Excess of Par—Common		465,000

Stock Dividends Distributable is not a liability account because *a stock dividend does not involve the distribution of the firm's assets*. Rather, it is a contributed capital account because the company will issue the new shares of common stock on the date of payment. The entry below shows how to record the distribution of the additional shares:

Stock Dividends Distributable	15,000	
Common Stock		15,000

"Large" Stock Dividends   A large stock dividend, one that is greater than 25 percent of the number of shares issued, requires the use of the par value rather than the market value of the stock to value the transaction. Using par value as opposed to market value is done for two reasons. First, the issuance of such a large number of additional shares usually reduces the market value of the stock and makes it difficult to determine the appropriate market price. Second, the total market value of such a large number of shares might reduce retained earnings to such an extent that it could impair the future dividend-paying ability of the firm.

To illustrate, assume that Cavanaugh Cardboard declared a 50 percent stock dividend; $75,000 of retained earnings would be transferred to common stock—that is, 75,000 new shares of common stock (150,000 × 0.50) multiplied by the $1 par value of common stock. The company would record the same sequence of entries it used for the small stock dividends excluding the Paid-in Capital in Excess of Par account. Note that if we had used even half of the market value of the stock to value the transaction (75,000 × $16 = $1,200,000), the balance in Cavanaugh's retained earnings would become a debit balance and eliminate the firm's ability to declare any dividends.

Stock dividends are called *interequity transactions* because the amount of the dividend is taken from one stockholders' equity account, Retained Earnings, and transferred into the Common Stock and Paid-in Capital in Excess of Par accounts of the contributed capital section of stockholders' equity.

HOW TO ACCOUNT FOR ADDITIONAL EQUITY EVENTS   LO 4

The following section discusses two equity events that are common to corporations. Treasury stock transactions and stock splits both affect stockholders' equity but do not fit into either the contributed capital or retained earnings categories discussed thus far.

Treasury Stock

Recall from Chapter 17 that treasury stock is a company's own stock reacquired with the intent of issuing it again at a later date. It should not be confused with a corporation's authorized but unissued shares or with investments in the stock of other companies.

Regardless of the reason a corporation buys its own stock, treasury stock is not an asset to the corporation. Rather, treasury stock represents the amount paid to liquidate one or more stockholders' interest in the corporation. The debit balance of the Treasury Stock account is reported as a contra equity account that reduces total stockholders' equity on a company's balance sheet.

Although transactions involving treasury stock affect stockholders' equity, these transactions cannot result in a gain or loss on the income statement because treasury stock is not an asset of the company. Because the company purchases its shares of stock with the intent of issuing them again at a later date, the shares are still considered issued but no longer outstanding. There are no cash dividends paid on treasury shares.

Purchase of Treasury Stock   When a firm purchases its own shares in the open market, the company debits the Treasury Stock account for the cost of those shares. For example, if Cavanaugh Cardboard purchased 100 shares of its own $1 par common stock for cash at $35 per share, the entry is:

Treasury Stock	3,500	
Cash		3,500

Exhibit 19.4 shows how to report treasury stock on Cavanaugh Cardboard Corporation's balance sheet. (Exhibit 17.5 shows how Ben & Jerry's reports its treasury stock.) Observe that the presentation of information about treasury stock contains the number of shares of treasury stock (100) and that the difference between the number of shares issued (150,000) and outstanding (149,900) is the number of treasury shares. Also note that the entire cost of the treasury shares is subtracted from total stockholders' equity.

EXHIBIT	19.4	Balance Sheet Presentation of Treasury Stock

CAVANAUGH CARDBOARD CORPORATION
Partial Balance Sheet
December 31, 1999

Stockholders' Equity

Common stock—$1 par value, 500,000 shares authorized, 150,000 shares issued, 149,900 shares outstanding	$ 150,000
Paid-in capital in excess of par—common	593,000
Total paid-in capital	$ 743,000
Retained earnings	438,000
Total stockholders' equity before treasury stock	$1,181,000
Less treasury stock (100 shares)	(3,500)
Total stockholders' equity	$1,177,500

Reissue of Treasury Stock　Assume that some time after the purchase of those 100 shares of treasury stock, Cavanaugh Cardboard sells 50 shares at $38 per share. Because Treasury Stock is a stockholders' equity account and is not an asset, the difference between the sales price ($38) and the purchase price ($35) is recorded in a contributed capital account rather than being recognized as a gain. **Paid-in Capital from Treasury Stock Transactions** is the account used to show the additional capital generated from the reissue of treasury stock:

Cash (50 shares × $38)	1,900	
Treasury Stock (50 shares × $35)		1,750
Paid-in Capital from Treasury Stock Transactions		150

On the balance sheet, the Paid-in Capital from Treasury Stock Transactions account is included with the other Paid-in Capital accounts.

When treasury stock is reissued at a price below its initial cost, then the difference between the market price and the initial cost is debited to the Paid-in Capital from Treasury Stock Transactions account. If the Paid-in Capital from Treasury Stock Transactions account has no balance, or if the balance is insufficient to offset the entire amount of the difference between the cost and the smaller reissue price, then it is necessary to subtract the remainder of the difference from Retained Earnings. For example, if the remaining 50 shares of Cavanaugh Cardboard's treasury stock were sold for $27 per share, the entry to record this transaction would be:

Cash (50 shares × $27)	1,350	
Paid-in Capital from Treasury Stock Transactions	150	
Retained Earnings	250	
Treasury Stock (50 shares × $35)		1,750

By reducing Retained Earnings rather than a contributed capital account, the corporation reduces its dividend-paying ability rather than the initial contributions of the owners. By maintaining the corporation's initial contributed capital and, instead, reducing the amount of stockholders' equity available for distribution as dividends, creditors' interest in the firm is protected.

Stock brokers typically view a stock split as a positive event and notify their clients when stock splits occur.

Stock Splits

Chapter 17 indicated that a stock split occurs when a corporation calls in all the shares issued, reduces the par value of the shares, and issues a larger number of new shares in their place. For example, if Stone Container's board of directors approved a two-for-one split, it would call in the old $0.01 par value shares and replace them with twice as many $0.005 par value shares.

PAUSE & REFLECT

In some cases corporations will issue a reverse stock split—that is, reduce the number of shares issued and outstanding by some multiple. Why would a company declare a reverse stock split? *(answer on page 668)*

Although a stock split, like a stock dividend, does not change the total amount of stockholders' equity, there is a difference in accounting for these two events. Recall that stock splits, unlike stock dividends, which are interequity transactions, do not change the balance in any stockholders' equity account; they merely change the par value of the stock and increase the number of shares authorized, issued, and outstanding. Therefore, no formal accounting entry is required.

HOW ARE CORPORATE EQUITY EVENTS REPORTED?

LO 5

Reporting on the status of a corporation's stockholders' equity is more involved than reporting on the same type of transactions for a sole proprietorship or partnership because a corporation has a wider variety of accounts. The information is relatively easy to organize if you keep in mind the two distinct parts of a corporation's stockholders' equity: contributed capital and retained earnings.

To illustrate how to report the equity events of a corporation, let's assume that Creative Paper Corporation is authorized to issue 50,000 shares of preferred and 200,000 shares of common stock. The preferred stock has a $50 par value, and the common stock is no par.

On January 1, 1999, Creative Paper Corporation has a balance in its Retained Earnings account of $1,575,000. Using this information, Exhibit 19.5 shows the statement of retained earnings and the stockholders' equity section of Creative Paper Corporation's balance sheet for 1999. We examine each of these statements next.

EXHIBIT 19.5 Retained Earnings and Stockholders' Equity

CREATIVE PAPER CORPORATION
Statement of Retained Earnings
For the Year Ended December 31, 1999

Retained earnings, 1/1/99		$1,575,000
Add net income		190,000
Less: Preferred stock dividends	$85,000	
Common stock dividends	35,000	(120,000)
Retained earnings, 12/31/99		$1,645,000

CREATIVE PAPER CORPORATION
Stockholders' Equity Section of Balance Sheet
December 31, 1999

Preferred stock—10%, $50 par value, 50,000 shares authorized, 17,000 shares issued and outstanding	$ 850,000	
Paid-in capital in excess of par—preferred stock	83,000	
Total paid-in capital—preferred stock		$ 933,000
Common stock—no par, 200,000 shares authorized, 132,000 shares issued, and 125,000 shares outstanding		990,000
Paid-in capital from treasury stock transactions		15,000
Donated capital—land		250,000
Total contributed capital		$2,188,000
Retained earnings		1,645,000
Total stockholders' equity before treasury stock		$3,833,000
Less treasury stock (common stock), 7,000 shares		(70,000)
Total stockholders' equity		$3,763,000

Statement of Retained Earnings

We know that the statement of retained earnings shows the effects of operating performance and dividend policy on the stockholders' interest in the corporation. For Creative Paper Corporation, the statement in Exhibit 19.5 reveals that, of the $190,000 of net income generated by the corporation, there was a distribution of dividends of $85,000 to the preferred stockholders and $35,000 to the common stockholders, with $70,000 of net income reinvested in the firm.

This information allows stockholders and other interested parties to evaluate corporate management's policy on reinvesting the earnings of the firm. Is corporate management's dividend policy appropriate, or should the corporation reinvest more or less of the firm's earnings? The ending balance on the statement of retained earnings, $1,645,000, is the amount of retained earnings reported in the stockholders' equity section of Creative Paper Corporation's balance sheet.

Stockholders' Equity

The contributed capital section of Creative Paper's stockholders' equity section reports the dollar amount of resources contributed to the corporation. Typically, an ownership interest is given in exchange for the contribution, but contributed capital also can include donations from governmental entities.

Creative Paper's stockholders' equity section in Exhibit 19.5 reports that it has issued 17,000 of the 50,000 shares of the authorized preferred stock and in exchange received $933,000 in assets. The $933,000 is a combination of the par value of the 17,000 shares issued, $850,000, and the Paid-in Capital in Excess of Par, $83,000. In addition, Creative Paper raised $990,000 by issuing 132,000 shares of its 200,000 authorized shares. However, only 125,000 shares of common stock are outstanding because 7,000 shares of common stock are held by Creative Paper as treasury stock.

The $15,000 of Paid-in Capital from Treasury Stock Transactions means that Creative Paper increased its assets by selling treasury stock for a price greater than the price paid to reacquire it. The Donated Capital—Land account reflects the market

On May 10, 1998 Stone Container (Stone) and Jefferson Smurfit Corporation (JSC) jointly announced they had signed a merger agreement and on November 18, 1998 the merger was consummated. The new company is called Smurfit-Stone Container Corporation and is listed on the NASDAQ exchange under the symbol SSCC. The companies felt the merger would accomplish the following:

1. Create one of the world's premier manufacturers of paperboard and paper-based packaging.

2. Serve as a catalyst to focus the product strategy of JSC and Stone.

3. Enable the companies to reduce debt through divestitures of non-core businesses and assets.

4. Enable the companies to provide their customers with better service and a broader range of paperboard and paper-based packaging products.

5. Create opportunities for significant synergies and cost reductions through the integration of the two companies' operations.*

One of the key factors motivating the merger was Stone Container's high leverage and inability to cover the interest on its debt. Stone's income for fiscal year 1997 and for the first six months of 1998 was insufficient to cover the interest on its debt:

Stone's dilemma began in 1989 when it made a strategic decision to expand its operations and to use debt rather than equity to finance the expansion. In 1988 Stone Container reported $765.1 million in long-term debt, stockholders' equity of $1,063.60 million, and had a debt to equity ratio of 1.25. By 1989 Stone had long-term debt of $3,536.9 million, stockholders' equity of $1,347.6 million, and a debt to equity ratio of 3.64. From 1989 to 1997 Stone's earning before interest and taxes were able to cover interest expense in only three of the nine years. By 1997 Stone's had long-term debt of $3,935.5 million, stockholders' equity had dropped to $276.9 million, and the debt to equity ratio was 20.

Both JSC and Stone are highly levered but believe that Smurfit-Stone Container Corporation's leverage will improve for two reasons. First, the company expects to sell some non-core businesses and assets and use the proceeds to reduce long-term debt. Second, they expect Smurfit-Stone to be more profitable because it will provide better products and services to its customers and reduce its operating cost by integrating the two firms' operations. The increased profitability should generate greater operating cash flows and improve the firm's ability to service its debt or retire more debt.

*Joint Proxy Statement/Prospectus, Jefferson Smurfit Corporation and Stone Container Corporation, Oct 8, 1998, page 24.

---

value of the land that Creative Paper received in exchange for locating a manufacturing plant in a particular city. Total contributed capital summarizes the dollar amount of the assets raised by Creative Paper in exchange for an ownership interest or other considerations.

The contributed capital and the retained earnings sections of stockholders' equity reflect the amount and source of stockholders' equity. Treasury stock, however, reduces the sum of total contributed capital and retained earnings because it represents the portion of total stockholders' equity that was liquidated with the repurchase of issued stock. While Creative Paper paid $70,000 to liquidate owners' interests in the corporation, it expects to reissue the treasury stock at a later date. However, until the company reissues the treasury stock, it will reflect the price paid as a contra equity account in the stockholders' equity section of the balance sheet.

Internal users, of course, have all of the information available to external users. In addition, management receives periodic reports from the company's stock agent outlining stock-related activity during the period.

Equity Events and the Cash Flow Statement

The statement of cash flows reports the impact equity events have on the firm's cash flows. The cash from net income is reported in the operating section of the statement, while all other equity events are reported in the financing section of the statement. To illustrate how equity events affect the cash flow statement, let's assume the following occurred during 1999:

Cash generated from Creative Paper Corporation's net income was $250,000.

The corporation purchased 10,000 shares of treasury stock for $10.

The corporation issued 20,000 shares of common stock for $240,000.

The corporation sold 3,000 shares of treasury stock for $12 per share.

The corporation declared and paid $85,000 in cash dividends to preferred stockholders and $35,000 in cash dividends to common stockholders.

The partial cash flow statement for Creative Paper in Exhibit 19.6 illustrates how these equity events are reported.

EXHIBIT 19.6	Creative Paper Corporation, Partial Cash Flow Statement

CREATIVE PAPER CORPORATION
Partial Cash Flow Statement
For the Year Ended December 31, 1999

Cash flows from operating activities:		
Net Cash from Operating Activities		$250,000
Cash flows from financing activities:		
Purchase of treasury stock	$(100,000)	
Initial issue of common stock	240,000	
Sale of treasury stock	36,000	
Dividends paid	(120,000)	
Cash flow from equity financing activities		56,000

PAUSE & REFLECT

Can you identify the cash flows from equity financing activities in Stone Container's statement of cash flows in Exhibit 19.7? (answer on page 668)

EXHIBIT 19.7	Stone Container's December 31, 1997, Partial Cash Flow Statement

Cash flows from financing activities			
Debt repayments	(475.6)	(376.2)	(826.3)
Payments by consolidated affiliates on non-recourse debt	(16.1)	(18.9)	(146.1)
Borrowings	931.6	587.7	515.8
Non-recourse borrowings of consolidated affiliates	.1	2.6	4.2
Proceeds from issuance of common stock	.1	.4	1.7
Cash dividends	(2.0)	(67.6)	(41.5)
Net cash provided by (used in) financing activities	438.1	128.0	(492.2)

SUMMARY

This chapter discusses how the accounting system captures and reports the changes in the ownership interest of a business enterprise. The accounting treatment reflects the respective characteristics of the sole proprietorship, partnership, and corporate forms of ownership. Sole proprietorships and partnerships use simple capital accounts to show their owners' interest because the organizations are not separate legal entities from the owners. The accounting treatment of a corporation's owners' equity reflects that it is a separate legal entity and that its owners have limited liability.

- Accounting for sole proprietorships and partnerships requires a permanent balance sheet account called the owner's capital account. A withdrawal by an owner represents a reduction in an owner's capital account and is not an expense of the business entity.

- A statement of owner's capital and the statement of partners' capital summarize and reflect the changes in the owners' capital accounts during the year.

- A new partner can buy an interest in the firm from a partner or make a direct investment in the firm in exchange for an ownership interest. In either case, the existing partners must approve the admission of the new partner.

- The stockholders' equity section of a corporation's balance sheet is divided into contributed capital and retained earnings sections. This allows creditors to determine whether any dividends paid are a distribution of earnings or a return of stockholders' contributions, which would place the owners' claims ahead of the creditors.

- Par value represents the minimum issue price of corporate stock, and any amount paid in excess of the par value is accounted for in the Paid-in Capital in Excess of Par account.

- Stock that is issued for noncash assets is valued at the fair market value of the asset or the stock, whichever is more reasonably determinable.

- Retained earnings typically represent the amount of earnings reinvested in the corporation. When the Retained Earnings account has a debit balance, it is referred to as a deficit in retained earnings.

- Dividends are usually either cash or stock dividends. Cash dividends reduce the assets of the firm as well as the amount of retained earnings. Stock dividends do not change the amount of total stockholders' equity because they increase contributed capital and reduce retained earnings. For this reason, stock dividends are called interequity transactions.

- The Treasury Stock account is considered a contra equity account and is reported as a reduction of total stockholders' equity. When a company reissues treasury stock, the difference between the initial cost paid to acquire the stock and the reissue price will either increase or decrease stockholders' equity.

- Stock splits reduce the par value of stock and increase the number of authorized, issued, and outstanding shares of stock. However, stock splits do not change the amount of contributed capital or retained earnings in stockholders' equity.

- The status of a corporation's stockholders' equity is reported in two sections of the balance sheet. Contributed capital reflects the type and amount of stock and the assets received from the issue of stock and donations by governmental units. The retained earnings section of the balance sheet describes the stockholders' claims to the firm's reinvested earnings.

KEY TERMS

deficit in retained earnings A negative or debit balance in the Retained Earnings account created when the cumulative total of net losses plus dividends declared exceeds the cumulative total of net income

Donated Capital An account that reflects the dollar value of the assets given by a governmental unit to a corporation that increases the contributed capital of the corporation's stockholders' equity but does not change the number of shares or shareholders

drawing account A contra equity account used in proprietorship and partnership accounting to summarize the dollar amount of assets withdrawn from the business entity for personal use

Paid-in Capital from Treasury Stock Transactions An account used to show the amount of additional capital generated from the reissue of treasury stock

statement of partners' capital A financial statement that presents the changes in the individual partners' capital balances that result from additional contributions, the firm's income or loss, and the partners' withdrawals from the firm over a specific period of time

Stock Dividends Distributable An account credited on the date of declaration of a stock dividend to show the par value of the shares the corporation will issue on the date of distribution

p. 657, When a corporation overvalues the assets in a noncash stock transaction it has issued *watered stock.* This overstates the value of the assets and the financial position of the stockholders.

A corporation creates *secret reserves* when it undervalues the assets in a noncash stock transaction. This understates the value of the assets and the financial position of the stockholders and creates a unreported buffer against negative effects of poor corporate performance.

Both watered stock and secret reserves are not appropriate because both distort the financial position of the corporation.

p. 658, By making no entry, the benefits of tax abatements are realized in the year the taxes are not paid or when they are realized. In the year the taxes are forgiven, net income is higher by the amount of the taxes not paid.

Those who argue that this future benefit should be recognized as an asset when the abatement is granted would make the following entry:

Tax Abatement	9,500,000	
Contributed Capital		9,500,000

The consumption of the benefit over the life of the abatement would create an expense that would lower net income in the years the tax abatement was granted:

Amortization Expense—Tax Abatement	950,000	
Tax Abatement		950,000

p. 659, While Kroger's stockholders have the right to vote and, therefore, to select the management team to run the corporation, they do not have an equity position financially because the firm's assets are less than the liabilities of the firm. At this point, only the creditors have a claim to Kroger's assets. However, because the firm is able to service the debt, the creditors cannot foreclose their debt and must allow the management selected by the board of directors (who are elected by the shareholders) to operate the company.

p. 663, In some cases, reverse stock splits are used to increase the price of the stock in the secondary market by reducing the number of shares of a company in the market. Management can also use a reverse stock split to take over a company. The Metropolitan Maintenance Co. used a 1-for-3,000 reverse stock split for such a takeover. The company issued one share of stock for every 3,000 shares held and cash was paid to those shareholders who did not have 3,000 shares. It was no coincidence that the only people with more than 3,000 shares were two of Metropolitan's top officers (*Forbes,* November 19, 1984, p. 54).

p. 666, In 1997, Stone Container raised $100,000 by issuing common stock and paid $2 million in dividends.

QUESTIONS

1. What accounting treatments are common to accounting for both sole proprietorships and partnerships?

2. What is the purpose of a drawing account in accounting for a sole proprietorship and a partnership? Why is the drawing account not an expense item used to determine net income?

3. What is the difference between the owners' equity sections of the balance sheets of sole proprietorships and partnerships?

4. Why don't sole proprietorships have an account for how much the owner has contributed and another for how much the company has earned and reinvested in the company?

5. What are the events that can make a sole proprietor's capital account increase? Decrease?

6. What are the events that can make a partner's capital account increase? Decrease?

7. When a partner withdraws from a firm, what are the alternatives for compensating the withdrawing partner for his or her interest in the company?

8. If an outside party directly buys the interest of a partner with the consent of all partners, is the price paid for the partnership interest included in the entry to record the admission of the new partner? Why?

9. If a partner withdraws from a partnership and is paid with partnership assets more or less than the balance in his or her partnership account, how is the difference accounted for in the partnership's accounting records?

10. How does a sole proprietor or a partner determine how much of his or her earnings have been reinvested in the business since the firm has started? How does a stockholder determine the earnings his or her corporation has reinvested?

11. Why is the par value rather than the market value recorded in a stock account?

12. How do journal entries reflect the market value of par value stock when the stock is first issued?

13. What distinguishes par value from no-par stock in the stockholders' equity section of the balance sheet?

14. Explain the basis for determining the issue price of shares of stock when the stock is exchanged for a noncash asset.

15. What event does the Donated Capital account represent?

16. What is the purpose of the Retained Earnings account, and what business events cause it to change during the year?

17. Why would a company buy treasury stock? How is it reported on a firm's financial statements?

18. What does the Paid-in Capital from Treasury Stock Transactions account represent? How is it reported on a firm's financial statements?

19. Explain the difference between a 100 percent stock dividend and a two-for-one stock split.

20. What does a deficit in Retained Earnings represent?

EXERCISES

E 19.1
LO 1

Harley Pottrof started his business in January 2000 with a contribution of $90,000 cash and a building he had recently purchased for $155,000. In August 2000, he withdrew $22,000 from the business's Cash account for his personal use. On December 31, 2000, his business had revenues of $300,000 and expenses of $192,000. Make the journal entries to record the following:
  a. His initial contributions
  b. His cash withdrawal
  c. The closing entries at December 31

E 19.2
LO 1

Given the information in E 19.1, prepare a statement of owner's equity for Harley Pottrof for his first year of business.

E 19.3
LO 1

Jeff Stanley and Craig Bezdek were both operating consulting services as sole proprietors when they decided to merge their businesses and form a partnership. Listed below are the balance sheets for both sole proprietorships before the merger as well as the current market value of the respective assets of the two businesses. Make the entry required to establish the partnership, given this information.

STANLEY CONSULTING

	Cost	Market
Cash	$10,000	
Accounts receivable	30,000	$ 28,000
Office equipment	60,000	56,000
Accounts payable	30,000	
Stanley, capital	70,000	

BEZDEK CONSULTING SERVICES

	Cost	Market
Cash	$ 7,000	
Accounts receivable	13,000	$ 12,500
Building	90,000	124,000
Accounts payable	40,000	
Bezdek, capital	70,000	

E 19.4
LO 1

Holly Elliott and Sally Larson are partners and have just completed their first year of business as Tescott Company. Their agreement is to divide profits and losses equally. The revenue and expense accounts have been closed, and the accounting records contain the accounts and balances shown below. Using these data, make the entries to complete the closing process.

	Debit	Credit
Revenues		$ 347,000
Expenses	$96,000	
Elliott, capital		297,000
Elliott, drawings	81,000	
Larson, capital		198,000
Larson, drawings	64,000	

E 19.5
LO 1

The partnership of Sloan, Traxel, and Ruble specifies a division of profits in a ratio of their respective capital balances at the start of the period. These balances are as follows:

Sloan	$56,400
Traxel	92,000
Ruble	48,000

Prepare the journal entry to close the Income Summary account if that account has (a) a credit balance of $125,000 and (b) a debit balance of $26,400.

E 19.6
LO 1

Supply the missing figure for each of the partners below.

Partner 1	
Partner 1's capital at the beginning of the year	$_____
Partner 1's capital at the end of the year	122,670
Partner 1's share of income for the year	58,000
Partner 1's drawings during the year	36,700
Partner 2	
Partner 2's capital at the beginning of the year	$ 97,480
Partner 2's capital at the end of the year	77,410
Partner 2's share of income for year	_____
Partner 2's drawings during the year	52,900
Partner 3	
Partner 3's capital at the beginning of the year	$108,600
Partner 3's capital at the end of the year	109,210
Partner 3's share of income for the year	39,240
Partner 3's drawings during the year	_____

E 19.7
LO 1

In their partnership agreement, McGuire, Sosa, and Junior agreed that McGuire should receive a salary allowance of $15,000 per year and that Sosa should receive a salary allowance of $6,000. Any remainder is divided equally among the three partners. Prepare the journal entry to divide the following: (a) net income of $39,000, (b) net income of $14,000, and (c) net loss of $24,000.

E 19.8
LO 1

Jenika Hlasney, who is a partner in Nontrad Company, has decided to sell her ownership interest in the firm. The balance in her capital account is $850,000. With the consent of the other partners, she sells two-thirds of her interest to Lisa Trout, an incoming partner, for $600,000 and the remaining one-third to Jason Ryan, an existing partner, for $300,000. If no partnership assets were used to buy Hlasney out, prepare the journal entry to record the transfer of ownership interest.

E 19.9
LO 1

Lochmiller and Birck, each of whom has a partnership capital balance of $157,000, admit Reno to a one-third interest in the firm upon Reno's payment of $170,000 to the partnership. If Lochmiller and Birck share profits and losses equally, record the entry to reflect the admission of Reno to the partnership.

E 19.10
LO 1

The firm of Schmidt and Massoth decided to admit Darnell to the partnership. Darnell paid $120,000 cash for a one-third interest in the firm. At the time Schmidt had a capital balance of $110,000, and Massoth had a balance of $100,000. They shared profits and losses equally. Record the entry to reflect the admission of Darnell to the partnership.

E 19.11
LO 1

Dibbern was invited to join an existing partnership. She paid $260,000 to the firm for a one-fourth interest. At that time the other two existing partners' capital balances were Waterman, $336,000; and Duncan, $388,000. Waterman and Duncan shared profits in a ratio of 5:3, respectively. Prepare the journal entry to record the admission of Dibbern to the partnership.

E 19.12
LO 1

Tom Grafton and John Alberry decided to accept Tammy Grove into their partnership because she has an established reputation as an excellent salesperson in the community. She was admitted with a one-third interest for $63,000 cash. Grafton and Alberry had capital balances of $70,500 and $69,000, respectively, and shared profits equally. Show the journal entry required to reflect the admission of Grove to the firm.

E 19.13
LO 1

The partnership of Merick and Lichti needs additional financial resources, and they have asked Marcus to join their company. Immediately prior to Marcus's admission, they reviewed their accounting records, and all parties agreed to the following changes: revalue inventory, which was maintained on a LIFO basis, upward by $36,000 and increase the allowance for doubtful accounts by $3,500. Merick and Lichti share profits and losses on a 3:2 basis, respectively.

Prepare the entry to revalue the partnership assets before the admission of Marcus to the partnership. Why is revaluation necessary?

E 19.14
LO 1

Marjie Butel has a capital balance of $720,000 in a partnership. The other two partners in the business have capital balances as follows: Pat Parks, $880,000; and Gwen Ziegler, $810,000. Profits and losses are shared equally. Prepare the journal entry to record Butel's withdrawal from the firm under each of the following circumstances:
a. She sold one-half of her interest to each of the other two partners for $460,000 (not the firm's cash).
b. She was paid $796,000 cash from the partnership assets.
c. She was paid $640,000 cash from the partnership assets.

E 19.15
LO 2

Dorchester, Inc., is authorized to issue 1,000,000 shares of $1 par value common stock and 400,000 shares of $100 par preferred stock. Prepare the journal entries to record the sale of 23,000 shares of common stock at $17.50 and 250 shares of preferred stock at $103 per share.

E 19.16
LO 2

Zeandale Corporation issued 5,100 shares of its no-par common stock for $28 per share and 500 shares of its $50 par value preferred stock for $52.50 per share. Prepare the journal entry to record the sale of the stock.

E 19.17
LO 2

Murphy Company's no-par common stock has a stated value of $5 per share. Journalize the entries for the following sales of Murphy's stock:
a. 11,200 shares at $6.50 per share.
b. 17,000 shares for a total of $115,000.

E 19.18
LO 5

Ogallah, Inc., is authorized to issue 5,000,000 shares of no-par common stock and 800,000 shares of $30 par value preferred stock. During its first year of operation, the company issued 1,200,000 shares of common stock for a total amount of $20,400,000 and 250,000 shares of preferred stock for a total of $8,750,000. The firm has net income of $1,335,000 for the year, but it declared no dividends.

Prepare the stockholders' equity section of the balance sheet as it would appear after the first year's operation.

E 19.19
LO 2

Scott Products issued 8,000 shares of its $1 par value common stock in exchange for some machinery. Prepare the journal entry for each of the following situations:
a. The machinery has a fair market value of $187,000.
b. The machinery has a list price of $215,000, but the stock sold earlier in the day for $26 per share.

E 19.20
LO 2   LO 4

Make the entries for the following events of the Goodland Corporation:
a. Sold 2,000 shares of a $30 par value preferred stock for $72,000.
b. Received a tract of land valued at $120,000 in exchange for promising to open a new plant in Astoria, Oregon.
c. Declared a two-for-one stock split on its $1 par value common stock. There are 1,600,000 shares of common stock authorized and 600,000 issued and outstanding.

E 19.21
LO 4

On March 20, 1999, Hiawatha Inc. purchased 2,400 shares of its own $1 par value common stock for $26 per share and held it as treasury stock. Six hundred of the treasury shares were reissued on June 10 for a total price of $16,800. On August 18, an additional 500 shares were reissued at $25 per share.
a. Prepare the entries to record the acquisition and reissue of the treasury stock.
b. If Hiawatha has 300,000 shares of common stock authorized and 50,000 shares of common issued before the treasury stock was purchased, how many shares of common stock are authorized, issued, and outstanding after these transactions? What reasons would Hiawatha possibly have for the acquisition?

E 19.22
LO 4

On July 1, 1999, Valarie Boyd Corporation purchased 2,000 shares of its $0.10 par common stock for $18 per share. Make the entries for the following treasury stock transactions:
a. On July 18, 1999, it sold 600 of the treasury shares for $19 per share.
b. On August 1, 1999, it sold 800 more shares for $15.50 per share.
c. On December 1, 1999, Boyd sold the remaining 600 shares for $20 per share.

E 19.23
LO 3

On June 20, 2000, the board of directors of Norton Company declared a $64,000 dividend for its common stockholders. The date of payment for the dividend is July 15, 2000, to stockholders of record on June 30, 2000. Record all the appropriate journal entries.

E 19.24
LO 3

Eric Oleson Corporation decided to pay a dividend of $2.40 per share. The corporation has 2,500,000 shares authorized, 800,000 shares issued, and 765,000 shares outstanding on the date of declaration. Make the entries necessary for the dividend on the following dates:

June 15, 2000	Date of declaration
July 13, 2000	Ex-dividend date
July 15, 2000	Date of record .
August 1, 2000	Date of payment

E 19.25
LO 3

Rimrock Inc. has 10,000,000 shares of $1 par value common stock authorized and 1,500,000 shares issued and outstanding. The stock had a fair market value of $16 per share on November 15, 1999, when the board of directors declared a 5 percent stock dividend to holders of record on November 27, 1999. The new shares were distributed on December 10, 1999.

Make the journal entries to record the declaration and distribution of the stock dividend. How are the par value per share, retained earnings, total stockholders' equity, and number of shares authorized, issued, and outstanding affected by the stock dividend?

E 19.26
LO 3

Using the information in E 19.25, how would your answer differ if Rimrock Inc. had declared a 50 percent stock dividend?

PROBLEMS

P 19.1
LO 1

Eleana Pilipicek has owned and operated her own business, U-Serve Tennis, for several years. On March 18, 2000, in order to expand her operations, she borrowed $100,000 using her personal residence as security for the loan. She placed $85,000 from the proceeds of the loan in her business account. At the start of 2000 her capital account had a credit balance of $259,200. A partial listing of accounts and related balances from the firm's general ledger on December 31, 2000, is shown below:

Sales	$429,600
Service revenue	35,300
Rental revenue	177,100
Cost of goods sold	376,300
Selling expenses	134,600
Administrative expenses	78,100
Pilipicek, drawings	81,800

Required

a. Journalize the closing entries for December 31, 2000.
b. Prepare a statement of owner's equity for 2000.

P 19.2
LO 1

R. J. Robertson holds a patent on a new golf club. Although the patent has an estimated fair market value of $122,000, he is unable to obtain sufficient financing to start his own manufacturing plant. He contacts James Smiley, who owns a building and equipment appropriate for manufacturing the new device.

The building is carried on Smiley's records as having an original cost of $215,000 less accumulated depreciation of $78,000, and the equipment has an original cost of $89,000 less accumulated depreciation of $43,000. Currently, the fair market value of the building is $164,000 and that of the equipment is $71,000.

R. J. Robertson contributes his patent and James Smiley his building and equipment to form a partnership. They are joined in the new partnership by Wilsy Robbins, who invests $64,000 in cash.

Required

Prepare the journal entry to record the contribution of each of the partners to the partnership.

P 19.3
LO 1

Baird, Kurtz, and Dobson agreed to divide partnership profits and losses as follows:
1. Annual salary allowance of $12,000 to Baird and $15,000 to Kurtz.
2. Interest allowance of 8 percent on beginning capital balances.
3. Remainder divided by Baird, Kurtz, and Dobson in a ratio of 5:3:2, respectively.

The beginning capital balances are Baird, $105,000; Kurtz, $47,000; and Dobson, $52,000.

Required   Make the entry to record the income or loss if the Income Summary account has the following balances:

a. Credit balance of $90,000
b. Debit balance of $18,000
c. Credit balance of $32,000

P 19.4
LO 1

The owners' capital balances and profit-sharing percentages of the B/D Company are shown below:

	Capital Balance	Profit Ratio
Wallin	$132,000	30%
Miller	148,000	30
Mitchell	96,000	30
Snyder	104,000	10

Wallin decides to withdraw from the firm and is paid from the partnership's assets.

Required   Prepare the journal entry to record Wallin's withdrawal assuming a payment from partnership cash of:

a. $132,000
b. $145,000
c. $120,000

P 19.5
LO 1

Prior to completing the closing procedures on December 31, 2000, the accounting records of Detroit Company contained the following accounts and balances:

	Debit	Credit
Income Summary		$142,000
Ekart, Capital		220,000
Ekart, Drawing	$62,000	
Nunley, Capital		110,000
Nunley, Drawing	48,000	

The profit and loss agreement provides the following: salary allowance of $24,000 to Ekart; 10 percent interest allowance on each partner's beginning capital balance; and the remainder divided in a ratio of 5:3, Ekart to Nunley, respectively.

Required   a. Prepare the journal entries to complete the closing process.
b. Prepare a statement of partners' capital for the year ended December 31, 2000.

P 19.6
LO 1

The partnership agreement of Billings and Dukas specifies a division of profits in a ratio of 2:1, Billings to Dukas, respectively. Prior to admitting Petrie to a one-fourth interest in the firm, the partnership hired an independent appraiser to determine the value of the partnership's assets.

The inventory is overvalued by $20,000 because it contains some obsolete items. The fair market value of the building is $48,000 greater than its book value, and the equipment's fair market value is $14,000 greater than its book value. Immediately before the revaluation of assets and admission of Petrie, the partners' capital balances were $174,000 for Billings and $186,000 for Dukas.

Required   a. Journalize the entry to record the revaluation of the assets.
b. Prepare the journal entry to record the admission of Petrie assuming payments of:
  1. $152,000
  2. $102,000

P 19.7
LO 1

Van Meter, Sorenson, and O'Connell form a partnership called the Trifecta Company. Van Meter contributes inventory having a fair market value of $60,000, Sorenson contributes a building currently appraised at a fair market value of $105,000, and O'Connell invests $43,000 in cash. They agree to divide profits and losses as follows: Van Meter receives a salary allowance of $20,000 because she operates the business full-time. Each partner receives a 10 percent interest allowance on the beginning balance of their respective capital accounts, and the residual is divided equally.

During the first period of operation, Van Meter withdraws $18,000, Sorenson also withdraws $18,000, and O'Connell does not withdraw anything.

Required	a. Prepare the journal entries to record the following:

a. Prepare the journal entries to record the following:
   1. The individual contributions by the partners
   2. The remaining closing entries, presuming that the Income Summary account has a credit balance of $69,000
b. Prepare a statement of partners' capital.

Immediately after the first year of operation, Rhodes buys out Sorenson's interest directly from her for $120,000. At this time, the three new partners, Van Meter, O'Connell, and Rhodes, agree that they will divide all future profits and losses in a ratio of 3:1:2—Van Meter, O'Connell, and Rhodes, respectively. At the end of that year's operation, income amounts to $88,000 and withdrawals are Van Meter, $11,000; O'Connell, $12,000; and Rhodes, $18,000.

Required
c. Record the transfer of Sorenson's share of the partnership.
d. Make the closing entries starting with closing the balance in the Income Summary account.

After the books are closed on the second year of operation, Kaus asks to buy into the partnership. All parties agree that he should pay $110,000 for a one-fourth interest. It is further agreed that all profits after Kaus's admission will be divided in the ratio of 2:1:2:2—Van Meter, O'Connell, Rhodes, and Kaus, respectively. Profits for the third year of operations are $72,000 and withdrawals are Van Meter, $21,000; O'Connell, $22,000; Rhodes, $22,000; and Kaus, $16,000.

Required
e. Record the admission of Kaus to the partnership.
f. Complete the closing entries starting with the Income Summary account.

At the start of the fourth year of operations, Van Meter decides to withdraw from the firm. All parties agree that she should receive $140,000 for her interest, and she is paid $20,000 cash at the time of the withdrawal and given a six-month, 10 percent note payable by the partnership for the $120,000 balance.

Required
g. Record Van Meter's withdrawal from the firm.
h. Determine the balance in each of the remaining partner's capital accounts.

P 19.8
LO 2 LO 3 LO 5

The charter of the BRHC Corporation authorizes the issue of 1,500,000 shares of no-par common stock and 500,000 shares of 8 percent, $50 par value, cumulative preferred stock. Events affecting stockholders' equity during the first year of operation are listed below:

1. 250,000 shares of common stock were sold for $15 per share.
2. 50,000 shares of preferred stock were sold at $52 per share.
3. A building with a fair market value of $560,000 was acquired for a cash payment of $150,000 and 17,000 shares of common stock.
4. 30,000 shares of common stock were issued for $690,000 cash.
5. A dividend of $1 per share for common and $4 per share for preferred stock was declared.

Required
a. Record the transactions described above.
b. Prepare the stockholders' equity section of the balance sheet for December 31 assuming that BRHC generated $945,000 of income.

P 19.9
LO 2 LO 4 LO 5

Meetz Corporation is authorized to issue 500,000 shares of $40 par value, 10 percent preferred stock and 2,000,000 shares of $0.01 par value common stock. The following transactions summarize the events affecting its capital stock accounts during its first year of operations:

1. The company issued 950,000 shares of common stock for cash of $20 per share.
2. 100,000 shares of preferred stock were sold for cash of $44 per share.
3. Meetz repurchased and held as treasury stock 10,000 shares of its own common stock at $19 per share.
4. 2,000 shares of the treasury stock were reissued at $23 per share.

Required
a. Make the entries to record these events.
b. Prepare the stockholders' equity section of Meetz's balance sheet assuming Retained Earnings has a credit balance of $276,000.

P 19.10

LO 2 LO 3 LO 4 LO 5

The stockholders' equity section of Watkins Company's balance sheet appeared as follows on August 15, 2000:

Common stock—$1 par value, 1,000,000 shares authorized, 400,000 shares issued and outstanding	$ 400,000
Paid-in capital in excess of par	500,000
Total contributed capital	$ 900,000
Retained earnings	606,000
Total stockholders' equity	$1,506,000

On August 15, 2000, the board of directors declared a 10 percent stock dividend. The date of distribution was September 25, 2000, to the stockholders of record on September 1, 2000. The stock was selling for $10.50 per share on the date of declaration.

On November 30, 2000, Watkins Company repurchased and held as treasury stock 2,000 shares of its common stock at $11 per share.

On December 15, 2000, the company received land with a fair market value of $240,000 in exchange for a promise to locate a new distribution facility in Minot, North Dakota.

Watkins generated $400,000 of net income in 2000.

Required

a. Make the entries to record these equity events.

b. Prepare the stockholders' equity section to reflect these events.

P 19.11

LO 2 LO 3 LO 4 LO 5

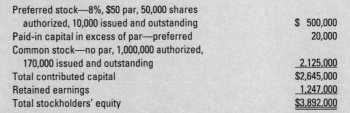

On December 31, 1999, the stockholders' equity section of Sasnak Inc.'s balance sheet was as follows:

Preferred stock—8%, $50 par, 50,000 shares authorized, 10,000 issued and outstanding	$ 500,000
Paid-in capital in excess of par—preferred	20,000
Common stock—no par, 1,000,000 authorized, 170,000 issued and outstanding	2,125,000
Total contributed capital	$2,645,000
Retained earnings	1,247,000
Total stockholders' equity	$3,892,000

During 2000, the following transactions affecting stockholders' equity took place:

Feb.	17	Sold 10,000 shares of common stock for $12.75 per share.
June	1	Declared a $1.20 per share dividend on common stock and $2 per share dividend on preferred stock. Dividends are payable on June 25 to stockholders of record on June 10.
	25	Paid the dividend declared on June 1.
July	15	Received a tract of land valued at $147,000 in consideration for locating a manufacturing plant in Ridings Cove, Virginia.
Aug.	12	Purchased and held in treasury stock 5,000 shares of common stock for $14 per share.
Sept.	18	Sold 2,000 shares of treasury stock at $15.50 per share.
Oct.	18	Sold 1,000 shares of treasury stock for $14.50 per share.
Nov.	1	Declared a 10 percent common stock dividend. New shares are distributable on November 20 to shareholders of record on November 14. The market value of the stock on November 1 was $14 per share.
	20	Distributed the common stock dividend.
Dec.	1	Declared a $1.40 per share dividend on common stock and a $2 per share dividend on preferred stock. Dividends are payable on December 28 to stockholders of record on December 10.
	28	Paid the dividend declared December 1.
	31	Closed the $910,000 credit balance in the Income Summary account.

Required

a. Give the journal entries to record these events.

b. Prepare the stockholders' equity section of Sasnak Inc.'s balance sheet.

CASES

C 19.1
LO 1

Brian Goolsby has operated his own business as a sole proprietorship for several years. Although the business is quite profitable, he believes profits would increase significantly if he expanded his operations by increasing the quantity of inventory, hiring an additional employee, and doing some remodeling in the production area. This would require a minimum investment of $80,000.

The company uses FIFO inventory costing and, with the exception of the equipment that the firm owns, the assets' values on the books are reasonably close to their fair market values. The equipment has a net book value of $37,000 and a fair market value of $44,000. Goolsby's capital balance is $180,000.

Travis Oaks is willing to contribute $90,000 for a one-third interest in the firm, providing he is allowed a 10 percent allowance on his beginning capital balance and the remaining profits are split on a 2:1, Goolsby to Oaks, basis. Since he is not very knowledgeable about Goolsby's business, he wants Goolsby to continue to manage the business.

Goolsby was offered a job by a larger firm at $60,000 per year, but he has a strong preference to continue his own business if he can acquire the additional capital necessary for the expansion.

Required

Prepare a brief report to Goolsby outlining your assessment of Oak's proposal. You should discuss the following:
a. What impact would the admission of Oaks as a partner have on his capital account?
b. What sort of income must the firm generate to reach Goolsby's goal of $60,000?
c. Do you recommend the proposal? If not, what counterproposal should Goolsby make?

C 19.2
LO 2 **LO 3**

Mark Semineau, your long-time friend, owns 2,000 shares of $1 par value common stock in Sports Stuff Inc. There are 1,000,000 shares of common stock authorized, and 800,000 shares are issued and outstanding.

Recently, the company was authorized to issue 200,000 shares of $50 par value preferred stock. These shares have a dividend rate of 8 percent based on par value, and they are cumulative. The company expects to sell 10,000 shares of the preferred stock in the near future to finance the acquisition of more production facilities.

Mark has studied the firm's annual reports in an effort to determine the impact the new stock issue will have on his dividends. He is confused because his $1 par value common stock has a market value of $50 per share. He has received a $5 dividend per share in recent years. The company has consistently maintained a policy of paying out 70 percent of its after-tax net income as dividends, a policy management expects to continue into the foreseeable future. Aside from being confused about the difference between par value and market value, Mark is concerned that the company will not make enough net income to maintain his $5 per share dividend.

Required

a. Explain to Mark in memo form the difference between par value and market value.
b. Show Mark how to compute the minimum amount of after-tax net income the company must earn in order for him to receive a $5 per share dividend if the 10,000 shares of preferred stock are sold.

CRITICAL THINKING

CT 19.1
LO 1

Mitch Holtus and Stan Weber are partners in a company called Sports Voice. Ron Paradise has approached the partners about joining the firm, and he wants to buy a 25 percent interest in the firm. Sports Voice has $100,000 in liabilities, and its assets are undervalued by $22,000.

Holtus has a capital balance of $80,000; Weber's capital balance is $92,000. They share profits and losses equally. How much money will Paradise have to contribute to the firm to obtain a 25 percent interest if the existing partnership revalues the assets?

CT 19.2
LO 2 **LO 3** **LO 5**

The Duckworth Corporation was authorized to issue 2,000,000 shares of $0.01 par value common stock and 200,000 shares of $50 par value, 10 percent preferred stock. To date, Duckworth has issued 600,000 shares of common stock and no preferred stock.

Duckworth is contemplating the acquisition of a new piece of equipment and wants to issue stock to raise the $200,000 cash to finance its acquisition. The company is trying to decide whether to issue 10,000 shares of common stock or 3,800 shares of preferred stock.

Required		*a.* Describe how the issue of each type of stock would affect the stockholders' equity of Duckworth Corporation.

a. Describe how the issue of each type of stock would affect the stockholders' equity of Duckworth Corporation.

b. If Duckworth generates about $3,600,000 of net income each year and the new machine can generate an additional $40,000 of after-tax income, how will the earnings of the common stockholders be affected if:

1. Preferred stock is issued.
2. Common stock is issued.

ETHICAL CHALLENGES

EC 19.1
LO 1

Larry Barton and Elvis Purinton are partners in a struggling business that is badly in need of cash. Kate Kohlrus has expressed an interest in buying a one-third interest in the partnership. Barton and Purinton know that the market value of the firm's assets is substantially lower than their book value. Purinton suggests that they not tell Kohlrus about this situation and not revalue the assets.

What are the financial and ethical ramifications of not revaluing the assets before Kohlrus is admitted to the partnership?

EC 19.2
LO 2

Le Miz Corporation's management expects the firm to have some financial difficulties in the next year. In fact, it expects the company's common stock, which is currently selling at $54 per share, to drop to about $19 per share as a result of these difficulties. One member of management suggests that the corporation buy the stock of selected stockholders now to spare them this loss of value. Discuss the ethics of this proposal.

COMPUTER APPLICATIONS

CA 19.1
LO 2   LO 4   LO 5

Using the EDGAR database, (www.sec.gov), find the following for five companies of your choice:
a. The par value of the corporation's common stock
b. The number of shares authorized, issued, and outstanding of common stock
c. The amount of contributed capital
d. The number of treasury shares and the amount paid for the treasury stock
e. The par value of preferred stock and the number of shares authorized, issued, and outstanding
f. How much cash was raised with the issue of preferred stock
g. The dollar amount of retained earnings and the percentage of total stockholders' equity that retained earnings represents

CA 19.2
LO 3

Utilitrade Corporation currently has 600,000 shares of $1 par value common stock outstanding. The market value of the stock is currently $35 per share.

Required

Use a computer spreadsheet package. Assume independent situations.
a. Determine the amounts to be used in the journal entry to record a 5 percent stock dividend.
b. Determine the amounts to be used in the journal entry to record a 15 percent stock dividend.
c. Determine the amounts to be used in the journal entry to record a 30 percent stock dividend
d. Determine the amounts to be used in the journal entry to record a 50 percent stock dividend.
e. Repeat requirements (**a**) through (**d**) assuming that the par value of the stock is only $0.01 per share.

CA 19.3
LO 5

Locate the 1998 10Ks for Stone Container Corporation and Jefferson Smurfit Corporation in the Edgar database (www.sec.gov) and find the sales, net income, total long-term debt, total stockholders' equity, debt-to-equity ratio, and times interest earned ratio for both corporations. Next locate the 1999 10K for Smurfit-Stone Container Corporation and find the same set of numbers. Discuss the impact the merger had on the two companies.

YOU ARE HERE

Chapter 20 considers the formal process of recording and communicating debt financing activities. In Chapter 18 we learned how businesses plan their debt financing activities. Now, in Chapter 20, we discuss the process of recording the initial liabilities, subsequent payments, and required adjusting entries for all three types of notes (periodic payment, lump-sum payment, and periodic and lump-sum payment, and periodic and lump-sum payment). We learn how companies record debt financing activities in the accounting system and report these activities on the financial statements. In addition, Chapter 20 considers other debt financing issues such as early retirement of debt and leasing.

LEARNING OBJECTIVES

LO 1 Explain how and why companies record and communicate activities concerning long-term periodic payment notes.

LO 2 Describe how and why companies record and communicate events pertaining to long-term lump-sum (noninterest-bearing) notes.

LO 3 Illustrate how and why companies record and communicate bond financing.

LO 4 Explain how and why companies record and communicate operating and capital leases.

Recording and Communicating Long-Term Debt Financing Activities

WAL-MART
www.wal-mart.com

Sam Walton understood how to meet the needs of retail customers. His company, Wal-Mart, has grown from a local store, to a regional force, and today to a national and international power in retail sales. Sam Walton for many is the modern-day icon of the self-made man. While his genius may have been anchored in retail sales, his ability to grow his company was closely tied to his ability to use long-term debt to finance his expansion. The Wal-Mart empire continues to grow in no small part because of its ability to acquire long-term assets with the prudent use of long-term borrowing and intelligent leasing arrangements. As of January 31, 1998, Wal-Mart had a debt-to-equity ratio of 1.45 and financed about 21 percent of its assets with long-term debt and capital leases. An 8.3 times interest earned ratio for the same period indicates Wal-Mart's conservative approach to debt financing minimizes its financial risk. Wal-Mart's modest leverage helped the firm generate a return on equity of 19 percent for the fiscal year ended January 31, 1998. How does Wal-Mart's accounting system capture these long-term debt financing events? How does Wal-Mart communicate its successful financing strategies to existing and potential stockholders and current and potential lenders?

ompanies like Wal-Mart use long-term debt to finance their operational infrastructure and generate higher returns for their stockholders. Companies using financial leverage are willing to accept the risks inherent in this type of financing.

Long-lived assets typically require sizable expenditures and are not converted into cash quickly. In Chapter 18 we learned that companies financing such assets with long-term debt plan to repay the debt with the cash flows generated by the long-term investments. For example, in 1997 Wal-Mart's cash flow statement indicated it raised $547 million by issuing long-term debt and may have used this to finance some of the $2,636 million it spent to acquire property, plant, and equipment.

In this chapter we describe how to account for long-term debt financing events and how the accounting system provides useful information related to these events for both internal and external decision makers. Chapter 18 introduced the three basic types of notes businesses use to acquire funds or other assets. Now we will discuss how the accounting system reflects information about these three types of long-term notes payable—periodic payment, lump-sum payment, and periodic payment and lump-sum notes—in the company records. In addition, the chapter describes how and why these notes payable appear in the financial statements of a firm. The chapter also addresses how to account for and report lease transactions, a special type of debt financing.

ACCOUNTING FOR LONG-TERM NOTES PAYABLE

Each type of long-term note payable promises a specific type of cash flow in exchange for cash or other assets. Recall from Chapter 18 that the periodic payment (installment) note includes a promise to make equal cash payments at equal intervals over a specified period of time. The lump-sum payment (noninterest-bearing) note is a promise to pay a specific cash amount—the note's face value—at a particular point in the future, the note's maturity date. The periodic payment and lump-sum (interest-bearing) note consists of a promise to make both periodic cash interest payments based on the face value of the note and a lump-sum payment of cash at a specific future date. The following discussion explains how the accounting system captures and reports information about each type of note.

Periodic Payment Long-Term Notes Payable

LO 1

Accounting for installment notes requires timely recognition of the interest expense on the notes and proper classification of the note itself as either a long-term or short-term liability. The following example illustrates how to account for an installment note.

Assume that on March 1, 1999, Wal-Mart arranged to purchase a $100,000 piece of equipment by making a 10 percent down payment ($10,000) and signing a three-year installment note with an 8 percent annual interest rate on the $90,000 balance. The loan document calls for six semiannual installments of $17,168.69 starting September 1, 1999. Exhibit 20.1, panel A, shows how to determine the amount of the payment, and the repayment schedule for the note is shown in panel B. The repayment schedule is useful because it acts as a road map for the note over its life.

The repayment schedule shows the portion of each payment that covers the interest on the loan (column 2) and the portion that reduces the principal of the note (column 3). The difference between the amount of the payment made (column 1) and the interest expense for a particular period (column 2) is the amount by which the payment reduces the principal of the note.

Home mortgages are typically long-term installment notes.

EXHIBIT 20.1 Installment Note—Wal-Mart

A. Determining the Installment Payment

Annuity	×	$P_{6,4\%}$	=	Present value of annuity
Annuity	×	5.2421	=	$90,000
		Annuity	=	$17,168.69

B. Repayment Schedule

Date	(1) Payment	(2) Interest Expense (0.04 × Loan Balance)	(3) Principal (1) – (2)	(4) Loan Balance
3/1/99				$90,000.00
9/1/99	$17,168.69	$3,600.00	$13,568.69	76,431.31
3/1/00	17,168.69	3,057.25	14,111.44	62,319.87
9/1/00	17,168.69	2,492.79	14,675.90	47,643.97
3/1/01	17,168.69	1,905.76	15,262.93	32,381.04
9/1/01	17,168.69	1,295.24	15,873.45	16,507.59
3/1/02	17,168.69	661.10*	16,507.59	–0–

*Rounded.

Exhibit 20.2 shows the entries recorded in conjunction with the note over its life. The cost of the equipment is the sum of the face value of the note, ($90,000) and the cash down payment ($10,000). The entry to record the first payment on September 1, 1999, mirrors the information in the repayment schedule. That is, interest expense of $3,600 is recorded, and $13,568.69 of principal is reduced with the required semiannual payment of $17,168.69.

EXHIBIT 20.2 Entries for Installment Note—Wal-Mart

Fiscal Year	2/1/99 to 1/31/00	2/1/00 to 1/31/01	2/1/01 to 1/31/02	2/1/02 to 1/31/03
March 1 Entries				
Equipment	100,000			
Cash	10,000			
Installment Note Payable	90,000			
Interest Expense		509.54	317.63	110.18
Interest Payable		2,547.71	1,588.13	550.92
Installment Note Payable		14,111.44	15,262.93	16,507.59
Cash		17,168.69	17,168.69	17,168.69
September 1 Entries				
Interest Expense	3,600.00	2,492.79	1,295.24	
Installment Note Payable	13,578.69	14,675.90	15,873.45	
Cash	17,168.69	17,168.69	17,168.69	
January 31 Entries				
Interest Expense	2,547.71	1,588.13	550.92	
Interest Payable	2,547.71	1,588.13	550.92	

Wal-Mart closes its books on January 31. To comply with the matching principle, Wal-Mart makes an adjusting entry at closing to record five months' interest (September through January) on the note (see Exhibit 20.3). The adjusting entry identifies the interest expense associated with the year in which it was incurred. At the same time, it reflects the obligation of the firm to pay the interest at year-end. As of January 31, 2000, the amount of accrued interest for the five months since September 1, 1999, is $2,547.71 [Unpaid loan balance ($76,431.31) × Annual interest rate (8%) × Percentage of year since the last payment (5/12)].

EXHIBIT 20.3 Interest Expense Allocation—Wal-Mart

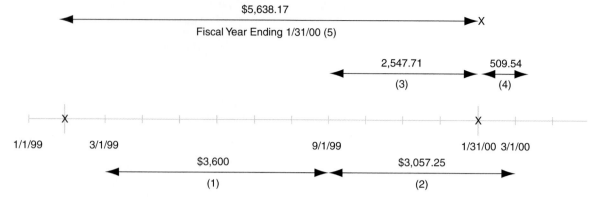

(1) Interest expense from 3/1/99 to 9/1/99.
(2) Interest expense from 9/1/99 to 3/1/00.
(3) Interest expense from 9/1/99 to 1/31/00 or ($3,057.25 x 5/6).
(4) Interest expense from 2/1/00 to 3/1/00 or ($3,057.25 x 1/6).
(5) Interest expense from 1/31/99 to 1/31/00, Wal-Mart's fiscal year, or [$3,600.00 (1) + $2,547.71 (3)].

Then on the next payment date, March 1, 2000, Wal-Mart would debit the Interest Payable account for $2,547.71 and record February 2000's interest expense of $509.54. The interest expense for February 2000 is the difference between the $3,057.25 of interest for the entire six-month period ending February 29, 2000, and the $2,547.71 of interest accrued from September 1, 1999 through January 31, 2000.

Even though the second payment occurs on March 1, 2000, Wal-Mart allocates the interest expense of $3,057.25 (footnote 2 in Exhibit 20.3) for the six-month period between two accounting periods—$2,547.71 (footnote 3 in Exhibit 20.3) accrued for the five months and $509.54 (footnote 4 in Exhibit 20.3) for the final month's interest expense in February 2000, the next accounting period. The time line in Exhibit 20.3 shows how the interest expense incurred during the first year of this note's life is allocated between the two accounting periods.

Exhibit 20.4 shows how this installment note impacts Wal-Mart's financial statements for 2000 to 2003. The income statement for 2000 shows the interest expense incurred during the year, which amounts to $6,147.71 ($3,600 + $2,547.71). The balance sheet shows the amount of interest accrued as of January 31, 2000, $2,547.71, as a current liability. As of January 31, 2000, Wal-Mart still owes $76,431.31 (see Exhibit 20.1) on the installment note. The portion of the installment note's principal due in 2000, $28,787.34 ($14,111.44 + $14,675.90 in Exhibit 20.1), is reported as a current liability. Wal-Mart classifies the remaining principal of the installment note, $47,643.97, as a long-term liability because it is due after 2000.

The issuance of the note does not affect the January 31, 2000, cash flow statement because the company received equipment rather than cash from the transaction. However, the company would report $3,600.00 of the first $17,168.69 payment as cash paid for interest in the operating section of the statement of cash flows, while the remaining $13,568.69 would appear as a reduction of the balance of the installment note payable in the financing section of the cash flow statement.[1]

Lump-Sum Payment Long-Term Notes Payable

LO 2

As we discussed in Chapter 18, the face value of a lump-sum payment note depends on the market rate of interest of the firm at the time the note is issued and the value of the asset acquired. The accountant's job is to ensure that the market rate used to value the

---
[1]There is also an investing cash flow of $10,000 shown on the cash flow statement due to the cash down payment.

EXHIBIT   20.4   Financial Statements for Installment Note—Wal-Mart

Fiscal Year	2/1/99 to 1/31/00	2/1/00 to 1/31/01	2/1/01 to 1/31/02	2/1/02 to 1/31/03
Income Statement				
Interest expense	$6,147.71	$4,590.46	$2,163.79	$110.18
Balance Sheet				
Current liabilities:				
Interest payable	2,547.71	1,588.13	550.92	
Installment Note				
Payable	28,787.34	31,136.38	16,507.59	
Long-term liabilities:				
Installment Note				
Payable	47,643.97	16,507.59	–0–	
Cash Flow Statement				
Operating section:				
Cash interest	3,600.00	5,550.04	3,201.00	661.10
Financing section:				
Cash paid on note	13,568.69	28,787.34	31,136.38	16,507.59
Investing section:				
Cash paid for				
equipment	10,000			

note is appropriate and to record the transaction so that the assets, liabilities, and interest on the note are presented fairly on the company's financial statements.

PAUSE &
REFLECT

Who determines the firm's market rate of interest on a noncash transaction? How subjective is this process? When is an interest rate used to determine the present value of the note considered unrealistic? *(answer on page 700)*

To illustrate, assume that on April 1, 2000, when the market interest rate was 8 percent Wal-Mart issued a four-year noninterest-bearing note to acquire a parcel of land with a market value of $500,000. Marcus Perry, one of Wal-Mart's controllers, calculated the $680,272.11 face value of the note in panel A of Exhibit 20.5 and set up the amortization table illustrated in panel B of Exhibit 20.5.

Because Wal-Mart was able to exchange the note for the land, the assumption here is that the value of the property is the same as the present value of the note. In other words, Wal-Mart could have gone to a bank with this $680,272.11 noninterest-bearing note and borrowed $500,000 in cash and then purchased the land. The entry to record the acquisition of land on April 1, 2000, should have been:

Land	500,000.00	
Discount on Note Payable	180,272.11	
Note Payable		680,272.11

The Discount on Note Payable account represents the difference between the market rate of interest, 8 percent, and the face rate of interest, 0 percent. In this case, it represents all of the interest that Wal-Mart will recognize over the life of the note. The discount account is a **contra liability** account because its debit balance offsets and, therefore, reduces a specific related liability account. In this case, the discount offsets the face value of the Note Payable account to reflect the note's carrying value, or amount of the liability reported on the firm's balance sheet. For example, on the date of the note's issuance, the carrying value or liability incurred by Wal-Mart was the $680,272.11 note payable less the $180,272.11 discount on the note payable, or $500,000.

Calculator:
PV = 500,000
c = 1
n = 4
r = 8
PMT = 0
FV = 680,244.48

EXHIBIT 20.5 Noninterest-Bearing Note—Wal-Mart

A. Determination of the Face Value of the Note

Present value	=	Face (Future) value	×	$P_{4,8\%}$
$500,000	=	Face (Future) value	×	0.7350
$500,000/0.7350	=	Face (Future) value		
$680,272.11	=	Face (Future) value		

B. Amortization of Discount

Date	(1) Cash Payment	(2) Interest Expense (0.08 × Carrying Value)	(3) Remaining Discount	(4) Carrying Value
4/1/00			$180,272.11	$500,000.00
4/1/01		$ 40,000.00	140,272.11	540,000.00
4/1/02		43,200.00	97,072.11	583,200.00
4/1/03		46,656.00	50,416.11	629,856.00
4/1/04		50,416.11*	–0–	680,272.11
4/1/04	$680,272.11			–0–

*Rounded.

The amortization table shown in panel B of Exhibit 20.5 shows the amount of interest expense recognized each year in the life of the note (column 2). The interest for the first year of this note, April 1, 2000, to April 1, 2001, is $40,000. Entries to reflect interest in the accounting records show a credit to the Discount on Note Payable account and a debit to Interest Expense. As the company reduces the Discount on Note Payable account, the carrying value of the note increases. The entry to record the interest for the fiscal year ending January 31, 2001 (April 1, 2000, through January 31, 2001) is:

Interest Expense ($40,000 × 10/12 of a year)	33,333.33	
Discount on Note Payable		33,333.33

Exhibit 20.6 illustrates the entries that Wal-Mart would make in its accounting records over the life of the note. During the 2001 fiscal year, the interest is $42,666.67, which consists of one-sixth of the note's interest in its first year ($40,000 × 2/12), plus five-sixths, or 10 months, of the note's second year of interest ($43,200 × 10/12). Wal-Mart will amortize the discount on the note until the company makes the final payment of the $680,272.11 face value on April 1, 2004.

EXHIBIT 20.6 Entries for Noninterest-Bearing Note—Wal-Mart

Fiscal Year	2/1/00 to 1/31/01		2/1/01 to 1/31/02		2/1/02 to 1/31/03		2/1/03 to 1/31/04		2/1/04 to 1/31/05	
April 1 Entries										
Land	500,000.00									
Discount on Note Payable	180,272.11									
Note Payable		680,272.11								
Note Payable									680,272.11	
Cash										680,272.11
January 31 Entries										
Interest Expense*	33,333.33		42,666.67		46,080.00		49,789.43		8,402.68	
Discount on Note Payable		33,333.33		42,666.67		46,080.00		49,789.43		8,402.68

*Interest expense calculation (use amounts from Exhibit 20.5, column 2):

2000: $40,000 × 10/12 = $33,333.33.

2001: ($40,000 × 2/12) + ($43,200 × 10/12) = $42,666.67.

2002: ($43,200 × 2/12) + ($46,656 × 10/12) = $46,080.00.

2003: ($46,656 × 2/12) + ($50,416.11 × 10/12) = $49,789.43.

2004: $50,416.11 * 2/12 = $8,402.68.

Exhibit 20.7 shows Wal-Mart's financial statement presentation of the note during its term. The interest reported on the income statement each year is recorded as part of Wal-Mart's adjusting entries on January 31. The carrying value of the note at January 31, 2001, is $533,333.33 and $576,000.00 for January 31, 2002. The note's carrying value increases each year because of the amortization of the Discount on Note Payable account each time the company records interest. On January 31, 2004, the carrying value of the note becomes a current liability because Wal-Mart will pay the note in full on April 1, 2004.

EXHIBIT 20.7	**Financial Statements for Noninterest-Bearing Note—Wal-Mart**				
Fiscal Year	2/1/00 to 1/31/01	2/1/01 to 1/31/02	2/1/02 to 1/31/03	2/1/03 to 1/31/04	2/1/04 to 1/31/05
Income Statement					
Interest expense	$ 33,333.33	$42,666.67	$46,080.00	$ 49,789.43	$ 8,402.68
Balance Sheet					
Current liabilities:					
Note Payable				$680,272.11	
Less discount on Note Payable				8,402.68	
Carrying value				$671,869.43	
Long-term liabilities:					
Note Payable	$680,272.11	$680,272.11	$680,272.11		
Less discount on Note Payable	146,938.78	104,272.11	58,192.11		
Carrying value	$533,333.33	$576,000.00	$622,080.00		
Cash Flow Statement					
Financing section:					
Cash paid on note					$680,272.11

As in the case of the installment note, the interest expense amounts and carrying values on the note's amortization schedule do not correspond to the amounts reported on Wal-Mart's income statement and balance sheet because the note's yearly cycle does not correspond to Wal-Mart's fiscal year. Because this is a noninterest-bearing note, the only cash flow reported during the life of the note is the cash payment of the face value of the note, $680,272.11, in the financing section of Wal-Mart's cash flow statement for the fiscal year ending January 31, 2005.

Periodic Payment and Lump-Sum Long-Term Notes Payable—Bonds LO 3

We use bonds as our example for the accounting treatment for periodic payment and lump-sum notes. Recall from Chapter 18 that bonds are a form of long-term debt designed to raise funds from public rather than private sources.

To illustrate how to account for periodic payment and lump-sum notes, assume that Wal-Mart is planning a $28,000,000 capital expenditure and has the authorization from its board of directors to issue $20,000,000 of 10-year bonds on March 1, 1999, to finance part of the project (as of January 31, 1998, Wal-Mart did not have any bonds issued). Thus Wal-Mart will issue 20,000 bonds, each with a face value of $1,000. The bonds have a 10 percent face rate that is paid semiannually on September 1 and March 1. Wal-Mart has a January 31 fiscal year-end.

Each payment on an installment consists of principal and interest.

Market Rate Equal to the Face Rate If the market rate of interest for Wal-Mart is 10 percent when it issues the bonds, the proceeds of the sale of the bonds will be $20,000,000, as panel A in Exhibit 20.8 shows. Because the market and face rate are the same, the bond issue has no discount or premium, and the interest expense equals the amount of cash interest paid, as shown in panel B of Exhibit 20.8.

Calculator:
FV = 20,000,000
PMT = 1,000,000
c = 2
n = 20
r = 10
PV = 20,000,000

EXHIBIT 20.8 Bonds Issued at Face Value—Wal-Mart

A. Present Value of Cash Flows

Cash flow 1:

Present value of annuity	=	Annuity	×	$P_{20,5\%}$
	=	$1,000,000	×	12.4622
	=	$12,462,200		

Cash flow 2:

Present value of lump sum	=	Future value	×	$p_{20,5\%}$
	=	$20,000,000	×	0.3769
	=	$7,538,000		

Present value of cash flow 1	$12,462,200
Present value of cash flow 2	7,538,000
Present value of note	$20,000,200*

B. Amortization Table

Date	Cash Interest (0.05 × Face Value)	Interest Expense (0.05 × Carrying Value)	Premium or Discount Amortized	Premium/ Discount	Carrying Value
3/1/99					$20,000,000
9/1/99	$1,000,000	$1,000,000	—	—	20,000,000
3/1/00	1,000,000	1,000,000	—	—	20,000,000
9/1/00	1,000,000	1,000,000	—	—	20,000,000
3/1/01	1,000,000	1,000,000	—	—	20,000,000

*This amount should equal $20,000,000; the present value factor is limited to four decimal places and results in the $200 rounding difference shown here.

Exhibit 20.9 presents the entries Wal-Mart will make in its accounting records for the first two years of the bond issue's life. Wal-Mart's adjusting entries on January 31 recognize the interest expense incurred from September 1 to January 31 as well as the obligation to pay $833,333 of cash interest as of that date (interest payable). On March 1 of the following year, when the company pays the cash interest due, it recognizes interest expense for February 2000 and removes the liability for the interest recognized at fiscal year-end January 31, 2000, from the company's records. Because the bonds were issued at their face value, the exhibit's entries are the same for each date over the life of the bonds.

EXHIBIT 20.9 Entries for Bonds Issued at Face Value—Wal-Mart

Fiscal Year	2/1/99 to 1/31/00		2/1/00 to 1/31/01	
March 1 Entries				
Cash	20,000,000			
Bonds Payable		20,000,000		
Interest Expense			166,667*	
Interest Payable			833,333	
Cash				1,000,000
September 1 Entries				
Interest Expense	1,000,000		1,000,000	
Cash		1,000,000		1,000,000
January 31 Entries				
Interest Expense	833,333**		833,333	
Interest Payable		833,333		833,333

*$1,000,000 × 1/6.

**1,000,000 × 5/6.

Exhibit 20.10 shows how to report the bonds on Wal-Mart's financial statements. The yearly interest expense is the balance in the Interest Expense account after recording the adjusting entries on January 31. The carrying value of the bonds on the balance sheet of Wal-Mart is $20,000,000 for each year of their life. Wal-Mart classifies the bonds as a long-term liability until January 31, 2009, when they become a current liability because they mature on March 1, 2009.

EXHIBIT 20.10	Financial Statements for Bonds Issued at Face Value—Wal-Mart	
For Fiscal Years	2/1/99 to 1/31/00	2/1/00 to 1/31/01
Income Statement		
Interest expense	$ 1,833,333*	$ 2,000,000**
Balance Sheet		
Long-term liabilities:		
Bonds payable	$10,000,000	$10,000,000
Cash Flow Statement		
Operating section:		
Cash interest paid	$(1,000,000)	$(2,000,000)
Financing section:		
Cash received from bond	20,000,000	

*$1,000,000 + $833,333 = $1,833,333.

**$166,667 + $1,000,000 + $833,333 = $2,000,000.

The cash reported on the cash flow statement is the same for each year of the bond issue's life except for the first and last years. Its January 31, 2000, cash flow statement shows the receipt of the $20,000,000 from the sale of the bonds in the financing section and $1,000,000 of cash interest Wal-Mart paid in the operating section of the cash flow statement. During the next eight years, Wal-Mart reports only the $2,000,000 of cash interest paid in the operating section of the cash flow statement. In 2009, the year the bonds mature, the cash flow statement reports the payment of $1,000,000 of cash interest in the operating section and the $20,000,000 payment of the face value to retire the bonds in its financing section of the cash flow statement.

Market Rate Greater than Face Rate   When the market rate of interest is greater than the face rate of the bond issue, the proceeds from the issuance of the bonds are smaller than the face value of the bonds. That is, the bonds are issued at a discount. Assume that Wal-Mart issued the 10 percent face rate bonds when the market rate of interest was 12 percent. Then the bonds' proceeds are $17,705,900, as panel A of Exhibit 20.11 illustrates. Panel B shows the bond amortization table for the first two years of the bond issue's life.

Exhibit 20.12 presents the entries for the first two fiscal years of the bonds' life. Wal-Mart has borrowed $17,705,900 but must repay the $20,000,000 face value on the maturity date. Therefore, the $2,294,100 difference represents the discount on bonds payable, or the amount of additional interest that Wal-Mart incurs to make these 10 percent bonds yield 12 percent interest. Because the discount represents the difference between the face rate of interest and the market rate of interest over the life of the bond issue, the company will amortize the discount over the life of the bonds.

On the first payment date, September 1, 1999, Wal-Mart pays $1,000,000 cash interest, as promised in the bond indenture (Exhibit 20.11, panel B, column 1). However, the actual interest expense for the six-month period is $1,062,354 (Exhibit 20.11, panel B, column 2), or $17,705,900 (amount borrowed) × 12 percent × 6/12 (six months of the year). The $62,354 difference between the cash interest paid ($1,000,000) and the interest expense ($1,062,354) is the amount by which the company will reduce or amortize the discount account. It represents the difference between the face rate of interest (10 percent) and the market rate of interest (12 percent).

EXHIBIT 20.11 Bonds Issued at a Discount—Wal-Mart

A. Present Value of Bonds' Cash Flows

Cash flow 1:

Present value of annuity	=	Annuity	×	$P_{20,6\%}$
	=	$1,000,000	×	11.4699
	=	$11,469,900		

Cash flow 2:

Present value of lump sum	=	Future value	×	$p_{20,6\%}$
	=	$20,000,000	×	0.3118
	=	$6,236,000		

Present value of cash flow 1 $11,469,900
Present value of cash flow 2   6,236,000
Present value of note $17,705,900

B. Bond Amortization Table

Date	(1) Cash Interest (0.05 × Face Value)	(2) Interest Expense (0.06 × Carrying Value)	(3) Discount Amortized	(4) Discount	(5) Bond Carrying Value
3/1/99				$2,294,100	$17,705,900
9/1/99	$1,000,000	$1,062,354	$62,354	2,231,746	17,768,254
3/1/00	1,000,000	1,066,095	66,095	2,165,651	17,834,351
9/1/00	1,000,000	1,070,061	70,061	2,095,590	17,904,410
3/1/01	1,000,000	1,074,265	74,265	2,021,325	17,978,675

EXHIBIT 20.12 Entries for Bonds Issued at a Discount—Wal-Mart

For Fiscal Years	2/1/99 to 1/31/00		2/1/00 to 1/31/01	
March 1 Entries				
Cash	17,705,900			
Discount on Bonds Payable	2,294,100			
Bonds Payable		20,000,000		
Interest Expense			177,683[a]	
Interest Payable			833,333	
Discount on Bonds Payable				11,016[b]
Cash				1,000,000
September 1 Entries				
Interest Expense	1,062,354		1,070,061	
Discount on Bonds Payable		62,354		70,061
Cash		1,000,000		1,000,000
January 31 Entries				
Interest Expense	888,413[c]		895,221[d]	
Discount on Bonds Payable		55,080[e]		61,888[f]
Interest Payable		833,333[g]		833,333

See Exhibit 20.11 for quantities used:

[a]$1,066,095 (3/1/00, col. 2) × 1/6.

[b]$ 66,095 (3/1/00, col. 3) × 1/6.

[c]$1,066,095 (3/1/00, col. 2) × 5/6.

[d]$1,074,265 (3/1/01, col. 2) × 5/6.

[e]$ 66,095 (3/1/00, col. 3) × 5/6.

[f]$ 74,265 (3/1/01, col. 3) × 5/6.

[g]$1,000,000 (3/1/00, col. 1) × 5/6.

The adjusting entries on January 31 reflect the recognition of the interest expense incurred from September 1 to January 31 and the obligation to pay $833,333 of cash interest as of that date. The interest expense, $888,413 ($1,066,095 × 5/6), is greater than the $833,333 entry made to the Interest Payable account. The $55,080 difference is the amount of the discount amortized for this five-month period ($66,095 × 5/6). On March 1, 2000, when the company pays the amount of cash interest due, it recognizes the interest expense of $177,683 ($1,066,095 × 1/6) for the first month of the next fiscal year and amortizes the $11,016 discount for the two-month period ($66,095 × 1/6). Wal-Mart also removes the related liability (interest payable) recognized on January 31, 2000, from its records. This adjusting process continues throughout the life of the bonds because the fiscal year does not correspond to the timing of the cash flows promised in the bond indenture.

**PAUSE &
REFLECT**

If the amounts Wal-Mart records in the January 31 adjusting entries in the Interest Expense and Discount accounts change each year, why does the amount of interest payable remain the same? *(answer on page 700)*

Exhibit 20.13 shows how to report bonds issued at a discount on Wal-Mart's financial statements for the first two years of the bonds' life. The interest expense of $1,950,787 in 2000 and $2,142,945 in 2001 is the balance in the Interest Expense account after recording the adjusting entries on January 31. The company reports the bonds on the balance sheet as a long-term liability and the accrued interest as a current liability. The contra liability account, Discount on Bonds Payable, is subtracted from the Bonds Payable account to show the bond issue's carrying value on the balance sheet date. As each year passes, the carrying value of the bonds becomes larger because the discount gets smaller as the bonds are amortized. On the maturity date of the bonds, the Discount on Bonds Payable account is fully amortized and the amount of Wal-Mart's liability for the bonds equals the face value of the bonds.

EXHIBIT 20.13	Financial Statements for Bonds Issued at a Discount—Wal-Mart	
Fiscal Years	2/1/99 to 1/31/00	2/1/00 to 1/31/01
Income Statement		
Interest expense	$ 1,950,767*	$ 2,142,965**
Balance Sheet		
Long-term liabilities:		
Bonds payable	$20,000,000	$20,000,000
Less discount	2,176, 666	2,033,701
	$17,823,334	$17,966,299
Cash Flow Statement		
Operating section:		
Cash interest paid	$(1,000,000)	$ (2,000,000)
Financing section:		
Cash received from bond	17,705,900	

*$1,062,354+ $888,413 from Exhibit 20.12.

**$177,683 + $1,070,061 + $895,221 from Exhibit 20.12.

In 1999 Wal-Mart's cash flow statement reflects the receipt of the bond proceeds, $17,705,900, in the financing section and $1,000,000 of cash interest paid in the operating section. However, from this point on, the amount of cash flows reported on the cash flow statement is the same as those for the bonds issued at their face value. That is, Wal-Mart will report $2,000,000 of cash interest paid in the operating section of the cash flow statement each year until the year the bonds mature. In that year, the cash flow statement will report the payment of cash interest of $1,000,000 in the operating section and the repayment of the $20,000,000 face value of the bonds in the financing section.

etting up a bond payment schedule on a spreadsheet requires a little planning, but the result is well worth the effort because the computer will do all the tedious calculations.

For example, let's set up a bond payment schedule for a 20-year bond issue with a $1,000,000 face value that pays 13 percent interest semiannually. Assume the bond was issued when the market rate of interest was 12 percent; therefore, the company received $1,075,231 for the bonds. Set up the spreadsheet with the following column headings in rows 1 and 2:

| Period | Cash Interest | Effective Interest | Premium Amortized | Carrying Value |

Then enter the current carrying value, $1,075,231 in column e, row 3. Use the fill command; then enter the number of periods from 1 to 40 in column a, starting with row 4. Next, you must decide how the cell amounts can be calculated using other cell amounts and the appropriate interest rates. In cell b4, enter: +1000000*.13*1/2 to calculate the semiannual cash interest amount. Then use the copy command to copy this cell to the other 39 periods. In cell c4, enter: +e3*.12*1/2 to calculate the semiannual interest expense amount. In cell d4, enter: +b4–c4 to calculate the amount of premium amortized each semiannual period. In cell e4, enter: +e3–d4 to calculate the new carrying value. Now use the copy command to copy cells c4, d4, and e4 to the remaining periods. Finally, format the cells for dollars with the desired number of decimal places. Remember, if you round to even dollars, you may have a small rounding error at the end.

Market Rate Less than Face Rate When the market rate is less than the face rate of interest on a bond issue, the proceeds from a bond issue exceed the face value of the bond issue, and the bonds are issued at a premium. If Wal-Mart's 10 percent bonds were issued when the market rate was 8 percent, the proceeds of the sale of the bonds would yield $22,718,300 as shown in panel A of Exhibit 20.14.

Exhibit 20.14, panel B, presents the first two years of the bonds' amortization schedule. Semiannual payments dictate that it is necessary to compound the 8 percent market rate of interest semiannually. The $2,718,300 premium on bonds payable is the amount of proceeds generated in excess of the bonds' face value. Wal-Mart does not have to pay this amount back to the holders of the bonds; rather, the premium reduces the amount of interest due on the note over its life. This, in effect, makes the bonds yield the 8 percent market rate of interest rather than the 10 percent face interest rate.

Calculator:
$FV = 20,000,000$
$PMT = 1,000,000$
$c = 2$
$n = 20$
$r = 8$
$PV = 22,718,065$

EXHIBIT 20.14 Bonds Issued at a Premium—Wal-Mart

A. Present Value of Bonds' Cash Flows

Cash flow 1:

Present value of annuity	=	Annuity	×	$P_{20,4\%}$
	=	$1,000,000	×	13.5903
	=	$13,590,300		

Cash flow 2:

Present value of lump sum	=	Future value	×	$P_{20,4\%}$
	=	$20,000,000	×	0.4564
	=	$9,128,000		

Present value of cash flow 1	$13,590,300
Present value of cash flow 2	9,128,000
Present value of note	$22,718,300

B. Bond Amortization Table

	(1) Cash Interest (0.05 × Face Value)	(2) Interest Expense (0.04 × Carrying Value)	(3) Premium Amortized	(4) Premium	(5) Bond Carrying Value
Date					
3/1/99				$2,718,300	$22,718,300
9/1/99	$1,000,000	$908,732	$91,268	2,627,032	22,627,032
3/1/00	1,000,000	905,081	94,919	2,532,113	22,532,113
9/1/00	1,000,000	901,285	98,715	2,433,398	22,433,398
3/1/01	1,000,000	897,336	102,664	2,330,734	22,330,734

Exhibit 20.15 illustrates Wal-Mart's journal entries for the first two fiscal years of this bond issue. On the first payment date, September 1, 1999, Wal-Mart recognizes interest expense of $908,732 (column 2, Exhibit 20.14) but pays $1,000,000 cash interest (column 1, Exhibit 20.14) as promised in the bond indenture. The interest expense for this six-month period is incurred because Wal-Mart borrowed $22,718,300 for six months. The difference between the amount of cash paid for interest and the interest expense, $91,268 (column 3, Exhibit 20.14), is the amount by which Wal-Mart will reduce (amortize) the Premium on Bonds Payable account. It represents the difference between the 10 percent face rate of interest and the 8 percent market rate of interest.

EXHIBIT 20.15	Entries for Bonds Issued at a Premium—Wal-Mart			
For Fiscal Years		2/1/99 to 1/31/00		2/1/00 to 1/31/01
March 1 Entries				
Cash	22,718,300			
Premium on bonds payable		2,718,300		
Bonds Payable		20,000,000		
Interest Expense			150,847[a]	
Interest Payable			833,333	
Premium on bonds payable			15,820[b]	
Cash				1,000,000
September 1 Entries				
Interest Expense	908,732		901,285	
Premium on bonds payable	91,268		98,715	
Cash		1,000,000		1,000,000
January 31 Entries				
Interest Expense	754,234[c]		747,780[d]	
Premium on bonds payable	79,099[e]		85,553[f]	
Interest Payable		833,333[g]		833,333

[a]$905,081 (3/1/00, col. 2) × 1/6.

[b]$ 94,919 (3/1/00, col. 3) × 1/6.

[c]$905,081 (3/1/00, col. 2) × 5/6.

[d]$897,336 (3/1/01, col. 2) × 5/6.

[e]$ 94,919 (3/1/00, col. 3) × 5/6.

[f]$102,664 (3/1/01, col. 3) × 5/6.

[g]$1,000,000 (3/1/00, col. 1) × 5/6.

The adjusting entries on January 31 shown in Exhibit 20.15 recognize the interest expense incurred on the bonds from September 1 to January 31 and the obligation to pay $833,333 of cash interest as of that date. For example, the interest expense on January 31, 2000, $754,234 ($905,081 × 5/6) is less than the $833,333 shown in the Interest Payable account. The $79,099 difference is the premium amortized for this five-month period ($94,919 × 5/6). On March 1, 2000, when the company pays $1,000,000 of cash interest due, it recognizes the interest expense of $150,847 ($905,081 × 1/6) for the first two months of 2000, amortizes the $15,820 ($94,919 × 1/6) premium for the one-month period, and removes the amount of interest payable of $833,333 recognized on January 31, 2000, from Wal-Mart's records.

Exhibit 20.16 shows the impact of this bond issue on Wal-Mart's financial statements at January 31, 2000 and 2001. The interest expense on Wal-Mart's income statement of $1,662,966 in 2000 and $1,799,912 in 2001 reflects balances in the Interest Expense account after adjusting entries. The carrying value of the bonds, that is, the amount reflected in the Bonds Payable account plus the balance in the Premium on Bonds Payable account, on January 31 appears on the balance sheet as a long-term liability. As each year passes, the carrying value becomes smaller as the premium account is amortized. On the maturity date, the premium account is amortized fully, and the carrying value of the bonds is their $20,000,000 face value.

EXHIBIT 20.16 Financial Statements of Bonds Issued at a Premium—Wal-Mart		
For Fiscal Years	2/1/99 to 1/31/00	2/1/00 to 1/31/01
Income Statement		
Interest expense	$ 1,662,966*	$ 1,799,912**
Balance Sheet		
Current liabilities:		
Interest payable	$833,333	$833,333
Long-term liabilities:		
Bonds payable	20,000,000	20,000,000
Add premium on bonds payable	2,547,933	2,347,845
	$22,547,933	$22,347,845
Cash Flow Statement		
Operating section:		
Cash interest paid	$(1,000,000)	$(2,000,000)
Financing section:		
Cash received from bond	22,718,300	

*$908,732 + $754,234 from Exhibit 20.15.

**$150,847 + $901,285 + $747,780 from Exhibit 20.15.

In 1999 the cash flow statement shows the receipt of the proceeds for the issuance of the bonds, $22,718,300 in the financing section and $1,000,000 of cash interest paid in the operating section. From this point on, the bonds' cash flows reported on the statement of cash flows for the remainder of the bonds' life are the same as those shown in the previous examples.

Periodic Payment and Lump-Sum Notes Payable—Private

Frequently, companies use periodic payment and lump-sum types of notes to acquire debt financing from nonpublic sources. When this occurs, determining the amount received for the note, the accounting entries, and the financial statement presentation for the long-term notes is the same as the procedures described for bonds. However, instead of using Bonds Payable as the account title, companies would use Note Payable.

EARLY RETIREMENT OF BONDS

Bonds contain provisions that allow a company to retire the debt before it matures. Retirement usually occurs in one of three ways: (1) buying the bonds in the secondary bond market, (2) using the bonds' call feature, and (3) converting bonds into stock. In this section we describe how to account for each of these events.

Buying Bonds in the Secondary Market

Firms can retire debt by buying their bonds in the secondary bond market where the bonds are traded among investors. Recall from Chapter 18 that the prices of bonds in the secondary market are quoted as a percentage of the bonds' face value, such as 101 1/2 (1.015 × Face value) or 89 3/4 (0.8975 × Face value). These prices change as the market interest rates change.

Some investors buy bonds so they can lock in a specific return for a long period of time. Other short-term investors buy bonds anticipating a decline in interest rates that would drive bond prices up, therefore, profiting when they sell the bonds.

The corporation that issues bonds is free to participate in the secondary bond market. If the market rate of interest on the bonds increases, bond prices decline. This presents an opportunity for the corporation to retire its debt early at a lower price.

Suppose that after Wal-Mart issued its bonds at a premium that yields 8 percent (Exhibit 20.14), the market interest rate for the company increased. By September 1, 2000, the market price of the bonds was 89 5/8. Assume that, at this point, Wal-Mart's management decides to buy one-half of the bond issue and retire it.

When the purchase price exceeds the bonds' carrying value, the company recognizes a loss because it is paying more than the liability due on that date. However, when the purchase price is less than the carrying value of the bonds, it recognizes a gain because the liability is being paid off for an amount less than the debt due on that date.[2]

Exhibit 20.17 shows that the gain on the bonds retirement of $2,254,199 is the difference between the carrying value of the bonds, $11,216,699 ($22,433,398/2), and its market price, $8,962,500. The entry below reflects the bonds' retirement on September 1, 2000:

9/1/00	Bonds Payable	10,000,000	
	Premium on Bonds Payable	1,216,699	
	Cash		8,962,500
	Gain on Retirement of Bonds		2,254,199

Notice that this entry removes *both* the *bonds payable* and the related *premium on bonds payable* from the accounting records.

EXHIBIT 20.17 Purchase of Bonds in the Secondary Market—Wal-Mart

Carrying Value of One-Half of Bond Issue, 9/1/00	
Bonds payable ($20,000,000/2)	$10,000,000
Add premium on bonds payable ($2,433,398/2)	1,216,699
Carrying value of bonds	$11,216,699
Gain on Retirement of the Bonds	
Carrying value of the bonds	$11,216,699
Price paid for bonds	8,962,500*
Gain on retirement of bonds	$ 2,254,199

*$10,000,000 × 0.89625, where the price of a bond, 89 5/8, is expressed as a percentage of the face value of the bond.

Using the Bonds' Call Feature

Chapter 18 introduced the concept of a call feature enabling the company to retire the bonds before their maturity date by paying the bondholders a specified call price. For example, if a bond issue has a call price of 106, the company can buy a $1,000 bond for $1,060, or 106 percent of the $1,000 face value ($1,000 × 1.06).

When a company calls bonds, it is paying off its debt obligation prior to the maturity date. The carrying value of the bonds when they are called usually differs from the call price. If the call price is greater than the carrying value, the company would record a loss on the redemption of the bonds, and, if the call price is less than the carrying value, it would record a gain. The following example describes how to account for called bonds.

Assume that Wal-Mart's bond indenture has a call price that can be exercised after two years at a call price of 101. If Wal-Mart issued the bonds at a discount, as shown in Exhibit 20.11, and the entire bond issue was called on March 1, 2001, the company would make the entry below:

3/1/01	Bonds Payable	20,000,000	
	Loss on Retirement of Debt	2,221,325	
	Discount on Bonds Payable		2,021,325
	Cash		20,200,000

---

[2]Both gains and losses on early retirement are considered extraordinary items, which we discuss in Chapter 23.

Because the price paid to retire the debt, $20,200,000, is greater than the carrying value of the debt, $17,978,675, when it is called on March 1, 2001 (Exhibit 20.11, panel B), the company would record a $2,221,325 loss. Remember that the carrying value is a combination of two accounts, Bonds Payable and Discount on Bonds Payable, and the entry must eliminate both of these accounts when the company calls the bonds.

Converting Bonds into Stock

As indicated in Chapter 18, convertible bonds allow the bondholders to convert their bonds into stock *at the bondholder's option.* When bondholders convert their bonds into common stock, they are exchanging creditors' equity in the firm for owners' equity in the firm. This is called, therefore, an **interequity transaction,** or an exchange of one type of equity in the firm for another. As a result, the debt of the firm is retired without a cash expenditure by the corporation.

Bondholders will convert their bonds into stock only when the value of the stock they will receive upon conversion exceeds the value of the bond. *Remember that the decision to convert rests with the bondholders and not with the corporation.* Therefore, it is unusual for all of a company's bondholders to convert all of a corporation's bonds at one point in time. When conversion of bonds occurs between the bonds' interest dates, the company accrues the interest to the date of conversion, but the converting bondholder forfeits the cash interest due at that date. As a result, most bonds are converted at or soon after their interest dates.

Corporations can use the call feature of a bond to force convertible bondholders to convert their bonds. For example, if Wal-Mart's $0.10 par value common stock reaches $35 a share, the value of the 50 shares of stock associated with the bond is $1,750. Wal-Mart could notify the bondholders that it intends to call the bonds, which means each bondholder would receive $1,010 in cash for their bonds on the next interest date. Then the bondholders have a choice of either converting their bonds into stock worth $1,750 or taking $1,010 in cash. Given the choice, most rational bondholders would convert their bonds into stock and, as a result, the corporation is able to reduce its debt through the conversion process rather than paying cash. The entry below reflects this interequity transaction for one bond with a $1,000 carrying value.

Bonds Payable	1,000	
Common Stock ($0.10 × 50)		5
Paid in Capital in Excess of Par		995

ACCOUNTING FOR LEASES

LO 4

We described the features of operating and capital leases in Chapter 18. This section describes how to account for capital leases, a type of long-term debt financing. Leases are a source of long-term debt whose features cause their accounting treatment to differ from the basic types of notes just discussed.

Reflecting Operating Leases in the Accounting Records

Operating leases typically are rental agreements for a period of time that is substantially shorter than the economic life of the asset. For example, suppose Wal-Mart signs a three-year lease agreeing to pay $250 each month for the use of a Dodge Caravan as a delivery vehicle for its pharmacy. Wal-Mart would debit the Rent Expense account when it makes each rental payment but would record no liability at any time during the life of the lease:

Rent Expense—Selling	250	
Cash		250

Reflecting Capital Leases in the Accounting Records

Recall that a capital lease is a rental agreement that confers to the lessee such a substantial interest in the leased asset that, in economic substance, the lessee owns the asset. When the lessee signs a capital lease, the lessee records an asset for the leased property and a related liability for the lease obligation in its accounting records. The amount of the lease obligation for the lessee is equal to the present value of the future lease payments, while the value of the asset on the lessee's records is the amount of the lease obligation plus any cash payments made when the lease is signed. The lessee records subsequent lease payments like those made for an installment note.

Assume that Wal-Mart signs a four-year lease on February 1, 1999, for a copier that has a four-year life. The terms of the lease call for Wal-Mart to pay $2,000 immediately and to make four payments of $4,321.39 each year starting January 31, 2000. Wal-Mart is responsible for all maintenance and repairs to the copier after the first two years. Wal-Mart's market rate of interest is 9 percent. This leasing agreement is clearly a capital lease because Wal-Mart has, in effect, purchased the machine.

<table>
<tr><td>Calculator:</td></tr>
<tr><td>PV = 14,000</td></tr>
<tr><td>c = 1</td></tr>
<tr><td>n = 4</td></tr>
<tr><td>r = 9</td></tr>
<tr><td>FV = 0</td></tr>
<tr><td>PMT = 4,321.36</td></tr>
</table>

EXHIBIT 20.18 Capitalization of Lease Payments—Wal-Mart

A. Determining the Installment Payment

$$\text{Present value of annuity} = \text{Annuity} \times P_{4,9}\%$$
$$= \$4,321.39 \times 3.2397$$
$$= \$14,000$$

B. Lease Payment Schedule

Date	Payment	Interest Expense (0.09 × Lease Balance)	Principal	Lease Balance
2/1/99				$14,000.00
1/31/00	$4,321.39	$1,260.00	$3,061.39	10,938.61
1/31/01	4,321.39	984.47	3,336.92	7,601.69
1/31/02	4,321.39	684.15	3,637.24	3,964.45
1/31/03	4,321.39	356.94*	3,964.45	–0–

*Rounded.

This capital lease creates a leased asset of $16,000, which is equal to the $2,000 cash paid and the $14,000 lease liability incurred to acquire the asset. The $14,000 lease liability is the present value of the four $4,321.39 lease payments (shown in Exhibit 20.18, panel A) using Wal-Mart's 9 percent borrowing rate. The lease liability takes the form of an installment note because each lease payment covers the amount of interest expense due and reduces a portion of the principal. The entry to record the lease is:

Copier	16,000	
Cash		2,000
Lease Payment Obligation		14,000

Exhibit 20.18, panel B, presents the lease payment schedule. The entries for the lease payments are the same as those made for installment notes. The entry below for the first lease payment reflects the interest expense of $1,260 and the reduction of the lease liability of $3,061.39 at January 31, 2000:

Interest Expense	1,260.00	
Lease Payment Obligation	3,061.39	
Cash		4,321.39

The liability account Lease Payment Obligation decreases each year as payments are made. As with the case of installment notes, the company classifies the portion of the principal due next year as a current liability and the remainder as a long-term liability for 2000 and 2001. The entire amount of the lease is classified as a current liability for 2002. Wal-Mart would report the associated cash flows of a lease on its cash flow statement in the same way it would for the cash flows of an installment note. Because Wal-Mart records a tangible, operating asset on the books at the time of signing the lease, it records depreciation expense on the leased asset at the end of the fiscal year.

A capital lease requires the recognition of a liability on the financial statements. Wal-Mart's balance sheet reports Long-Term Obligations Under Capital Leases of $2,483,000,000 in 1998 and $2,307,000,000 in 1997 (See Exhibit 20.19). Exhibit 20.20 is note 8, "Long-Term Lease Obligations," from Wal-Mart's financial statements that describes in more detail Wal-Mart's lease obligations. Note that the note not only gives more detail about the nature of Wal-Mart's leases but also describes the future cash flows for both operating and capital leases through 2002.

CONSOLIDATED BALANCE SHEETS

(Amounts in millions)

January 31,	1998	1997
Current Liabilities:		
Accounts payable	$ 9,126	$ 7,628
Accrued liabilities	3,628	2,413
Accrued income taxes	565	298
Long-term debt due within one year	1,039	523
Obligations under capital leases due within one year	102	95
Total Current Liabilities	14,460	10,957
Long-Term Debt	7,191	7,709
Long-Term Obligations Under Capital Leases	2,483	2,307

2 Commercial Paper and Long-term Debt

At January 31, 1998 and 1997, there were no short-term borrowings outstanding. At January 31, 1998, the Company had committed lines of credit of $1,873 million with 77 banks and informal lines of credit with various banks totaling an additional $1,950 million, which were used to support short-term borrowings and commercial paper. Short-term borrowings under these lines of credit bear interest at or below the prime rate.

Long-term debt at January 31, consists of (amounts in millions):

		1998	1997
8.625%	Notes due April 2001	$ 750	$ 750
5.875%	Notes due October 2005	597	597
5.614%	Notes due February 2010 with biannual put options	500	–
7.500%	Notes due May 2004	500	500
9.100%	Notes due July 2000	500	500
6.125%	Notes due October 1999	500	500
7.800%-8.250%	Obligations from sale/leaseback transactions due 2014	458	466
6.500%	Notes due June 2003	454	454
7.250%	Notes due June 2013	445	445
7.000% - 8.000%	Obligations from sale/leaseback transactions due 2013	306	314
6.750%	Notes due May 2002	300	300
8.500%	Notes due September 2024	250	250
6.750%	Notes due October 2023	250	250
8.000%	Notes due September 2006	250	250
6.125%	Eurobond due November 2000	250	250
6.875%	Eurobond due June 1999	250	250
6.375%	Notes due March 2003	228	228
6.750%	Eurobond due May 2002	200	200
5.500%	Notes due March 1998	–	500
5.125%	Eurobond due October 1998	–	250
7.000%	Eurobond due April 1998	–	250
	Other	203	205
		$ 7,191	$ 7,709

Of Interest Sale-Lease Back

ale-Leasebacks at first glance seem like a paradox. Why would a company that owns a building sell it to another person or entity and then immediately lease it back from that entity? The sale-leaseback is a common transaction in business because it is financially advantageous for both parties. For the company selling the property there are two main advantages. The first advantage is that by selling the property the company can raise cash to invest in daily operations that would otherwise be tied up in the cost of the building. The second advantage occurs when debt used to acquire the property is retired with the proceeds from its sale and, therefore, improves the firm's debt-to-equity ratio. A sale-leaseback is advantageous to the company buying the property because it is making a relatively low-risk investment that will provide secure cash flows, a *return of* its investment, and a satisfactory *return on* its investment.

To illustrate lets assume that Wal-Mart completes construction of a building for a new store that cost $1,500,000 on January 1, 2000 and has financed $700,000 of the cost by issuing a 10 year 10% note payable. Upon completing the building, Wal-Mart immediately sells the building to the Millenium Leasing Company for $1,500,000 and then signs a 10 year operating lease with Millenium Leasing Company for the use of the building. Wal-Mart's lease payments will be $265,477 a year starting January 1, 2001 for the next ten years. Wal-Mart uses the proceeds of the sale to pay off its $700,000 note and uses the remaining proceeds to acquire inventory for the new store. Wal-Mart benefits from the transaction because it improves its debt-to-equity ratio by paying off its debt. However, the most important aspect of the transaction is that Wal-Mart now has $800,000 to invest in inventory that can generate a much higher return for the company than if it were tied up in the building.

For Millenium Leasing the lease is a safe investment with a satisfactory return. The lease will provide Millenium with a return of its investment in ten years and a 12 percent return on its investment over the life of the lease. At the end of the lease Millenium could sign another lease with Wal-Mart, sell the building, or lease it to another company.

Some firms want to avoid capital leases because the liability increases the firm's debt-to-equity ratio, which could have an adverse effect on the interest rates available to the firm. For this reason, firms signing lease agreements may structure the lease to qualify as an operating lease, thus getting the use of the leased asset without recording an asset or a liability. If significant, however, the company must disclose the future cash outflows they are obligated to make as a result of the operating leases. We have illustrated this disclosure to the financial statements for both Wal-Mart (Exhibit 20.20) and Sprint (Exhibit 18.11).

INFORMATION PROVIDED FOR DECISION MAKERS

External and internal decision makers who are interested in a firm's long-term debt find the information described in this chapter quite useful. External decision makers want to know the amount, type, and cost of a firm's long-term debt, as well as its related cash flows. A firm's financial statements and notes to the statements (see Exhibit 20.19 for Wal-Mart) provide external decision makers with useful information about the composition and features of a firm's long-term debt and its ability to service the debt. The cash flow statement gives the reader some idea how much cash was raised by issuing long-term debt and what was acquired with the funds. A firm's financial statements provide the information external decision makers need to assess the risks

8 Long-term Lease Obligations

The Company and certain of its subsidiaries have long-term leases for stores and equipment. Rentals (including, for certain leases, amounts applicable to taxes, insurance, maintenance, other operating expenses and contingent rentals) under all operating leases were $596 million, $561 million and $531 million in 1998, 1997 and 1996, respectively. Aggregate minimum annual rentals at January 31, 1998, under non-cancelable leases are as follows (in millions):

Fiscal year	Operating leases	Capital leases
1999	$ 404	$ 347
2000	384	345
2001	347	344
2002	332	343
2002	315	340
Thereafter	2,642	3,404
Total minimum rentals	$ 4,424	5,123
Less estimated executory costs		73
Net minimum lease payments		5,050
Less imputed interest at rates ranging from 6.1% to 14.0%		2,465
Present value of minimum lease payments		$ 2,585

Certain of the leases provide for contingent additional rentals based on percentage of sales. Such additional rentals amounted to $46 million, $51 million and $41 million in 1998, 1997 and 1996, respectively. Substantially all of the store leases have renewal options for additional terms from five to 25 years at comparable rentals.

The Company has entered into lease commitments for land and buildings for 38 future locations. These lease commitments with real estate developers provide for minimum rentals for 20 to 25 years, excluding renewal options, which if consummated based on current cost estimates, will approximate $38 million annually over the lease terms.

and rewards created by debt financing and provide a basis for deciding among investment alternatives.

Internal decision makers are in a position to influence the amount and type of the firm's long-term debt. They use information on the financial statements and internal reports as a basis for making their decisions about long-term debt. Their goal is to balance the risk and reward of using long-term debt and to incur the smallest cost possible for the use of the funds obtained by issuing debt.

In addition to balancing the risk and reward of long-term debt financing, internal decision makers must understand the amount and timing of cash flows associated with their debt financing decisions. This means they must understand the characteristics of the debt financing alternatives at their disposal. We discussed the factors these managers must consider when planning long-term debt financing in Chapter 18. Once the long-term debt instruments are issued, financial managers have reports prepared that compare the cash flows mandated by their debt financing decisions and the cash flows generated by the project that was financed by the debt. These internal reports help identify potential problems in meeting the cash flow obligations required by the firm's long-term debt. This in turn reduces the chance of the firm defaulting on its long-term debt.

EXHIBIT **20.20** *Continued*

The Company has agreed to observe certain covenants under the terms of its note agreements, the most restrictive of which, relates to amounts of additional secured debt and long-term leases.

The Company has entered into sale/leaseback transactions involving buildings while retaining title to the undering land.

These transactions were accounted for as financings and are included in long-term debt and the annual maturities schedules above. The resulting obligations are amortized over the lease terms. Future minimum lease payments for each of the five succeeding years, as of January 31, 1998, are (in millions):

In fiscal 1998, the Company borrowed $500 million due in 2010 with put options imbedded. Beginning in 2000, and every second year, thereafter until 2010, the holders of the debt may require the Company to repurchase the debt at face value.

Long-term debt is unsecured except for $202 million, which is collateralized by property with an aggregate carrying value of approximately $349 million. Annual maturities of long-term debt during the next five years are (in millions):

Fiscal year ending January 31,	Annual maturity
1999	$ 1,039
2000	815
2001	2,018
2002	52
2003	559
Thereafter	3,747

Fiscal years ending January 31,	Minimum rentals
1999	$ 76
2000	104
2001	100
2002	94
2003	98
Thereafter	817

At January 31, 1998 and 1997, the Company had letters of credit outstanding totaling $673 million and $811 million, respectively. These letters of credit were issued primarily for the purchase of inventory.

Under shelf registration statements previously filed with the Securities and Exchange Commission, the Company may issue debt securities aggregating $251 million.

SUMMARY

Long-term debt is a means of raising large amounts of cash typically used to acquire a firm's operational investments. Each of the three types of notes used to raise these funds receives a slightly different accounting treatment because the cash flows specified by the notes differ according to the form of the note. The resources acquired depend upon how the market rates affect the cash flows promised by the notes. A firm's accounting records reflect the long-term obligation created by these notes as well as the cost of using long-term debt financing.

- Each type of long-term note used to obtain funds or resources—periodic payment, lump-sum payment, and periodic payment and lump-sum notes—is recorded and reported in a manner consistent with its respective cash flow characteristics and the matching principle.

- A periodic payment note has a portion of the note reported as a current liability and a portion reported as a long-term liability.

- The discount on a lump-sum or noninterest-bearing note represents the interest over the entire life of the note and is reported as a contra liability on the balance sheet.

- Premiums and discounts on bonds represent the difference between the face rate of interest and the market rate of interest on the bond. Amortization of premiums results in interest expense reported on the income statement that is less than the amount of cash interest reported on the cash flow statement. Amortization of discounts causes effective interest reported on the income statement to be greater than the amount of cash interest reported on the cash flow statement.

- Early retirement of bonds occurs when bonds are purchased in the secondary market or when they are called, or converted. Gains and losses are recorded when the carrying value of the bonds differs from the market price of the bonds at the time of retirement.

- Operating and capital leases are another source of debt financing.

KEY TERMS

contra liability An account that has a debit balance that reduces the amount of a specific related liability account to show its carrying value

interequity transaction A transaction that reflects the exchange of one type of equity in a firm for another

ANSWERS TO THE PAUSE & REFLECTS

p. 683, The market interest rate on noncash transactions is set by the management of a company. It is a fairly subjective process but should be based on the incremental borrowing rate of the firm. That is, the interest rate that a firm would incur to borrow cash on a long-term basis at the time of the noncash transaction. However, because the firm is not actually borrowing cash at the time of the transaction, management makes an informed judgement about its incremental borrowing rate. Any interest rate that is less than two-thirds of a firm's incremental borrowing rate is considered unrealistic. In applying the 2/3 test, the incremental borrowing rate is determined by an independent third party rather than management.

p. 689, The interest payable account remains the same because it is a portion of the cash interest established by the bond indenture. The amount of cash interest is the same each year and is determined by multiplying the face interest rate times the face or maturity value of the bond.

QUESTIONS

1. Why does management finance a company's operational infrastructure with long-term debt?
2. What two accounts are debited when a company makes a payment on an installment loan?
3. When is an adjusting entry recorded for an installment note? Why is it necessary?
4. When is an installment note classified as both a current liability and a long-term liability?
5. Describe what the Discount on Note Payable represents.
6. Describe why and how the Discount on Note Payable is reported on the balance sheet.
7. How does the entry to record the issuance of a bond at a premium differ from a bond issued at a discount?
8. How should a company report a premium on bonds payable on its balance sheet?
9. What constitutes the carrying value of a noninterest-bearing note? A bond?
10. Explain why and how the Premium and Discount on Bonds Payable affect interest expense.
11. How does the adjusting entry for a noninterest-bearing note differ from a periodic payment and lump-sum note (bond)? Why are they different?
12. What impact does amortization have on the carrying value of bonds issued at a premium? At a discount?
13. Describe the difference in cash flows between two identical bonds when one is issued at a discount and the other is issued at a premium.
14. If a company repurchases its bonds in the secondary market, under what circumstances would the company record a gain?
15. How is the cash paid to call a bond determined?
16. Describe what happens to a company's balance sheet when a convertible bond is converted to common stock.

17. When a bond is converted into common stock, it is called an *interequity transaction*. What does this mean?

18. Compare and contrast accounting for a called bond and a converted bond.

19. What are the differences between the entries to record an operating and a capital lease? Why do these differences exist?

20. Describe the difference between how an operating lease and a capital lease are reported on the income statement, the balance sheet, and the statement of cash flows for the lessor.

EXERCISES

E 20.1

LO 1 LO 2 LO 3

The schedules below describe three notes:

Schedule 1

Date	Cash Payment	Interest Expense	Principal	Loan Balance
2/1/99				$40,000
8/1/99	$8,135	$2,400	$ 5,735	34,265
2/1/00	8,135	2,056	6,079	28,186
8/1/00	8,135	1,691	6,444	21,742
2/1/01	8,135	1,305	6,830	14,912
8/1/01	8,135	895	7,240	7,672
2/1/02	8,135	463	7,672	–0–

Schedule 2

Date	Cash Payment	Interest Expense	Discount	Carrying Value
4/1/98			$364,500.00	$ 635,500.00
4/1/99		$ 76,260.00	288,240.00	711,760.00
4/1/00		85,411.20	202,828.80	797,171.20
4/1/01		95,660.54	107,168.26	892,831.74
4/1/02		107,168.26	–0–	1,000,000.00
4/1/02	$1,000,000			–0–

Schedule 3

Date	Cash Interest	Interest Expense	No Discount or Premium	Carrying Value
3/1/98				$10,000,000
9/1/98	$500,000	$500,000		10,000,000
3/1/99	500,000	500,000		10,000,000
9/1/99	500,000	500,000		10,000,000
3/1/00	500,000	500,000		10,000,000

a. Which schedule describes a periodic payment and lump-sum note?
b. Which schedule describes a lump-sum payment note?
c. Which schedule describes a periodic payment note?
d. What are the annual interest rates on each of the notes?
e. Assuming each note was issued for cash, show the entry to record the issuance of each of the notes.

E 20.2

LO 1 LO 2 LO 3

Presented below is a partial schedule for a note payable of the Denver Broncos Company:

Date	Cash Payment			
3/1/98				$50,000
6/1/98	$3,058	$1,000	$2,058	47,942
9/1/98	3,058	958	2,100	45,841
12/1/98	3,058	916	2,142	43,700
3/1/99	3,058	874	2,184	41,516
6/1/99	3,058	830	2,228	39,288

a. Is this a periodic payment, a lump-sum payment, or a periodic payment and lump-sum note?
b. What is the note's annual market interest rate?

c. If the note was used to pay for a truck, make the entry for the acquisition of the truck.

d. Make the entry for the 6/1/98 payment.

E 20.3

LO 1

Using the data in E 20.2 and assuming that Denver Broncos Company has a June 30 fiscal year-end, make the appropriate adjusting entry for June 30, 1998. Describe how the company would report this note on its balance sheet, income statement, and statement of cash flows for the year ended June 30, 1998.

E 20.4

LO 2

On September 1, 1999, Hale/Bop Telescopes borrowed $92,000 cash at 7 percent on a four-year installment note. Annual payments starting on September 1, 2000, are $27,161. Prepare an installment loan repayment schedule for the first two years of the note. Make the entries for the first year of the note assuming that Hale/Bop has a December 31 fiscal year-end.

E 20.5

LO 1

The payment schedule below is for a $75,000 note the Colby Jones Corporation issued for cash on August 1, 1999. If Colby Jones Corporation has a December 31 fiscal year-end, make the entries for the issuance of the note and through December 31, 2000.

Date	Cash Payment	Interest Expense	Principal	Loan Balance
8/1/99				$75,000.00
2/1/00	$14,776.29	$3,750.00	$11,026.29	63,973.71
8/1/00	14,776.29	3,198.69	11,577.60	52,396.11
2/1/01	14,776.29	2,619.81	12,156.48	40,239.63
8/1/01	14,776.29	2,011.98	12,764.31	27,475.32

E 20.6

LO 1

Using the information in E 20.5, show how the installment note is reported on Colby Jones Corporation's income statement, balance sheet, and statement of cash flows for the years ended December 31, 1999 and 2000.

E 20.7

LO 2

On November 1, 2000, Bryce Lynd, the chief financial officer of the Collyer Corporation, raised $2,382,100 by issuing a five-year, $3,500,000 noninterest-bearing note. The amortization table for the note is presented below. Make the entries for the note from November 1, 2000, to December 31, 2001.

Date	Cash Payment	Interest Expense	Discount	Carrying Value
11/1/00			$1,117,900	$2,382,100
11/1/01		$190,568	927,332	2,572,668
11/1/02		205,813	721,519	2,778,481

E 20.8

LO 2

Using the information in E 20.7, show how Collyer Corporation's income statement and balance sheet report the impact of this note for the years ended December 31, 2000, and December 31, 2001.

E 20.9

LO 2

Kovar Furnace Company purchased equipment from Quirin Pipe and Fittings on January 1, 1999, by issuing a four-year noninterest-bearing note with a face value of $245,000. If Kovar Furnace has a December 31 fiscal year-end, prepare the journal entries for the acquisition of the equipment and the first two years of the note. Assuming that Kovar's market rate of interest is 10 percent, how much interest will Kovar report on its 1999 income statement? How would Kovar report the note on its balance sheet at December 31, 1999? How does the note affect Kovar's statement of cash flows in 1999?

E 20.10

LO 2

On June 1, 2000, Buseman Corporation purchased a piece of equipment with a list price of $300,000 and signed a two-year noninterest-bearing note. Given the amortization schedule below for the note and the fact that Buseman has a December 31 fiscal year-end, make the entries necessary for the life of the note.

Date	Cash Payment	Interest Expense (0.08 × Carrying Value)	Discount	Carrying Value
6/1/00			$42,810.00	$257,190.00
6/1/01		$20,575.20	22,234.80	277,765.20
6/1/02		22,234.80	–0–	300,000.00
6/1/02	$300,000			–0–

E 20.11

LO 2

Using the information in E 20.10, show how much interest Buseman Corporation will report on its income statement in 2000, 2001, and 2002. How would Buseman report the note on the balance sheets on December 31, 2000 and 2001? What are the cash flows reported on the cash flow statements for 2000, 2001, and 2002?

E 20.12
LO 3

The Wyndam Company borrowed $670,000 cash and signed a $670,000, 8 percent, four-year note payable dated May 1, 1999. Interest on the note is payable semiannually on November 1 and May 1 each year. The company closes its books annually on December 31. Prepare the entries for the issuance of the note and for events related to the note during the first year of the note's life. How is the note reported on Wyndam's balance sheet, income statement, and cash flow statement for the year ended December 31, 1999?

E 20.13
LO 3

Ross Greenwood, the chief financial officer of Moose Corporation, issued for cash a $4,200,000, 11 percent, three-year note payable on September 1, 1999, that pays interest annually. Moose Corporation has a December 31 fiscal year-end. Make the entries for the first year of the note's life if the market rate of interest is 9 percent.

E 20.14
LO 3

Hanson Corporation issued $55,000,000 of bonds for cash on June 1, 1999, and prepared the amortization schedule shown below. Given this information, make the entries for the first year of the bond issue's life if Hanson Corporation has a December 31 fiscal year-end. Show how Hanson reports the bond issue on its income statement, balance sheet, and cash flow statement for the year ended December 31, 1999.

Date	Cash Interest	Interest Expense	Discount Amortized	Discount	Carrying Value
6/1/99				$6,308,775	$48,691,225
12/1/99	$2,750,000	$2,921,424	$171,424	6,137,351	48,862,649
6/1/00	2,750,000	2,931,759	181,759	5,955,582	49,044,418

E 20.15
LO 3

Lichti Oil Corporation issued $4,000,000 of 10-year, 6 percent bonds on September 1, 1999, that pay interest semiannually on March 1 and September 1 each year. The bonds will yield an 8 percent effective rate of interest. Prepare the journal entries for the first year of the bonds' life if Lichti Oil has a June 30 fiscal year-end.

E 20.16
LO 3

DeMers Corporation is authorized to issue 6,000 10-year, 9 percent bonds. Each bond has a $1,000 face value, is convertible into 50 shares of DeMers' no-par common stock, and has a call price of 105. DeMers issued the bonds on March 1, 1999, at a discount and prepared the amortization schedule shown below. On March 1, 2000, the market price of DeMers' stock had risen to $42 per share, and bondholders had turned in 2,000 bonds for conversion to stock. Make the entry for the conversion of the bonds on March 1, 2000.

Date	Cash Interest	Interest Expense	Discount Amortization	Bond Discount	Carrying Value
3/1/99				$1,032,326	$4,967,674
9/1/99	$270,000	$298,060	$28,060	1,004,266	4,995,734
3/1/00	270,000	299,744	29,744	974,522	5,025,478
9/1/00	270,000	301,528	31,528	942,994	5,057,006
3/1/01	270,000	303,420	33,420	909,574	5,090,426

E 20.17
LO 3

Using the information in E 20.16, make the entry for DeMers Corporation assuming it called the entire bond issue on September 1, 2000.

E 20.18
LO 3

Given the amortization table shown in E 20.16, assume that the market price of DeMers' bond had dropped to 90 3/4 on March 1, 2000, and DeMers purchased 2,000 of the bonds in the secondary market. Make the entry for DeMers' purchase of the bonds. After the bonds are purchased, what is the entry to record the interest on the bond issue on September 1, 2000?

E 20.19
LO 4

On September 1, 2000, a capital lease was signed by Sando Industries in which it agreed to lease machinery with a fair market value of $26,585 for a five-year period, which is the machine's useful life. Annual payments of $6,585 are to be made at the beginning of each year, and Sando's interest rate is 12 percent. Given the lease payment schedule below, make the entries for the lease payments for the first two years of the lease if Sando has a December 31 fiscal year-end.

Date	Lease Payment	Interest	Principal	Lease Obligation
9/1/00				$26,585
9/1/00	$6,585			20,000
9/1/01	6,585	$2,400	$4,185	15,815
9/1/02	6,585	1,898	4,687	11,128

E 20.20

LO 4

On May 1, 1999, Smoke Corporation signed a lease for a delivery truck that called for seven lease payments of $2,500. Smoke Corporation could borrow funds at an 8 percent rate of interest when the lease was signed. The first lease payment is made when the lease is signed, and the remaining payments are made every six months. If this is considered an operating lease and Smoke Corporation has a December 31 fiscal year-end, make the entries for the first year of the lease.

E 20.21

LO 4

The Chad Parker Corporation signed a three-year capital lease for a copier on June 1, 2000. The lease calls for four annual payments of $1,800. The first payment was made when the lease was signed. Make the entries for the first two years of the lease if Chad Parker Corporation's interest rate for the lease is 11 percent and it has a December 31 fiscal year-end. How would the company report the lease on its balance sheet, income statement, and cash flow statement for the year ended December 31, 2001?

PROBLEMS

P 20.1

LO 1 LO 2 LO 4

Millennium Products had the following transactions during 1999:

May 1	Borrowed $140,000 on a three-year, 10 percent installment note with quarterly payments.
June 15	Signed a four-year operating lease for additional equipment. Semiannual lease payments are $3,500 and the first payment was made when the lease was signed.
Aug. 1	Made the first quarterly installment payment on the May 1 installment loan.
Sept. 1	Issued a $200,000 noninterest-bearing note that is due in two years in exchange for a piece of equipment. Millennium's market rate of interest is 10 percent.
Nov. 1	Paid the second quarterly installment on the May 1 loan.
Dec. 15	Made the semiannual lease payment.

Required

a. Prepare the journal entries for the events described at Millennium.
b. Make the necessary adjusting entries on December 31, the company's fiscal year-end.
c. Show how Millennium reports the notes on its December 31, 1999 balance sheet.
d. How much interest is reported on Millennium's income statement in 1999?
e. Does the cash paid for interest in 1999 differ from the amount reported on its income statement? Explain.
f. How much cash was paid to reduce principal on the notes?

P 20.2

LO 3

The New Corporation made the following transactions in 1999 when its market rate of interest was 8 percent. New has a December 31 fiscal year-end.

Apr. 1	Purchased $42,000 of office equipment from Office World by paying $5,000 down and signing a three-year note with a face interest rate of 8 percent that is paid annually.
July 1	Purchased a piece of equipment with a list price of $62,000 and signed a two-year noninterest-bearing note for that amount.

Required

a. Make the entries to record the transactions above.
b. Make the appropriate adjusting entries for the notes.
c. Show how the notes are reported on the December 31, 1999 balance sheet.
d. How much interest was reported on the 1999 income statement?
e. Does the cash paid for interest differ from the amount reported on the income statement? Explain.
f. How much cash was paid to reduce the principal of the notes?

P 20.3

LO 3

Roger Smith Corporation has an 8 percent market interest rate and a December 31 fiscal year-end. During 2000 the following notes were issued to acquire equipment:

Mar. 1	Issued a $140,000, two-year, noninterest-bearing note for a conveyor system.
May 1	Issued a $140,000, two-year, 8 percent installment note for two trucks. The payments are due semiannually on November 1 and May 1.
June 1	Issued a $140,000, two-year, 6 percent note for a fabrication machine. The face interest is paid semiannually on December 1 and June 1.

Required

a. Make the entries for the issuance of each of these notes.
b. Make the entries for the notes through December 31, 2000.
c. Show how the notes are reported on the December 31, 2000, balance sheet.
d. What is the interest expense reported on the 2000, income statement?
e. How much cash interest was paid in 2000, and does this differ from the interest expense recognized in 2000? Explain.

P 20.4

LO 3

Metroplex Industries' board of directors authorized the issue of $60,000,000 in 10-year, 9 percent bonds. The bonds are dated November 1, 1999, and interest is paid semiannually on May 1 and November 1. Metroplex closes its books on June 30 each year. The bonds were issued on November 1, 1999, when the market rate of interest was 8 percent.

Required

a. How many individual bonds make up the bond issue?
b. Prepare the journal entries for the issuance of the bonds and the first year of the bonds' life.
c. Describe how the bonds are reported on Metroplex's income statement, balance sheet, and statement of cash flows for the year ended June 30, 2000.

P 20.5

LO 3

On April 1, 1999, South Port Supply issued $50,000,000 in 15-year, 10 percent bonds that pay interest annually on April 1. The bonds were issued on April 1, 1999, when the market interest rate was 11 percent. South Port's fiscal year ends December 31.

Required

a. Prepare the journal entries for the first two years of the bond issue's life.
b. Show how South Port Supply reports the events involving the bond issue on its income statement, balance sheet, and statement of cash flows for the years ended December 31, 1999, and December 31, 2000.

P 20.6

LO 3

Kahn Corporation has a market interest rate of 10 percent and is authorized to issue $50,000,000 in 10-year debentures on June 1, 1999. The face interest rate on the bonds will be paid semiannually.

Required

a. Make the entries for the bond issue and for the first year of the debenture's life if the face interest rate is 8 percent.
b. Make the entries for the bond issue and for the first year of the bond's life if the face interest rate is 12 percent.
c. Given the two possible face rates above, which one generates the most cash? In terms of rate of interest, which one is the least expensive for Kahn Corporation?

P 20.7

LO 3

Precious Stones is authorized to issue $40,000,000 in 10-year, 8 percent bonds on September 1, 1999. The bonds pay interest annually on August 1, and Precious Stone's fiscal year-end is on December 31.

1999
Aug. 1   Issued the bonds when the market rate of interest was 9 percent.
Dec. 31   Recorded the adjusting entry for the bond interest.

2000
Aug. 1   Made the first interest payment.

Required

a. Prepare the journal entries for the events above.
b. Determine the amount of interest expense incurred in 1999.
c. How much cash was paid in interest in 1999? How does this relate to your answer in (**b**) and why?
d. Show how to report the liabilities associated with the bonds on the December 31, 1999 balance sheet.

P 20.8

LO 3

On June 1, 2000, Sooner Corporation issued 180,000 10-year bonds each with a $1,000 face value. The bonds have a face rate of 10 percent and pay interest semiannually on December 1 and June 1. The bonds have a 50:1 conversion feature; that is, the bondholders can exchange one bond for 50 shares of Sooner's no-par common stock.

On June 1, 2001, bondholder Bruce Derr converted 20 of his bonds. The carrying value of all the bonds on Sooner's books at the time of conversion was $179,800,000.

Required

a. Prepare the entry for Sooner Corporation to record the conversion of the 20 bonds.
b. Why would an investor want to convert the bonds?
c. Why would Sooner put a conversion feature on the bonds?
d. What is the carrying value of the remaining bonds after the conversion?

P 20.9

LO 3

Using the same facts as in P 20.8, assume that on June 1, 2001, Sooner purchased 10,000 of its bonds in the bond market when the price was 98.

Required

a. Prepare the necessary journal entry for the purchase of the bonds.
b. Why would Sooner take such an action?
c. Assuming this is Sooner's only bond transaction, what is the carrying value of the remaining bonds after the purchase?

P 20.10

LO 3

Assume the Sooner bonds in P 20.8 were issued with a call feature of 105 and that on June 1, 2001, Sooner called 2,000 bonds when the market price of the bonds was 108.

Required
    a. Make the journal entry to record the calling of the bonds on June 1, 2001.
    b. Why would Sooner call these bonds?
    c. Assuming this is Sooner's only bond transaction, what is the carrying value of the remaining bonds after the bonds are called?

P 20.11
LO 3

On March 1, 1999, the Burke Corporation issued $60,000,000 of 10-year, 8 percent, convertible bonds. The bonds have a call price of 105, and interest is paid semiannually on September 1 and March 1. Each $1,000 bond is convertible into 60 shares of Burke's no-par common stock. The bond was issued to yield an effective rate of interest of 6 percent. Burke Corporation has a December 31 fiscal year-end.

Required
    a. Make the entry to record the issuance of the bonds.
    b. Set up an amortization table for the first four interest payments of the bond issue.

Treat each of the following as independent events.

    c. Show the entry if 1,000 bonds are converted on March 1, 2000, when the stock is selling for $30 per share. Explain why the bondholders would convert these bonds.
    d. Show the entry if the company calls 1,000 bonds on March 1, 2000. Why would Burke call its bonds?
    e. Make the entry if the company buys 1,000 bonds in the secondary bond market for 98 3/4 on March 1, 2000.

The following requirements assume that (**c**), (**d**), and (**e**) have all occurred.

    f. Make the entry to record the interest on the remaining bonds on September 1, 2000, and December 31, 2000.
    g. How would the remaining bonds be reported on Burke's December 31, 2000 balance sheet?

P 20.12
LO 4

Barton Leasing Service recently purchased equipment for $140,000 and leased it to Willamina Machine and Foundry on April 1, 1999. The equipment has an estimated useful life of five years. Willamina has leased the equipment for five years with an option to purchase it for $1 at the end of the fifth year. During the period of the lease, Willamina is responsible for all repairs and maintenance of the leased property. Willamina will make five annual lease payments of $33,020; the first is due on the date of the lease. Willamina's interest rate is 9 percent and it closes its books annually on December 31.

Required
    a. Is this a capital or operating lease?
    b. Make Willamina's April 1, 1999, entry for the lease.
    c. Prepare the appropriate adjusting entries at December 31, 1999.
    d. Describe how Willamina would report information regarding this lease on its income statement, balance sheet, and cash flow statement for the year ended December 31, 1999.
    e. Record the second annual lease payment on April 1, 2000.

CASES

C 20.1
LO 4

Note 8 of Wal-Mart's annual report for 1998 describes the leasing activity of the company as shown in Exhibit 20.20. What is management's incentive to structure leases so they qualify as operating rather than capital leases?

C 20.2
LO 1 **LO 2** **LO 3** **LO 4**

Using the annual report of a company of your choice, describe the firm's long-term notes (bonds, etc.). You should describe the following:
    a. Type of debt instruments used
    b. Cost of using debt financing
    c. Existence of capital leases and operating leases
    d. How the long-term debt instruments are reported in the annual report

CRITICAL THINKING

CT 20.1
LO 1 **LO 2**

Wayne's Furniture World is offering "interest-free financing for two full years—just divide the price of the furniture by 24 months to determine the monthly payment." Watkins Company purchased $16,800 of office furniture under this plan on November 15, 1999.

Required
    a. Make the entry to record Watkin's purchase if the company usually borrows money at 12 percent.
    b. Make the entry for the first $700 payment on December 15, 1999.

c. Make the adjusting entry on December 31, Watkin's fiscal year-end.

d. Make the entry for the second payment on January 15, 2000.

e. How is this lease reported on Watkin's December 31, 1999, balance sheet? Why?

f. How are the cash flows associated with this note reported on the cash flow statement?

CT 20.2
LO 1   LO 2

Dan Short, the promotions manager of Waterbed Bonanza Company, is interested in running a "36 months, no interest sale." He wants to offer customers the opportunity to buy waterbeds and to finance the purchase by merely dividing the price of the waterbed by 36 to determine the customer's monthly payment. However, he realizes that the "sale price" must somehow include the 12 percent interest usually charged to finance credit purchases. He has asked you to show him how to determine the "sale price" of a waterbed that normally sells for $1,000.

CT 20.3
LO 3

Sermier Corporation wants to raise $20,000,000 by issuing zero-coupon (noninterest-bearing) bonds that are due in 10 years. How many $1,000 zero-coupon bonds must it issue if the company's market rate is 8 percent? How would Sermier Corporation record the issuance of these bonds?

ETHICAL CHALLENGES

EC 20.1
LO 3

When the Beto Corporation issues long-term notes for noncash assets, it uses a face interest rate on the notes that is 2 percent less than the company's market interest rate at the time and records the notes at their face values. The corporation's chief financial officer argues that, because the notes are not issued to a bank for cash, they are secured with the assets of the company and, therefore, have less risk than if the company were borrowing cash from the bank to buy these assets. Do you agree or disagree with this reasoning? Why or why not? Why would management bonuses tied to net income create an incentive for following this course of action? What is the impact of this policy on Beto's income statement and balance sheet?

EC 20.2
LO 1

The Hacker Corporation has a considerable amount of long-term installment notes. The company controller has made it a company policy to report the entire amount of these installment notes as long-term liabilities. The controller argues that because the notes are all for long periods of time, they constitute long-term debt. Do you agree or disagree with this policy? Why or why not? What is the incentive for Hacker Corporation to follow this policy?

COMPUTER APPLICATIONS

CA 20.1
LO 3

Titanic Marine plans to issue $2 million of 10 percent, 20-year bonds. The market rate of interest at the time of issue is 9 percent. The bonds are issued on June 30, 1998 and pay interest semiannually. Titanic Marine has a December 31 year-end.

Required   Use a computer spreadsheet.

a. Determine the amount of cash Titanic will receive when the company issues the bonds, assuming they are issued on an interest payment date.

b. Prepare a bond amortization schedule that indicates the amounts of cash, interest expense, amortization, and bond carrying value on each interest payment date.

CA 20.2
LO 3

Refer to CA 20.1. Assume that the market rate of interest at the time of issue is 12 percent.

Required   Use a computer spreadsheet.

a. Determine the amount of cash Titanic will receive when the bonds are issued assuming they are issued on an interest payment date.

b. Prepare a bond amortization schedule that indicates the amounts of cash, interest expense, amortization, and bond carrying value on each interest payment date.

CA 20.3
LO 1   LO 2   LO 3   LO 4

Locate Wal-Mart's Web site and answer the following:

a. When and where was Wal-Mart founded?

b. How many Wal-Mart stores are there today?

c. Name five countries other than the United States that have Wal-Mart stores.

d. Locate the firm's financial statements and find Wal-Mart's net income for the past three years.

e. What are Wal-Mart's debt-to-equity ratios for the past two years?

f. Describe at least two recent news releases found on Wal-Mart's Web site.

PART SIX

YOU ARE HERE

Chapter 21 builds on the concepts developed in Chapter 15. In Chapter 15 we looked at the processes used by businesses to determine whether capital expenditures should be made. Chapter 21 adds to this discussion as we explore the process of recording asset acquisition, use, and disposal. Chapter 21 looks at recording and reporting operational investment activities (those involving operating assets). We explore the process of recording the initial acquisition of the asset, subsequent use of the asset (depreciation), and the disposal of the asset. Chapter 21 examines physical assets, intangible assets, and natural resources.

LEARNING OBJECTIVES

LO 1 Describe the issues involved in determining the cost of plant assets.

LO 2 Explain the nature of depreciation and related issues regarding the use of plant assets.

LO 3 Determine the financial impact of plant asset disposals.

LO 4 Describe the characteristics of natural resources and the process of depletion.

LO 5 Explain the characteristics of intangible assets and the process of amortization.

LO 6 Illustrate how to communicate events involving operational investments to external and internal users.

Recording and Communicating Operational Investment Activities

AMERICAN SKIING COMPANY
www.peaks.com

In November 1997 the American Skiing Company, headquartered in Newry, Maine, completed a very successful initial public offering (IPO), issuing just under 14 million shares of stock to investors at an offer price of $18 per share. The company now advertises itself as the "largest operator of alpine ski, snowboard and golf resorts in the United States."[1] The many resorts it owns and operates include familiar names such as Steamboat in Colorado, Killington and Sugarbush in Vermont, Sunday River and Sugarloaf in Maine, and Heavenly in both California and Nevada.

In 1997 American Skiing initiated its most ambitious project to date—the acquisition and development of The Canyons, a resort located just outside of Salt Lake City, Utah, site of the 2002 Winter Olympics. On April 9, 1998, people stood in line to put down deposits on 150 units of its "Sundial Lodge" condominium project, projected to sell for a total of $42.6 million. Additional real estate plans are in the works. On top of that, American Skiing has already installed a new high-speed gondola and has plans for additional new lifts and other developments that will make The Canyons the largest ski resort in Utah.

[1]<www.peaks.com>

American Skiing regularly makes huge investments in plant and equipment and other intangible assets. At July 26, 1998 (its most recent year-end), it reported total assets of $781 million, of which $521 million (67%) represented long-term investments in property and equipment and $100 million (13%) represented intangibles.[2] For the year ended July 26, 1998, expenses resulting from the use of these assets totaled $38 million.

The successful utilization of plant and equipment and intangibles is vital to the success of most companies. Some companies, such as mining and paper companies, also make significant long-term investments in natural resources. Thus it is important to understand what these assets are, as well as the accounting principles companies follow to record and report them to investors and creditors.

[2]Form 10-K filed by American Skiing Company with the SEC for its year ended July 26, 1998. The figure for intangibles includes $76 million of goodwill, which we define in this chapter.

n this chapter we discuss **operational investments,** which are long-term investments made to acquire the facilities necessary to conduct basic business activities. Operational investments fall into three major categories, which we discuss in turn: (1) plant assets, (2) natural resources, and (3) intangible assets.

The benefits derived from investments in plant assets, natural resources, and intangible assets represent an important factor in the successful operation of most companies. Because of the importance of operational investments, it is vital that we understand not only what these assets represent, but also how companies record and report their acquisition, use, and disposal.

PLANT ASSETS

LO 1

Plant assets, often referred to as *property, plant, and equipment,* are tangible assets acquired by a company primarily for use in the business over a time span covering more than one accounting period. This category includes land, buildings, and equipment employed to help create and deliver goods and services to customers. It represents the basic infrastructure of the business, without which successful business operations would be impossible.

Determining whether to categorize any tangible, long-term asset as a plant asset depends on its intended use. For example, if the American Skiing Company acquires a parcel of land as the site for a new skiing resort, the land is a plant asset because of its intended use as a place to carry on the company's business. However, if the company acquires the same piece of land because it plans to hold the land vacant for several years and then sell it at a profit, it is not a plant asset because the company will not use the land to create any of the goods or services it provides. In this second case, the company would report the land as a long-term investment.

There are three stages to consider when describing the accounting process for plant assets: (1) acquisition, (2) use, and (3) disposal. Users of financial statements should understand the recording process at each stage in order to meaningfully analyze the activities involved in plant asset purchase, use, and disposal.

ACQUISITION OF PLANT ASSETS

To understand why certain expenditures are added to or excluded from the acquisition cost of a plant asset, we must understand the difference between capital and revenue expenditures. A **capital expenditure** creates the expectation of future benefits that apply beyond the current accounting period. Because companies use plant assets for more than one accounting period, an expenditure to acquire any plant asset is a capital expenditure, which companies **capitalize,** or add to the cost of the plant asset rather than expensing it immediately. On the other hand, a **revenue expenditure** provides benefits exclusively during the current accounting period. Revenue expenditures include the costs of annual repairs and maintenance, as well as real estate taxes, utility bills, and most other day-today operating costs. Because revenue expenditures provide current benefits, companies generally expense them when incurred.

The capital expenditures added to the cost of any particular purchased plant asset include all normal, reasonable, and necessary expenditures to acquire the asset and prepare it for its intended future use. As discussed in Chapter 15, the cost of a building normally includes its purchase price as well as related legal fees and any broker's commissions paid. These are all considered normal, necessary costs of acquiring real estate. If the building is constructed rather than purchased, all normal costs incurred during the period of construction must be accumulated and added to the cost of the building.

The accounting for construction costs helps illustrate the difference between capital and revenue expenditures. Remember that assets represent economic resources with expected future benefits and that assets become expenses as they are used up to generate current benefits. During construction of a building, *all* normal, necessary costs incurred provide future benefits and, therefore, are capital expenditures added to the cost of the building. These costs include labor and materials directly associated with construction, permits, architect's fees, and taxes paid. They also include indirect costs, such as wages paid to security personnel, insurance payments, and interest costs on money borrowed during construction. However, once a company begins to use the completed building, it derives current benefits from the asset's use; therefore, expenditures for normal repairs and maintenance to maintain these current benefits are revenue expenditures, which the company reflects as expenses as they are incurred.

To illustrate this point, Note 2 of the American Skiing Company's financial statements for the year ended July 26, 1998, included the following statement:

> The Company capitalizes as real estate developed for sale the original acquisition cost of land, direct construction and development costs, property taxes, interest incurred on costs related to real estate under development, and other related costs (engineering, surveying, landscaping, etc.) until the property reaches its intended use.

The cost of land, like that of a building, includes its purchase price and any related legal and broker's fees paid. When purchasing land, frequently the buyer also pays for a survey and title search, title insurance, and various other fees that are necessary to transfer ownership. The buyer adds all of these expenditures to the cost of the land. If it is necessary to level out uneven sections of the land or to remove existing structures on the land before using it for its intended purpose, the buyer would include all of these expenditures as part of the cost of the land.

PAUSE & REFLECT

When insurance and interest costs are incurred during the course of a long-term construction project, they are added to the cost of the asset. If insurance and interest costs continue after the asset is completed and placed in service, should a company continue to add these expenditures to the cost of the asset? If not, how should they be treated? *(answer on page 736)*

Often a buyer pays one price to purchase land and a building together. When this occurs, the buyer must allocate the total purchase price between the two, because buildings and equipment are depreciable assets, whereas land is not. Allocation frequently occurs based on the relative dollar amount of separate appraisals completed for each asset. Or, to save money, small businesses may use real estate tax bills showing values assigned to the land and building by local tax assessors.

To demonstrate how this allocation works, assume the American Skiing Company paid $380,000 for a building sitting on one acre of land. An appraisal paid for by the company immediately prior to the transaction indicated that the land and building were worth $100,000 and $300,000, respectively. American Skiing might allocate the total purchase price based on the following two-step calculation:

1. Calculate the percentage of the total appraised values applicable to each asset:

	Appraised Value	Percentage of Total Appraised Value
Land	$100,000	$100,000/$400,000 = 25%
Building	300,000	$300,000/$400,000 = 75%
Total	$400,000	

2. Use the percentages calculated in step 1 to allocate the purchase price between the acquired assets:

	Percentage of Total Appraised Value	×	Total Purchase Price	=	Portion of Total Purchase Price Allocated to Each Asset
Land	25%	×	$380,000	=	$ 95,000
Building	75%	×	$380,000	=	285,000
Total	100%				$380,000

As a result of the allocation, the recorded cost of the land is $95,000, and the cost of the building is $285,000. These two amounts sum to the total purchase price of $380,000.

PAUSE & REFLECT

When land and buildings are purchased together for one price, a company might look for a justification to assign the smallest possible portion of the purchase price to the land. Why would it do this? *(answer on page 736)*

The cost of equipment normally includes the purchase price, freight charges, sales taxes paid, and installation costs. Any other normal, necessary costs, such as assembly and testing before use, are added to the cost of the equipment, and any discounts allowed, such as those for prompt payment, are deducted from the cost.

An interesting issue may arise when purchasing used equipment. What if a company paid $6,000 to purchase a used automobile with a remaining useful life of four years, and the company also paid $250 for a necessary tune-up before placing the auto in service? Assuming that the tune-up is a necessary, normal cost of readying the asset for use, the company would capitalize the cost of the tune-up as part of the total cost of the auto. However, if the company pays an additional $250 for a second tune-up one year later to maintain the car in good working order, the second payment is not added to the cost of the auto. Rather, this cost would be charged to repairs and maintenance expense for that time period. In the first case, the tune-up was a capital expenditure because it helped prepare a newly acquired asset for use during future accounting periods. In the second case, the tune-up was a revenue expenditure because it simply maintained a working asset in good condition for use in the current accounting period.

If a company purchases a used car, any service required prior to use would be capitalized.

Finally, many companies choose not to capitalize certain capital expenditures on the grounds that the dollar amount involved is insignificant. For example, if a company purchases a screwdriver for $5, even though the screwdriver may last for many years and is, therefore, theoretically a plant asset, the company will probably charge the $5 to an expense account. This is an application of the accounting concept of **materiality,** which relates to whether an item's dollar amount or its inherent nature is significant enough to influence a financial statement user. When a company prepares financial statements in accordance with generally accepted accounting principles, the goal is to prepare statements that are free of material errors. However, accountants have much latitude regarding the recording and reporting of immaterial items because, by definition, these items will not affect decisions made by users of the financial statements.[3] Therefore, most companies have capitalization policies stating that any expenditure less than some specified dollar amount will be expensed regardless of whether it is capital in nature or not.

Now that we understand the factors affecting their recorded acquisition cost, let's examine how to account for the use of plant assets.

USE OF PLANT ASSETS

LO 2

After placing a plant asset in service, a company begins to receive benefits from its use and must recognize the cost of these benefits as an expense over the useful life of the asset. Recall from Chapter 7's discussion of the matching principle that the proper determination of net income requires the recording of expenses in the period when benefits are received.

We also know from our previous discussions in Chapters 7 and 8 that the expense associated with using plant assets is called *depreciation* and that companies record it as follows:

Depreciation Expense	XXX	
Accumulated Depreciation		XXX

There is a separate accumulated depreciation account maintained for each asset or group of assets. Each separate accumulated depreciation account serves as a contra asset account and appears on the balance sheet as a deduction from the asset (or a group of assets) to which it relates. Whereas the depreciation expense account is closed out to income summary and owners' equity at the end of each period, accumulated depreciation is a permanent account, just like its related asset account. Its balance carries over and "accumulates" from one year to the next. Therefore, if a piece of equipment costing $10,000 was depreciated $1,000 per year for three full years, at the end of the third year it would appear on the balance sheet as follows:

Equipment (at cost)	$10,000	
Less accumulated depreciation	(3,000)	$7,000

Recall that the $7,000 figure is variously referred to as the *carrying value, book value,* or *remaining undepreciated cost* of the equipment.

Many individuals operate under the mistaken impression that accountants use depreciation to reflect the decline in value of an asset. It is important to emphasize that depreciation is actually a process whereby accountants systematically allocate the net cost of a plant asset to the various periods receiving benefits from the use of that asset to obtain a proper matching of revenue and related expense. *Depreciation is not an attempt to measure declining value.* Thus the carrying value of any plant asset shown on the balance sheet represents the remaining undepreciated cost of the asset—not its fair market value.

---

[3]Further discussion of the concept of materiality is beyond the scope of this text. However, students may find it interesting to look at the report of independent accounts (the auditor's report) included in companies' annual reports to shareholders. In the auditor's report, the use of the word *material* is in accordance with the discussion in this text. Accountants do not generally attempt to prepare financial statements that are free of all errors. The goal is to prepare statements that are free of material errors and omissions.

In fact, at the same time that companies record depreciation on buildings they own, many of those buildings are increasing in value due to inflation and other factors.

Because of the impact of inflation, it is possible that a 20-year-old building that originally cost $100,000 might be fully depreciated on a company's balance sheet, even though it is currently worth $1,000,000. What problems does this cause for the user of financial statements? What problems would be created if businesses were required to report the current values of all of their plant assets? *(answer on page 736)*

Factors Affecting Depreciation Calculations

Before calculating depreciation for any given plant asset, it is necessary to know the following:

- Cost of the asset
- Estimated useful life of the asset
- Estimated salvage value of the asset
- Method of depreciation

We have already discussed those expenditures included in the cost of plant assets, but the useful life, salvage value, and method of depreciation require further explanation.

Useful Life

Useful life is the period of time over which a business expects to obtain economic benefits from the use of a plant asset or any other operational investment. Of necessity, it is an estimate based on information available to management at the date the company places an asset in service.

With the exception of land, the useful life of operational investments is limited due to two factors: (1) physical wear and tear resulting from use of the asset or the passage of time and (2) obsolescence.

Obsolescence results from changing technology, tastes, and/or preferences. For example, businesses generally replace computers because improved hardware is available, not because the computers no longer function for their originally intended purpose. Or, even though an automobile could be used for seven to 10 years, a company may have a policy of buying a new automobile every three years simply because of a preference for newer automobiles.

Useful life can be expressed as a period of time or defined as the total number of units of output expected over the useful life of the asset, such as the estimated total miles an automobile will be driven.

Salvage Value

The expected fair market value of a plant asset at the end of its useful life is referred to as the **salvage value,** or **residual value,** of the asset. The portion of a plant asset's total cost that will be depreciated over its useful life, which is called its **depreciable cost,** is calculated as follows:

$$\text{Cost} - \text{Salvage value} = \text{Depreciable cost}$$

As in the case of useful life, the salvage value is based on an estimate made at the time an asset is placed in service.

Students often wonder about the accuracy of a depreciation expense figure calculated using an "estimated" useful life and salvage value. How can a company possibly know what a piece of equipment will be worth at the end of its useful life? Even more difficult, imagine estimating what a building will be worth at the end of an estimated useful life of 30 years! One should always remember that accounting is not an exact science. The matching principle requires that there be an honest attempt to record expenses in the period when related benefits are derived. A company could wait and record depreciation only after an asset is sold, at which time both its useful life and salvage value would be known with certainty. However, that would violate the matching principle and would result in improper determination of income during every period of the asset's life. Depreciation is just one of many examples demonstrating that amounts reported in financial statements are frequently based on estimates involving individual judgment.

METHODS OF DEPRECIATION

Three common methods exist for calculating the amount of depreciation reported in financial statements: (1) the straight-line method; (2) the units-of-production method; and (3) accelerated methods. We discuss each method in turn.

Straight-Line Depreciation

The **straight-line depreciation** method reflects the calculation of annual depreciation by allocating the depreciable cost of the asset to depreciation expense equally over its useful life. We calculate straight-line depreciation as follows:

$$\text{Annual depreciation expense} = \frac{\text{Cost} - \text{Salvage value}}{\text{Estimated number of years in useful life}}$$

For example, assume a delivery truck purchased by CDL Company for a total cost of $22,000 has an anticipated useful life of five years and a salvage value estimated at $2,000. The company would calculate annual straight-line depreciation expense for the truck as follows:

$$\frac{\$22,000 - \$2,000}{5 \text{ years}} = \$4,000 \text{ per year}$$

Exhibit 21.1, panel A, shows annual straight-line depreciation expense (column 1), as well as the resulting accumulated depreciation (column 2) and asset carrying value (column 3) at the end of each year of the truck's useful life. Notice that the annual depreciation expense shown in column 1, which is deducted in calculating income each year, is a constant figure, while the amount of accumulated depreciation shown in column 2 increases by the amount of depreciation expense taken each year. The balance of accumulated depreciation at the end of each year is subtracted from the asset's cost to obtain the year-end carrying value shown in column 3 to be reported in the plant asset section of the company's balance sheet.

Straight-line depreciation is based on the assumption that benefits derived from an asset are constant during each year of its use. This justifies recording the same dollar amount of expense annually. When this assumption is not valid, companies may employ one of the other methods of depreciation.

Units-of-Production Depreciation

Units-of-production depreciation is a way of calculating annual depreciation expense based on actual usage rather than the passage of time. Instead of defining the useful life of an asset in terms of years, this depreciation method expresses an asset's useful life in terms of total expected units of output. For example, a company might expect a piece of manufacturing equipment to last for a total of 20,000 hours of operating use. Or the company may assign an automobile a useful life of 100,000 miles. Thus the depreciable cost of the asset is divided by the expected total units of output to determine the depreciation rate per unit of output. This rate is used to calculate annual depreciation based on the actual output for the period.

Units-of-production depreciation involves calculating depreciation expense in two steps:

1. $\dfrac{\text{Cost} - \text{Salvage value}}{\substack{\text{Estimated total output} \\ \text{over life of asset}}}$ = Depreciation per unit of output

2. $\substack{\text{Depreciation per unit} \\ \text{of output (from step 1)}} \times \substack{\text{Actual output} \\ \text{for current year}} = \substack{\text{Depreciation expense} \\ \text{for current year}}$

EXHIBIT 21.1 Comparison of Various Depreciation Methods

Assumptions

Asset description	Delivery truck
Cost of asset	$22,000
Useful life	5 years
Salvage value	$2,000

Panel A. Straight-Line Depreciation

Year	(1) Annual Depreciation Expense[a]	(2) Accumulated Depreciation as of Year-End	(3) Carrying Value as of Year-End
1	$4,000	$ 4,000	$18,000
2	4,000	8,000	14,000
3	4,000	12,000	10,000
4	4,000	16,000	6,000
5	4,000	20,000	2,000

Panel B. Units-of-Production Depreciation

Year	(1) Annual Depreciation Expense[b]	(2) Accumulated Depreciation as of Year-End	(3) Carrying Value as of Year-End
1	$0.20 × 14,000[c] = $2,800	$ 2,800	$19,200
2	0.20 × 23,000 = 4,600	7,400	14,600
3	0.20 × 18,700 = 3,740	11,140	10,860
4	0.20 × 21,300 = 4,260	15,400	6,600
5	0.20 × 23,000 = 4,600	20,000	2,000
	100,000 miles		

Panel C. Double-Declining-Balance (DDB) Depreciation
(rounded to nearest whole dollar)

Year	(1) Annual Depreciation Expense[d]	(2) Accumulated Depreciation as of Year-End	(3) Carrying Value as of Year-End
1	$22,000 × 0.40 = $8,800	$ 8,800	$13,200
2	13,200 × 0.40 = 5,280	14,080	7,920
3	7,920 × 0.40 = 3,168	17,248	4,752
4	4,752 × 0.40 = 1,901	19,149	2,851
5	851[e]	20,000	2,000

[a]Annual depreciation expense = ($22,000 − $2,000)/5 years.

[b]Annual depreciation calculated in two steps:
1. ($22,000 − $2,000)/100,000 miles = $0.20/mile
2. $0.20/mile × Actual miles driven each year

[c]The mileage figures shown for each year are assumed.

[d]Annual depreciation expense calculated as follows:
1. Straight-line rate = 20%
   Double-declining-balance rate = 2 × 20% = 40%
2. Depreciation for each year is equal to:
   Carrying value at beginning of year × 0.40

[e]In year 5, the depreciation calculation yields the following: $2,851 × 0.40 = $1,140. However, if this amount is used, total depreciation taken over the useful life of the asset will exceed the $20,000 of total depreciation allowed. This is a common problem of DDB depreciation. When this happens, companies simply record the final year's depreciation as the amount that will bring total accumulated depreciation to the amount desired ($20,000, in this case).

If the CDL Company from the prior example expects its delivery truck to have a useful life of 100,000 miles, and it was actually driven 14,000 miles in its first year of use, depreciation expense for year 1, calculated using the units-of-production method, is:

1. $\dfrac{\$22,000 - \$2,000}{100,000 \text{ miles}}$ = $0.20 depreciation per mile of use

2. $0.20/mile × 14,000 miles = $2,800 depreciation for year

The units-of-production depreciation method results in depreciation expense with each mile driven.

Exhibit 21.1, panel B, shows the calculation of depreciation expense for each year of the truck's use, based on the following assumptions:

Year	Actual Miles Driven
1	14,000
2	23,000
3	18,700
4	21,300
5	23,000

The advantage of the units-of-production method of depreciation is that it allows a company to record varying amounts of depreciation expense each year, as illustrated in Exhibit 21.1, panel B, to properly match the amount of expense recognized with actual rates of usage. In our example, the rate of asset use and the corresponding benefit derived from that use are measured in terms of miles driven each year.

Accelerated Depreciation

Even when the use of a plant asset is expected to be at a constant rate over its useful life, many accountants believe that the benefits derived from the use of a new asset are greater than the benefits from the use of the same asset as it ages. For example, a new computer functions at "state-of-the-art" efficiency, but, after just a few years, the computer may no longer provide the same relative degree of benefit to the company. Also, a brand new automobile benefits a company by providing not only transportation, but also a certain image of success. As the automobile ages, it still provides adequate transportation, but it no longer carries the same prestige and "image" value that it conveyed when new. Additionally, as it gets older, it is much more likely to need repairs to keep it running properly.

If benefits derived from the use of an asset tend to decline over time, then the matching principle justifies using one of various **accelerated depreciation** methods designed to recognize relatively greater expense in early years of asset use and progressively less expense as time passes.

Declining-balance depreciation is a type of accelerated depreciation that reflects depreciation expense for each year based on a constant percentage of a declining balance equal to the remaining undepreciated cost of the asset at the start of each year. The asset's undepreciated cost is its original cost less the total of any depreciation taken in prior years. The multiplication of a constant rate by this declining balance yields the greatest amount of depreciation in the asset's first year of use and a declining amount in each subsequent year; thus the depreciation expense recorded each year declines along with the declining benefits of asset use.

To "accelerate" the amount of depreciation expense taken each year, companies multiply the asset's beginning-of-year undepreciated cost by a constant percentage that exceeds the rate applicable for straight-line depreciation. In the case of the delivery truck purchased by CDL Company, the amount of annual straight-line depreciation resulted from dividing the depreciable cost of the asset by five years (the asset's useful life), which is the same as multiplying by one-fifth, or 20 percent. Using the declining-balance method, the company would compute annual depreciation expense by multiplying the truck's undepreciated cost at the start of each year by some multiple of this rate. **Double-declining-balance depreciation** (DDB) is a specific type of declining-balance depreciation that reflects annual depreciation expense using a constant percentage equal to twice the straight-line rate of depreciation. For example, the double-declining-balance method would use a depreciation rate of 40 percent per year ($2 \times 20\%$) in this case.[4]

---

[4]In addition to 200 percent declining-balance depreciation, 150 percent declining-balance depreciation is also possible, as are various other percentages, each of which uses a stated multiple of the straight-line rate of depreciation, ranging up to 200 percent.

The complete set of steps to calculate double-declining-balance depreciation follows:

1. Determine the straight-line rate of depreciation for the asset and double it.

2. Calculate depreciation for the first year by multiplying the rate determined in step 1 by the *original* cost of the asset. (Note: Do not reduce the cost by the salvage value of the asset.)[5]

3. Determine depreciation for the second and all subsequent years by multiplying the rate from step 1 by the undepreciated cost (Cost – Accumulated depreciation) of the asset as of the beginning of the year, continuing until the asset's remaining undepreciated cost equals its salvage value.

Exhibit 21.1, panel C, illustrates this calculation for each year of the useful life of CDL Company's delivery truck.

Although the depreciation expense in the early years of an asset's life is greater, accelerated depreciation does not increase the total amount of depreciation taken over the life of the asset, which is always limited to depreciable cost (Cost – Salvage value) of the asset. Notice in Exhibit 21.1 that total depreciation recorded under each of the three methods equals $20,000 ($22,000 original cost – $2,000 salvage value).

Because of this requirement, it is generally necessary to modify DDB depreciation taken during the last portion of an asset's useful life. In Exhibit 21.1, panel C, depreciation calculated for year 5 under the DDB formula requires us to multiply $2,851 (the remaining undepreciated cost of the truck at the beginning of the year) by 40 percent, which would result in year 5 depreciation equal to $1,140. However, this amount would cause total accumulated depreciation to exceed $20,000 (and the remaining undepreciated cost would be less than the $2,000 salvage value), so we must limit the amount of depreciation expense in year 5 to $851, the amount that will bring total accumulated depreciation to $20,000. It is usually necessary to adjust the amount of double-declining-balance depreciation expense taken in the final portion of an asset's life so that total accumulated depreciation taken over the life of the asset equals the estimated net depreciable cost of the asset.

Partial-Year Depreciation

What if a company with a December 31 year-end purchases or disposes of a plant asset on April 5, 2000? If it uses the units-of-production depreciation method, the timing of the disposal is not an issue, because depreciation for any period is based on actual output or use for that period. But if the company uses either straight-line or accelerated depreciation, both of which define useful life in terms of years, the fact that the asset was not used for a full 12-month period in 2000 will normally require a modification in the amount of depreciation expense recorded for that year.

There are several ways to deal with this issue. Companies making numerous plant asset purchases and disposals spread out evenly during the course of the fiscal year frequently use the **midyear convention** which reflects depreciation expense for each asset as if it were purchased or disposed of exactly halfway through the company's fiscal year. This avoids the expense of tracking the exact date that the business places each asset in service, and, so long as acquisitions and disposals of assets occur uniformly, it yields an annual depreciation expense that is not significantly different from the result that would have been obtained by tracking each asset individually.

Other companies record depreciation based on the actual number of months an asset was in service during the year. When following this approach, businesses that acquire

---

[5]The curious student may wonder why we do not use the asset's depreciable cost ($20,000) as we did for the other depreciation methods. Although the depreciable cost represents the total amount of depreciation to take over the life of the asset, if we take 40 percent of $20,000 in year 1, 40 percent of the remainder in year 2, and so on, the depreciation calculated for each of the five years will sum to less than $20,000. Use of the asset's original cost helps solve this problem.

assets on or before the 15th of each month record depreciation expense for these assets as if they were in service for the entire month. They treat assets acquired after the 15th of any month as being placed in service at the start of the next month. Similarly, assets disposed of after the 15th of any month get a full month's depreciation, while those disposed of on or before the 15th receive no depreciation for the month.[6]

To illustrate, if CDL Company has a December 31 year-end, purchased its delivery truck in April 2000, and expects to dispose of it five years later in April 2005, straight-line depreciation for each fiscal year of use would be as follows:[7]

Year Ended	Number of Months Used			Depreciation Expense		
12/31/00	9	9/12	×	$4,000*	=	$ 3,000
12/31/01	12	12/12	×	4,000	=	4,000
12/31/02	12	12/12	×	4,000	=	4,000
12/31/03	12	12/12	×	4,000	=	4,000
12/31/04	12	12/12	×	4,000	=	4,000
12/31/05	3	3/12	×	4,000	=	1,000
Total						$20,000

*Full 12-month year of depreciation expense = ($22,000 − $2,000)/5 = $4,000.

Selection of Depreciation Method

Each depreciation method discussed is acceptable for financial statement reporting purposes. Companies should select the one that, in their view, most closely matches the cost of derived benefits with revenues earned in all periods. However, when choosing which method of depreciation to use for tax reporting purposes, other issues come into play.

Depreciation for Tax Purposes   It is important to begin a discussion of tax depreciation with an understanding of these points:

• A primary objective of financial statement reporting is to properly measure and communicate income earned during a given time period. On the other hand, the major

---

[6]To illustrate yet another approach, Note 1 of the American Skiing Company's 1998 financial statements included this statement: "Due to the seasonality of the Company's business, the Company records a full year of depreciation relating to its operating assets over the second and third quarters of its fiscal year." These are the quarters corresponding to the skiing season.

[7]Although not illustrated in the text, declining-balance depreciation can also be calculated based on the number of months an asset is actually used during a fiscal year.

objective of taxing authorities is to collect necessary taxes in a manner designed to promote certain desirable social, political, or economic consequences. The goal of company managers and accountants is to legally minimize the company's tax liability.

- There is no requirement that the amount of depreciation expense reported to shareholders in a company's annual financial report equal the amount of depreciation deducted on that company's annual tax returns. In fact, because the tax statutes passed by legislatures of some states have established depreciation rules that are different from those required by the federal government, some companies use one method of depreciation for their annual report to shareholders, another for a required state tax return, and still another for the return filed each year with the Internal Revenue Service.

How Businesses Benefit from Tax Depreciation   As we already know, depreciation expense is different from most other expenses. Wages, electricity, advertising, and most other expenses usually require cash payments. However, depreciation expense does not.

As explained in Chapter 15, although a business makes no cash payment when recording depreciation, this expense still reduces taxable income and thus serves as a "tax shield" that reduces income taxes paid by the business. *Therefore, instead of requiring a current cash outflow, depreciation generally puts money back in the hands of the company.*

If the federal government desires to stimulate the economy, one effective approach it uses is to give companies more generous tax depreciation deductions. For example, in the early 1980s, when the United States was in a recession, Congress, at the urging of President Reagan, enacted laws establishing the accelerated cost recovery system (ACRS). These laws included the following changes, all designed to increase the amount of depreciation allowable:

- The period of time over which tax laws allowed assets to be depreciated was reduced, thus accelerating the rate of depreciation allowed.

- For all assets, companies generally were instructed to use a salvage value equal to zero, thus increasing the total amount of depreciation expense allowed over the life of an asset.

- Companies were allowed to deduct a full year of depreciation expense for any newly acquired plant asset, regardless of the timing of asset acquisition and placement in service.

Our current tax depreciation system is referred to as the **modified accelerated cost recovery system (MACRS).** It is much less stimulative in nature than its predecessor, ACRS, because it lengthens the depreciable lives for many assets and is more restrictive regarding the use of accelerated depreciation.

The MACRS classifies assets according to the period of time over which the Internal Revenue Code requires those assets to be depreciated. For example, three-year property, which must be depreciated over a three-year time period, includes race horses that are more than two years old when placed in service. (Yes, even horses are sometimes treated as depreciable assets!) The IRS considers automobiles, trucks, computers, and typewriters to be five-year property. The normal depreciation period allowed for office desks and files is seven years, and for residential buildings the period is 27.5 years. All assets other than real property (real estate) are generally depreciated using the midyear convention discussed earlier in the chapter, and real property requires the use of a mid-month convention whereby the asset is assumed to be placed in service halfway through the first month of its use. For example, if a company places a building in service on any day in February 2000, there will be 10.5 months of depreciation included on the company's 2000 tax return.

Exhibit 21.2 shows the method of depreciation allowed for selected categories of assets. The truck purchased by CDL Company is five-year property, so it can be depreciated using 200 percent declining-balance depreciation.

EXHIBIT 21.2 Method of Depreciation Allowable under MACRS

Type of Property	Depreciation Method Allowable*
3-, 5-, 7-, and 10-year	200% declining balance
15- and 20-year	150% declining balance
Residential and nonresidential real estate	Straight-line depreciation (accelerated depreciation not allowed)

*Depreciation method shown represents the most accelerated form allowed. Straight-line depreciation and units-of-production depreciation are also allowed for the categories shown.

Using the prescribed method of depreciation, companies can determine annual depreciation expense by using the methods described in this chapter, or they can use IRS tables designed to simplify the calculations, such as those shown in Exhibit 21.3. Although this exhibit shows tables for only three-, five-, and seven-year property, similar tables exist for all types of property shown in Exhibit 21.2. Companies use these tables to calculate annual depreciation expense by multiplying the original cost of an asset by the appropriate percentage shown for each year.

EXHIBIT 21.3 Tax Depreciation Tables for Three-, Five-, and Seven-Year Property*

Year	Three-Year Property	Five-Year Property	Seven-Year Property
1	33.33%	20.00%	14.29%
2	44.45	32.00	24.49
3	14.81	19.20	17.49
4	7.41	11.52	12.49
5		11.52	8.93
6		5.76	8.92
7			8.93
8			4.46

*Table based on 200 percent declining-balance depreciation, using the midyear convention and switching to straight-line depreciation during the last half of asset life. Depreciation for each year is calculated by multiplying appropriate percentage by the original cost of the asset.

Exhibit 21.4 illustrates the calculation of depreciation expense for the delivery truck purchased by CDL Company. The left-hand side of this table shows the calculation of 200 percent declining-balance depreciation using the standard technique described in this chapter. Note that only one-half year of depreciation is allowed in the first year because of the midyear convention and that the company switches to straight-line depreciation in the last half of the asset's life.[8] The right side of the table shows the calculation of the

EXHIBIT 21.4 Calculation of 200 Percent Declining-Balance Depreciation

Standard Calculation*			Tax Table Calculation		
$22,000 × 0.40 × 1/2	=	$ 4,400.00	$22,000 × 0.2000	=	$4,400.00
17,600 × 0.40	=	7,040.00	22,000 × 0.3200	=	7,040.00
10,560 × 0.40	=	4,224.00	22,000 × 0.1920	=	4,224.00
6,336/2.5 years	=	2,534.40	22,000 × 0.1152	=	2,534.40
6,336/2.5 years	=	2,534.40	22,000 × 0.1152	=	2,534.40
6,336/2.5 years × 1/2	=	1,267.20	22,000 × 0.0576	=	1,267.20
	Total	$22,000.00			$22,000.00

*Standard calculation based on 200 percent declining-balance, midyear convention, a five-year useful life, zero salvage value, and switching to straight-line depreciation with 2.5 years remaining.

---

[8]The MACRS provides for a switch to straight-line depreciation when that method results in a larger expense than accelerated depreciation. When making the switch, the company calculates depreciation for each remaining year by dividing the remaining undepreciated cost of the asset by its remaining useful life.

same annual depreciation expense by multiplying the original cost of the truck ($22,000) by the IRS-provided percentages shown in Exhibit 21.3. The "tax table calculation" shown in the exhibit yields amounts identical to the "standard calculation," and most individuals find it easier to use.

OTHER ISSUES RELATED TO THE USE OF PLANT ASSETS
Revision of Estimates

The original useful life and salvage value assigned to any plant asset for financial reporting purposes are estimates. Due to the principle of materiality, companies do not worry if these projections are marginally inaccurate, as is normally the case. But what happens if a company originally assigns a useful life of seven years to a computer and, one year after the date of purchase, realizes that it will have to replace the computer after a total of three years? When it becomes clear that there were significant mistakes of judgment in estimating the useful life and/or salvage value of any asset, companies usually do the following: *Depreciate the remaining undepreciated cost of the asset over the asset's revised remaining useful life using the appropriate depreciation method and, when deemed necessary, a revised salvage value.*

To illustrate, assume that on January 1, 2000, a company purchases and begins to use office equipment costing $12,000, with an expected useful life of 10 years and a salvage value of $2,000. Assuming the business uses the straight-line method of depreciation for the asset, accumulated depreciation at December 31, 2002, would be $3,000 [($12,000 − $2,000)/10 × 3 years]. The remaining undepreciated cost of the asset at that time would be $9,000 ($12,000 − $3,000). If, during the following year, the company realizes that the equipment will last only four more years, after which its estimated salvage value will be $3,000, then depreciation expense for each of the remaining four years of the asset's useful life would be calculated as follows:

$$\frac{\text{Remaining undepreciated cost of asset} - \text{Revised salvage value}}{\text{Remaining useful life}} = \text{Depreciation expense}$$

$$\frac{\$9,000 - \$3,000}{4 \text{ years}} = \$1,500 \text{ year}$$

This change in depreciation is prospective—that is, it will only affect the current and future year financial statements.

Continued Use of Fully Depreciated Asset

The fact that an asset is fully depreciated does not mean that a company must stop using it. However, because total costs associated with the use of any asset cannot exceed the total cost of the asset (reduced by its salvage value), the company must stop recording annual depreciation expense.

PAUSE & REFLECT

How do fully depreciated assets appear on the balance sheet? Should companies report them or not? Why? *(answer on page 737)*

Extraordinary Repairs and Betterments

After placing a plant asset in service, businesses record expenditures to maintain the asset in normal operating condition as expenses in the period incurred. However, some expenditures relating to the continued use of the asset may be capital in nature. These are classified as either extraordinary repairs or betterments. **Extraordinary repairs** are capital expenditures that extend the remaining useful life of an operational asset, and **betterments** represent capital expenditures to improve the asset's performance capabilities.

When making such capital expenditures for a plant asset already in use, the company would add the amount of the expenditure to the depreciable cost of the asset and then depreciate it over the asset's remaining useful life. For example, $30,000 spent to add a new room onto an existing building with a remaining useful life of 15 years will increase straight-line depreciation expense by $2,000 ($30,000/15 years) per year for each of the last 15 years of the building's life, assuming the improvement does not change the building's expected salvage value.

We have discussed the acquisition and use of operational investments. Now we look at their disposal.

DISPOSAL OF PLANT ASSETS

LO 3

Eventually, it is necessary to dispose of depreciable assets, either because they have worn out or because management has determined that disposal is an economically desirable course of action. The asset may be discarded, sold, or exchanged for other assets. Whatever the method, the entries made to record disposals must generally accomplish the following:

- Record partial-year depreciation expense up to the date of disposal.
- Remove both the cost of the asset and its related accumulated depreciation from the accounting records.
- Record any gain or loss, calculated as the difference between the carrying value of the disposed asset and the fair market value of any assets received in return.

Recall from Chapters 9 and 10 that gains and losses result from events that are incidental to the ongoing activity of a business. Gains increase owners' equity and are recorded as credit entries. Losses reduce owners' equity and are, therefore, recorded as debits.

Discard Plant Assets

Sometimes an asset with little or no value will be disposed of, with nothing at all received in return. When this happens, it is necessary to record a loss equal to the carrying value of the asset at the date of disposal. For example, discarding equipment that cost $5,000, with $4,200 of accumulated depreciation at the date of disposal, results in a loss of $800 (its carrying value), recorded as follows:

Loss on Disposal of Equipment	800	
Accumulated Depreciation—Equipment	4,200	
Equipment		5,000

Any amount paid to discard the asset would be added to the amount of the recorded loss.

Sell Plant Assets

Plant assets may be sold for an amount equal to, less than, or greater than their carrying value. Terms of sale might require a cash payment of the selling price or an agreement in the form of a promissory note obligating the purchaser to make specified future cash payments.

To illustrate the accounting for the various possibilities, assume that a company sells the following piece of equipment:

Cost of asset	$8,000
Accumulated depreciation through date of sale	(6,000)
Carrying value at date of sale	$2,000

The following accounting entries illustrate the three different possibilities:

Sales Price Equal to Carrying Value

Cash (Assumed Sales Price)	2,000	
Accumulated Depreciation—Equipment	6,000	
Equipment		8,000

Sales Price Greater Than Carrying Value

Cash (Assumed Sales Price)	2,700	
Accumulated Depreciation—Equipment	6,000	
Equipment		8,000
Gain on Sale of Equipment		700

Cash (Assumed Sales Price)	1,600	
Loss on Sale of Equipment	400	
Accumulated Depreciation—Equipment	6,000	
Equipment		8,000

Each of the above entries assumed the receipt of cash at the date of sale. In those cases where the buyer signs a promissory note at the date of sale, the selling company would debit Notes Receivable instead of Cash.

Exchange Plant Assets

Companies occasionally exchange plant assets for other noncash assets. Sometimes these exchanges involve partial cash payments; other times they do not. For example, a business might trade in an old automobile as part of the purchase price of a new vehicle, making a cash payment for the remaining amount owed. Or a business might make an even trade of two different pieces of equipment or two different parcels of land, with no cash changing hands.

The exchanged assets can be dissimilar or similar in nature. An exchange of a building in return for a stock investment held by another company represents an exchange of dissimilar assets. We define similar productive assets as those that are of the same general type, that perform the same function, or that are employed in the same line of business.[9] A trade-in of an old automobile as part of the purchase price of a new one involves the exchange of similar assets.

In this section, we discuss the financial accounting rules companies must follow to account for exchanges of dissimilar and similar plant assets. Then we briefly discuss related tax issues, pointing out how tax law differs from financial accounting for exchanges. Exhibit 21.5, which the student should refer to after reading the complete discussion, summarizes the different rules.

Exchanges of Dissimilar Assets When a business disposes of a plant asset via an exchange of dissimilar assets, it calculates and records a gain or loss on the transaction as the difference between the carrying value of the asset given up and whichever of the following two values it can determine more objectively:

- Fair market value of the asset received in the exchange
- Fair market value of the asset given up in the exchange

Whichever value the company uses to calculate the gain or loss becomes the recorded "cost" of the newly acquired asset.

To illustrate, assume the American Skiing Company exchanges the following building for 10,000 shares of stock held by another company as an investment:

Cost of building	$100,000
Accumulated depreciation at date of exchange	(75,000)
Carrying value at date of exchange	$ 25,000

Assume further that the fair market value of the building on the date of the exchange is difficult to determine, but that the stock received is selling for $4 per share. The entry to record the transaction is:

Investment in Stock (10,000 × $4)	40,000	
Accumulated Depreciation—Building	75,000	
Building		100,000
Gain on Exchange		15,000

---

[9]The discussion of the accounting for exchanges of similar and dissimilar assets is based on principles enunciated in *Accounting Principles Board Opinion No. 29,* paragraph 3.

The entry to record any exchange of dissimilar assets follows essentially the same rules governing the sale of an asset for cash. Accountants view the exchange of one asset for a fundamentally different type of asset, whether it be cash or a noncash asset, as the completion of an earnings process requiring the recognition of gain or loss.

Exchanges of Similar Assets The accounting treatment applicable to exchanges of similar assets represents an exception to the general rule requiring recognition of gains and losses. The exception stems from the fact that accounting authorities do not view the exchange of similar assets as the culmination of an earnings process. If two stores, for example, exchange items from their inventory to enable one of the stores to sell a particular product to a customer, the earnings process is complete only upon final sale to the customer, not when the stores exchange the merchandise. Likewise, if the Boston Celtics and the Los Angeles Lakers exchange player contracts, neither has "earned" anything as either of the teams would have if it sold a player's contract to another franchise for a fixed sum of money.

Because we do not view exchanges of similar assets as completed earnings processes, accountants rely on the principle of conservatism when they record these events. Thus accountants do not record any gain determined by comparison of the fair market value and carrying value of the asset given up, yet they do record any loss on the exchange.

To illustrate, assume that Company A, which is headquartered in Oregon, plans to close down a factory building it owns in Michigan and move this operation to California. The 10-year-old building has a carrying value of $100,000 (cost of $500,000 less accumulated depreciation of $400,000) and has a current market value of $800,000. Company B owns a one-year-old building just outside of San Francisco with a carrying value of $950,000 (cost of $1,000,000 less accumulated depreciation of $50,000). This building also has a current market value of $800,000. Companies A and B swap buildings.

Company B has a $150,000 loss calculated as the difference between the fair market value of the company's building ($800,000) and its carrying value on the date of the exchange ($950,000). Company B makes the following entry to record this loss:

Loss on Exchange	150,000	
Building (Acquired in Exchange)	800,000	
Accumulated Depreciation—Building (Given up in Exchange)	50,000	
Building (Given up in Exchange)		1,000,000

On the other hand, the same transaction results in a gain of $700,000 for Company A, calculated as the difference between the $800,000 fair market value of its building and its $100,000 carrying value, which it does not record. Instead, it removes the carrying value of the old building from its books and assigns this same carrying value, not the fair market value, to the cost of the new building acquired in the exchange. The entry is:

Building (Acquired in Exchange)	100,000	
Accumulated Depreciation—Building (Given up in Exchange)	400,000	
Building (Given up in Exchange)		500,000

The fact that this new building has the same carrying value that the old building had on Company A's books ensures that Company A will eventually recognize the implied gain from the disposal of the old building, plus or minus any additional gain or loss from changes in the value of the new building, when and if the company sells the new building for cash.[10] That is, if Company A turned around and immediately sold this newly acquired

---

[10]When similar assets are exchanged, it is rare that both assets have exactly equal values. When the values of exchanged assets are different, some cash also will probably change hands at the date of the exchange. If cash (or a promissory note) is received as part of an exchange of similar assets, the company receiving the cash must immediately record the portion of any gain attributable to this cash receipt. A description of the calculation of this recognized gain is beyond the scope of this text.

building for its current value of $800,000, the earnings process would finally be complete, and the company would recognize the full $700,000 gain that would have been recorded if its original building had been sold for cash rather than exchanged for the new building.

In the previous example, Company A did not record the implied gain of $700,000. Accountants often say that this unrecorded gain will be recognized through use of the asset. Does this make sense? How much depreciation will Company A record over the life of the newly acquired building? Would this amount have been different if the company recognized the $700,000 gain at the date of the exchange and added the recognized gain to the recorded value of the new asset? (answer on page 737)

Trade-Ins   A trade-in of an old asset as part of the purchase price of a new, similar asset is by far the most commonly encountered example of an exchange involving similar assets. Cars and trucks are often traded in partial payment for a new vehicle, as are computers and many other categories of equipment. Most trade-ins involve giving up an old, used asset plus an additional amount of cash in exchange for the new asset.

Gain or loss on disposal of the old asset (the one traded in) is measured as the difference between the carrying value of the old asset and the trade-in allowance assigned to it in the exchange transaction. As with any other exchange involving similar assets, losses are recognized; gains are not. When assigning a value to the new asset acquired as a result of the trade-in transaction, the new asset's carrying value is increased by the amount of any cash given up.

Illustration of Accounting for Trade-Ins   To illustrate the accounting for trade-ins, assume a company approaches a computer dealer offering to trade in an old computer system as part of the purchase price of a new one. The old computer system cost $25,000 and at the trade-in date has $15,000 of accumulated depreciation, yielding a carrying value of $10,000.

Loss on Exchange   If the negotiated price for the new computer system is $28,000, and the dealer grants a trade-in allowance of $8,000 on the old computer system, the company will recognize a $2,000 loss on the trade-in of the old computer system, and it will have to make an additional $20,000 payment to acquire the new computer system. The $2,000 loss results from the difference between the trade-in allowance and the carrying value of the old computer system ($8,000 − $10,000). The cash payment is calculated as the difference between the purchase price of the new computer system and the trade-in allowance on the old one ($28,000 − $8,000). The transaction is recorded as follows:

Computer System (New)	28,000	
Loss on Exchange	2,000	
Accumulated Depreciation—Computer System (Old)	15,000	
Computer System (Old)		25,000
Cash		20,000

Gain on Exchange   Recall that gains on the exchange of similar assets are not recognized. If the negotiated price of the new computer system is $28,000, but the dealer grants a trade-in allowance of $12,000 on the old computer system, the company will have a $2,000 gain on the trade-in, which it will not record. This gain results from the difference between the $12,000 trade-in allowance and the $10,000 carrying value of the old computer system. The company will have to pay $16,000 in cash, calculated as the difference between the purchase price of the new computer system and the trade-in allowance ($28,000 − $12,000).

The new computer system will be assigned a cost of $26,000. This amount can be calculated in either of two ways: (1) reduce the $28,000 purchase price of the new computer system by the $2,000 of unrecognized gain, or (2) add the $10,000 carrying value of the old computer system to the $16,000 cash given in the exchange. The $2,000 reduction in the value assigned to the new computer system is necessary to offset the $2,000 of unrecognized gain. The resulting entry is:

Computer System (New)	26,000	
Accumulated Depreciation—Computer System (Old)	15,000	
Computer System (Old)		25,000
Cash		16,000

Tax Issues Relative to Exchanges   When businesses exchange dissimilar assets, they include all resulting gains and losses when calculating the amount of income reported to the Internal Revenue Service. However, when companies exchange similar productive assets, they *do not include the gain or loss* resulting from the exchange on their tax returns. These procedures represent one of the primary reasons why companies, when they want to dispose of assets that have appreciated in value, sometimes consider an exchange for a similar asset the company needs, rather than a cash sale of the asset.

To illustrate the potential tax benefit from an exchange of similar assets, assume that Company A in the foregoing illustration sold its building in Michigan for $800,000. Assuming the carrying value of the building for financial accounting and tax purposes was the same, the company would have had a taxable gain of $700,000 (selling price of $800,000 less the asset's $100,000 carrying value). Assuming a tax rate of 30 percent, the company would have paid $210,000 in taxes as a result of this gain, leaving it with $590,000 cash (selling price of $800,000 less taxes of $210,000), not enough to purchase the $800,000 building in California. The exchange of assets enabled Company A to accomplish two things: defer the payment of $210,000 of taxes and obtain the California building that the company needed for its operations.

Exhibit 21.5 summarizes the financial accounting and tax rules for recording gains and losses on exchanges of dissimilar and similar assets. Note that financial accounting and tax rules are exactly the same for gains, but tax law, unlike the financial accounting rules, does not allow the recognition of losses from exchanges of similar assets.

EXHIBIT 21.5	Summary of Financial Accounting Rules versus Tax Requirements for Recording Exchanges of Similar and Dissimilar Assets

Exchange Results In	Gain	Loss
Reason	Trade-in allowance or other fair value received exceeds carrying value of asset given up.	Trade-in allowance or other fair value received is less than carrying value of asset given up.
Rules for Financial Accounting and Reporting		
Dissimilar Assets	Record the gain and assign cost to new asset equal to total fair value of cash plus noncash assets given up.	Record the loss and assign cost to new asset equal to total fair value of cash plus noncash assets given up.
Similar Assets (Includes Trade-ins)	Do not record the gain. Cost assigned to new asset is reduced by amount of unrecorded gain.	Record the loss and assign cost to new asset equal to total fair value of cash plus noncash assets given up.
Rules for Tax Reporting		
Dissimilar Assets	Record the gain and assign cost to new asset equal to total fair value of cash plus noncash assets given up.	Record the loss and assign cost to new asset equal to total fair value of cash plus noncash assets given up.
Similar Assets (Includes Trade-ins)	Do not record the gain. Cost assigned to new asset is reduced by amount of unrecorded gain.	Do not record the loss. Cost assigned to new asset is increased by amount of unrecorded loss.

NATURAL RESOURCES

LO 4

Natural resources are nonrenewable assets such as coal mines and oil rights. A company's investment in natural resources is determined according to the same general rules established for assigning costs to plant assets; typically, the cost includes the purchase price of the asset and related legal fees, as well as items such as surveying and various development costs.

As with plant assets, the benefits associated with natural resources dissipate with use. Once coal or oil reserves are exhausted, they cannot be renewed. Therefore, the cost of these assets also must be allocated as an expense over the periods they benefit. This process is called **depletion,** and, because benefits from natural resources usually correlate with usage rather than the passage of time, it is generally calculated using the units-of-production method.

To illustrate, assume that a company paid $1,400,000 for a mine estimated to contain 2,000,000 tons of ore. The residual value of the land after extraction of all the ore is estimated at $100,000. The depletion charge per ton of extracted ore is:

$$\frac{\$1,400,000 - \$100,000}{2,000,000 \text{ tons}} = \$0.65 \text{ per ton}$$

If this company mines 300,000 tons of ore during a given accounting period, total depletion will be $195,000 ($0.65 × 300,000 tons), recorded as follows:

Depletion—Mine	195,000	
Accumulated Depletion—Mine		195,000

The company does not expense the recorded depletion immediately. Instead, it adds the amount of depletion to the cost of the company's inventory of extracted ore. Therefore, as long as the ore remains on hand, the depletion is a cost of the inventory reported on the balance sheet. When the company sells the ore, the depletion, along with all other costs of the ore, becomes part of cost of goods sold reported as an expense on the company's income statement.

PAUSE & REFLECT

When depreciation was recorded earlier in the chapter, it resulted in an expense on the income statement. The amount of depletion on the mine in the preceding example was added to the cost of inventory. Why was one expensed while the other became part of the cost of an asset? Can you think of any situations where depreciation would be added to the cost of inventory rather than being immediately expensed? *(answer on page 737)*

INTANGIBLE ASSETS

LO 5

As introduced in Chapter 3, intangible assets, unlike plant assets and natural resources, have no tangible or visible physical presence. However, they convey to their owner a legal right or benefit that is often vital to successful operations. Therefore, intangible assets usually represent some of the most important and valuable assets owned by a company. Let's look at some examples.

Patents

A **patent** is an intangible asset giving its owner the exclusive legal right to the commercial benefits of a specified product or process. For instance, Microsoft obtained a patent to ensure the exclusive right to produce and sell Windows 98.

In the United States, the U.S. Patent Office issues patents that last for a period of 17 years. However, even though they exist for 17 years, the economically useful life of patents may be much shorter if technological developments render the patented product or process obsolete.

Microsoft Windows 98 was the result of R&D that was expensed as incurred.

The determination of a patent's cost raises an interesting question. Virtually all accountants agree that the normal and necessary expenditures made to buy an existing patent from another entity, as well as legal costs directly incurred to obtain a patent, should be added to the cost of the patent. But what about costs involved when a company spends money on research and development (R&D) to create a process or product that it hopes will lead to a patent?

One could argue that all R&D costs, whether successful or not, should be accumulated and added to the cost of any patents obtained as a result. Since patents, like any asset, do not generate expenses until the periods when they are used, this approach would postpone the expensing of R&D costs. Such expense postponement would tend to increase a company's current reported income. On the other hand, since it is questionable whether money spent on R&D will ever provide any future benefits, one could argue that these expenditures should be expensed immediately as incurred. This more conservative approach would yield more current expenses and, therefore, less current income.

Generally accepted accounting principles, taking the more conservative view, require that companies expense most research and development costs in the period incurred.[11] As a result, a company that develops its own products often owns extremely valuable patents that it does not report, or that it reports at a very low dollar amount on its balance sheet.

Copyrights

A **copyright** is an intangible asset that gives its owner an exclusive legal right to the reproduction and sale of a literary or artistic work. Copyrights last for the life of the creator plus 50 years. However, their economically useful life is almost always substantially less and, therefore, not significant for financial statement users.

Because the fee to initially establish a copyright is minimal, businesses usually write this cost off as an expense. However, when a company purchases a copyright from the original owner, the expenditure is often substantial; therefore, the company must capitalize the cost as an intangible asset. For example, the Academy Award-winning movie *Titanic* is a copyright owned by Paramount Pictures and Twentieth Century-Fox.

Paramount Pictures and Twentieth Century Fox own the copyright to Titanic.

---

[11]*SFAS No. 2,* issued in October 1974, established this requirement.

Franchises

A **franchise** is an intangible asset representing the exclusive right to operate or sell a brand name product in a specified territory. A franchise is granted by one entity, called the *franchisor,* to another party, called the *franchisee.* Burger King and McDonald's are examples. If the franchisee pays an up-front fee for this right, it has an intangible asset to report on the balance sheet.

PAUSE &
REFLECT

How much would you be willing to pay for a franchise giving you the exclusive right to provide cable TV service in your hometown? How much do you think it would be worth to be the only individual able to open a Burger King where you live? *(answer on page 737)*

Leaseholds and Leasehold Improvements

A **leasehold** is an intangible asset conveyed by a lease to use equipment, land, and/or buildings for a specified period of time. Periodic payments made on operating leases are generally expensed when paid.[12]

Some leases require a down payment at the inception of the lease. For example, a car lease might require payments of $399 per month, plus an initial $2,000 down payment. If the amount of the down payment is material, companies will capitalize it by debiting an intangible asset account called Leasehold. This asset has a useful life equal to the term of the lease.

Additionally, the amount paid to a lessee to purchase the rights to a lease creates an intangible asset, also referred to as a *leasehold,* with a useful life that equals the remaining life of the lease. To illustrate, assume that Bob Smith has a lease to rent 3,000 square feet of prime space in a mall at an attractive rate for the next five years. Bob has been in business for years and now wants to retire. A company that operates fast-food restaurants immediately approaches Bob and offers to purchase the rights to this lease for $10,000 because there is no other space available in the mall. If Bob sells the lease, the restaurant company will record a $10,000 leasehold with a useful life of five years.

Any amounts paid by a lessee to make physical improvements constituting an integral part of leased property are recorded as an intangible asset referred to as a **leasehold improvement.** Accountants consider this asset to be intangible because, although the improvement represents tangible property, the lessee possesses only the legal right to *use* the improvement during the remaining life of the lease.

Goodwill

Goodwill is an intangible asset representing the value assigned to a company's ability to generate an above-average return on invested capital. This may result from a combination of many factors, including efficient management, good labor relations, superior product quality, and brand name recognition. Companies record goodwill only if they pay an identifiable amount of money to acquire it. Thus businesses generally record goodwill only when they pay for it as part of the purchase price to acquire another company. The amount of goodwill recorded in connection with the purchase of another company is the difference between the total price paid to purchase the company and the value of the purchased company's underlying net assets (all identifiable assets minus liabilities).

To illustrate, assume the Progressive Grocery Corporation wants to purchase the Healthy-Deli Company, a small delicatessen supply firm, and is willing to pay $250,000. The Healthy-Deli has net identifiable assets (excluding goodwill) with an appraised value of $210,000. If the offer is accepted, Progressive will record $40,000 of goodwill on its books, calculated as follows:

Total purchase price	$250,000
Less appraised value of Healthy-Deli's net identifiable assets	210,000
Amount of goodwill	$ 40,000

---

[12]As discussed in Chapter 18, there are two types of leases: operating leases and capital leases. The majority are operating leases whose required periodic payments are expenses when made.

Users of financial statements should understand that unless a company purchases another company, goodwill is not recorded. Therefore, internally generated goodwill is a noncapitalized asset (see Chapter 16) that goes unreported on balance sheets.

PAUSE & REFLECT

Goodwill is often "purchased" as part of the price paid to acquire another business. What attributes must goodwill possess before it can be sold? For example, if a doctor wants to sell a medical practice and retire, can the doctor sell the goodwill associated with his or her name? Why or why not? *(answer on page 737)*

USE OF INTANGIBLE ASSETS

As they do for plant assets and natural resources, companies must expense the cost of intangible assets over the periods they benefit. This process, called **amortization,** is calculated as follows:[13]

1. Use the straight-line method.[14]

2. Amortize the full cost of the asset without reduction for any salvage value, because intangibles generally have no significant economic value once their useful life is complete.

3. Utilize a useful life that does not exceed 40 years. Accountants base this number on the assumption that it is impossible to predict economic usefulness past a certain point in the future. Thus, even though a copyright has a legal life in excess of 40 years, its useful life for calculating amortization is the lesser of (a) the period of time its owner expects it to yield economic benefits or (b) 40 years.

To illustrate, assume Purinton Corporation paid $3,000,000 for a patent on a device that reduces acid rain pollutants produced during certain manufacturing operations. Although 15 years of the patent's legal life remain, the company believes that new technology will render the patent obsolete after 10 years. Amortization expense for the year is $300,000 ($3,000,000/10 years), recorded as follows:

Amortization Expense—Patent	300,000	
Patent		300,000

Note that, unlike depreciation and depletion, there is no "accumulated amortization" account. Instead, companies typically deduct the amount of amortization directly from the Patent, or other intangible asset, account.

We have now seen how to account for operational investments. In the final portion of the chapter, we turn our attention to reporting issues related to these types of investments.

REPORTING OPERATIONAL INVESTMENTS LO 6

Operational investment activities result in assets, expenses, and cash flows. These activities are communicated to both internal and external stakeholders.

Internal Reporting

Every company operates differently and, therefore, has its own unique system of accounting for plant assets. However, with regard to the recording and communicating of operational investments, every good system of internal control must provide adequate documents and records. For each plant asset, managers want to know the original cost, any additional capital expenditures made, and accumulated depreciation taken to date for both financial statement and tax return purposes.

---

[13]*APB Opinion No. 17,* issued in August 1970, spells out the rules for amortization of intangible assets.

[14]Although generally used, the straight-line method is not required. For some intangibles, such as copyrights, the units-of-production method is also common.

Therefore, in addition to the general ledger, which keeps track of the *total* for each category of plant assets, companies maintain a detailed subsidiary ledger that includes a separate record for each individual asset. In the absence of such a subsidiary ledger, companies might continue to depreciate fully depreciated assets and would not know the amount of gain or loss to record on the disposal of any specific asset.

To help safeguard their plant assets, some companies even place a unique identification (ID) number on each individual asset. This helps companies perform periodic checks to verify the physical location and proper utilization of plant assets. Periodic comparison of these ID numbers with assets actually on hand helps keep records accurate and deters theft. Companies must also maintain similar records for all natural resources and intangible assets.

External Reporting

When analyzing a company's financial statements, one of the first things external stakeholders should determine is the method of depreciation used. In accordance with requirements for full disclosure of all relevant data, companies usually give this information (as well as related information regarding any material amount of depletion of natural resources and amortization of intangible assets) in one of the first notes attached to the financial statements.

For instance, the American Skiing Company reported the following information in notes to its financial statements:

Property and Equipment

Property and equipment are carried at cost, net of accumulated depreciation. Depreciation is calculated using the straight-line method over the assets' estimated useful lives which range from 9 to 40 years for buildings, 3 to 12 years for machinery and equipment, 10 to 50 years for leasehold improvements and 5 to 30 years for lifts, lift lines and trails.

Intangible Assets

Intangible assets consist of goodwill and various other intangibles. . . . Intangible assets are recorded net of accumulated amortization in the accompanying consolidated balances sheet and are amortized using the straight-line method over their estimated useful lives as follows:

Goodwill	40 years
Tradenames	40 years
Other intangibles	16–20 years

The method of depreciation, useful lives, and salvage values selected can have a significant impact on the amount of operating income for the year. All else equal, straight-line depreciation results in a higher reported income, and accelerated depreciation in a lower income. A change to longer useful lives and higher salvage values reduces depreciation expense, while shorter lives and lower salvage values increase it.

For instance, in a note included in its 1995 annual report, Royal Caribbean Cruises, Ltd., one of the world's largest cruise lines, disclosed the following:

Property and Equipment

Depreciation of property and equipment . . . is computed using the straight-line method over useful lives of primarily 30 years for vessels and three to ten years for other property and equipment. The Company revised its depreciation policy to recognize extended estimated service lives from 25 to 30 years and higher residual values on certain of its vessels effective January 1, 1994. The change in vessel depreciation reduced depreciation expense and increased net income by approximately $10.0 million, or $0.16 per share, during 1994.

When comparing reported income of two competitor companies, one should remember that the utilization of different depreciation methods distorts the comparison process. When comparing two consecutive income statements for the same company, look for disclosure of any changes in depreciation policy that will affect the amount of income reported from one year to the next. Unless otherwise stated in the notes, the consistency principle requires the use of the same method and policies from one year to the next.

Financial statement users also need to remember that the MACRS generally allows companies to deduct an amount of depreciation expense on their tax returns that exceeds the amount deducted in their annual reports to shareholders. Because depreciation expense reduces taxes, companies benefit from this excess tax depreciation. However, recall that total depreciation taken over the life of an asset is the same regardless of the method used. As a result, the excess tax depreciation initially allowed under the MACRS is eventually offset by lower depreciation taken toward the end of an asset's life and, therefore, the MACRS only serves to postpone taxes that companies will have to pay later on. Companies report this "deferred tax" as a liability on their balance sheets.[15] At July 26, 1998, the long-term liability section of American Skiing Company's balance sheet included the following:

	Thousands of Dollars	
	July 27, 1997	July 26, 1998
Deferred income taxes	$28,514	$22,719

Balance Sheet: Reporting Operational Investments

The July 26, 1998, balance sheet of American Skiing Company (with 1997 figures included for comparative purposes) reported operational investments under the following headings:

	Thousands of Dollars	
	July 27, 1997	July 26, 1998
Property and equipment, net	$252,346	$521,139
Goodwill	10,664	76,301
Intangible assets	—	23,706

Note 4 of the financial statements detailed the property and equipment as follows:

Property and equipment consists of the following (in thousands):

	July 27, 1997	July 26, 1998
Buildings and grounds	$ 69,635	$159,841
Machinery and equipment	61,218	108,046
Lifts and lift lines	60,769	158,074
Trails	11,667	36,072
Land improvements	18,096	24,612
	221,385	486,645
Less accumulated depreciation and amortization	36,940	69,817
	184,445	416,828
Land	49,160	73,755
Construction-in-progress	18,741	30,556
Property and equipment, net	$252,346	$521,139

Income Statement: Gains and Losses from Operational Investments

We already know that companies report gains and losses as "nonoperating" items on the income statement. If any individual gain or loss is material, the income statement may show it as a separate line item. However, income statements usually lump all gains and losses together with various other categories of nonoperating income and include them as one line item.

The 1998 income statement of American Skiing Company did not report any gains or losses. However, to illustrate the way companies report the disposal of operational

---

[15]Depreciation is one of several factors contributing to the postponement of taxes. The subject of deferred taxes is discussed in more detail in Chapter 24.

investments, let's look at the comparative income statement in Union Pacific's 1993 annual report. On a line immediately following the calculation of Operating Income, it showed:

	Millions of Dollars		
	1993	1992	1991
Other Income, Net (note 13)	$ 89	$146	$122

The reference to note 13 reveals:

13. Other Income—Net
Other Income—Net includes the following:

	Millions of Dollars		
	1993	1992	1991
Rental income	$ 33	$ 38	$ 45
Net gain on property dispositions	18	36	51
Interest on tax settlements	38	17	11
Total	$ 89	$146	$122

The $18 million net gain on property dispositions reported in 1993 represented 3.4 percent of Union Pacific's total of $530 million reported net income for 1993.

Statement of Cash Flows: Acquisition and Disposal of Operational Investments

The Investing Activities section of the statement of cash flows reports the amount of cash used and provided by the acquisition and disposal of operational investments. Investing activities often represent a significant portion of a company's total cash flows. For instance, the statement of cash flows in American Skiing Company's 1998 financial statements showed the following:

	Thousands of Dollars	
	July 27, 1997	July 26, 1998
Cash flows from investing activities:		
Payments for purchases of businesses, net of cash acquired	$ (6,959)	$(291,773)
Long-term investments	836	1,110
Capital expenditures	(23,267)	(106,917)
Proceeds from sale of property & equipment	2,627	7,227
Cash payments on note receivable	250	100
Proceeds from sale of businesses	14,408	5,702
Other	(1,964)	248
Net cash used in investing activities	$(122,583)	$(384,303)

The dollar amounts shown for the "purchases of businesses" and "capital expenditures," both of which represent significant operational investments (i.e., expenditures to obtain facilities necessary for basic business activities) are by far the largest cash flows reported in the investing activities section of the statement of cash flows.

Errors in Reporting

Whether a company reports an expenditure as a capital or a revenue expenditure is an important and sometimes controversial decision. Publicly owned corporations, which are required to issue annual reports to shareholders, are mindful of the stock market's reaction to published earnings reports. Because of the potential market reaction, companies may have a predisposition to improperly capitalize expenditures as a means of postponing expenses and thereby increasing reported profits. On the other hand, privately held businesses owned by a small group of closely related individuals frequently do not have to make their earnings a matter of public record. When earnings are confidential, a business may prefer to treat all expenditures as current expenses in order to reduce the amount of taxable income reported to the Internal Revenue Service. This is especially true in the case of sole proprietorships and partnerships where the owners are personally responsible for payment of the taxes on the business's income.

Operational investments represent some of the most significant long-term uses of a company's capital. This chapter presented information about plant assets, natural resources, and intangible assets and introduced some of the fundamental principles that determine how accountants record the acquisition, use, and disposal of these assets. Finally, we discussed and illustrated the manner in which companies report information regarding operational investments to stakeholders.

- Operational investments are capital expenditures made to acquire the facilities necessary for the conduct of basic business activities. They include investments in plant assets, natural resources, and intangible assets.

- Plant assets are investments in property, plant, and equipment used for business operations over a time span covering more than one accounting period.

- The cost of a plant asset includes all the normal, reasonable, and necessary expenditures to acquire the asset and make it ready for its intended use.

- Depreciation is the process of systematically allocating the net cost of a plant asset to the various periods benefiting from the use of that asset. For financial statement reporting, depreciation can be calculated using the (1) straight-line method, (2) units-of-production method, or (3) accelerated methods.

- For federal tax purposes, depreciation is calculated using the modified accelerated cost recovery system (MACRS). When preparing tax returns, businesses benefit from depreciation deductions because they reduce taxes without requiring any current cash outlay.

- The gain or loss on the disposal of plant assets is the difference between the carrying value of the asset (Cost – Accumulated depreciation) and the fair market value of any assets received in return. When a business sells assets for cash or exchanges dissimilar noncash assets, it records and reports all resulting gains and losses. For financial reporting purposes, when there is an exchange of similar assets, companies record losses but not gains. For tax purposes, no gains or losses are reported upon the exchange of similar assets.

- Natural resources are a company's investment in nonrenewable assets such as coal mines and oil rights. The expense resulting from the cost of these assets is called *depletion* and is usually calculated using the units-of-production method.

- Intangible assets have no physical presence that can be seen or touched. They convey a legal right or benefit to their owner. Examples include patents, copyrights, franchises, leaseholds, and goodwill. The cost of intangible assets is amortized, generally by the straight-line method, over the expected useful life of the assets or their legal lives, whichever is shorter.

- Information regarding operational investments must be reported to internal and external stakeholders. Internal stakeholders require detailed information about individual assets. External stakeholders prefer summarized data about events pertaining to the acquisition, use, and disposal of operational investments. Companies report this information on their balance sheet, income statement, and statement of cash flows and frequently include additional detail in attached notes.

KEY TERMS

accelerated depreciation A method of depreciation that recognizes relatively greater expense in early years of asset use and progressively less expense as time passes

amortization The process of allocating the cost of intangible assets to an expense over the periods they benefit

betterments Capital expenditures that improve an asset's performance capabilities

capital expenditure An expenditure that creates the expectation of future benefits that apply beyond the current accounting period

capitalize To add an expenditure to the cost of an asset, rather than expensing it immediately

copyright An intangible asset that gives its owner the exclusive legal right to the reproduction and sale of a literary or artistic work

declining-balance depreciation A type of accelerated depreciation that reflects depreciation expense for each year based on a constant percentage of a declining balance equal to the remaining undepreciated cost of the asset at the start of each year

depletion The process of allocating the cost of natural resources to an expense over the periods they benefit

depreciable cost The portion of a plant asset's total cost that will be depreciated over its useful life

double-declining-balance depreciation A specific type of declining-balance depreciation that reflects annual depreciation expense using a constant percentage equal to twice the straight-line rate of depreciation

extraordinary repairs Expenditures that extend the remaining useful life of an operational investment

franchise An intangible asset representing the exclusive right to operate or sell a brand name product in a specified territory

goodwill An intangible asset representing the value assigned to a purchased company's ability to generate an above-average return on invested capital

leasehold An intangible asset conveyed by a lease to use equipment, land, and/or buildings for a specified period of time

leasehold improvement An intangible asset representing the amounts paid by a lessee to make physical improvements that are an integral part of leased property

materiality An accounting concept that relates to whether an item's dollar amount or its inherent nature is significant enough to influence a financial statement user

midyear convention The convention that reflects depreciation expense for each asset as if it were purchased or disposed of exactly halfway through the company's fiscal year

modified accelerated cost recovery system (MACRS) The laws that currently govern the calculation of depreciation for federal tax purposes

natural resources Nonrenewable assets such as coal mines and oil rights

operational investments Long-term investments made to acquire the facilities necessary for the conduct of basic business activities

patent An intangible asset giving its owner the exclusive legal right to the commercial benefits of a specified product or process

plant assets Tangible assets acquired primarily for use in a business over a time span covering more than one accounting period

residual value See salvage value

revenue expenditure An expenditure that provides benefits exclusively during the current accounting period

salvage value The expected fair market value of a plant asset at the end of its useful life; also referred to as *residual value*

straight-line depreciation A method of calculating annual depreciation by allocating the depreciable cost of the asset to depreciation expense over its useful life

units-of-production depreciation A method of calculating annual depreciation based on actual usage rather than the passage of time

useful life The period of time over which a business expects to obtain economic benefits from the use of an operational investment

ANSWERS TO THE PAUSE & REFLECTS

p. 711, *SFAS No. 34* specifically requires the capitalization of interest costs incurred during construction of certain assets. Insurance and other costs incurred as part of the costs of a long-term construction project are also capitalized if incurred during construction. However, once construction is complete and the asset is placed in service, the same interest and insurance costs are revenue expenditures which are expensed as incurred. *SFAS No. 34,* paragraph 18, states that the capitalization period for interest ends "when the asset is substantially complete and ready for its intended use." The same would apply to other indirect costs such as insurance.

The reason for the rule is simple. Interest and insurance costs incurred during construction will provide future benefits and are therefore capital expenditures, but once the asset is in use, interest and insurance expenditures provide current benefits.

p. 712, Companies generally want to maximize depreciation deductions on their tax returns in order to minimize tax payments. Because land cannot be depreciated, companies benefit from assigning the smallest possible portion of the total purchase price to the land.

p. 714, The fact that plant assets are often reported on the balance sheet at carrying values substantially below their current fair market values causes at least two major problems:

1. It is not easy for investors and creditors to determine the real net worth of the business, especially for companies where operational investments represent a majority of the dollar amount of reported assets and many of the assets may be older.

2. It is difficult to compare the real net worth of related companies when one company may own relatively new assets with carrying values relatively close to their current fair market values, while the other may own older assets with carrying values significantly different than their current fair market values.

If businesses were required to report current fair market values for all plant assets, the values would be somewhat subjective. This fact can easily be demonstrated by asking several students to state what they think various well-known buildings might be worth.

In addition, during the period that *SFAS No. 33* was in effect (which required some companies to present supplementary information regarding the impact of changing prices), the Financial Accounting Standards Board found that financial statement users often did not fully understand the information presented and, therefore, it was not considered particularly useful for many of the users.

p. 722, Fully depreciated plant assets, like any plant asset, are reported on the balance sheet at their carrying value (original cost less accumulated depreciation)—even if this carrying value equals zero. Companies must report them as part of an effort to fully disclose the company's financial position (including *all* plant assets owned) in accordance with GAAP. Assets are removed from the balance sheet if and when the company disposes of them, not simply because they are fully depreciated.

p. 726, In the example used in the chapter to illustrate the exchange of similar assets, the entry to record the exchange (without recognizing the gain) was:

Building (Acquired in Exchange)	100,000	
Accumulated Depreciation—Building	400,000	
Building (Given up in Exchange)		500,000

The newly acquired building will generate $100,000 of depreciation over its useful life (assuming a salvage value equal to zero), which will reduce income by a total of $100,000.

If the $700,000 gain were recorded, the new building would have been assigned a cost equal to its current fair market value of $800,000. The entry would have been:

Building (Acquired in Exchange)	800,000	
Accumulated Depreciation—Building	400,000	
Building (Given up in Exchange)		500,000
Gain on Exchange		700,000

The gain would have increased income by $700,000, but resulting depreciation over the useful life of the new asset would have been $800,000. Thus the net effect on income would still have been a reduction of $100,000, the same as when the gain was not recorded.

Therefore, we can say that the unrecorded gain on exchanges of similar assets is recognized in the form of *reduced depreciation* over the life of that asset, and the final impact is essentially the same as if the gain had been recognized.

p. 728, Expense recognition requires the realization of the benefit that corresponds with the expense. When we recorded depreciation, we assumed we were getting current benefits from using the plant asset. However, in the case of depletion we assumed the depletion was part of the cost of producing a natural resource and that this resource had not yet been sold (which is necessary to get any benefit from its production).

If depreciation is directly associated with the cost of manufacturing inventory (such as depreciation on a factory building and manufacturing equipment), it should be added to the cost of the inventory rather than expensed as incurred.

p. 730, There is no one answer for these two questions. They are intended to stimulate discussion designed to point out that a franchise can be a very valuable asset.

p. 731, This question is designed to make you think about the characteristics that goodwill must possess for it to be a saleable commodity.

For a company to be able to acquire goodwill as part of the purchase of another business, the goodwill must be attached to the business or the business's product, not the prior owner of the business.

If a sole practitioner doctor sells his or her business and retires, the doctor cannot generally sell any goodwill because the goodwill cannot be separated from the individual who is retiring. When the retiring doctor leaves the practice, he or she cannot leave behind any goodwill for the benefit of the new doctor. The same is true for accountants, lawyers, and other professionals. This point has been established over the years in a number of court cases relating to professionals who attempted to "sell" goodwill in order to take advantage of applicable tax benefits.

However, if the doctor practices as part of a clinic, or some other group practice, and the goodwill attaches to the reputation of the clinic, rather than any individual doctor, it might be possible to purchase goodwill as part of the purchase of the clinic.

QUESTIONS

1. What three characteristics define a plant asset?

2. What factors do companies consider in determining the cost of plant assets?

3. Distinguish between capital and revenue expenditures and give an example of each.

4. Should the cost of paving a parking lot be treated as a capital expenditure or a revenue expenditure? Why?

5. Crandall Company's purchasing agent was presented with an offer he couldn't refuse and purchased 5,000 number 2 lead pencils for $800. The pencils will last the company at least five years. How should Crandall Company record this transaction and why?

6. What special problem exists when a company purchases several assets for one lump sum of money? How is it solved?

7. Is the following statement true or false? Depreciation is the opposite of appreciation and represents the asset's decline in value. Explain your answer.

8. What four factors affect the calculation of depreciation? Which factors are merely estimates involving individual judgment?

9. Why is land not depreciated? Are there any other plant assets whose costs are not allocated over their useful life?

10. What is meant by the term *depreciable cost* and how is it determined?

11. Identify the various methods of depreciation mentioned in the chapter. In your opinion, which method is the easiest to calculate? Which method do you think is most likely to be used by the majority of companies in preparing their financial statements? Why?

12. Explain how the choice of a depreciation method might affect the financial statements of a company.

13. What is the midyear convention and why do companies use it?

14. Explain the term *MACRS*. When is it used, by whom, and for what purpose?

15. Identify the two factors involved in determining the amount of gain or loss on the sale of a plant asset.

16. Give an example of a dissimilar asset exchange as well as a similar asset exchange. Is a gain or loss always recorded for both types of transactions? Explain.

17. What are natural resources? Where do they appear on the financial statements? Are they depreciated?

18. Explain the term *intangible asset* and provide three examples. What is the maximum possible useful life for each of your examples? Where do intangible assets appear on the financial statements?

19. How do companies reflect plant assets on their financial statements? What specific disclosures are required?

20. Worldwide Resources, Inc., purchased a delivery truck and immediately expensed the $24,800 cost. Do you agree with this treatment? Why or why not? What effect will this transaction have on the financial statements?

EXERCISES

E 21.1

LO 1

For each of the situations described below, indicate whether it is a capital (**C**) or revenue (**R**) expenditure.

_____ *a.* Purchased land and a building at a cost of $750,000 by paying $200,000 down and signing a two-year note payable for the remainder.

_____ b. Spent $325 on a tune-up for a truck used in making deliveries.

_____ c. The owner of a restaurant paid a plumber $400 to install a new dishwasher in the kitchen.

_____ d. Paid $1,300 in sales tax on a new delivery van when registering the van at the Registry of Motor Vehicles.

_____ e. A new machine was damaged during installation. The uninsured cost to repair the machine was $1,250.

E 21.2

LO 1

For each of the situations described below, what account would be debited to record the expenditure?

a. Constructed a warehouse for storing merchandise.

b. Purchased 300 reams of 8 1/2-by-11-inch paper for the fax machine.

c. Purchased a parcel of land in a nearby town because of rumors that a new mall would be built on adjoining land. Management expects to sell the land in three years at a substantial profit.

d. Bought 20 used desks and 30 used chairs to be utilized at corporate headquarters in the accounting office.

e. Paid for a new battery installed in the delivery truck.

E 21.3

LO 1

Professional Cleaning Systems (PCS) purchased a new van to expand its business. The invoice price of the van was $25,400, with additional costs of $350 for dealer prep and $275 in destination charges. PCS also had the dealer install special roof racks at a cost of $1,430 and paid $1,300 in sales tax, $85 in registration fees, and $50 for the title. The annual insurance bill totaled $1,960, and PCS opted for an extended warranty package costing $935. Within one month's time, PCS spent $230 for gasoline. Determine the dollar amount that PCS should debit to the Vehicles account.

E 21.4

LO 1

Cabletron Communications purchased land, a building, and several pieces of equipment for $2,400,000. An appraisal of the purchased items estimated the value of the land at $662,500, the building at $1,590,000, and the equipment at $397,500. Determine the portion of the total purchase price applicable to each asset.

E 21.5

LO 2

Micron Electronics recently acquired a new machine at a cost of $54,000. The machine has an estimated useful life of eight years or 24,000 production hours, and salvage value is estimated at $6,000. During the first two years of the asset's life, 2,700 and 3,100 production hours, respectively, were logged by the machine. Calculate the depreciation charge for the first two years of the asset's life using the (a) straight-line method, (b) units-of-production method, and (c) double-declining-balance method.

E 21.6

LO 2

Lanourette Industries purchased a copier with a cost of $37,000 and a salvage value estimated at $5,000. It was expected that the copier would last four years, over which time it would produce 6,400,000 copies. The copier actually produced 1,500,000 copies in year 1, 1,800,000 copies in year 2, 1,700,000 copies in year 3, and 1,400,000 copies in year 4. Calculate the depreciation expense and carrying value of the asset at year-end for each of the four years using the following methods: (a) straight-line method, (b) units-of-production method, and (c) double-declining-balance method.

E 21.7

LO 2

In each of the following situations, determine the age of each asset in either years or units, whichever is appropriate.

a. Equipment appears on the balance sheet at a cost of $28,500 with accumulated depreciation of $14,100. The salvage value was estimated at $5,000, the useful life was estimated at five years, and the straight-line method of depreciation is used.

b. The cost of the truck is $21,800 with $17,100 of accumulated depreciation. Salvage value was estimated at $2,800, and the truck would most likely be driven for 100,000 miles. The company uses the units-of-production method of depreciation.

c. Machinery was purchased for $64,500 and, at present, has accumulated depreciation of $23,220. The useful life was estimated at 10 years, with a salvage value of $9,500. The double-declining-balance method of depreciation is used.

E 21.8

LO 2

Computer Chip Company (CCC) purchased several cash registers on April 2, 2000, at a total cost of $4,350. Estimated useful life of the registers is five years, and their total expected salvage value is $600. CCC uses the straight-line method of depreciation and has a December 31 year-end. Determine the amount of depreciation expense in 2000 assuming, alternatively, that (a) depreciation is calculated to the nearest month and (b) CCC uses the midyear convention.

E 21.9

LO 2

Waltham Industries purchased a computer for $35,000 on January 2, 2000. Its useful life is estimated at five years, with a salvage value of $2,500. Waltham uses straight-line depreciation for its own books and follows the MACRS for tax purposes, taking advantage of the most accelerated method allowed. Waltham's year-end is December 31. Compute the book and tax depreciation for the first three years of the computer's life. Use Exhibits 21.2 and 21.3 as a reference.

E 21.10

LO 2

Sun Limited purchased a building 12 years ago at a price of $650,000. At that time, useful life was estimated at 25 years with a $75,000 salvage value, and straight-line depreciation was used. After recording depreciation for the 12th year, Sun decided that for future years it would revise its original estimate of the building's useful life from 25 to 39 years and salvage value from $75,000 to $50,000. Calculate the depreciation expense that Sun should record for each of the remaining years of the building's life.

E 21.11

LO 2

Bullegato Interiors owns a computer that it purchased two years ago at a total cost of $9,250. At that time it was estimated that the company would use the computer for six years and then sell it for $850. Recently, Bullegato upgraded the computer at a cost of $4,500. This upgrade did not extend the life of the computer, nor did it change the estimated salvage value. Prepare journal entries to record the cost of the upgrade and the depreciation expense for the third year assuming that Bullegato uses straight-line depreciation.

E 21.12

LO 3

Conduit Corporation owns a delivery van with an original cost of $18,400 and accumulated depreciation of $13,750. Determine the amount of gain or loss on the sale of the van under each of the following situations:

a. The van is sold for $5,300 cash.

b. The van is sold for $4,180 cash.

c. The van is sold for $1,500 cash plus a six-month $3,150 note receivable with a stated 10 percent interest rate.

E 21.13

LO 3

Spectrum Products closes its books on October 31 and prepares depreciation adjustments annually. On July 27, 2000, Spectrum sold some equipment with an original cost of $26,250 for $8,500. The equipment was purchased on November 4, 1995, and was depreciated using the straight-line method and had an estimated useful life of eight years and a salvage value of $650. Prepare the entries to update the depreciation and record the sale of the equipment.

E 21.14

LO 3

On July 1, 2000, Federated Supply Company exchanged a warehouse and some land for 50,000 shares of Geico Corporation stock. The stock was selling for $12 per share, and a recent appraisal of the land and warehouse set their total value at $650,000. The warehouse and land originally cost $450,000 and $225,000, respectively. Accumulated depreciation on the warehouse was $320,000. Prepare the entry to record the exchange. What value did you assign to the stock acquired in the transaction? Why?

E 21.15

LO 3

Willow & Company exchanged a building it owned in Wichita for a building in Kansas City owned by Candid Corporation. The buildings were both valued at $575,000, so there was no cash transferred between the companies. Just prior to the exchange, Willow's accounts showed the cost of the original building as $425,000, with accumulated depreciation of $260,000. Candid's Kansas City building was on its books with a cost of $750,000 and accumulated depreciation of $160,000. Determine the gain or loss that each company should recognize. What dollar amount should each company assign to the building it acquired?

E 21.16

LO 3

Adventure World is trading in its old computer system for a new model. The old computer system is on the books at a cost of $270,000 with accumulated depreciation of $185,000. The new model has a list price of $450,000, but the manufacturer has agreed to reduce this amount by $75,000 in return for Adventure's old computer system. Prepare the journal entry to record the acquisition of the new computer system.

E 21.17

LO 4

Harah Minerals owns oil reserves in Texas. The reserves were originally purchased for $14,900,000 and were estimated to contain 3,500,000 barrels of oil. The salvage value of the property was established at $200,000. Production for the current period amounted to 850,000 barrels, all of which are still on hand. Determine the depletion cost per barrel and prepare the journal entry to record the depletion for the current period. How would your entry have changed if one-half the barrels of oil had been sold as of the end of the period?

E 21.18

LO 5

Rega Forest paid $96,000 for the right to operate a Copy Master store in her hometown for the next eight years. Copy Master specializes in printing and copying jobs, both large and small. Prepare journal entries to record the purchase of the franchise and the amortization expense for the first full year.

E 21.19

LO 6

Refer to the financial statements of the Walt Disney Company introduced in Chapter 7. For the most recent fiscal year shown, find the total plant assets, intangible assets, and natural resources, if any. Calculate the percentage of total assets represented by each category above. Compare these percentages to those mentioned in the opening vignette for the American Skiing Company. Were you surprised by the results? Explain.

E 21.20

LO 6

Frontier Express recently repaved its parking lot at a total cost of $60,000. The estimated useful life of the parking lot is five years with zero salvage value, and Frontier uses the straight-line method of depreciation for all plant assets. Assuming Frontier treats this as a revenue expenditure, what effect will it have on income? Assuming Frontier treats it as a capital expenditure, what effect will it have on income?

PROBLEMS

P 21.1

LO 1

Riviera Industries recently completed several transactions relating to plant assets. For each transaction described, determine the dollar amount to be capitalized as well as the account title to be used.

a. Riviera purchased a parcel of land on which it will construct a manufacturing facility. The purchase price of $155,000 included survey fees of $2,700, a title document costing $800, and brokers' fees of $7,500. Riviera also incurred $10,500 in blasting costs to prepare the land for construction of the building.

b. Riviera constructed the manufacturing facility referred to in (**a**) above. Materials and labor costs amounted to $278,000, the architect's fee was $18,500, and the necessary permits totaled $3,600. Insurance carried during the construction was $2,300, and interest on the construction loan amounted to $14,200.

c. Riviera purchased the machinery and office furniture of a company that was going out of business. The total package price was $90,000. Appraisers valued the machinery at $83,000 and the office furniture at $17,000.

d. Riviera paid the following bills relating to the use of its plant assets: (1) annual real estate taxes, $14,250; (2) annual insurance premiums, $8,380; (3) annual mortgage payments, $124,800, of which $61,700 was interest; and (4) painting of the outside of the buildings, $7,200.

e. Riviera purchased a new computer system for $437,000 and paid $3,600 for a three-year service contract. The company also paid $650 to send one of its employees to computer training school to learn how to use the new computer.

P 21.2

LO 2

Priority Corporation purchased a computer system at a total cost of $375,000. As the accountant for the company, you estimated a useful life of four years or 40,000 hours of operation, with a salvage value of $55,000. The president of the company wants to know what impact this capital expenditure will have on income over the next four years. (Assume the computer is used 7,000 hours the first year and that its usage increases 20 percent in each succeeding year.)

Required

a. Prepare a schedule showing the depreciation expense and year-end carrying value of the asset for each of the next four years under each of the following methods of depreciation:
1. Straight-line method
2. Units-of-production method
3. Double-declining-balance method

b. Which method produces the highest income in year 1? Which produces the lowest income in year 1?

P 21.3

LO 2

Zesti Travel, whose year-end is December 31, purchased $36,500 worth of office furniture on January 7, 2000. The company uses straight-line depreciation for financial statement purposes based on an estimated useful life of five years and a salvage value of $3,500. Zesti's tax return preparer follows the MACRS rules for income tax purposes using the most accelerated method allowed.

Required

a. Calculate depreciation expense for financial statement purposes for each year of the asset's life.

b. Calculate depreciation expense for tax purposes for each year of the asset's life. Use Exhibits 21.2 and 21.3 as a reference.

c. Why is it appropriate to use two different methods of depreciation for the same asset?

P 21.4

LO 2

Almeda, Inc., whose year-end is December 31, purchased a delivery truck on May 2, 2000. The invoice price was $43,600 and included dealer prep and destination charges of $875. Almeda also paid sales tax of $2,200, registration fees of $95, and a $100 fee to obtain a title. On May 5, 2000, the company installed air conditioning in the truck at a cost of $1,850. On January 10, 2003, the company installed a new transmission in the truck at a cost of $3,700 and paid $375 for a tune-up of the engine. Almeda uses straight-line depreciation and the midyear convention. The estimated useful life of the truck is eight years with a $6,000 salvage value.

Required

a. Determine the dollar amount that should be capitalized to the Truck account in May 2000.

b. Calculate the depreciation expense to be recorded for 2000.

c. Should Almeda account for the expenditures made in January 2003 as capital or revenue expenditures?

d. If the useful life of the truck was extended two years by the installation of the new transmission, calculate the depreciation expense for 2003, assuming that the salvage value did not change.

P 21.5

LO 2   LO 3

CATCO Laboratories owns various types of equipment used in its research labs. The company, whose year-end is June 30, uses straight-line depreciation calculated to the nearest whole month. On June 30, 2000, the accounting records showed the following:

Equipment	Cost	Salvage Value	Estimated Life	Accumulated Depreciation
Microscope	$ 5,300	$ 800	5 years	$2,025
Autoclave	12,800	1,500	7	5,670
Refrigerator	7,500	900	10	2,420

The following events took place in fiscal 2001:

Aug. 29   The microscope was stolen, and CATCO received a check from the insurance company for $3,000.

Nov. 5   The autoclave was sold for $7,300 cash.

Dec. 17   The refrigerator was sold for $2,300 cash plus a one-year, $2,000 note receivable with a stated interest rate of 12 percent.

Required

a. Update the depreciation expense through the date of disposal for each piece of equipment.

b. Prepare the journal entry to record the disposal of each piece of equipment.

P 21.6

LO 3

Peoples Medical Center owns a CAT scan machine that it wants to dispose of. The original cost of the machine was $245,000, and depreciation of $192,500 has been recorded to date. The purchasing manager is contemplating the following alternatives to dispose of the machine. (Treat each alternative independently.)

1. Mainland Medical Supply is willing to take the old machine and give Peoples a $45,000 trade-in allowance toward the purchase of a new CAT scan machine with a list price of $310,000. The balance of the price must be paid in cash.

2. Cornell Medical Supply is willing to give Peoples a $65,000 trade-in allowance on a new CAT scan machine with a list price of $325,000, the balance to be paid in cash.

3. Century Medical Center is willing to make an even exchange. Century will exchange a parcel of land worth $50,000 for Peoples' CAT scan machine.

4. Saxony Medical Center is willing to give Peoples an ambulance worth $65,000 for Peoples' CAT scan machine plus $10,000 cash.

Required

a. Prepare Peoples' required journal entry to record each of the above alternatives for financial statement purposes.

b. Was the gain/loss recognized for each of the above alternatives? If not, why not?

P 21.7

LO 3

Olympic Touring Company owns a luxury motorcoach it uses in long-distance tours. The motorcoach originally cost the company $285,000, and depreciation taken to date amounts to $227,000.

Olympic's president is considering several alternative methods of disposing of the motorcoach and is concerned about the financial statement impact. The alternative methods of disposal available are as follows. (Treat each alternative independently.)

1. The motorcoach will be sold for $65,000 cash.

2. The motorcoach will be exchanged for a stock investment in Recreation, Ltd. The value of the stock is estimated at $67,500.

3. The motorcoach will be traded in on a new model valued at $325,000. A trade-in allowance of $55,000 will be granted by the manufacturer with the balance paid in cash.

4. The motorcoach will be traded in on a new model valued at $370,000. A trade-in allowance of $73,000 will be granted by the manufacturer with a cash down payment of $50,000 and the balance on a two-year note payable.

Required

a. Determine the amount of gain or loss to be recognized in each of the above alternatives.

b. Calculate the net increase/decrease in total assets for each of the above alternatives.

P 21.8

LO 4

Replenish Corporation owns a coal mine, an oil field, and a tract of timberland. Information regarding these assets follows:

1. The coal mine was purchased several years ago at a total cost of $865,000. The mine was estimated to contain 200,000 tons of ore and to have a $35,000 salvage value. During the current year, 53,000 tons of ore were mined.
2. The oil field was acquired in exchange for stock and was initially valued at $12,600,000. It was estimated to contain 500,000 barrels of oil and to have a salvage value of $100,000. During the current year, 127,000 barrels of oil were extracted.
3. The timberland was obtained through a land swap and was initially recorded at $1,350,000. The number of board feet of timber estimated to be available amounted to 120,000, and the salvage value of the land was estimated at $150,000. During the current year, 21,000 board feet of timber were cut.

Required

a. Assuming Replenish uses the units-of-production method of depletion, determine the depletion rate per ton, barrel, and board foot.
b. Compute the amount of depletion for each of the assets for the current year.
c. Will the depletion charge appear on the financial statements as depletion expense? If not, where would it most likely appear?

P 21.9

LO 5

Chandler Recording Company acquired the following assets during 2000:

1. The patent to manufacture a revolutionary compact disc. The purchase price was $2,300,000, and there are 16 years remaining in the legal life of the patent.
2. The copyright to an album by the newest country western group, Best of the West. The total amount spent to obtain the copyright was $480,000. The album is expected to be produced for three years, but royalties from the album are expected to continue for 10 years.
3. The copyright to a music video by the hottest new female vocalist, Flamingo. Chandler paid $1,000,000 to Flamingo for this right. The video is expected to be produced for two years. However, royalties from the video are expected to continue for six years.

Required

a. Assuming Chandler uses the straight-line method of amortization, determine the amortization expense for 2001 for each of the assets above.
b. Give the journal entry to record the 2001 amortization expense for the patent.

P 21.10

LO 6

In each of the following situations, determine if the appropriate action was taken. If not, describe the financial statement impact of the error.
a. Recorded the $50,000 purchase of land acquired for investment purposes as a debit to the Land account.
b. A $450 tune-up to the delivery truck was capitalized to the Truck account.
c. Land to be used as the site for a new warehouse was purchased for $250,000 plus a broker's commission of $12,500. The Land account was debited for $250,000, and the $12,500 broker's commission was recorded as commission expense.
d. The $650 cost to install a new water heater was charged to plumbing repairs expense.
e. A patent was purchased for $475,000 and recorded in the Equipment account.
f. Depletion relating to the extraction of 200,000 barrels of oil was not recorded because the oil is still sitting in inventory and has not been sold.

CASES

C 21.1

LO 2   LO 6

Using the annual report you obtained as a Chapter 1 assignment, review the financial statements and accompanying notes. For the most recent fiscal year shown, identify the types and amounts of plant assets, natural resources, and intangible assets, if any, as well as any related accumulated depreciation or depletion accounts.
a. How much depreciation, depletion, or amortization expense did the company report?
b. Which method of depreciation, depletion, or amortization did the company use?

C 21.2

LO 1   LO 6

Review the financial statements and accompanying notes of three companies in the same industry. Which depreciation method does each company use? Would you expect them to be the same? Explain.

For each company, calculate total property, plant, and equipment as a percentage of total assets. Can you explain the similarities or the differences in this percentage among the three companies? Are your results consistent with your expectations? Why or why not?

C 21.3

LO 6

(This is a continuation of C 8.4.) In December 1986, the Financial Accounting Standards Board issued *SFAS No. 89.* This statement superseded *SFAS No. 33* and its subsequent amendments, and, although it encouraged the disclosure of supplementary current cost/constant purchasing power information, it no longer required it.

Required

a. Obtain a copy of *SFAS No. 89,* and read paragraphs 1 through 4.
b. Prepare a report on the dissenting opinions given by three board members. Be prepared to discuss your findings in class.

CRITICAL THINKING

CT 21.1

LO 2 **LO 3**

International Communications recently exchanged a warehouse it owned in Boston, Massachusetts, for a warehouse owned by Austin Tea Company in Austin, Texas. The market value of the Boston warehouse was $730,000 and the market value of the Austin warehouse was $850,000. To make the deal work, International paid Austin Tea $120,000 cash. Prior to the exchange, International's original warehouse was on its books at a cost of $275,000, with accumulated depreciation of $92,000.

Required

a. Record the exchange on the books of International Communications assuming the gain is recognized.
b. Record the exchange on the books of International Communications assuming the gain is not recognized.
c. Prepare separate depreciation schedules for alternatives (**a**) and (**b**) above, using straight-line depreciation, a zero salvage value, and a useful life of five years.
d. Accountants sometimes claim that any unrecorded gain resulting from an exchange of similar assets is recognized over the useful life of the acquired asset. Does your answer to requirement (**c**) give any justification for this belief?

CT 21.2

LO 1 **LO 6**

For one lump-sum payment of $2,500,000, Delta Industries recently purchased a parcel of land with a building on it, as well as some equipment located in the building. What special problem exists with lump-sum purchases? How would you determine the dollar value to assign to each of the three individual assets in Delta's accounting records?

Do the following individuals have any incentive to over/understate the value of any one of the three assets acquired? Explain.

a. Delta's president, who receives an annual bonus equal to 5 percent of net income
b. The owners of the company

ETHICAL CHALLENGES

EC 21.1

LO 1 **LO 6**

The president of your company paid you a visit today. He believes that the financial statements misrepresent the financial condition of the company and you, as the accountant, have the job to rectify these mistakes. As an example, he pointed out that the land and buildings have a carrying value on the books of $350,000 but were recently appraised for insurance purposes at $900,000. In addition, he knows for a fact that the company has generated large amounts of goodwill over the years as the result of its dependable service to customers. Yet there is no goodwill listed in the asset section of the balance sheet.

He has asked you to estimate the amount of goodwill and record it on the books. He also wants you to increase the value of all plant assets to their appraised values. He stresses the importance of these changes to the company's ability to obtain a much needed bank loan next week.

Required

a. Identify the accounting and ethical issues in the above scenario.
b. As the accountant for the company, what would you do?

EC 21.2

LO 2

Southwest Manufacturers is having one of its worst years ever. Profits are plummeting, and the controller has approached you, the plant asset accountant, with a proposal. She wants you to reduce depreciation expense by increasing the salvage values on all plant assets and lengthening their useful lives. In this way, she says, the company can end up reporting current year income that is not much lower than in prior years. If need be, the company can change back to the original salvage values and useful lives in future accounting periods. She states, "No one gets hurt and, anyway, no one will even notice the change."

Required

a. Identify the accounting and ethical issues in the above scenario.
b. As the plant asset accountant, what would you do?

COMPUTER APPLICATIONS

CA 21.1

LO 2

Calcutta Corporation purchased five new assets at the beginning of its accounting period. The cost, salvage value, and estimated useful lives of these assets appear below:

Asset	Cost	Salvage Value	Useful Life
1	$45,000	$3,500	7 years
2	14,400	0	3
3	25,200	1,200	6
4	28,900	1,900	6
5	38,200	2,500	5

Required

Use a computer spreadsheet package.
a. Your spreadsheet package's financial functions should include a function to calculate depreciation. Use this function to calculate the straight-line depreciation on each asset for the first year.
b. Repeat requirement (**a**) using the double-declining-balance method.

CA 21.2

LO 2

Cierno Company purchased an asset for $125,000. It has an expected useful life of 10 years and no salvage value. Cierno uses the double-declining-balance depreciation method.

Required

Use a computer spreadsheet package.
a. Prepare a schedule that indicates the depreciation expense, ending balance of accumulated depreciation, and ending book value of each year of the asset's life. (Do not be alarmed if you still have a book value at the end of 10 years.)
b. Because double-declining-balance does not balance to zero, particularly when the cost of the asset is high and the salvage value is low, companies often switch to straight-line depreciation some time during the life of the asset. Determine when Cierno should switch to the straight-line method and prepare a schedule as indicated in requirement (**a**).

CA 21.3

LO 6

Find American Skiing Company's latest financial statements and answer the following:
a. What is the depreciation expense for the year?
b. Is it still using the same method?
c. Does it report any amortization expense? If so, how much?
d. Did it buy or sell any long-term assets during the year? If so, how much cash was given/received?

YOU ARE HERE

Chapter 22 investigates non-operational investment activities, that is, investments made for the return they can generate or for the influence the investor can generate over the investee. This discussion relies on your understanding of cash management issues discussed in Chapter 6 as well as the issues of risk and return explored in Chapter 14. In addition, an understanding of the issues involved when a company issues equity or debt securities (Chapters 17–20) is important. We examine the process of recording investments in equity and debt securities and how these securities are classified by management.

LEARNING OBJECTIVES

LO 1 Describe how to account for investments that give a corporation significant influence or control over another corporation.

LO 2 Explain why investments are classified as trading securities and how to account for and communicate transactions involving these investments.

LO 3 Describe why investments are classified as available-for-sale securities and how to record and communicate transactions involving these investments.

LO 4 Explain the importance of investments in debt securities and how to account for and communicate transactions involving these investments.

LO 5 Illustrate how companies report their investment activities to interested users.

Recording and Communicating Nonoperational Investment Activities

Some people claim that biotechnology has the potential to do more for the quality of human life than the computer chip. That's a giant claim! But many who follow the biotech industry believe that it is true. One of the leaders in this burgeoning industry is Genentech, Inc., a

GENENTECH
www.genentech.com

biotechnology company founded in 1976 in San Francisco, California. It describes itself as a company that discovers, develops, manufactures, and markets human pharmaceuticals internationally. In his letter to stockholders in 1997, Genentech's president and chief executive officer said, "[W]e purposely target our science to produce products that not only represent significant medical advances, but also could yield a strong growth rate for our company and our investors."[1]

In 1998 Genentech opened the world's largest biotech manufacturing facility for the large-scale production of pharmaceutical proteins. Yet the company has a significant portion of its financial resources in assets that are not directly involved in the research and development of new products or in the marketing and production of its existing products. Genentech's 1997 balance sheet reports that 41 percent of its assets consist of short-term (23 percent) and long-term (18 percent) investments in

[1]Genentech, Inc., *Annual Report,* 1997, p. 10.

debt and equity securities. These investments generated $69,160,000 of interest revenue, which represented 6.8 percent of total revenues and almost 55 percent of the firm's net income in 1997.

Why would a company like Genentech make such nonoperating investments? How does the company account for the events involving the acquisition and disposal of these nonoperating investments? How does the accounting system present information about the cost, type, market value, and earnings of these investments to internal and external parties who have an interest in the firm? And, most important, why are these types of investments significant?

n previous chapters, we discussed the nature of debt and equity securities and described how to account for them from the perspective of the issuing company. This chapter addresses the nature of debt and equity securities from the perspective of the buyer of these securities (that is, the investor).

WHY INVEST?

Among the things for which management is responsible are generating a satisfactory return on investments and making sure that funds are available when needed by the company. Genentech's management teams are responsible for deciding which projects to move to the marketplace and for generating profitable growth. Some projects have potential for high return, but at a higher risk than management might otherwise consider. Others may have lower potential for return, but also lower risk. Of course, management makes a priority of those with low relative risk and high potential for return. The result is a balanced mix offering good opportunity for significant return with reasonable risk.

For Genentech, Inc. and other companies, investing in debt and equity securities allows them to generate returns on funds that they plan to use at a later date. Firms use these funds to meet short-term objectives like buying inventory or to accomplish long-term objectives such as developing new products or increasing the firm's productive capacity.

For some companies, excess cash accumulates at certain points in the operating cycle. For example, toy retailers like Toys "R" Us make a majority of their sales in the few months before Christmas. They could restock their inventory in January and February, but that investment would not provide much return. In fact, restocking early in the year requires the company to incur additional storage costs, thereby incurring a negative return on the funds tied up in the inventory. Instead, Toys "R" Us can invest its excess cash in debt and equity securities of other companies that generate a greater return than it would have by allowing the cash to remain in a checking account until the time to buy more inventory.

Cash generated from the firm's profits is either distributed to the shareholders as dividends or reinvested in the firm. Many firms reinvest some of this cash in debt and equity securities on a long-term basis. These long-term investments can accumulate and thus allow firms to finance the expansion of existing capacity or to develop new products without incurring more debt or issuing more stock. When firms need the funds for a new project, they can sell their long-term investments. In discussing its long-range plan, Genentech states that it will "use its solid cash position to build value through product or company acquisitions or value-enhancing financial strategies."[2]

This chapter begins with an overview of the ways that investor companies account for their investments in the equity securities of other corporations. Next we explain how to account for investments in the stock of another company when the investing company has either significant influence or control over the investee company. Then we discuss two methods used to account for the acquisition and disposal of equity securities where the investor does not have significant influence or control. Following this, we show how accounting methods are applied to investments in debt securities. The chapter concludes with a discussion of how to summarize events involving debt and equity securities in both external and internal reports.

---

[2]Genentech, Inc., *Annual Report,* 1997, p. 10.

What factors do companies consider when they are deciding to invest in debt and equity securities instead of assets that directly impact their ability to produce goods or services?
(answer on page 767)

EQUITY INVESTMENTS: THE BIG PICTURE

Recall that a corporation is a legal entity and as such it can own stock in another corporation just like an individual can. To get an overview of equity investments by one corporation in another corporation, the first question that we must answer is "How much of an owner is the investor company?" This may seem like a strange question, but the extent of ownership by one corporation in another determines how the investor accounts for its investment. Three categories of ownership are used to determine the appropriate accounting for investments in another corporation: (1) control, (2) significant influence, and (3) ownership with neither control nor significant influence.

As we show in Exhibit 22.1, the percentage of the investee's outstanding voting stock determines the ownership category of the investment. If an investor owns less than 20 percent of the investee's stock, the investment is one where neither influence nor control exists; the investor must account for these investments using a market-based method. For investments where the percentage is between 20 and 50 percent, an accounting method known as the equity method must be used. Finally, when the investor's percentage of ownership exceeds 50 percent, the investor is assumed to have control over the investee corporation and must use the equity method; the two entities must also consolidate their financial statements. In the following sections of the chapter we explain how investors account for their investments in the equity securities of another corporation.

EXHIBIT 22.1

Accounting for Equity Investments

Extent of investment in another corporation's voting stock determines the appropriate method of accounting and reporting.

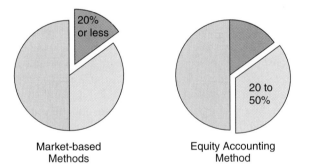
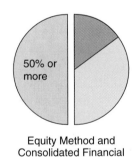

| Market-based Methods | Equity Accounting Method | Equity Method and Consolidated Financial Statements |

ACCOUNTING FOR CONTROL OF ANOTHER CORPORATION

LO 1

When the investment of one company in the voting stock of another company exceeds 50 percent, the investing company has effective control of the investee firm. The controlling company is known as the **parent company,** and the investee firm is called the **subsidiary company.** The investment account on the parent company's books is maintained using the equity method described below. When this type of extensive financial interrelationship exists, the legal distinction between the parent and subsidiary is usually ignored for reporting purposes, and consolidated financial statements for the companies are required. **Consolidated financial statements** are combined financial statements of the parent and subsidiary companies. That is, the operating results, financial position, and cash flows of the two companies are reported as if the companies were one economic entity.

Consider, for example, Ford Motor Company, which has a number of subsidiaries including Hertz, a car rental company. Assume that Ford owns all the voting stock of Hertz, so Hertz is a wholly-owned subsidiary of Ford. Because Ford owns more than 50 percent of Hertz, Ford and Hertz must consolidate their financial statements. The consolidation

Hertz's rental revenues are combined with Ford's income on Ford's consolidated income statement.

process does not result in adjustments recorded in either company's accounting records; instead, the adjusted trial balances of the two companies are combined solely for external reporting purposes. Exhibit 22.2 shows a simplified example of how the consolidation of Ford's and Hertz's financial statements might occur. Ford owns all the assets and liabilities of Hertz because it owns all the outstanding stock of Hertz. To show the assets and liabilities of the consolidated Ford, the assets and liabilities of Hertz should be added to those of unconsolidated Ford. But not all of the assets and liabilities should be added together. Consolidation requires that the two entities be seen as one. Therefore, transactions between them should be effectively canceled, or eliminated, by the consolidation process.

Assume that Ford appropriately carries its investment in Hertz for $200 million.[3] Because an entity cannot invest in itself, showing Ford's investment in Hertz makes no sense. Thus the $200 million investment in Hertz shown in the column representing Ford's unconsolidated balance sheet must be eliminated from Ford's consolidated balance sheet. Because Hertz's stockholders' equity is the same as its net assets (assets minus liabilities), adding the equity of Hertz to the equity of unconsolidated Ford would be adding Hertz's net assets twice. So the stockholders' equity of Hertz is eliminated in the consolidation process. By eliminating both unconsolidated Ford's investment in Hertz and the stockholders' equity of Hertz, the last column in Exhibit 22.2 shows that the consolidated Ford has assets as well as liabilities and stockholders' equity equal to $10,400 million. In a similar way, the actual consolidation of Ford and Hertz eliminates other assets and liabilities that arise from transactions between these two companies.

To arrive at a consolidated income statement, the effects of operating events such as sales and purchases between Ford and Hertz must be eliminated. Recall that when one sells to the other, the transaction is a sale for one and a purchase for the other. Assume that Hertz buys $40 million in cars from Ford—that is, consolidated Ford has sold $40 million worth of cars to itself. Both the sale recorded by the unconsolidated Ford and the cost of sales[4] recorded by Hertz should be eliminated in the consolidation process. Exhibit 22.2 shows the elimination of $40 million in sales from Ford to Hertz. The remaining $25 million of Hertz's $65 million cost of sales must have been purchased from other companies. Therefore, that $25 million should be included on the consolidated Ford income statement.

Most large corporations today have subsidiaries that require accounting procedures to reflect their consolidation. In essence, the accounting procedures transfer the relevant balance sheet and income statement balances to the parent company in order to consolidate, or bring together, the information from two or more companies.

---

[3]We assume that the book value of Hertz's equity is equal to the fair value of its net assets. Otherwise, the asset and liability values and possibly the intangible asset goodwill could complicate the example.

[4]We consider Hertz's rental income to be sales and the amounts paid for those cars to be the cost of sales.

EXHIBIT 22.2 Consolidating the Financial Statements of Ford and Hertz

Balance Sheet Consolidation (in millions)

	Ford Motor Company (unconsolidated)	Hertz Corp.	Eliminating the Effects of Transactions between Ford and Hertz	Ford Motor Company (consolidated)
Investment in Hertz	$ 200	$ —	$(200)	$ —
Other assets	9,000	1,400		10,400
Total assets	$9,200	$1,400		10,400
Liabilities	2,400	$1,200		$ 3,600
Stockholders' equity	6,800	200	$(200)	6,800
Total liabilities and stockholders' equity	$9,200	$1,400		$10,400

Income Statement Consolidation

	Ford Motor Company (unconsolidated)	Hertz Corp.	Eliminating the Effects of Transactions between Ford and Hertz	Ford Motor Company (consolidated)
Sales	$ 800	$ 110	$(40)	$ 870
Cost of sales	500	65	40	525
Other expenses	200	25		225
Net income	$ 100	$ 20		$ 120

Accounting for Significant Influence over Another Company

When a company has a significant influence over another company due to stock ownership (20 to 50 percent), the investee company is viewed as an extension of the investor's operations. The investor company uses the equity method to account for these investments. The equity method violates the historical cost principle, but it is used because it better reflects the investor's changing financial interest in the investee corporation's net assets. It also recognizes that once an investor achieves significant influence, the investor can affect when dividends are paid by the investee. If investment income is determined by the receipt of investee dividends, as it is when the investor doesn't have significant influence, the investor potentially can affect its own income by dictating when the investee company declares its dividends.

The **equity method** of accounting for an investment reflects increases and decreases in the investment account of the investor company in proportion to the changes in the investee's stockholders' equity (net assets of the investee company). The investment, which is an asset for the investor, mirrors the investee's stockholders' equity. Just as net income increases the investee's stockholders' equity, under the equity method, the investor records its *proportionate* share of the investee's net income as an increase in the value of its investment account. Dividends, which decrease the equity of the investee, also decrease the investment account of the investor.

For example, assume that Genentech, Inc., purchases 35 percent of the voting stock of Cell Research Corporation (CRC) for a total of $700,000. CRC's net income for the period in which Genentech acquires CRC's stock is $50,000, and CRC pays dividends of $30,000. Since Genentech, Inc., owns 35 percent of CRC's voting stock, its proportionate share of the net income is $17,500 ($50,000 × 0.35), and it receives dividends of $10,500 ($30,000 × 0.35). The entries to record the purchase of the stock and the recognition of Genentech's proportionate share of CRC's net income and dividends follow:

```
Investment in CRC Stock          700,000
     Cash                                   700,000
(Purchase of CRC stock)


Investment in CRC Stock          17,500
     Investment Income                      17,500
(Recording Genentech's proportionate share of CRC's income)


Cash                             10,500
     Investment in CRC Stock                10,500
(Recording Genentech's receipt of dividends from CRC)
```

Genentech records its share of CRC's net income in the Investment in CRC Stock account based on its percentage of ownership in CRC. Thus Genentech's investment account reflects the increase in CRC's stockholders' equity generated by net income and a decrease in CRC's stockholders' equity because of CRC's declared dividends. Exhibit 22.3 shows how the equity method causes the investor's investment account to mirror the investee's stockholders' equity.

Consider what the total amount of CRC's equity must have been when Genentech purchased the stock. Genentech paid $700,000 for 35 percent of CRC's stock, which means that the book value of CRC's equity must have been $2,000,000.[5] During the year, CRC had income of $50,000 and paid dividends of $30,000. Thus, at the end of the year, CRC's equity was $2,020,000 ($2,000,000 plus the $50,000 net income less the $30,000 dividends that it paid to its stockholders), and 35 percent of $2,020,000 is $707,000. Genentech's Investment in CRC Stock began at $700,000 then increased by its 35 percent share of CRC's income ($17,500) and decreased by the portion of CRC's dividends that it received ($10,500), which means that the investment accounted for using the equity method had a balance of $707,000. As you can see, an investment accounted for under the equity method equals the investor's share of the investee's stockholders' equity.

EXHIBIT 22.3	Genentech's Investment in CRC Using the Equity Method			

Equity Events for CRC During 1999

	Beginning of 1999	1999 Net Income	Dividends Paid by CRC in 1999	End of 1999
Assets	$2,000,000			$2,520,000
Liabilities	$ –0–			$ 500,000
Stockholders' equity	2,000,000	$50,000	$ (30,000)	2,020,000
	$2,000,000			$2,520,000

Investment Events for Genentech During 1999

	Beginning of 1999	1999 Net Income	Dividends Paid by CRC in 1999	End of 1999
Investment in CRC	$700,000	$17,500	$(10,500)	$707,000

If, at a subsequent date, Genentech decides to sell some or all of its stock in CRC, the gain or loss on the sale will be determined by comparing the net proceeds from the sale to the carrying (book) value of the stock in the investment account at the time of the sale.

PAUSE & REFLECT

"Significant influence" includes an investor's ability to influence the amount and timing of dividends paid by an investee. Assuming that the equity method is not available, what are the motives of the investor company's management to influence the investee's dividend payments? How does the equity method diminish the investor company's incentives to influence the investee's dividend payments? *(answer on page 767)*

Market Value: Neither Influence nor Control

Often companies invest in stocks where the portion of the investee that they own is too small for the investor to have influence or control over the investee. For accounting purposes, these equity investments are classified on the investor's balance sheets as either trading securities or available-for-sale securities. These investments are shown on the balance sheet of the investor at their market value as of the date the statements were issued. Reporting securities at market value violates the historical cost principle by valuing

---

[5]We assume that the investor pays the book value of the investee's equity. Otherwise, the accounting becomes even more complicated, which is beyond the scope of this text.

the securities not at what the company paid for the securities but at the amount for which the securities could be sold.

We use market values rather than historical cost to account for investments in financial instruments because it is possible to accurately verify the market value of these securities. Financial publications such as the *Wall Street Journal* and *Barron's* report on the activities of the financial markets and give financial statement users reasonable assurance that the market values of a company's investments are objectively and fairly determined. Mark-to-market accounting for investments in equity (and debt) securities helps financial statement users get a more realistic assessment of the value of a company's investments. It also helps both internal and external financial statement users evaluate the effectiveness of a company's investment policies.

Securities classified as **trading securities** are those that companies purchase with the intent of selling them after holding them for a short period of time. Therefore, the balance sheet reflects a company's trading securities as current assets. Trading securities have little associated risk because companies can readily convert them into cash and typically hold them for no more than a few months. While the bulk of such temporary investments is made in U.S. government securities, prime commercial paper, and other types of debt securities, companies also make short-term investments in equity securities of other companies.

Companies purchase certain securities in order to maintain a portfolio of securities that management can sell, as needed, to raise cash for particular projects. These investments are classified as **available-for-sale** (AFS) **securities.** Such investments typically appear on the balance sheet as long-term assets, but individual securities that qualify are classified as current assets. Each classification requires a distinct accounting treatment that reflects the nature of the particular investment, as the next two sections of the chapter show.

TRADING SECURITIES (EQUITY)

LO 2

Companies invest in equity securities because they expect to generate a return on their short-term investment from dividends and the appreciation of the purchased stock. When a company buys the stock of other companies, the cost of the securities includes the brokerage fees paid to acquire the stock. For example, assume Genentech purchased 1,000 shares of American Electric Power (AEP) common stock at $19 per share and paid $570 in brokerage fees. The cost per share of AEP common stock is $19.57 ($19,570/1,000 shares), and the entry to record this transaction is:

Trading Securities—AEP Common Stock	19,570	
Cash		19,570

Income from Equity Investments

Investors in stock receive earnings from their investments in the form of dividends declared by the investee company. These investors record cash dividends when they are received. Unlike investments accounted for using the equity method, investors whose investments give them neither significant influence nor control account for dividends received as income. Considering the short period of time that trading securities are held, the investor company often receives no dividends during the time that it holds the investment. However, if AEP declared and paid a quarterly dividend of $0.50 per share while Genentech held the stock, it would record the event on its books with the entry below:

Cash (1,000 shares × $0.50)	500	
Dividend Revenue		500

Gains and Losses from the Sale of Equity Investments

Companies compute gains and losses realized through the sale of equity investments on the basis of the cost of the securities held compared to the net proceeds they receive from the sale. The sale of an equity trading security is recorded by a debit to Cash and a credit to the specific trading security equity account.[6] If the net proceeds from the sales

---

[6]Companies keep records of their investments in individual stocks but show only a single account, such as Trading Securities, on their balance sheet. This is similar to the way that they account for accounts receivable.

exceed the carrying cost of the equity security, there is a gain on the sale of trading securities; if the net proceeds are less than the carrying cost, a loss on the sale of trading securities results.

For example, assume that Genentech sells 100 shares of AEP stock for $2,500 less a broker's fees of $60. The net proceeds, $2,440 ($2,500 – $60), less the cost of the AEP stock, $1,957 ($19.57 × 100 shares), generate a gain of $483 that Genentech records as shown in the following entry:

Cash	2,440	
Gain on Sale of Trading Securities		483
Trading Securities		1,957

Adjusting Trading Securities to Their Market Value

Equity trading securities change in value over time, and the market value of a firm's portfolio of trading securities is of interest to many financial statement users. Recall that market value, or fair market value, is the amount at which a security could be exchanged in a current transaction between willing parties. Therefore, we use a method of investment valuation called **mark-to-market** to show the market value of the entire portfolio of trading securities on the balance sheet without altering the cost of the individual securities. That is, a company reflects its investment portfolio at the equivalent market value at the time it issues its financial statements.

When the market value of all the trading securities held at the balance sheet date differs from the total cost of those securities, the reporting company creates a **market adjustment account.** This balance sheet account reflects adjustments made to the total cost of the trading securities to show the total market value of the securities.

Assume, for example, that on December 31, 1999, Genentech, Inc., had trading securities with a total cost of $185,325,000 and a total fair market value of $185,311,000. In order to report the market value on the balance sheet, Genentech would create a valuation account called *Market Adjustment—Trading Securities* to reflect the difference between the cost and market value of its trading securities at that date. Because the market value of its trading securities is below their cost, Genentech credits the market adjustment account and subtracts the $14,000 amount from the total cost figure on the balance sheet to reflect the $185,311,000 market value of the trading security portfolio. The offsetting debit is made to an income statement account called *Unrealized Loss—Trading Securities*. This represents a decrease in the market value of the portfolio of trading securities that Genentech still holds; therefore, the "loss" has not yet been recognized in the accounts (that is, it is unrealized).

The entry below shows how Genentech, Inc., records the difference between the cost and market value of its portfolio of trading securities for 1999:

Unrealized Loss—Trading Securities	14,000	
Market Adjustment—Trading Securities (TS)		14,000

Genentech's 1999 balance sheet would reflect the market value of the portfolio of trading securities using one of two acceptable approaches. Genentech could simply report the portfolio of trading securities (net) which would show the trading securities at their market value. Alternatively, Genentech could show the portfolio of trading securities at their cost and subtract the market adjustment to illustrate the market value of the portfolio. Either format is acceptable as shown below:

Trading securities at market value (net)	$135,311,000

or

Trading securities	$135,325,000
Less market adjustment	14,000
Trading securities at market value	$135,311,000

When the market value of the trading securities is more than the cost of the securities, the market adjustment account would have a debit balance and the company would record a corresponding Unrealized Gain, which is also an income statement account, in its accounting records. The balance sheet would show trading securities at more than their cost.

Entries made to Market Adjustment—Trading Securities reflect the market value of the entire portfolio of trading securities, and they are made only at the end of the accounting period prior to issuing financial statements. The purchases and sales of individual debt and equity securities during the year do not affect the market adjustment account. Rather, by the end of the next accounting period, most, if not all, of the securities held as trading securities at the previous balance sheet date probably have been sold and replaced with a new portfolio of debt and equity securities. Nevertheless, at the end of each accounting period, it is necessary to adjust the balance in the market adjustment account to reflect the difference between total cost and total market value of the trading securities at that point in time.

Suppose that on December 31, 2000, Genentech, Inc., has a portfolio of trading securities that cost $175,603,000 with a market value of $175,605,000. The market adjustment account still has the $14,000 credit balance that was established at the prior year's balance sheet date. Therefore, to adjust the portfolio of trading securities from cost to market value on the December 31, 2000, balance sheet date, the market adjustment account needs to have a $2,000 debit balance. This is accomplished with the following entry:

Market Adjustment—Trading Securities	16,000	
Unrealized Gain—Trading Securities		16,000

The related unrealized gain on the trading securities would be reported on the income statement for 2000, and the trading securities for 2000 would be reported in the current asset section of the balance sheet at their market value in either form shown below:

Trading securities at market value (net)	$175,605,000

or

Trading securities	$175,603,000
Add market adjustment	2,000
Trading securities at market value	$175,605,000

AVAILABLE-FOR-SALE SECURITIES (EQUITY)

LO 3

Management expects to sell available-for-sale (AFS) equity securities, but not in the near future. Because management expects to sell these securities, the market value of the available-for-sale securities portfolio is reported on the balance sheet under the investments classification. However, individual debt and equity securities that qualify are classified as current assets.

Accounting for the purchase and sale of individual equity securities classified as available-for-sale securities is the same as accounting for trading securities except they are labeled *AFS*. However, the process of adjusting the portfolio of available-for-sale securities differs from trading securities in a very important way. *The gains and losses that result from the adjustment of available-for-sale securities to market value are not shown as part of net income on the income statement.* Instead, those gains and losses are shown as part of comprehensive income, often in the statement of stockholders' equity. Thus the gains and losses that result from trading securities affect a company's current net income, while those that result from available-for-sale securities do not affect current net income. (We discuss comprehensive income in Chapter 23.)

Adjusting Available-for-Sale Securities to Their Market Value

Companies report available-for-sale equity (and debt) securities on a market value basis. As in the case of presenting trading securities, companies use a market adjustment account to reflect the adjustment of the total cost of the available-for-sale portfolio to its market value. In order to indicate the required balance in the market adjustment account, it is necessary to compare the total cost of the available-for-sale portfolio to the market value of the portfolio. An adjusting entry changes the existing market adjustment account balance to the desired balance. For available-for-sale securities, a **Net Unrealized Gain**

or Loss account reflects the adjustments made to total stockholders' equity to correspond to the balance in the market adjustment account for available-for-sale securities on the balance sheet. The adjustment is not considered a gain or loss and, therefore, is not part of net income.

Assume that on December 31, 1999, Genentech, Inc., reported that it held available-for-sale securities at a cost of $385,304,000 that had a market value of $459,577,000. The entry to record the required adjustment of $74,273,000 (cost of $385,304,000 to market value of $459,577,000) is:

Market Adjustment—Available-for-Sale Securities	74,273,000	
Net Unrealized Gain or Loss		74,273,000

The debit balance in the market adjustment account is added to the cost of the available-for-sale portfolio and reported in the investments section of the balance sheet in either of these ways:

Available-for-sale securities at market value (net)	$459,577,000

or

Available-for-sale securities	$385,304,000
Add market adjustment	74,273,000
Available-for-sale securities at market value	$459,577,000

Genentech would report the unrealized gain on its AFS securities as a $74,273,000 addition to stockholders' equity on its balance sheet.

If, at December 31, 2000, the market value of the portfolio of available-for-sale securities was $488,900,000 and the cost of the portfolio was $405,304,000, the following entry would be made:

Market Adjustment—Available-for-Sale Securities	9,323,000	
Net Unrealized Gain or Loss		9,323,000

The difference between the market value and cost of the portfolio is $83,596,000 ($488,900,000 − $405,304,000). However, the existing balances in both the Market Adjustment—AFS and the Net Unrealized Gain or Loss accounts are $74,273,000 (see the December 31, 1999, journal entry). Therefore, the December 31, 2000, entry changes the Market Adjustment—AFS account to its desired balance of $83,596,000 ($83,596,000 − $4,273,000) and increases the Net Unrealized Gain or Loss account to the same amount.

We show the balance sheet presentation for the available-for-sale portfolio in the investments section of the 2000 balance sheet below. The $83,596,000 balance in the Net Unrealized Gain or Loss account would be reported as an addition to Genentech's stockholders' equity in the same way it was on the 1999 balance sheet.

Available-for-sale securities at market value (net)	$488,900,000

or

Available-for-sale securities	$405,304,000
Add market adjustment	83,596,000
Available-for-sale securities at market value	$488,900,000

WHY DISTINGUISH BETWEEN TRADING AND AVAILABLE-FOR-SALE SECURITIES?

The rationale for dividing investments in equity securities into trading securities and available-for-sale securities may not be obvious. To understand the reasoning, you have to think about the different motives that managers have for investing. The overriding motive that managers have is to provide a return to the company and its stockholders. But that motive can be achieved either directly or indirectly. Directly, managers can provide returns by investing in securities that pay dividends (interest in the case of debt securities) or appreciation in the security's price. Indirectly, managers can earn a return by building good relationships between the company and its customers, suppliers, or other important companies, such as partners in product development. This difference in motives for ownership results in different methods of accounting for the two types of investments. Trading securities are very short term in nature and bought almost exclusively for the return that they generate. Small holdings of stocks that are held for a few days or a few months are not useful in building or maintaining relationships. Therefore, managers' only purpose in making these investments is for the return that they provide. *If the reason for owning these securities is to generate a return, then that return ought to be included in the company's net income, which is an important measure of corporate performance.*

On the other hand, investments that build or support relationships are not made to produce a direct return. Genentech has a number of investments in companies that it wants to support in product development or that it believes offer important distribution channels, even though Genentech does not have sufficient levels of ownership to be considered to have significant influence or control. If a company does not buy the stock of another to provide a direct return, does it make sense to include the gains and losses on the holdings of those investments in net income? The FASB's answer to that question is no. So when a company invests for an indirect return, the changes in the market value of available-for-sale securities do *not* go through the current period's income but instead are part of comprehensive income and are shown as increases or decreases in the investor's stockholders' equity.

As an example of the difference in these two approaches, assume that two companies (Trader Company and Partner Company) each make investments of $450,000 in Third Company. Trader Company bought Third Company's stock as a short-term investment and intends to sell it very soon, while Partner Company views the investee as a potential co-developer of a new product and, thus, doesn't intend to sell the stock in the foreseeable future. Trader classifies its investment as a trading security and Partner classifies its investment as available-for-sale. Next, assume that in Year 1, the first year of ownership, the market value of their investments rise to $500,000. Exhibit 22.4 shows how the balance sheets and income statements of Trader and Partner would be affected by the acquisition and the Year 1 change in market value. Both report the investment at its market value, though Trader considers it a current asset and Partner includes the investment as a long-term asset in the investments section of its balance sheet. Trader reports net income that is $50,000 higher than Partner's, due to the unrealized gain that is included in Trader's net income but reported by Partner in its stockholders' equity.[7] If the market price fell to $375,000 in the second year, Trader would report a loss of $125,000 on its income statement, while Partner, which accounts for its investment using the available-for-sale method, does not. For both companies, the market values would be reported as before. Finally, in the third year, assume that both sold their investments for $475,000. The sale in Year 3 is a real exchange transaction, and just like any sale the net proceeds are compared to the net carrying value of the asset to determine a gain or loss that goes on the income statement regardless of how the investment was classified.

Notice that the carrying value of both investments is $375,000 when they are sold. But Partner, which classified the security as available-for-sale, has a $75,000 unrealized loss in its stockholders' equity that it eliminates by debiting the Market Adjustment—AFS account and crediting the Net Unrealized Gain or Loss account. That leaves the original $450,000 as Partner's adjusted carrying value (which equals the original cost when accounting for available-for-sale investments). The gain for Partner is $25,000 because the proceeds ($475,000) exceed the adjusted carrying value of $450,000. The $100,000 realized gain for Trader is simply the proceeds ($475,000) less the carrying value of $375,000. An important outcome to notice is that the net gain each reports on its income statement over the three-year period relating to its investment is the same! Partner reports a $25,000

---

[7]For simplicity, we ignore the impact of income taxes. That assumption doesn't change the idea that holding securities classified as trading securities has more impact on net income during the time the securities are held than if the securities were considered to be available-for-sale securities.

EXHIBIT 22.4 Comparing the Reporting Using AFS and Trading Classifications

Partner Company

	Year 1	Year 2	Year 3	Net Gain from Holding Third Company Stock
Balance Sheet				
Investments:				
Investment in Third Company	$450,000	$450,000	$450,000	
Market Adjustment—AFS	–0–	50,000	(75,000)	
Investments at market value	$450,000	$500,000	$375,000	
Stockholders' equity:				
Net unrealized gain or loss	$ –0–	$ 50,000	$ (75,000)	
Income Statement				
Realized gain			$ 25,000	$25,000

Trader Company

	Year 1	Year 2	Year 3	Net Gain from Holding Third Company Stock
Balance Sheet				
Current assets:				
Trading securities	$450,000	$450,000	$ 450,000	
Market adjustment—TS	–0–	50,000	(75,000)	
Trading securities at market value	$450,000	$500,000	$ 375,000	
Income Statement				
Net unrealized gain or loss		$ 50,000	$(125,000)	
Realized gain			$ 100,000	$25,000

gain on its income statement only in Year 3, and the sum of the gains and losses Trader reports over the three years is a $25,000 gain (Year 1 has a $50,000 unrealized gain, Year 2 has a $125,000 unrealized loss, and Year 3 has a $100,000 realized gain).

Preferred Stock

You may be asking "Where does preferred stock fall?" Preferred stock is not affected by the rules that determine how equity investments should be accounted for because preferred stock does not have voting rights. Thus the important difference between preferred stock and other equity investments is that it does not grant its holder ownership rights as common stock does, so the percentage of the outstanding preferred stock that a company owns is irrelevant. Therefore, preferred stock is classified as either trading or available-for-sale depending on management's intent and accounted for as we described previously.

We have discussed how investors account for their investments in equity securities. But investors also can invest in debt securities. Most of the methods of accounting for investments in debt securities are the same as for equity securities. In the next section, we describe the areas of accounting for debt securities that differ from investments in equity securities.

DEBT SECURITIES AS INVESTMENTS

LO 4

Investors can invest in a variety of debt instruments, such as U.S. Treasury bills and corporate bonds. One important difference between debt and equity securities is that when debt securities are bought at prices where the effective interest rate differs from the stated interest rate, they have either a premium or discount. Accounting for the premium or discount makes investments in debt securities different from equity investments.

Another way that accounting for debt securities differs from equity securities is that debt matures—debt has a "due date." This feature allows a third classification of investments beyond trading and available-for-sale securities: held-to-maturity securities. **Held-to-maturity securities** are debt securities that firms purchase with the intent of holding until maturity. These debt securities are considered long-term assets and appear in the investments section of the balance sheet. However, if individual debt securities are due to mature within the next accounting period, they are classified as current assets.

In the next two sections, we discuss how to determine the investor's cost of interest-bearing debt securities and some of the unique features of debt securities when they are considered trading securities. Then we show how to account for an investment in debt securities that has a premium or discount. Finally, we describe how to account for debt investments classified as held-to-maturity securities.

Determining the Cost of Debt Securities

Whether the investor classifies interest-bearing debt securities as trading, available-for-sale, or held-to-maturity, their cost is determined the same way. Recall that bond prices are quoted on the market on the basis of 100. In addition to the basic price of the debt security, two other factors may affect the amount of cash paid for the debt instrument: (1) the broker's commission or fee and (2) the accrued interest. The amount of any commission or fee paid to a broker when purchasing securities is included in the cost of the investment because it is a reasonable and necessary cost of acquiring the asset. However, interest accrued on the note is paid to the seller of the note and is not included in the cost of the security. The purchasing company excludes the accrued interest from the cost of the investment because it will receive the accrued interest as part of the cash interest at the next interest payment date.

Assume that Genentech purchases Quintico Manufacturing bonds with a face value of $10,000 on May 1 through a security broker. The bonds have a 12 percent face rate that is paid semiannually on March 1 and September 1. The price of the bonds is 101, and the broker's fee is $90. The computation of the cost of the bonds and the total cash paid is as follows:

Basic price of the bonds ($10,000 × 1.01)	$10,100
Broker's fee	90
Cost of bonds	$10,190
Accrued interest (10,000 × 0.12 × 2/12)	200
Total cash paid	$10,390

Genentech must pay the seller the interest from the last interest date to the time of the purchase (March and April). If Genentech does not pay the interest, the seller would not receive the interest due for the two months it held the bonds, and Genentech would receive six months' interest even though it held the bonds for only four months. The entry to record this transaction is as follows:

Trading Securities—Quintico Mfg. Bonds	10,190	
Interest Receivable	200	
Cash		10,390

When Genentech receives the semiannual interest payment of $600 on September 1, it will record the event as follows:

Cash ($10,000 × 0.12 × 1/2)	600	
Interest Receivable		200
Interest Revenue		400

Of the $600 Genentech receives, $200 relates to the interest paid to the seller when Genentech purchased the bonds; the remaining $400 is the amount of cash interest earned on the bond.

Trading Securities: Debt Instruments

Equity investments in other companies' capital stock normally present a greater risk of price change than do investments in debt securities. Although the prices of debt securities change in response to changes in interest rates and economic conditions, they are not subject to the rapid increases and decreases in prices experienced by equity securities. Thus debt securities like U.S. Treasury bills and commercial paper are often purchased for a short-term return on idle cash and are classified as trading securities. Below we discuss accounting for debt securities considered to be trading securities.

Noninterest-Bearing Notes Recall that noninterest-bearing notes do not have a face interest rate. The purchaser of the note pays an amount that is less than the note's face value based on the present value of the promised future cash flows at the market interest rate. Upon maturity, the investor receives the full amount of the face value of the note. The purchaser of a noninterest-bearing note does not use a discount account to show the difference between the face value and the sales price of the debt security, as the company would if it issued the note.

The amount of interest earned on noninterest-bearing notes is the difference between the note's purchase price and its face value upon maturity. However, if the investor sells the note before its maturity date, the difference between the purchase price and the proceeds from the sale is considered a gain or loss on the sale of the security. If the company sells a noninterest-bearing note before its maturity date, it reflects the difference between the proceeds of the sale and the cost of the note as either a gain or a loss.

For example, if Genentech purchased U.S. Treasury bills with a maturity, or face, value of $10,000 for $9,500, the company would make the following entry to record the purchase:

Trading Securities—U.S. Treasury Bills	9,500	
Cash		9,500

Notice that Genentech does not use a discount account as it would if it issued the note. When the Treasury bills mature, the entry made to reflect this event will show the amount of interest earned as the difference between the $9,500 cost and the $10,000 maturity value:

Cash	10,000	
Trading Securities—U.S. Treasury Bills		9,500
Interest Revenue		500

If Genentech sells the Treasury bills for $9,600 before they mature, it would make the following entry to record the event:

Cash	9,600	
Trading Securities—U.S. Treasury Bills		9,500
Gain on Sale of U.S. Treasury Bills		100

Interest-Bearing Notes Companies also record their investments in interest-bearing debt securities, such as U.S. Treasury notes, at the cost of those securities rather than the amount of their face value. Therefore, they do not record the effective interest rate of the note. These securities may be issued at a premium or a discount, depending upon whether the market interest rate at the time of the investment is greater or less than the face interest rate. Companies do not amortize the discount when they receive cash interest payments because they do not intend to hold such notes to maturity. At the end of an accounting period, companies with interest-bearing notes held as trading securities accrue only the amount of cash interest with no recognition of any premium or discount.

Assume that Genentech, Inc., purchased U.S. Treasury notes with a face value of $15,000 at a total cost of $14,850. Further assume that the face interest rate is 10 percent and that it is paid semiannually. Therefore, the investment pays $750 of cash interest every six months ($15,000 × 0.10 × 1/2). The entries shown below illustrate how Genentech would reflect the acquisition of the securities and the subsequent receipt of one semiannual interest payment in its records:

Trading Securities—U.S. Treasury Notes	14,850	
Cash		14,850
Cash	750	
Interest Revenue		750

Note that Genentech does not record the $150 discount ($15,000 − $14,850) on the U.S. Treasury note separately. In addition, Genentech does not amortize the discount when it receives the cash interest payment because the company intends to hold the note for a short period of time. Therefore, Genentech will not record the effective interest rate of the note. At the end of the accounting period, Genentech would accrue only the amount of cash interest on its interest-bearing notes held as trading securities.

If Genentech sold interest-bearing debt securities on an interest payment date, the difference between the proceeds and the cost of the investment would determine the gain or loss. For example, if the proceeds from the sale of the U.S. Treasury note were $14,900 on any given interest payment date, the entry would reflect a $50 gain on that transaction as shown below:

Cash	14,900	
Trading Securities—U.S. Treasury Notes		14,850
Gain on Sale of U.S. Treasury Notes		50

Available-for-Sale Debt Investments

Available-for-sale debt securities usually consist of bonds, and the process of recording their acquisition is the same as that described for trading securities. However, because firms buying available-for-sale bonds do not intend to sell these bonds in the near future, they are interested in the effective interest rate of these debt instruments. For this reason, these investments usually consist of corporate and government bonds. Firms amortize the premiums and discounts on these bonds and maintain each debt security on an amortized cost basis.

As we explained earlier, when a company purchases bonds as an investment, the price paid for the bonds is determined by finding the present value of the remaining cash flows of the bond using the market interest rate. The bond is purchased at a premium if the market rate of interest is less than the face rate of interest and at a discount if the market rate is greater than the face interest rate.

For example, assume that on July 1, 1999, Genentech, Inc., purchased 20, $1,000 bonds of the Chappuy Corporation that are due in five years and that have a face interest rate of 12 percent. Interest is paid on June 30 and December 31 of each year. Genentech purchased the bonds for $21,544 when the market interest rate was 10 percent. The entry to record the acquisition of the bonds appears below:

Available-for-Sale Securities—Chappuy Bonds	21,544	
Cash		21,544

Exhibit 22.5 shows how to determine the market price of the bonds (panel A) and presents the premium amortization table for the first year of the bonds' life (panel B). The company records the bonds at their cost in the available-for-sale investment account. Typically, companies do not use a separate premium or discount account when reflecting investments in debt instruments.

The entry for the first interest payment presented here shows that the premium is amortized by decreasing the carrying value of the Available-for-Sale Securities—Chappuy Bonds account and that the company recognizes the effective interest for

EXHIBIT 22.5 Investment in AFS Bonds

Calculator:
PMT = 1,200
FV = 20,000
c = 2
n = 10
r = 10
PV = 21,544.35

A. Market Price Determination

Cash flow 1:

Present value of annuity	=	Annuity	×	$P_{10,5\%}$
	=	$1,200	×	7.7217
Cash flow 2:	=	$9,266		
Present value	=	Future value	×	$P_{10,5\%}$
	=	$20,000	×	0.6139
	=	$12,278		

Present value of cash flow 1	$ 9,266
Present value of cash flow 2	12,278
Price of bond	$21,544

B. Premium Amortization Schedule

Date	Cash Interest (0.06 × Face Value)	Effective Interest (0.05 × Carrying Value)	Amortized Premium	Premium	Carrying Value
7/1/99				$1,544	$21,544
12/31/99	$1,200	$1,077	$123	1,421	21,421
6/30/00	1,200	1,071	129	1,292	21,292

the six-month period. When the bonds mature in five years, the Available-for-Sale Securities—Chappuy Bonds account will equal the face value of the bonds, or $20,000.

Cash	1,200	
Available-for-Sale Securities—Chappuy Bonds		123
Interest Revenue		1,077

When a company purchases bonds between interest dates, the purchaser must pay the seller of the bond the amount of cash interest accrued from the last interest date. The accounting treatment for this is the same as that illustrated earlier in determining the cost of debt trading securities. At the date of purchase, the purchaser would record any accrued interest as interest receivable and not as part of the cost of the bond.

Companies acquire long-term investments as a means of funding capital expenditures to enhance the productivity of the firm's operations. Companies sell their available-for-sale bonds when they need cash to fund these types of capital expenditures. The entry to record the sale of available-for-sale bonds is the same as the entry made for trading securities except that the cost of the bond is the amount of its amortized cost on the date of the sale rather than its original cost. For example, suppose that Genentech, Inc., sold five of its 20 Chappuy bonds on June 30, 2000, at 108 1/2. The amortized cost of five of the bonds on the sale date is $5,323 ($21,292 × 1/4). The following entry records the sale:

Cash ($5,000 × 1.085)	5,425	
Available-for-Sale Securities—Chappuy Bonds		5,323
Gain on Sale of Investment in Bonds		102

Held-to-Maturity Securities

Held-to-maturity securities consist of debt securities, usually bonds, that a firm buys with the intent of holding them until they mature. The purchaser amortizes any premium or discount on individual debt instruments to generate the effective interest earned during an accounting period, as is the practice with available-for-sale securities. Therefore, the entries to acquire and hold held-to-maturity securities are the same as those for available-for-sale debt securities.

However, companies do not report held-to-maturity securities on the balance sheet at their market value. Rather, they appear at their amortized cost because they are not expected to be sold before their maturity dates and, therefore, the current market value is irrelevant. Typically, these securities appear in the investments section of the balance sheet. However, when individual held-to-maturity securities mature within the next fiscal year, companies classify them as current assets. For example, in Genentech, Inc.'s Investment Securities note it reports that in 1997 it had $193,295,000 of held-to-maturity securities, all of which would mature within one year and, therefore, are classified as current assets.

PAUSE &
REFLECT

Companies invest in bonds in the expectation of generating a return on their investment. How can an investor company lose money on a bond? *(answer on page 767)*

HOW DO COMPANIES REPORT THEIR INVESTMENTS?

LO 5

Information about a company's investment in debt and equity securities is important to both external and internal users of financial information. External users, such as investors and creditors, are interested in the liquidity of the investments, the return they generate, and the reason why the investments are being made. Such users obtain most of their information from the firm's general purpose financial statements.

Internal users, such as cash flow managers, members of the finance department, and strategic planners who are responsible for financing and investing decisions, need reports designed specifically to meet their respective needs. These users are interested in the timing of the cash flows, whether the return on investments reflects the risk assumed, and whether the investments are compatible with the company's short- and long-term goals.

External Reporting: The Financial Statements

The balance sheet, income statement, and cash flow statement provide information to external users about the firm's short-term and long-term nonoperational investments.

Balance Sheet   The balance sheet classification of a firm's investments in debt and equity securities includes current and long-term investments. Trading securities are reported at their market value as current assets. The held-to-maturity and available-for-sale debt securities that mature in the coming fiscal year, as well as individual available-for-sale equity securities that qualify, are also classified and are reported as current assets. For example, Genentech, Inc.'s December 31, 1997, balance sheet reports that the company had $588,853,000 of short-term investments. The Investment Securities note tells the financial statement user that these investments consist of $193,295,000 of held-to-maturity securities that will mature in the next fiscal year, $5,079,000 of accrued interest, available-for-sale securities maturing within one year of $137,852,000, and trading securities with a market value of $252,627,000. While the company could list each of these classifications separately as current assets, Genentech chooses to aggregate this information and, as most companies do, present the detailed information about the short-term investments in a note to the financial statements.

The investments section, which is located immediately after the current assets section of the balance sheet, reports the long-term investments of a firm. It shows the market value of available-for-sale investments, the amortized cost of the held-to-maturity investments, and the carrying value of the investments where the investor has a significant influence over the investee. Each of these classifications could be reported separately. Available-for-sale securities would reflect the market value of the debt and equity securities in the company's portfolio, while held-to-maturity securities would reflect investments at their amortized cost. Genentech, however, aggregates the available-for-sale and held-to-maturity classifications on the balance sheet but reports the amount of available-for-sale and held-to-maturity securities in the Investment Securities note. For example, the 1997 balance sheet reports long-term marketable securities of $453,188,000, which the note says consists of available-for-sale securities with a market value of $447,054,000 and accrued interest of $6,134,000. The note reveals that there are no held-to-maturity securities included in the long-term marketable securities reported on the balance sheet.

The amounts associated with investments accounted for using the equity method represent neither the cost nor the market value of the stock. Rather, the balance in these accounts represents the investor firm's dollar amount of its interest in the stockholders' equity of the investee corporation.

In contrast, as the market value of a company's investment in available-for-sale securities changes, its stockholders' equity will increase or decrease depending on whether the market value of the portfolio is greater or less than its cost. When the market value is greater (less) than the securities cost, stockholders' equity increases (decreases) by the difference.

Exhibit 22.6 summarizes these various investment categories. It indicates how companies classify and value each of them on the balance sheet, and it describes their impact on the income statement.

EXHIBIT 22.6	Summary of Financial Statement Presentation of Investments	
Classification of Investment	Balance Sheet	Income Statement
Trading Securities		
All debt and equity securities	Current assets reported at market value	Dividends and interest and unrealized gains and losses included in income
Available-for-Sale Securities		
Debt securities maturing in next fiscal year	Current assets reported at market value	Dividends and interest included in income
All other debt and equity securities	Investments reported at market value	Dividends and interest included in income
	Unrealized gains and losses for both current and long-term assets are reported as a separate item of stockholders' equity	
Held-to-Maturity Securities		
Debt securities maturing in next fiscal year	Current asset reported at amortized cost	Interest revenue included in income
All other debt securities	Investments reported at amortized cost	
Significant Influence in Another Corporation		
Ownership of 20% to 50% of common stock of another company	Investments reported at cost adjusted for investee's income, losses, and dividends (equity method)	Proportionate share of investee's income or loss included in investor's income
Control of Subsidiary		
Ownership of more than 50% of common stock of subsidiary company	Assets, liabilities, and stockholders' equity of parent and subsidiary are combined	Revenues, expenses, gains and losses of parent and subsidiary are combined

Income Statement A company's investments can affect its income statement in two common ways. First, any sales of securities held as investments during the period result in realized gains and losses measured by the differences between the amount that the company originally paid and the amount received when they were sold. In 1997, Genentech sold $410.4 million of its available-for-sale securities resulting in $13.2 million in realized gains and $2.1 million in realized losses, which were included in net income for the period. The second common way that investments affect the income statement involves the unrealized gains and losses on trading securities. Genentech reported net unrealized losses of $3.8 million in 1997. A third, less common way for investments to affect the income statement is through permanent declines in value for available-for-sale securities. That is, declines in the market values of stocks that are not expected to be recovered. In 1997, Genentech included in the computation of net income declines in the value of certain biotechnology stocks that amounted to $4.0 million.

It's not always true that the investments shown on the balance sheet actually exist. Here's a tale of one company's misguided efforts to improve its balance sheet through creative accounting.

Remember the well-muscled, beach-tanned "gladiators" on the popular television show *American Gladiators* who pummeled a series of often hapless opponents that included accountants, package delivery drivers, and government employees? Diamond Entertainment Inc. was a company whose only asset was the right to stage live performances of the show in a tent next to the Imperial Palace casino in Las Vegas. In 1994 Diamond merged with Eagle Automotive Inc., which was listed on the NASDAQ. Shortly before the merger, however, Eagle divested itself of all its assets, leaving it as flabby financially as the gladiators were fit, and later changed its name to Chariot Entertainment.

In 1998 the U.S. Securities and Exchange Commission filed a lawsuit in U.S. District Court. It claimed that in order to maintain Chariot's NASDAQ listing and to raise money for its proposed shows, a scheme was cooked up by Michael Carnicle, a Salt Lake City promoter who essentially controlled the operations of the company, and Robert Cord Beatty, Chariot's president. Along with three other defendants—Hillel Sher, Amotz Frenkel, and Nili Frenkel—they artificially inflated the company's assets by acquiring $5 million in certificates of deposit, ostensibly issued by a Russian bank.

The certificates, the SEC said, were actually created by Sher at a Kinko's copy shop in Hollywood, Florida. To finance the acquisition of the bogus certificates, the defendants arranged to have Chariot issue stock to a California corporation that one of the defendants controlled. The stock was then sold to pay for the certificates.

All the battles fought by the Gladiators were real, some of the assets on their balance sheet were not.

In its complaint, the SEC asked that the defendants be ordered to disgorge their allegedly ill-gotten gains. And it wanted them barred from selling unregistered securities in the future.

This episode of financial chicanery and the SEC's response highlights the watchdog role of the SEC. Using laws enacted by Congress, the SEC works to ensure that the information provided to investors is accurate and reliable so that assets really exist and aren't just printed out at Kinko's.

Source: "SEC Says 'Fake!' at Utah Firm's Gladiator Show; SEC Charges Utah's Chariot Was Fake Show," *Salt Lake Tribune*, August 12, 1998.

Cash Flow Statement   The investing section of the cash flow statement reflects the amounts of cash paid and received as a result of a company's investing activities. For example, Genentech, Inc.'s cash flow statement points out that, in 1997, the company purchased $304,932,000 of held-to-maturity securities and spent $512,727,000 to buy available-for-sale securities. Also, during 1997, it received $455,317,000 in cash from held-to-maturity securities that matured and received cash proceeds of $410,395,000 from the sale of available-for-sale securities. Presenting the specific cash inflows and outflows associated with particular investments helps external users evaluate how the firm's investing activities affect a firm's cash flows.

Internal Reporting

The content of internal reports depends upon the needs of the decision maker. While external reports aggregate and classify data, internal reports help financial managers make decisions about specific securities as well as portfolios of securities.

The accounting system reflects information about the cost of each security purchased and its performance. Portfolio managers need this information to decide whether to keep or sell particular securities. Accounting information helps assess whether portfolios of securities are performing as expected.

For example, a manager who is responsible for investing idle cash needs to know whether short-term debt instruments mature when cash is needed at some point in the future and whether the return that the investment is generating is satisfactory. Accounting information also helps decision makers identify the securities that have performed well or poorly in the past.

For managers who are responsible for making long-term investments, the accounting information helps them assess whether the risk they have assumed is justified by the returns being generated by the investment. These managers must also consider whether funds invested in debt and equity securities would generate a better return if invested in operating assets that increase or improve the operating capacity of the firm.

SUMMARY

Companies make long-term investments because of the opportunity to enhance the investing firm's overall net income directly through interest and dividends, or indirectly through exerting significant influence or control over the investee's operations. The circumstances surrounding the type of securities purchased and the existence of influence or control over the investee's operations determine how a company reports these investments.

- Investment criteria rest on the timing of the firm's needs for cash and the risk of loss associated with the related investment. Trading securities are usually short-term, low-risk government or corporate noninterest-bearing or interest-bearing notes. Generally, short-term investments are made in debt securities rather than in the common stock of other companies because of the risk of rapid price changes of equity securities. The portfolio of a firm's trading securities is reported at its fair market value.

- Firms invest in debt and equity securities in order to manage their short-term cash flows, provide funds to finance future long-term operational projects, or to influence or control another corporation.

- An investor company prepares consolidated financial statements when it owns a controlling interest in an investee company (50 percent or more of the investee's common stock). Consolidation includes reporting the income statements, balance sheets, and cash flow statements of two separate legal entities as one economic entity.

- An investor company uses the equity method if it owns enough of an investee company's common stock (usually 20 to 50 percent) to have a significant influence on the company. When using the equity method, the investor increases its investment account based on increases in the stockholders' equity of the investee company due to the recognition of income. Also, the investor's investment account would decrease when the investee declares dividends. The equity method violates the historical cost principle in an effort to reflect the investor's interest in the investee's stockholders' equity.

- Trading securities, available-for-sale securities, and held-to-maturity securities, are classifications that identify investments in debt securities and equity securities that are less than 20 percent of a corporation's voting stock.

- Trading securities are considered current assets and are reported at their market value.

- Available-for-sale securities, except for those individual securities that qualify as current assets, are classified as long-term assets. Both current and long-term AFS securities are reported at their market value.

KEY TERMS

available-for-sale securities Debt and equity securities bought with the intent of maintaining a portfolio of securities that management can sell, as needed, to raise cash for particular projects

consolidated financial statements The combined financial statements of the parent and subsidiary companies

equity method The accounting method used by an investor company that exercises a significant influence over an investee company's operations which reflects increases and decreases in the investment account of the investor company in proportion to the investee's stockholders' equity

held-to-maturity securities Debt securities the firm buys with the intent of holding them until they mature

market adjustment account A balance sheet account that reflects adjustments made to the total cost of trading securities and available-for-sale securities to show the market value of the securities portfolio

mark-to-market A method of showing the market value of the entire portfolio of trading securities and available-for-sale securities on the balance sheet without altering the cost of the individual securities

Net Unrealized Gain or Loss account A balance sheet account that reflects the adjustments made to total stockholders' equity to correspond to the balance in the market adjustment account for available-for-sale securities

parent company An investor company that owns more than 50 percent of another corporation's voting stock

subsidiary company An investee company that has more than 50 percent of its voting stock owned by another company

trading securities Debt and equity securities bought with the intent of selling the securities after holding them for a short period of time

ANSWERS TO THE PAUSE & REFLECTS

p. 749, Three main factors affect the investment decision: potential return, uncertainty, and timing. Managers' primary objective is to earn the highest return possible, so they weigh their alternatives and choose the one with the highest return. Managers also face a great deal of uncertainty about all facets of business. Sometimes it makes sense to invest in assets like securities, which the company can get into and out of quickly and easily, until it can resolve any uncertainties. In other situations, managers know what they want to do, but the time is not right, so they invest in securities until the right time arises to make other investments.

p. 752, If the equity method were not available as a reporting option, managers could influence when the investee's dividends were paid. They could affect when they had reportable income for both financial and tax purposes. Under the equity method, income is recognized by the investor when it is considered earned by the investee. Therefore, the timing of dividends is not relevant to income recognition.

p. 759, The price of debt securities changes primarily with the change in interest rates. The price of equity securities changes with investors' expectations about future earnings of a corporation. Expectations about future earnings are affected by factors such as interest rates, the health of the national economy, consumer demand for the corporation's products, quality of the corporation's management, and the corporation's prior earnings performance. There are more factors that impact a firm's earnings performance, so the stock price is more volatile than the bond price.

p. 763, An investor company can lose money on its investment in another company's bonds in two ways:

1. An investor company can lose when it sells bonds at a price lower than when it originally invested. The bond price in the secondary market will decline if the market interest rate rises. Therefore, if a bond holder sells the bonds before they mature, it is possible for the price to drop below the purchase price and for the bondholder to sell at a loss.

2. If an investor company intends to hold the bonds of another company until maturity, it can lose money on the bond if the issuing company defaults on the bond issue. That is, the company fails to pay the cash flows promised by the bond indenture.

QUESTIONS

1. What are consolidated financial statements and why do companies prepare them?
2. Explain what impact the investor's ability or inability to exercise significant influence or control over the investee's operations has on how to account for long-term investments in equity securities.
3. When and why do companies use the equity method to account for an investment?

4. Why do firms make short-term investments in debt and equity securities?

5. Why do firms make long-term investments in debt and equity securities?

6. How do you determine whether an investment should be classified as a trading security?

7. How do you determine whether an investment should be classified as an available-for-sale security?

8. What items are included in or excluded from the cost of an investment in debt securities?

9. Why are discounts and premiums on trading debt securities not amortized?

10. When a noninterest-bearing note that is a trading security matures, the amount of cash received is greater than the cost of the investment. How does the accounting system reflect this difference?

11. Why are the market values of trading securities and available-for-sale securities reported on the financial statements?

12. Why are held-to-maturity securities not shown at their market value?

13. What is the distinction between realized gains and losses and unrealized gains and losses on trading securities?

14. Why are discounts and premiums on available-for-sale debt securities amortized when discounts and premiums on trading securities are not amortized?

15. When premiums and discounts are amortized on long-term investments in bonds, which of these makes interest income greater than the amount of cash interest received? Why?

16. Can a company that owns a large number of debt securities of another company have the same level of influence as a company that holds 20 percent or more of a company's stock? Why?

17. What is the role of the Net Unrealized Gain or Loss account for available-for-sale securities?

18. Explain how the sale of individual trading or available-for-sale securities affects the market adjustment account.

19. What information about investments in debt and equity securities appears on the cash flow statement?

20. How do internal reports on investments in debt and equity securities differ from external financial statements?

EXERCISES

E 22.1

LO 1   LO 2   LO 3   LO4

Match the following terms with the descriptions below:
a. Equity method
b. Trading security investments
c. Consolidated financial statements
d. Available-for-sale investments
e. Equity security investments
f. Held-to-maturity investments
g. Debt security investments
h. Mark-to-market

_____ 1. Investments in the stock of another company
_____ 2. The financial statements that reflect the control of one corporation over another
_____ 3. Used when one company has a significant influence over another company
_____ 4. Debt and equity securities that will be sold in the near term
_____ 5. Reporting the market value of a company's portfolio of investments
_____ 6. Investments in debt securities held until they mature
_____ 7. Debt and equity securities of another company that could be sold but that management does not expect to sell in the near future
_____ 8. Securities that describe a creditorship relationship between the holder of a note and the maker of the note

E 22.2

LO 1   LO 5

Match the following balance sheet classifications with the type of security described below:

a. Current assets
b. Investments
c. Included in consolidated balance sheet

_____ 1. Investment in 30 percent of another company's common stock
_____ 2. Trading securities
_____ 3. Available-for-sale securities
_____ 4. Investment in 60 percent of another company's common stock
_____ 5. Held-to-maturity securities
_____ 6. Held-to-maturity securities that mature in the next year

E 22.3

LO 4

On February 1, the Dunn Corporation purchased for $49,450 a U.S. Treasury bill with a $50,000 face value that was due in two months. Dunn collected the $50,000 when the Treasury bills matured on April 1. Make the entries for Dunn's Treasury bill transactions.

E 22.4

LO 4

SKP Company purchases a $50,000 face value U.S. Treasury bill issued on a discounted basis for $48,400 and paid brokerage fees of $100. Four months later when it needed the cash, SKP Company sold the investment for $29,300. Prepare the journal entries to record the purchase and sale of this trading security.

E 22.5

LO 4

Brooks Manufacturing Corporation purchased interest-bearing U.S. Treasury notes with a face value of $60,000 on August 1, 1999, as a trading security. The purchase price of $57,500 included $800 in accrued interest.

On December 1, 1999, Brooks received a check for $2,400 for six months' interest. On February 28, 2000, the investment was sold for $58,200 including accrued interest of $1,200. Assuming that Brooks has a December 31 fiscal year-end, journalize all transactions related to Brook's investment in U.S. Treasury notes.

E 22.6

LO 4

Kwan, Inc., paid $20,560 to purchase $20,000 face value 9 percent bonds issued by Kavco Products as a temporary investment on May 31. The purchase price included brokerage fees and interest accrued on the bonds since March 1, the most recent interest payment date. Kavco pays interest on March 1 and September 1 each year. Kwan sold the investment on September 30. The proceeds from the sale, including accrued interest, amounted to $20,700. Prepare all journal entries required for Kwan's investment in the bonds.

E 22.7

LO 2

Brother Industries' accounting records are maintained on a calendar-year basis. On May 15 the firm purchased 1,500 shares of French Company's common stock at $42 per share plus brokerage fees of $350. Brother Industries expected to hold the shares for less than three months. On July 1 Brother Industries received a cash dividend of $1.50 per share from the stock. The shares were sold on August 4 at $42.50 per share. Brokerage fees on the sale were $370. Prepare all journal entries required in relation to Brother Industries' investment in the stock of French Company.

E 22.8

LO 2

On February 15, 2000, the Snowbird Corporation purchased 300 shares of Park Corporation's common stock for $26 per share plus $200 in brokerage fees. Snowbird expects to sell the stock within three months. On April 2 Snowbird received a $0.20 per share dividend. On May 8 it sold 100 of the shares for $36.75 per share less brokerage fees of $80. On June 1 it sold the remaining shares for $36, less brokerage fees of $120. Make the entries necessary for these transactions.

E 22.9

LO 2

Smokey Enterprises had the following trading securities on December 31, 2001:

	Historical Cost	Current Market Value
U.S. Treasury bills	$17,515	$18,000
U.S. Treasury notes	41,700	41,830
Adams Company bonds	33,080	32,900
Quincy Corporation bonds	76,140	76,150

The current market value amount represents the market value of the securities on December 31, 2001. Make the entry to adjust these trading securities to their market value assuming that the market adjustment account does not have a balance as of the end of the fiscal year. Show how the firm's trading debt securities are reported on Smokey's balance sheet. Why are these securities shown at their market value?

E 22.10

LO 2

Hamilton Company occasionally buys and sells shares of stock in various other companies as a part of its cash management program. The total cost and market value of its trading securities at the end of 1999 and 2000 are shown below. For each year, prepare the necessary entries to adjust the portfolio from cost to market and show how Hamilton's trading securities would appear on the balance sheet for each year. At the start of 1999, Hamilton had no balance in its market adjustment account.

Year	Cost	Market Value
1999	$24,200	$32,800
2000	63,950	83,600

E 22.11

LO 3

Using the data in E 22.10, make the mark-to-market entries necessary and show the balance sheet presentation assuming that these are available for-sale securities.

E 22.12

LO 2

On December 31, 2000, Darrell Corporation had trading securities that cost $250,000 and had a market value of $268,000. Included in Darrell Corporation's investments are 200 shares of Allen Products common stock acquired at a total cost of $11,128. Those 200 shares had a market value of $12,700 at the end of 2000. Early in 2001, the investment in Allen Products was sold. The net proceeds from that sale were $10,830. Prepare the journal entry to record the sale of Allen Products common stock by Darrell Corporation.

E 22.13

LO 2

The Garden Corporation had the following portfolio of trading securities at its fiscal year-end, December 31, 2000:

	Cost	Market
100 shares InPal common stock	$25,000	$25,350
200 shares COBA preferred stock	13,500	13,450
10, $1,000 Gyro Corporation bonds	9,980	10,200

Make the entry to record Garden's mark-to-market adjustment on December 31, 2000, and show how Garden's portfolio of trading securities is reported on its balance sheet. On January 15, 2001, Garden sold 50 of the COBA shares at $68 per share. Make the entry to record the sale of the COBA shares.

E 22.14

LO 4

On August 1, 2000, Roads Company purchased bonds with a face value of $5,000 and a face interest rate of 9 percent that is paid on August 1 and February 1. The bonds were initially issued by the Shaw Corporation in 1992 and had a 10-year life. Roads purchased the bonds to yield an effective rate of interest of 6 percent and considered them to be an available-for-sale security. What price did Roads pay for the Shaw bonds? Given that Roads Corporation has a December 31 fiscal year-end, make the entries for the Shaw bonds on Roads' books from August 1 to the first interest date of February 1, 2001. If the bonds were the only available-for-sale security Roads owned and had a market price of 101¾ on December 31, 2000, show how Roads would report these bonds on its December 31, 2000 balance sheet.

E 22.15

LO 4

Stromb's Manufacturing purchased bonds of Dixie Products on May 1, 1999, that had a face value of $30,000 and a face rate of interest of 6 percent that is paid annually. The bonds mature on May 1, 2002, and Stromb's is going to hold the bonds to maturity. Make the entry to record the bonds for the period from May 1, 1999, to May 1, 2000, if the bonds were purchased to yield an effective rate of interest of 7 percent. Show how Stromb's balance sheet would report the bonds on December 31, 1999, if the bonds had a market value of 102.

E 22.16

LO3

On July 10, 1999, Alabama Distributors purchased 10,000 shares of San Antonio Manufacturing common stock at 23¼ plus brokerage fees of $600. This investment represents 5 percent of the common stock of San Antonio. Alabama also purchased 1,000 shares of Dallas Corporation common stock for 32¼ plus brokerage fees of $100 on September 1, 1999. On November 15, Alabama sold 500 shares of San Antonio for $25⅜ less brokerage fees of $80. The market price of San Antonio's and Dallas's common stock on December 31, 1999, Alabama's fiscal year-end, was 22⅝ and 35, respectively.

Prepare the entry to record Alabama's purchase and sale of these available-for-sale equity securities. Make the mark-to-market adjusting entry on December 31 assuming the market adjustment account has a zero balance.

E 22.17

LO 5

Given the information in E22.16, show the balance sheet presentation of Alabama Corporation's available-for-sale equity securities on December 31, 1999.

E 22.18

LO 1   LO 5

Color Corporation has an investment in the common stock of Playtime Company. The investment is accounted for on the equity basis because Color owns 35 percent of Playtime's common stock and exercises significant influence over its investee. On August 1, 1999, Color received a dividend check for $15,000 from Playtime. After closing its books on September 30, 1999, Playtime reports a total net income of $250,000 to its investors. Prepare the journal entries to be made on Color Corporation's books on August 1, 1999, and on September 30, 1999. How would Color report its investment in Playtime on its balance sheet?

E 22.19

LO 1   LO 5

On July 1, 2000, Dahl Corporation purchased 30 percent of Savnot Corporation's voting common stock for $750,000 plus a commission of $8,000. During the year Savnot declared and paid $18,000 of dividends and reported that for its fiscal year ended December 31, 2000, it had incurred a loss of $20,000. What is the ending balance in Dahl's Investment in Savnot Corporation account? Show how Dahl will report its investment on its balance sheet. What impact will Dahl's investment in Savnot Corporation have on its income statement in 2000?

E 22.20

LO 5

Tooele Corporation owns the following securities at December 31, 2000:

	Cost	Market
Jones Corporation common stock	$81,225	$82,126
U.S. Treasury bills	19,850	19,950
Ellsworth Corporation preferred stock	5,750	5,544
Eining Corporation bonds	43,950	45,180
AT&T Bonds	19,950	19,865
Superscope common stock	6,775	5,605
Cushing Corporation common stock	50,350	51,439

If Tooele classifies its securities as described below, show how it will report these securities on its December 31, 2000, balance sheet.

Trading securities:
   U.S. Treasury bills
   Ellsworth preferred stock
Available-for-sale securities:
   Superscope common stock
   Cushing Corporation common stock
   AT&T bonds
   Jones Corporation common stock
Held-to-maturity securities:
   Eining Corporation bonds

PROBLEMS

P 22.1

LO 4

On February 1, 2001, Barta Corporation purchased bonds of Washburn Foundry, Inc., as trading securities for 102¼ plus a brokerage fee of $1,000. The bonds have a face value of $150,000 and a face interest rate of 9 percent that is paid on April 1 and October 1; they mature 20 years from the date of purchase.

Required

a. How much cash did Barta Corporation pay to acquire the bonds?
b. Prepare the journal entries to record the following:
     1. Acquisition of the bonds
     2. Receipt of the cash interest on April 1, 2001 and October 1, 2001
     3. Adjusting entry for the December 31 fiscal year-end
c. What is the cost of the investment in the bonds on December 31, 2001?

P 22.2

LO 4

On September 1, 2000, Holiday Corporation purchased bonds of Ross Products as an available-for-sale investment. The bonds have a face value of $100,000, bear a 10 percent face interest rate that is paid on March 1 and September 1, and mature on September 1, 2002. No brokerage fees were involved.

Required

a. What price did Holiday Corporation pay for these bonds if the bonds will yield 8 percent?
b. Prepare the journal entries to record the following:
     1. Acquisition of the bonds
     2. Accrual of the interest on the bonds on December 31, 2000
     3. Receipt of the interest on March 1, 2001
c. What is the cost of the bonds as of Holiday's fiscal year-end?

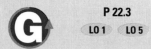

P 22.3

LO 1　LO 5

Clint, Inc., owns 100,000 shares of Weber Enterprises common stock, which represents 40 percent of Weber's outstanding shares. Clint accounts for the long-term investment using the equity method. On December 31, 2000, the balance in the investment account was $900,000, and the market value per share was 9¼.

In 2001, Weber Enterprises paid dividends totaling $87,500 and reported net income of $500,000. Market value per share on December 31, 2001, was 8⅞. Weber Enterprises reported a net loss of $50,000 in 2002. Dividends of $25,000 were declared and paid during the year. Market value per share of Weber's common stock was 9⅜ on December 31, 2002.

Required

a. Prepare the journal entries for Clint, Inc., for 2001 and 2002.
b. Describe how the investment is reported on Clint's balance sheet on December 31, 2001, and December 31, 2002.

P 22.4

LO 3　LO 5

Wood Industries owns 40,000 shares of common stock in Avis Company. This represents a 15 percent interest in Avis's outstanding shares that Wood considers an available-for-sale security. The balance in the investment account on December 31, 1999, was $2,400,000. Market value per share of Avis Company was 66¼ on that date. The Avis Company stock is Wood's only available-for-sale security.

During 2000, Avis Company paid dividends to common stockholders totaling $150,000, and its net income for the year was $660,000. Market value of the stock on December 31, 2000, was 68½.

On January 1, 2001, Wood Industries sold 20,000 shares of the Avis Company stock for $68 per share less a $10,000 brokerage fee. In 2001 Avis Company paid dividends to the common stockholders totaling $120,000, and the firm had a net loss for the year of $130,000. The market value of the stock on December 31, 2001, was 65¾ per share.

Required

a. Prepare the journal entries for Wood Industries for 2000 and 2001.
b. Give Wood's balance sheet presentation of these securities for 1999, 2000, and 2001.

P 22.5

LO 2　LO 4

In the month of March, Far West Company had the following transactions in its trading securities classification:

Mar. 5　Sold U.S. Treasury notes for $103,000 including accrued interest. The notes are carried at a cost of $101,800. Unrecorded interest of $1,600 had accrued on the notes up to the date of sale.

10　Purchased $25,000 face value of Mountain Power Company's bonds for 100 7/8 plus accrued interest of $800 and brokerage fees of $150.

17　Purchased U.S. Treasury bills with a face value of $30,000 for $29,650.

22　Received interest of $1,500 on U.S. Treasury notes. No interest was accrued when the notes were purchased.

28　Sold the U.S. Treasury bill purchased on March 17. The sales price was $29,635.

Required　Prepare the necessary journal entries to record the March transactions.

P 22.6

LO 2　LO 4

During August, Fowles Company had the following transactions related to its trading securities:

Aug. 3　Received a check for $1,800 for interest on the investment in Independence Company bonds. Of the total received, $500 is accrued interest that had been paid for when the bonds were purchased. Brokerage fees of $80 were already deducted from the check.

6　Purchased U.S. Treasury notes with a face value of $100,000 for $100,200 plus brokerage fees of $360 and accrued interest of $3,500.

11　Received dividends of $450 on an investment in common stock of Inland Gas and Oil Corporation.

14　Sold 600 shares of Wadley Company stock for $13,820 less brokerage fees of $140. The stock is carried in the accounts at a cost of $13,385.

18　Sold U.S. Treasury certificates with a face value of $20,000, which were purchased at a total cost of $19,250 for net proceeds of $19,600.

20　Purchased 300 shares of Colony Corporation stock for $56 per share plus brokerage fees of $200.

24　Sold Carlston Corporation bonds, which are carried at a cost of $32,650. The cash received of $31,600 included accrued interest to the date of sale of $730 less brokerage fees of $1,200.

31　Received $4,000 for six months' interest on U.S. Treasury notes purchased on August 6.

Required　Prepare the necessary journal entries to record August's transactions.

P 22.7

LO 2 LO 3 LO 4 LO 5

The Ray-Beam Corporation has calculated the total cost and the market values of its investments below:

	Cost	Market Value
Trading securities	$ 214,300	$ 213,600
Available-for-sale securities	2,156,000	2,159,000
Held-to-maturity securities	532,450	359,000

Before the year-end adjustment was made, the market adjustment account for trading securities had a debit balance of $1,900, while the market adjustment account for available-for-sale securities had a credit balance of $1,800. The held-to-maturity securities account had $20,000 of bonds that will mature in the next year.

Required

a. Make the adjusting entries for Ray-Bean's investments.
b. Prepare the balance sheet presentation of these investments.

P 22.8

LO 3 LO 5

At the end of 1999, Gillam & Company's asset accounts included the following:

Available-for-sale investments	$621,980
Less market adjustment account	4,525
	$617,455

During 2000, the firm sold securities that cost $45,400 for $46,250. It also purchased additional securities costing a total of $61,300. The market value of the available-for-sales securities at December 31, 2000, totaled $655,850. Securities costing $23,670 were sold in 2001. Proceeds from that sale totaled $23,450. No additional transactions occurred in 2001. The market value of all securities held at the end of 2001 amounted to $624,770.

Required

a. Prepare the journal entries to record the sales and acquisitions of securities each year.
b. Prepare the adjusting entry at the end of each year to value the securities at their market value.
c. Show how the available-for-sale investments are presented on Gillam & Company's balance sheet on December 31, 2000 and 2001.

P 22.9

LO 3 LO 5

The following accounts and balances appeared in the asset section of Lincoln Company's balance sheet at the end of 2000:

Investments:	
Available-for-sale securities	$103,760
Less market adjustment	2,140
Investments at market	$101,620

During 2001, Lincoln sold securities that cost $26,890 for $28,120. It also purchased additional securities so that at the end of the year it held available-for-sale securities costing $113,400 whose market value was $110,980.

More available-for-sale securities were purchased in 2002, and the company sold some of its investments that cost $48,720 for $46,950. The available-for-sale securities held at the end of 2002 had a cost of $96,390 and a market value of $99,200. On December 30, 2002, Lincoln purchased a held-to-maturity bond for $10,220.

Required

a. Prepare the journal entries to record the sale and purchase of the securities for 2001.
b. Prepare the adjusting entry necessary to value the securities at their market value for 2001.
c. Show the balance sheet presentation for 2001.
d. Prepare the journal entries to record the sale and purchase of the securities for 2002.
e. Prepare the adjusting entry necessary to value the securities at their market value for 2002.
f. Show the balance sheet presentation for 2002.

P 22.10

LO 2 LO 4 LO 5

Peters Company's cash management policy is to invest idle cash in trading securities and to sell those securities as the company approaches its peak season when it needs funds. On December 31, 1999, the end of the fiscal year, Peters had the following information related to its trading securities:

U.S. Treasury bills, maturing on March 12, 2000, face value of $10,000 (market value, $9,850)	$ 9,815
Kim Corporation 8% bonds, face value of $50,000 (market value, $49,200)	48,860
Interest receivable on Kim Corporation bonds	1,000
Hirschi, Inc., common stock, 200 shares (market value, $18,625)	18,485
Union Products Company common stock, 200 shares (market value, $7,350)	7,570

The market adjustment account had a credit balance of $380 before the mark-to-market adjusting entry was made in 1999.

During 2000, Peters Company had the following transactions related to its trading securities:

Mar. 12   The U.S. Treasury bills matured and were converted to cash.

18   Purchased 300 shares of Hancock Corporation stock at $72 per share plus brokerage fees of $85.

Apr. 1   Collected six months' interest on Kim Corporation bonds.

May 3   Sold 200 shares of Union Products Company stock at $34.75 per share. Total brokerage fees on the sale were $65.

June 3   Purchased $30,000 face value Hasak Company 8 percent bonds for $30,650, including brokerage fees of $175 and accrued interest of $200. The bonds pay interest on June 1 and December 1. (They are accounted for on a cost basis.)

July 8   Purchased $40,000 in U.S. Treasury bills at a total cost of $39,920.

Aug. 27   Sold 200 shares of Hirschi, Inc., stock for net proceeds of $18,690.

Sept. 17   The U.S. Treasury bills purchased on July 8 matured and were converted to cash.

Oct. 1   Collected six months' interest on Kim Corporation bonds and sold the bonds for 99¼.

17   Purchased 400 shares of Midwest, Inc., common stock at $58 per share plus brokerage fees of $170.

Dec. 1   Collected six months' interest on Hasak Company bonds.

On December 31, 2000, the market value of Hancock Company common stock was $75.50 per share, and the Midwest, Inc., common stock was $58.25 per share. The Kim Corporation bonds had a market value of $48,500 and the Hasak Company bonds had a market value of $30,530.

Required a. Make the entry to record the mark-to-market adjustment for 1999.
b. Record the entries for the transactions in 2000.
c. Prepare the necessary adjusting entries for December 31, 2000.
d. Show how to report the trading securities on the December 31, 1999 and 2000, balance sheets.

P 22.11
LO 4   LO 5

On June 1, 2001, Bush Corporation purchased 100 Wildcat Corporation bonds that had a total face value of $100,000. The bonds had a face rate of 8 percent and paid interest semiannually on December 1 and June 1; they were issued to yield a 6 percent market rate of interest. The bonds had a 10-year life when Wildcat issued them on June 1, 1994. Bush Corporation intends to hold the bonds to maturity and has a December 31 fiscal year-end.

Required a. Make the entry to record the acquisition of the bonds.
b. Make the entry to record the receipt of the cash interest on December 1, 2001.
c. Make the entry(ies) necessary on December 31, 2001, assuming that the market price of the bonds is 101¾ and Bush only owns the Wildcat bonds.
d. Show how the bonds are reported on Bush's balance sheet at December 31, 2001.
e. Give the entry to record the receipt of the cash interest on June 1, 2002.
f. Give the entry assuming that Bush sold 10 of the Wildcat bonds for 102 on June 1, 2002.

CASES

C 22.1
LO 1   LO 5

Mark Bardsley, president of Brown, Inc., is conducting the annual stockholders' meeting. After he completes his remarks on the company's objectives for the coming year, which include introducing a new product line, he asks you, the financial vice president, to answer stockholders' questions on the financial statements contained in the firm's annual report. Kelly Harper, who owns a substantial number of shares of common stock, makes the following statement:

I'm not going to quote a bunch of numbers, but I see the company has a lot of money tied up in short-term investments and there is some kind of market adjustment account that lowers them to market. Does that mean we have lost money on those investments? Besides that, the income statement shows we have interest income, losses on the sale of investments, and some kind of unrealized gain. How can the company have an unrealized gain when the market value of these investments is less than their cost? Anyway, why don't you just put all of those gains and losses and the investment income together in one amount and be done with it? Furthermore, if the company has so much extra cash that you can play around investing it, I'd just as soon you increase the dividends and give that cash to the stockholders.

Required Answer the specific questions Kelly Harper has raised and respond to her comment about the extra cash.

C 22.2

LO 5

Using the financial statements of the Walt Disney Company, find the following information about Disney's short-term and long-term investments:
a. What is the cost and market value of Disney's trading securities?
b. What is the cost and market value of its available-for-sale securities?
c. What is the dollar value of the bonds held to maturity?
d. How much cash was generated by the sale of investments? How much cash was paid to acquire investments?
e. Does Disney have a significant influence on another company?
f. Does Disney have a controlling interest in other corporations?

CRITICAL THINKING

CT 22.1

LO 2   LO 5

It is possible for a corporation to report an unrealized gain on trading securities on its income statement when the market value of its portfolio of trading securities is less than its cost. How could this occur? Is it possible to have an unrealized loss or gain on the income statement if a corporation does not have any trading securities at the end of a fiscal year? Explain.

CT 22.2

LO 2   LO 5

Accounting principles require companies to report the unrealized gains and losses associated with their portfolio of trading securities on the income statement, but not the unrealized gains and losses from available-for-sale securities. Why do you think these unrealized gains and losses are reported differently?

ETHICAL CHALLENGES

EC 22.1

LO 2   LO 3
LO 4   LO 5

Uinta Corporation has a practice of moving its investments from the long-term to the short-term investment classification whenever their current ratio becomes too low. Once the current ratio becomes high enough, the company reclassifies the short-term investments back to the long-term classification.

Required   Comment on this practice. What are the implications for financial statement readers?

EC 22.2

LO 4   LO 5

The management of Cook Corporation is very concerned because it anticipates that 2001's income is going to be its lowest in five years. Darla Fry, the corporation's president, has suggested a unique solution to this problem. She realizes that the company holds a large number of bonds purchased in 1988 that are classified as held-to-maturity securities. Because the interest rates have decreased dramatically since the bonds were purchased, their market value greatly exceeds their cost. She suggests that the company reclassify the bonds as trading securities. In this way, the bonds will be adjusted to their market value and the unrealized gain will appear on the income statement and boost this year's earnings. Once the current crisis is over, she suggests the bonds be reclassified as held-to-maturity. Fry defends this action because she says that the increase in the bonds' value is hidden from the investors. She contends that this action will actually show a more realistic picture of the company's financial position.

Required   Comment on the advisability of Fry's proposal.

COMPUTER APPLICATIONS

CA 22.1

LO 4

Woodbury Company purchased a $1 million bond issue on the interest payment date when the market rate of interest was 9 percent. The bonds pay interest semiannually at the rate of 10 percent. There are 15 years remaining in the 20-year life of the bonds.

Required   Use a computer spreadsheet package.
a. Determine how much Woodbury paid to obtain these bonds.
b. Assuming that Woodbury intends to hold these bonds until maturity, prepare a schedule that indicates the amounts needed for journal entries on each semiannual interest payment date.

CA 22.2

LO 4

Tech Enterprises plans to purchase a $500,000 bond issue on the interest payment date when the market rate of interest is 11 percent. The bonds in question pay interest semiannually at a 9 percent rate. The bonds mature in eight years.

Required   Use a computer spreadsheet package.

    a. Determine how much Tech must pay to obtain the bond issue.

    b. Assume that Tech plans to hold the bonds until maturity. Prepare a schedule that shows the amount of cash received, the change in the investment account, the interest revenue, and the carrying value of the bonds on each interest payment date.

CA 22.3

LO 5

Find the investment portion of Quicken.com's Web site (<www.quicken.com/investments/stocks/>). Enter the ticker symbols under "Quotes" for each of the following companies: Walt Disney (symbol: DIS), Procter & Gamble (PG), and Sprint (PCS). The first screen that you will see after you click on the Go button will include the most recent stock price and will have an item on the menu at the left (Financials) that allows you to view the firm's condensed financial statements. For each of the three companies, determine what portion of their assets are in "Securities." For these three companies, how does the portion of assets invested in securities compare with Genentech's? Pick a few companies with which you are familiar and make the same comparison.

PART SEVEN

THE ROAD TRAVELED

Chapters 19–22 explored the role of the accounting system during the performing phase of the investing and financing cycles. Chapter 19 considered recording and reporting equity financing activities and Chapter 20 looked at debt financing activities. Then, Chapters 21 and 22 examined the recording and reporting of investing activities.

YOU ARE HERE

Now that you completed the planning and performing phases for all three cycles (operating, financing, and investing), it is time to investigate the financial statements and financial statement analysis, in depth. These final chapters are comprehensive and rely on information you have learned in Chapters 1–22. Chapter 23 examines the profitability reporting. We look at the reporting requirements for the income statement and the statement of retained earnings (statement of owners' equity) for external users. We consider internal reporting issues including an examination of absorption, variable, and throughput accounting.

THE ROAD AHEAD

Chapters 24–26 build on Chapter 23 as we explore the balance sheet and the external auditor's report (Chapter 24), the statement of cash flows (Chapter 25), and comprehensive financial statement analysis (Chapter 26). Thus, these final chapters rely heavily on materials presented in Chapters 1–22.

LEARNING OBJECTIVES

LO 1 Explain the importance of the components of earnings (income from continuing operations) to users.

LO 2 Describe what is important about the components of nonowner changes in equity and cumulative accounting adjustments.

LO 3 Explain the importance of other comprehensive items of income.

LO 4 Explain how companies determine earnings per share and what information it provides to users.

LO 5 Identify the elements of the statement of retained earnings.

LO 6 Calculate return on investment for business segments.

LO 7 Describe the differences among absorption, unit-variable, and throughput accounting income reports used internally.

LO 8 Explain why companies use product line (divisional) income reports.

Firm Performance: Profitability

PepsiCo, Inc., is one of the most successful beverage and snack companies in the world, with 1997 profits of $2 billion and over 140,000 employees. Although many of PepsiCo's brand names are over 100 years old, PepsiCo was founded in 1965 through the merger of Pepsi-Cola Company and Frito-Lay, Inc. Today, PepsiCo actively markets such well-known products as Pepsi, Diet Pepsi, Mountain Dew, 7UP, Fritos corn chips, Lay's potato chips, Doritos tortilla chips, and Rold Gold pretzels.[1]

PEPSICO
www.pepsico.com

In 1997 PepsiCo spun off its restaurant divisions consisting of Taco Bell, Kentucky Fried Chicken, and Pizza Hut. These businesses are now operated as an independent, publicly owned company called TRICON Global Restaurants, Inc.

In 1998 PepsiCo introduced WOW! potato chips made from Olean, developed by Procter & Gamble (see Chapter 5). It has plans to produce additional low-fat snack chips in the future. How will PepsiCo determine whether its new low-fat snack chips are successful? How will PepsiCo's stockholders and creditors determine whether PepsiCo is successful? This chapter examines one measure of a company's success—profitability.

[1]<www.pepsico.com/corp/overview>.

hroughout this text, we have talked about business events that affect a company's profitability and that are reported on the income statement. In this chapter, we look at the income statement in its entirety, exploring issues such as what information the income statement and its related notes actually provide to users and some reporting issues income statement users should consider. We also examine the statement of retained earnings (or statement of owners' equity), which provides the link between the income statement and the balance sheet. Finally, we introduce other ways of reporting profitability for internal users.

To illustrate all the components of comprehensive income, we use a company called LaGrande Beverage. Then we relate these ideas to the financial statements and related notes of PepsiCo.

WHAT IS THE PURPOSE OF THE INCOME STATEMENT?

The purpose of the income statement is to reflect the earnings (income) generated by the company during the accounting period. It is vital for both internal and external users to comprehend the components of reported earnings.

Recall from Chapter 1 that the FASB's conceptual framework states that the three objectives of financial reporting are to provide information that is (1) useful for making investment and credit decisions; (2) useful for assessing cash flow prospects; and (3) relevant to evaluating enterprise resources, claims to those resources, and changes in the resources.

The income statement helps fulfill these three objectives by disclosing information about the earnings of the company during the current fiscal year. Investors and creditors use current earnings information to assess the future earnings potential of the firm. Such assessment of earnings also provides information that allows external users to evaluate the amounts, timing, and uncertainty of future cash flows from dividends or interest. The income statement also provides important information about changes in the company's resources (assets) and claims to those resources (equities) due to the operating activities of the company. Investors and creditors use this type of past operating performance information to predict the future performance of the company.

The income statement is the most widely quoted of the financial statements, yet it is relatively new compared to the balance sheet. The income statement did not become popular until corporations became widespread in the late 1800s. As you know, the corporate form of business made income reporting necessary because corporations are separate legal entities and, therefore, generate taxable profits. In addition, the income statement, which reports the earnings performance of an entity for a period of time, was (and is) vitally important to both absentee owners and to creditors for evaluating the company. Finally, the existence and publication of periodic income statements facilitated the purchase and sale of stock because interested parties can assess the current operating performance of the company as part of the negotiation process.

HOW DO GAAP AFFECT THE INCOME STATEMENT?

Generally accepted accounting principles (GAAP) require that externally reported income comply with the comprehensive concept of income. **Comprehensive income** reported externally should reflect all changes in owners' equity during the period except those resulting from investments by, or distributions to, owners and those resulting from the correction of errors made in previous periods. (We present a discussion of the latter items in the section on the statement of retained earnings later in this chapter.) The elements of comprehensive income are illustrated below:

```
+    Revenues
−    Expenses
+    Gains
−    Losses
=    Earnings (income from continuing operations)
+/−  Other nonowner changes in equity
+/−  Cumulative accounting adjustments
=    Net income
+/−  Other comprehensive income items
=    Comprehensive income
```

Comprehensive income often is not the same as earnings. **Earnings** represent income from continuing operations and consists of revenues minus expenses, and gains minus losses. Earnings are recurring, whereas the events included in comprehensive income are not necessarily recurring. Rather, they are reported as part of comprehensive income so that financial statement users have a complete picture of both the operating and other nonowner activities that caused changes in owners' equity during the period.

Comprehensive income is important because it reflects both the recurring and nonrecurring aspects of the firm's earnings. This gives financial statement users a better idea of how to predict future earnings and cash flows as well as how to evaluate management's actions for the current period. We discuss this issue in more detail as we explore the components of earnings and comprehensive income next.

Exhibit 23.1 shows the multistep income statement for LaGrande Beverage, which we will use as our road map for this chapter. We discuss the income statement in four sections: (1) earnings; (2) other nonowner changes in equity, which are discontinued operations and extraordinary items; (3) cumulative accounting adjustments, which are changes in accounting principles; and (4) other comprehensive income items, which are adjustments

EXHIBIT 23.1	Multistep Income Statement

LAGRANDE BEVERAGE
Income Statement
For the Year Ended December 31, 1999
(in thousands except per share data)

Sales	$3,687,240
Cost of goods sold	2,629,226
Gross margin	**$1,058,014**
Selling and administrative expenses	636,204
Income from operations	**$ 421,810**
Other revenues and gains:	
Interest income	920
Dividend income	302
Other expenses and losses:	
Interest expense	(675)
Loss on sale of equipment	(150)
Income from continuing operations before income taxes	**$ 422,207**
Income tax expense	189,993
Income from continuing operations	**$ 232,214**
Discontinued operations:	
Income from operations of division, net of applicable taxes	180
Loss on disposal of division, net of applicable taxes	2,175
Income before extraordinary items and cumulative effect of accounting change	**$ 230,219**
Extraordinary loss from flood, net of applicable taxes	1,650
Cumulative effect of change in depreciation method, net of applicable taxes	1,320
Net income	**$ 227,249**
Other comprehensive income items:	
Unrealized gain on available-for-sale securities, net of applicable taxes	$ 210
Comprehensive income	**$ 227,459**
Earnings per share:	
Income from continuing operations	$7.44
Discontinued operations	−0.07
Income before extraordinary items and cumulative effect of accounting change	7.37
Extraordinary loss	−0.06
Cumulative effect of accounting change	−0.04
Net income	$7.27
Diluted earnings per share:	
Income from continuing operations	$6.35
Discontinued operations	−0.06
Income before extraordinary items and cumulative effect of accounting change	6.29
Extraordinary loss	−0.05
Cumulative effect of accounting change	−0.03
Net income	$6.21

resulting from changes in the relative value of foreign currency, pension liability adjustments, and unrealized holding gains or losses. Following this discussion we look at the reporting of earnings per share.

What Is Reported as Earnings?

LO 1

The earnings of the firm include its revenues minus expenses plus gains and minus losses. The business activities that result in income from continuing operations are assumed to be recurring. Revenue and expense events clearly are recurring events because they take place daily. Likewise, many gains and losses such as those from selling property, plant, and equipment occur often enough to be considered recurring events. Other gains and losses, such as those regarding discontinued operations, are not recurring events and are reported as other nonowner changes in equity. The recurring events are important to statement users because they can be used to predict future earnings of the company.

As discussed in Chapter 10, the income statement is shown in either a multistep or single-step format. Exhibit 23.1 is an example of a multistep income statement that shows subdivided earnings (income) based on the types of company activities reported. Note that all amounts are shown in thousands except for per share data. In a multistep income statement, cost of goods sold ($2,629,226,000) is subtracted from sales ($3,687,240,000), which results in gross margin ($1,058,014,000). Gross margin, then, is the overall profitability of the company's products. Selling and administrative expenses ($636,204,000) are subtracted from gross margin to derive income from operations ($421,810,000). Income from operations reflects the overall profitability of the company's operating activities.

Other revenues and gains ($920,000 and $302,000) are added and other expenses and losses ($675,000 and $150,000) are subtracted to calculate income from continuing operations before income taxes ($422,207,000). After taxes ($189,993,000) are subtracted, the resulting amount is called *income from continuing operations* ($232,214,000). Income from continuing operations represents the profitability of the company's ongoing activities.

Take a moment to examine the consolidated statement of income for PepsiCo in Exhibit 23.2. PepsiCo shows 1997 net sales of $20,917 million, an operating profit (income from operations) of $2,662 million, and income from continuing operations of $1,491 million. Notice that although some of the headings used are not exactly the same as La-Grande Beverage, you can determine their meaning once you understand the format of the income statement.

The notes to the financial statements are required because they provide valuable information for income statement users. For example, looking at the income statement of PepsiCo in Exhibit 23.2, we cannot tell what costing approach (i.e., FIFO or LIFO) was used to determine its cost of goods sold or what depreciation method was used. However, this information is available in the notes to the financial statements. Note 1 to the PepsiCo statements indicates that it determines its cost of goods sold using FIFO and calculates depreciation using the straight-line method.

What Is Reported as Nonowner Changes in Equity?

LO 2

Nonowner changes in equity resulting from discontinued operations and extraordinary items appear net of taxes after income from continuing operations, which is the basis for a company's income tax calculation. See Exhibit 23.1, which illustrates income from continuing operations before these items on the income statement. We discuss discontinued operations and extraordinary items in turn.

Discontinued Operations   **Discontinued operations** are the result of a company selling or disposing of a segment of its business. The results of these types of events are presented separately on the income statement because they are unique and infrequent and, thus, not a regular part of ongoing operations. However, discontinued operations do have ramifications on the future earnings potential and cash flows of the company and, therefore, provide useful information to income statement users.

When a segment of a business is discontinued, two items are reported, either on the income statement itself or in the notes to the financial statements. The first is the income or loss generated based on the operations of the segment from the beginning of the account-

EXHIBIT 23.2 PepsiCo's Consolidated Statement of Income

Consolidated Statement of Income

($ in Millions except per share amount) PepsiCo, Inc. And Subsidiaries Fiscal Years ended December 27, 1997 December 28, 1996 and December 30, 1995	1997	1996	1995
Net Sales	**$20,917**	$20,337	$19,067
Costs and Expenses, net			
Cost of Sales	8,525	8,452	8,054
Sellings, general & administrative expenses	9,241	9,063	8,133
Amortization of intangible assets	199	206	208
Unusual items	290	576	66
Operating Profit	2,662	2,040	2,606
Interest expense	(478)	(565)	(629)
Interest income	125	91	114
Income from Continuing Operations Before Income Taxes	2,309	1,566	2,091
Provision for Income Taxes	818	624	669
Income from Continuing Operations	1,491	942	1,422
Income from Discontinued Operations, net of tax	651	207	184
Net Income	**$ 2,142**	**$ 1,149**	**$ 1,606**
Income Per Share – Basic			
Continuing Operations	$ 0.98	$ 0.60	$ 0.90
Discontinued Operations	0.42	0.13	0.12
Net income	**$ 1.40**	$ 0.73	$ 1.02
Average shares outstanding	1,528	1,564	1,576
Income Per Share – Assuming Dilution			
Continuing Operations	$ 0.95	$ 0.59	$ 0.88
Discontinued Operations	0.41	0.13	0.12
Net income	**$ 1.36**	$ 0.72	$ 1.00
Average shares outstanding	1.570	1,606	1,608

ing period through the disposal date. The second item reported is the gain or loss resulting from the disposal of the segment's net assets. Separating these items allows income statement readers to assess management's actions concerning the current and future aspects of disposing of the segment.

To illustrate how discontinued operations appear on the income statement, assume that during 1999 LaGrande Beverage disposed of a segment of its operations that had income of $327,273 before taxes. Assuming a 45 percent tax rate, the income from operations, net of tax, reported on the income statement, is $180,000, as shown below:

Income from operations of division	$327,273
Less applicable taxes (45%)	147,273
Income from operations of division, net of applicable taxes	$180,000

The loss incurred by LaGrande Beverage to dispose of the segment was $3,954,546 before taxes. The amount of the loss from disposing of the segment, net of tax, reported on the income statement is $2,175,000, as shown below:

Loss from disposal	$3,954,546
Less tax savings (45%)	1,779,546
Loss from disposal of division, net of applicable tax	$2,175,000

Take a moment to locate these items in Exhibit 23.1. They are added and subtracted, respectively, from "income from continuing operations" to determine "income before extraordinary items and cumulative effect of accounting change."

In 1997, Pizza Hut was spun off from PepsiCo.

Typically, companies report a single line item, called *discontinued operations,* on the face of the income statement and provide additional information concerning the disposal in the notes, as mentioned earlier. For example, PepsiCo's income statement (Exhibit 23.2) shows income from discontinued operations, net of tax, of $651 million in 1997. Note 4 (Exhibit 23.3) indicates that this income resulted from the spin-off of Pizza Hut, Taco Bell, and Kentucky Fried Chicken.

Extraordinary Items **Extraordinary items** are events that occurred during the accounting period that are both unusual and infrequent. Extraordinary events are often the result of a major casualty, such as assets that are expropriated by a foreign government, losses sustained from a disaster, or material gains and losses from early extinguishment of debt. Extraordinary items are important because they may have current and/or future cash flow implications. In addition, a financial statement user should evaluate the effect of an extraordinary item when predicting future earnings.

EXHIBIT	23.3	PepsiCo's Discontinued Operations Disclosure

Note 4—Discontinued Operations

The Restaurants segment was composed of the core restaurant businesses of Pizza Hut, Taco Bell and KFC, PepsiCo Foods Systems (PFS), the restaurant distribution operation, and several non-core U.S. restaurant businesses. In 1997, PepsiCo announced its intention to spin off its restaurant businesses to its shareholders as an independent publicly traded company (Distribution) and sell PFS separately. The spin-off was effective as a tax-free Distribution on October 6, 1997 (Distribution Date). Owners of PepsiCo capital stock as of September 19, 1997 received one share of common stock of TRICON Global Restaurants, Inc. (TRICON), the new company, for every ten shares of PepsiCo capital stock. Just prior to the Distribution Date, PepsiCo received $4.5 billion in cash from TRICON as repayment of certain amounts due and a dividend. PFS and the non-core U.S. restaurant businesses were sold prior to the Distribution Date resulting in after-tax cash proceeds of approximately $1.0 billion.

Income from discontinued operations:

	1997	1996	1995
Net sales	$ 8,375	$11,441	$11,328
Costs & expenses	(7,704)	(10,935)	(10,946)
PFS gain	500	–	–
Interest expense, net	(20)	(25)	(40)
Provision for income taxes	(500)	(274)	(158)
Income from discontinued operations	$ 651	$ 207	$ 184

The above amounts include costs directly associated with the spin-off but do not include an allocation of PepsiCo interest or general and administrative expenses.

It is not always easy to determine if a particular event is an extraordinary item. For example, a California company's loss due to an earthquake is not an extraordinary item because earthquakes in that region are not unusual. On the other hand, a Tennessee company's loss due to an earthquake would probably be an extraordinary item because earthquakes are rare in that region of the United States.

Extraordinary items appear net of taxes, the details of which are often found in the notes. To illustrate extraordinary items, assume that LaGrande Beverage suffered an uninsured loss from a flood during 1999. The total loss was $3,000,000; however, the amount shown on the income statement (see Exhibit 23.1) is only $1,650,000 due to the tax savings resulting from the loss, as calculated below:

Loss due to flood	$3,000,000
Less tax savings (45%)	1,350,000
Extraordinary loss, net of applicable taxes	$1,650,000

An examination of PepsiCo's income statement (Exhibit 23.2) reveals that no extraordinary events occurred from fiscal 1995 through 1997.

What Are Cumulative Accounting Adjustments?

Cumulative accounting adjustments are modifications made to the accounting records that result from changes in accounting principles. These events occur when the company switches from one generally accepted accounting method to another (for example, from straight-line to double-declining-balance depreciation), or when the company adopts a new accounting standard requiring a change in the way some event is reported.

Regardless of management's reasons for making an accounting principle change, the statements presented for the current accounting period will not be prepared on the same basis as previous financial statements. This results in a lack of consistency between statements for consecutive reporting periods, which could mislead financial statement users. Therefore, it is necessary to disclose the reasons for the inconsistent presentation of events. The cumulative effect of the accounting change is shown because it is impractical to go back and restate all previous years' financial statements to make them comparable to the current period's statements. Since cumulative effects of accounting changes are not recurring, they are shown separately on the income statement, net of tax.[2]

For example, assume that LaGrande Beverage has assets with a 10-year useful life and no salvage value that were originally purchased in 1997 for $15 million. During 1997 and 1998, these assets were depreciated using the straight-line method. In 1999 management decided to switch to the double-declining-balance depreciation method. The difference in the depreciation expense for 1997 and 1998, respectively, using straight-line versus double-declining-balance is shown below:

	1997	1998	Total
Double-declining-balance depreciation	$3,000,000	$2,400,000	$5,400,000
Straight-line depreciation (former method)	1,500,000	1,500,000	3,000,000
Excess over straight-line	$1,500,000	$ 900,000	$2,400,000

If the company had used double-declining-balance depreciation in 1997 and 1998, the reported income before taxes would have been $1,500,000 and $900,000 lower, respectively, for each year. But the increased depreciation expense, which would have created lower income, also would have reduced the amount of income tax expense. Assuming a 45 percent income tax rate, the tax savings resulting from the increased amount of depreciation expense are shown below:

	1997	1998	Total
Increased depreciation expense	$1,500,000	$900,000	$2,400,000
Tax rate	0.45	0.45	0.45
Tax savings	$ 675,000	$405,000	$1,080,000

---

[2] Special rules apply when a company switches its method of accounting for inventories to or from LIFO. If a company changes from LIFO to FIFO, it must restate its income for any years shown on the comparative financial statements. If a company changes to LIFO from FIFO, this restatement is not required because it is impractical to ascertain the LIFO inventory numbers.

Therefore, the 1999 cumulative effect of this accounting change, net of taxes, is an increase in expenses and, therefore, a reduction in income of $1,320,000 as shown below:

	1997	1998	Total
Increased depreciation expense	$1,500,000	$900,000	$2,400,000
Decreased tax expense	675,000	405,000	1,080,000
Net increase in expenses	$ 825,000	$495,000	$1,320,000

The $1,320,000 of net reduction is shown on the face of the income statement (see Exhibit 23.1). The company would report the details of this calculation as well as management's reasons for making the change from one depreciation method to the other in the notes to the financial statements.

Take a moment to determine whether PepsiCo reported any cumulative accounting changes in 1997. We notice no such reporting by PepsiCo. Therefore, after adding income from discontinued operations ($651 million) to its income from continuing operations ($1,491 million), PepsiCo reports net income of $2,142 million in 1997.

What Is Included as Other Comprehensive Income Items?

LO 3

SFAS No. 130 requires that companies report comprehensive income in addition to net income. Items included in comprehensive income include foreign currency translation adjustments, minimum pension liability adjustments, and unrealized gains and losses from certain debt and equity transactions.

Foreign currency translation adjustments may be required for companies operating in more than one country due to changes in currency exchange rates relative to the value of the U.S. dollar. Minimum pension liability adjustments may be required for companies that delay the recognition of their pension liabilities. Both of these subjects are beyond the scope of this text.

The final item of other comprehensive income is unrealized gains and losses from certain debt and equity transactions. Recall from Chapter 22 that unrealized gains and losses from available-for-sale securities are reported in the current period. That reporting is part of comprehensive, not net, income. For example, assume that LaGrande Beverage had the following available-for-sale securities at the end of 1999:

	Cost	Market Value
Common stocks	$546,998	$ 940,655
Bonds	221,347	209,508
Total	$768,345	$1,150,163

Based on this information, LaGrande Beverage has an unrealized gain before income taxes of $381,818. Assuming a 45 percent tax rate, the after-tax unrealized gain shown on the income statement is determined as shown below:

Unrealized gain before income taxes	$381,818
Less applicable taxes (45%)	171,818
Unrealized gain, net of applicable taxes	$210,000

Exhibit 23.1 shows that this gain is added to "net income" to determine "comprehensive income."

Note: Although other comprehensive income items are shown on the income statement, they are not closed to Retained Earnings at the end of the period. Rather, these items are disclosed as separate items within the stockholders' equity section on the balance sheet and are adjusted from year to year as appropriate.

PepsiCo reports its other comprehensive income items on the consolidated statement of shareholders' equity that we will examine later in this chapter. It reports the cumulative effect of these items on the balance sheet as a separate item, "currency translation adjustment," in the shareholders' equity section.

Now that you understand the components of comprehensive income, we look at how to report income on a per share basis.

WHAT DOES EARNINGS PER SHARE REPRESENT?

LO 4

Fundamentally, **earnings per share** is a common-size measure of a company's earnings
performance that allows financial statement users to compare the operating performance
of large and small corporations on a per share basis. Earnings per share is the most frequently quoted measure of firm performance in the financial press, and it is a required
disclosure on the face of the income statement. It reflects the amount of the company's
earnings belonging to each shareholder on a per share basis. Earnings per share is *not* the
amount that each stockholder will receive as dividends because, as you know, companies
typically do not pay out all their earnings in dividends.

Calculating Earnings per Share

In its basic form, earnings per share is the current period's net income reported on a per
share basis, or the net income of the current period available to common shareholders divided by the weighted-average number of common shares outstanding. It is calculated as
shown below:

$$\text{Earnings per share} = \frac{\text{Net income} - \text{Preferred stock dividends}}{\text{Weighted-average number of common shares outstanding}}$$

Take a closer look at this formula. First, it is necessary to reduce net income by the
amount of required preferred stock dividends because preferred stockholders have a pre-
specified first claim on the earnings of the firm if any of those earnings are paid out as
dividends. The remaining amount is known as *earnings available to common stockholders.* Second, the company uses the weighted-average number of common shares outstanding to measure the average number of shares held outside the company during the entire
accounting period. It reflects an adjustment made for issuances and repurchases of shares
during the period.

For example, suppose that on January 1, 1999, LaGrande Beverage had 28.8 million
common shares outstanding. On June 1, 1999, it issued an additional 5,700,000 shares
and on October 1, 1999, it repurchased 9,000,000 shares to hold as treasury stock through
the end of the year. Using this information, we calculate the weighted-average number of
shares outstanding below:

Time Period, 1999	Shares	Partial-Year Ratio	Weight
Jan. 1–May 31	28,800,000	5/12	12,000,000
June 1–Sept. 30	34,500,000	4/12	11,500,000
Oct. 1–Dec. 31	25,500,000	3/12	6,375,000
Weighted-average number of shares outstanding			29,875,000

Assuming that net income is $227,249,000 (see Exhibit 23.1) and that preferred dividends are $10,000,000, the earnings per share is calculated as follows:

$$\frac{\$227,249,000 - \$10,000,000}{29,875,000} = \$7.27$$

This indicates to financial statement users that stockholders earned, on average, $7.27 per share held. Take a moment to examine Exhibit 23.1 and locate the earnings per share of $7.27.

Calculating Diluted Earnings per Share

How do securities that can be converted into common stock, such as convertible preferred stock and convertible bonds, affect earnings per share? What about stock options? Because earnings per share is often used as an indication of future earnings, it is necessary to show the amount of dilution, or decrease, in earnings per share that would occur as a result of activities like conversions and the exercise of stock options. This figure is referred to as **diluted earnings per share.** While diluted earnings per share reflects an indication of dilution, it does not represent full dilution of earnings. This subject is complicated and beyond the scope of this text. For illustrative purposes, we look at a simple example of diluted earnings per share.

Assume that LaGrande Beverage offers its employees stock options as additional compensation. Further suppose that if all these stock options were exercised, the weighted-average number of shares outstanding would be 35,000,000 (versus the 29,875,000 calculated previously). Using this information, the diluted earnings per share would be:

$$\frac{\$227,249,000 - \$10,000,000}{35,000,000} = \$6.21$$

Take a moment to locate the amount of diluted earnings per share in Exhibit 23.1 and notice that it is lower than the amount of earnings per share because the existing stockholders' interests will be diluted if the options are exercised.[3] Diluted earnings per share also appear on the income statement with some details regarding the calculation disclosed in the notes to the financial statements.

Other Earnings per Share Disclosures

Companies must show the per share effects of extraordinary items and accounting changes so that users can assess, on a per share basis, the effects of these items on net income. For example, the income statement of LaGrande Beverage (see Exhibit 23.1) indicates that earnings per share from continuing operations was $7.44 [($232,214,000 – $10,000,000)/29,875,000] and that income before extraordinary items and cumulative effect of accounting change on a per share basis was $7.37 [($230,219,000 – $10,000,000)/29,875,000]. The per share effects of the extraordinary loss and cumulative effect of accounting change were 6 and 4 cents, respectively ($1,650,000/29,875,000 = $0.06 and $1,320,000/29,875,000 = $0.04). This information is important because it allows shareholders and others to evaluate on a common-size basis, the impact of specific items on earnings per share.

Exhibit 23.1 indicates that diluted earnings per share from continuing operations was $6.35 [($232,214,000 – $10,000,000)/35,000,000] and that income before extraordinary items and cumulative effect of accounting change on a diluted per share basis was $6.29 [($230,219,000 – $10,000,000)/35,000,000].

PepsiCo reports income per share (basic) of $1.40 in 1997 and diluted income per share of $1.36 (see Exhibit 23.2). Note 5 (Exhibit 23.4) provides additional information concerning the calculation of earnings per share.

---

[3]If a company has dilutive, convertible securities, two adjustments are necessary. First, the weighted-average number of common shares outstanding is adjusted. Second, the income available to common shareholders must be adjusted to reflect the fact that preferred dividends would not be required if preferred stock is converted into common stock. Or, in the case of convertible bonds, income must be adjusted by the amount of interest (net of tax) that would not be paid if the convertible bonds were converted into common stock.

EXHIBIT 23.4   PepsiCo's Earnings Per Share Disclosure

Note 5—Income Per Share

PepsiCo adopted the provisions of Statement of Financial Accounting Standards No. 128, "Earnings Per Share," in 1997. Application of its provisions results in disclosure of two income per share measures, basic and assuming dilution, on the face of the Consolidated Statement of Income.

PepsiCo's reported net income represents its net income available to common stockholders for purposes of computing both measures. The following reconciles shares outstanding at the beginning of the year to average shares outstanding used to compute both income per share measures.

	1997	1996	1995
Shares outstanding at beginning of year	1,545	1.576	1,580
Weighted average shares issued during the year for exercise of stock options	14	13	9
Weighted average shares repurchased	(31)	(25)	(13)
Average shares outstanding - basic	1,528	1,564	1,576
Effect of dilutive securities			
Dilutive shares contingently issuable upon the exercise of stock options	151	169	151
Shares assumed to have been purchased for treasury with assumed proceeds from the exercise of stock options	(109)	(127)	(119)
Average shares outstanding - assuming dilution	1,570	1,606	1,608

PAUSE &

REFLECT

Examine the income statement (Exhibit 23.2) and Note 5 (Exhibit 23.4) of PepsiCo. Does PepsiCo have any preferred stock? *(answer on page 802)*

OTHER REQUIRED INCOME STATEMENT DISCLOSURES

Companies with multiple business segments usually report income on a combined basis; that is, the incomes of the various business units are combined and reported on one income statement. GAAP require that such companies report segment information based on how management has organized the company. The company must report information about its products, geographic markets, and major customers. In addition, for any identifiable segment, the following items must be disclosed:

- Revenues from external customers
- Revenues from internal customers (other segments of the same company)
- Interest revenue and/or expense
- Depreciation, depletion, and amortization expense
- Income tax expense
- Segment profit or loss
- Extraordinary items
- Identifiable segment assets
- Expenditures for segment assets

Beverages are a primary industry segment for PepsiCo.

EXHIBIT 23.5 PepsiCo's Segment Disclosure

Note 17 (cont.)
INDUSTRY SEGMENTS

	1997	1996	1995
NET SALES			
Beverages	$ 10,541	$10,587	$10,467
Snack Foods	10,376	9,750	8,600
	$ 20,917	$20,337	$19,067
OPERATING PROFIT (a)			
Beverages	$ 1,114	$ 890	$ 1,309
Snack Foods	1,695	1,608	1,432
Combined Segments	2,809	2,498	2,741
Equity Income/(Loss)	84	(274)	38
Unallocated Expenses, net	(231)	(184)	(173)
Operating Profit	$ 2,662	$ 2,040	$ 2,606
Amortization of Intangible Assets			
Beverages	$ 155	$ 165	$ 167
Snack Foods	44	41	41
	199	206	208
Depreciation Expense			
Beverages	$ 444	$ 440	$ 445
Snack Foods	394	346	304
Corporate	7	7	7
	$ 845	$ 793	$ 756

	1997	1996	1995
Identifiable Assets			
Beverages	$ 9,752	$ 9,816	$10,032
Snack Foods	6,998	6,279	5,451
Investments in Unconsolidated Affiliates	1,201	1,147	1,253
Corporate	2,150	468	1,464
Net Assets of Discontinued Operations	–	4,450	4,744
	$ 20,101	$22,160	$22,944
Capital Spending			
Beverages	$ 618	$ 648	$ 563
Snack Foods	873	973	768
Corporate	15	9	34
	$ 1,506	$ 1,630	$ 1,365
United States	$ 996	$ 1,109	$ 928
International	510	521	437
	$ 1,506	$ 1,630	$ 1,365
Acquisitions and Investments in Unconsolidated Affiliates			
Beverages	$ 43	$ 75	$ 318
Snack Foods	76	–	82
	$ 119	$ 75	$ 400
United States	$ 3	$ 15	$ 37
International	116	60	363
	$ 119	$ 75	$ 400

For example, PepsiCo reported two industry segments in 1997—beverages (Pepsi-Cola, Diet Pepsi, Mountain Dew, 7UP, etc.) and snack foods (Frito-Lay, etc.). Note 17 shown in Exhibit 23.5 reports net sales, operating profits, identifiable assets, and depreciation of these two segments. In addition, PepsiCo reports geographic information concerning net sales and operating profits.

EXHIBIT   23.5   *Continued*

Note 17 (cont.)
GEOGRAPHIC AREAS (b)

	Net Sales			Segment Operating Profit (c)		
	1997	1996	1995	**1997**	1996	1995
Europe	**$ 2,327**	$ 2,513	$ 2,451	**$ (133)**	$ (88)	$ (7)
Canada	**941**	946	889	**105**	116	94
Mexico	**1,541**	1,314	1,204	**214**	105	135
United Kingdom	**859**	810	751	**106**	159	139
Other	**1,371**	1,346	1,371	**(50)**	(342)	103
Total International	**7,039**	6,929	6,666	**242**	(50)	464
United States	**13,878**	13,408	12,401	**2,567**	2,548	2,277
Combined Segments	**$20,917**	$20,337	$19,067	**$2,809**	$2,498	$2,741

Investments in Unconsolidated Affiliates
Corporate
Net Assets of Discontinued Operations

(b) The results of centralized concentrate manufacturing operations in Puerto Rico and Ireland have been allocated based upon sales to the respective geographic areas.
(c) The unusual items reduce combined segment operating profit by $290 (United States - $74, Europe -$96, Mexico - $(17), United Kingdom - $53, Other - $84) in 1997, $576 (Europe - $69, Mexico - $4, Other - $503) in 1996 and $66 (Europe - $62, Other - $4) in 1995.

WHAT IS THE PURPOSE OF THE STATEMENT OF RETAINED EARNINGS?

LO 5

For corporations, the statement of retained earnings indicates the changes that occurred in the Retained Earnings account during the period. These changes arise from three sources: (1) net income or loss, (2) cash or stock dividends declared, and (3) prior period adjustments. Previously, we discussed how the balance of Retained Earnings increases or decreases during the closing process to reflect the net income or net loss of the period. In Chapter 19 we examined the effect of cash and stock dividends on retained earnings. Recall that the statement of retained earnings may be presented as part of a broader statement of stockholders' equity. Here we will discuss prior period adjustments.

A **prior period adjustment** is a correction of a previously undetected material error that affected the net income or loss of a previous accounting period. The correction is made to beginning Retained Earnings because net income or loss is closed to Retained Earnings. Therefore, the beginning balance of Retained Earnings would be incorrect if an error affecting net income occurred in a previous accounting period. When the error is discovered in the current year, companies report the impact of the error on Retained Earnings as an adjustment, net of tax.

For example, assume that LaGrande discovered in 1999 that land costing $60,000,000 was incorrectly recorded as depreciation expense rather than land in 1998. Thus La-Grande's 1998 expenses were overstated and its income, total assets, and retained earnings were understated. If the entry had been made correctly, 1998 expenses would have been less, and assets would have been larger by $60,000,000 each, as shown below:

	Depreciation Expense	Land
Amounts actually recorded in error	$ 60,000,000	$ –0–
Amounts that should have been recorded	–0–	60,000,000
Correction needed	$(60,000,000)	$60,000,000

However, because depreciation expense was incorrectly recorded, the tax expense was smaller due to the smaller net income, so the 1998 tax expense and taxes payable were understated by $27,000,000 each ($60,000,000 × 0.45).

Because both the Depreciation Expense and Tax Expense accounts were closed into Retained Earnings at the end of 1998, the 1999 beginning balance of Retained

Earnings must be increased by $33,000,000 ($60,000,000 – $27,000,000) as a result of the information shown below:

Error	Correction to Retained Earnings
1998 depreciation expense overstated	Increase $60,000,000
1998 tax expense understated	Decrease 27,000,000
Net correction	Increase $33,000,000

Exhibit 23.6 shows LaGrande Beverage's statement of retained earnings. Notice that the beginning Retained Earnings balance is corrected for the $33,000,000 net error, which is a prior period adjustment. Then the balance is increased by the amount of net income generated during 1999 and decreased by the dividends declared in 1999.

EXHIBIT 23.6 Statement of Retained Earnings

LAGRANDE BEVERAGE
Statement of Retained Earnings
For the Year Ended December 31, 1999
(in thousands)

Retained earnings, December 31, 1998	$250,000
Prior period adjustment	33,000
Adjusted balance	$283,000
Add net income	227,249
	$510,249
Less dividends declared	
Preferred stock	10,000
Common stock	67,685
Retained earnings, December 31, 1999	$432,564

Exhibit 23.7 illustrates PepsiCo's consolidated statement of shareholders' equity. Notice that it shows the changes in capital stock and treasury stock in number of shares and in dollars. It also shows the changes in capital in excess of par value and retained earnings. The highlighted Currency Translation Adjustment column is the disclosure for PepsiCo's other comprehensive income. Thus PepsiCo applies *SFAS 130* by reporting other comprehensive income on the statement of shareholders' equity rather than the income statement.

EXHIBIT 23.7 PepsiCo's Consolidated Statement of Shareholders' Equity

Consolidated Statement of Shareholder's Equity

	Capital Stock							
	Issued		Treasury					
	Shares	Amount	Shares	Amount	Capital in Excess of Par Value	Retained Earnings	Currency Translation Adjustment	Total
Shareholders' Equity Dec 31, 1994	1,726	$29	(146)	$(1,361)	$920	$7,739	$ (471)	$6,856
1995 Net Income	–	–	–	–	–	1,606	–	1,606
Cash dividends declared (per share –$0.39)	–	–	–	–	–	(615)	–	(615)
Currency translation adjustment	–	–	–	–	–	–	(337)	(337)

EXHIBIT 23.7 *Continued*

Share repurchases	–	–	(24)	(541)	–	–	–	(541)
Stock option exercises, including tax benefits of $ 91	–	–	20	218	125	–	–	343
Other	–	–	–	1	–	–	–	1
Shareholders' Equity Dec 30 1995	1,726	$29	(150)	$(1,683)	$1,045	$8,730	$(808)	$7,313
1996 Net Income	–	–	–	–	–	1,149	–	1,149
Cash dividends declared (per share –$.445)	–	–	–	–	–	(695)	–	(695)
Currency translation adjustment	–	–	–	–	–	–	40	40
Share repurchases	–	–	(54)	(1,651)	–	–	–	(1,651)
Stock option exercises, including tax benefits of $ 145	–	–	23	310	158	–	–	468
Other	–	–	–	1	(2)	–	–	(1)
Shareholders' Equity Dec 28, 1996	1,726	$ 29	(181)	$(3,023)	$1,201	$9,184	$(768)	$6,623
1997 Net Income	–	–	–	–	–	2,142	–	2,142
Cash dividends declared (per share –$.49)	–	–	–	–	–	(746)	–	(746)
Currency translation adjustment	–	–	–	–	–	–	(220)	(220)
Share repurchases	–	–	(69)	(2,459)	–	–	–	(2,459)
Stock option exercises, including tax benefits of $ 173	–	–	25	488	88	–	–	576
Spin-off Restaurant businesses	–	–	–	–	–	987	–	987
Other	–	–	1	8	25	–	–	33
Shareholders' Equity Dec 27 1997	1,726	$29	(224)	$(4,986)	$1,314	$11,567	$(988)	$6,936

WHAT ARE THE REPORTING ISSUES CONCERNING THE INCOME STATEMENT?

No discussion of the income statement is complete without reference to its potential reporting issues. Because the income statement of a publicly held company is based on historical costs, and, for manufacturing firms, full-absorption costing, it is subject to certain assumptions that users must understand. We examine three reporting issues next: historical cost and conservatism, cost allocations, and full-absorption costing.

Historical Cost and Conservatism

We have discussed the concepts of return of and return on investment throughout the second part of this text. Investment pertains to the amount of capital invested in assets, and determining the return on investment depends on how capital is defined. When a company prepares its financial statements, it recognizes gains (profits) on inventory and property, plant, and equipment only when they are realized.

Therefore, if a company has a building with a carrying value of $400,000 and a market value of $600,000, it will report the building on the balance sheet at $400,000 and will *not* report the unrealized gain of $200,000. Likewise, if the market value of the company's inventory is greater than its cost, it will report the inventory on the balance sheet at cost and will not report the unrealized gain. However, if the market value of the company's inventory is less than its cost, it will report the inventory on the balance sheet at its market value and will report the unrealized loss. This seeming inconsistency is due to the concept of conservatism that obligates companies to anticipate losses but not gains. As you have learned, however, exceptions do exist. Companies now report unrealized gains and losses on trading securities.

Cost Allocations

Another income statement issue that external users need to understand concerns cost allocations. Depreciation (depletion and amortization) expense does not measure the economic deterioration of assets; it is merely the allocation of the cost of the asset over its expected useful life. As you learned in Chapter 21, a variety of methods are available to allocate the cost of depreciable assets to the income statement. Therefore, readers of financial statements must look to the notes accompanying the financial statements to determine which depreciation method a company uses in order to compare companies.

Because companies use assets in different ways, alternatives are necessary to allow companies to describe and best reflect their operations. Therefore, knowing how management chooses to estimate its cost allocation is as important as knowing the actual amount of the estimate. Financial statement users must be aware that different companies use different allocation methods and should take this into account when reading financial statements and other information. Cost allocation information is normally disclosed only in the notes to the financial statements, so users should investigate note information when comparing companies. Likewise, users should determine the inventory costing method used by companies before comparing them.

Full-Absorption Costing

As discussed in Chapter 11, full-absorption costing, the required costing method for external reporting, assigns all production costs, such as direct materials, direct labor, and unit-related, batch-related, product-sustaining, and facility-sustaining manufacturing overhead, to the units produced during the period. The cost of goods sold, then, is the amount of beginning finished goods inventory plus the cost of goods manufactured minus the amount of ending finished goods inventory.

When a manufacturing company prepares an income statement for external users, it often calculates cost of goods manufactured and cost of goods sold by applying overhead to production based on the number of units produced. We know from earlier chapters, however, that many overhead cost items do not vary with the number of units produced. Therefore, distortions in income can result when overhead costs are treated as though they vary with the level of production.

To illustrate this issue, consider a very simple situation where two companies (Company A and Company B) in their first year of operations (1999) have only two types of overhead—unit-related and facility-sustaining. These companies are identical except that Company A produced 15,000 units and Company B produced 30,000 units during 1999. Relevant operating data for the two companies are shown in Exhibit 23.8.

EXHIBIT   23.8   Company A and Company B Data

	Company A	Company B
Units produced	15,000	30,000
Units sold	12,000	12,000
Selling price per unit	$ 100.00	$ 100.00
Direct materials cost per unit	$ 4.25	$ 4.25
Direct labor cost per unit	$ 1.75	$ 1.75
Unit-related overhead per unit	$ 6.50	$ 6.50
Variable selling cost per unit	$ 2.00	$ 2.00
Facility-sustaining overhead per year	$750,000	$750,000
Fixed selling cost per year	$175,000	$175,000

Exhibit 23.9 shows the results of operations for Company A. Take a moment to study this exhibit. Using absorption costing, the cost of goods sold consists of all production costs on a per unit basis. Thus it includes an amount of facility-sustaining overhead per unit, $50 ($750,000 incurred/15,000 units produced) in this case.

EXHIBIT   23.9   Company A Income Statement

COMPANY A
Income Statement
For the Year Ended December 31, 1999

Sales (12,000 x $100)		$1,200,000
Less cost of goods sold:		
Direct materials (12,000 x $4.25)	$ 51,000	
Direct labor (12,000 x $1.75)	21,000	
Unit-related overhead (12,000 x $6.50)	78,000	
Facility-sustaining overhead* (12,000 x $50)	600,000	750,000
Gross margin		$ 450,000
Less other operating costs:		
Variable selling costs (12,000 x $2.00)	$ 24,000	
Fixed selling costs	175,000	199,000
Net income		$ 251,000

*$750,000 overhead/15,000 units produced = $50.

Full-absorption costing implies that facility-sustaining overhead varies with the number of units produced rather than with a facility-related cost driver. What problems can result from this? Companies can increase income simply by increasing the number of units produced during the period, even if the number of units sold remains the same!

To illustrate, look at Exhibit 23.10, which shows the income statement for Company B. Notice that although the sales ($1,200,000), selling expenses ($24,000), and administrative expenses ($175,000) are the same as Company A's (compare Exhibit 23.9 to Exhibit 23.10), the gross margin and net income are each $300,000 greater due solely to an increase in production of 15,000 units! For Company B, cost of goods sold includes an amount of facility-sustaining overhead per unit of only $25 because more units were produced during the period ($750,000 incurred/30,000 units produced).

EXHIBIT 23.10 Company B Income Statement

COMPANY B
Income Statement
For the Year Ended December 31, 1999

Sales (12,000 x $100)		$1,200,000
Less cost of goods sold:		
Direct materials (12,000 x $4.25)	$ 51,000	
Direct labor (12,000 x $1.75)	21,000	
Unit-related overhead (12,000 x $6.50)	78,000	
Facility-sustaining overhead* (12,000 x $25)	300,000	450,000
Gross margin		$ 750,000
Less other operating costs:		
Variable selling costs (12,000 x $2.00)	$ 24,000	
Fixed selling costs	175,000	199,000
Net income		$ 551,000

*$750,000 overhead/30,000 units produced = $25.

• This $300,000 difference in income is due to the difference in the company's cost of ending inventory. Company A, which has only 3,000 units in ending inventory, shows a cost per unit of $62.50 ($4.25 direct materials + $1.75 direct labor + $6.50 unit-related overhead + $50.00 facility-sustaining overhead). Company B, however, which has 18,000 units in ending inventory, reports a cost per unit of $37.50 ($4.25 direct materials + $1.75 direct labor + $6.50 unit-related overhead + $25.00 facility-sustaining overhead). Therefore, Company A and Company B do not have a permanent difference in income; rather, the difference in this year's income is represented as an asset on the balance sheet. Does this imply that Company B's inventory is worth more per unit than Company A's inventory? Absolutely not—the same costs were incurred by each company.

This simplified example illustrates that users must evaluate the change in cost of goods sold in relation to the change in inventory levels to judge whether the gross margin and ending inventory are larger than expected based on the past performance of the company. If the gross margin and ending inventory are larger than expected, this may indicate that the number of units produced far exceeded the number of units sold. Because inventories are costly to hold, a manager of a company that produces more than the amount sold may not be utilizing the company resources in an efficient and effective manner. This would be important for financial statement users to know because it has implications for the future earnings and cash flows of the company.

Now that we have looked at the reporting issues concerning the income statement, we turn to the topic of internal reporting of earnings.

INCOME REPORTS FOR INTERNAL USERS

LO 6

Internally, management needs to know not only the company's total income but also the revenues, costs, and profits of the company's various divisions, segments, and locations. These various portions of the total business are often evaluated as one of four types of responsibility centers:

- **Cost center**—responsible for controlling costs and providing a good or service in an efficient manner; example: manufacturing department

- **Revenue center**—responsible for generating revenues and promoting the company's products and services effectively; example: marketing department

- **Profit center**—responsible for making a profit, it must effectively generate revenues and efficiently control costs; example: major product line

- **Investment center**—responsible for using assets in an effective and efficient manner to generate profits; example: overseas branch operation

Notice that each of these centers is responsible for, and evaluated on, different items. Cost centers are evaluated on costs only and revenue centers are evaluated on revenues only. But profit centers and investment centers are evaluated on profits. Therefore, two issues arise: how to measure profits internally and how to measure the profits of the division. We examine each of these issues below.

PAUSE &
REFLECT

What analysis tools are available to evaluate cost and revenue centers? (Refer to Chapter 13 if you are unsure.) *(answer on page 803)*

Unit-Variable and Throughput Accounting Income Reports

Previously, we explored how a company can increase its reported income simply by producing more units. Why might management have an incentive to do such a thing? Recall from Chapter 16 that management's bonuses are often based on net income. Thus managers might have an incentive to manage earnings in order to get or increase bonuses. One way to decrease this incentive is to report income internally (and compute bonuses) in a different manner.

One way of reporting income internally is known as the **unit-variable accounting method,** where only costs that vary with the number of units produced are included in cost of goods sold. Using this method, batch-related, product-sustaining, and facility-sustaining overhead costs are expensed, in total, in the period incurred. Another way of reporting income internally is with the **throughput accounting method,** where only direct materials are included in cost of goods sold. All other production costs (labor and all types of overhead) are expensed, in total, in the period incurred.

To illustrate the differences among absorption, unit-variable, and throughput accounting, we will again compare Company A and Company B introduced earlier. Relevant data are reproduced in Exhibit 23.11. Recall that using absorption costing, Company A and Company B reported the following (see Exhibits 23.9 and 23.10):

	Company A	Company B
Cost of goods sold	$750,000	$450,000
Net income	251,000	551,000
Ending inventory	187,500	675,000

EXHIBIT 23.11 Company A and Company B Data

	Company A	Company B
Units produced	15,000	30,000
Units sold	12,000	12,000
Selling price per unit	$ 100.00	$ 100.00
Direct materials cost per unit	$ 4.25	$ 4.25
Direct labor cost per unit	$ 1.75	$ 1.75
Unit-related overhead per unit	$ 6.50	$ 6.50
Variable selling cost per unit	$ 2.00	$ 2.00
Facility-sustaining overhead per year	$750,000	$750,000
Fixed selling cost per year	$175,000	$175,000

Now let's see what happens if we use unit-variable costing to determine profit. Under unit-variable costing, cost of goods sold includes only costs that vary with the number of units produced (direct materials, direct labor, and unit-related overhead). All other production costs (facility-sustaining overhead) are expensed in the year incurred. Therefore, a contribution margin format income report is frequently used.

Exhibit 23.12 shows the unit-variable income reports of Company A and Company B. Notice that both Company A and Company B report the same contribution margin ($1,026,000) and the same profit ($101,000). Why does this occur? Because Company A and Company B have the same unit-variable costs per unit and the same total facility-sustaining overhead, they will have the same contribution margin and profit. However, Company B shows a much larger ending inventory amount because it produced 30,000 units compared to the 15,000 units produced by Company A. Also notice that the profit reported using unit-variable costing is lower than that determined using absorption costing for both Company A ($101,000 versus $251,000) and Company B ($101,000 versus $551,000). This happens because the number of units produced was greater than the number of units sold. Because absorption costing calculates a higher unit cost, including facility-sustaining overhead in the cost figure, more costs are held in inventory. Managers whose bonuses are based on unit-variable income will not be rewarded for overproducing inventory because facility-sustaining costs will be expensed regardless of how many units are produced.

EXHIBIT   23.12   Unit-Variable Income Reports

COMPANY A
Unit-Variable Income Report
For the Year Ended December 31, 1999

Sales (12,000 × $100)		$1,200,000
Less unit-variable costs:		
Direct materials (12,000 × $4.25)	$ 51,000	
Direct labor (12,000 × $1.75)	21,000	
Unit-related overhead (12,000 × $6.50)	78,000	
Variable selling costs (12,000 × $2.00)	24,000	174,000
Contribution margin		$1,026,000
Less other operating costs:		
Facility-sustaining overhead	$750,000	
Fixed selling costs	175,000	925,000
Operating profit		$ 101,000
Ending inventory (3,000 × $12.50)		$ 37,500

COMPANY B
Unit-Variable Income Report
For the Year Ended December 31, 1999

Sales (12,000 × $100)		$1,200,000
Less unit-variable costs:		
Direct materials (12,000 × $4.25)	$ 51,000	
Direct labor (12,000 × $1.75)	21,000	
Unit-related overhead (12,000 × $6.50)	78,000	
Variable selling costs (12,000 × $2.00)	24,000	174,000
Contribution margin		$1,026,000
Less other operating costs:		
Facility-sustaining overhead	$750,000	
Fixed selling costs	175,000	925,000
Operating profit		$ 101,000
Ending inventory (18,000 × $12.50)		$ 225,000

If we use throughput accounting to determine profit, the results are even more dramatic. Exhibit 23.13 shows the throughput accounting income reports for Company A and Company B. Using throughput accounting, the costs of direct materials are subtracted from sales to determine the throughput margin. Then all other operating costs *incurred* during the period are subtracted to determine profit. Note that other operating costs are subtracted, in total, to determine profit. None of these costs are assigned to inventory.

Using throughput accounting, Company A and Company B report the same throughput margin ($1,149,000), but their profits are vastly different. Company A subtracts operating costs of $1,072,750 from its throughput margin, resulting in an operating profit of

EXHIBIT 23.13 Throughput Income Reports

COMPANY A
Throughput Income Report
For the Year Ended December 31, 1999

Sales (12,000 x $100)		$1,200,000
Less direct materials (12,000 x $4.25)		51,000
Throughput margin		$1,149,000
Less other operating costs:		
Direct labor (15,000 x $1.75)	$ 26,250	
Unit-related overhead (15,000 x $6.50)	97,500	
Facility-sustaining ove. ead	750,000	
Variable selling costs (12,000 x $2.00)	24,000	
Fixed selling costs	175,000	1,072,750
Operating profit		$ 76,250
Ending inventory (3,000 x $4.25)		$ 12,750

COMPANY B
Throughput Income Report
For the Year Ended December 31, 1999

Sales (12,000 x $100)		$1,200,000
Less direct materials (12,000 x $4.25)		51,000
Throughput margin		$1,149,000
Less other operating costs:		
Direct labor (30,000 x $1.75)	$ 52,500	
Unit-related overhead (30,000 x $6.50)	195,000	
Facility-sustaining overhead	750,000	
Variable selling costs (12,000 x $2.00)	24,000	
Fixed selling costs	175,000	1,196,500
Operating profit		$ 47,500
Ending inventory (18,000 x $4.25)		$ 76,500

$76,250. On the other hand, Company B must subtract operating costs of $1,196,500 from throughput margin, resulting in an operating profit of only $47,500. Company B had higher operating costs because it produced more units and, using throughput accounting, these costs are not held in inventory.

Company B shows a larger ending inventory value than does Company A ($76,500 versus $12,750). Also notice that throughput accounting results in the lowest reported profit compared to absorption and unit-variable costing. This is because throughput assigns the fewest costs to inventory and, therefore, expenses the greatest costs during the period. Throughput accounting, even more than unit-variable accounting, discourages managers from overproducing inventory. Because the only costs held in inventory are direct materials, a manager who produces excess inventory will show more expenses on the income statement for labor and overhead. Clearly, there is no incentive for management to increase production if bonuses are based on throughput accounting.

Proponents of unit-variable costing believe it is superior because it determines contribution margin that can be used in cost-volume-profit analysis (see Chapter 4). Proponents of throughput costing believe it is superior because it determines cost of goods sold based only on direct materials, which according to many is the only truly variable cost. Which method a company uses internally reflects its philosophy concerning variable versus non-variable costs.

Product Line (Divisional) Income Reports

LO 8

Product line (divisional) income reports are specific-purpose reports designed to provide more detailed information than general-purpose segment disclosures of the results of operations for a product line or company division.

Internally, product line or divisional managers are often evaluated and rewarded as profit or investment centers. These product lines or divisions may not require external segment disclosure, but they may warrant internal disclosure. The goal of a good reward and control system is to assign responsibility for those items for which the manager has control (recall our related discussion in Chapter 13). These income reports, then, are prepared to eliminate costs assigned to the product or division that the manager cannot control as well as to overcome the problems associated with full-absorption costing.

Exhibit 23.14 illustrates LaGrande Beverage's income report on a divisional basis. Notice that there are many divisions of earnings, such as contribution margin (sales less variable costs), product margin (contribution margin less batch-related and product-sustaining overhead), and segment margin (product margin less facility-sustaining and other costs that are controllable by the manager).

EXHIBIT 23.14	Product Line Income Report			

LAGRANDE BEVERAGE
Product Line Income Report
For the Year Ended December 31, 1999
(In thousands)

	Segment 1	Segment 2	Segment 3	Company Total
Sales	$1,399,893	$1,234,394	$1,052,953	$3,687,240
Less unit costs:				
Direct materials	349,974	138,750	189,531	678,255
Direct labor	203,421	207,675	132,672	543,768
Unit-related overhead	5,898	270,571	39,801	316,270
Unit selling costs	87,493	61,470	59,178	208,141
Contribution margin	**$ 753,107**	**$ 555,928**	**$ 631,771**	**$1,940,806**
Less batch and product costs:				
Batch-related overhead	46,664	27,751	78,972	153,387
Product-sustaining overhead	146,937	27,796	236,913	411,646
Product margin	**$ 559,506**	**$ 500,381**	**$ 315,886**	**$1,375,773**
Less other controllable costs:				
Advertising	12,750	11,250	7,800	31,800
Market analysis	1,838	1,650	1,125	4,613
Segment margin	**$ 544,918**	**$ 487,481**	**$ 306,961**	**$1,339,360**
Less noncontrollable costs:				
Facility-sustaining costs				525,900
Other corporate overhead				391,650
Income from operations				**$ 421,810**

As Exhibit 23.14 shows, the segment margins of the three divisions are $544,918,000; $487,481,000; and $306,961,000, respectively. Also notice that other fixed costs are deducted from the total segment margin of the company, not from the segment margins of the respective product lines or divisions. In this case, facility-sustaining overhead and other corporate expenses are not allocated to the divisions because their respective managers cannot control these costs. Therefore, the income from operations of the company is not the sum of the segment margins. Rather, it is the sum of the segment margins less the costs that were not assigned to the divisions.

Finally, notice that these internal income reports, although based on absorption costing, do not use the comprehensive income concept used for external parties. That is, they do not reflect discontinued operations, cumulative accounting adjustments, or other comprehensive income items that are assumed to be beyond the control of product line or divisional managers.

If the division is evaluated as a profit center, the segment margins determined in the product-line income report are sufficient. However, if the division is evaluated as an investment center, it is responsible for assets as well as profits. In these cases, it is necessary to determine the assets for which the divisional manager is responsible. Then we can calculate the return on investment for the division as shown on the following page:

$$\frac{\text{Profit of the division}}{\text{Assets of the division}} = \text{Return on investment}$$

For example, assume that LaGrande Beverage has determined that the manager of Segment 1 is responsible for $5,000,000 of assets, while the managers of Segments 2 and 3 are responsible for $3,500,000 and $1,500,000 of assets respectively. The return on investment of each segment is determined as follows:

	Segment 1	Segment 2	Segment 3
Profit (segment margin)	$ 544,918	$ 487,481	$ 306,962
Assets	5,000,000	3,500,000	1,500,000
Return on investment	10.9%	13.9%	20.5%

Snack foods is a primary industry segment for PepsiCo.

Thus, although Segment 1 was the most profitable segment, Segment 3 generated the largest return on investment. Return on investment is a common measure of divisional performance because it reflects not only profits but also amounts that are invested in the division's operations.

We can calculate the return on investment for both of PepsiCo's identifiable segments. Recall that Note 17 (Exhibit 23.5) reports identifiable assets and operating profits of each segment. Using this information, we determine the return on investment for 1997 for the beverage division to be 11.4 percent ($1,114 million/$9,752 million), while the return on investment for the snack foods division is 24.2 percent ($1,695 million/$6,998 million). Thus it appears that the snack foods segment is more profitable than the beverage segment. However, financial statement users must be careful when comparing segments in this manner. Some segments require greater investments in assets and, therefore, may show a lower return on investment. Some segments may have older, more depreciated assets and, therefore, may show a higher return on investment. These are some of the issues involved when using return on investment as a measure of divisional performance. More advanced accounting and finance courses discuss additional issues involved in performance measurement.

SUMMARY

The income statement is vitally important to both external and internal users in order to evaluate a company's operating activities. It is important for users to understand the actual components of income presented as well as the limitations of the income statement itself. Internally, these limitations are often corrected by preparing more detailed income reports.

- Comprehensive income is reported to external users to provide them with a complete picture of the recurring operating activities of the company during the period as well as other nonowner changes in equity that occurred during the period.

- Discontinued operations, extraordinary items, and cumulative accounting adjustments are shown on the income statement after income from continuing operations. These items appear net of tax because income tax expense is based on income from continuing operations.

- Other comprehensive income items are shown, net of tax, after net income on the income statement. These items are not closed to retained earnings at the end of the accounting period.

- Earnings per share is shown on the income statement as a common-size measure of company performance. Companies often report diluted earnings per share, which indicates the decrease in earnings per share if additional shares were outstanding.

- Companies are also required to disclose certain segment information in the notes to the financial statements.

- The statement of retained earnings indicates the changes that occurred in the Retained Earnings account during the period due to net income or loss, cash and stock dividends, and prior period adjustments.

- Using full-absorption costing, income increases with increases in production because all production costs are assigned to inventory.

- Internally, different profit-reporting formats and product line income reports are often used to provide additional information for decision making.

KEY TERMS

comprehensive income Income that reflects all changes in owners' equity during the period except those resulting from investments by, or distributions to, owners and those resulting from errors made in previous periods

cost center A center that is responsible for controlling costs and providing a good or service in an efficient manner

cumulative accounting adjustments Modifications made to the accounting records that result from changes in accounting principles that occur when a company switches from one generally accepted method of accounting to another or when a company adopts a new accounting principle

diluted earnings per share Earnings per share that reflect the amount of decrease in earnings per share that would occur as a result of activities like conversions and the exercise of stock options

discontinued operations The result of a company selling or disposing of a segment of its business

earnings Income from continuing operations; consisting of revenues minus expenses and gains minus losses

earnings per share A common-size measure of a company's earnings performance; the reported net income of the company less preferred dividends for the period divided by the weighted-average number of common shares outstanding

extraordinary items Events that occurred during the accounting period that are both unusual and infrequent

investment center A center that is responsible for using assets in an effective and efficient manner to generate profits

prior period adjustment A correction of a previously undetected material error that affected the net income or loss from a previous accounting period

product line (divisional) income reports Specific-purpose internal reports designed to provide more detailed information than general-purpose income statements regarding the results of operations for a product line or company division

profit center A center that is responsible for making a profit; it must effectively generate revenues and efficiently control costs

revenue center A center that is responsible for generating revenues and promoting the company's products and services effectively

throughput accounting method A method of determining profits in which only direct materials are included in cost of goods sold and all other production costs are expensed as incurred

unit-variable accounting method A method of determining profits in which only costs that vary with the number of units produced are included in cost of goods sold and batch-related, product-sustaining, and facility-sustaining overhead costs are expensed as incurred

ANSWERS TO THE PAUSE & REFLECTS

p. 784, Often a company will discontinue a segment that is profitable in order to invest its resources in something else. For example, when PepsiCo spun off Pizza Hut, Kentucky Fried Chicken, and Taco Bell, it reinvested those resources in other segments of PepsiCo's operations.

p. 789, Based on the available information, it appears that PepsiCo does not have any preferred stock. If you take the net income on the 1997 income statement ($2,142 million) and divide it by the average shares outstanding—basic (1,528 million), you get earnings per share of $1.40.

Because this is the amount shown as income per share—basic, preferred dividends were $0. Because most preferred stock is cumulative, we can infer that PepsiCo has no preferred stock. (You can verify this by examining PepsiCo's balance sheet.)

p. 797, Both cost and revenue centers can be evaluated using variances such as those calculated in Chapter 13. In addition, nonfinancial performance measures such as quality and time measures are often used to evaluate cost and revenue centers.

QUESTIONS

1. Explain the difference between earnings and comprehensive income. Why is this important?

2. What are the two types of nonowner changes in equity? Why are they important?

3. Explain cumulative accounting adjustments. Why are they important?

4. Why are discontinued operations, extraordinary items, and cumulative accounting changes shown net of tax on the income statement?

5. Why are other comprehensive income items shown on the income statement? Why are they presented net of tax?

6. Why is the income (loss) from discontinued operations shown separately from the gain (loss) on disposal of a segment? Where is this information usually found? Why?

7. Is a Georgia company's loss from a tornado an extraordinary item? Why or why not?

8. When a company changes its method of accounting for inventories from FIFO to LIFO, does it restate the prior years' financial statements? Why or why not?

9. What is earnings per share and how can it be diluted?

10. What is a prior period adjustment and why is it important?

11. Why is a prior period adjustment shown net of tax?

12. Assume a company with a 45 percent tax rate forgot to record $100,000 of expenses in 1999. How would this error be shown on the 2000 retained earnings statement?

13. Explain why the historical cost and conservatism concepts are important to income statement users.

14. Explain how a company can increase net income by increasing production even though sales remain the same.

15. Explain how cost, revenue, profit, and investment centers, respectively, are evaluated.

16. Explain the advantages of a product line income report for internal users. Do you think this information would be useful for external users? Why or why not?

17. Explain how production and nonproduction costs are treated using absorption costing.

18. Explain how unit-variable and nonvariable costs are treated using unit-variable accounting method.

19. Explain how direct materials and other operating costs are treated using throughput accounting method.

20. If a company produces more units than it sells in its first year of operations which method (absorption, unit-variable, or throughput) reports the highest profit? Why?

EXERCISES

E 23.1
LO 1

The accounts below are from the André Company. Show how this information is presented on a multistep income statement and explain the benefits of this format.

Cost of goods sold	$110,000
Sales	405,000
Selling expenses	45,000
Administrative expenses	35,000
Depreciation expense	20,000
Loss on sale of equipment	8,000
Sales returns	10,000

E 23.2
LO 1

Refer to E 23.1. Chapter 10 illustrated a single-step income statement where total revenues were subtracted from total expenses to determine net income. Show how the information in E 23.1 is presented on a single-step income statement and explain the benefits of this format.

E 23.3

LO 1 LO 2

The Cecil Corporation has the following information available on December 31, 1999. The tax rate is 40 percent. Show how this information is presented to external users in a multistep format.

Interest expense	$ 36,000
Sales salaries	228,000
Rental revenue	8,000
Accounts receivable	101,000
Administrative salaries	300,000
Sales	2,483,000
Depreciation (40% selling, 60% administrative)	130,000
Dividends paid	48,000
Cost of goods sold	841,000
Sales returns and allowances	45,000
Loss due to meteor damage	700,000
Gain on sale of equipment	79,000

E 23.4

LO 2

Metzler's Sporting Goods decided to sell its children's toy division during 1999. The following relevant information is available. Use this information to determine the income (loss) from operations of the division and the income (loss) upon disposal of the division.

Loss from operations of toy division	$900,000
Gain on disposal of toy division	600,000
Effective tax rate	40%

E 23.5

LO 2

Refer to E 23.4. How does your answer change if the toy division showed a profit from operations of $900,000 and if Metzler experiences a loss on disposal of $600,000? Show your calculations.

E 23.6

LO 2

The Specialty Stores Corporation calculated its income before taxes and the extraordinary loss but wants you to advise it on how to present this information to external users. Determine the extraordinary loss, net of tax; calculate the net income for the year; and explain in a brief memo to the owners how to present this information on the income statement.

Earnings before income taxes and extraordinary items	$950,000
Tax rate	30%
Extraordinary loss due to earthquake in Kansas	$250,000

E 23.7

LO 2

Schmelner Corporation repurchased $1,000,000 of its 12 percent interest, subordinated debenture bonds during 1999 and experienced an extraordinary gain on the repurchase of $300,000. Schmelner's income tax rate is 45 percent. What is the extraordinary gain (loss) shown on the income statement for 1999? Show your calculations.

E 23.8

LO 3

Dody, Inc., has the following available-for-sale securities in its portfolio at the end of 2000. Dody's tax rate is 25 percent. How would this information be reported on Dody's 2000 income statement?

	Cost	Market Value
Common stocks	$456,900	$504,000
Preferred stocks	324,560	321,450
Bonds	125,000	150,000

E 23.9

LO 3

Schneider Enterprises has determined that the cost of its available-for-sale securities exceeds the market value by $80,000. If Schneider is subject to a 30 percent tax rate, how is the information presented on the income statement?

E 23.10

LO 2

Griff Corporation is going to change from the double-declining-balance method of depreciation to straight-line depreciation in 2001. The differences in the two depreciation methods for the years affected are presented below. The tax rate is 30 percent. Determine the cumulative accounting change. What information should Griff disclose in the notes to its financial statements?

Year	Double-Declining-Balance Depreciation	Straight-Line Depreciation
1996	$400,000	$200,000
1997	360,000	200,000
1998	324,000	200,000
1999	291,600	200,000
2000	262,440	200,000

E 23.11
LO 2

Castillon Company has $10,000,000 of equipment with a $500,000 salvage value and a 10-year life. The equipment was purchased four years ago and has been depreciated using straight-line depreciation. Castillon plans to switch to the double-declining-balance depreciation method this year. The income tax rate is 45 percent. Determine the cumulative accounting change. What information should Castillon disclose in the notes to its financial statements?

E 23.12
LO 4

Haigh Company has 500,000 shares of common stock issued and 250,000 shares of common stock outstanding. Determine the earnings per share for 1999 if its net income is $100,000.

E 23.13
LO 4

Hipsher Corporation has 50,000 shares of common stock outstanding and 10,000 shares of $100 par value, 6 percent preferred stock outstanding. Determine the earnings per share for 1999 if net income is $150,000.

E 23.14
LO 4

Shupick Enterprises had 200,000 shares of common stock outstanding on January 1, 2000, and issued an additional 50,000 shares on March 1, 2000. Determine the earnings per share for 2000 if net income was $225,000.

E 23.15
LO 4

Potter Company had 200,000 shares of common stock outstanding on January 1, 1999, and repurchased 60,000 shares of common stock on March 31, 1999. Determine the earnings per share for 1999 if net income was $350,000.

E 23.16
LO 5

In 1999 Politis Corporation failed to record depreciation expense of $30,000. The accountant discovered this error in 2000. Politis Corporation is subject to a 40 percent income tax rate. What is the effect of this error on the 2000 statement of retained earnings? What other accounts must be corrected in Politis Corporation's accounting records? Explain.

E 23.17
LO 5

In 2000 Kirkwood Company, which is subject to a 35 percent tax rate, recognized interest revenue of $15,000. On January 16, 2001, the accountant discovered that the correct amount of interest revenue for 2000 was $25,000. What is the effect of this error on the 2001 statement of retained earnings? What other accounts must be corrected in Kirkwood Company's accounting records? Explain.

E 23.18
LO 6

Lopez, Inc., evaluates its divisions as investment centers. The sales, income, and assets of its three divisions are shown below. Calculate return on investment for each division. Which division is best?

	Division A	Division B	Division C
Sales	$1,000,000	$2,350,000	$4,000,000
Income	100,000	157,000	200,000
Assets	500,000	8,900,000	6,000,000

E 23.19
LO 6

Davis Clothing Store has three segments: Women's Wear, Men's Wear, and Children's Wear. The sales, cost of goods sold, operating expenses, and identifiable assets of these segments are shown below. Determine the return on investment of each segment.

	Women's Wear	Men's Wear	Children's Wear
Sales	$4,000,000	$2,500,000	$8,000,000
Cost of goods sold	1,000,000	1,250,000	3,200,000
Operating expenses	200,000	200,000	200,000
Assets	500,000	400,000	800,000

E 23.20
LO 6

Refer to E 23.19. Assume the operating expenses are allocated from corporate headquarters and are not controllable by the segment managers. Determine the return on investment of each segment.

E 23.21
LO 7

Peterson Enterprises, in its first year of operations, reported the following information:

Selling price per unit	$125
Direct materials per unit	5
Direct labor per unit	1
Unit-related overhead per unit	6
Selling cost per unit	2
Batch-related overhead for the year	$500,000
Facility-sustaining overhead for the year	800,000
Fixed administrative cost for the year	650,000
Units produced	20,000
Units sold	15,000

What is Peterson's absorption costing gross margin and profit?

E23.22
LO 7

Refer to E23.21. What is Peterson's unit-variable contribution margin and profit?

E23.23
LO 7

Refer to E23.21. What is Peterson's throughput margin and profit?

E23.24
LO 7

Refer to E23.21 through E23.23. What is Peterson's ending inventory using absorption, unit-variable, and throughput accounting?

PROBLEMS

P 23.1
LO 1   LO 2   LO 4   LO 5

Thalhammer Equipment Corporation provided the following relevant information for its fiscal year ending September 30, 2000:

Sales	$2,280,000
Cost of goods sold	1,231,600
Sales returns	41,000
Depreciation on sales equipment	6,500
Sales commissions	103,000
Sales salaries	62,300
Administrative salaries	98,200
Depreciation on office equipment	8,500
Bond interest expense	22,000
Selling expenses	168,900
Administrative expense	134,600
Gain on disposal of marine products division	280,000
Marine products division operating income	100,000
Dividend income	4,000
Entertainment expense	23,100
Dividends declared on preferred stock	14,000

On October 1, 1999, Thalhammer's Retained Earnings balance was $238,790. The tax rate for Thalhammer Equipment Corporation is 30 percent. There are 85,000 shares of common stock outstanding. In addition, in 2000 the company discovered that a $10,000 piece of equipment with a five-year useful life was expensed when purchased on October 2, 1998. Thalhammer uses straight-line depreciation.

Required

a. Prepare a multistep income statement for fiscal 2000.
b. Calculate the earnings per share for 2000.
c. Prepare a statement of retained earnings for fiscal 2000.

P 23.2
LO 1   LO 2

The income statement below was prepared by Bob's Bookkeeping Service for the Atlas Corporation:

ATLAS CORPORATION
Income Statement
At December 31, 1999

Sales	$1,250,000
Interest income	5,000
Less sales returns	9,000
Net sales	$1,246,000
Cost of goods sold	740,000
Gross margin	$ 506,000
Gain on sale of equipment	40,000
Total revenue inflows	$ 546,000
Administrative expenses	120,000
Selling expenses	45,000
Loss on sale of land	10,000
Operating income	$ 371,000
Interest expense	9,000
Extraordinary loss on building, net	20,000
Income from continuing operations	$ 342,000
Tax expense	102,600
Net income	$ 239,400

a. Make a list of all the errors found on this income statement and briefly describe what is wrong.

b. Prepare a correct multistep income statement for Atlas Corporation.

P 23.3

LO 1   LO 2   LO 3   LO 4

Refer to the income statement of Anheuser-Busch.

Required

a. What was the income from operations during the year?
b. What was the income from continuing operations during the year?
c. What was the net income?
d. Did the company discontinue any operations during the year? If so, what were they?
e. Did the company experience any extraordinary events during the year? If so, what were they?
f. Did the company have a cumulative accounting change during the year? If so, what was the change?
g. What were the earnings per share for the year?
h. Based on the income statement, would you advise someone to invest in Anheuser-Busch? Why or why not?

P 23.4

LO 1   LO 2   LO 3   LO 4

Refer to the income statement of the Walt Disney Company.

Required

a. What was the income from operations during the year?
b. What was the income from continuing operations during the year?
c. What was the net income?
d. Did Disney discontinue any operations during the year? If so, what were they?
e. Did Disney experience any extraordinary events during the year? If so, what were they?
f. Did Disney have a cumulative accounting change during the year? If so, what was the change?
g. What were the earnings per share for the year?
h. Based on the income statement, would you advise someone to invest in Disney? Why or why not?

P 23.5

LO 5

Refer to the consolidated statement of common shareholders' equity of the Walt Disney Company.

Required

a. How is this statement different from a statement of retained earnings?
b. Did the company declare any dividends during the year? If so, what were they?
c. Did the company report any prior period adjustments? If so, what were they?

P 23.6

LO 7

Devault Company began operations in 1999. Its operating information is presented below:

Selling price per unit	$200
Direct materials cost per unit	40
Direct labor cost per unit	10
Unit-related overhead per unit	15
Unit selling cost	5
Batch-related overhead per year	$ 55,000
Product-sustaining overhead per year	125,000
Facility-sustaining overhead per year	850,000
Fixed selling and administrative costs	400,000
Units produced	50,000
Units sold	40,000

Required

a. Using absorption accounting, determine Devault's gross margin and profit for the year.
b. Using unit-variable accounting, determine Devault's contribution margin and profit for the year.
c. Using throughput accounting, determine Devault's throughput margin and profit for the year.
d. Determine the differences in ending inventory using absorption, unit-variable, and throughput costing.

P 23.7

LO 6   LO 8

College Publishers produces three textbooks for various college campuses: *Introductory Marketing,* *Introductory Management,* and *Introductory Accounting.* Each book sells for $60. The manager of College Publishers is concerned that *Introductory Marketing* appears to be losing money. The most recent income report is shown on the next page:

	Marketing	Management	Accounting	Total
Sales	$ 400,000	$500,000	$900,000	$1,800,000
Less expenses:				
Printing	160,000	200,000	360,000	720,000
Commissions	40,000	50,000	90,000	180,000
Warehousing	48,000	48,000	48,000	144,000
Salaries	34,000	34,000	34,000	102,000
Depreciation 1	36,000	36,000	36,000	108,000
Depreciation 2	24,000	24,000	24,000	72,000
Miscellaneous	34,000	34,000	34,000	102,000
Advertising	8,000	8,000	8,000	24,000
Shipping	48,000	60,000	108,000	216,000
Net income (loss)	$ (32,000)	$ 6,000	$158,000	$ 132,000

An analysis of the records reveals that printing, commissions, and shipping costs are traced directly to the product lines, while the remaining costs are allocated equally to the three product lines. Further analysis reveals the following:

1. The warehouse consists of 60,000 square feet of which 30,000 square feet are used for accounting books, 16,000 are used for management, and the remaining square feet are used to house marketing texts.
2. Depreciation 1 is depreciation on production equipment. During the past year, the production equipment operated a total of 2,500 hours, of which 1,250 hours were used to produce accounting texts, 750 hours were used for management texts, and 500 hours were used to produce marketing texts.
3. Depreciation 2, salaries, advertising, and miscellaneous costs cannot be traced to any particular product line.
4. College Publishers estimates that its investments in its introductory books are $50,000, $100,000, and $80,000, respectively, for *Introductory Marketing, Introductory Management,* and *Introductory Accounting.*

Required a. Prepare a product line income report.
b. Should College Publishers drop the marketing text? Why or why not?

P 23.8
LO 8

Refer to P 23.7. Assume that management decides to drop the marketing text.

Required a. Determine the net income of the company.
b. Determine the product margins of the accounting and management texts.
c. Analyze your results.

P 23.9
LO 7

Vinson Products produces specialty alarm clocks that it sells to novelty stores throughout the mid-Atlantic. During the current period, the following results were obtained:

Sales	650,000 clocks at $40
Cost of goods manufactured	700,000 clocks at $28
Variable selling cost	650,000 clocks at $ 9
Fixed selling and administrative costs	$645,000
Cost of goods manufactured consists of:	
Direct materials	$ 5
Direct labor	2
Unit-related overhead	8
Other nonvariable overhead	13
	$28

Other nonvariable overhead consists of depreciation on machinery and buildings, insurance, and other items that do not vary with the number of clocks produced during the period. The unit cost is calculated by dividing the total nonvariable overhead for the period by the number of clocks produced in the period as shown below:

$$\frac{\$9,100,000}{700,000} = \$13 \text{ per clock}$$

Required a. Determine the profit for the period using full-absorption accounting.
b. Determine the profit for the period using unit-variable accounting.
c. Determine the profit for the period using throughput accounting.

d. Determine the cost of ending inventory using each of the accounting methods in parts (a) through (c).

P 23.10

LO 1 LO 2 LO 3

Use the following information (in millions) to determine Agassi's comprehensive income:

Interest expense	$ 221.4
Interest income	3.3
Marketing expense	2,370.3
Administrative expense	565.0
Cost of goods sold	7,784.4
Sales	13,733.5
Sales discounts	1,679.7
Cumulative effect of accounting change loss, net of tax	76.7
Extraordinary gain, net of tax	5.6
Dividend income	2.1
Income taxes	391.4
Unrealized gain on available-for-sale securities, net of tax	1.0
Discontinued operations, loss net of tax	2.3

CASES

C 23.1

LO 1 LO 2 LO 3

LO 4 LO 5

Use the annual report you obtained in Chapter 1 to answer the following questions:
a. What was the income from operations during the year?
b. What was the income from continuing operations during the year?
c. What was the net income for the year?
d. Did the company discontinue any operations during the year? If so, what were they?
e. Did the company experience any extraordinary events during the year? If so, what were they?
f. Did the company have a cumulative accounting change during the year? If so, what was the change?
g. Did the company show any "other comprehensive income items"? If so, what were they?
h. What were the earnings per share for the year?
i. Did the company declare any dividends during the year? If so, what were they?
j. Did the company report any prior period adjustments? If so, what were they?
k. Based on this information, would you advise someone to invest in this company? Why or why not?

C 23.2

LO 2 LO 5

By consulting NEXIS, Disclosure, or a similar annual report database, determine the following:
a. How many companies reported discontinued operations during the period?
b. Of the companies that reported discontinued operations, did they report gains or losses?
c. How many companies reported extraordinary items during the period?
d. Of the companies that reported extraordinary items, did they report gains or losses?
e. How many companies reported cumulative accounting changes?
f. Of the companies that reported cumulative accounting changes, what were the two most common changes reported?
g. Of the companies that reported cumulative accounting changes, did the changes result in gains or losses?
h. How many companies reported a loss per share?
i. How many companies declared both common and preferred stock dividends during the period?
j. How many companies reported prior period adjustments during the period?
k. How many companies reported other comprehensive income?

CRITICAL THINKING

CT 23.1

LO 7

In the first year of operations, Naivete Company experienced a $500,000 net loss even though it sold 250,000 units. Management was very concerned about this outcome, so it hired an efficiency expert to turn the company's operations around. The efficiency expert guaranteed the company a profitable second year. The expert stressed, "I agree to work for you for one year at no salary. At the end of the year, if your net income is not at least $500,000, you pay me nothing. If your income is $500,000 or more, you pay me $500,000."

Naivete's income statement for the first year of operations is shown below:

Sales (250,000 units at $16)		$4,000,000
Cost of goods sold:		
Beginning inventory	$ –0–	
Cost of goods manufactured	3,750,000	
Cost of goods available	$3,750,000	
Ending inventory	–0–	3,750,000
Gross margin		$ 250,000
Selling and administrative expenses		750,000
Net loss		$ (500,000)

Cost of goods manufactured is composed of the following:

Direct materials	$ 750,000
Direct labor	500,000
Unit-related overhead	1,000,000
Other nonunit related overhead	1,500,000
	$3,750,000

In the second year of operations, the same number of units were sold, but the company produced 750,000 units. The selling price and costs remained constant, which resulted in the following income statement:

Sales (250,000 units at $16)		$4,000,000
Cost of goods sold:		
Beginning inventory	$ –0–	
Cost of goods manufactured	8,250,000	
Cost of goods available	$8,250,000	
Ending inventory	5,500,000	2,750,000
Gross margin		$1,250,000
Selling and administrative expenses		750,000
Income before bonus		$ 500,000
Bonus		500,000
Net income		$ –0–

Required Explain to the managers of Naivete Company, in detail, what happened to operations in the second year.

CT 23.2
LO 7

Barrett, Inc., produced 175,000 units and prepared the following income report using absorption costing:

Sales (100,000 units)		$15,000,000
Less cost of goods sold:		
Direct materials	$1,200,000	
Direct labor	300,000	
Unit-related overhead	900,000	
Other overhead	4,000,000	6,400,000
Gross margin		$ 8,600,000
Less other operating costs:		
Variable selling and administrative costs		600,000
Fixed selling and administrative costs		2,000,000
Profit		$ 6,000,000

Required
 a. Determine Barrett's profit using unit-variable costing.
 b. Determine Barrett's profit using throughput costing.
 c. Which method do you think presents the most realistic picture of current earnings? Why?

ETHICAL CHALLENGES

EC 23.1
LO 1 LO 4

Earnings management is a common practice. Some argue that it is unethical, if not illegal, while others argue that earnings management is necessary to avoid large fluctuations in income that could confuse stockholders. Perform library research on this subject and write a two- to three-page paper supporting or refuting the practice of earnings management.

EC 23.2
LO 3

The practice of including unrealized gains and losses on debt and equity securities on the income statement is relatively new. Some argue that unrealized gains and losses are misleading to external users because they have not been incurred and do not follow historical cost. Others argue that unrealized gains and losses support the FASB's *Concepts Statements* (Chapter 1). Do you think unrealized gains and losses should be included on the income statement? Do you think unrealized gains and losses should be reported for other assets such as inventory and property, plant, and equipment? Why or why not?

COMPUTER APPLICATIONS

CA 23.1
LO 1   LO 4   LO 5

The following list of items (accounts) was obtained from an annual report of Braun's Fashions Corporation:

Depreciation and amortization	$ 2,052,707
Interest expense	210,678
Merchandise, buying, and occupancy expenses	56,406,679
Provision for income taxes	1,615,931
Selling, publicity, and administrative expenses	18,679,253
Net sales	81,301,766

The following additional information is available:
1. The beginning balance of Retained Earnings was a deficit of $(14,536,277).
2. Braun's has 3,664,625 common shares outstanding.
3. No dividends were declared during the period.

Required

Use a computer spreadsheet.
a. Determine net income.
b. Determine the ending balance of Retained Earnings.
c. Determine the earnings per share.
d. Assume that in the following year, net sales were 15 percent greater, merchandise and taxes remained at the same percentage rate, and all other expenses remained at the same dollar amount. What would be the amount of net income for this period?
e. Refer to part (*d*). What would be the amount of the ending Retained Earnings balance in this period?

CA 23.2
LO 4

Use a computer spreadsheet program to determine earnings per share in each of the following independent situations. Assume a calendar year-end in each situation.
a. Net income is $500,000. There are 250,000 shares of common stock and 50,000 shares of $10 par, 8 percent preferred stock outstanding.
b. Net income is $600,000. There were 200,000 shares of common stock outstanding on January 1. On March 31, 100,000 additional shares were issued. On September 1, 50,000 additional shares were issued.
c. Net income is $250,000. There were 300,000 shares of common stock outstanding on January 1. On July 31, 50,000 shares of common stock were repurchased and held as treasury stock.
d. Net income is $425,000. There were 200,000 shares of common stock and 100,000 shares of $100 par, 6 percent preferred stock outstanding on January 1. On May 1, 60,000 shares of common stock were issued. On October 31, 10,000 shares of common stock were issued.

CA 23.3
LO 1   LO 2   LO 3
LO 4   LO 5

In this chapter we used PepsiCo's fiscal 1997 income statement and statement of shareholders' equity. Go to PepsiCo's Web site and locate its most recent financial information. Answer the following questions:
a. What is PepsiCo's current net sales?
b. What is PepsiCo's current operating profit?
c. What is PepsiCo's current net income?
d. What is PepsiCo's current income per share and diluted income per share?
e. What item(s) does PepsiCo report as other comprehensive income and where are they reported?
f. What is the balance in retained earnings?

PART SEVEN

YOU ARE HERE

Chapter 24 explores the balance sheet, (the statement of financial position). We look at the GAAP requirements for the balance sheet and why classification on the balance sheet is important. Chapter 24 also discusses the audit report and what it does and does not tell financial statement users. Then, we consider internal reporting issues. You must understand Chapters 1–23 before studying Chapter 24.

LEARNING OBJECTIVES

LO 1 Explain the implications of classifying assets and liabilities as short term or long term.

LO 2 Describe the proper classifications of assets, liabilities, and equity items on the balance sheet.

LO 3 Describe some of the additional financial disclosures beyond the financial statements themselves.

Firm Performance: Financial Position

QUAKER OATS
www.quakeroats.com

On December 31, 1997, Quaker Oats had more than $2,697 billion in assets. Those assets were located around the world, as were the holders of the 168 million shares of Quaker's common stock. Quaker's assets represent the company's resources available to generate future profits. The company's liabilities and owners' equity represent the claims on those assets and accumulated profits.

By carefully examining Quaker's balance sheet, readers can combine the information presented with other available information to predict how the company will perform over the next few years. For example, balance sheets issued for 1995 and 1996 included a $1.7 billion investment in Snapple, a tea and fruit-beverage company, that Quaker purchased in November 1994. Quaker saw this investment as an opportunity to enhance its return on investment

because it felt that Snapple complemented its very successful sports drink, Gatorade. Things didn't work out for Quaker and sales of Snapple declined during the time that Quaker owned it. In May 1997 Quaker sold Snapple for $300 million, suffering a $1.4 billion loss. When Quaker bought Snapple, most of the purchase price was goodwill, an intangible asset shown on the balance sheet. In 1997 the Snapple sale caused Quaker's intangible assets to drop from $2,237.2 million to $350.5 million. The Snapple ordeal seriously affected Quaker's profitability and led to the resignations of William Smithburg, chairman and CEO, and Phillip Marineau, former president.

Not only should statement readers examine the numbers on the balance sheet, but they also should understand the nature of the assets that underlie those numbers in order to appreciate the performance potential they represent. The balance sheet, along with its related disclosures, provides a great deal of information about the resources a company has and where it might use future operating profits. Understanding the nature of those resources helps to predict how profitable the company might be, how easily the company can pay its debts, and how likely stockholders are to receive dividends.

The balance sheet (the statement of financial position) reports the amount and type of assets the firm controls and the claims the owners and creditors have on those assets on the last day of a reporting period. This financial statement is an important means of communication with parties outside the business.

In this chapter, the emphasis is on the external reporting rules embodied in generally accepted accounting principles as they apply to a company's reporting practices. While we have described these rules throughout the book, here we provide a comprehensive overview of the balance sheet and expand upon previous discussions of the reporting rules for balance sheet items. In addition, we discuss other disclosures required to communicate transactions and events of the business to external stakeholders.

WHAT DOES FINANCIAL POSITION TELL US?

We know that a company's financial position is the summary of the relationship between its assets and the claims of its creditors, owners, and other suppliers of goods and services to those assets at a certain point in time. The concept of financial position conveys information about the nature of the company's resources and obligations, its ability to meet its obligations, and its prospects for future profitability. Measuring financial position differs from measuring profitability, as discussed in Chapter 23, because firms measure financial position at a point in time, while they measure profit over a period of time.

How does financial position reveal future profit potential? Assets, reported as part of financial position, are the economic resources that the company will have in the future to operate and generate future profits. Information about the quantities and types of assets a company has communicates the profit potential of the company. In addition, information about the claims on those assets by owners, creditors, and others reveals how the firm might use its future profits. Possible uses could include providing a return to creditors in the form of interest, repaying amounts borrowed from creditors, or, for owners, either receiving a return in the form of dividends or reinvesting in additional assets.

In earlier chapters, we explained that the principal role of financial statements is to communicate economic information about the company to outside parties like creditors and investors. Management and other insiders, too, use financial statements, but, in addition, they use many other sources of information about the company. Some of these other sources are internal reports, which differ from published financial statements in two important ways: (1) they are more detailed and contain proprietary information that companies would prefer that competitors not know, and (2) they are not constrained by GAAP that apply to asset valuation and cost allocation methods used in determining product costs.

The simplest balance sheet consists of the same number reported twice, once for total assets and once for total liabilities and owners' equity. A company with $100 million in assets, $65 million in liabilities, and $35 million in owners' equity would report a balance sheet with $100 million for both total assets and the total of liabilities and owners' equity. That type of balance sheet, however, does not reveal meaningful information about a company's financial position. At the other extreme, consider a balance sheet that lists every permanent account found in a company's general ledger. For most major manufacturers like Quaker Oats, this could involve more than 2,000 accounts, which would make such a detailed type of presentation cumbersome for the readers of the statement. However, the users of financial statements who take the time to analyze such detailed content on the balance sheet could learn more company information than management is required, or might prefer, to reveal. A properly classified balance sheet fits somewhere between these two extremes. It aggregates related accounts into line items such as those shown on the balance sheet of Quaker Oats in Exhibit 24.1.

This chapter begins by describing the way that companies organize assets, liabilities, and equity accounts on the balance sheet, and it includes other disclosures required by GAAP. Then it discusses other types of information included in the annual reports of corporations. The chapter concludes with a discussion of the different approaches to asset valuation that companies use on their internal balance sheets.

EXHIBIT 24.1 Quaker Oats' Balance Sheet

Consolidated Balance Sheets

December 31	1997	1996
Assets		
Current Assets		
Cash and cash equivalents	$ 84.2	$ 110.5
Trade accounts receivable – net of allowances	305.7	294.9
Inventories		
Finished goods	172.6	181.8
Grains and raw materials	59.0	62.1
Packaging materials and supplies	24.5	31.0
Total inventories	256.1	274.9
Other current assets	487.0	209.4
Total Current Assets	1,133.0	889.7
Property, Plant and Equipment		
Land	29.1	29.6
Buildings and improvements	417.2	389.5
Machinery and equipment	1,466.8	1,524.2
Property, plant and equipment	1,913.1	1,943.3
Less accumulated depreciation	748.4	742.6
Property – Net	1,164.7	1,200.7
Intangible Assets – Net of Amortization	350.5	2,237.2
Other Assets	48.8	66.8
Total Assets	$2,697.0	$4,394.4

EXHIBIT **24.1** *(Continued)*

Dollars in Millions

December 31	1997	1996
Liabilities and Shareholders' Equity		
Current Liabilities		
Short-term debt	$ 61.0	$ 517.0
Current portion of long-term debt	108.4	51.1
Trade accounts payable	191.3	210.2
Accrued payroll, benefits and bonus	132.3	111.3
Accrued advertising and merchandising	123.0	130.2
Income taxes payable	73.8	42.4
Other accrued liabilities	255.9	292.5
Total Current Liabilities	945.7	1,354.7
Long-term Debt	887.6	993.5
Other Liabilities	578.9	558.9
Deferred Income Taxes	36.3	238.4
Preferred Stock, Series B, no par value, authorized 1,750,000 shares; issued 1,282,051 of $5.46 cumulative convertible shares (liquidating preference of $78 per share)	100.0	100.0
Deferred Compensation	(57.2)	(64.9)
Treasury Preferred Stock, at cost, 245,147 and 187,810 shares, respectively	(22.3)	(16.1)
Common Shareholders' Equity		
Common stock, $5 par value, authorized 400 million shares	840.0	840.0
Additional paid-in capital	29.0	—
Reinvested earnings	431.0	1,521.3
Cumulative translation adjustment	(82.4)	(68.2)
Deferred compensation	(91.0)	(103.4)
Treasury common stock, at cost	(898.6)	(959.8)
Total Common Shareholders' Equity	228.0	1,229.9
Total Liabilities and Shareholders' Equity	$2,697.0	$4,394.4

WHAT DOES "CURRENT" TELL THE FINANCIAL STATEMENT READER ABOUT AN ITEM?

LO 1

Amounts appearing on a balance sheet are intended to provide statement users with enough information to make good assessments of the firm's financial position without revealing more about the operations of the business than the company believes it should. One important assessment that external stakeholders make, particularly creditors, is the status of a company's short-term liquidity. That is, how likely is the company to pay its obligations for the next year? Classifying assets and liabilities as current and noncurrent helps to answer that question.

A firm reflects its short-term liquidity and solvency on the balance sheet by the relationship of its current assets to its current liabilities. Recall that *liquidity* refers to the time required for a firm to convert its assets to cash, and *solvency* is simply the ability to meet obligations when they are due.

You already know that current assets include cash and other assets a firm expects to convert into cash, sell, or use in one year or in the business's operating cycle, whichever is longer. Also recall that the operating cycle is the length of time it takes to (1) invest cash in the acquisition or production of inventory, (2) sell the inventory, and (3) collect the cash from the sale.

Current liabilities are obligations that will become due in one year or within the operating cycle and will be paid with current assets or replaced with another current liability. Note that this definition includes not only the element of time, but also the means by which the firm will liquidate the debt. If a liability is due within one year and management intends to pay for it with noncurrent assets or refinance it with some form of long-term debt, the liability would be considered long term. Thus obligations due within one year may be classified as long term, depending on the means management intends to liquidate the debt. For example, the classification of available-for-sale securities as either long or short term depends on whether management intends to sell the securities within the coming fiscal year. It is a violation of GAAP for management of a firm to reclassify marketable securities held as long-term investments as available-for-sale securities, if it does not intend to sell the securities in the coming fiscal year. Such a reclassification would mislead statement readers because it would increase the firm's current assets, and, therefore, falsely make the firm appear to be more liquid than it actually is.

The decision to classify a liability as either short term or long term also affects how investors and creditors perceive the solvency of the firm. Classification of liabilities may seem straightforward, but managers must exercise care when doing this. For example, firms often sign one-year notes knowing that at the end of the year they will pay all of the accrued interest, but only part of the note's principal, and will then refinance the unpaid balance with another one-year note. To illustrate, assume that on June 30, 2000, Quaker Oats gives a one-year, $500 million, 10 percent note to the Minneapolis National Bank. Both Quaker Oats and the bank are aware that Quaker Oats does not intend to pay off the entire note at the end of one year. Instead, Quaker Oats intends to pay $175 million of the $500 million due, and the bank expects to accept another one-year note. The $175 million will cover the $50 million accrued interest payable ($500 million at 10 percent) and will reduce the principal of the note to $375 million ($500 million less $125 million).

Should management classify all or part of this note as a short- or long-term liability on Quaker Oats' December 31, 2000, balance sheet? If Quaker Oats can perform as intended, then it would classify $125 million of the note as short term and $375 million as long term on the December 31, 2000, balance sheet. This classification is based on the substance of the transaction, not on its form. That is, the transaction's form indicates that the company will repay this debt within one year, which would imply that Quaker should classify the debt as short term. However, management's intention to repay the debt in more than one year using a series of one-year notes overrides the consideration of the form of the note and determines the substance of the transaction. Therefore, Quaker should classify the note as long term. If there is a doubt about Quaker Oats' ability to refinance the note, management should classify the entire note as a current liability.

Proper classification of current items also affects the assessment of short-term solvency ratios, such as the current and quick ratios (explained in Chapter 12). Assume that before Quaker Oats borrowed the $500 million by issuing the note, total current assets were $1,257 million and current liabilities were $1,209 million. Thus, before the loan, the current ratio was 1.04 ($1,257/$1,209).

If management classifies $125 million as a current liability and $375 million of the note as a long-term liability, current liabilities would then total $1,334 ($1,209 + $125) million. The current ratio would increase to 1.32 due to both the $500 million received in cash, which increases current assets to $1,757 million, and the $125 million in additional current liabilities ($1,757/$1,334). However, if the company classified the entire note as current, total current liabilities would be $1,709 million, and the current ratio would decrease slightly from its initial position to 1.03 ($1,757/$1,709). Thus the proper classification of the note is an effective means to communicate management's intent regarding conversion of assets or debt payment to outsiders who are assessing the short-term cash flows of the firm.

Management's decision to classify assets and liabilities as long term or short term is subjective. Keep in mind that a firm's management realizes that reporting more assets as current and classifying liabilities as long term rather than short term enhances the appearance of the firm's liquidity and solvency. Thus statement readers must consider the implications of such management decisions regarding the classification of current assets and liabilities as they study a firm's balance sheet.

Classifying assets and liabilities as current and noncurrent is one way to classify assets. We describe other classifications that communicate information to external stakeholders next.

IS THERE INFORMATION TO BE GAINED FROM BALANCE SHEET CLASSIFICATIONS?

LO 2

Those who use financial statements as their source of information about companies want to know more than the firm's liquidity and short-term solvency. They also want to know useful information about the nature of the firm's assets and its capital structure. One way accountants provide this information is by summarizing the accounts and recommending appropriate account classifications. See Exhibit 24.2 for the most common currently used balance sheet classifications.

Firms are not required to use these specific classifications and may use alternatives to make the balance sheet more descriptive, as noted previously when discussing management's classification of assets and liabilities. Next we describe each of the major asset classifications and the related additional disclosures.

EXHIBIT 24.2	Balance Sheet Classifications		
Assets =	**Liabilities** +		**Stockholders' Equity**
Current assets	Current liabilities		Contributed capital
Investments	Long-term debt		Donated capital
Property, plant, and equipment	Other long-term liabilities		Valuation capital*
Intangible assets			Retained earnings
Other assets			

*These terms are discussed more completely later in the chapter.

ASSETS

Companies classify assets according to their purpose and /or useful life. Thus, most companies use 5 classifications: (1) current assets, (2) investments, (3) property, plant, and equipment, (4) intangible assets, and (5) other assets.

Current Assets

Asset classifications are listed on properly classified balance sheets in order of their liquidity, which is how quickly the firm will convert them to cash or consume them as part of operations. Assets found within the current asset classification are listed in the order of their liquidity, too. They include cash, short-term investments in marketable securities, accounts and notes receivable, inventory, and prepaid expenses.

Cash Companies carry cash on the balance sheet at its stated value, assuming it is readily available to meet any current obligation. Companies should not classify as cash any deposits that are restricted for a particular use. For example, some banks require that a

PAUSE & REFLECT

When a check marked *NSF* (not sufficient funds) is returned by the bank to the company that deposited it, should the company classify the check as cash? If not cash, where should it classify this check? Do returned NSF checks belong on the balance sheet at all?
(answer on page 837)

NSF checks are returned to the depositor because the balance in the payor's account was lower than the amount of the check.

company borrowing from the bank maintain a compensating balance in a checking account at the bank. A **compensating balance** is a minimum cash balance that the company (depositor) must maintain either to continue to earn interest on the amount deposited in the bank account or to avoid certain fees from the bank, such as service charges. Compensating balances may also be required by banks in order to maintain lines of credit or similar short-term lending arrangements.

Assume Quaker Oats has a checking account with Minneapolis National Bank and has a $10 million line of credit from the bank. As part of the agreement, the bank requires Quaker to maintain a minimum of $500,000 in its checking account as a compensating balance. Therefore, if at the end of the year, the cash in the checking account was $830,000, only $330,000 would be classified as cash on the balance sheet. This reflects the restriction on the $500,000, which Quaker must keep as a compensating balance. Quaker, instead, classifies the $500,000 properly as a long-term investment rather than cash.

Marketable Securities Short-term investments in marketable securities is the second item under the current assets classification. As we discussed in Chapter 22, these securities are temporary investments that companies intend to convert to cash when needed, and they can be either trading or available-for-sale securities. Because they are trading or available-for-sale securities, the securities appear on the balance sheet at their market value. This helps the reader understand the amount of cash that the company would realize if it sold the securities immediately.

Accounts and Notes Receivable Accounts and notes receivable appear after marketable securities on the balance sheet. As we explained in Chapter 10, companies show accounts receivable at their net realizable value, which represents the amount of accounts receivable currently due that the firm estimates is collectible. When the company reports only the net accounts receivable on the balance sheet, it would disclose the amount of the allowance for doubtful accounts in the notes to the financial statements. If accounts and notes receivable arise from persons who bought goods and services from the company, it should label them as trade receivables. Companies must disclose the total amount of trade receivables as a separate item either on the balance sheet or in the notes.

Exhibit 24.3 contains the note to Quaker Oats 1997 financial statements that presents information about Quaker's trade accounts receivable. The provision for doubtful accounts is the amount of Quaker's allowance for uncollectible accounts. The company also discloses the provision for the amount of sales discounts and allowances that it expects in the future for items sold before the end of 1997. By showing the amount of accounts written off and discounts and allowances taken in 1997, Quaker provides statement readers with all the information needed to explain the changes in the two provision accounts.

Exhibit 24.3 also includes the effects of exchange rate fluctuations for receivables generated by transactions conducted in currencies other than U.S. dollars. For example, if the U.S. currency (dollars) strengthens against the German mark, a transaction denominated in German marks will require fewer U.S. dollars to settle. Since accounts receivable on Quaker Oats financial statements are reported in dollars, receivables recorded in a foreign currency against which the dollar is strengthening, such as German marks, have a lower dollar value, which is what happened to Quaker in each of the two years shown. A weakening U.S. dollar would result in higher receivables on the balance sheet.

EXHIBIT **24.3** **Quaker Oats' 1997 Trade Accounts Receivable Note**

Note 4

Trade Accounts Receivable Allowances

Dollars in Millions	1997	1996
Balance at beginning of year	$ 29.3	$ 26.8
Provision for doubtful accounts	4.2	12.3
Provision for discounts and allowances	25.0	32.2
Write-offs of doubtful accounts – net of recoveries	(5.5)	(8.4)
Discounts and allowances taken	(26.5)	(28.0)
Effect of divestitures	(3.8)	(5.3)
Effect of exchange rate changes	(0.4)	(0.3)
Balance at end of year	$ 22.3	$ 29.3

Inventory Inventory follows the receivables in the current asset section of the balance sheet. The balance sheet or related notes must disclose the inventory method used to determine the cost of the inventory (for example, FIFO or LIFO). If a company has an inventory of raw materials or goods in process, it can show these amounts separately, although frequently the amounts are included with the inventory of merchandise available for sale.

In addition, the firm must disclose whether it reports the inventory amount at its cost or its market value, whichever is lower at the end of the period. For example, consider a company that sells computers and records the purchase of those computers at the price paid, which is referred to as cost. Before the fiscal year-end, the manufacturer introduces a new production process, which means that any computer the company buys in the future will be much cheaper. GAAP requires that the company report that inventory at the price it will have to pay to replace the computers in inventory. This rule says that the cost may have to be lowered to an amount equal to the price that the company can sell the old computers less its costs to make the sale. Companies are required to show inventory on the balance sheet at the lower of cost or market, where market is the amount required to replace the old inventory. This rule is applied to individual inventory items, classes of items like computers or furniture, or the inventory as a whole.

Descriptions of the accounting principles and methods the company has chosen to use are part of the accompanying notes to the financial statements. A company's annual report includes a section often called **summary of significant accounting policies** that includes a discussion of any accounting methods where the company has a choice among alternatives, such as the method of computing inventory values and depreciation methods. The following is an excerpt from the December 31, 1997, summary of significant accounting policies of Quaker Oats that describes its inventory reporting policies:

Inventories. Inventories are valued at the lower of cost or market using various cost methods, and include the cost of raw materials, labor, and overhead. The percentage of year-end inventories valued using each of the methods was as follows:

December 31	1997	1996
Last-in, first-out (LIFO)	65%	53%
Average quarterly cost	15	39
First-in, first-out (FIFO)	5	8

If the LIFO method of valuing inventories was not used, total inventories would have been $8.6 and $15.3 million higher than reported at December 31, 1997 and 1996, respectively.

This note shows that Quaker, like many large companies, uses more than one method of accounting for inventories. As shown on its balance sheet in Exhibit 24.1, Quaker Oats had $256 million of inventory at December 31, 1997, reported in three categories: finished goods, grains and raw materials, and packaging materials and supplies. It is likely that Quaker uses the inventory method it finds most appropriate for each category depending on the ease of application and the effects on tax and financial income determination. Recall that LIFO usually produces inventory values that are significantly lower than the current market value, and income determined under LIFO is typically lower than income determined under other methods.

Prepaid Expenses   Prepaid expenses are classified as current assets because they support the operating activities of the firm and are usually consumed during the operating cycle. They appear as current assets because they will be used up or consumed within the next year. Furthermore, prepayments made for items such as insurance and rent are considered current because, if the contract for either item is canceled, the firm will receive a cash refund. If the prepaid item is not refunded when canceled, the portion that applies to periods of more than one year is considered long term and is reported as an other asset.

Investments

Following the current assets section on the balance sheet is the investments section. The investment classification on the balance sheet describes the type and extent of the company's long-term, nonoperational investments. Acquiring long-term, nonoperational investments, such as stock or bonds of other companies, is an alternative to investing in operational assets such as production plants or equipment. Sometimes investing in nonoperating assets is a better management strategy because investing in operating assets might increase the firm's productive capacity beyond the demand for the products and services the firm provides. In Chapter 22 we described various long-term investments available to the firm, why companies acquire them, and how companies record them. For financial statement users, a relatively detailed description of a company's long-term investments is often included in the notes to the financial statements.

Property, Plant, and Equipment

Property, plant, and equipment follows the investments section and shows the tangible operational investments that support the infrastructure of the firm. This balance sheet classification typically has the largest dollar amounts of any of the asset classifications and represents the largest and most diverse group of assets. The classifications found most typically in property, plant, and equipment are land, buildings, and equipment.

Land in the property, plant, and equipment section represents the land acquired to provide a site for the firm's operational activities, while land held for speculative gains would be considered an investment. The building's classification summarizes the cost of the various structures used by the firm to conduct its operations. Some firms subdivide this classification into more specific classifications such as manufacturing plants, office buildings, or retail outlets if such distinctions are deemed useful to the financial statement users. Buildings are depreciable assets and, therefore, companies show buildings at their book or carrying values—that is, net of their accumulated depreciation. This is accomplished either by showing the original cost of the buildings less the accumulated depreciation or by showing the net book value. Regardless of how net book value is shown on the balance sheet, details such as major categories of property, plant, and equipment and the related amounts of accumulated depreciation are disclosed in the notes.

Exhibit 24.1 shows the total of Quaker Oats' property, plant, and equipment at December 31, 1997, as $1,164.7 million. At that time, Quaker Oats operated 55 manufacturing plants in 18 states and 14 foreign countries, and it owned or leased distribution centers, warehouses, and sales offices in 21 states and 21 foreign countries.[1]

---

[1]Quaker Oats Company, *Annual Report,* 1997.

Leased Assets   As discussed in Chapters 18 and 20, leasing assets is an alternative to buying them. Recall that assets leased under capital leases appear on the lessee's balance sheet as property, plant, and equipment. There are other types of lease agreements, operating leases, that are simply rental agreements whose obligation is not recorded in a company's accounting records. For capital leases, the economic substance of the lease agreement implies that the asset was purchased instead of leased, thus overriding the legal form of the lease itself.

Quaker appropriately includes its capital leases as part of property, plant, and equipment. Exhibit 24.4 shows that Quaker had significant commitments under its operating leases. Quaker does not reflect the amount of its property under its capital leases and the fixed payments under those agreements because they were not large enough to warrant separate reporting.

EXHIBIT   24.4   Quaker Oats' Disclosure for Leases

Note 12

Lease and Other Commitments

Certain equipment and operating properties are rented under non-cancelable and cancelable operating leases. Total rental expense under operating leases was $38.0 million, $36.4 million and $36.3 million for the years ended December 31, 1997, 1996 and 1995, respectively. The following is a schedule of future minimum annual rentals on non-cancelable operating leases, primarily for sales offices, distribution centers and corporate headquarters, in effect as of December 31, 1997.

Dollars in Millions	1998	1999	2000	2001	2002	Thereafter	Total
Total payments	$27.5	$24.8	$23.4	$22.4	$17.5	$41.1	$156.7

The Company enters into executory contracts to obtain inventory and promote various products. As of December 31, 1997, future commitments under these contracts amounted to $145.8 million.

Natural Resources   Quaker Oats had no significant investments in natural resources, which, as you know from Chapter 21, are nonrenewable resources such as mineral, timber, or oil rights. If it had such an investment, Quaker would report it in the property, plant, and equipment classification on a classified balance sheet. Recall that as natural resources are consumed, the original cost of the asset is depleted. The original cost of the natural resource usually is maintained on the balance sheet, and the depletion taken to date is reported as a contra asset, accumulated depletion. A company can also show the net book value of the natural resource on the balance sheet and report accumulated depletion in the notes. Companies reveal the rate of depletion and how they determine its amount in the summary of significant accounting policies.

Intangible Assets   Intangible assets are operational investments that a firm has acquired and that appear following property, plant, and equipment on a company's balance sheet. Intangibles have no physical substance but are expected to generate some economic benefit for the firm in the future. Companies report intangible assets on the balance sheet at the original cost less the amortization taken on the assets up to that point in time.

Exhibit 24.5 shows Quaker's disclosure of its intangible assets for 1997 and 1996. Note the drastic reduction in intangible assets from 1996 to 1997. Much of that reduction arose from Quaker's divestiture of Snapple, which it purchased for $1.7 billion in late 1994. The intangible asset goodwill is recorded when the purchase price of an acquired company exceeds the fair value of the acquired company's identifiable assets, such as inventory and fixed assets. Companies amortize goodwill over a period of up to 40 years. When Quaker sold Snapple, it wrote off the unamortized goodwill which was included when Quaker calculated its $1.4 billion loss from the sale of Snapple.

EXHIBIT   24.5   Quaker Oats' Disclosure for Intangibles

Intangibles – Intangible assets consist principally of excess purchase price over net tangible assets of businesses acquired (goodwill) and trademarks. Intangible assets are amortized on a straight-line basis over periods ranging from two to 40 years.

Intangible assets, net of amortization, and their estimated useful lives consist of the following:

Dollars in Millions	Estimated Useful Lives (In Years)	1997	1996
Goodwill	10 to 40	$ 500.6	$ 1,887.1
Trademarks and other	2 to 40	20.4	586.8
Intangible assets		521.0	2,473.9
Less: accumulated amortization		170.5	236.7
Intangible assets – net of amortization		$ 350.5	$ 2,237.2

Other Assets

Firms use the last asset classification, other assets, for unusual items that do not fit in the previous asset classifications. The items found in this classification vary in practice and include items such as noncurrent receivables and special funds. Many accountants consider other assets to be too general a description and, therefore, recommend that items found in this classification be placed in another, more specific asset classification.

Deferred charges (deferrals) frequently are found in the other asset classification. Such charges are long-term prepayments that companies amortize over various lengths of time, depending on how long management believes the firm will benefit from the expenditures. For example, the account, Organizational Costs, which represents the money spent for starting a business, including licenses and attorney fees, is an example of a deferred charge typically found in the other asset classification. Organizational costs are amortized on a straight-line basis over a minimum of five to a maximum of 40 years depending on management's view of the period they benefit.[2]

Now we have described the major classifications of assets found on most balance sheets. The other side of the balance sheet generally reflects the means by which a company has chosen to finance its assets. This portion of the balance sheet includes a company's obligations to creditors and other outside parties as well as its investments from owners. In the next section, we discuss the major classifications found in the liabilities section of the balance sheet.

LIABILITIES: DEBT AND OTHER OBLIGATIONS

There are three basic classifications of liabilities on the balance sheet: current liabilities, long-term debt, and other long-term liabilities. The latter two classifications differ from each other in that long-term debt refers to obligations to creditors from borrowing, and

---

[2]The maximum of 40 years is determined by GAAP.

long-term liabilities include obligations that arise from means other than borrowing, such as obligations under capital leases and pension obligations.

Current Liabilities

Current liabilities are listed first in the liabilities section of the balance sheet. They result from one of four events: (1) the receipt of loan proceeds by the firm, (2) the purchase of goods and services using credit to defer payment for them, (3) the receipt of prepayments for goods and services promised to be provided subsequently by the firm, and (4) the reclassification of the portion of long-term debt that becomes due within the coming fiscal year.

The acquisition of goods and services on credit creates the most common type of current liability. Accounts payable, notes payable, wages and salaries payable, interest payable, and even taxes payable all reflect short-term obligations to pay for goods, services, or other obligations of the firm. When the firm receives payments in advance, it is required to either perform the prepaid service or provide the goods promised or return the cash advanced. The accounts associated with this type of obligation include unearned rent, unearned subscription revenue, and deposits made by customers to hold merchandise for future delivery. The balance sheet for Quaker Oats (Exhibit 24.1) shows current liabilities, as of December 31, 1997, of $945.7 million, $108.4 million of which was the current portion of long-term debt.

As discussed earlier, firms must classify as current any portion of a long-term debt that comes due within the time frame established for current liabilities. The exception to this rule occurs regarding those liabilities a firm expects to either pay with a noncurrent asset or refinance with another long-term debt agreement. Installment notes, lease obligations, bonds, and mortgage notes can appear as both a current liability and a long-term liability if part of the debt meets the current liability criteria. If the entire amount of the debt meets the current liability criteria, it is properly classified, in total, as a current liability. As part of its 1997 note for short-term debt, Quaker explained that its "(s)hort-term debt consists primarily of commercial paper borrowings in the United States and notes payable to banks in foreign countries."[3]

Long-Term Debt

Long-term liabilities are not expected to come due within one year or the operating cycle, whichever is longer. However, as we discussed earlier, the classification, long-term liabilities, also can include those liabilities that will come due within the next fiscal year. In the latter case, the company expects to pay for these liabilities with noncurrent assets, or the company expects to refinance them with another long-term debt instrument. Chapters 18 and 20 discussed the different types of long-term debt instruments and their accounting treatments.

Most long-term debt instruments specify the terms promised by the borrower as well as the restrictions imposed for the benefit of the lender. Companies disclose these details in the notes to the financial statements.

A long-term note payable reflects a firm's debt agreement with an individual or institution. A long-term note commonly found on the balance sheet is the mortgage note payable, which shows the amount of borrowing secured with the real estate of the borrower.

As you know, bonds payable differ from long-term notes payable in that the firm typically is borrowing the needed funds from the public and not from a specific individual or institution. Recall that firms amortize any premium or discount because interest expense shown on the income statement differs from the amount of cash interest paid. The unamortized premium or discount is shown either as an adjustment to the bond's face value on the balance sheet or in the notes to the statements where the bonds appear at their carrying value.

---

[3]Quaker Oats Company, *Annual Report,* 1997, p. 49.

The amount of information about a bond issue presented on the face of the balance sheet is limited. Companies often show detailed information about bond issues, such as the life of the bond, its effective interest rate, and whether it was secured, in the notes to the financial statements. The notes to the financial statements also include a description of any other features of the bonds, such as conversion rates, call prices, and the restrictions the bond indebtedness places on the corporation.

Exhibit 24.6 shows the detailed information about the long-term debt of Quaker Oats at December 31, 1997, and December 31, 1996. The two debt issues listed first represent funds borrowed to buy stock, which Quaker will distribute as part of its employee stock ownership plan (ESOP). The term *senior* used to describe the ESOP notes means that those notes have preference over another unsecured debt in the event of a company's liquidation. The order of preference begins with secured debt, followed by the senior unsecured debt, and then other unsecured debt. Recall that all debt holders have preference over stockholders.

Since the noninterest-bearing installment note does not have an explicit interest rate, Quaker explained the payments and interest rates of that debt as follows:

The non-interest bearing installment note for $55.5 million has an unamortized discount of $48.5 million and $49.4 million as of December 31, 1997 and 1996, respectively, based on an imputed interest rate of 13 percent.

EXHIBIT 24.6 Quaker Oats' Disclosure for Long-term Debt

Long-term Debt – The carrying value of long-term debt, including current maturities, as of December 31, 1997 and 1996 is summarized below.

Dollars in Millions	1997	1996
7.76% Senior ESOP notes due through 2001	$ 57.2	$ 64.9
8.0% Senior ESOP notes due through 2001	82.5	100.3
7.75%-7.9% Series A medium-term notes due through 2000	41.5	41.5
8.63%-9.34% Series B medium-term notes due through 2019	178.7	185.6
6.5%-7.48% Series C medium-term notes due through 2024	200.0	200.0
6.45%-7.78% Series D medium-term notes due through 2026	400.0	400.0
6.63% Deutsche mark swap matured in 1997	—	18.1
11.7% Chinese renmimbi notes due 2001	4.8	—
5.7%-6.63% Industrial Revenue Bonds due through 2009, tax-exempt	19.4	24.9
Non-interest bearing installment note due 2014	7.0	6.1
Other	4.9	3.2
Subtotal	996.0	1,044.6
Less: current portion of long-term debt	108.4	51.1
Long-term debt	$ 887.6	$ 993.5

The fair value of long-term debt, including current maturities, was $1.06 billion and $1.07 billion as of December 31, 1997 and 1996, respectively, and was based on market prices for the same or similar issues or on the current rates offered to the Company for similar debt of the same maturities.

Other Long-Term Liabilities

Companies classify long-term obligations other than amounts explicitly borrowed, such as pension and lease obligations, as other long-term liabilities. Recall from Chapter 18 that, for capital leases, firms report the present value of the future lease payments as a long-term liability. Firms disclose other lease terms, including minimum payments for the next five years, in the notes to the financial statements. This disclosure helps statement users predict how these lease agreements will affect the firm's future cash flows.

Companies also include the liability under their pension plans as another long-term liability. Chapter 16 indicated that defined benefit pension plans require companies to base the pension benefits paid to employees on factors including estimates of the time employees will work and their expected lives. This makes accounting for these plans very complicated, including the calculation of the amount that companies should record as pension liability. Though we have not dealt with the details of these calculations or shown the complexity of determining other postretirement benefit obligations, you should know that these obligations are reported under this liability classification.

Deferred income tax liability is another long-term liability reported on most corporate balance sheets. Due to the complexities surrounding this account, discussion of this account was delayed to this point. The brief discussion that follows presents basic information to provide a fundamental understanding of why this account exists. A more detailed discussion of this topic is found in more advanced accounting textbooks.

Deferred income tax liabilities (and assets) result from differences between computing income using generally accepted accounting principles and computing taxable income using tax laws. Remember that accounting principles are designed to measure and reflect business events on an objective basis, whereas tax laws are designed to raise money for the government and encourage, or discourage, particular types of business transactions. Because firms must comply with both accounting principles and tax laws, the resulting tax calculations can differ from the financial accounting treatment of a particular business event. Such differences create a deferred income tax amount that appears on the balance sheet.

To illustrate how a deferred tax liability arises, assume that Quaker Oats has a tax rate of 34 percent and signs a contract on December 15, 2000, for $1 million, which is considered revenue for financial accounting purposes. Assume that for tax purposes, however, this amount is not considered taxable income until Quaker receives the cash in payment of the contract on January 15, 2001. Note that both Quaker and the IRS consider the $1 million as revenue, but they differ about the time period in which to recognize it.

To comply with GAAP, Quaker recognizes the $1 million as revenue and reflects the related tax expense of $340,000 ($1 million × 34%) for the fiscal year ended December 31, 2000. When it recognizes the tax expense, a related Deferred Income Tax Liability account appears on its balance sheet, indicating that the taxes are due from Quaker. Quaker will actually be paid when the IRS recognizes the $1 million as taxable income in 2001. In this case, Quaker would report a deferred tax liability of $340,000 on its year 2000 balance sheet.

There are numerous differences between tax law and GAAP that cause taxable income and accounting income to differ. The important differences result from recognizing certain revenues and expenses for tax purposes at different times than they are recognized for financial accounting purposes, which creates deferred income tax assets and liabilities. Exhibit 24.7 shows Quaker Oats's deferred assets and liabilities in 1997 and 1996 along with a list of accounting events that produced them. Postretirement benefits gave rise to deferred assets because the financial expense preceded the deductibility for tax purposes. On the other hand, the tax deductions for depreciation and amortization were greater than the related financial expenses of the period for most assets. This means that taxable income was lower than financial income and that Quaker has an obligation, or a liability, for the difference.

EXHIBIT 24.7 Quaker Oats' Deferred Tax Disclosure

Deferred tax assets and deferred tax liabilities were as follows:

Dollars in Millions	1997		1996	
	Assets	Liabilities	Assets	Liabilities
Depreciation and amortization	$ 20.3	$218.9	$ 56.9	$ 400.1
Postretirement benefits	129.8	—	100.3	—
Other benefit plans	50.2	5.7	60.8	9.2
Accrued expenses including restructuring charges	92.5	11.5	80.3	7.9
Loss carryforwards	328.5	—	14.5	—
Other	4.1	15.9	13.3	33.2
Subtotal	625.4	252.0	326.1	450.4
Valuation allowance	(319.2)	—	(14.2)	—
Total	$306.2	$252.0	$ 311.9	$ 450.4

As of December 31, 1997, as a result of the loss on divestiture of Snapple, the Company had approximately $790 million of capital loss carryforwards available to reduce future capital gains in the United States for up to five years. A valuation allowance has been provided for the full value of the deferred tax assets related to these loss carryforwards.

PAUSE & REFLECT

Because long-term obligations do not require payment within the next year, why is it necessary to distinguish between long-term debt and other long-term obligations? In what important ways are they different? What useful information can a statement reader glean from the distinction? *(answer on page 837)*

Off-Balance-Sheet Financing

Some financial reporting rules for liabilities, such as capital lease obligations, allow the substance of the transaction to override its form, so companies are obligated to record the amounts of the related debt and reflect them in their financial statements. These reporting rules arose in response to managers' attempts to borrow money in ways that would avoid having to record such borrowings on the balance sheet (known as **off-balance-sheet financing**).

When a company leases an asset under a long-term noncancellable lease, it is obligated to reflect the lease payments on the financial statements as if the company had borrowed the money and bought the asset. Without such obligations created by GAAP, the noncancellable lease obligation would not be reported on the company's balance sheet.

When balance sheets omit reflecting the sources of off-balance-sheet financing, such as long-term leases classified as operating leases (even though there are substantial obligations to make future lease payments), it affects how balance sheet readers perceive the risk and financial health of the business. Not recording such liabilities affects indicators of financial risk, such as the current ratio and the debt-to-equity ratio, by making them appear better than if the obligation was recorded.

Understanding the nature of current liabilities, long-term debt, and other long-term liabilities helps financial statement readers assess the nature of the obligations that the company faces. Next we describe the classifications in the stockholders' equity section.

STOCKHOLDERS' EQUITY

Here we review some important points about stockholders' equity. Dividing the stockholder's equity section into contributed capital (often called *paid-in capital*) and retained earnings reflects the resources provided by the owners and the claims generated by retaining the corporation's profits, respectively. Retained earnings is also called the *undistributed earnings of the corporation.*

Contributed Capital

Chapter 19 discussed the equity financing events that create the accounts found in the contributed capital section of stockholders' equity on the balance sheet. The following discussion focuses on how the balance sheet reports these events. (Refer to the stockholders' (shareholders') equity section of the Quaker Oats balance sheet in Exhibit 24.1 to find the parts of the equity section we discuss.)

Quaker has chosen to separate the preferred stock section of equity from the common stockholders' equity. This presentation reflects the idea that the nature of preferred stock is like debt because preferred stockholders cannot vote in shareholder meetings. In addition, as you know, the preferred stock dividends usually are set at a fixed amount, and preferred stock has preference over common stock regarding the receipt of dividends and in liquidation. On more traditional balance sheets, preferred stock typically appears as the first item in the contributed capital section because of its preference.

In the case of Quaker, its preferred stock was no par; consequently, it had to disclose the liquidation value of its preferred stock ($78 per share). This represents the minimum amount that Quaker would pay for each share of preferred stock held before the common stockholders could receive any distribution in the event of a liquidation.

Quaker adopted a new Shareholder Rights Plan in 1996 "designed to deter coercive or unfair takeover tactics and to prevent a person or group from gaining control of the Company without offering a fair price to all the shareholders."[4] Under this plan, all shareholders receive the right to a share of redeemable preferred stock exercisable during any merger or other business combination not determined to be fair by the company's independent directors. When exercised, these rights entitle the holder to receive shares of the acquiring company or surviving company with a market value up to twice the exercise price of each right. This ensures that Quaker's stockholders will receive fair compensation for their stock in the case of a takeover.

Donated Capital

Donated capital is a type of contributed capital shown in the contributed capital section. Recall that corporations use this classification when they receive assets from governmental entities but give no ownership interest in exchange. For example, it is common for a city to give a corporation land or buildings in exchange for its locating a production plant or corporate headquarters in that city. When this occurs, the company would record the asset at its fair market value and would increase the donated capital account by the same amount; the city receives no ownership interest in the corporation.

Valuation Capital

Appearing between the contributed capital and retained earnings sections[5] of stockholders' equity if it is a credit balance or after retained earnings if it is a debit balance is a valuation capital section representing components of the company's comprehensive income. The most common source of valuation capital comes from fluctuations in market value for investments in securities classified as available-for-sale (discussed in Chapter 22). Recall that available-for-sale securities are those that management does not intend to sell in the next year. Usually management has purchased these types of securities in order to

---

[4]Quaker Oats Company, *Annual Report,* 1997, p. 53.

[5]There are no rigid rules regarding where in the equity section valuation capital is placed. It can go either before or after retained earnings.

have control over or influence on another corporation rather than for short-term returns. Since the principal reason corporations hold these securities is not for short-term returns, fluctuations in their market value might distort current income. Therefore, by requiring that companies show these fluctuations as part of stockholders' equity, GAAP ensure that the corporation can show the market value of its investments without affecting the current period's reported income.

Retained Earnings

Recall that retained earnings represents the earnings that have been reinvested in the firm and have not been distributed to the stockholders. In fact, as you can see in Exhibit 24.1, Quaker has chosen to call its retained earnings *reinvested earnings*.

Corporations may restrict retained earnings, which limits the dividend-paying ability of the corporation. Any restriction on retained earnings means that the corporation may not pay the entire amount of retained earnings as dividends. A restriction is often placed on retained earnings when a corporation issues bonds and the bonds' covenants restrict the dividend-paying ability of the corporation to protect the bondholders. When the retained earnings of the firm are restricted, corporations disclose the amount of and reason for the restriction in a note.

One common retained earnings restriction occurs when corporations purchase treasury stock. They restrict retained earnings by the amount paid for the treasury stock. Because the purchase of treasury stock represents the amount paid to former stockholders, both common and preferred, the purchase liquidates owners' interest. Therefore, creditors of the company want to limit the dividend-paying ability of the corporation to protect them from further distribution of the firm's assets to stockholders. As the corporation sells treasury stock, it removes any related restrictions.

Treasury Stock

Treasury stock is shown after retained earnings in the stockholders' equity section of the balance sheet. Note that treasury stock is not a reduction in the amount of retained earnings; rather, it reflects a reduction in the total amount of stockholders' equity. Because corporations assume that they will reissue treasury shares, they treat treasury stock as a temporary reduction in stockholders' equity, which they eliminate when they reissue the shares.

Notice in Exhibit 24.1 that Quaker Oats had treasury stock for both preferred and common stock. It chose to report each type of treasury stock separately with the related type of stock rather than as a total at the bottom of the stockholders' equity section. Quaker held these shares to distribute as part of its employee stock ownership plan. The debt that Quaker issued to obtain the money to buy these shares of treasury stock appears as part of the long-term debt shown in Exhibit 24.6.

PAUSE & REFLECT

Corporations often buy their outstanding shares of stock as treasury stock to issue as part of stock option plans. Why should they buy their outstanding stock rather than simply issue authorized but unissued stock? *(answer on page 837)*

THERE IS MORE TO ANNUAL REPORTS THAN FINANCIAL STATEMENTS

LO 3

Corporations usually issue financial statements to outside parties, particularly stockholders and potential investors, as part of the annual report. An annual report not only includes the financial statements but also reflects other disclosures that management wants to communicate, along with some supplementary required disclosures. This section discusses other important items found in corporate annual reports.

Reconsider here the essential components of a company's annual report. Included in the annual reports distributed by corporations are topics that management wants to present to stakeholders, including descriptions of new products or markets, as well as

management's views of the business's outlook. Annual reports also include the report that external auditors issue on the financial statements as well as other disclosures about the business.

Management's View of the Business

Most major corporations are run by professional managers whose actual ownership may be only a small portion of the company's outstanding stock. The annual report is the principal way that managers communicate their assessment and perception of the company. Much of the information that managers want to communicate appears in the management's **letter to stockholders.** This written report gives an overview of the items other than financial statements in the annual report and highlights important aspects of financial performance.

Business Segment Information

In addition to financial statements, annual reports provide details about the performance of the company. One important disclosure for large corporations includes **segment data.** Large corporations usually are involved in several lines of business that often are spread around the globe. Recall from Chapter 23 that companies must disclose segment activities as part of the annual report in certain circumstances. Whenever a segment, which can be an identifiable geographic region or an identifiable product line, accounts for 10 percent or more of total company sales or assets, related segment data must appear as part of the annual report. By revealing this information, stakeholders can assess major parts of the business. Using 10 percent as the threshold for disclosure, the amount of data is limited and assures interested parties that the information disclosed concerns parts of the business that are big enough so that significant effects on a segment will also have an effect on the firm.

Exhibit 24.8 shows the two types of segment data for Quaker Oats in 1997. The geographic disclosure shows that Quaker Oats had most of its 1997 segment assets in the United States and Canada. Exhibit 24.8 also shows the two product categories. Notice that the amounts attributable to Snapple for 1996 and 1995 are segregated from the ongoing business operations. Elsewhere in its 1997 annual report, Quaker reported that Gatorade had $1.5 billion in sales and was distributed in 47 countries. Disclosures like these help investors assess the prospects of future sales and earnings associated with specific product categories.

EXHIBIT   24.8   Quaker Oats' Segment Disclosure

Industry Segment and Geographic Area Information

	Identifiable Assets		
Year Ended December 31	**1997**	1996	1995
Industry Segment Information			
Foods	**$ 1,636.7**	$1,705.2	$1,728.2
Beverages	**544.6**	537.8	490.6
Total Ongoing Businesses	**2,181.3**	2,243.0	2,218.8
Divested Businesses *(a)*	**—**	1,930.6	2,133.0
Total Businesses	**2,181.3**	4,173.6	4,351.8
Corporate *(b)*	**515.7**	220.8	268.6
Total Consolidated	**$2,697.0**	$4,394.4	$4,620.4

	Identifiable Assets		
Year Ended December 31	**1997**	1996	1995
Geographic Area Information			
United States and Canada	**$ 1,672.3**	$1,689.0	$1,673.9
Latin America	**289.3**	339.6	331.5
Europe and Asia/Pacific	**219.7**	214.4	213.4
International	**509.0**	554.0	544.9
Total Ongoing Businesses	**2,181.3**	2,243.0	2,218.8
Divested Businesses *(a)*	**—**	1,930.6	2,133.0
Total Businesses	**2,181.3**	4,173.6	4,351.8
Corporate *(b)*	**515.7**	220.8	268.6
Total Consolidated	**$2,697.0**	$4,394.4	$4,620.4

(a) Includes the following Divested Businesses: 1997 (Snapple beverages, certain food service businesses); 1996 (Snapple beverages, certain food service businesses, U.S. and Canadian frozen foods and Italian products); 1995 (Snapple beverages, certain food service businesses, U.S. and Canadian frozen foods, U.S. and Canadian pet food, U.S. bean and chili, Italian products, European pet food, Mexican chocolate and Dutch honey).

(b) Identifiable assets include corporate cash and cash equivalents, short-term investments and miscellaneous receivables and investments.

Periodic Reports— More Timely Reporting

Because investors and stockholders want to know how the business is faring more often than once a year, companies often issue quarterly financial statements. Issuing statements at three-month intervals provides stockholders and investors with timely information to use in decision making. Exhibit 24.9 shows Quaker Oats' 1997 quarterly reports, which it included as part of the annual report. Unlike some businesses, Quaker's business activity is fairly constant across the four quarters. While Quaker's business activity was fairly constant, it reported a net loss in the first quarter when the $1.4 billion loss from the sale of Snapple was recorded. Quaker also includes the amount of quarterly cash dividends it declared each quarter ($0.285 per share each quarter) and the market price range, high and low, of the common stock during each quarter.

Contingent Liabilities

Some events, such as lawsuits or claims by customers for defective products, may affect the business negatively. However, in some cases, the actual events that create the specific losses have not occurred at the end of the reporting period, such as a judgment in a lawsuit

EXHIBIT   24.9   Quaker Oats' Quarterly Data Disclosure

Note 18

Quarterly Financial Data (Unaudited)

Dollars in Millions (Except Per Share Data)

1997	First Quarter(a)	Second Quarter(b)	Third Quarter(c)	Fourth Quarter(d)
Net sales	$ 1,201.7	$1,395.5	$1,370.7	$1,047.8
Cost of goods sold	627.7	704.1	674.1	559.0
Gross profit	$ 574.0	$ 691.4	$ 696.6	$ 488.8
Net (loss) income	$ (1,109.8)	$ 75.8	$ 77.5	$ 25.6
Per common share:				
Net (loss) income	$ (8.15)	$ 0.57	$ 0.58	$ 0.20
Net (loss) income – assuming dilution	$ (8.15)	$ 0.57	$ 0.58	$ 0.20
Cash dividends declared	$ 0.285	$ 0.285	$ 0.285	$ 0.285
Market price range:				
High	$ 40⅜	$ 45⅛	$ 53	$ 55⅛
Low	$ 34⅜	$ 35⅞	$ 44⅜	$ 42 1/16

(a) Includes a $1.40 billion pretax impairment loss ($1.14 billion after-tax or $8.39 per share) for the Snapple beverages business.

(b) Includes a $10.6 million pretax loss ($5.5 million after-tax or $.02 per share) for the sale of the Snapple beverages business and pretax restructuring charges of $11.8 million ($7.9 after-tax or $.06 per share) for plant consolidations in the International Foods business and the closing of an International beverages office.

(c) Includes a $4.8 million pretax net charge ($3.4 million after-tax or $.02 per share) for an impairment loss partly offset by a litigation settlement in the International Foods business and pretax restructuring charges of $46.9 million ($28.2 million after-tax or $.19 per share) for plant consolidations in the U.S. and Canadian Foods business and staffing reductions.

(d) Includes a $5.8 million combined pretax loss ($1.9 million after-tax or an immaterial per share impact) for the sale of certain food service businesses and pretax restructuring charges of $7.2 million ($4.3 after-tax or $.02 per share) for manufacturing reconfigurations in the U.S. and Canadian Foods and Beverages business.

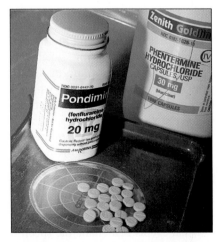

Companies must recognize in their annual reports amounts that represent future losses for events such as product-liability judgements.

that is filed but not settled. Outside stakeholders want to know about these potential events, and companies are required to disclose them under certain conditions. These potential losses are called **contingent liabilities,** which represent events that could create negative financial results for a company at some future point. Companies must actually record losses when the related event is considered probable and when the company can estimate its monetary effect on the financial statements.

Even when corporations cannot estimate the impact of the events or whether the likelihood of such events is less than probable, they must disclose the existence of contingent liabilities as part of the notes that accompany the financial statements. Exhibit 24.10 shows the note that Quaker Oats included in its 1997 annual report to disclose contingent liabilities. Quaker disclosed its victory in a lawsuit against Borden, Inc., in which it was awarded $35 million. Though Quaker has a number of lawsuits against it outstanding, none appear to meet the criteria for recording as a contingent loss.

EXHIBIT   24.10   Quaker Oats' Contingent Liability Disclosure

Note 16

Litigation

On November 1, 1995, the Company filed suit against Borden, Inc. in Federal District Court in New York related to the Company's November 1994 acquisition of a Brazilian pasta business. The suit was settled in August 1997 for $35.0 million.

The Company is also a party to a number of lawsuits and claims, which it is vigorously defending. Such matters arise out of the normal course of business and relate to the Company's past acquisition activity and other issues. Certain of these actions seek damages in large amounts. While the results of litigation cannot be predicted with certainty, management believes that the final outcome of such litigation will not have a material adverse effect on the Company's consolidated financial position or results of operations. Changes in assumptions, as well as actual experience, could cause the estimates made by management to change.

The Auditor's Report

One other important disclosure included in annual reports is the auditor's report. Recall that CPAs provide an opinion about the fairness of the financial statements using GAAP as the criteria. There are four kinds of reports issued (given) by external auditors: unqualified, qualified, and adverse opinions, and a disclaimer of opinion. When an auditor issues an **unqualified opinion,** it means that the financial statements are fair representations of the business's financial position, cash flows, and reported income and that, in the auditor's opinion, the company has applied GAAP appropriately. A **qualified opinion** indicates that either the auditor found parts of the company's financial statements not in accordance with GAAP or the auditor's ability to examine the underlying records used to develop the financial statements was limited. Qualified opinions mean that, overall, the statements are fair representations of the business's financial position and reported income but that certain parts of the statements, as indicated by the auditor as a portion of his or her report, are not disclosed as specified by GAAP.

CPAs rarely issue the other two kinds of audit reports. An **adverse opinion** indicates that the external auditor believes that the financial statements are not fair representations of the company's financial position or income. The financial statements are management's representations, and an adverse opinion means that the CPA finds that management's financial statements do not comply with GAAP and, therefore, are not fair representations of the company's financial position or performance. A **disclaimer of opinion** means that the auditor was not able to gather sufficient evidence to support an opinion or that the auditor was not sufficiently independent of the company to issue an opinion.

The auditor's report is an important part of the annual report because it provides assurance that the financial statements meet the reporting standards represented by GAAP. When CPAs state that financial statements, considered as a whole, are materially correct, they believe that if any remaining errors were considered together, such errors would not change the outcome of decisions (such as whether to buy or sell the company's stock or whether to lend the company money) made by an informed reader of the statements.

Exhibit 24.11 shows that the auditors found Quaker's 1997 financial statements to "present fairly" the financial position of the company. Note that they remind readers of

EXHIBIT   24.11   Quaker Oats' Audit Report

Report of Independent Public Accountants

To the Shareholders of The Quaker Oats Company:

We have audited the accompanying consolidated balance sheets of The Quaker Oats Company (a New Jersey corporation) and subsidiaries as of December 31, 1997 and 1996, and the related consolidated statements of income, common shareholders' equity and cash flows for the years ended December 31, 1997, 1996 and 1995. These financial statements are the responsibility of the Company's management. Our responsibility is to express an opinion on these financial statements based on our audits.

We conducted our audits in accordance with generally accepted auditing standards. Those standards require that we plan and perform the audits to obtain reasonable assurance about whether the financial statements are free of material misstatement. An audit includes examining, on a test basis, evidence supporting the amounts and disclosures in the financial statements. An audit also includes assessing the accounting principles used and significant estimates made by management, as well as evaluating the overall financial statement presentation. We believe that our audits provide a reasonable basis for our opinion.

In our opinion, the financial statements referred to above present fairly, in all material respects, the financial position of The Quaker Oats Company and subsidiaries as of December 31, 1997 and 1996, and the results of their operations and their cash flows for the years ended December 31, 1997, 1996 and 1995 in conformity with generally accepted accounting principles.

Arthur Andersen LLP

Chicago, Illinois
February 4, 1998

the report that the statements are the representations of management. Also note that the report states that the examination was done on a test basis, which means that there was no audit, or verification, of every transaction. Auditors attempt to gain sufficient evidence to support their opinion that the statements are materially correct. They do not attempt to find every error because they rely upon the principle of materiality.

We have discussed many of the rules that guide how balance sheet information is reported to external parties and what additional disclosures are necessary to complete the picture of the firm's financial position. There is no need to limit internal users to n 1932 the aggregate value of the stocks offered on the New York Stock Exchange was $15 billion—a drop of $74 billion since the fall of 1929. In investigating the securities industry following this massive decline, Congress found that "during the post-war decade, some 50 billion of new securities were floated in the United States. Fully half or $25,000,000,000 worth of securities floated during this period have been proved to be worthless."* A critical outcome of this investigation was the Securities Exchange Act of 1934 which established the SEC.

Now, as then, the principal role of the SEC is to ensure "full and fair" disclosure regarding securities offered for public investment. In a speech made in September 1998, SEC Chairman Arthur Levitt blasted the current financial reporting process as being a "game of nods and winks." He labeled five key illusions poisoning the financial reporting process as accounting "hocus-pocus." The five reporting illusions were "big bath" restructuring charges, creative acquisition accounting, "cookie jar reserves," "immaterial" misapplications of accounting principles, and the premature recognition of revenue. Levitt offered a plan as a solution to the financial disclosure problem including the following:

- The SEC staff will require well-detailed disclosures about the impact of changes in accounting assumptions including a supplement to the financial statement showing beginning and ending balances.

- The SEC will implore the accounting profession through the AICPA to clarify the auditing of purchased R&D, and to augment existing guidance on restructurings, large acquisition write-offs, and revenue recognition practices.

- The concept of materiality will no longer be an excuse for deliberate misstatement of performance. Levitt stated that "materiality is not a bright line cutoff of three or five percent.

It requires consideration of all relevant factors that could impact an investor's decision."

- SEC staff will consider interpretive accounting guidance on the "do's and don'ts of revenue recognition."

- The SEC's review and enforcement teams will reinforce these regulatory initiatives formally targeting reviews of public companies that announce restructuring liability reserves, major write-offs, or other practices that appear to manage earnings.

- Stating that "we cannot permit thorough audits to be sacrificed for re-engineered approaches that are efficient, but less effective," Levitt proposed that the Public Oversight Board will review the way audits are performed and assess the impact of recent trends on the public interest.

- Levitt reported that the New York Stock Exchange and the National Association of Securities Dealers have agreed to sponsor a "blue-ribbon" panel to develop a series of far-ranging recommendations intended to "empower audit committees and function as the ultimate guardian of investor interests and corporate accountability."

- Levitt challenged corporate management and Wall Street to reexamine the current environment, reminding corporate managers the financial reporting system is directly related to the long-term interests of a corporation. While the temptations are great, and the pressures strong, illusions in numbers are only that—ephemeral, and ultimately self-destructive.

*The House Committee on Interstate and Foreign Commerce, *Federal Supervision of Traffic in Investment Securities in Interstate Commerce,* Report No. 85, 73d Cong., 1st Sess. (Washington, D.C.: U.S. Government Printing Office, 1934), p. 2.

Source: Adapted from "Arthur Levitt Addresses 'Illusions,' " *Journal of Accountancy,* December 1998, pp. 12–13.

the same data reported on statements issued to external parties. In the next section we describe some of the data included on balance sheets for internal users.

BALANCE SHEETS USED FOR INTERNAL REPORTING

Balance sheets issued to external parties are limited in their usefulness for internal decision makers because of their use of historical cost asset valuation. The assets of most companies are at least a few years old, and many include buildings that are 30 and 40 years old. The use of historical cost valuation understates firms' investments because the assets are shown at these old prices. This means that the firms appear to have much lower investments in assets than they actually have.

Reporting property, plant, and equipment at their historical cost is required by GAAP, but internal users do not face this same restriction when formulating their reports. An alternative to using historical cost valuation is using current replacement cost. Current cost valuation of assets means that long-lived assets values are adjusted to their replacement cost at the balance sheet date. Companies can obtain current cost data by obtaining catalogues that report average recent prices for certain types of equipment or by having their assets appraised by independent appraisers.

To explain the decision-making usefulness of current cost valuation, consider the steel industry during the middle of the twentieth century. Steel manufacturers had large investments in buildings and equipment like blast furnaces. When the return earned by these companies was measured using historical cost, they appeared to be earning sufficient return. However, the return that they were earning was not sufficient to replace the equipment as technology changed and their equipment became obsolete. If the equipment had been valued at its replacement cost, which was higher than its historical cost, then the denominator of the return calculation (Return on investment = Net income/Average investment) would have been larger, and the calculated return would have been lower. The lower return on investment based on replacement costs would have indicated that higher prices were necessary to earn the return they thought they were getting, and that replacement of the equipment with more efficient equipment would have been a good decision.

Current cost valuation presents two problems that led GAAP to adopt historical cost valuation. First, obtaining current cost data can be costly, and the benefits of collecting that data need to exceed its cost. The other problem with current cost data is that the data are subjective. Different appraisers rarely appraise an asset at exactly the same value, and if a published value is used to value the asset, the condition of the asset is probably not the same as the assumed condition of the asset with the published price.

The subjectivity inherent in replacement cost valuation allows a range of potential values, any of which can be justified as the asset's replacement value. When managers report to outside parties, they may bias the information to influence someone to invest or lend by choosing from the set of possible valuations the one that makes the company appear better. In contrast, the subjectivity of the replacement cost is less of a problem for internal users because they want to use it to make better decisions and have less motivation to bias the information through their choice of replacement values.

As you can see, there is much more important information to consider when reviewing a company's financial statements than the statements themselves. Readers must be careful to assess not only the financial statements but also the other related informative disclosures as well.

SUMMARY

A company's assets, along with the claims to those assets by owners and creditors, represent its financial position, which the balance sheet presents. Classifying assets, liabilities, and equity accounts allows readers to assess the nature of the significant items in each category. Understanding the meaning of balance sheet classifications facilitates the communication process between managers and external stakeholders.

- Proper classification of assets and liabilities as current and noncurrent facilitates assessment of a firm's solvency and liquidity. Management intends to convert assets classified as current to cash within a year. Companies expect to liquidate liabilities classified as current with current assets or to refinance them with current liabilities within a year.

- Proper classification of assets allows statement readers to assess the nature of a firm's assets. This allows financial statement readers to determine the firm's prospects for profitability and future cash flows.

- Proper classification of liabilities allows the financial statement reader to assess some of the uses of future profits and cash flows. Specifically, the level of current assets relative to current liabilities shows the firm's short-term solvency. Long-term obligations require the use of current assets or additional long-term assets sometime in the future.

- Corporate annual reports include financial statements as well as other disclosures, such as the management letter and the auditor's report, that help external stakeholders interpret those statements.

KEY TERMS

adverse opinion The report issued by an external auditor that indicates that the financial statements are not fair representations of the company's financial position or income

compensating balance A minimum cash balance that the depositor (company) must maintain either to continue to earn interest on the amount deposited in the bank account or to avoid certain fees, such as service charges

contingent liabilities Events that could create negative financial results for a company; required to be recorded when the event is probable and estimable in terms of its monetary effects

deferred charges Long-term prepayments frequently found in the other assets classification that companies amortize over various lengths of time, depending on how long the company will benefit from the expenditures; also called *deferrals*

disclaimer of opinion The report issued by an external auditor that indicates that the auditor was not able to gather sufficient evidence to support an opinion or that the auditor was not sufficiently independent of the company to issue an opinion

letter to stockholders Management's written report that presents an overview of the items in the annual report other than financial statements and highlights important aspects of financial performance

off-balance-sheet financing Borrowing money in ways that would avoid having to record the obligation on the balance sheet

qualified opinion The report issued by an independent auditor stating that parts of the financial statements are not in accordance with GAAP or that the auditor's ability to examine the underlying records used to develop the financial statements was limited

segment data Part of the annual report that discloses financial information for product lines or identifiable geographic regions that account for 10 percent or more of total company sales or assets

summary of significant accounting policies Part of the accompanying notes to the financial statements that describes the accounting principles and methods the company has chosen to use

unqualified opinion The report issued by an independent auditor stating that the financial statements are fair representations of the business's financial position and reported income and that the company has applied GAAP appropriately

ANSWERS TO THE PAUSE & REFLECTS

p. 818, These checks were taken by the company in payment for another's obligation to it. Since the checks did not liquidate the debt, the firm should record receivables instead of cash. It should record the amount of the check plus any fees that its bank assessed as a result of the NSF check. If the company believes that the receivable is uncollectible, then it is inappropriate to record it as a receivable and it does not belong on the balance sheet.

p. 827, Long-term debt represents contractual obligations between the company and its debt holders. Other long-term liabilities include pension obligations and deferred taxes. Thus, the legal obligation to make cash payments differs between the two classifications, since funding of pensions and the payments for deferred taxes are much less certain than the principal and interest payments required in a debt agreement. Making the distinction allows statement readers to better estimate the legal obligations to make payments and the risk of violating debt covenants, which may lead to bankruptcy.

p. 829, Legally corporations can issue authorized but unissued stock, or they can issue treasury stock. They might reacquire stock rather than issuing additional stock in order to avoid changing ownership control or further diluting the ownership of the net assets.

QUESTIONS

1. What is meant by the term *financial position,* and what is the purpose of the statement of financial position?

2. How is financial position related to profit potential?

3. What is a current asset? Give three examples for a manufacturing firm.

4. What is a current liability? Give three examples for a service firm.

5. Explain the effects on the current ratio if long-term liabilities are mistakenly classified as current liabilities.

6. Explain why a long-term note is classified as current if the fiscal year ends during the last year of the note's life.

7. In what order are current assets listed on the balance sheet? Why is this order important?

8. What does the term *valued* mean as it relates to the accounts shown on the balance sheet?

9. Why is a prepaid insurance policy with a three-year life often listed as a current asset?

10. Explain how each of the following current assets is valued on the balance sheet: (1) accounts receivable, (2) inventory, and (3) prepaid insurance.

11. How can a reader of the financial statements determine how the company's current assets are valued?

12. How are investments valued on the balance sheet? Why?

13. How are property, plant, and equipment accounts valued on the balance sheet? Why?

14. How are intangible assets valued on the balance sheet? Why?

15. What is an other asset? Give two examples.

16. In what order are current liabilities listed on the balance sheet? Why is this order important?

17. How are current liabilities valued on the balance sheet? Why?

18. How are long-term liabilities such as bonds payable valued on the balance sheet? Why?

19. What are other long-term liabilities? Give two examples.

20. What is the order of the items included in the stockholders' equity section of the balance sheet? Why is this order important?

21. What is donated capital? How is it different from contributed capital?

22. What are the differences among the following audit opinions: an unqualified opinion, a qualified opinion, an adverse opinion, and a disclaimer of opinion?

EXERCISES

E 24.1

LO 2

For each of the following accounts, determine its classification on the balance sheet using the following classifications. Put the letters in the spaces provided.

CA	Current assets
INV	Investments
PPE	Property, plant, and equipment
INT	Intangibles
OA	Other assets
CL	Current liabilities
LTL	Long-term liabilities
OL	Other liabilities
CC	Contributed capital
RE	Retained earnings
OOE	Other owners' equity

_____ 1. Common Stock

_____ 2. Wages Payable

_____ 3. Building

_____ 4. Land Held for Speculation

_____ 5. Cash

_____ 6. Bonds Payable

_____ 7. Accumulated Depreciation

_____ 8. Accounts Payable

_____ 9. Treasury Stock

_____ 10. Marketable Securities

E 24.2

LO 2

For each of the following accounts, determine its classification on the balance sheet using the following classifications. Put the letters in the spaces provided.

CA   Current assets

INV   Investments

PPE   Property, plant, and equipment

INT   Intangibles

OA   Other assets

CL   Current liabilities

LTL   Long-term liabilities

OL   Other liabilities

CC   Contributed capital

RE   Retained earnings

OOE   Other owners' equity

_____ 1. Deferred Income Tax Payable

_____ 2. Mining Property

_____ 3. Bonds Payable Due Next Year

_____ 4. Goodwill

_____ 5. Donated Land

_____ 6. Common Stock Dividend Distributable

_____ 7. Allowance for Uncollectible Accounts

_____ 8. Mortgage Payable

_____ 9. Accumulated Depletion

_____ 10. Discount on Bonds Payable

Use the following information for E 24.3 through E 24.9:

Ramsey Manufacturing Company has just completed its first year of operation. It has the following accounts in the general ledger. The bookkeeper is unsure which accounts to show on the balance sheet and which accounts to report on the income statement.

Accounts Receivable
Accounts Payable
Accumulated Depreciation, Building
Accumulated Depreciation, Machinery
Additional Paid-In Capital
Allowance for Uncollectible Accounts
Bonds Payable
Building
Cash
Common Stock
Copyright
Cost of Goods Sold
Deferred Income Taxes Payable

Discount on Bonds Payable
Dividends Payable
Finished Goods
Income Tax Expense
Income Taxes Payable
Insurance Expense
Interest Expense
Land
Land Held for Speculation
Machinery
Marketable Securities (trading)
Notes Payable, Due in 90 Days
Petty Cash
Preferred Stock
Prepaid Insurance
Prepaid Rent
Purchases Discounts
Raw Materials Inventory
Rent Expense
Retained Earnings
Sales
Sales Discounts
Sales Returns and Allowances
Selling and Administrative Expenses
Supplies
Wages Payable
Work-in-Process Inventory

E 24.3 **LO 2** Prepare a list of all the accounts that will not appear on the balance sheet.

E 24.4
LO 1 **LO 2** Determine the accounts that will appear in the current asset section of the balance sheet and the order in which they should be listed.

E 24.5
LO 1 **LO 2** Determine the accounts that will appear in the long-term assets section of the balance sheet and the order in which they should be listed.

E 24.6
LO 1 **LO 2** Determine the accounts that will appear in the current liability section of the balance sheet and the order in which they should be listed.

E 24.7
LO 1 **LO 2** Determine the accounts that will appear in the long-term liability section of the balance sheet and the order in which they should be listed.

E 24.8
LO 2 Determine the accounts that will appear in the stockholders' equity section of the balance sheet and the order in which they should be listed.

E 24.9 **LO 2** Determine the accounts that will appear in the statement of stockholders' equity.

E 24.10
LO 2 Simmon Company has provided you with the following information concerning its stockholders' equity:

- Common stock, $1 par value, 1,000,000 shares authorized, 600,000 shares issued, 550,000 shares outstanding. The average additional paid-in capital was $30 per share when the shares were issued.

- Preferred stock, $100 par value, 500,000 shares authorized, 300,000 shares issued and outstanding. There is no additional paid-in capital on preferred shares. The preferred stock pays a 6 percent dividend and is cumulative.

- The beginning balance of retained earnings was $1,455,000. Dividends were declared during the year. The common stock dividend was $1.50 per share. The net income for the period was $5,980,500. Treasury stock was purchased during the year for $20 per share.

Prepare the stockholders' equity section of the balance sheet for Simmon Company.

E 24.11
LO 3 Locate the annual report of the Walt Disney Company. Describe management's responsibilities as they relate to communication of financial results.

E 24.12 LO 3 Locate the annual report of the Walt Disney Company. What type of audit report was issued? Why?

E 24.13 LO 3 Compare and contrast the four types of audit opinions.

E 24.14 LO 3 Using Lexis/Nexis or a similar database, find a company that received a qualified opinion. What was the cause of the qualification? How was the audit report written to reflect the qualification?

E 24.15 LO 3 Describe the role of the auditor in communicating financial information to external users.

PROBLEMS

P 24.1 LO 2 The following list of accounts was provided by Daniel Transportation Corporation, which has a September 30 fiscal year-end. Using these accounts, prepare a balance sheet for Daniel Transportation Corporation for fiscal 2000.

Accounts payable	$ 231,200
Accounts receivable	251,300
Accumulated depreciation, barges	114,900
Accumulated depreciation, buildings	133,600
Accumulated depreciation, tugboats	1,560,100
Allowance for uncollectible accounts	9,400
Barges	281,000
Buildings	275,000
Common stock	500,000
Cash	79,300
Installment note payable, long-term	685,400
Interest payable	34,300
Investment in BR, Inc., common stock	75,000
Land	115,700
Mortgage payable	88,300
Trade notes payable	157,000
Payroll taxes payable	14,900
Prepaid insurance	36,500
Retained earnings	?
Salaries and wages payable	26,800
Supplies	17,800
Temporary investments (trading securities)	121,500
Tugboats	2,785,400

P 24.2 LO 2 Presented below is a list of accounts taken from the general ledger of Bastia Electric Company. Prepare a balance sheet for the fiscal year ended December 31, 2000. Ignore income taxes.

Cash	$ 234,000
Sales	16,600,000
Marketable securities (trading)	306,000
Cost of goods sold	10,200,000
Investment in Ford Motor Company bonds	558,000
Investment in General Motors Company common stock	664,000
Notes payable, due in 120 days	180,000
Accounts payable	950,000
Selling and administrative expenses	5,800,000
Interest revenue	74,560
Land	620,000
Buildings	2,080,000
Dividends payable	320,000
Dividend revenue	61,440
Accrued liabilities	172,000
Accounts receivable	870,000
Accumulated depreciation, buildings	304,000
Allowance for uncollectible accounts	50,000
Interest expense	422,000
Inventory	1,194,000
Gain on sale of equipment	160,000
Prior period adjustment of underreported expenses (net of tax of $84,000)	196,000
Long-term notes payable	1,800,000
Discount on notes payable	20,000

Equipment	1,200,000
Bonds payable	2,200,000
Premium on bonds payable	45,000
Accumulated depreciation, equipment	80,000
Copyrights and patents	675,000
Treasury stock	382,000
Retained earnings (January 1, 1996)	404,000
Preferred stock	800,000
Common stock	1,180,000
Additional paid-in capital	160,000
Prepaid assets	120,000

P 24.3

LO 1   LO 2   LO 3

Refer to the annual report of Gap, Inc., and answer the following questions:
a. What is the total amount of current assets, and what types of assets are classified as current?
b. What is the total amount of long-term assets, and what types of assets are classified as long term?
c. What is the total amount of current liabilities, and what types of liabilities are classified as current?
d. What is the total amount of long-term liabilities, and what types of liabilities are classified as long term?
e. How did the Gap value its inventories?
f. What depreciation method did the Gap use?
g. Did the Gap report any items as other assets or other liabilities? If so, what are they?
h. Is the Gap's financial position better or worse than last period? Why or why not?
i. Is the Gap a good investment? Why or why not?

P 24.4

LO 1   LO 2   LO 3

Refer to the annual report of the Walt Disney Company, and answer the following questions:
a. What is the total amount of current assets, and what types of assets are classified as current?
b. What is the total amount of long-term assets, and what types of assets are classified as long term?
c. What is the total amount of current liabilities, and what types of liabilities are classified as current?
d. What is the total amount of long-term liabilities, and what types of liabilities are classified as long term?
e. How did Disney value its inventories?
f. What depreciation method did Disney use?
g. Did Disney report any items as other assets or other liabilities? If so, what are they?
h. Is Disney's financial position better or worse than last period? Why or why not?
i. Is Disney a good investment? Why or why not?

P 24.5

LO 1   LO 2   LO 3

Refer to the annual report of Wal-Mart, and answer the following questions:
a. What is the total amount of current assets, and what types of assets are classified as current?
b. What is the total amount of long-term assets, and what types of assets are classified as long term?
c. What is the total amount of current liabilities, and what types of liabilities are classified as current?
d. What is the total amount of long-term liabilities, and what types of liabilities are classified as long term?
e. How did Wal-mart value its inventories?
f. What depreciation method did Wal-mart use?
g. Did Wal-mart report any items as other assets or other liabilities? If so, what are they?
h. Is Wal-mart's financial position better or worse than last period? Why or why not?
i. Is Wal-mart a good investment? Why or why not?

P 24.6

LO 1   LO 2   LO 3

Refer to the annual report of Anheuser-Busch, and answer the following questions:
a. What is the total amount of current assets, and what types of assets are classified as current?
b. What is the total amount of long-term assets, and what types of assets are classified as long term?
c. What is the total amount of current liabilities, and what types of liabilities are classified as current?
d. What is the total amount of long-term liabilities, and what types of liabilities are classified as long term?
e. How did Anheuser-Busch value its inventories?
f. What depreciation method did Anheuser-Busch use?

g. Did Anheuser-Busch report any items as other assets or other liabilities? If so, what are they?

h. Is Anheuser-Busch's financial position better or worse than last period? Why or why not?

i. Is Anheuser-Busch a good investment? Why or why not?

P 24.7

LO 1   LO 2   LO 3

Refer to the Intel annual report and answer the following questions:

a. What is the total amount of current assets, and what types of assets are classified as current?

b. What is the total amount of long-term assets, and what types of assets are classified as long term?

c. What is the total amount of current liabilities, and what types of liabilities are classified as current?

d. What is the total amount of long-term liabilities, and what types of liabilities are classified as long term?

e. How did Intel value its inventories?

f. What depreciation method did Intel use?

g. Did Intel report any items as other assets or other liabilities? If so, what are they?

h. Is Intel's financial position better or worse than last period? Why or why not?

i. Is Intel a good investment? Why or why not?

P 24.8

LO 1   LO 2

Assume you have recently been hired to provide investment advice to the manager of Cushing Company. The company has excess cash that it needs to invest. The manager, Jenny Lyn, is concerned that she does not understand how to read financial statements. Write a memo to Jenny Lyn describing how to read and interpret a balance sheet.

P 24.9

LO 3

Refer to P 24.8. Write a memo to Jenny Lyn describing how to read and interpret an auditor's report.

P 24.10

LO 3

Using Disclosure or a similar database, find a company that was issued a qualified audit opinion and determine why the qualification was necessary.

CASES

C 24.1

LO 1   LO 2   LO 3

Refer to the annual report of the company you selected in Chapter 1 (C 1.1), and answer the following questions:

a. What is the total of current assets, and what types of assets are classified as current?

b. What is the total of long-term assets, and what types of assets are classified as long term?

c. What is the total of current liabilities, and what types of liabilities are classified as current?

d. What is the total of long-term liabilities, and what types of liabilities are classified as long term?

e. How did this company value its inventories?

f. What depreciation method did this company use?

g. Did this company report any items as other assets or other liabilities? If so, what are they?

h. Is this company's financial position better or worse than last period? Why?

i. Is this company a good investment? Why?

C 24.2

LO 2

The balance sheet of Zimbleman Company shown below, for fiscal 2000 contains several errors. Identify each of the errors and determine how to correct them.

ZIMBLEMAN COMPANY
Statement of Finances
For the Period Ending December 31, 2000

Debits

Current assets:	
Cash	$ 12,000
Accounts receivable, net	29,000
Prepaid rent	6,000
Total current assets	$ 47,000
Long-term assets:	
Land	50,000
Patents, net	45,000
Inventory	75,000
Buildings	280,000
Investment in Durk bonds	59,000
Discount on bonds payable	20,000
Silver mine	261,000
Total long-term assets	$790,000
Total assets	$837,000

Credits	
Current liabilities:	
Accounts payable	$ 35,000
Note payable, due June 1, 2003	50,000
Income tax payable	28,000
Total current liabilities	$113,000
Long-term liabilities:	
Accumulated depreciation, buildings	32,000
Mortgage payable	65,000
Accumulated depletion	26,000
Bonds payable	250,000
Total long-term liabilities	$373,000
Owners' equity:	
Common stock	200,000
Additional paid-in capital	125,000
Retained earnings	51,000
Treasury stock	25,000
Total owners' equity	$401,000
Total liabilities and owners' equity	$887,000

CRITICAL THINKING

CT 24.1
LO 3
Throughout this textbook you have seen examples regarding the relationships among the income statement, statement of retained earnings, and balance sheet. Write a paper describing, in detail, how these three statements are related.

CT 24.2
LO 2
Historical cost is a basic concept of accounting. Describe the concept of historical cost, and evaluate each of the items found on a typical balance sheet to determine if it is reported at historical cost.

ETHICAL CHALLENGES

EC 24.1
LO 1 **LO 2** **LO 3**
Assume you are an auditor and have significant doubts about whether your client is a going concern. According to the auditing standards, you must issue an adverse opinion. If you issue this adverse opinion and the company pulls through, the management will probably sue you. However, if you do not issue an adverse opinion and the company fails, the creditors and stockholders will probably sue you. What should you do in this situation?

EC 24.2
LO 2 **LO 3**
Assume you are an auditor and are concerned about how a client is reporting its marketable securities. You know that under certain circumstances marketable securities must be marked to market. In addition, you realize that if the marketable securities are classified as trading securities, any unrealized gains are shown on the income statement while unrealized gains on available-for-sale securities are disclosed in the owners' equity section of the balance sheet. Your client has recently reclassified a large amount of marketable securities from available-for-sale to trading securities. This reclassification increased its current ratio from 1.9 to 2.3. The company has a large loan outstanding that requires a current ratio of 2.0. How will you determine if the securities are correctly classified? How will the various stakeholders be affected by your decision?

COMPUTER APPLICATIONS

CA 24.1
LO 2
The following list of accounts was taken from the 1999 annual report of Chavez Fashions Corporation:

Accounts payable	$4,669,902
Accounts receivable	664,065
Accrued liabilities	1,639,292
Accrued rent obligation long-term	861,421
Accrued store closing costs	1,134,714
Accumulated depreciation and amortization	8,783,914
Additional paid-in capital	25,032,637
Cash	261,394

Common stock	37,688
Construction in progress	904,560
Deferred tax asset	478,200
Furniture and fixtures	4,727,134
Leasehold improvements	10,633,116
Leasehold interests, net	953,645
Long-term debt	2,200,000
Merchandise inventory	13,134,317
Other assets	65,005
Other equipment	1,432,871
Prepaid expenses	493,148
Retained deficit	10,612,113

Required Use a computer spreadsheet program.

a. Arrange the accounts in proper balance sheet order and show the equality of assets with liabilities and stockholders' equity. Hint: If you are unfamiliar with some of the accounts, use the balance sheet equation as an aid.

b. Determine the total dollar amount of current assets.

c. Determine the total dollar amount of long-term assets.

d. Determine the total dollar amount of current liabilities.

e. Determine the total dollar amount of long-term liabilities.

f. Determine the total dollar amount of stockholders' equity.

g. Repeat requirements (**a**) through (**f**) above assuming that all accounts increase by 15 percent.

CA 24.2

LO 2

The following list of accounts was adopted from the 2000 annual report of Johnsons Department Stores, Inc. Amounts are shown in thousands.

Accumulated depreciation	$ 911,996
Additional paid-in capital	622,634
Buildings and leasehold improvements	1,162,120
Buildings under capital leases	29,416
Buildings under construction	13,977
Capital lease obligations	31,621
Cash and cash equivalents	51,244
Commercial paper current	145,276
Common stock, class A	1,090
Common stock, class B	40
Current portion of capital lease obligation	2,242
Current portion of long-term debt	65,061
Deferred income taxes	282,648
Federal and state income taxes	54,011
Furniture, fixtures, and equipment	1,583,380
Investments and other assets	52,110
Land and land improvements	44,573
Long-term debt	1,238,293
Merchandise inventories	1,299,944
Other current assets	8,976
Preferred stock	440
Retained earnings	1,457,443
Trade accounts receivable, net	1,096,530
Trade and other accounts payable	529,475

Required Use a computer spreadsheet program.

a. Prepare a classified balance sheet and prove that total assets equal total liabilities plus total stockholders' equity. (*Hint:* If you are unfamiliar with some of the accounts, use the balance sheet equation as an aid.)

b. Determine the balance in retained earnings if total assets decrease by 5 percent, total liabilities remain the same, and stockholders' equity other than retained earnings remains the same.

CA 24.3

LO 2

Using Quicken.com or a similar online financial information service, find the condensed balance sheet for the Quaker Oat Company's most recent fiscal year. Compare the balance sheet you find on the Internet with the one shown in Exhibit 24.1. What significant changes do you find?

PART SEVEN

YOU ARE HERE

Chapter 25 examines the statement of cash flows. We learn how the statement is prepared using both the direct and indirect methods and how the statement can be analyzed both internally and externally. We examine cash flows from operating, investing, and financing activities as well as non-cash financing and investing activities. Chapter 25 relies on knowledge gained in Chapters 1–24.

LEARNING OBJECTIVES

LO 1 Describe the information companies provide users through the statement of cash flows.

LO 2 Discuss how companies determine and analyze cash flows from operating activities using the direct format.

LO 3 Discuss how companies determine and analyze cash flows from operating activities using the indirect format.

LO 4 Explain how companies determine and analyze cash flows from investing activities.

LO 5 Explain how companies determine and analyze cash flows from financing activities.

Firm Performance: Cash Flows

The Reebok brand of athletic shoes originated from the Joseph William Foster family, four generations past. Joseph was an avid runner who desperately wanted a pair of spiked running shoes. But, alas, none were found in Boston in the late 1800s. So Joseph made his own. By 1900, Joseph began his own business

REEBOK
www.reebok.com

(Fosters) making handmade running shoes for local athletes. Joseph and his wife lived over the workshop where their two sons, John William and James William, were born. As the boys grew into men, the company also grew and became J.W. Foster & Sons, experts in making running shoes. Reebok, named after the African gazelle, was formed in 1958 by two sons of James William.

Today, Reebok is a major competitor in the field of athletic shoes and apparel. Its fiscal

1997 net sales were $3.6 billion, notwithstanding a troubled industry. As Paul Fireman, chairman and CEO, said, "The athletic footwear and apparel industry is experiencing some very difficult conditions due to a slowdown in consumer demand which has resulted in a retail inventory back-up and a highly promotional environment." He went on to state, "We believe our Reebok footwear technologies—DMX and 3D UltraLite—represent true breakthroughs in athletic footwear. We will focus in 1998 on continuing to lead those technologies through impactful direct-to-the-consumer marketing campaigns . . . designed to separate Reebok from the competition and build consumer pull." In addition, Reebok plans to focus resources on its Rockport, Ralph Lauren, and Greg Norman brands. It also plans to market its products to lovers of all sports, young and old, men and women.[1]

In order for Reebok to achieve its goals it must generate cash flows in addition to profits. How can Reebok's management, stockholders, and creditors determine whether and from what sources cash is being generated and/or used?

[1]www.reebok.com/corp

In previous chapters, we examined the income statement, the statement of retained earnings, and the balance sheet. In this chapter, we examine the fourth financial statement required by the FASB—the statement of cash flows. The statement of cash flows provides an additional link between the accrual-based income statement and the balance sheet because the statement of cash flows shows the changes in cash from operations. Users need to comprehend the elements included on the cash flow statement so that they can make informed decisions regarding the liquidity and solvency of the reporting company.

GAAP AND THE STATEMENT OF CASH FLOWS

LO 1

Comparatively speaking, the statement of cash flows is a new statement. Prior to its adoption in 1987, companies prepared a statement of changes in financial position. That statement was designed to show the sources and uses of working capital (current assets minus current liabilities) provided to, or used by, a company during the period of time covered by the income statement. Due to the variety of methods used to prepare the statement of changes in financial position and the resulting confusion that existed among statement users, the Financial Accounting Standards Board determined that a statement that showed cash flows would be more useful.

The following classic example shows how cash flow information is more useful than working capital information. In 1975, when W.T. Grant Company declared bankruptcy, it was the nation's 17th largest retailer competing with companies such as Kmart and J.C. Penney. It achieved this growth by expanding its product line into durable goods, marketing its products to lower-income consumers, and offering easy financing through a credit card system. Most customers were allowed 36 months to pay the balances they owed Grant with a $1 minimum payment per month. Thus W.T. Grant showed large amounts of both inventory (due to the expanded product line) and accounts receivable (due to the easy financing) on its financial statements.

In the 10 years prior to Grant's bankruptcy declaration, the company showed positive net income and working capital. As Exhibit 25.1 shows, beginning in 1973, its net income and working capital position began to deteriorate. However, the cash flows of the company began to decline much earlier (in 1969), falling off sharply in 1972. This was due to the large amount of uncollectible receivables on the books of W.T. Grant. Eventually, credit was denied Grant; the company was unable to pay its debts, and it ceased to be a going concern. If W.T. Grant had presented and relied upon the information included in a statement of cash flows instead of a statement of changes in financial position, its management, stockholders, and creditors would have been warned of its impending doom much sooner and, perhaps, Grant could have been saved.

What Is the Purpose of the Statement of Cash Flows?

The statement of cash flows has four primary purposes. According to the FASB, the statement of cash flows is useful to:

- Assess the entity's ability to generate positive future net cash flows. Operating activities must provide sufficient net cash flows to support the firm's future

EXHIBIT 25.1

Cash versus Working Capital Flows

W. T. Grant Company Net Income, Cash Flows from Operations, and Working Capital from Operations for the Years Ended January 31, 1966 to 1975

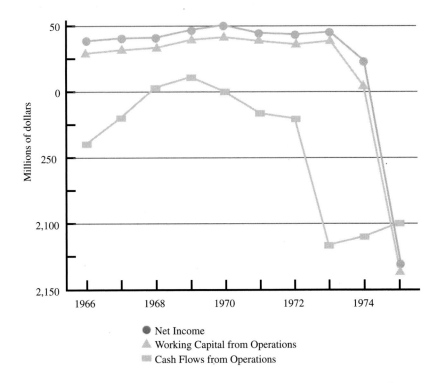

● Net Income
▲ Working Capital from Operations
▪ Cash Flows from Operations

operations. The relationship between sales and the operating cash flows from year to year provides insights into the firm's ability to sustain positive net cash flows.

- Assess the entity's ability to meet its obligations and pay dividends, and its need for external financing. The statement of cash flows provides a clear picture of the sources and uses of a company's cash flows. It indicates whether the firm has the ability to generate the cash needed to meet its obligations to its creditors and owners.

- Assess the reasons for differences between income and associated cash receipts and payments. The statement of cash flows provides information that highlights the specific reasons for the difference between accounting income and cash flows from operations.

- Assess both the cash and noncash aspects of the entity's investing and financing transactions during the period. The statement of cash flows specifically identifies and discloses significant noncash investing and financing activities undertaken by the firm to provide complete information about the events that have future cash flow implications.

Why Are the Sections of the Statement of Cash Flows Important?

Recall from previous chapters that the statement of cash flows is divided into three distinct sections: operating, investing, and financing. These sections represent the basic and significant functions of any business enterprise and the amounts of cash flowing in and out of the enterprise as a result of the business activities. In addition, the information contained in these sections achieves the four purposes of the statement of cash flows presented previously. Exhibit 25.2 shows the basic functions of business and how they are classified on the statement of cash flows. We look at each of the cash flow sections in turn.

Operating Activities As Exhibit 25.2 illustrates, operating activities involve transactions that result from the earnings process of the company. Cash inflows from operating activities are primarily from customers, but cash also increases due to interest and

EXHIBIT 25.2 Cash Inflows and Outflows

Business Activities	Inflows	Outflows
Operating activities	Collections from customers Collections of interest Collections of dividends	Payments to suppliers of goods and services Payments to employees Payments for interest Payments for taxes
Investing activities	Proceeds from sales of long-term assets Collections of loans made to other entities	Purchases of long-term assets Loans made to other entities Purchases of short-term investments
Financing activities	Proceeds from sales of short-term investments Proceeds from issuance of debt Proceeds from issuance of stock	Payment of long-term debt Purchase of treasury stock Payment of cash dividends

dividends received by the company. Cash outflows from operating activities result from payments made for operating expenses, including the purchase of inventory.

Notice that cash received from dividends is an operating activity, but cash paid for dividends is a financing activity. Dividends received are earned income from investments, while dividends paid are not expenses of the business; that is, they are not incurred in an attempt to generate revenues. Rather, dividends paid reflect the company's decision about when and how to distribute its earnings.

The presentation of the operating section of the statement of cash flows allows readers to (1) assess the entity's ability to generate positive future cash flows and (2) assess the reasons for differences between a company's accounting income and its associated cash receipts and payments. The ability of a company to generate cash from operations is crucial. If cash is not generated by operations, then the ability of the company to pay its current liabilities is questionable. Recall our discussion of liquidity in Chapter 12.

Investing Activities   Investing activities usually involve acquiring and disposing of property, plant, and equipment; other long-term investments; and short-term or temporary investments that are not considered cash equivalents. For example, Reebok defines cash equivalents as "highly liquid investments with maturities of three months or less at date of purchase." Other short-term investments owned by Reebok would not be considered "cash equivalents." Exhibit 25.2 shows that disposing of these assets results in cash inflows, while purchasing them results in cash outflows.

Analyzing the investing activities section of the statement of cash flows allows users to assess the entity's ability to continue to operate and pay dividends, as well as its need for external financing. Because the company needs assets to operate, and because long-term assets are normally financed with long-term debt or equity, analyzing the investing activities of the company provides users with insight into both the future investing and the future financing needs of the company.

Financing Activities   Financing activities involve borrowing from and repaying creditors, raising funds from owners, and distributing funds to owners that are either a return on, or a return of, investment. Exhibit 25.2 shows that issuing debt and issuing stock both result in cash inflows, while repayment of debt and equity result in cash outflows.

Analyzing financing activities of the statement of cash flows also allows users to assess the entity's ability to pay dividends as well as its ability to invest in additional assets. For example, if a company issues long-term debt in the current period, it can use the funds to finance assets. Users should also analyze financing cash flows because, typically, the borrowing of money requires interest payments, which, in turn, may require additional cash flows from operations.

Noncash Investing and Financing Activities In addition to the types of cash flow events shown in Exhibit 25.2, companies also present noncash investing and financing events either on the statement of cash flows or in the notes to the financial statements. For example, if Reebok issues 100,000 shares of its common stock in exchange for a building, this would be reported as a noncash investing/financing event.

It is necessary to show financial statement users the noncash means of financing that the company uses to acquire its assets because of their future cash flow impact. The example above may have cash flow implications because of the related dividends that Reebok may pay in the future. Or, if a company buys land by issuing a lump-sum payment note, the note will require a cash outflow in the future.

Now that you understand the purpose of the statement of cash flows, we focus attention on the determination and analysis of cash flows. Externally, cash flows are evaluated by analyzing the statement of cash flows in conjunction with the income statement, statement of retained earnings, and balance sheet. Internally, management uses cash flow statement information plus additional information it has available concerning the amounts and timing of cash flows.

DETERMINATION AND ANALYSIS OF OPERATING CASH FLOWS

The events represented in the operating activities section of the statement of cash flows may be presented in either the direct or indirect format. The **direct format** shows the actual cash inflows and outflows of operating activities. The **indirect format** shows the differences between accrual-based net income and cash flows from operations. Note that the only difference between the direct and indirect formats concerns the operating activities section and that regardless of the format used, the amount of net cash flows from operating activities is the same.

To illustrate all the components and calculations of cash flows, we will use a company called Cowboy Boots and Shoes. Then we will relate this discussion to Reebok. Exhibit 25.3 shows Cowboy Boots and Shoes' statement of cash flows prepared using the direct format, while Exhibit 25.4 shows the statement of cash flows using the indirect format. The corresponding income statement, statement of retained earnings, and balance sheets of Cowboy Boots and Shoes are illustrated in Exhibits 25.5, 25.6, and 25.7, respectively. You may want to flag these exhibits as we will refer to them throughout this chapter.

Take a moment to examine Exhibits 25.3 through 25.7. Notice that the amount shown as net income on the income statement in Exhibit 25.5 is also shown as an increase to retained earnings on the statement of retained earnings in Exhibit 25.6. The amounts shown as the beginning and ending balances of retained earnings on the statement of retained earnings are also shown on the comparative balance sheets in Exhibit 25.7. How does the statement of cash flows fit with the other three financial statements? It indicates the difference between accrual-based net income and cash flows from operations, and it shows

EXHIBIT   25.3   Statement of Cash Flows—Direct Method

COWBOY BOOTS AND SHOES
Statement of Cash Flows (Direct Method)
For the Year Ended December 31, 1999
(in thousands)

Net cash flows from operating activities:

Cash received from customers	$100,500
Cash received from renters	7,500
Cash paid for inventory	(58,125)
Cash paid for insurance	(2,700)
Cash paid for wages	(4,800)
Cash paid for miscellaneous expenses	(4,200)
Cash paid for income taxes	(6,075)
Cash paid for interest	(960)
Net cash flows from operating activities	$ 24,390

Net cash flows from investing activities:

Cash received from sale of trading securities	$ 1,950
Cash received from sale of equipment	800
Cash paid for building	(25,650)
Cash paid for equipment	(6,050)
Net cash flows from investing activities	$(28,950)

Net cash flows from financing activities:

Cash received from short-term note payable	$ 150
Cash received from bond issues	14,100
Cash paid for treasury stock	(12,500)
Cash paid for dividends	(5,000)
Net cash flows from financing activities	$ (3,250)

Net change in cash during 1999	$ (7,810)
Add beginning balance of cash	42,250
Ending balance of cash	$ 34,440

Other investing and financing activities not requiring cash:

Purchase of building with preferred stock	$ 12,150

Reconciliation of net income to cash flows from operations:

Net income	$ 13,650

Adjustments to reconcile net income to net cash flows from operations:

Depreciation expense—buildings	5,850
Depreciation expense—equipment	3,150
Amortization expense—patent	1,050
Gain on sale of trading securities	(900)
Loss on sale of equipment	2,250
Amortization of discount on note payable	15
Increase in accounts receivable, net	(8,100)
Increase in inventory	(600)
Decrease in prepaid insurance	300
Increase in accounts payable	8,175
Increase in rent received in advance	150
Decrease in wages payable	(300)
Decrease in interest payable	(75)
Decrease in taxes payable	(225)
Net cash flows from operating activities	$ 24,390

the change in the Cash account on the balance sheet due to operating, investing, and financing activities.

As Exhibit 25.3 illustrates, one advantage of the direct format is that it clearly shows the amounts of cash received by or paid for operating activities. However, one disadvantage is that the FASB requires companies to disclose, either on the statement or in the

EXHIBIT   25.4   Statement of Cash Flows—Indirect Method

COWBOY BOOTS AND SHOES
Statement of Cash Flows (Indirect Method)
For the Year Ended December 31, 1999
(in thousands)

Net cash flows from operating activities:	
Net income	$13,650
Adjustments to reconcile net income to net cash flows from operations:	
Depreciation expense—building	5,850
Depreciation expense—equipment	3,150
Amortization expense—patent	1,050
Amortization of discount on note payable	15
Gain on sale of trading securities	(900)
Loss on sale of equipment	2,250
Increase in accounts receivable, net	(8,100)
Increase in inventory	(600)
Decrease in prepaid insurance	300
Increase in accounts payable	8,175
Increase in rent received in advance	150
Decrease in wages payable	(300)
Decrease in interest payable	(75)
Decrease in taxes payable	(225)
Net cash flows from operating activities	$24,390
Net cash flows from investing activities:	
Cash received from sale of trading securities	$ 1,950
Cash received from sale of equipment	800
Cash paid for building	(25,650)
Cash paid for equipment	(6,050)
Net cash flows from investing activities	$28,950
Net cash flows from financing activities:	
Cash received from short-term note payable	$150
Cash received from bond issues	14,100
Cash paid for treasury stock	(12,500)
Cash paid for dividends	(5,000)
Net cash flows from financing activities	$ (3,250)
Net change in cash during 1999	$ (7,810)
Add beginning balance of cash	42,250
Ending balance of cash	$34,440
Other investing and financing activities not requiring cash:	
Purchase of building with preferred stock	$12,150
Additional disclosures:	
Cash paid for interest	$ 960
Cash paid for taxes	$ 6075

notes, a reconciliation of accrual-based net income to the amount of cash flows from operations to achieve the fourth purpose of the statement of cash flows. This reconciliation (shown on the bottom of Exhibit 25.3) is essentially the same information shown in the indirect format for the statement of cash flows in Exhibit 25.4. Therefore, one advantage of the indirect format is that it clearly shows the difference between net income and cash flows from operations.

Although the FASB suggests the use of the direct format for presenting cash flows from operations, *Accounting Trends and Techniques* reports that 97.5 percent of companies use the indirect format. We examine the direct and indirect formats of reporting operating cash flows in more detail next.

EXHIBIT 25.5   Income Statement

COWBOY BOOTS AND SHOES
Income Statement
For the Year Ended December 31, 1999
(in thousands)

Sales		$109,500
Cost of goods sold		65,700
Gross margin		$ 43,800
Operating expenses:		
Wages	$4,500	
Insurance	3,000	
Uncollectible accounts	900	
Miscellaneous	4,200	
Depreciation—building	5,850	
Depreciation—equipment	3,150	
Amortization—patent	1,050	22,650
Operating income		$ 21,150
Other revenues and gains:		
Rent revenue	$ 600	
Gain on sale of trading securities	900	1,500
Other expenses and losses:		
Interest expense	$ 900	
Loss on sale of equipment	2,250	$ (3,150)
Income from continuing operations		$ 19,500
Income tax expense		5,850
Net income		$ 13,650

EXHIBIT 25.6   Statement of Retained Earnings

COWBOY BOOTS AND SHOES
Statement of Retained Earnings
For the Year Ended December 31, 1999
(in thousands)

Retained earnings, January 1, 1999	$85,385
Add net income	13,650
	$99,035
Less dividends declared	4,950
Retained earnings, December 31, 1999	$94,085

Determination of Operating Cash Flows: Direct Format

LO 2

As Exhibit 25.3 illustrates, the direct format indicates the amounts of cash received from customers and the other sources of operating cash, such as dividends and interest. In addition, it shows how much cash the company paid for interest, taxes, and other operating activities. Throughout the text, we have shown calculations of cash flows using the direct format. We review this process of determining operating cash flows next.

To determine the cash flows for a particular operating item on the income statement, it is necessary to relate that item to a balance sheet account because the income-generating and cash flow activities of the company cause changes in the operating, balance sheet accounts of the company. For example, if a company had no sales on account, it would not have an accounts receivable account. But companies that have sales on account must have an accounts receivable account because of the timing difference between sales and collections of sales. Companies use the beginning and ending balances of a given balance sheet account, along with the related revenue or expense amount from the income statement, to determine the related cash flows for the period.

EXHIBIT 25.7 Comparative Balance Sheets

COWBOY BOOTS AND SHOES
Balance Sheets
December 31, 1999 and 1998
(in thousands)

	1999	1998
Assets		
Cash	$ 34,440	$ 42,250
Trading securities, net	750	1,800
Accounts receivable, net	22,410	14,310
Inventory	20,100	19,500
Prepaid insurance	450	750
Building	150,450	112,650
Accumulated depreciation, building	(45,900)	(40,050)
Equipment	51,900	50,850
Accumulated depreciation, equipment	(16,650)	(15,450)
Patent, net	11,700	12,750
Total assets	$229,650	$199,360
Liabilities and Owners' Equity		
Liabilities:		
Accounts payable	$ 24,225	$ 16,050
Notes payable	300	150
Rent received in advance	600	450
Interest payable	225	300
Taxes payable	425	650
Wages payable	750	1,050
Dividends payable	100	150
Long-term notes payable	750	750
Discount on notes payable	(60)	(75)
Bonds payable	13,500	0
Premium on bonds payable	600	0
Total liabilities	$ 41,415	$ 19,475
Owners' Equity:		
Preferred stock	$ 36,500	$ 30,000
Additional paid-in capital, preferred stock	14,600	8,950
Common stock	23,000	23,000
Additional paid-in capital, common stock	32,550	32,550
Retained earnings	94,085	85,385
Treasury stock	(12,500)	0
Total owners' equity	$188,235	$179,885
Total liabilities and owners' equity	$229,650	$199,360

Why Don't Revenues Equal Cash Inflows? Remember that a company's revenues shown on its income statement might differ from its cash inflows from operations for two reasons: (1) the revenue is earned before the cash is collected or (2) the cash is collected before the revenue is earned.

Revenues, Current Assets, and Cash Inflows For example, Cowboy Boots and Shoes allows its customers to charge purchases on account (accounts receivable) and it accepts rent payments in advance from customers (rent received in advance), as noted on its balance sheets in Exhibit 25.7. Thus we would expect the cash inflows from customers to be different from the amount of revenues earned during the period because revenues would be recognized before the cash is actually received, when customers charge on account, and after cash is received when customers pay in advance.

The accounts receivables on the balance sheets are shown net of related allowance for doubtful accounts, so cash receipts from customers is calculated as shown below:

> Beginning balance of Accounts Receivable, net
> \+ Sales on account during the period
> = Maximum amount of cash owed by customers
> − Uncollectible accounts expense
> − Sales discounts
> − Sales returns and allowances
> − **Cash collections from customers during the period**
> = Ending balance of Accounts Receivable, net[2]

Using the information in Exhibits 25.5 and 25.7 and solving for the unknown cash collection results in the following:

$ 14,310,000	Beginning balance (Exhibit 25.7)
109,500,000	Sales (Exhibit 25.5)
$123,810,000	Maximum collectible
(900,000)	Uncollectible accounts (Exhibit 25.5)
(100,500,000)	**Cash received from customers (Exhibit 25.3)[3]**
$ 22,410,000	Ending balance

Therefore, cash collections from customers equal $100,500,000. Take a moment to locate these items in the appropriate exhibits. Companies follow this type of approach to determine the amount of cash received from other operating sources such as dividends, interest, and rent.

PAUSE & REFLECT

Reebok reported net sales of $3,643,599 (in thousands) in 1997, and its beginning and ending balances of accounts receivable, net were $590,504 (in thousands) and $561,729 (in thousands), respectively. What is your estimate of cash collected from customers?[4] *(answer on page 872)*

Revenues, Current Liabilities, and Cash Inflows In addition to cash receipts from accounts receivable customers, Cowboy Boots and Shoes also receives rent from customers. We determine the amount of cash received from rental customers as shown below:

> Beginning balance of Rent Received in Advance
> \+ **Cash received from renters during the period**
> = Maximum rent owed to renters
> − Rent revenues earned during the period
> = Ending balance of Rent Received in Advance

---

[2]If the Accounts Receivable account is separate from an Allowance for Doubtful Accounts, then the following is used:

> Beginning Accounts Receivable
> \+ Sales on account
> = Maximum amount due from customers
> − Accounts written off during the period
> − Sales discounts
> − Sales returns and allowances
> − Cash collections from customers
> = Ending Accounts Receivable

[3]We determine the amount of cash received from customers as $123,810,000 − $900,000 − $22,410,000 = $100,500,000. Throughout this chapter you must use algebra to determine the missing amounts.

[4]<www.sec.edgar.gov/reebok>.

Using the information in Exhibits 25.5 and 25.7 and solving for the unknown cash amount, we determine cash received from rental customers as shown below:

$ 450,000	Beginning balance (Exhibit 25.7)
750,000	**Cash received from renters (Exhibit 25.3)**[5]
$1,200,000	Maximum rent owed
(600,000)	Rent revenue (Exhibit 25.5)
$ 600,000	Ending balance (Exhibit 25.7)

Take a moment to locate these amounts in the appropriate financial statements.

Why Don't Expenses Equal Cash Outflows?   Recall that a company's expenses can differ from the actual amounts of cash paid for expense items for two reasons: (1) the expenses are incurred before the cash is paid or (2) the expenses are incurred after the cash is paid.

Expenses, Current Assets, and Cash Outflows   Cowboy Boots and Shoes pays for its insurance in advance and, therefore, has a current asset called Prepaid Insurance. We determine the amount of cash paid for insurance using the following format:

	Beginning balance of Prepaid Insurance
+	**Cash paid for insurance during the period**
=	Maximum insurance rights available
−	Insurance expense during the period
=	Ending balance of Prepaid Insurance

Using the information from Exhibits 25.5 and 25.7 and solving for the unknown cash amount results in the following:

$ 750,000	Beginning balance (Exhibit 25.7)
2,700,000	**Cash paid for insurance (Exhibit 25.3)**[6]
$3,450,000	Maximum insurance available
(3,000,000)	Insurance expense (Exhibit 25.5)
$ 450,000	Ending balance (Exhibit 25.7)

Take a moment to locate these numbers in the appropriate financial statements.

Expenses, Current Liabilities, and Cash Outflows   Many expenses are incurred prior to the cash payment. For example, Cowboy Boots and Shoes's employees earn wages prior to payment; therefore, Cowboy has a Wages Payable account. To determine the amount of cash paid for wages, we use the following format:

	Beginning balance of Wages Payable
+	Wages expense during the period
=	Maximum amount of cash owed to employees
−	**Cash paid to employees during the period**
=	Ending balance of Wages Payable

Using the information from Exhibits 25.5 and 25.7, we find that Cowboy Boots and Shoes paid $4,800,000 in wages during the year:

$1,050,000	Beginning balance (Exhibit 25.7)
4,500,000	Wages expense (Exhibit 25.5)
$5,550,000	Maximum owed to employees
(4,800,000)	**Cash paid to employees (Exhibit 25.3)**[7]
$ 750,000	Ending balance (Exhibit 25.7)

---

[5]We determine cash received from renters as $600,000 + $600,000 = $1,200,000; $1,200,000 − $450,000 = $750,000.

[6]We determine cash paid for insurance as $450,000 + $3,000,000 = $3,450,000; $3,450,000 − $750,000 = $2,700,000.

[7]Cash paid to employees is calculated as $5,550,000 − $750,000 = $4,800,000.

Likewise, cash paid for income taxes is determined as follows:

Beginning balance of Taxes Payable
+ Tax expense during the period
= Maximum amount of cash owed for taxes
− **Cash paid for taxes during the period**
= Ending balance of Taxes Payable

Based on this relationship, we can determine cash paid for income taxes using the information from Exhibits 25.5 and 25.7 as follows:

$ 650,000	Beginning balance (Exhibit 25.7)
5,850,000	Tax expense (Exhibit 25.5)
$6,500,000	Maximum taxes owed
(6,075,000)	**Cash paid for taxes (Exhibit 25.3)[8]**
$ 425,000	Ending balance (Exhibit 25.7)

Determining the amount of cash paid for interest is a little more complicated. Recall that interest expense can be greater than or less than the cash paid for interest due to discounts and premiums on long-term debt. Therefore, to determine the amount of cash paid for interest, we must analyze the Interest Payable account as well as the premium or discount accounts associated with long-term debt. For example, Cowboy Boots and Shoes has a note payable that was issued at a discount. Recall that when a note is issued at a discount, the amount of interest expense is greater than the amount of cash interest paid. Based on this information, we analyze the Interest Payable account as shown below:

Beginning balance of Interest Payable
+ Interest expense less discount amortization
= Maximum amount of cash owed for interest
− **Cash paid for interest during the period**
= Ending balance of Interest Payable

Let's locate this information in Exhibits 25.5 and 25.7. In Exhibit 25.5 we notice that interest expense for the period is $900,000. From Exhibit 25.7 we determine that discount amortization (decrease in Discount on Notes Payable) is $15,000. Therefore, the cash paid for interest during the period is:

$ 300,000	Beginning balance (Exhibit 25.7)
885,000	($900,000 − $15,000)
$1,185,000	Maximum interest owed
(960,000)	**Cash paid for interest (Exhibit 25.3)[9]**
$ 225,000	Ending balance (Exhibit 25.7)

---

[8]Cash paid for taxes is calculated as $6,500,000 − $425,000 = $6,075,000.

[9]We calculate cash paid for interest as $1,185,000 − $225,000 = $960,000.

Expenses, Current Assets, Current Liabilities, and Cash Outflows Because inventory is typically purchased on account, determining the amount of cash paid for inventory involves an analysis of both the Inventory and Accounts Payable accounts. For example, Cowboy purchases its inventory on account (Accounts Payable), which it records as an asset (Inventory) until it is sold. Therefore, to determine the amount of cash paid for inventory, we must determine the changes in both accounts. We know the following relationships:

	Beginning balance of Inventory
+	Purchases during the period
=	Maximum amount of inventory available for sale
−	Purchase returns and allowances
−	Cost of goods sold
=	Ending balance of Inventory

	Beginning balance of Accounts Payable
+	Purchases during the period
=	Maximum amount of cash owed for inventory
−	Purchase returns and allowances
−	**Cash paid for inventory during the period[10]**
=	Ending balance of Accounts Payable

Using the information in Exhibits 25.5 and 25.7, we find cash paid for inventory during the period in two steps as shown below. First, determine the amount of purchases made during the period by solving for the unknown amount in the Inventory analysis. Then find the cash paid for inventory by solving for the unknown amount in the Accounts Payable analysis.

$19,500,000	Beginning balance (Exhibit 25.7)
__66,300,000__	**Purchases made during the period[11]**
$85,800,000	Maximum inventory available
(65,700,000)	Cost of goods sold (Exhibit 25.5)
$20,100,000	Ending balance (Exhibit 25.7)
$16,050,000	Beginning balance (Exhibit 25.7)
__66,300,000__	Purchases made during the period (above)
$82,350,000	Maximum owed for inventory
(58,125,000)	**Cash paid for inventory (Exhibit 25.3)[12]**
$ 24,225,000	Ending balance (Exhibit 25.7)

Take a moment to locate these amounts in the appropriate exhibits.

PAUSE & REFLECT

Reebok reported cost of sales (cost of goods sold) of $2,294,049 (in thousands) for fiscal 1997. Its beginning and ending balances of Inventory and Accounts Payable (in thousands) were as follows:[13]

	Beginning	Ending
Inventory	$544,522	$563,735
Accounts payable	196,368	192,142

What is your estimate of cash paid for inventory during 1997? *(answer on page 872)*

There is one more operating item on the income statement that we must analyze. Miscellaneous expense incurred during the period is $4,200,000. How much cash was paid for miscellaneous expense during the year? Because we have analyzed all the current,

---

[10]If we had Discounts lost during the period it would be added to this amount because payments would have been more than the recorded liability.

[11]We determine purchases as $20,100,000 + $65,700,000 = $85,800,000; $85,800,000 − $19,500,000 = $66,300,000.

[12]Cash paid for purchases is determined as $82,350,000 − $24,225,000 = $58,125,000.

[13]<www.sec.edgar/gov/reebok>.

operating assets and current, operating liabilities, we can assume that the amount of cash paid for miscellaneous expense is the same amount as the expense; $4,200,000. Take a moment to locate this amount on both the income statement (Exhibit 25.5) and statement of cash flows (Exhibit 25.3). The remaining items on the income statement are noncash items. Therefore, we have fully explained the cash flows from operating activities as Exhibit 25.3 illustrates.

Analysis of Cash Flows from Operating Activities: Direct Format

An analysis of cash flows from operations should compare the current period's cash flows to prior periods. This enables the user to assess trends in cash inflows and outflows for various activities. In addition, users should compare the cash flows of the company to others in the same industry. This comparison allows assessment of the cash flows of the company relative to others.

When companies present operating cash flows using the direct format, users can analyze operating cash flows to determine if cash inflows are large enough to cover cash outflows. Users can also assess whether the company is collecting revenue and paying current obligations in a timely fashion. Although the exact timing of cash flows is unknown to external users, they can get a general idea of the timing by examining the amounts of cash inflows and outflows compared to the total amounts due.

For example, Cowboy Boots and Shoes collected 81 percent of the amount due from accounts receivable customers during this period as shown below:

$$\frac{\text{Cash collected from customers}}{\text{Beginning accounts receivable} + \text{Sales}} = \frac{\$100,500,000}{\$14,310,000 + \$109,500,000} = 81\%$$

Cowboy also paid 71 percent of the total amount due to inventory suppliers during the period as indicated by the following calculation:

$$\frac{\text{Cash paid to inventory suppliers}}{\text{Beginning accounts payable} + \text{Purchases}} = \frac{\$58,125,000}{\$16,050,000 + \$66,300,000} = 71\%$$

These ratios, together with the information generated from the accounts receivable and inventory turnovers, provides information about the amount and timing of cash generated from customers and paid to suppliers of inventory.

Determination of Operating Cash Flows: Indirect Format

LO 3

As Exhibit 25.4 illustrates, the indirect format for the statement of cash flows presents the amount of cash generated from operations by adjusting the net income for items that cause cash from operations to differ from accrual-based net income. To present cash flows in the indirect format, also called the *reconciliation format,* companies begin with the amount of accrual-based net income and apply a series of adjustments to convert net income to cash from operations.

The four adjustments made to net income to determine cash flows from operations using the indirect format are:

- Adjustments for noncash income statement items
- Adjustments for gains and losses
- Adjustments for changes in noncash current operating assets
- Adjustments for changes in current operating liabilities

Adjustments for Noncash Income Statement Items   Noncash income statement items increase or decrease income but do not affect operating cash flows. Therefore, for any noncash expenses that reduce income but do not reduce operating cash flows, it is necessary to add them back to net income in order to convert net income to cash from operations. For any noncash revenues that increase net income but do not increase operating cash flows, it is necessary to deduct them from net income to convert the net income to cash from operations.

We discuss two common noncash adjustments next: (1) depreciation and amortization and (2) interest adjustments due to premiums or discounts. These items affect the amount of accrual-based net income but do not require the use or receipt of cash.

Depreciation, Depletion, and Amortization Items such as depreciation of plant assets and amortization of intangibles are added back to net income to derive cash flows because they do not require an outlay of cash but they do reduce net income.

For example, Exhibit 25.5 indicates that Cowboy Boots and Shoes's depreciation expense for buildings was $5,850,000, depreciation expense for equipment was $3,150,000, and amortization of patents expense was $1,050,000. These amounts are added back to net income to determine cash flows from operations, as shown in Exhibit 25.4.

Interest Adjustments The portion of interest expense related to amortization of discounts on notes and bonds payable is also added back to net income to determine cash flows from operations. The expense is different from the actual amount of cash outflow, thus requiring a net income adjustment. This type of adjustment is necessary when a company pays interest on a note issued at a discount (premium) because the amount of interest expense is greater (less) than the actual amount of cash paid.

For example, as discussed previously, Cowboy Boots and Shoes has a note payable that was issued at a discount. Therefore, the amount of interest expense that reduces net income is greater than the cash impact of the interest. Therefore, Cowboy must add back the $15,000 difference to net income to determine operating cash flows, as shown in Exhibit 25.4.[14]

Adjustments for Gains and Losses
The events that generate gains and losses may affect the cash flows of the firm, but these events are either investing or financing events and are reported as such on the statement of cash flows. Therefore, it is important to remove the impact of gains and losses from accrual-based net income when converting income to cash from operations using the indirect format. Because gains increase reported net income, they must be subtracted as a net income adjustment to determine cash flows from operations. On the other hand, losses decrease reported net income and, therefore, must be added as a net income adjustment to determine cash flows from operations.

For example, as shown in Exhibit 25.5, Cowboy has a $900,000 gain from the sale of trading securities and a loss of $2,250,000 from the sale of equipment. On the statement of cash flows, the gain is subtracted from net income because it increased net income but did not provide operating cash flows, while the loss is added to net income because it decreased income but did not use operating cash flows (see Exhibit 25.4).

Adjustments for Changes in Noncash Current Operating Assets
The indirect format uses the changes in noncash current operating asset accounts to adjust accrual-based net income. **Noncash current operating assets** are noncash accounts that represent operating activities. Note that not all current asset accounts fall into this category. For example, trading securities, which are not cash equivalents, and nontrade notes receivables reflect investing events and, therefore, the cash flows associated with these events appear in the investing activities section of the statement of cash flows.

An increase in a noncash current operating asset during the period indicates one of two things: (1) the revenue associated with the account was greater than the amount of cash inflow or (2) the expense associated with the account was less than the cash outflow. Because the related revenues and expenses are reflected in net income at the end of the period, the increase in a noncash current operating asset must be deducted from accrual-based net income to derive the amount of cash flows from operations. Conversely, the decrease in a noncash current operating asset must be added to accrual-based net income.

---

[14]For creditors, the amount of interest income due to the amortization of discounts on notes receivables and investments in bonds is subtracted from accrual-based net income because the amount of cash received by the company is less than the interest income it earned during the period. Conversely, the amount of interest income due to the amortization of premiums on notes receivables and investments in bonds is added to net income because the amount of cash received is greater than the interest income earned during the period. (Note that Cowboy did not require any adjustments for interest income during the period.)

Analysis of Noncash Current Operating Assets Related to Revenues When a noncash current operating asset such as accounts receivable is related to revenue, an increase in the account implies that revenues were greater than cash receipts from customers. On the other hand, a decrease indicates that the amount of revenues was less than the cash receipts from customers. Therefore, the amount of increase in the account must be deducted from net income, while the amount of decrease in such an account must be added to net income to determine cash flows from operations.

For example, Cowboy's Accounts Receivable account increased by $8,100,000 from the beginning to the end of the year (Exhibit 25.7). Therefore, we must deduct $8,100,000 from net income to determine cash flows from operations as shown in Exhibit 25.4. This adjustment is necessary because net income increased by the amount of sales ($109,500,000—Exhibit 25.5) and decreased by the amount of uncollectible accounts expense ($900,000—Exhibit 25.5), while net cash flows increased only by the amount of cash received from customers ($100,500,000), which we calculated previously (see page 856). The increase in net income was $8,100,000 greater than the increase in net cash flows from operations, so this difference must be deducted from accrual-based net income to derive net cash flows from operations.

Analysis of Noncash Current Operating Assets Related to Expenses When a noncash current operating asset such as prepaid insurance is related to an expense, an increase in the account implies that the cash paid was greater than the amount of expense. On the other hand, a decrease indicates that the amount of expense was greater than the cash payment. Thus the amount of increase in the account must be deducted from net income, while the amount of decrease must be added to net income to determine cash flows from operations. For example, Cowboy's Prepaid Insurance account decreased by $300,000 during 1999 (Exhibit 25.7). Thus we must add this amount to net income to determine cash flows from operations as shown in Exhibit 25.4. This adjustment is necessary because net income decreased by the amount of insurance expense ($3,000,000—Exhibit 25.5), while net cash flows decreased only by the amount of cash paid for insurance ($2,700,000), which we calculated earlier (see page 857). The decrease in net income was $300,000 greater than the decrease in net cash flows from operations, so this difference must be added to accrual-based net income to derive net cash flows from operations.

Based on the above analysis, we can determine the net income adjustment needed due to the change in inventories. Because the Inventory account is related to an expense (cost of goods sold), the increase in the account must be deducted from net income to determine cash flows from operations.

Adjustment for Changes in Current Operating Liabilities As in the case of current assets, the indirect format adjusts accrual-based net income for changes in current operating liabilities to derive cash flows from operating activities. **Current operating liabilities** are accounts representing operating obligations. Nontrade notes payable, bank loans payable, and dividends payable are generally excluded from this category because they represent financing events and appear in the financing section of the cash flow statement.

When a current operating liability increases during the period, it indicates one of two things: (1) the revenue associated with the account was less than the cash inflow or (2) the expense associated with the account was greater than the cash outflow. Because the related revenues and expenses are reflected in net income at the end of the period, the amount of the increase in a current operating liability must be added to net income to determine cash flows from operations.

Analysis of Current Operating Liabilities Related to Revenues When a current operating liability such as rent received in advance is related to revenue, an increase in the account implies that revenues earned were less than cash receipts from customers. On the other hand, a decrease indicates that the amount of revenues was more than the cash receipts from customers. Therefore, the amount of increase in the account must be added to net income, while the amount of decrease in such an account must be deducted from net income to determine cash flows from operations. For example, Cowboy's Rent Received in Advance account increased by $150,000 from the beginning to the end of the year (Exhibit 25.7). Therefore, we must add $150,000 to net income to determine cash flows from operations as shown in Exhibit 25.4. This adjustment is necessary because net income increased by the amount of rent revenue ($600,000—Exhibit 25.5), while net cash flows increased by the amount of cash received from renters ($750,000), which we calculated previously (see page 857). The increase in net income was $150,000 less than the increase in net cash flows from operations, so this difference must be added to accrual-based net income to derive net cash flows from operations.

Analysis of Current Operating Liabilities Related to Expenses   When a current operating liability such as taxes payable is related to an expense, an increase in the account implies that expenses were greater than cash payments. On the other hand, a decrease indicates that the amount of expense was less than the amount of cash paid. Thus the amount of increase in the account must be added to net income, while the amount of decrease in such an account must be deducted from net income to determine cash flows from operations. For example, Cowboy's Taxes Payable account decreased by $225,000 during 1999 (Exhibit 25.7). Thus we must deduct $225,000 from net income to determine cash flows from operations as shown in Exhibit 25.4. This adjustment is necessary because net income decreased by the amount of tax expense ($5,850,000—Exhibit 25.5), while net cash flows decreased by the amount of cash paid for taxes ($6,075,000), as we determined previously (see page 858). The decrease in net income was $225,000 less than the decrease in net cash flows from operations, so this difference must be deducted from accrual-based net income to derive net cash flows from operations.

Based on the above analysis, we can determine the net income adjustment needed due to the changes in accounts payable, interest payable, and wages payable. Because these accounts are all related to expenses, any increases must be added to net income, while decreases would be deducted from net income to determine cash flows from operations. Exhibit 25.7 indicates that accounts payable increased $8,175,000, while interest payable and wages payable decreased by $75,000 and $300,000, respectively. Exhibit 25.4 shows that the increase in accounts payable was added to net income, while the decreases in interest and wages payable were deducted from net income to determine net cash flows from operating activities.

Notice that the amount of net cash flows from operating activities is the same regardless of whether the direct or indirect method is used. Exhibit 25.8 summarizes the adjustment process when using the indirect format for the operating section of the statement of cash flows.

Note: The FASB requires two additional disclosures when using the indirect method to present operating activities. Companies must disclose either on the statement of cash flows itself or in the accompanying notes the amounts of cash paid for interest and for taxes.

EXHIBIT 25.8	Net Income Adjustments	
Change in Account	**Adjustment to Net Income**	**Reasoning**
Increase in current asset	Subtract the amount of the increase	Revenue > Cash inflows, or Expense < Cash outflows
Decrease in current asset	Add the amount of the decrease	Revenue < Cash inflows, or Expense > Cash outflows
Increase in current liability	Add the amount of the increase	Expense > Cash outflows, or Revenue < Cash inflows
Decrease in current liability	Subtract the amount of the decrease	Expense < Cash outflows, or Revenue > Cash inflows

Reebok prepares its operating section using the indirect format as shown in Exhibit 25.9. Notice that this statement begins with net income, which is then adjusted for such items as depreciation and amortization, along with the changes in operating assets and liabilities. Reebok's net cash provided by operating activities was $126,925,000 in fiscal 1997. Also note that Reebok paid $59,683,000 for interest and $115,985,000 for taxes during fiscal 1997.

EXHIBIT 25.9 Reebok's Statement of Cash Flows

REEBOK
Consolidated Statements of Cash Flows
(amounts in thousands)

Year Ended December 31	1997	1996	1995
Cash flows from operating activities:			
Net income	$ 135,119	$ 138,950	$ 164,798
Adjustments to reconcile net income to net cash provided by operating activities:			
Depreciation and amortization	47,423	42,927	39,579
Minority interest	10,476	14,635	11,423
Deferred income taxes	(17,285)	(6,333)	(1,573)
Special charges	55,697		62,743
Changes in operating assets and liabilities, exclusive of those arising from business acquisitions:			
Accounts receivable	(13,915)	(107,082)	16,157
Inventory	(47,937)	77,286	(29,531)
Prepaid expenses	(28,613)	22,650	7,841
Other	24,458	11,042	(18,830)
Accounts payable and accrued expenses	20,759	67,769	(25,327)
Income taxes payable	(59,257)	18,419	(55,553)
Total adjustments	(8,194)	141,313	6,929
Net cash provided by operating activities	126,925	280,263	171,727
Cash flows from investing activities:			
Payments to acquire property and equipment	(23,910)	(29,999)	(63,610)
Proceeds from business divestitures		6,887	
Net cash used for investing activities	(23,910)	(23,112)	(63,610)
Cash flows from financing activities:			
Net borrowings (payments) of notes payable to banks	27,296	(36,947)	2,426
Proceeds from issuance of common stock to employees	17,163	13,362	11,216
Dividends paid		(20,922)	(23,679)
Repayments of long-term debt	(156,966)	(1,209)	(112,445)
Net proceeds from long-term debt		632,108	230,000
Proceeds from premium on equity put options		717	3,233
Dividends to minority shareholders	(3,900)	(7,426)	(2,885)
Repurchases of common stock	————	(686,266)	(225,470)
Net cash used for financing activities	(116,407)	(106,664)	(117,604)
Effect of exchange rate changes on cash	(9,207)	1,485	5,944
Net increase (decrease) in cash and cash equivalents	(22,599)	151,972	(3,543)
Cash and cash equivalents at beginning of year	232,365	80,393	83,936
Cash and cash equivalents at end of year	$ 209,766	$ 232,365	$ 80,393
Supplemental disclosures of cash flow information:			
Interest paid	$ 59,683	$ 38,738	$ 23,962
Income taxes paid	115,985	77,213	152,690

Refer to Exhibit 25.9. Did Reebok's accounts receivable (net) increase or decrease during fiscal 1997? *(answer on page 873)*

Analysis of Cash Flows from Operating Activities: Indirect Format

As is true when the statement of cash flows is prepared using the direct format, the first step to analyzing the statement prepared using the indirect format is to compare the current period with prior periods. This comparison is done to detect trends in cash flows. Then the user should compare the cash flows of the company to others in the same industry.

When companies present cash flows from operations using the indirect format, external users can also evaluate how much cash is generated by operations by calculating the ratio of cash flows from operations to net income. However, it is difficult for external users to analyze actual cash inflows and outflows.

For example, Cowboy Boots and Shoes's cash flows from operations to net income ratio is:

$$\frac{\$24,390,000}{\$13,650,000} = 1.79$$

This indicates that Cowboy's cash flows from operations are 1.79 times larger than its net income. It is possible to use this ratio to compare Cowboy to other companies in the same industry. (We discuss ratio analysis and industry evaluation in more detail in Chapter 26.)

Comparison of Direct and Indirect Formats

Exhibit 25.10 illustrates the direct and indirect operating activities sections of the statement of cash flows of Cowboy Boots and Shoes. As you can see, the net cash provided by operating activities is the same. Therefore, it doesn't matter which statement a company uses. The direct format indicates the amounts of cash received and paid for various items. The indirect format indicates the reconciliation of net income to cash flows

EXHIBIT 25.10	Comparison of Direct and Indirect Cash Flows from Operations

Net cash flows from operating activities—direct method (in thousands)	
Cash received from customers	$100,500
Cash received from renters	750
Cash paid for inventory	58,125
Cash paid for insurance	2,700
Cash paid for wages	4,800
Cash paid for miscellaneous expenses	4,200
Cash paid for income taxes	6,075
Cash paid for interest	960
Net cash flows from operating activities	$ 24,390

Net cash flows from operating activities—indirect method (in thousands)	
Net income	$13,650
Adjustments to reconcile net income to net cash flows from operations:	
Depreciation expense—buildings	5,850
Depreciation expense—equipment	3,150
Amortization expense—patent	1,050
Amortization of discount on note payable	15
Gain on sale of trading securities	(900)
Loss on sale of equipment	2,250
Increase in accounts receivable, net	(8,100)
Increase in inventory	(600)
Decrease in prepaid insurance	300
Increase in accounts payable	8,175
Increase in rent received in advance	150
Decrease in wages payable	(300)
Decrease in interest payable	(75)
Decrease in taxes payable	(225)
Net cash flows from operating activities	$ 24,390

from operations. Whichever statement you prefer, remember that most companies prepare their statements using the indirect method. However, a thorough understanding of the direct format should help you understand the reconciliation process used in the indirect format.

DETERMINATION AND ANALYSIS OF CASH FLOWS FROM INVESTING ACTIVITIES LO 4

Determination of Cash Flows from Investing Activities

Cash flows from investing activities are associated with the company's long-term assets and its current nonoperating assets, such as nontrade notes receivable and trading securities. Recall that investing activities may result in cash inflows and cash outflows.

The cash flows from the investing activities section of the statement of cash flows reflects the amount of cash received from sales of long-term and current nonoperating assets and the amount of cash paid to purchase these assets.

For example, assume the following additional information concerning Cowboy Boots and Shoes:

- A building was obtained at the end of 1999 with preferred stock and cash.

- Equipment was purchased for cash at the end of 1999.

- Equipment costing $5,000,000 was sold during 1999.

First, let's analyze the change in the Trading Securities account. Changes in the Trading Securities account are determined as follows:

> Beginning balance in Trading Securities, net
> + Trading securities purchased during the period
> = Maximum amount of trading securities available
> − Trading securities sold during the period
> −/+ Market adjustment
> = Ending balance in Trading Securities, net

This account decreased during the year, indicating that overall securities (1) were sold or (2) declined in value.[15]

Next examine the income statement for further information concerning trading securities. Specifically, we are looking for a gain or loss on the sale of securities or an unrealized loss due to the decline in value. According to the income statement, Cowboy Boots and Shoes had a $900,000 gain on the sale of trading securities but there is no information indicating any decline in value. Therefore, we can analyze the change in the Trading Securities account as follows:

$1,800,000	Beginning balance (Exhibit 25.7)
−0−	Securities purchased during the period
$1,800,000	Maximum amount of trading securities available
(1,050,000)	**Trading securities sold during the period**[16]
−0−	Market adjustment
$ 750,000	Ending balance (Exhibit 25.7)

Based on this information, we determine that the *cash received* from the sale of securities is $1,950,000 ($900,000 gain + $1,050,000 decrease in trading securities). (Recall that a gain implies that the resources received were greater than the book value of the resources given up in the sale or exchange.) Take a moment to find "cash received from sale of trading securities" in Exhibits 25.3 and 25.4.

Next we must consider the changes in the Buildings account. When analyzing assets that are depreciated, we must also consider the changes in the accompanying Accumulated Depreciation accounts.

---

[15]It is possible that securities were both purchased and sold during the period. However, the fact that the account decreased during the year implies that more securities were sold than were purchased.

[16]The cost of securities sold during the period is determined as $1,800,000 − $750,000 = $1,050,000.

Of Interest   Net Income versus Cash Flows

Many people confuse net income and cash flows from operations. As you have seen, they are not the same. Nor does it follow that a company with positive (negative) net income will show positive (negative) cash flows from operations. It is entirely possible that a company with positive (negative) cash flows from operations could have negative (positive) change in cash and cash equivalents for the period. To illustrate this point, the table below shows the net income, cash flows from operations, and the change in cash and cash equivalents of many of the companies featured in the text for a recent fiscal period. Note, for example, that Intel shows positive net income and cash flows from operations but a decrease in cash and cash equivalents. On the other hand, Stone Container and Quaker Oats both show a net loss, but positive cash flows from operations.

Company	Net Income	Cash Flows from Operations	Change in Cash and Cash Equivalents
Intel	$6,945,000,000	$10,008,000,000	$ (63,000,000)
Mattel	285,184,000	481,854,000	144,676,000
Procter & Gamble	3,780,000,000	4,885,000,000	(801,000,000)
Sherwin-Williams	260,614,000	439,530,000	(1,650,000)
Disney	1,850,000,000	5,115,000,000	(190,000,000)
Unitog	12,519,215	36,626,656	1,464,413
Boeing	(178,000,000)	2,100,000,000	(104,900,000)
Anheuser-Busch	1,169,200,000	1,816,600,000	53,700,000
The Gap	533,901,000	844,651,000	428,525,000
3M	212,100	1,716,000	(353,000)
Goodyear	558,700,000	1,067,800,000	20,100,000
Microsoft	2,195,000,000	3,719,000,000	644,000,000
Ben & Jerry's	3,896,000	17,639,000	11,214,000
Sprint	952,500,000	3,379,000,000	(1,048,900,000)
Stone Container	(132,000,000)	391,000,000	(30,000,000)
Wal-Mart	3,526,000,000	7,123,000,000	564,000,000
PepsiCo	1,491,000,000	3,419,000,000	1,621,000,000
Quaker Oats	(930,900,000)	490,000,000	(26,300,000)
Dell	944,000,000	1,592,000,000	205,000,000

Source: Company annual reports taken from Web sites and EDGAR. Annual reports of most recent period as of January 12, 1999.

Beginning balance of Building account
+ Cost of building purchased during the period
= Maximum amount of building available
− Cost of building sold during the period
= Ending balance of Building account

Beginning balance of Accumulated Depreciation
+ Depreciation expense for the period
= Maximum amount of accumulated depreciation
− Depreciation removed from records due to sale of asset
= Ending balance of Accumulated Depreciation

Using these relationships, let's see what we know about Cowboy Boots and Shoes's buildings. The Buildings account increased during the period, indicating that Cowboy Boots and Shoes purchased a building; the additional information given above indicates that both preferred stock and cash were used in the transaction. However, before we conclude that the value of the building purchased is equal to the increase in the Building account, we must analyze the change in the Accumulated Depreciation account. If this account increased by the amount of depreciation expense, we can conclude that no buildings were sold during the period. (Recall that when a depreciable asset is sold or exchanged, the cost of the asset and the accumulated depreciation on the asset are removed from the accounting records.)

Let's analyze Cowboy's Accumulated Depreciation account:

$40,050,000	Beginning balance (Exhibit 25.7)
5,850,000	Depreciation expense (Exhibit 25.5)
$45,900,000	Maximum amount of accumulated depreciation
–0–	**Depreciation removed from records**
$45,900,000	Ending balance (Exhibit 25.7)

Cowboy's Accumulated Depreciation—Building account increased by $5,850,000 during 1999. Because the amount of Depreciation Expense shown on the income statement is also $5,850,000, we conclude that no buildings were sold.

Now we can analyze the change in the Buildings account.

$112,650,000	Beginning balance (Exhibit 25.7)
37,800,000	**Cost of building purchased during the period[17]**
$150,450,000	Maximum amount of building
–0–	Cost of building sold during the period
$150,450,000	Ending balance (Exhibit 25.7)

To determine the amount of cash used in purchasing the building, we must determine the change in the Preferred Stock and Additional Paid-in Capital—Preferred Stock accounts.[18] These accounts increased by a total of $12,150,000. Therefore, we surmise that $12,150,000 of preferred stock was used to purchase the building(s). Because the Building account increased by $37,800,000, the cash used was $25,650,000 ($37,800,000 – $12,150,000). Take a moment to locate the "cash paid for building" and the "purchase of building with preferred stock" in both Exhibits 25.3 and 25.4.

Finally, we must analyze the changes in the Equipment and Accumulated Depreciation—Equipment accounts using the same relationships as we used for the Building and Accumulated Depreciation—Building accounts. The Accumulated Depreciation—Equipment account increased by $1,200,000 during 1999. Is this the same as the Depreciation Expense shown on the income statement? No; therefore, we conclude that equipment was sold during 1999. To determine the amount of accumulated depreciation associated with the sale of the asset, we calculate the following:

$15,450,000	Beginning balance (Exhibit 25.7)
3,150,000	Depreciation expense (Exhibit 25.5)
$18,600,000	Maximum amount of depreciation
(1,950,000)	**Depreciation removed from the records[19]**
$16,650,000	Ending balance (Exhibit 25.7)

The income statement shows that Cowboy incurred a loss on the sale of equipment ($2,250,000). Thus the amount of cash received was less than the carrying value of the equipment. Based on the analysis of the Accumulated Depreciation account and the additional information given previously, we determine the carrying value of the equipment sold was $3,050,000:

$5,000,000	Cost of equipment
(1,950,000)	Accumulated depreciation on equipment
$3,050,000	Book (carrying) value of equipment

Thus the *cash received* from the sale of equipment was $800,000 as shown below:

$3,050,000	Book (carrying) value of equipment
(2,250,000)	Loss on the sale of equipment (Exhibit 25.5)
$ 800,000	Cash received from sale of equipment

When buildings are sold for or purchased with cash the amount(s) are shown in the investing section of the Statement of Cash Flows.

[17]Cost of buildings purchased is determined as $150,450,000 + $0 = $150,450,000; $150,450,000 – $112,650,000 = $37,800,000.

[18]Our additional information indicated that the increase in the Preferred Stock account represents preferred stock issued to buy the building.

[19]The depreciation removed is determined as $18,600,000 – $16,650,000 = $1,950,000.

Take a moment to locate "cash received from sale of equipment" in Exhibits 25.3 and 25.4.

We determine that $6,050,000 cash was paid for equipment during the period as shown below:

$50,850,000	Beginning balance (Exhibit 25.7)
6,050,000	**Cost of equipment purchased**[20]
$56,900,000	Maximum amount of equipment available
(5,000,000)	Cost of equipment sold (additional information)
$51,900,000	Ending balance (Exhibit 25.7)

Because we have no additional information about this purchase, we conclude that it was transacted in cash. Locate "cash paid for equipment" in Exhibits 25.3 and 25.4.

Now look at Reebok's investing cash flows. As Exhibit 25.9 shows, Reebok had a net cash outflow from investing activities of $23,910,000. This cash outflow was a payment to acquire property, plant, and equipment.

Analysis of Cash Flows from Investing Activities

Financial statement users evaluate investing cash flows to determine if a company is making adequate investments in long-term assets and other investments. Users compare the investing cash flows of a particular company, both over time and with other companies in the same or similar industries.

For example, Cowboy Boots and Shoes shows a net cash outflow from investing activities of $28,950,000, indicating that it purchased more assets than it sold. This trend is common, but investors should be aware that long-term assets can be costly to maintain, so the amount and timing of the purchase and sale of investments is crucial. In addition, a net cash outflow from investing activities may signal that management is expanding or replacing assets, while a net cash inflow may signal that management is selling off assets.

DETERMINATION AND ANALYSIS OF FINANCING CASH FLOWS

LO 5

Cash flows from financing activities are associated with long-term liabilities; current nonoperating liabilities, such as nontrade notes payable and dividends payable; and the owners' equity of the company. Financing activities include the issuance and repayment of notes and bonds, the sale and repurchase of stock, and the distribution of the company's earnings. Financing activities do not include the change in owners' equity caused by the company's net income. That change is accounted for by cash flows from operations.

Determination of Financing Cash Flows: Nonowner

The amounts shown on the statement of cash flows represent the cash flows that occurred as a result of increases or decreases in the long-term and current nonoperating liabilities (excluding dividends payable, which relates to owner financing) during the period.

For example, assume the following additional information concerning Cowboy Boots and Shoes:

- Bonds were issued at the end of 1999.

- Short-term notes were issued during 1999.

First, we analyze Notes Payable using the relationship shown below:

	Beginning balance of Notes Payable
+	Notes issued during the period
=	Maximum debt due to notes payable
−	Cash paid on principal of notes payable
=	Ending balance of Notes Payable

---

[20]The cost of the equipment purchased is calculated as $51,900,000 + $5,000,000 = $56,900,000; $56,900,000 − $50,850,000 = $6,050,000.

The Notes Payable account increased by $150,000 during 1999, so it appears that notes were issued during the period. We can then determine the amount of cash received as follows:

$150,000	Beginning balance (Exhibit 25.7)
150,000	**Notes issued during the period**
$300,000	Maximum debt due to notes payable
–0–	Cash paid on principal of notes payable
$300,000	Ending balance (Exhibit 25.7)

Next look at Bonds Payable using the same relationship as shown for Notes Payable. This account increased by $13,500,000 during 1999, so we assume that bonds were issued during the period. But remember, bonds are often issued for more or less than their face values. Because the Premium on Bonds Payable account increased by $600,000, we conclude that $14,100,000 of cash ($13,500,000 + $600,000) was raised by issuing bonds. Take a moment to locate both "cash received from short-term note payable" and "cash received from bond issues" in Exhibits 25.3 and 25.4.

Determination of Financing Cash Flows: Owner

The amounts on the statement of cash flows show the cash flows that resulted from changes in owners' equity and the Dividends Payable account during the period.

For example, assume the following additional information concerning Cowboy Boots and Shoes:

- Treasury stock was purchased during 1999.
- Dividends were paid during 1999.

The Treasury Stock account is analyzed as follows:

	Beginning balance of Treasury Stock
+	Treasury stock purchased during the period
=	Maximum amount of treasury stock
–	Treasury stock reissued during the period
=	Ending balance of Treasury Stock

First, we notice on the balance sheet (see Exhibit 25.7) that the Treasury Stock account increased by $12,500,000, so we assume that overall more treasury stock was purchased than was reissued. We, therefore, conclude that $12,500,000 was paid to buy treasury stock during 1999 as shown below:[21]

$ –0–	Beginning balance (Exhibit 25.7)
12,500,000	**Treasury stock purchased during the period**
$12,500,000	Maximum amount of treasury stock
–0–	Treasury stock reissued during the period
$12,500,000	Ending balance (Exhibit 25.7)

Next examine the Dividends Payable account and Exhibit 25.6. To determine the cash paid for dividends during 1999, use the following relationships:

	Beginning balance of Dividends Payable
+	Dividends declared during the period
=	Maximum dividends owed
–	Dividends paid during the period
=	Ending balance of Dividends Payable

Using the information from the balance sheet and statement of stockholders' equity, we determine the cash paid for dividends as shown below:

$ 150,000	Beginning balance (Exhibit 25.7)
4,950,000	Dividends declared (Exhibit 25.6)
$5,100,000	Maximum dividends owed
(5,000,000)	**Dividends paid**
$ 100,000	Ending balance (Exhibit 25.7)

---

[21]If the Treasury Stock account had decreased during the period, it would indicate that treasury stock had been reissued. To determine the amount of cash received, determine the decrease in the Treasury Stock account and the increase in the Paid-in Capital from Treasury Stock account and/or additional information.

Take a moment to locate both "cash paid for treasury stock" and "cash paid for dividends" in Exhibits 25.3 and 25.4.

Now examine Reebok's financing cash flows (Exhibit 25.9). Reebok had a net cash outflow from financing activities of $116,407,000, due largely to a debt repayment of $156,966,000.

Analysis of Cash Flows from Financing Activities

Financial statement users evaluate financing cash flows to determine if the company is obtaining adequate amounts of cash to enable it to invest in long-term assets. Financial statement users compare the financing cash flows of a particular company, both over time and against other companies in the same or similar industries.

For example, Cowboy Boots and Shoes shows a net cash outflow from financing activities of $3,250,000 (Exhibit 25.3), indicating that it paid off more obligations than it incurred or that its owner-related transactions resulted in a cash outflow. Users must determine whether these actions were appropriate given the current economic climate. Cowboy also repurchased stock during the period. If this was done to make the stock available for stock options, users might infer that the company is making a long-term commitment to its employees.

DETERMINATION AND ANALYSIS OF OTHER INVESTING AND FINANCING ACTIVITIES

Cash flows associated with the operating, investing, and financing activities of the firm are the only required disclosures on the face of the statement of cash flows. Other significant noncash investing and financing events that are important to readers of the cash flow statement are reported either on the statement itself or in the notes to the financial statements. The following are typical noncash events that are reported:

- Acquisition of assets by issuing debt or equity securities
- Exchanges of assets
- Conversion of debt or preferred stock to common stock
- Issuance of common or preferred stock to retire debt

It is important for readers to analyze these events because of their future cash flow implications. If a company acquires assets by issuing debt, for example, it will need cash in the future to make the required periodic payments of interest and principal. If a company retires debt by issuing stock, it is relieved from the periodic payments on the debt but may face future dividend payments.

PAUSE & REFLECT

Reebok shows a net decrease in cash during 1997. Does this imply that Reebok had a net operating loss during 1997? Why or why not? *(answer on page 873)*

Take a moment to locate Cowboy Boots and Shoes's disclosure of its other investing and financing activities on the statement of cash flows.

At this point, we have analyzed all the noncash accounts on the balance sheet and income statement. We determined the following:

Cash flows from operating activities	$ 24,390,000
Cash flows from investing activities	(28,950,000)
Cash flows from financing activities	(3,250,000)
Net change in cash	$ (7,810,000)
Add beginning balance of cash	42,250,000
Ending balance of cash	$ 34,440,000

CASH FLOW ANALYSIS: INTERNAL USERS

Internal financial statement users have additional information concerning cash flows that, for reasons of privacy, is not available to external users. For example, internal users have information concerning the timing of cash receipts from customers and cash payments to suppliers, which they would not want competitors to know. In addition, insiders have knowledge about the cash flows generated by different divisions within the company. Finally, managers know the level of cash flows expected at the beginning of the period and can compare it to the actual level of cash flows to determine whether or where problems might exist.

SUMMARY

The statement of cash flows supplements the accrual-based accounting information illustrated in the income statement, balance sheet, and statement of retained earnings. Its purpose is to illustrate the cash flows arising from operating, investing, and financing activities, respectively.

- According to the Financial Accounting Standards Board, the statement of cash flows is useful to (1) assess the entity's ability to generate positive future net cash flows, (2) assess the entity's ability to meet its obligations and pay dividends and its need for external financing, (3) assess the reasons for differences between income and associated cash receipts and payments, and (4) assess both the cash and noncash aspects of the entity's investing and financing transactions during the period.

- The operating activities section of the statement of cash flows may be prepared using either the direct or indirect format. The direct format illustrates the actual amounts received or paid for operating activities, while the indirect format requires adjustments to accrual-based net income to determine cash flows from operations.

- The investing and financing sections of the statement of cash flows indicate the cash received from or paid for investing and financing events, respectively. The events are further reflected by changes in current nonoperating assets and liabilities, noncurrent assets and liabilities, and owners' equity accounts.

KEY TERMS

current operating liabilities Accounts representing operating obligations

direct format The format of the statement of cash flows that shows the actual cash inflows and outflows of operating activities

indirect format The format of the statement of cash flows that shows the differences between accrual-based net income and cash flows from operations

noncash current operating asset A noncash account that represents operating activities

ANSWERS TO THE PAUSE & REFLECTS

p. 856, Cash collections can be estimated as follows:

$ 590,504,000	Beginning Accounts Receivable
+ 3,643,599,000	Net sales
$ 4,234,103	Maximum Accounts Receivable
− 561,729,000	Ending Accounts Receivable
$ 3,672,374	Cash collections from customers

p. 859, Cash paid for inventory can be estimated as follows:

$ 544,522,000	Beginning Inventory
+2,313,262,000	Purchases
$2,857,784,000	Maximum inventory available
−2,294,049,000	Cost of goods sold
$ 563,735,000	Ending Inventory

$ 196,368,000	Beginning Accounts Payable
+2,313,262,000	Purchases (determined above)
$2,509,630,000	Maximum accounts payable
− 192,142,000	Ending Accounts Payable
$2,317,488,000	Cash paid for inventory

p. 865, The change in accounts receivable was subtracted from net income to determine cash flows from operations. Therefore, the Accounts Receivable account decreased during fiscal 1997.

p. 871, No. As reported on the statement of cash flows, Reebok had a net income of $135,119,000 during fiscal 1997. Cash flows are not equivalent to profits. That is why both the income statement and the statement of cash flows are necessary.

QUESTIONS

1. Explain the objectives of the cash flow statement.

2. Explain how the cash flow statement, in conjunction with the other financial statements, is useful for external users.

3. Explain the importance of the sections of the statement of cash flows.

4. Explain the difference between the direct and indirect formats for presenting the statement of cash flows.

5. If accounts receivable decreases during the period, which is greater, collections from customers or sales on account? Why?

6. Rent expense as shown on the income statement is $120,000, while cash paid for rent is shown on the statement of cash flows at $135,000. Did prepaid rent increase or decrease during the period? By what amount?

7. Accounts payable for services decreased $67,000 during the year. The statement of cash flows indicates that cash paid for services was $568,000. What was the amount of the related expense shown on the income statement?

8. If the Subscriptions Received in Advance account decreases during the period, which is greater, cash received in advance from customers or subscription revenue? Why?

9. Company A's inventory decreased by $10,000 during the period, while its accounts payable for inventory increased by $6,000. Which is greater, cost of goods sold or cash paid for inventory? Why?

10. If the interest expense for the period is $1,500 and the Premium on Bonds Payable account decreases during the period by $50, how much is the cash paid for interest? Why?

11. In the indirect method of presentation of operating cash flows, why is net income adjusted for depreciation, depletion, and amortization?

12. If a bond payable is issued at a discount, is the resulting amortization added to, or deducted from, net income to determine cash flows from operations in the indirect method? Why?

13. If an investment in bonds is purchased at a discount, is the resulting amortization added to, or deducted from, net income to determine cash flows from operations in the indirect method? Why?

14. Where and how do gains and losses appear on the statement of cash flows on an indirect basis? Why?

15. When the indirect method is used for the statement of cash flows, how and why is net income affected by changes in current operating assets to determine cash flows from operations?

16. When the indirect method is used for the statement of cash flows, how and why is net income affected by changes in current operating liabilities to determine cash flows from operations?

17. If a company sells a building for $65,000 that cost $150,000 and that has $80,000 of accumulated depreciation, how does the company reflect this event on the statement of cash flows? Why?

18. Does the amount shown on the statement of retained earnings always equal the amount shown on the statement of cash flows for dividends? Why or why not?

19. If a company exchanges common stock for a building, should it disclose this event on the statement of cash flows? Why or why not?

20. Explain why managers have cash flow information that they do not wish to disclose to external users.

EXERCISES

E 25.1

LO 1

A variety of transactions is shown below. Identify each transaction as an operating (**O**), investing (**I**), financing (**F**), or other noncash (**NC**) event. Put the correct letter(s) in the space provided.

_____ a. Loan from a bank or other financial institution

_____ b. Payment of accounts payable

_____ c. Purchase of machinery and equipment

_____ d. Collection of an accounts receivable

_____ e. Declaration of dividends to stockholders

_____ f. Sale of land and building

_____ g. Purchase of inventory

_____ h. Sale of common stock

_____ i. Interest received on available-for-sale securities

_____ j. Payment of insurance for one year in advance

E 25.2

LO 1

A variety of transactions is shown below. Identify each transaction as an operating (**O**), investing (**I**), financing (**F**), or other noncash (**NC**) event. Put the correct letter(s) in the space provided.

_____ a. Borrowed $50,000 on a long-term note payable.

_____ b. Made a sale for $2,500 on open account.

_____ c. Reclassified as a short-term liability the long-term notes payable of $30,000 now due within one year.

_____ d. Purchased a building for $120,000 with a $20,000 cash down payment and signed a long-term note payable for the balance.

_____ e. Paid the maturity value of $1,050 on a short-term note payable with a face value of $1,000.

_____ f. Wrote off $500 in uncollectible accounts receivable.

_____ g. Paid the liability for accrued wages payable of $700 as well as the current period's wages of $4,500.

_____ h. Paid $2,000 on accounts payable.

_____ i. Sold marketable securities that cost $12,000 for $12,750.

_____ j. Issued 200 shares of $5 par value common stock in payment for equipment having a fair market value of $17,400.

E 25.3

LO 2

Anderson Company reveals the following information for the past fiscal period:

	Ending Balance	Beginning Balance
Accounts receivable	$ 54,300	$45,600
Inventory	34,000	50,000
Prepaid insurance	8,000	6,400
Accounts payable	82,100	74,560
Taxes payable	15,400	10,500
Wages payable	23,600	32,875
Sales	560,500	
Cost of goods sold	392,350	
Insurance expense	5,000	
Tax expense	8,200	
Wage expense	50,000	

Use the direct format to determine Anderson's cash flows from operating activities for the period.

E 25.4

LO 2

Wright Company reveals the following balances in selected accounts:

	May 31, 1999	May 31, 1998
Accounts receivable	$108,600	$ 96,200
Inventory	68,000	100,000
Prepaid rent	16,000	13,200
Accounts payable—inventory	52,100	44,560
Accounts payable—services	25,300	28,700
Wages payable	12,500	14,400
Sales	970,000	
Cost of goods sold	582,000	
Rent expense	78,000	
Miscellaneous expenses	125,600	
Wage expense	144,000	

Determine the operating cash flows using the direct format.

E 25.5
LO 2

For the year ended December 31, 1999, Chicago Service, Inc., reported net income of $175,000 on the accrual basis of accounting. Using the information supplied below, convert the accrual-based net income to the cash basis.
a. The liability for unearned service revenue increased by $12,500 during 1999.
b. The liability for equipment rental decreased $5,100 during the year.
c. The inventory for supplies on hand increased by $1,700 during 1999.

E 25.6
LO 3

During 2000, World Tours Company generated a $56,750 net income. Using the information below, determine the adjusted net income.
a. Equipment was sold during the period at a loss of $5,000.
b. Trading securities (not cash equivalents) were sold during the period at a gain of $2,400.
c. Patent amortization expense was $1,800 for the period.
d. Bonds were retired at a loss of $3,500.

E 25.7
LO 3

During 1999, Barrett Company recorded interest expense on bonds payable of $15,800 and decreased the premium on bonds payable by $200. If net income was $44,600 during 1999, what is Barrett's net income adjustment shown on the statement of cash flows?

E 25.8
LO 3

Refer to E 25.7. Assume your company purchased Barrett's bonds when issued and held them during 1999. If your net income is $34,500, what is the net income adjustment to your statement of cash flows?

E 25.9
LO 4

Thalhammer Products had a beginning balance in Furniture and Fixtures, net of depreciation, of $186,500. The ending balance in that account was $192,000. Depreciation expense for that period was $18,700, and there were no sales of furniture or fixtures during the period. What was the amount of furniture and fixtures purchases?

E 25.10
LO 4

DeVault's Specialty Meats had $45,900 in its Equipment account at the beginning of 1999. The beginning balance of Accumulated Depreciation—Equipment was $9,000 at that time. During 1999, DeVault recorded depreciation expense of $9,000 and sold a piece of equipment for $2,500 resulting in a gain of $500. At the end of 1999, the Equipment account had a balance of $63,100 and the balance in the Accumulated Depreciation—Equipment account was $14,000. What was the amount of equipment purchases that DeVault's made during 1999?

E 25.11
LO 3   LO 4

Storey Company purchased a machine on January 1, 2000, for $75,000 in cash. On June 30, 2000, Storey sold the machine at a gain of $5,000. Accumulated depreciation as of June 30, 2000, was $18,250. What is the cash flow shown in the investing section of the statement of cash flows? What adjustment is needed to the net income in the operating section of the statement of cash flows?

E 25.12
LO 5

On March 1, 1999, Dody Incorporated issued 10-year bonds with a face value of $600,000 and a face interest rate of 10 percent that was paid semiannually. The bonds were sold to yield a market rate of 8 percent. What is the cash inflow shown in the financing section of the statement of cash flows for the year ended December 31, 1999?

E 25.13
LO 2

Refer to E 25.12. Assuming this is Dody's only debt, what is the amount shown on the cash flow statement for the year ended December 31, 1999, as cash paid for interest using the direct method?

E 25.14
LO 5

During 2001, Grey Incorporated issued a long-term note for $50,000. In this same time period, Grey paid off another long-term note of $30,000. How would Grey reflect these events on the statement of cash flows? Why? In what section do these events appear?

E 25.15
LO 5

During 1999, Smith Motors' Common Stock and Additional Paid-in Capital accounts increased by $25,000 and $37,500, respectively. If no common stock was retired during 1999, what is the amount shown on the statement of cash flows with respect to common stock? In what section is this disclosed?

E 25.16
LO 5

Ross Rustproofing had a beginning balance in Retained Earnings of $36,790. During the year, it generated a net income of $5,320. At the end of the year, the Retained Earnings account had a balance of $39,110. In addition, Ross Rustproofing's Dividends Payable account increased by $500 during the year. What is the total amount shown on the statement of cash flows as "cash paid for dividends"? In what section is this disclosed?

E 25.17
LO 4

During the year, Fairbanks Company sold trading securities costing $6,500 for a gain of $600. What amount of cash did Fairbanks raise from this transaction, and where would Fairbanks report it on the statement of cash flows?

E 25.18

LO 5

During the year, Shafer, Inc., issued 50,000 shares of $1 par value common stock in exchange for land. The appraised value of the land was $580,000. Shafer's common stock was trading at $12 per share at the time of the exchange. Where, and in what amount, would Shafer report this transaction on the statement of cash flows for the period?

PROBLEMS

P 25.1

LO 1   LO 2   LO 3
LO 4   LO 5

The financial statements of Hopkin's Store are presented below:

HOPKIN'S STORE
Income Statement
For the Year Ended September 30, 1999

Sales		$485,000
Expenses:		
Cost of goods sold	$331,000	
Salaries	87,000	
Rent	16,000	
Depreciation	7,000	
Other operating expenses	20,000	461,000
Net Income		$ 24,000

HOPKIN'S STORE
Balance Sheet
September 30, 1999 and 1998

	1999	1998
Current assets:		
Cash	$ 23,000	$ 16,000
Accounts receivable	36,000	28,000
Inventory	120,000	135,000
Prepaid rent	4,000	–0–
Total current assets	$183,000	$179,000
Long-term assets:		
Furniture and fixtures	148,000	148,000
Accumulated depreciation	(88,500)	(81,500)
Total long-term assets	$ 59,500	$ 66,500
Total assets	$242,500	$245,500
Current liabilities:		
Accounts payable	$ 28,000	$ 25,000
Salaries payable	5,000	5,500
Accrued liabilities—operating expenses	7,500	4,000
Notes payable	35,000	–0–
Total current liabilities	$ 75,500	$ 34,500
Long-term liabilities:		
Notes payable	–0–	35,000
Total liabilities	$ 75,500	$ 69,500
Owner's equity:		
Hopkins, capital	167,000	176,000
Total liabilities and owner's equity	$242,500	$245,500

Required

a. Prepare Hopkin's statement of cash flows using the indirect method.
b. Prepare Hopkin's operating activities section of the statement of cash flows using the direct method.
c. Determine the percentage of cash collections and cash payments for inventory and the cash flows from operations to net income ratio. What do these indicate?
d. Which statement do you feel provides the most relevant information for external users? For internal users? Why?

P 25.2

LO 1   LO 2   LO 3
LO 4   LO 5

The financial statements of Scott, Inc., are shown below:

SCOTT, INC.
Income Statement
For the Year Ended December 31, 2000

Sales		$576,000
Cost of goods sold		392,000
Gross margin		$184,000
Operating expenses:		
Depreciation	$ 6,500	
Other operating expenses	155,900	162,400
Net income		$ 21,600

SCOTT, INC.
Balance Sheet
December 31, 2000 and 1999

	2000	1999
Current assets:		
Cash	$ 12,800	$ 15,400
Accounts receivable	21,700	20,300
Inventory	32,100	34,600
Total current assets	$ 66,600	$ 70,300
Property, plant, and equipment:		
Furniture and fixtures	$ 68,700	$ 51,200
Less accumulated depreciation	(29,400)	(22,900)
Total property, plant, and equipment	$ 39,300	$ 28,300
Total assets	$105,900	$ 98,600
Current liabilities:		
Accounts payable—merchandise	$ 16,800	$ 18,300
Accounts payable—operating expenses	13,400	5,100
Total current liabilities	$ 30,200	$ 23,400
Long-term liabilities:		
Notes payable	25,000	30,000
Total liabilities	$ 55,200	$ 53,400
Stockholders' equity:		
Common stock	$ 40,000	$40,000
Retained earnings	10,700	5,200
Total stockholders' equity	$ 50,700	$ 45,200
Total liabilities and stockholders' equity	$105,900	$ 98,600

Required

a. Prepare Scott's statement of cash flows using the indirect method.

b. Prepare Scott's operating section of the statement of cash flows using the direct method.

c. Determine the percentage of cash collections and cash payments for inventory and the cash flows from operations to net income ratio. What do these indicate?

d. Which statement do you feel provides the most relevant information for external users? For internal users? Why?

P 25.3

LO 1 LO 2 LO 3
LO 4 LO 5

Refer to Mattel's statement of cash flows and answer the following questions:

a. Is this statement prepared on the direct or indirect basis? How can you tell?

b. Are net cash flows from operating activities greater than or less than net income?

c. What is shown on the statement of cash flows regarding changes in current operating assets during the period?

d. What is shown on the statement of cash flows regarding changes in current operating liabilities during the period?

e. How much cash did Mattel pay for interest during the period? Where did you find this information?

f. How does the company define cash equivalents? Where did you find this information?

g. How much cash did Mattel pay for income taxes during the period? Where did you find this information?

h. What were the principal investing events during the year?

i. What were the principal financing events during the year?

j. Did the company report any noncash investing/financing events during the year? If so, where did you find this information?

k. If you were an investor, would you be interested in Mattel? Why or why not?

P 25.4

LO 1 LO 2 LO 3
LO 4 LO 5

Refer to the Walt Disney Company's statement of cash flows and answer the following questions:

a. Is this statement prepared on the direct or indirect basis? How can you tell?

b. Are net cash flows from operating activities greater than or less than net income?

c. What is shown on the statement of cash flows regarding changes in current operating assets during the period?

d. What is shown on the statement of cash flows regarding changes in current operating liabilities during the period?

e. How much cash did Disney pay for interest during the period? Where did you find this information?

f. How does the company define cash equivalents? Where did you find this information?

g. How much cash did Disney pay for income taxes during the period? Where did you find this information?

h. What were the principal investing events during the year?

i. What were the principal financing events during the year?

j. Did the company report any noncash investing/financing events during the year? If so, where did you find this information?

k. If you were an investor, would you be interested in Disney? Why or why not?

P 25.5

LO 1 LO 2 LO 3
LO 4 LO 5

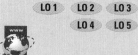

Refer to Anheuser-Busch's statement of cash flows and answer the following questions:

a. Is this statement prepared on the direct or indirect basis? How can you tell?

b. Are net cash flows from operating activities greater than or less than net income?

c. What is shown on the statement of cash flows regarding changes in current operating assets during the period?

d. What is shown on the statement of cash flows regarding changes in current operating liabilities during the period?

e. How much cash did Anheuser-Busch pay for interest during the period? Where did you find this information?

f. How does the company define cash equivalents? Where did you find this information?

g. How much cash did Anheuser-Busch pay for income taxes during the period? Where did you find this information?

h. What were the principal investing events during the year?

i. What were the principal financing events during the year?

j. Did the company report any noncash investing/financing events during the year? If so, where did you find this information?

k. If you were an investor, would you be interested in Anheuser-Busch? Why or why not?

P 25.6

LO 1 LO 2 LO 3
LO 4 LO 5

Refer to Intel's statement of cash flows and answer the following questions:

a. Is this statement prepared on the direct or indirect basis? How can you tell?

b. Are net cash flows from operating activities greater than or less than net income?

c. What is shown on the statement of cash flows regarding changes in current operating assets during the period?

d. What is shown on the statement of cash flows regarding changes in current operating liabilities during the period?

e. How much cash did Intel pay for interest during the period? Where did you find this information?

f. How does the company define cash equivalents? Where did you find this information?

g. How much cash did Intel pay for income taxes during the period? Where did you find this information?

h. What were the principal investing events during the year?

i. What were the principal financing events during the year?

j. Did the company report any noncash investing/financing events during the year? If so, where did you find this information?

k. If you were an investor, would you be interested in Intel? Why or why not?

P 25.7

LO 1 LO 2 LO 3
LO 4 LO 5

Refer to PepsiCo's statement of cash flows and answer the following questions:

a. Is this statement prepared on the direct or indirect basis? How can you tell?

b. Are net cash flows from operating activities greater than or less than net income?

c. What is shown on the statement of cash flows regarding changes in current operating assets during the period?

d. What is shown on the statement of cash flows regarding changes in current operating liabilities during the period?

e. How much cash did PepsiCo pay for interest during the period? Where did you find this information?

f. How does the company define cash equivalents? Where did you find this information?

g. How much cash did PepsiCo pay for income taxes during the period? Where did you find this information?

h. What were the principal investing events during the year?

i. What were the principal financing events during the year?

j. Did the company report any noncash investing/financing events during the year? If so, where did you find this information?

k. If you were an investor, would you be interested in PepsiCo? Why or why not?

The financial statements of Hoppal Corporation are presented below:

HOPPAL CORPORATION
Balance Sheet
December 31, 1999 and 2000
(in thousands)

	2000	1999
Cash and cash equivalents	$ 8,328	$ 6,458
Short-term investments, at market	8,893	10,557
Receivables	6,920	5,255
Inventories	4,637	1,848
Prepaid expenses	2,775	1,426
Property, plant, and equipment	137,094	98,690
Accumulated depreciation	(16,883)	(11,156)
Total assets	$151,764	$113,078
Current notes payable	$ 1,996	$ 1,212
Accounts payable	9,509	8,500
Accrued expenses	13,636	9,153
Accrued dividends	1,269	879
Accrued income taxes	1,510	2,199
Long-term notes payable	26,624	8,749
Common stock	257	256
Additional paid-in capital	68,946	63,245
Retained earnings	28,962	19,734
Unrealized loss on short-term investments	(96)	–0–
Treasury stock	(849)	(849)
Total liabilities and stockholders' equity	$151,764	$113,078

HOPPAL CORPORATION
Income Statement
For the Year Ended December 31, 2000
(in thousands)

Sales	$208,527
Less cost of goods sold	153,951
Gross margin	$ 54,576
Less operating expenses:	
Depreciation expense	5,757
General expenses	22,432
Income from operations	$ 26,387
Other revenue items:	
Investment income	1,259
Other expense items:	
Loss on sale of equipment	(861)
Interest expense	(1,227)
Income before taxes	$ 25,558
Income tax expense	9,778
Net income	$ 15,780

Additional information:

1. No short-term investments were purchased during the year.
2. Equipment costing $956 (thousand) was sold during the year

Required   *a.* Prepare the operating section of the statement of cash flows using the direct method.
b. Prepare the statement of cash flows using the indirect method.

The financial statements of Romness Enterprises are presented below:

ROMNESS ENTERPRISES
Balance Sheet
December 31, 2000 and 2001
(in millions)

	2001	2000
Cash and cash equivalents	$ 330.7	$ 226.9
Short-term investments	1,157.4	1,573.8
Accounts and notes receivable, net	2,050.9	1,883.4

Inventories	970.0	924.7
Prepaid expenses	563.2	499.8
Property, plant, and equipment, net	9,882.8	8,855.6
Intangibles, net	9,837.0	9,741.6
Total assets	$24,792.0	$23,705.8
Accounts payable	$ 1,451.6	$ 1,390.0
Interest payable	753.5	726.0
Short-term borrowings	678.5	2,191.2
Income taxes payable	671.7	823.7
Accrued marketing expense	546.2	400.9
Other current liabilities	1,168.9	1,043.1
Long-term debt	12,665.5	10,608.3
Capital stock at par	14.4	13.4
Capital in excess of par value	934.4	879.5
Retained earnings	7,739.1	6,541.9
Unrealized loss on sale of securities	(470.6)	–0–
Treasury stock	(1,361.2)	(912.2)
Total liabilities and shareholders' equity	$24,792.0	$23,705.8

ROMNESS ENTERPRISES
Income Statement
For the Year Ended December 31, 2001
(in millions)

Sales	$28,472.4
Less cost of goods sold	13,715.4
Gross margin	$14,757.0
Less operating expenses:	
Selling and general expense	10,011.3
Depreciation and amortization expense	1,576.5
Income from operations	$ 3,169.2
Other revenue (expense):	
Interest income	108.2
Interest expense	(645.0)
Income before income taxes	$ 2,632.4
Provision for income taxes	880.4
Net income	$ 1,752.0

Additional information:

1. No short-term investments or property, plant, and equipment were sold during the year.
2. Amortization of intangibles was $139.3 (million) for the year.

Required a. Prepare the operating section of the statement of cash flows using the direct method.
b. Prepare the statement of cash flows using the indirect method.
c. Discuss the relative benefits of the indirect method.

P 25.10 The financial statements of Kirsch, Inc., are presented below:

LO 1 LO 2 LO 3
LO 4 LO 5

KIRSCH, INC.
Balance Sheet
December 31, 1999 and 2000
(in thousands)

	2000	1999
Cash	$ 2,180	$ 6,071
Accounts receivable	78,213	82,266
Inventories	158,330	160,894
Prepaid expenses	11,955	10,340
Investments held for sale	4,879	5,523
Land	42,753	41,571
Buildings	222,576	208,513
Equipment	11,069	3,935
Accumulated depreciation	(155,546)	(144,192)
Total assets	$376,409	$374,921

Notes payable to banks	$ 10,000	$ 5,000
Trade accounts payable	14,152	19,087
Accrued payroll items	11,786	11,775
Accrued insurance	15,283	15,839
Accrued income taxes	2,141	2,769
Other accrued expenses	8,424	9,359
Dividends payable	1,071	1,089
Long-term debt	63,573	74,254
Common stock	69,674	69,674
Capital in excess of par value	30,290	30,290
Retained earnings	161,932	141,111
Treasury stock	(11,917)	(5,326)
Total liabilities and shareholders' equity	$376,409	$374,921

KIRSCH, INC.
Income Statement
For the Year Ended December 31, 2000
(in thousands)

Sales	$461,448
Less cost of goods sold	300,842
Gross margin	$160,606
Selling, general, and administrative expenses	99,281
Depreciation expense	16,089
Income from operations	$ 45,236
Other revenue (expense) items:	
Interest expense	(5,032)
Gain on sale of investment	167
Income before taxes	$ 40,371
Income taxes	14,720
Net income	$ 25,651

Additional information:

1. A building with a cost of $8,286 (thousand) was sold at book value.
2. No equipment was sold during the period.

Required

a. Prepare the operating section of the statement of cash flows using the direct method.
b. Prepare the statement of cash flows using the indirect method.
c. Discuss the relative benefits of the direct method.

CASES

C 25.1

LO 1 LO 2 LO 3
LO 4 LO 5

Refer to the annual report of the company you selected in Chapter 1 (C 1.1), and answer the following questions:

a. Is this statement prepared on the direct or indirect basis? How can you tell?
b. Are net cash flows from operating activities greater than or less than net income?
c. What is shown on the statement of cash flows regarding changes in current operating assets during the period?
d. What is shown on the statement of cash flows regarding changes in current operating liabilities during the period?
e. How much cash did the company pay for interest during the period? Where did you find this information?
f. How does the company define cash equivalents? Where did you find this information?
g. How much cash did the company pay for income taxes during the period? Where did you find this information?
h. What were the principal investing events during the year?
i. What were the principal financing events during the year?
j. Did the company report any noncash investing/financing events during the year? If so, where did you find this information?
k. If you were an investor, would you be interested in this company? Why or why not?

C 25.2

LO 1 LO 2 LO 3

Using a database such as LEXIS/NEXIS or NAARS, determine how many companies prepared their statement of cash flows on an indirect basis and how many prepared their statement of cash flows on a direct basis during the current year. Do the companies in each category have anything in common? Describe what you discovered.

CRITICAL THINKING

CT 25.1

LO 2 LO 3 LO 4 LO 5

The statement of cash flows shown below is incorrectly presented. Analyze this statement and explain the problems you found. Do not prepare a new statement.

PURCELL COMPANY
Statement of Cash Flows
As of December 31,1999

Sources (inflows) of cash:		
Net income	$ 88,000	
Add (deduct) items to convert from the accrual to cash basis:		
Depreciation	15,800	
Inventory increase	10,000	
Prepaid expense increase	(4,000)	
Extraordinary gain on land	(36,000)	
Extraordinary loss on bonds	(2,000)	
Accounts receivable increase	(60,000)	
Accounts payable increase	30,000	
Amortization of bond discount	200	
Wages payable decrease	3,000	
Cash inflows from operations	$ 45,000	
Sales of land	106,000	
Issuance of bonds	10,000	
Total sources of cash		$171,000
Uses (outflows) of cash:		
Cash dividends	$ 30,000	
Machinery purchased	20,000	
Common stock issued to retire bonds	42,000	
Preferred stock issued to purchase building	20,000	
Purchase of trading securities	10,000	
Total uses of cash		122,000
Increase in cash		$ 39,000

CT 25.2

LO 1 LO 2 LO 3
LO 4 LO 5

Prior to the issuance of *SFAS No. 95*, companies commonly prepared a "funds" statement that reported the changes in working capital during the period. We present a funds statement below. Analyze this statement and describe its strengths and weaknesses as a communication tool.

LEONARD ENTERPRISES
Statement of Changes in Financial Position—Working Capital Basis
For the Year Ended December 31, 1981

Sources of working capital:		
Income from continuing operations:		
Net income		$ 132,000
Add (deduct) items to convert to working capital:		
Depreciation expense	$ 23,700	
Amortization of bond discount	300	
Gain on sale of equipment	(54,000)	
Loss on sale of land	3,000	
Working capital from operations		105,000
Sale of equipment		159,000
Sale of land		15,000
Total working capital sources		$ 279,000
Uses of working capital:		
Cash dividends paid		$ 45,000
Machinery purchased		30,000
Trading securities exchanged for note payable		12,000
Total uses of working capital		$ 87,000
Increase in working capital during 1981		$ 192,000

ETHICAL CHALLENGES

EC 25.1

LO 1

M. Potter is the manager of Masson Company. Potter receives an annual salary plus a bonus of 15 percent of net income before taxes. Masson Company uses the LIFO inventory costing method. During 1999 when prices were increasing, M. Potter switched to the FIFO inventory method.

Required

Prepare an example that illustrates the effect on the income statement of switching from LIFO to FIFO. In addition, show the effect of the switch on the balance sheet and the statement of cash flows.
  a. Did net income increase or decrease?
  b. Did ending inventory increase or decrease?
  c. Did cash flows increase or decrease?
  d. Could a change in inventory methods entitle M. Potter to a larger bonus than she was otherwise entitled to? Explain.
  e. In this situation, was the change economically beneficial to the Masson Company? Explain.

EC 25.2

LO 1

K. Poe is the manager of Mystea Enterprises. Poe receives an annual salary and a bonus of 20 percent of net income before taxes. Mystea uses the FIFO inventory costing method. During 2000, the prices of inventory began to rise and K. Poe suggested that the firm switch to the LIFO inventory method. This change was made during 2000. At the end of the year, K. Poe was very upset because her year-end bonus was small. She argues that her bonus should be increased because she saved Mystea Enterprises money.

Required

Prepare an example that illustrates the effect on the income statement of switching from FIFO to LIFO. In addition, show the effect of the switch on the balance sheet and the statement of cash flows.
  a. Did net income increase or decrease?
  b. Did ending inventory increase or decrease?
  c. Did cash flows increase or decrease?
  d. Could a change in inventory methods prevent K. Poe from receiving as large a bonus? Explain.
  e. In this situation, was the change economically beneficial to Mystea Enterprises? Explain.
  f. Was K. Poe treated fairly? Explain.

COMPUTER APPLICATIONS

CA 25.1

LO 2

Peterson Company wants you to prepare a spreadsheet to answer the following questions:
  a. Sales for the period were $500,000. The beginning accounts receivable balance was $40,000. The ending balance was $35,000. Sales discounts of $5,000 were given. No accounts were written off and no sales returns and allowances were given. How much cash was received from customers?
  b. Cash collections from customers during the period were $800,000. The ending balance of accounts receivable was $12,000. The beginning balance of accounts receivable was $23,000. Sales discounts of $4,000 were given during the period. Sales returns and allowances during the period were $1,500. An account with a $5,000 balance was written off during the period. What is the amount of the sales for the period?
  c. Sales for the period were $350,000, while cash collections from customers were only $300,000. Sales discounts of $3,500 and sales returns and allowances of $1,000 were granted during the period. The beginning balance of accounts receivable was $10,000. No accounts were written off during the period. What is the ending balance of accounts receivable?

CA 25.2

LO 2

Schneider Enterprises wants you to prepare a spreadsheet to answer the following questions:
  a. Purchases (net of discount) of inventory were $500,000 during the period. The beginning balance of accounts payable was $40,000, while the ending balance was $25,000. A purchase of $4,000 (net) was returned during the period. How much cash was paid for inventory during the period?
  b. Cash paid for inventory during the period was $400,000. The beginning and ending balances of accounts payable were $10,000 and $12,000, respectively. Cash discounts of $2,500 were lost

during the period. No purchase returns were made during the year. What was the amount of purchases (net of discount) made during the period? Hint: When cash discounts are lost, cash decreases by more than accounts payable.

c. Purchases of inventory (net of discount) were $800,000, while cash paid for inventory was $950,000 during the period. A purchase of $5,000 (net) was returned during the period. If the ending balance of accounts payable was $35,000, what was the beginning balance?

CA 25.3

LO 1   LO 3   LO 4   LO 5

www

In this chapter we examined Reebok's fiscal 1997 statement of cash flows. Go to Reebok's Web site and locate its most recent financial information. Answer the following questions:

a. How much cash was generated (used) by operating activities?
b. How much cash was generated (used) by investing activities?
c. How much cash was generated (used) by financing activities?
d. Has Reebok's cash position improved? Why or why not?

PART SEVEN

YOU ARE HERE

Chapter 26 completes the business cycle. Now that you understand how accounting information is used in the planning, performing, and evaluating phases of business, we take one final look at the role accounting plays in the market for information. Chapter 26 investigates financial statement analysis for external users. We explore the role of capital and information markets and external sources of financial statement comparison information. Chapter 26 illustrates how ratios can be used by external stakeholders to evaluate the business.

LEARNING OBJECTIVES

LO 1 Describe the relationships among product and service markets, capital markets, and information markets.

LO 2 Use financial statement analysis to assess a company's profitability and its short-term and long-term risk.

LO 3 Explain why and how financial information and market information can be used to assess a company's investment potential.

Firm Performance:
A Comprehensive Evaluation

DELL COMPUTER
www.dell.com

In 1975 there was virtually no personal computer industry. However, the ever-increasing computing power and functionality of personal computers have made them indispensable in the workplace and commonplace in homes. Companies that manufacture computers, like Dell and Gateway, plus those that supply the

components, like Intel, have grown astronomically. By the end of 1998, Dell had reported record revenues for 37 of the previous 39 quarters.

Dell Computer Corporation was among the early personal computer manufacturers, and it continues to be a major force in the industry today. In 1998 Dell became the second-largest personal computer manufacturer and marketer in the United States and the third largest worldwide.

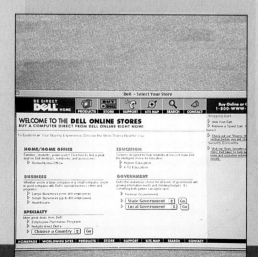

The secret to Dell's success is the way that it sells its computers. It doesn't have stores where customers shop. Dell's customers buy computers directly from Dell either by phone or over the Internet. This strategy makes Dell a very efficient company in a variety of ways. By selling directly to customers, Dell doesn't have to keep a large inventory of computers. It ended fiscal 1998 with seven days of inventory on hand, compared with 80 days for indirect-selling competitors and their resellers. The direct approach also makes Dell very adaptable to the changing needs of customers both at the time of purchase and afterward with its on-line customer service.

Dell grew from a small company to a strong contender in the personal computer industry because Dell Computer had products that consumers wanted and a very efficient way of manufacturing and delivering them. It is critical that Dell was able to attract investors who provided the capital for the company to expand its capacity as consumer demand grew. The investors used financial statement analysis as part of their investment decisions.

WHY ANALYZE?

In Chapter 15 we discussed how businesses choose among investment alternatives. Creditors and investors face the decision of whether to provide capital to businesses. The entire group of creditors and investors who provide capital to business make up the **capital market,** in which businesses find financing for their investments. Creditors and investors choose the businesses in which to invest based on their perception of the risk and potential return for each business. How do creditors and investors find out what they need to know? They use financial statements issued by companies as their principal source of information.

Also note that there is another important use for financial statement information as a means for managers to report how they have used the capital acquired from creditors and investors. Current creditors with outstanding loans to the company want to know how managers have handled the capital they have provided. As you know, creditors often include restrictions called *debt covenants* as part of the lending agreement on instruments such as bonds or mortgages. By requiring that a company maintain or have certain account balances or financial ratios, debt covenants attempt to ensure that managers do not jeopardize loan repayment or interest payments by paying investors prior to meeting the business's credit obligations. Creditors use financial statements to obtain information about whether management has violated such agreements.

Current stockholders want to know how managers are using the stockholders' investments. Stockholders have the option of selling a company's stock if they do not approve of its management's activities. This action resembles an investment decision. Though current creditors and stockholders face slightly different evaluation problems, the financial statement analysis they conduct is essentially the same.

This chapter begins with a discussion of the nature of the decisions that creditors and investors make and how capital markets function in allocating investment capital. Then financial statement analysis is applied to the financial statements of Dell Computer to show how external parties might assess Dell's risk and potential return. Finally, the chapter shows how analysts combine the information found on financial statements with other information to assess the overall performance of firms.

EXTERNAL STAKEHOLDERS' DECISION: WHETHER TO INVEST

Throughout the text we have discussed the economic interests of external stakeholders in business activities. In the broadest sense, many external parties face the decision about whether to invest in a company.[1] We focus on the decisions of two groups of external stakeholders: creditors and investors. Creditors loan money to the business and expect to receive interest payments plus repayment of the loaned money in return. Investors[2] invest money in companies expecting return in the form of dividends and/or higher prices for the stock they hold.

---

[1]Employees invest their time and effort, and, although they are compensated, they have a vested interest in seeing the company succeed. Their investment typically is less tangible than that of external parties, yet they have given part of their lives to the company and, in return, expect jobs in the future.

[2]Throughout this chapter, we use the term *investors* to describe both current stockholders or potential stockholders. It can also apply to partners and prospective partners in a partnership.

Different Investment Perspectives: Lenders and Investors

There are important differences in the ways that creditors and investors view any investment decision. Creditors lend a fixed amount of money over a limited term as part of a loan agreement. For example, banks and other financial institutions often lend money for periods ranging from a few days to 30 or 40 years. The fixed term and return (cash flows) aspects of debt make the risk of not receiving interest payments or principal repayment a major concern of creditors when they assess an investment prospect. On the other hand, investors have no limited or fixed term when it comes to their investments. They commit funds to a business until the business ceases to operate or until they sell their stock to another investor.[3]

Another important difference between creditors and investors is the legal nature of the risk they face. Creditors usually have legal documents like promissory notes, bonds, and mortgages that give them legal recourse in recovering their investment from the businesses to which they lend. Investors, however, have few guarantees for the money that they invest. The Securities Acts of 1933 and 1934 passed by Congress following the stock market crash of 1929 provide some recourse for investors. However, the principal thrust of the Securities Acts is to ensure that investors have sufficient reliable information on which to base their investment decisions.

Stepping back from the analysis of individual investments to look at the capital market as a whole gives an important perspective on its role in society. Creditors and investors are the owners of society's capital, and capital markets serve as a way of allocating that capital for investment in business. Next we briefly describe how capital markets serve as a mechanism to allocate capital.

Societal Role of Capital Markets

LO 1

In a **free market economy,** consumer demand determines the nature of businesses that exist and how much of a given product or service is available. Free market economies do not rely on a government dictating what kinds of businesses there should be and the level of investment that businesses should receive. As shown on the left side of Exhibit 26.1, a free market economy creates a product market (goods and services) where consumers, whether they are individuals, households, other businesses, or governments, determine the types of goods and services they need and want. This demand for products, in turn, creates opportunities for providers of goods and services to meet consumers' needs.

EXHIBIT 26.1

The Relationship between Product and Capital Markets

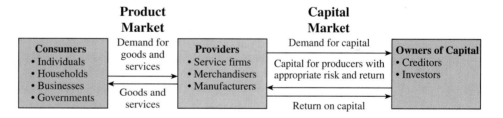

How does society decide where to invest its resources? The capital market serves an important role in the decision about what kinds of businesses receive the capital necessary to expand and succeed. The capital market exists between those who provide goods and services and the creditors and investors who own the capital, as shown on the right side of Exhibit 26.1. Providers whose product or service is in demand by consumers seek to expand, or new providers of that product or service want to begin business. How do they finance the necessary investment? The owners of capital are the principal source of funds for the providers. In return for the use of the capital, owners want the highest return possible, as long as the related level of investment risk is not too high.

---

[3]As you know, another possibility is that the corporation can buy back stock and either retire it or hold it as treasury stock.

The capital market determines which businesses get the capital they need as follows. The level of consumer demand determines the price and the profitability of products. The higher the demand for certain products, the higher the prices consumers are willing to pay, making products that are in high demand more profitable than those in low demand (for a given cost). Providers with more profitable products can afford to pay more, or provide a higher return, for the use of the capital they need to allow them to expand. Because the amount of capital is limited, capital owners choose to invest in providers that offer them the highest return. Thus consumer demand for products indirectly determines the businesses and industries that receive capital in a free market economy.

For example, consider the effect of the greater numbers of people working outside their homes since about 1970. This shift in the work force created demand for convenience foods and daycare for children. As these demands have risen, it has become more profitable for some businesses to provide meals that are either ready to eat with little preparation, or no preparation as in the case of fast-food restaurants. In addition, the expansion of the work force has resulted in the opening of chains of daycare centers. The resulting increased profitability of these types of businesses induced providers of daycare services to expand and encouraged other new providers of such services to enter the market. Because these types of services have become more profitable, their providers can compete for capital in the capital market by offering sufficient return to attract investors away from other investments.

Trading in Capital Markets

Any market is comprised of buyers and sellers who choose whether to buy or sell. Whether the market is for gold coins, food, or autos, it brings together those people who want a product with those who want to sell it. Capital markets function like other markets. Those individuals or businesses with capital and those in need of capital come together and agree on terms allowing the owners of capital (creditors and investors) to exchange the use of their capital for some return. For creditors, that return is the interest rate charged to the borrower. For debt that is not held to maturity, the return to creditors also includes the amount of change in the market value of the debt. Return for investors consists of the dividends they receive in addition to the change in the value of stocks they hold.

We need to be clear that there is not one big capital market where all the owners of capital and all those needing capital physically come together to trade. The capital market is segmented into different markets by factors like geography or size of transactions. A small local retailer who needs a loan to remodel the interior of a store is likely to view its capital market as the banks and savings and loan companies in its town. On the other hand, a large multinational company seeking a major expansion would consider as its capital market large banks in major cities or its own ability to issue bonds or stocks on a large scale.

In capital markets, owners of the capital have choices among alternatives. Not all potential investments offer the same risk and return. And not all creditors and investors share the same investment goals, nor do they have the same tolerance for risk. Creditors and investors use the information available from financial statements and other sources to assess firms' liquidity, long-term debt-paying ability, and profitability. Then they try to find investments with characteristics that match their investment goals and risk preferences.

For example, a retired couple whose active earning years are over is likely to have the investment goals of steady income and low risk of losing their capital. Thus they focus on finding investments that offer lower risk, even if that means a commensurately lower return. A young, successful professional might, on the other hand, be willing to accept more risk with the prospects of higher potential earnings. The young professional might look for high potential returns even though the risk of losing some or all of the investment is higher.

Information for Capital Markets

In order for creditors and investors to make good decisions, they need to answer certain questions about the businesses to which they might provide capital. Creditors want to know: Will I receive interest payments when they are due? Will I recover the principal loaned to the borrower? The situation with investors is a bit different. Because investors are not guaranteed dividends, they need to answer the questions: What return will the dividends I receive and the change in stock price provide? What is the risk that this investment will provide a lower return than I expect?

Unlike managers who have ready access to lots of information about the activities within a business, external investors and creditors cannot observe business activities firsthand, nor do they have much information about those activities. As Exhibit 26.2 shows, this creates another market for financial information. Owners of capital create the demand for accurate financial information on which to base their investment decisions. Providers (businesses) supply information to investors and creditors using GAAP to determine the necessary level of information disclosure. As we explain below, independent auditors play an important role in the financial information market by attesting, or indicating, that there is fair representation of the information communicated between businesses and investors.

EXHIBIT 26.2

Market for Financial
Information within
the Capital Market

Financial Information Market

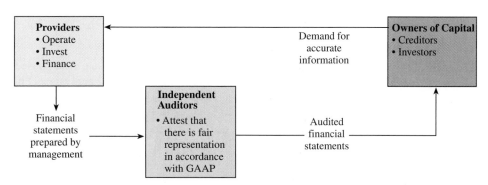

There are two problems with this market for financial information. One problem is that once information is published, anyone can use it. Annual reports issued by corporations, which include the four required financial statements plus other information like management's forecast of sales, are available to anyone. Because consumers receive this information for free, it is impossible to use price to determine the quantity of information demanded. The information market does not work as a typical product market in which price determines the quantity demanded. Therefore, the Securities and Exchange Commission mandates certain disclosures in order to maintain standards and consistency of public information. The content of these disclosures is determined by GAAP.[4]

The other problem with the financial information market is that investors cannot tell whether the information that management reports is accurate. Investors cannot see the events about which management reports and, in addition, investors tend to believe that managers bias their reports to reflect well on management. Investors can either assume that the information that managers provide is at least partially wrong and, as a result, they can subjectively adjust for the expected bias, or they can hire someone to help ensure the information's accuracy.

Many financial analysts publish newsletters that provide investment advice, which they sell to investors. What factors would you consider when deciding whether to subscribe to one of these newsletters? *(answer on page 912)*

---

[4]In 1994, the American Institute of Certified Public Accountants issued a special report, *Improving Business Reporting: A Customer Focus,* that called for financial reporting to include more information about the plans, opportunities, risks, and uncertainties that businesses face. It also called for more nonfinancial information indicating how key business processes are performing.

The Role That Auditors Play

An important role for independent auditors is to provide the users of financial statements with assurance that the financial statement information is a fair representation of the economic circumstances of the company that issues it.[5] Recall the audit report for Quaker Oats in Chapter 24. That report told the readers of Quaker's financial statements that Quaker had followed the accepted rules for financial reporting, GAAP. Independent auditors can issue other kinds of reports that serve as cautions to the readers that the financial statements should be read with extra care (qualified opinions) or that GAAP was not followed sufficiently (adverse opinions). By serving as a knowledgeable and objective third party, independent auditors help the market for financial information function and they indirectly aid the efficiency of the capital markets.

We have explained the nature of creditor and investor decisions in capital markets. In addition, we have shown why information from financial statements, as well as other sources, is critical for making good investment decisions. The next section of this chapter refers to the financial statements of Dell Computer to show how creditors and investors might use ratio analysis to evaluate Dell as an investment opportunity.

STATEMENT ANALYSIS FOR EXTERNAL USERS

LO 2

Chapter 12 indicates that those who evaluate firms based on financial statements generally use a combination of three methods of analysis: (1) horizontal analysis, which examines the changes in one financial statement item over time, either in dollars, as a percentage, or both; (2) vertical analysis, which shows each item on a financial statement as a percentage of one particular item on the statement; and (3) ratio analysis, which expresses two or more selected items on the statements in relation to one another.

Recall that horizontal and vertical analyses use changes in items on financial statements and the relative importance of those items to reflect a company's performance. Applications of these two methods of analysis are essentially the same whether they are used to evaluate a company's operating activities or its overall performance. In this chapter we extend the ratio analysis introduced in Chapter 12 by focusing on ratios that external analysts use to evaluate lending and investment decisions. We organize the discussion around four important dimensions: (1) activity, (2) liquidity, (3) long-term debt-paying ability, and (4) profitability. First we present some general points to remember when analyzing a company.

Studying the Statements

The first step in financial statement analysis is to carefully read the comparative financial statements. Comparative financial statements report two or more years of financial statements side-by-side in columnar form. The purpose of studying comparative financial statements is to become familiar with the firm's reporting practices, the accounts and classifications it uses, and the general range of amounts it reflects. Analysts must observe the company in the total context of its comparative statements before they can examine intelligently the specific aspects of its operations. Using comparative financial statements to study a firm's performance is a well-established practice, and published annual reports of large companies frequently contain comparative data for as many as 10 years.

A careful evaluation of the changes in reported financial data over time helps determine the general trend of operations and assists in deciding whether the company is better

---

[5]Often stockholders represented by the audit committee of the board of directors hire the independent auditor, though the auditor's fee is paid by the company. Banks also request audited financial statements before making major loans.

or worse off than in previous periods. It also enables the analyst to see trends as they develop. Creditors, actual or potential, may obtain the same information from their analysis and can use it as a factor when making decisions about the amount of credit to extend to a firm.

Obviously, analysts should not project historical trends indiscriminately into the future. Nonetheless, historical trends provide an excellent starting point for financial statement analysis because the more that is known about a company's past, the greater the chances of predicting its future accurately. A major thrust of financial statement analysis is to use what has transpired in the past to predict the future.

The 1997 and 1998 Dell Computer comparative balance sheets, income statements, and statements of cash flows are shown in Exhibits 26.3, 26.4, and 26.5, respectively. We will use these to analyze Dell as an investment prospect.

EXHIBIT 26.3 Dell Computer's Consolidated Statement of Financial Position

ASSETS

(in millions)	February 1, 1998	February 2, 1997
Current assets:		
Cash	$ 320	$ 115
Marketable securities	1,524	1,237
Accounts receivable, net	1,486	903
Inventories	233	251
Other	349	241
Total current assets	3,912	2,747
Property, plant and equipment, net	342	235
Other	14	11
Total assets	$ 4,268	$ 2,993

LIABILITIES AND STOCKHOLDERS' EQUITY

	February 1, 1998	February 2, 1997
Current liabilities:		
Accounts payable	$ 1,643	$ 1,040
Accrued and other	1,054	618
Total current liabilities	2,697	1,658
Long-term debt	17	18
Deferred revenue on warranty contracts	225	219
Other	36	13
Commitments and contingent liabilities	—	—
Total liabilities	2,975	1,908
Put options	—	279
Stockholders' equity:		
Preferred stock and capital in excess of $.01 par value; shares issued and outstanding: none	—	—
Common stock and capital in excess of $.01 par value; shares issued and outstanding: 644 and 692, respectively	747	195
Retained earnings	607	647
Other	(61)	(36)
Total stockholders' equity	1,293	806
	$ 4,268	$ 2,993

EXHIBIT   26.4   Dell Computer's Consolidated Statement of Income

Consolidated Statement of Income

(in millions)	February 1, 1998	Fiscal Year Ended February 2, 1997	January 28, 1996
Net revenue	$ 12,327	$ 7,759	$ 5,296
Cost of revenue	9,605	6,093	4,229
Gross margin	2,722	1,666	1,067
Operating expenses:			
Selling, general and administrative	1,202	826	595
Research, development and engineering	204	126	95
Total operating expenses	1,406	952	690
Operating income	1,316	714	377
Financing and other	52	33	6
Income before income taxes and extraordinary loss	1,368	747	383
Provision for income taxes	424	216	111
Income before extraordinary loss	944	531	272
Extraordinary loss, net of taxes	—	(13)	—
Net income	944	518	272
Preferred stock dividends	—	—	(12)
Net income available to common stockholders	$ 944	$ 518	$ 260
Basic earnings per common share (in whole dollars):			
Income before extraordinary loss	$ 1.44	$ 0.75	$ 0.36
Extraordinary loss, net of taxes	—	(.02)	—
Earnings per common share	$ 1.44	$ 0.73	$ 0.36
Diluted earnings per common share (in whole dollars):			
Income before extraordinary loss	$ 1.28	$ 0.68	$ 0.33
Extraordinary loss, net of taxes	—	(.02)	—
Earnings per common share	$ 1.28	$ 0.66	$ 0.33
Weighted average shares outstanding:			
Basic	658	710	716
Diluted	738	782	790

The accompanying notes are an integral part of these consolidated financial statements.

Business and trade publications are important sources of business information.

EXHIBIT 26.5   Dell Computer's Consolidated Statement of Cash Flows

Consolidated Statement of Cash Flows

(in millions)	February 1, 1998	Fiscal Year Ended February 2, 1997	January 28, 1996
Cash flows from operating activities:			
Net income	$ 944	$ 518	$ 272
Adjustments to reconcile net income to net cash provided by operating activities:			
Depreciation and amortization	67	47	38
Other	24	29	22
Changes in:			
Operating working capital	529	659	(195)
Non-current assets and liabilities	28	109	38
Net cash provided by operating activities	1,592	1,362	175
Cash flows from investing activities:			
Marketable securities:			
Purchases	(12,305)	(9,538)	(4,545)
Maturities and sales	12,017	8,891	4,442
Capital expenditures	(187)	(114)	(101)
Net cash used in investing activities	(475)	(761)	(204)
Cash flows from financing activities:			
Purchase of common stock	(1,023)	(495)	—
Repurchase of 11% Senior Notes	—	(95)	—
Issuance of common stock under employee plans	88	57	48
Cash received from sale of equity options	38	—	—
Preferred stock dividends and other	(1)	—	(14)
Net cash (used in) provided by financing activities	(898)	(533)	34
Effect of exchange rate changes on cash	(14)	(8)	7
Net increase in cash	205	60	12
Cash at beginning of period	115	55	43
Cash at end of period	$ 320	$ 115	$ 55

The computer industry is competitive and constantly changing. So, while published financial statements are an important source of information, they are not the only source. Industry trade publications and government statistics can reveal broader economic factors not related specifically to the business being analyzed. Exhibit 26.6 lists a few of the trade publications for the computer industry compiled by Standard & Poor's *Industry Surveys.* Some of the publications, like *Computerworld,* are sources of technological information about computer-related products and their performance. Others, like *Electronic News,* are oriented more toward the business aspects of the computer industry. For example, in these publications creditors and investors can find information about Dell Computer and its competitors which they can use along with financial information prepared by the company they are interested in to project financial performance of the firms.

EXHIBIT 26.6   Some Trade Publications in the Computer Industry

Publication	Frequency of Publication	Publisher	Content
Computer Reseller News	Weekly	CMP Publications Inc.	News coverage of the computer hardware and software industries
Computerworld	Weekly	Kevin McPherson	Computer hardware and software updates
Datamination	Bimonthly	Cahners Publishing Co.	News on all aspects of the information service industries
Electronic Business	Bimonthly	Cahners Publishing Co.	Computer hardware and software news
Electronic News	Weekly	Fairchild Publications	News coverage of the computer hardware and software industries
Information Week	Weekly	CMP Publications Inc.	News and features on the computer hardware and software industries
InfoWorld	Weekly	InfoWorld Publishing Co.	Coverage of the computer hardware and software industries
PC Week	Weekly	Ziff-Davis Publishing	News and developments in the desktop computing area

Source: Standard & Poor's, *Industry Surveys,* November 24, 1994.

A Basis for Evaluation

Without some standard for judgment, there is not a good basis for making evaluations about whether the firm is a good or bad investment. Remember that sources for external standards are available in college and public libraries. Generally, external standards provide both an average and a range of quantitative values for ratios of firms in the same or similar industries. This information is useful in making comparisons among investment alternatives.

Sources of Comparative Standards

We stated previously that amounts reported in financial statements are difficult to interpret without external standards against which they can be compared. Below we discuss a few additional sources of external standards.

Moody's Investor Services issues a number of publications, including *Moody's Handbook of NASDAQ Stocks* and *Moody's Handbook of Common Stocks.* These handbooks provide one-page summaries of the history and principal products as well as detailed financial tables for many of the companies whose stock is traded in the United States. Value Line Publishing, Inc. publishes another popular source of financial data to which investors can subscribe. Value Line not only publishes historical data, but it also makes forecasts of earnings and particular earnings components such as tax rates and operating margins. Exhibit 26.7 shows the Value Line summary of Dell Computer. As you can see, it lists financial data for 10 years and estimates for 1998 and 1999. It also includes a discussion of developments that are likely to affect Dell's performance in the near future.

Another source of financial information is a menu-driven database distributed on compact disk by Standard & Poor's Compustat Services, Inc. The information in this database is taken from the reports that companies are required to file with the Securities and Exchange Commission. A company's financial statements as well as data on ownership and information on 29 key financial ratios are available for the companies on Compustat.

The *RMA Annual Statement Studies* (published by Robert Morris Associates) summarizes financial information by industry using the Standard Industry Classification (SIC), which groups companies based on the nature of their business (e.g., service companies, manufacturers) and by the types of product they produce. Dell Computer is grouped into the electronic computer manufacturers industry (SIC #3571).

EXHIBIT 26.7 Value Line's Report on Dell Computer

DELL COMPUTER NDQ-DELL

RECENT PRICE	**91**	
P/E RATIO	**30.4**	(Trailing: 39.2 / Median: NMF)
RELATIVE P/E RATIO	**1.77**	
DIV'D YLD	**Nil**	
VALUE LINE	**1091**	

TIMELINESS 1 Highest
(Relative Price Perform-ance Next 12 Mos.)

SAFETY 3 Average
(Scale: 1 Highest to 5 Lowest)

BETA 1.30 (1.00 = Market)

2000-02 PROJECTIONS
	Price	Gain	Ann'l Total Return
High	105	(+15%)	4%
Low	70	(-25%)	-6%

Insider Decisions
	F	M	A	M	J	J	A	S	O
to Buy	0	1	0	0	0	0	0	0	0
Options	0	7	0	4	6	0	5	1	0
to Sell	1	9	0	7	8	0	9	12	0

Institutional Decisions
	1Q'97	2Q'97	3Q'97
to Buy	148	152	159
to Sell	121	147	187
Hld's(000)	213732	182929	166755

Percent shares traded: 90.0 / 60.0 / 30.0

High: 1.1 0.9 1.6 3.0 6.0 6.2 5.9 12.3 32.2 103.9
Low: 0.6 0.4 0.4 1.3 1.9 1.7 2.4 4.9 5.8 24.9

2-for-1 split
2-for-1 split
2-for-1 split
11.5 x "Cash Flow" p sh
3-for-2 split
Relative Price Strength
Shaded area indicates recession

Target Price Range 2000 2001 2002

Options: PHLE

Dell Computer Corp., originally incorporated in May, 1984, sells high-performance personal computers through specialized distribution channels (direct mail, direct sales) designed to facilitate direct end-user relationships. Completed initial public offering June 22, 1988, selling 48.304 million shares (adjusted for splits), at $0.71 per share, through Goldman, Sachs. In a secondary stock offering completed in April 1991, Dell sold an additional 45.6 million shares at $2.42 each.

CAPITAL STRUCTURE as of 11/2/97

Total Debt None

Leases, Uncapitalized Annual rentals $24.0 mill.
Pension Liability None - No defined benefit plan.
Pfd Stock None

Common Stock 326,435,775 shs. (100% of Cap'l)
outstanding at 12/1/97

CURRENT POSITION ($MILL.)
	1995	1996	11/2/97
Cash Assets	646.0	1352.0	1615.0
Receivables	726.0	903.0	1350.0
Inventory (FIFO)	429.0	251.0	301.0
Other	156.0	241.0	341.0
Current Assets	1957.0	2747.0	3607.0
Accts Payable	466.0	1040.0	1488.0
Debt Due	.5	--	--
Other	472.5	618.0	891.0
Current Liab.	939.0	1658.0	2379.0

ANNUAL RATES
of change (per sh)	Past 10 Yrs.	Past 5 Yrs.	Est'd '94-'96 to '00-'02
Sales	45.5%	46.0%	33.0%
"Cash Flow"	55.5%	48.0%	35.5%
Earnings	54.0%	51.0%	38.5%
Dividends	--	--	Nil
Book Value	60.5%	32.5%	37.5%

QUARTERLY SALES ($ mill.)
Fiscal Year Begins	Apr.Per	Jul.Per	Oct.Per	Jan.Per	Full Fiscal Year
1994	766.6	791.5	884.5	1033	3475.3
1995	1136	1206	1415	1539	5296.0
1996	1638	1690	2019	2412	7759.0
1997	2588	2814	3188	3510	12100
1998	3600	3900	4300	4700	16500

EARNINGS PER SHARE A B
Fiscal Year Begins	Apr.Per	Jul.Per	Oct.Per	Jan.Per	Full Fiscal Year
1994	.05	.08	.11	.15	.39
1995	.16	.17	.19	.17	.69
1996	.21	.29	.39	.50	1.35
1997	.54	.59	.69	.73	2.55
1998	.77	.80	.83	.95	3.35

QUARTERLY DIVIDENDS PAID
Calendar	Mar.31	Jun.30	Sep.30	Dec.31	Full Year
1994					
1995		NO DIVIDENDS			
1996					
1997		BEING PAID			
1998					

	1987	1988	1989	1990	1991	1992	1993	1994	1995	1996	1997	1998	© VALUE LINE PUB., INC.	00-02
Sales per sh A	1.20	1.15	1.72	2.35	3.11	6.83	9.47	10.95	14.17	22.42	37.05	50.55		87.25
"Cash Flow" per sh	.08	.07	.05	.16	.23	.41	d.02	.55	.82	1.67	3.05	4.00		6.25
Earnings per sh A B	.06	.07	.02	.11	.18	.32	d.13	.39	.69	1.35	2.55	3.35		5.75
Div'ds Decl'd per sh	--	--	--	--	--	--	--	--	--	--	Nil	Nil		Nil
Cap'l Spending per sh	.02	.03	.06	.04	.11	.16	.16	.20	.27	.33	.60	1.05		1.00
Book Value per sh	.07	.34	.35	.48	.96	1.25	1.13	1.65	2.59	3.14	4.00	6.70		16.75
Common Shs Outst'g C	132.04	223.82	225.47	232.14	286.41	294.86	303.43	317.44	373.79	346.09	326.40	326.40		326.40
Avg Ann'l P/E Ratio	--	12.5	26.0	8.3	13.2	11.1	--	10.4	11.6	12.6	Bold figures are Value Line estimates			15.0
Relative P/E Ratio	--	1.04	1.97	.62	.84	.67	--	.68	.78	.79				1.05
Avg Ann'l Div'd Yield	--	--	--	--	--	--	--	--	--	--				Nil
Sales ($mill) A	159.0	257.8	388.6	546.2	889.9	2013.9	2873.2	3475.3	5296.0	7759.0	12100	16500		28500
Operating Margin	11.4%	9.7%	4.8%	10.0%	9.3%	7.9%	NMF	8.1%	7.8%	9.8%	11.5%	11.0%		9.5%
Depreciation ($mill)	1.0	2.1	5.9	9.0	13.8	19.6	30.7	33.1	38.0	47.0	65.0	85.0		150
Net Profit ($mill)	9.4	14.4	5.1	27.2	50.9	101.6	d35.8	149.2	272.0	531.0	930	1225		1875
Income Tax Rate	38.0%	31.8%	38.2%	37.5%	30.6%	29.1%	--	30.0%	29.0%	28.9%	31.0%	31.0%		31.0%
Net Profit Margin	5.9%	5.6%	1.3%	5.0%	5.7%	5.0%	NMF	4.3%	5.1%	6.8%	7.7%	7.4%		6.6%
Working Cap'l ($mill)	26.7	63.1	57.9	95.2	282.7	359.0	510.4	719.0	1018.0	1089.0	1240	1855		3315
Long-Term Debt ($mill)	1.0	5.5	6.0	4.2	41.5	48.4	100.0	113.4	113.0	18.0	13.0	13.0		13.0
Net Worth ($mill)	29.7	75.2	79.8	112.0	274.2	369.2	471.1	651.7	973.0	1085.0	1300	2180		5440
% Earned Total Cap'l	--	18.1%	7.1%	23.8%	16.3%	25.3%	NMF	20.3%	25.7%	48.5%	71.0%	56.0%		34.5%
% Earned Net Worth	--	19.2%	6.4%	24.3%	18.6%	27.5%	NMF	22.9%	28.0%	48.9%	71.5%	56.0%		34.5%
% Retained to Com Eq	--	--	6.4%	24.3%	18.6%	27.5%	NMF	26.8%	27.9%	48.9%	71.5%	56.0%		34.5%
% All Div'ds to Net Prof	--	--	--	--	--	--	NMF	6%	1%	--	Nil	Nil		Nil

BUSINESS: Dell Computer Corp. makes notebook and desktop computers, servers, and workstations compatible with industry standards. Markets to corp., governmental, & educational customers via sales teams; markets to individuals & smaller institutional buyers through direct marketing. Provides on-site service through BancTec Service and Digital Equipment Corp. and lease financing through Newcourt Credit. Plants in Texas, Ireland & Malaysia. Fgn. sales.: 32% of total; R&D, 1.1%. '96 depr. rate: 13%. Est'd plant age: 3 yrs. Has abt. 8,400 empls., 3,526 stkhldrs. Michael S. Dell owns 16.0% of stk.; other off./dir., 2.0%; FMR Corp., 5.4%; (6/97 Proxy). Chrmn. & C.E.O.: M.S. Dell. Inc.: DE. Addr.: One Dell Way, Round Rock, TX 78682. Tel.: 512-338-4400. Internet: http://www.dell.com.

Dell Computer continues to forge ahead. Revenues for the fiscal third quarter (ended November 2, 1997) were up 58%, year over year, with share net rising an impressive 77%. Unit shipments grew 64%, slightly more than three times the average industry growth rate. Note, though, that Dell has not grabbed market share from Compaq Computer and Hewlett-Packard, which have been growing at near-parity rates. Rather, all three may be taking share from second-tier PC vendors. **Operating margins have widened ...** That's thanks, in part, to an improving product mix, with high-margin PC servers and workstations representing a rising percentage of sales. Too, margins have gained from the company's build-to-order manufacturing model, which results in a small finished-goods inventory. This, in turn, has allowed Dell to expand into next-generation products and incorporate declining component costs faster than rivals selling through third parties, pluses for both margins and market share. **... but we think they'll soon begin to decline,** especially as other PC makers have been adopting build-to-order business models. And even though Dell does not sell PCs in the sub-$1,000 price category, it has become more price competitive in recent months to hold its own against these low-end PCs. Also, the PC maker has been investing more in support services. Nonetheless, margin erosion should be gradual, as long as the sales mix continues to improve and the company further fine-tunes its manufacturing and distribution processes. We may also see marketing costs decline as a percentage of revenues as sales via the Internet climb faster than other modes of merchandising.

Timely Dell shares have become more volatile, given investors' worries about slowing PC demand, especially in Asia. It's too soon to gauge the impact of that region's financial turmoil on the company's overall future growth rate, but we think it will be modest, as Dell should easily find other sales opportunities. Meantime, its gross margins stand to gain from lower component costs, as most of the PC maker's materials come from Asia. All told, despite the shares' recent pullback, appreciation potential remains negligible.
Phillip M. Seligman   January 23, 1998

(A) Fiscal years end around Jan. 31st of following calendar year. Co. adopted 52-53 week fiscal year in fiscal 1988. Quarters are 13 weeks. (B) Primary egs. until 5/1/94; dil. egs. there-after. '96 egs. do not add due to changes in dil. shs. outstanding. Excl. charge for conversion of preferred stock: '95, 3¢. Excl. charge for repurchase of $68 mill. in 11% Senior Notes: '96, 3¢. Next earnings report due late January. (C) In millions, adjusted for stock splits.

Company's Financial Strength A+
Stock's Price Stability 10
Price Growth Persistence 95
Earnings Predictability 25

External sources of comparative financial standards, like many published financial statements, use some titles and descriptions that differ from those used in this book. For example, the *RMA Annual Statement Studies* uses *net worth* instead of *stockholders' equity*. These differences can be confusing initially, but, with some effort, it is easy to understand them.

Vertical Analysis

The right-hand column of Exhibit 26.8 shows the condensed common-size (vertical analysis) statements for manufacturers of electronic computers in 1997 compiled from Compustat. These percentages reflect the averages across all the companies classified as part of the industry. The middle two columns in Exhibit 26.8 show the common-size statements of Dell compiled from Quicken.com, an online financial service.

EXHIBIT 26.8	Condensed Common-Size Statements for Dell Computer and the Personal Computer Industry for 1997		
	Dell Computer*		Industry Average for Manufacturers of Electronic Computers (SIC #3571)
	1997	1998	
Cash and equivalents	45.1%	43.2%	16.3%
Trade receivables	30.1	34.8	33.4
Inventory	8.4	5.5	25.1
Other current assets	8.1	8.2	3.5
Total current assets	91.7%	91.7%	78.3%
Fixed assets	7.9	8.0	12.9
Intangibles (net)	0.0	0.0	3.2
Other noncurrent assets	0.4	0.3	5.6
Total assets	100.0%	100.0%	100.0%
Notes payable short term	0.0%	0.0%	8.6%
Current maturity of long-term debt	0.0	0.0	0.8
Trade payables	34.8	38.5	22.2
Income taxes payable	0.0	0.0	0.7
Other current liabilities	20.6	24.7	12.0
Total current liabilities	55.4%	63.2%	44.3%
Long-term debt	0.6	0.4	3.8
Deferred taxes	0.0	0.0	0.6
Other noncurrent liabilities	7.8	6.1	4.0
Net worth	36.2	30.3	47.3
Total liabilities and net worth	100.0%	100.0%	100.0%
Net sales	100.0%	100.0%	100.0%
Gross profit	22.1%	21.5%	46.7%
Operating profit	10.7%	9.2%	5.4%

*Dell's 1998 and 1997 year-ends were February 1, 1998, and February 2, 1997, respectively.

Comparing Dell's statements with the averages that represent the typical firm with sales over $25 billion in its industry reveals important differences. Throughout the chapter, we compare Dell's 1998 results with the 1997 results of the industry and other firms because 11 of the 12 months reported in Dell's 1998 financial statements were in 1997. For example, in 1998[6] Dell had a higher proportion of total current assets (91.7 percent versus 78.3 percent) than the average for the industry. This is due to the significantly higher percentage of its assets in cash and equivalents (43.2 percent versus 16.3 percent). Having more cash means that Dell is in a stronger position to meet its near-term obliga-

---

[6]Dell's 1998 and 1997 year-ends were February 1, 1998, and February 2, 1997, respectively.

tions. The higher percentage invested in cash more than offsets the lower percentage in inventory that Dell has (5.5 percent) versus the industry (25.1 percent). Dell's lower-than-average level of inventory implies that it is making computers as the customers demand them, thus having a substantially lower investment in inventory.

Dell's current liabilities include a higher proportion of trade accounts payable than the average for the industry. This seems to be an artifact of the small amount of long-term financing, reflected in the relatively low amounts of long-term debt (0.4 percent versus 3.8 percent for the industry) and net worth (30.3 percent versus 47.3 percent for the industry).

Comparing Dell's income statement items with those of the industry reveals cause for concern about Dell's profitability. Dell's gross profit is only 21.5 percent compared with the 46.7 percent industry average. This suggests that the price of Dell's computers does not exceed production cost by as much as others in the computer industry, which means that Dell does not have as much flexibility in price competition. On the other hand, Dell enjoys much higher operating profit (9.2 percent) than the industry (5.4 percent). This difference in operating profit is due to the direct way that Dell sells its computers—it avoids much of the selling and administrative costs that others in the industry must incur.

RATIO ANALYSIS FOR LENDING AND INVESTING

To demonstrate how ratio analysis is used as an aid in lending and investing decisions; we chose eight companies (including Dell) from a broad set of industries. Exhibit 26.9 presents a table of their 1997 financial ratios. We chose pairs of companies in four industries to illustrate how companies in the same industry tend to be more similar to each other than companies in other industries. As we discuss the various ratios throughout the remainder of the chapter, we will refer to Exhibit 26.9 to compare Dell's ratios to those of the other companies selected.

EXHIBIT 26.9	Ratio Comparison for 1997							
	Dell***	Gateway***	Safeway*	Albertsons***	Du Pont*	Dow***	Netscape	Microsoft
Current	1.45	1.54	0.80	1.28	0.84	1.18	1.94	2.87
Quick	1.23	1.14	0.10	0.18	0.49	0.52	1.66	2.76
Inventory turnover	39.69	19.79	11.10	8.61	6.78	6.03	—	—
Accounts receivable turnover	10.32	13.11	131.60	133.91	8.53	6.41	4.04	14.03
Total asset turnover	3.40	3.39	3.20	2.96	1.16	0.82	0.91	0.93
Gross profit margin	22.1%	17.1%	28.5%	26.4%	43.5%	13.6%	84.7%	90.4%
Return on assets	26.0%	5.9%	7.9%	10.4%	6.0%	7.4%	NA	28.2%
Return on equity	89.9%	26.9%	33.4%	22.1%	22.0%	22.8%	NA	41.4%
Interest coverage before taxes[1]	1006.88	352.55	5.46	10.14	8.29	6.37	NA	0.00
Long-term debt to equity[2]	0.01	0.01	1.42	0.47	0.53	0.54	0.00	0.00
Total debt to total assets	0.70	0.60	0.75	0.54	0.77	0.68	0.32	0.27
Earnings per share	$1.44	$0.71	$1.35	$2.08	$2.12	$7.81	($1.34)	$2.63

[1]Equivalent to times interest earned

[2]Equivalent to debt to equity for measuring long-term risk

*uses reported interest expense

*** uses long term debt times 8%

As you know, careful analysis of current and past financial statements helps provide some of the answers about why things happened in certain companies the way they did. Ratio analysis makes it easy to compare relationships (1) for a firm over time, (2) of different firms, and (3) with standards such as industry averages. Exhibit 26.10 shows some of the ratios commonly used in analyzing financial statements.

EXHIBIT 26.10 Important Financial Ratios

What Is Measured	Ratios	Means of Calculation
Activity	Accounts receivable turnover	$\dfrac{\text{Net credit sales}}{\text{Average net accounts receivable}}$
	Inventory turnover	$\dfrac{\text{Cost of goods sold}}{\text{Average inventory}}$
	Payables turnover	$\dfrac{\text{Total cash expenses}}{\text{Average current liabilities (except bank loans)}}$
Liquidity	Current ratio	$\dfrac{\text{Current assets}}{\text{Current liabilities}}$
	Cash flow per share	$\dfrac{\text{Cash flow from operations} - \text{Preferred dividends}}{\text{Weighted-average number of shares of common stock}}$
	Quick ratio	$\dfrac{\text{Cash} + \text{Temporary investments} + \text{Accounts receivable}}{\text{Current liabilities}}$
Long-term debt-paying ability	Times interest earned	$\dfrac{\text{Net income before interest and taxes}}{\text{Interest expense}}$
	Debt to equity	$\dfrac{\text{Total liabilities}}{\text{Total shareholders' equity}}$
Profitability	Gross margin ratio	$\dfrac{\text{Gross margin}}{\text{Net sales}}$
	Return on sales	$\dfrac{\text{Net income}}{\text{Net sales}}$
	Return on assets*	$\dfrac{\text{Net income}}{\text{Average total assets}}$
	Return on owners' equity	$\dfrac{\text{Net income}}{\text{Average owners' equity}}$
	Return on common equity	$\dfrac{\text{Net income} - \text{Preferred stock dividends}}{\text{Stockholders' equity} - \text{Liquidating value of preferred stock}}$
	Asset turnover	$\dfrac{\text{Net sales}}{\text{Average total assets}}$
	Du Pont ROI (ROA)	$\dfrac{\text{Net sales}}{\text{Average total assets}} \times \dfrac{\text{Net income}}{\text{Net sales}}$ or Asset turnover $\times$ Return on sales
	Earnings per share	$\dfrac{\text{Net income} - \text{Preferred dividends}}{\text{Weighted-average number of shares of common stock outstanding}}$
	Dividend payout ratio	$\dfrac{\text{Dividends paid to common stockholders}}{\text{Earnings available to common stockholders}}$
	Price-earnings ratio	$\dfrac{\text{Current market price}}{\text{Earnings per share}}$
	Dividend yield	$\dfrac{\text{Dividends paid per share of stock}}{\text{Market price per share of stock}}$

*Note: As discussed in Chapter 18 many companies use net income before interest and taxes in the numerator to measure the income generated regardless of financing and taxes. We use the simpler formula here.

**Note: As discussed in Chapter 12 many companies use income from continuing operations in the numerator to measure income generated by operating activities. We use the simpler formula here.

Activity Ratios

Creditors and investors ask the important question about whether the normal flow of funds from cash to inventory to accounts receivable and back to cash is sufficient and regular enough for the firm to pay its debts on time or to pay dividends. One means of assessing business operations is by using activity ratios, which are financial ratios that are helpful in judging a firm's efficiency in using its current assets and liabilities.

We use the accounts receivable turnover as an example of how creditors and investors might apply activity ratios to assess a potential investment. Recall from Chapter 12 that the accounts receivable turnover represents the relationship between accounts receivable and credit sales, and it measures how many times the company collected the average accounts receivable balance in the period.

Using the data from Exhibits 26.3 and 26.4, we calculate Dell's accounts receivable turnover for 1998 as follows:

$$\text{Accounts receivable turnover} = \frac{\text{Net credit sales}^{7}}{\text{Average net accounts receivable}} = \frac{\$12,327}{\$1,194.5^{8}} = 10.32$$

Comparing the 1998 accounts receivable turnover ratio with those of the other seven firms in Exhibit 26.9, we see that Dell's accounts receivable turnover ratio of 10.32 is slightly below Gateway's, which is also in Dell's industry, and not as high as the world's largest software manufacturer, Microsoft.

We do not include the accounts receivable turnover ratios of Safeway or Albertsons because they report only total sales, the combination of both cash and credit sales. Most of a retail grocer's sales are cash sales, so when its average accounts receivable balance (which is low) is divided into its total sales, it appears that the receivables turnover is incredibly high. Credit instead of total sales is the appropriate numerator to use in computing this ratio. Because credit sales for a grocer are much lower than total sales, the accounts receivable turnover ratio would be much lower than the 130 times that would result from using total sales to find the ratio for Safeway and Albertsons.

This leads us to raise two notes of caution about the computation of the accounts receivable turnover ratio. First, using total net sales assumes that all the sales were made on open account. If this is not the case, the numerator in the turnover ratio should be net credit sales, not total net sales.

Second, care must be exercised in using the average of beginning and ending accounts receivable balances. Many businesses are seasonal and have periods of high sales accompanied by large receivable balances. Ideally, the average accounts receivable balance should be the average of the beginning balances for each of the 12 months in the fiscal year. Keep in mind that the managers of the corporation who perform financial statement analysis have access to the data necessary to make these computations accurately. However, when the detailed data on credit sales and monthly balances are not available, the analyst needs to understand the potential deficiencies involved. When only total sales data are available, and the analyst believes the proportion of credit sales is low, then the accounts receivable turnover ratio should be used with caution. Using year-end balances rather than monthly data means that seasonal businesses with unusually high (low) accounts receivable balances at year-end appear to have an accounts receivable turnover that is slower (faster) than it is.

Inventory turnover and payables turnover discussed in Chapter 12 are also activity ratios. Investors use these ratios to assess management's operating efficiency with respect to the purchasing and payment activities. Dell's inventory turnover for 1998 was 39.69, which is an incredible number of times to sell inventory in a year. Recall from Chapter 12 that for 1997 the Gap, Inc.'s, inventory turned over 6.19 times during the period. Comparatively, Dell's inventory turnover is phenomenal and due in large part to its direct selling approach, which requires very low inventory levels while still meeting customer demand. For 1998 Dell's payables turnover ratio of 8.47[9] is much closer to that of the Gap,

---

[7]Most companies do not separate sales into cash and credit sales. We will explain the implications of this later in the chapter.

[8]The $1,194.5 denominator is the average of Dell's 1998 and 1997 accounts receivable [$1,486 (1998 balance) + $903 (1997 balance)]/2].

[9]To find Dell's cash expenses include cost of revenue; selling, general, and administrative expenses; research, development, and engineering; and provision for income taxes less depreciation and amortization. Its 1998 payables turnover ratio is calculated as $11,368/[($1,643 + 1,040)/2] = 8.47.

which had a payables turnover of 7.36 times during the year. The efficiencies that Dell has in purchasing and processing inventory do not appear to translate into paying short-term obligations. But that's not necessarily bad because paying too early would mean that Dell loses the use of its money before it needs to.

Assessing Short-Term Liquidity and Solvency

When assessing a business as a potential investment, its liquidity is an important consideration, particularly for creditors whose return relies exclusively on cash flows from the company. Recall that liquidity refers to the cash position of a company and its ability to generate cash inflows through normal operations. Firms rarely have sufficient cash on hand to pay off all their liabilities. Therefore, they depend on the timing of cash inflows in relation to the timing needs of the outflows to pay liabilities. Liquidity and solvency analysis is concerned with cash flows and the adequacy of current assets to meet current liabilities. In Chapter 12 we discuss two ratios commonly used for liquidity, or solvency, analysis: current and quick ratios. Using the amounts from Exhibit 26.3, we compute Dell's current ratio at the end of 1998 as follows:

$$\text{Current ratio} = \frac{\text{Current assets}}{\text{Current liabilities}} = \frac{\$3{,}912}{\$2{,}697} = 1.45$$

The quick ratio provides a stricter test of the adequacy of current assets to meet current liabilities because it excludes, in the numerator, current assets that are not readily convertible to cash, such as inventory and prepaid items. Dell's 1998 quick ratio of 1.23 was calculated by dividing readily convertible-to-cash assets of $3,330 million (cash, $320 million; marketable securities, $1,524 million; and accounts receivable, $1,486 million) by current liabilities of $2,697 million.

We evaluate Dell's liquidity based on its current and quick ratios (1.45 and 1.23, respectively) by comparing them to the ratios of the other firms listed in Exhibit 26.9. Dell appears to be in the middle of the other seven companies in terms of liquidity. Microsoft appears to be in the strongest liquidity position, with current and quick ratios of 2.87 and 2.76, respectively, well above the rest. Note the very low quick ratios for Safeway and Albertsons (0.10 and 0.18). This occurs because inventory is the major component of the current assets of grocers, and inventory is not part of the quick ratio calculation. Grocers like Safeway and Albertsons rely on selling inventory quickly, so their inventory could be considered more liquid than that of other types of firms. Thus we do not consider the liquidity positions of Safeway and Albertsons to be unusual for their industry.

Analysts also can use cash flows from the statement of cash flows to assess a firm's liquidity.[10] One such measure is **cash flow per share,** which we calculate as follows:

$$\text{Cash flow per share} = \frac{\text{Cash flows from operations} - \text{Preferred dividends}}{\text{Weighted-average number of shares of common stock}}$$

Using the amounts shown in Exhibits 26.4 and 26.5, we find that Dell's cash flow per share was $2.42 ($1,591[11]/658 million shares). Notice that the denominator in the ratio is the number of common and common equivalent shares used to calculate the basic earnings per share shown on Dell's income statement (Exhibit 26.4). Dell's 1998 cash flow per share supports the adequate liquidity indicated by its quick and current ratios.

Long-Term Debt Repayment

You already know that investors have an interest in a company's long-term ability to repay debt, but the creditors, both current and potential, have the risk of not recovering their funds. They, therefore, want to know about the firm's debt structure and how that will affect the firm's ability to meet both its short- and long-term debt obligations. We discuss three ratios typically used by creditors to evaluate a firm's creditworthiness: times interest earned; debt-to-equity; and long-term debt-to-equity.

---

[10]See Charles A. Carslaw and John R. Mills, "Developing Ratios for Effective Cash Flow Statement Analysis," *Journal of Accountancy,* November 1991, pp. 63–70.

[11]$1,592 million in net cash inflows from operating activities less preferred stock dividends of $1 million.

Of Interest   Using Cash-Based Ratios to Test for Solvency

Because creditors and lenders are mainly concerned about a company's ability to meet its payment commitments they use cash flow ratios to assess solvency. These ratios compare how much cash was generated over time with a company's near-term obligations, which helps to measure whether the company can pay loans with interest on time. The *operating cash flow ratio* is calculated by dividing the cash flow from operations taken from the Statement of Cash Flows by the current liabilities found on the Balance Sheet (Cash Flow from Operations/Current liabilities). This measures a company's ability to meet its current liabilities, and as with all ratios, needs to be compared with ratios from the company's industry peers. Another measure of a company's ability to pay its obligations is the *funds flow coverage ratio* (FFC). The numerator of this ratio is earnings before interest and taxes plus depreciation and amortization, which differs from the cash flow from operations in that it excludes cash paid for interest and taxes. The denominator of the funds flow coverage ratio is interest plus tax-adjusted debt repayment plus tax-adjusted preferred dividends. So, the denominator represents the unavoidable expenditures associated with the financing of the company: interest, preferred stock dividends

and debt repayment. This ratio highlights the company's ability to meet interest and tax commitments. If the FFC is at least 1.0, the company can meet its most immediate financial commitments—just barely. A ratio of 1.0 doesn't allow any room for maintaining its physical plant or growth. A third cash-based ratio is the cash current debt coverage debt ratio, which divides the retained operating cash flow by the current debt, debt maturing within one year. To find the company's retained operating cash flow start with the company's operating cash flows from its Statement of Cash Flows and subtract the cash dividends. This ratio is more revealing than comparing a company's current earning to its currently maturing debt because it links management's dividend policy to its ability to pay for its currently maturing debt. Why use cash flows instead of earnings? The income statement contains many arbitrary noncash allocations such as depreciation and amortization. Are cash flow ratios substitutes for traditional ratios? No, the best ratio analysis includes many ratios that measure similar underlying ideas like solvency and liquidity.

Adapted from "The power of cash flow ratios," *Journal of Accountancy*; New York; Oct 1998; John Mills; Jeanne H Yamamura; Volume 186 Issue: 4 Start Page: 53, 55+.

Times Interest Earned   Creditors, especially long-term creditors, judge the ability of a borrower to pay interest based on the relationship of the borrower's before-interest earnings to the amount of the interest charges for the period. As you know from Chapter 18, the times interest earned ratio compares earnings before deducting interest and taxes to the amount of the interest charges. A company whose income before interest is barely sufficient to cover its interest expense is riskier from a creditor's point of view than one with a high times interest earned ratio. We calculate Dell's 1998 times interest earned ratio as follows:

$$\text{Times interest earned} = \frac{\$944 + \$1.36^{12} + \$424}{\$1.36}$$
$$= \frac{\$1,369.36}{\$1.36}$$
$$= 1,006.88 \text{ times}$$

Of the firms we are comparing, Dell has the highest times interest earned ratio among those with any meaningful amount of debt, which indicates that it presents creditors with less risk than the other seven firms. The unusually high interest coverage before taxes for Dell and Gateway, another computer manufacturer, is due to their high earnings with very low interest expense. The two software companies, Microsoft and Netscape, have virtually no interest expense and, thus, present no risk of failing to pay interest to creditors.

The Internet is a good source for both financial and nonfinancial data.

Debt-to-Equity Ratio   Recall that the debt-to-equity ratio expresses the total liabilities as a percentage of the total owners' or shareholders' equity and, thus, measures a company's

---

[12] We estimated Dell's 1998 interest expense by assuming an interest rate on long-term debt of 8 percent.

risk as an investment by the extent to which it relies on debt rather than ownership financing. Using the amounts from Exhibit 26.3, we calculate Dell's 1998 debt-to-equity ratio as follows:

$$\text{Debt-to-equity ratio} = \frac{\text{Total liabilities}}{\text{Total shareholders' equity}} = \frac{\$2,975}{\$1,293} = 2.3$$

This means that at the end of fiscal 1998 almost 70 percent [$2,975/$4,268] of Dell's financing came from liabilities.

Long-Term Debt-to-Equity   A similar way of measuring risk is by comparing long-term debt-to-equity. The focus on long-term debt instead of total liabilities is a measure of the extent to which long-term financing comes from debt. The use of total liabilities would also include the proportion of debt that comes from operations (short-term) and financing from other long-term liabilities like pension obligations.

At the end of its 1998 fiscal year, Dell had only about $17 million of long-term debt, which is a very small amount of long-term debt. Its long-term debt-to-total-equity ratio was only 1.3 percent ($17/$1,293). Safeway's long-term debt-to-total-equity ratio of 1.42 suggests that it is the most risky of the firms we compare. But Safeway is a long established company with good cash flow and significant financial resources. It can be very misleading to rely on one measure of risk when analyzing a company. Other measures of risk like debt-to-total-assets show that Safeway is not too risky. That is, Safeway does not have a high debt level relative to its assets; instead, Safeway is highly leveraged with a large portion of its assets coming from debt rather than owner financing. Microsoft and Netscape present virtually no risk associated with the extent of long-term debt in their capital structure because their respective ratios are 0!

 **PAUSE & REFLECT**   **Many of the risk measures we have discussed focus on the risk to creditors of not receiving cash flows from their debtors. What is the nature of the economic risk that stockholders face? Can it be measured the same way as creditors' risk? If not, how can it be measured? (answer on page 912)**

Profitability: The Source of a Firm's Value

Our analysis and evaluation to this point have been concerned with the company's ability to pay its debts on time. In a broader, more long-term sense, if the company is not profitable, it eventually will not meet its maturing obligations. Thus profitability is important to lenders. However, future profitability is also central to investors' analyses of a firm's value as an investment because both the value of the company and the potential for dividend payments depend on a firm's profitability.

Profitability is the return on funds invested by the owners and achieved by the efforts of management. Profitability results from numerous operating, investing, and financing decisions over different periods of time. Effectively measuring profitability requires more than examining the amount of net income in a particular period. The absolute dollar amount of profits in one period reveals very little about the effectiveness of operations and a company's long-term prospects.

Both current and potential owners of a business are interested in the business's long- and short-term profitability. They also are interested in the firm's disposition of its earnings, which could be either distributed to them as dividends or reinvested in the firm. If the company's stock is publicly traded, owners are concerned also with the stock market's perception of the firm's profitability and its dividend policy. We discuss the role of market price in providing investors with a return on their investment later in the chapter. Now we describe a few of the financial ratios that investors use to evaluate a firm's profitability.

Gross Margin Ratio   Chapter 12 describes how to use ratios to assess management's product pricing decisions, which directly affect profitability. If management prices a product too high, it will sell fewer units. On the other hand, a price that is too low may

Even within the same industry, comparisons between companies such as Dow (left) and DuPont (right) can be complicated by differences in their product markets.

not provide the firm with a sufficient gross margin to cover operating expenses. Thus we use the gross margin ratio as a measure of profitability.

Using the amounts from Exhibit 26.4, we calculate Dell's gross margin ratio of 22.1 percent as shown here:

$$\text{Gross margin ratio} = \frac{\text{Gross margin}}{\text{Sales}} = \frac{\$2,722}{\$12,327} = 22.1\%$$

Dell's gross margin ratio indicates that after it pays for the cost of the items it sells, the company has 22.1 cents of every sales dollar available to meet other expenses, like administrative and advertising expenses, and to provide net profit. Comparing Dell's gross margins with those of the other seven firms in Exhibit 26.9 reveals that Dow has the lowest gross margin ratio (13.6 percent). Comparing gross margins with and between industries shows that the production process that is unique to an industry is a strong determinant of a firm's gross margin. As you look at the pairs of firms in the same industry, like Microsoft and Netscape, you find that the gross margins within an industry are more similar to each other than to companies in other industries. The exception to this industry effect is Dow and Du Pont, which suggests that, while they are both chemical companies, they differ substantially in the nature of the products they sell and the markets in which those products are sold. Many of Dow's products are sold at the retail level where the number of competitors forces prices lower, while Du Pont sells chemicals to manufacturers where the competitive forces on prices is different.

Return on Assets   Many analysts consider the return on assets (ROA) ratio singularly important because it includes the two fundamental profitability elements—earnings and investments in assets. The investment-in-assets element represents the total investment of the business, and the ratio of net income to those assets measures the effectiveness of management in utilizing the resources at its command. Because a company earns net income over a span of time, meaningful analysis compares net income to the firm's average amount of investments over that same time period, as shown below:

$$\text{Return on assets} = \frac{\text{Net income}}{\text{Average total asssets}}$$

Using the amounts from Exhibits 26.3 and 26.4, we compute Dell's 1998 return on assets as follows:

$$\text{ROA} = \frac{\$944}{(\$4,268 + \$2,993)/2} = \frac{\$944}{\$3,630.5} = 26.0\%$$

Comparing Dell's 1998 return on assets with the seven other firms in Exhibit 26.9, we find that Dell's 26.0 percent ROA is second only to Microsoft (28.2 percent). Software companies are likely to have fewer resources invested in fixed assets due to the easy-to-manufacture nature of the products they produce. Comparing Gateway and Dell is interesting because they are both established computer manufacturers. The difference in their ROAs is due, in part, to Gateway's lower gross margin (17.1 percent versus Dell's 22.1 percent) and its higher operating cost as reflected in its lower earnings per share.

Return on Owners' Equity   Another measure of profitability is return on owners' equity (ROE), which measures the return earned (net income) relative to the portion of the firm that belongs to the owners. Return on owners' equity is computed as follows:

$$\text{Return on owners' equity} = \frac{\text{Net income}}{\text{Average owners' equity}}$$

We calculate Dell's 1998 return on owners' equity using the amounts from Exhibits 26.3 and 26.4 as follows:

$$\text{ROE} = \frac{\$944}{(\$1,293 + \$806)/2} = \frac{\$944}{\$1,049.5} = 89.9\%$$

When comparing Dell's 1998 return on owners' equity of 89.9 percent with the seven other firms shown in Exhibit 26.9, we see that Dell is far more profitable than any of the others. We do not calculate either of the two return measures for Netscape because it reported a loss in 1997, and negative returns are not meaningful in comparisons with positive returns.

Return on equity is generally computed for the common stockholders only resulting in **return on common equity.** If there is preferred stock outstanding, adjustments are made for preferred dividend components of the calculation, as shown below, to derive a return on common equity:

$$\text{Return on common equity} = \frac{\text{Net income} - \text{Preferred stock dividends}}{\text{Stockholders' equity} - \text{Liquidating value of preferred stock}}$$

The net income in the numerator is reduced by the amount of preferred stock dividends, and the denominator is reduced by the liquidating value of the preferred stock,[13] which is the amount that the corporation would have to pay to purchase all the preferred stock from the preferred stockholders. Because Dell does not have any preferred stock, there is no difference between its return on equity and its return on common equity.

Asset Turnover   The **asset turnover ratio** is an activity ratio that measures profitability because it relates a firm's ability to generate sales to the amount of assets that the firm employs. The ratio involves dividing net sales by the average total assets for the period. A high ratio indicates that management is utilizing the assets under its control well.

$$\text{Asset turnover} = \frac{\text{Net sales}}{\text{Average total assets}}$$

---

[13]For preferred stock that is publicly traded, the liquidating value is the current market value per share times the number of shares outstanding. For the large stock exchanges, the *Wall Street Journal* publishes the closing prices of those stocks daily.

Using the amounts from Exhibits 26.3 and 26.4, we calculate Dell's asset turnover ratio for 1998 as follows:

$$\text{Asset turnover} = \frac{\text{Net sales}}{\text{Average total assets}} = \frac{\$12,327}{(\$4,268+\$2,993)/2} = \frac{\$12,327}{\$3,630.5} = 3.40$$

Comparing Dell's 1998 asset turnover ratio (3.4), with those of the other firms in Exhibit 26.9 shows that the pairs of firms in the computer manufacturing and retail grocery industries had the best asset turnover ratios. Three of the remaining four (Dow, Netscape, and Microsoft) did not generate sales that exceeded their average investment in assets.

Du Pont Method of Return on Investment The Du Pont Company was one of the early examples of a very diversified company. It produced a number of different products requiring different raw materials and production processes. In order to assess the profitability of various production facilities, Du Pont developed a return on investment (ROI) measure that is a combination of return on sales, a profitability measure, and the asset turnover ratio, an activity measure.

For our purposes, return on investment is the same as return on assets, which we discussed earlier. The Du Pont return on investment (return on assets) is calculated as follows:

$$\text{DuPont ROI} = \frac{\text{Net sales}}{\text{Average total assets}} \times \frac{\text{Net income}}{\text{Net sales}}$$
$$= \text{Asset turnover} \times \text{Return on sales}$$

By breaking the return on assets expression into two components, we can look at two potential causes for changes in a company's return on assets from period to period. We calculated Dell's return on assets for 1998 to be 26.0 percent. Using amounts from Dell's 1997 and 1996 financial statements,[14] we calculate that in 1997 its return on assets was 20.2 percent. Was this improvement in ROA from 1997 to 1998 due to changes in utilization of assets or profitability?

Using the Du Pont method, we can isolate the asset utilization measured by the asset turnover ratio from profitability measured by return on sales. Earlier we calculated Dell's 1998 asset turnover ratio to be 3.4 and calculated that Dell had an asset turnover ratio of 3.02 in 1997. We calculate Dell's return on sales for 1998 and 1997 as follows:

$$1998 \text{ Return on sales}^{15} = \frac{\$944}{\$12,327} = 7.66\%$$

$$1997 \text{ Return on sales} = \frac{\$518}{\$7,759} = 6.68\%$$

Looking at the components of Dell's ROA for 1998 and 1997, we see that the improvement in ROA from 1997 to 1998 was driven by both an improvement in profitability (return on sales) and an improvement in asset utilization. The calculations supporting this observation are as follows:

		ROA	=	Asset turnover	×	Return on sales
1998	=	26.0%	=	3.40	×	7.66%
1997	=	20.2%	=	3.02	×	6.68%

---

[14]In order to calculate Dell's average total assets, we went to Dell's 1996 balance sheet to find that its total assets at the end of fiscal 1996 were $2,148 million. Dell's return on assets of 20.2 percent for 1997 is calculated as $518/[($2,993 + $2,148)/2].

[15]Recall from Chapter 12 that the return on sales ratio is the ratio of income from operations to net sales. Many companies calculate return on sales using income from continuing operations; that is, income before interest and taxes, rather than net income.

Earnings per Share   We know that earnings per share (EPS) is such an important measure of profitability that it is required to be presented as part of the income statement. Dell's 1998 EPS is calculated below:

$$\text{Earnings per share} = \frac{\text{Net income} - \text{Preferred stock individuals}}{\text{Weighted-average number of common shares outstanding}}$$

In 1998 Dell's $1.44 EPS was about average for the seven firms we compare, while Dow had the highest EPS of $7.81 per share (Exhibit 26.9). From the stockholders' perspective, the EPS of the firms in which they invest are best evaluated relative to the market price of the firms' stock. Later we discuss how analysts use a stock's market price to assess earnings.

Dividends: Cash Flows for Investors

As part of their financing and operating decisions, some firms pay dividends to their stockholders, while others do not. Investors differ in their investment objectives, and not all investors want to receive dividends. Part of investors' evaluation of a potential investment is assessing the corporation's dividend policy.

The **dividend payout ratio** reveals a firm's dividend payment philosophy. The dividend payout ratio relates the amount of dividends paid to the period's earnings. As shown below, this is determined only for common stockholders:

$$\text{Dividend payout ratio} = \frac{\text{Dividends paid to common stockholders}}{\text{Earnings available to common stockholders}}$$

The dividend payout ratio enables financial statement users to assess the prospects for future cash flows paid directly to them by the corporation, which is not the same as the amount of cash flows received by the business. Rather, dividend payout shows the portion of the firm's assets distributed to the common stockholders as well as the remaining portion of earnings that is reinvested in the firm. Therefore, the dividend payout ratio gives the financial statement reader an indication of management's policy on reinvesting the earnings of the firm. Dell's statement of cash flows (Exhibit 26.6) shows that it did not pay common stock dividends in 1998.

Exhibit 26.11 shows the dividend and market-related data for the eight companies we have discussed in this chapter. (We discuss dividend yield on page 910). Comparing Dell's dividend payout to the other seven firms reveals some interesting differences in dividend policy among the firms. The three other high-tech companies, Gateway, Netscape, and Microsoft, do not pay dividends either. One explanation for this is that the nature of high-tech industries is characterized by strong growth in markets and products. These industries face increased prospects for higher incomes and good opportunities for the companies themselves to invest internally in high-return projects. Rather than payout dividends, they reinvest the money themselves. Safeway does not face the same sort of opportunities and its management apparently has made the decision not to pay dividends, while Albertsons, which is also in the retail grocery industry, does. Du Pont and Dow are in industries where growth opportunities are more limited; their managements have adopted the policy of paying dividends.

EXHIBIT 26.11   1997 Dividend and Market-Related Data for Eight Companies

	Dell	Gateway	Safeway	Albertsons	Du Pont	Dow	Netscape	Microsoft
Dividend payout	N/A	N/A	N/A	$0.64	$1.23	$3.36	N/A	N/A
Dividend yield	N/A	N/A	N/A	30.77%	59.24%	43.02%	N/A	N/A
Market price at the end of the fiscal year	$99.44	$32.75	$63.25	$47.75	$60.06	$101.50	$24.38	$126.375

We have shown how creditors and investors use information presented in a company's financial statements to assess activity, liquidity and solvency, long-term debt-paying ability, and profitability for companies, in addition to dividend policies. But external stakeholders use information about the market value of their investments as well as the information they receive from a company's financial statements. In the next section, we describe how investors use market information when evaluating companies.

USING STOCK PRICE INFORMATION FOR INVESTING

LO 3

Stock markets are an important part of the world's capital markets. They allow numerous transactions involving the purchase and sale of corporate stock on a daily basis. In addition to offering investors a place to exchange stock, stock markets provide corporations with a place to sell additional stock to raise capital and to repurchase their stock easily. In addition to the NYSE, AMEX, and NASDAQ in the United States, there are major stock exchanges throughout the world in places like London and Tokyo.

Organized Stock Markets

One important feature of stock exchanges is that the buyers and sellers are rarely present. Sales are made by brokers who represent the parties in the transaction. This allows large volumes of trades to occur. The typical volume on the NYSE alone is between 200 million and 400 million shares on an average day.

Another important feature of these exchanges is that they set trading rules to protect buyers and sellers. Because the parties to the buy and sell transactions are not present at the time of the transaction, they would be reluctant to trade if there was not some protection for their cash and investments.

Stock Prices

In the stock market, investors buy and sell ownership interest in corporations (stock) at a mutually agreeable price. When there are prospects for a firm to be more profitable and, thus, more valuable, stock prices go up. In such circumstances, the price the holders of stock demand and the price the buyers of that stock offer both go up. When the prospects for firm performance take a downturn, the opposite happens. This process results in the establishment of the market price of a stock.

Exhibit 26.12 shows the portion of the *Wall Street Journal* (WSJ) that includes Dell's price information for October 26, 1998. Dell is traded on the NASDAQ exchange. Dell is listed as Dell. Notice that Dell's stock ended the day (close) selling for $58.25 per share. The highest price for its stock in the preceding 52 weeks was $69.25, and the lowest price was $17.50. Also note that Dell's closing price on the previous trading day was 5/8 of a dollar ($0.625) higher. The range of prices and the daily changes allow investors to assess the risk of the stock as measured by the volatility of, or change in, its price.

Using Information from Stock Markets

Investors use the price-earnings and the dividend yield ratios to evaluate the stocks they are considering. Both of these ratios use the market price of the stocks as part of the calculation. The **price-earnings (PE) ratio** reflects the relationship between the current market price of the firm's common stock and the earnings of the firm. It appears below:

$$\text{Price-earnings ratio} \frac{\text{Current market price}}{\text{Earnings per share}}$$

The importance of the price-earnings ratio is reflected by the fact that it is included in the stock listings of the *Wall Street Journal*. Keep in mind that the PE ratio changes frequently as the price of the stock changes each day, or as annual earnings are announced.

PAUSE & REFLECT

What are the PE ratios for the eight firms in Exhibit 26.11? Why do you think there is such a wide range of P/Es among these firms? *(answer on page 912)*

The price-earnings ratio is an overall approximation of the market's assessment of a company's prospective earnings performance. A high PE ratio suggests that the market anticipates higher earnings for the firm in the future.

EXHIBIT 26.12 Market Disclosures from the *Wall Street Journal*, October 26, 1998.

Hi, Lo, Close and Net Chg refer to the day's trading for the stock.

Yld% and PE are based on the most recently reported annual earnings and the day's closing price.

Symbols that represent the stocks are found on the stock ticker, where prices are reported (almost) as they occur on stock exchanges.

	52 Weeks Hi	52 Weeks Lo		Stock	Sym	Div	Yld %	PE	Vol 100s	Hi	Lo	Close		Net Chg
	9 3/8	2		DeckrsOutdr	DECK		...	7	366	3 1/2	3 1/4	3 1/4	−	1/2
n	12	6		Decomafnt g	DECAF	.06e	...	...	4	6 29/64	6 29/64	6 29/64	−	1/4
$	8 1/4	3 3/8		Decorafnd	DECO		...	13	297	6 1/15	5 1/2	5 13/16	+	3/8
	10 1/4	6 1/4		Defiance	DEFI	.16	2.3	10	130	7 1/8	7	7 1/16	+	1/16
	12 7/8	6 1/8		DelGloblTch	DGTC		...	13	243	9 9/16	9 3/16	9 9/16	+	3/16
	32	4 1/8		dELIA's	DLIA		...	20	1876	9 3/8	7 11/16	8	+	1/4
$	69 1/4	17 1/2		DellCptr	DELL		...	6926	2440	59 15/16	58	58 1/4	−	5/8
n	17 15/16	5		DelphiInt	DLTDF		...	...	11	7 3/8	6 7/8	7 3/8		...
	24 1/2	14 7/8		DelphosBcp	DCBI	.18e	1.0	...	12	17 1/2	17 1/4	17 1/2	+	1/4
	19 1/2	16 7/16		DeliaNG	DGAS	1.14	6.2	18	56	18 1/4	17 1/2	18 1/4	+	1
	25 1/4	13 1/2		DellekSys	DLTX		...	35	1594	16 3/8	15 1/8	16 1/4	+	1 1/4
n	18 3/8	9 3/8		Denali	DNLI		...	15	307	12 1/4	11 1/4	11 1/2	−	1/2
$	28 5/16	7 13/16		DendritaInt	DRTE		...	61	4043	24 1/2	22 1/4	22 5/8	−	2 5/16
	4 7/8	17/32		Denspac	DPAC		...	dd	1827	1 15/32	1 1/8	1 11/32	+	1/4
$	15 3/4	7 7/8		DptlCrAllnc	DENT		...	38	22	18 1/4	10 1/8	10 1/4	+	1/2
$	35 1/8	20		DENTSPLY	XRAY	.21	.9	20	1710	22 7/8	22 1/2	22 7/8	+	1/4
	15 7/8	1 1/32	♣	DepoTch	DEPO		...	dd	931	1 15/32	1 3/16	1 15/32	+	5/32
	37	21		DsrtCmntyBk	DCBK	.14	.6	...	3	23 7/8	23 7/8	23 7/8	−	1 7/8
	4 9/16	1/8		DesignsInc	DESI		...	dd	811	13/16	3/4	3/4		...
	25 3/4	6		Deswell	DSWLF	1.05e	11.7	4	311	9	8 1/2	8 15/16	+	3/16
	19 7/8	7 7/8	♣	DetectnSys	DETC		...	33	119	9 15/16	9 1/2	9 15/16	+	7/16
	5 1/4	1 3/4		Deventnt	DEVC		...	dd	55	2	2	2	+	3/16
	4 9/16	3/8	♣	DeVliegBul	DVLG		...	dd	2109	21/32	17/32	19/32	+	1/16
	11 3/4	4 1/4		Diacrin	DCRN		...	dd	135	6	5 13/16	5 7/8	+	7/8
	14 1/8	2 7/16		DiagHlth	DHSM		...	16	315	3 5/16	3 1/4	3 1/4	−	1/16
	16 1/4	8 1/2		Dialog ADS	DIALY		...	dd	5	9 1/2	9 1/2	9 1/2	−	7/8
	47 1/8	17 1/2	♣	Dialogic	DLGC		...	9	1036	19 1/2	18 7/8	19 1/4	−	...
	9	2 15/16		Diametrics	DMED		...	dd	1139	3 9/16	3 1/4	3 1/4	−	1/8
	8 3/4	3 1/4		DiamondHm	DHMS		...	14	350	3 3/4	3 5/8	3 3/4		...
	16 1/2	2 7/8		DiamndMltl	DIMD		...	dd	5164	4 3/8	3 11/16	3 3/4	−	3/16
	31 1/2	7 1/2		DiamondTchA	DTPI		...	23	3754	12 7/8	11 3/4	12 5/8	−	2 1/4
	11 1/4	5 1/4		DianonSys	DIAN		...	14	128	6 1/4	5 3/4	6 1/4	+	3/8
	11 1/8	4 1/2		Diatide	DITI		...	dd	393	7 3/8	6 1/8	7 1/8	+	5/8

The price-earnings ratio is often referred to as the **earnings multiple** and is a measure used by investors to decide whether to buy, sell, or hold a particular stock. For example, if the price-earnings multiple is considered to be low by an investor, then the investor would view the stock price as low relative to its earnings potential and might buy the security. On the other hand, if an investor holds a company's stock that has an earnings multiple the investor considers too high, then the investor might sell the stock in anticipation of the decline in its market price.

The earnings multiple can vary widely by industry and by company. Determining whether a PE ratio is too high or too low is based on the belief of the investor making the investment decision.

Dividend Yield The **dividend yield ratio** measures the return that an investor would receive on a company's stock at the current price, if dividends paid in the recent past continue into the foreseeable future. It is applied to both preferred and common stock.

The dividend yield does not measure the return from appreciation of the stock price. Rather, it measures the cash return as a percentage of the stock's current price. It is calculated by dividing the dividend per share of stock by the current market price of the stock.

$$\text{Dividend yield} = \frac{\text{Dividends paid per share of stock}}{\text{Market price per share of stock}}$$

Comparing the companies shown in Exhibit 26.11, we see that Dell and the other firms whose managements have adopted the policy of not paying dividends have no dividend yield. The other three firms pay out from 30.77 percent of earnings (Albertsons) to 59.24 percent (Du Pont).

For companies with established dividend policies, the dividend yield is an important component of the return that investors expect. For example, preferred stock typically has a specified dividend amount, and investors who buy preferred stock realize that this set dividend yield will provide most of their return. If the amount of the specified dividend, which is the principal source of return on preferred stock, is not satisfactory, the investor will not buy the preferred stock.

It is important to remember that the information provided in a company's financial statements is only part of the information that prudent creditors and investors need. In addition to sources of industry and economic information, investors should include in their assessment the value that a stock's market price implies.

SUMMARY

Creditors and investors own the capital that businesses need to finance their investments. Financial statement analysis provides creditors and investors with important information they need to choose businesses in which they will invest their capital. However, the data from financial statements are not sufficient for a thorough understanding of investment opportunities.

- Consumer demand for products indirectly determines which businesses will be able to attract the capital they need from the capital markets. Creditors and investors need reliable information on which to base their investment decisions.

- Financial statement analysis requires a thorough understanding of the statements themselves and the accounting classifications used by the business. A careful reading of the statements should precede the computations of analytical ratios.

- The ratios used as part of financial statement analysis are classified into these categories: activity, liquidity and solvency, long-term debt-paying ability, and profitability. Activity ratios focus on the efficiency with which management uses the company's current assets and liabilities. Liquidity and solvency ratios reveal the firm's ability to pay its current debts on time. Assessing long-term debt-paying ability requires ratios that measure the risk of not receiving interest or principal repayment. Profitability ratios focus on the long-term earnings potential of a business.

- Stock markets are places where buyers and sellers of the stock of many companies typically engage in transactions through brokers. Stock markets provide information about the value of a firm that investors use in addition to the information from financial statement analysis to make their investment decisions.

KEY TERMS

asset turnover ratio An activity ratio that measures profitability by relating a firm's ability to generate sales to the amount of assets that the firm employs

capital market The entire group of creditors and investors who provide capital to

businesses to allow them to finance their investments

cash flow per share A measure of a firm's liquidity using the amount of cash flows from operations less preferred dividends on a per share basis

dividend payout ratio A ratio that reveals a firm's dividend payment philosophy by relating the amount of dividends paid to the period's earnings

dividend yield ratio A ratio that measures the return an investor would receive on a company's stock at the current price if recent dividend payments continue into the foreseeable future

earnings multiple A measure used by investors to decide whether to buy, sell, or hold a particular stock

free market economy An economy in which consumer demand determines the nature of businesses that exist and how much of a given product or service is available

price-earnings (PE) ratio A ratio that reflects the relationship between the current market price of the firm's stock and the earnings of the firm

return on common equity A profitability ratio for common stockholders that adjusts the ratio of net income to stockholders' equity for their respective preferred dividend components

ANSWERS TO THE PAUSE & REFLECTS

p. 891, Foremost, you should consider their "track record." How have they done at predicting firm performance or industry trends in the past? In addition, you should consider whether they have any industry specific expertise or insight that fits your investment plans. Cost should also be considered.

p. 904, The risks that stockholders face result principally from potential declines in stock prices while they own the stock. Stockholders can use diversification of their investments as a way of avoiding the risk of price fluctuations of individual stocks. They still face the effects of changes that affect the whole stock market. One measure of the risk of an individual stock's risk is its beta, which measures the covariation of that stock's price with the rest of the stock prices. Betas higher than one represent stocks that are more risky than the market in general.

p. 909,

	Dell	Gateway	Safeway	Albertsons	Du Pont	Dow	Netscape	Microsoft
P/E	69.06	46.13	46.85	22.96	28.33	13.00	N/A	48.05
Market Price at the end of the fiscal year	$99.44	$32.75	$63.25	$47.75	$60.06	$101.50	$24.38	$126.375
Earnings per share	$1.44	$0.71	$1.35	$2.08	$2.12	$7.81	($1.34)	$2.63

The variation of PEs among this group reflects the different expectations the market has about the firms ability to sustain increased earnings in the future.

QUESTIONS

1. Who are the major user groups of financial statements, and how do their perspectives on the analysis of financial statements differ?

2. What is meant by comparative financial statements and how are they used in horizontal analysis?

3. What is the advantage of analyzing a company's financial statements over a series of years rather than just for the current period?

4. Name three sources of external standards to which a firm may be compared.

5. What is a financial ratio?

6. Briefly explain what is meant by liquidity analysis, and state why it is important.

7. If you know a company has a current ratio of 2 to 1, why is that not enough information to judge its liquidity?

8. Explain what is meant when it is stated that a company has a quick ratio of 1.75.

9. What do activity ratios measure?

10. Explain why the following items are omitted from the calculation of the payables turnover:
   a. Depreciation expense
   b. Notes payable to the bank

11. What is meant by profitability analysis?

12. When a firm's return on assets increases and its asset turnover decreases, has the return on sales increased, decreased, or remained constant? Explain.

13. Why is there a difference between return on assets and return on owners' equity?

14. What is meant by earnings per share?

15. What is meant by the price-earnings ratio?

16. Does the dividend payout ratio tell you anything different from the information included in the computation for dividends per share?

17. Why do analysts use ratios to evaluate firm performance?

18. Explain why an analyst would want to use more than one ratio that measures the same characteristic of a firm, such as liquidity or profitability.

19. The market price of its stock is something that a firm has very little control over. Why is it an important part of analyzing a firm's performance?

20. Explain why dividend yield measures profitability from the stockholders' perspective rather than the firm's perspective.

EXERCISES

E 26.1

LO 2

Using the data in the abbreviated income statements below, prepare a horizontal analysis showing both the dollar amount and percentage change from year 1 to year 2.

	Year 2	Year 1
Sales	$432,000	$360,000
Cost of goods sold	264,000	220,000
Gross margin	$168,000	$140,000
Operating expenses	127,200	110,000
Net income	$ 40,800	$ 30,000

E 26.2

LO 2

Prepare a vertical analysis (common-size statement) for the condensed balance sheet of Fastake, Inc., shown below:

	Year 2	Year 1
Cash	$ 60,000	$ 56,000
Accounts receivable	142,500	136,000
Inventory	195,000	178,000
Property, plant, and equipment	352,500	252,000
Total assets	$750,000	$622,000
Accounts payable and accrued liabilities	$127,500	$160,000
Long-term liabilities	150,000	–0–
Stockholders' equity	472,500	462,000
Total liabilities and stockholders' equity	$750,000	$622,000

E 26.3

LO 2

Using the balance sheet information from Fastake, Inc., in E 26.2, compute the current ratio for each year.

E 26.4

LO 2

The summarized data below were obtained from the accounting records of Thomas Company at the end of its fiscal year, September 30:

	2000	1999
Cash	$ 24,180	$ 27,240
Accounts receivable	119,500	128,160
Inventory	143,390	111,690
All other assets	348,780	333,580
Accounts payable	95,340	99,590
Bank note payable, due in 90 days	48,000	36,000
Note payable, due in 8 years	27,500	27,500
Sales	940,240	888,240
Cost of goods sold	689,590	651,780
Operating expenses (includes depreciation of $7,160 in both years)	28,510	26,330

Compute the following for 2000:
a. Current ratio
b. Quick ratio

E 26.5

LO 2

Make the appropriate computations for each situation described below:
a. The firm's average days per receivable turnover is 44, and its sales are $676,300. What is the average Accounts Receivable balance?
b. If a company maintains an average inventory of $600,000, which it plans to turn over every 54 days, what will be the amount of its cost of goods sold?

E 26.6

LO 2

Refer to the information for Thomas Company in E 26.4 and compute the following for 2000:
a. Return on sales
b. Return on assets
c. Asset turnover
d. Ratio of debt to equity
e. Return on owners' equity

E 26.7

LO 2

The following three independent situations concern return on sales, asset turnover, and return on assets:
a. The return on sales is 10 percent, and the asset turnover is 1.7. What is the return on assets?
b. The return on assets is 12 percent, and the asset turnover is 2.8. What is the return on sales?
c. The return on sales is 6 percent, and the return on assets is 8 percent. What is the asset turnover?

E 26.8

LO 2

Maurice Products has $960,000 in total assets at the beginning of the period. The firm expects to declare and pay $90,000 in dividends during the year. The forecasted net income is $200,000, and it expects to show a 15 percent return on average total assets. Determine the expected amount of year-end assets assuming no changes in total liabilities.

E 26.9

LO 2

After a fire destroyed the accounting records and most of the offices of Park Company, the owner decided to ask the bank for a short-term loan to supplement the insurance settlement. The owner remembers the following information and asks you to determine the current ratio so that she may give that information in her loan application:

Current assets	$ 40,000
Long-term liabilities	80,000
Net income	32,000
Return on assets	8%
Ratio of debt to equity	0.3333

E 26.10

LO 2

Levitt Company has total liabilities of $150,000 and total owners' equity of $200,000. The firm had net income of $26,000 after deducting interest expense of $9,000. This is a proprietorship and, as such, does not pay income tax on its net income. Compute the return on assets and the return on owners' equity. What is the debt-to-equity ratio? What is the times interest earned ratio?

E 26.11

LO 2

Using the information shown below, determine the missing amounts:

	Case 1	Case 2	Case 3
Assets	$400,000	?	$100,000
Sales	$600,000	?	?
Net income	?	$ 45,000	?
Return on sales	6%	?	?
Return on assets	?	15%	20%
Asset turnover	?	3	5

E 26.12

LO 3

Yamamoto Imports has total stockholders' equity of $1,098,000 on September 30, 2000. The firm issues only no-par common stock and had 300,000 shares outstanding on that date. During the fiscal year ended September 30, 2000, the firm earned net income of $146,600 and paid dividends totaling $67,700. The stock was selling for $15 per share. Compute the following:
a. Return on common equity
b. Dividend payout ratio
c. Earnings per share
d. Price-earnings ratio
e. Dividend yield

PROBLEMS

P 26.1

LO 2

Smith Products presently has a current ratio of 2.0 to 1 and a quick ratio of 1.8 to 1. For each of the following transactions, specify the effect of the transaction on these two ratios. Use **I** for increase, **D** for decrease, and **NC** for no change. Consider each transaction separately.

	Current	Quick
a. Collection of an account receivable	_____	_____
b. Recording accrued but unpaid interest	_____	_____
c. Purchase of inventory on account	_____	_____
d. Payment of an account payable	_____	_____
e. Borrowing from the bank on a short-term note	_____	_____
f. Purchase of temporary investments	_____	_____
g. Payment of insurance premium of six months in advance	_____	_____
h. Additional contributions of cash made by owners	_____	_____
i. Purchase of equipment with a cash down payment and long-term note payable	_____	_____
j. Made a cash refund to a customer for merchandise returned	_____	_____

P 26.2

LO 2

For each transaction or change listed below, determine the effect on the return on sales, asset turnover, and return on assets. Consider each event by itself and fill in the blanks with **I** for increase, **D** for decrease, and **NC** for no change.

	Return on Sales	Asset Turnover	Return on Assets
a. Pay long-term liability.	_____	_____	_____
b. Purchase equipment for cash.	_____	_____	_____
c. Increase gross margin percentage.	_____	_____	_____
d. Increase average inventory by purchase on open account.	_____	_____	_____
e. Decrease operating expenses as a percentage of sales.	_____	_____	_____
f. Issue additional capital stock for cash.	_____	_____	_____
g. Decrease number of units sold.	_____	_____	_____
h. Purchase buildings with partial payment and issue a mortgage payable for the balance.	_____	_____	_____

P 26.3

LO 2 **LO 3**

Mountain Crest, Inc., had $1,000,000 in net income for 2001 after deducting interest expense of $220,000 and income taxes of $340,000. The price of the stock at the fiscal year-end was $32. The firm's stockholders' equity is presented below:

Common stock, $5 par value, authorized 1,000,000 shares,	
700,000 shares issued and outstanding	$3,500,000
Preferred stock, 6%, $10 par value, authorized 200,000 shares,	
50,000 shares issued and outstanding	500,000
Paid-in capital in excess of par, common stock	900,000
Total contributed capital	$4,900,000
Retained earnings	1,754,000
Total stockholders' equity	$6,654,000

Required

a. Determine the times interest earned.
b. Compute the earnings per share.
c. Calculate the return on common equity.
d. Determine the price-earnings ratio at the fiscal year-end.

P 26.4

LO 2

Summarized data from the records of Wyndham Enterprises at the end of the fiscal year appear below:

	2001	2000
Cash	$ 205,140	$ 213,860
Temporary investments	–0–	520,370
Accounts receivable	2,925,540	2,589,950
Inventory	3,480,210	3,684,970
All other assets	4,219,750	2,494,730
Accounts payable	1,054,950	1,142,630
Other current liabilities from operations	658,160	517,320
Current bank loans payable	1,580,000	1,073,880
Long-term liabilities	2,000,000	2,000,000
Sales	22,838,400	23,804,700
Cost of goods sold	18,910,190	20,543,450
Operating expenses (includes depreciation of $296,500 in each year)	2,986,995	2,323,870

Required

Calculate the following:
a. Current ratio
b. Quick ratio
c. Return on sales

d. Return on assets

e. Asset turnover

f. Ratio of debt to equity.

g. Return on owners' equity

P 26.5
LO 2

A condensed, common-size income statement and some other information for Cybil Company are presented below:

Income Statement	
Sales	100%
Cost of goods sold	62
Gross margin	38
Operating expenses	32
Net income	6
Operating expenses	$144,000
Asset turnover	2.5
Ratio of debt to equity	0.5
Current ratio	1.8

Required

a. Determine the dollar amount for all items shown on the income statement.

b. Compute the dollar amounts for the following balance sheet items:
1. Current assets
2. Property, plant, and equipment
3. Total assets
4. Current liabilities (there are no long-term liabilities)
5. Owners' equity
6. Total liabilities and owners' equity

P 26.6
LO 2

The following information is a condensed set of financial statements for Eccles Company:

ECCLES COMPANY
Statement of Financial Position
September 30

	1999	1998	1997
Cash	$ 35,400	$ 21,500	$ 16,800
Accounts receivable, net	78,600	80,000	87,150
Inventory	97,200	99,500	107,100
Prepaid expenses	13,800	10,500	4,200
Long-term assets, net	375,000	415,500	446,250
Total assets	$600,000	$627,000	$661,500
Current liabilities*	$ 95,000	$120,000	$110,500
Long-term liabilities	65,000	87,000	105,000
Owners' equity	440,000	420,000	446,000
Total liabilities and owners' equity	$600,000	$627,000	$661,500

*Does not include a note payable; all current liabilities result from operations.

ECCLES COMPANY
Income Statement
For the Years Ended September 30

	1999	1998	1997
Sales	$800,000	$820,000	$870,000
Cost of goods sold	545,000	580,000	590,000
Gross margin	$255,000	$240,000	$280,000
Operating expenses*	180,000	190,000	210,000
Net income	$ 75,000	$ 50,000	$ 70,000

*Includes depreciation expense of $48,000 for each of the three years and interest expense of $7,600 for 1999 and $9,500 for 1998 and 1997.

Required

a. Make the following financial statement analysis calculations for 1999 and 1998:
1. Current ratio
2. Quick ratio
3. Gross margin

4. Return on sales
5. Asset turnover
6. Return on assets
7. Return on owners' equity
8. Ratio of debt to equity
9. Times interest earned

P 26.7 LO 2   Refer to the financial statement information for Eccles Company in P 26.6.

Required   *a.* Prepare a vertical analysis of the financial statements for the three years shown.
b. Prepare a horizontal analysis of the financial statements for the three years shown.

P 26.8   The following information was taken from the accounting records of Spencer Company for the years ended December 31:

	2001	2000	1999
Current assets:			
Cash	$ 35,000	$ 38,000	$ 10,000
Trading securities	12,000	11,000	62,000
Accounts receivable	175,000	166,000	112,000
Inventories	225,000	209,000	269,000
Prepaid expenses	5,000	10,000	4,000
Total current assets	$452,000	$434,000	$457,000
Property, plant, and equipment:			
Land	$ 50,000	$ 50,000	$ 50,000
Building, net of depreciation	141,000	149,000	157,000
Equipment, net of depreciation	68,000	74,000	72,000
Total property, plant, and equipment	$259,000	$273,000	$279,000
Total assets	$711,000	$707,000	$736,000
Current liabilities:			
Accounts payable	$ 69,000	$ 67,000	$ 60,000
Notes payable	40,000	60,000	60,000
Other current liabilities	52,000	41,000	19,000
Total current liabilities	$ 161,000	$ 168,000	$ 139,000
Long-term liabilities	88,000	92,000	132,000
Total liabilities	$ 249,000	$ 260,000	$ 214,000
Owners' equity	462,000	447,000	436,000
Total liabilities and owners' equity	$ 711,000	$ 707,000	$ 736,000
Sales	$1,920,000	$2,085,000	$1,880,000
Cost of goods sold	1,152,000	1,209,000	1,110,000
Gross margin	$ 768,000	$ 876,000	$ 770,000
Operating expenses	698,000	731,000	688,000
Net income	$ 70,000	$ 145,000	$ 82,000

Required   *a.* Prepare a vertical analysis of the balance sheet accounts for the years 2001 and 2000.
b. Using the ratios in the chapter, analyze the liquidity position of the company for 2001 and 2000.
c. Compare the results of your vertical analysis with the results of the ratio and turnover calculations and point out areas that reveal essentially the same information or where the information from the calculations supplements each other.

P 26.9 LO 2   Use the information in P 26.8 for Spencer Company.

Required   *a.* Prepare a vertical analysis of the income statement accounts for the years 2001 and 2000.
b. Using the appropriate formulas discussed in the chapter, analyze the profitability of the company for 2001 and 2000.
c. Compare the results of your vertical analysis in this and the previous problem with the results of your profitability calculations and point out areas that reveal essentially the same information or where the information from the calculations supplements each other.

P 26.10 LO 2   Use the information in P 26.8 for Spencer Company.

Required   *a.* Perform a horizontal analysis on the statements.
b. Discuss any trends that appear to be significant. If you have worked P 26.8 and P 26.9 for the Spencer Company, compare your trends from the horizontal analysis with the ratios and turnovers from the other two problems to determine where similar information is revealed.

P 26.11

LO 2   LO 3

The condensed financial statements of Kelly-Lee Company for 1998 and 1999 are shown below:

KELLY-LEE COMPANY
Income Statement
For the Years Ended December 31

	1999	1998
Sales	$380,000	$360,000
Cost of goods sold:		
Inventory, 1/1	$ 32,700	$ 30,500
Purchases	266,000	253,000
Goods available for sale	$298,700	$ 283,500
Inventory, 12/31	33,500	32,700
Total cost of goods sold	$265,200	$ 250,800
Gross margin	$114,800	$ 109,200
Operating expenses*	89,000	88,200
Income before taxes	$ 25,800	$ 21,000
Income tax expense	5,600	3,900
Net income	$ 20,200	$ 17,100

*Includes $10,000 of depreciation expense.

KELLY-LEE COMPANY
Statement of Financial Position
December 31

	1999	1998
Assets		
Cash	$ 19,800	$ 18,400
Accounts receivable	38,200	37,600
Inventory	45,300	42,700
Property, plant, and equipment	158,700	149,300
Total assets	$262,000	$248,000
Liabilities and Stockholders' Equity		
Current liabilities	$ 44,200	$ 49,500
Long-term liabilities	142,000	132,000
Stockholders' equity	75,800	66,500
Total liabilities and stockholders' equity	$262,000	$248,000

Additional information:
Ending balances, December 31, 2000:
  Accounts receivable, $37,200
  Total assets, $263,000
  Stockholders' equity, $61,800
Common stock issued and outstanding: 50,000 shares
Market price of the stock: 12/31/1999, $23; 12/31/1998, $18
Dividends paid: 1999, $10,000; 1998, $15,000

Required

a. Prepare common-size income statements for 1998 and 1999.
b. Prepare the ratios that managers, owners and potential owners, and creditors would prepare if they were interested in the Kelly-Lee Company.

CASES

C 26.1

LO 2   LO 3

Select a company listed on the New York Stock Exchange and conduct a ratio analysis on the company. Organize the analysis from the perspective of management, common or potential stockholders, and creditors. Once the ratios are calculated, use either Dun & Bradstreet's *Key Business Ratios* or Robert Morris Associates' *Annual Statement Studies* to compare your company's results with other companies with similar operations.

C 26.2

LO 2   LO 3

The original Pan American Airlines went out of business. Determine when the airline went out of business and then find the annual reports for Pan American for the last three years of its existence. From these annual reports, calculate the ratios listed below, and then describe the trends in these ratios:
a. Return on assets
b. Return on common equity
c. Debt-to-equity ratio
d. Quick ratio
e. Earnings per share
f. Price-earnings ratio

Explain whether investors knew about Pan American's bankruptcy before it happened.

CRITICAL THINKING

CT 26.1

LO 1 LO 2 LO 3

Consider the differences between the investment decisions of internal stakeholders and those of external stakeholders. Describe any differences in the nature of their investment objectives. Relate those differences to the types of information they would use to make investment decisions.

CT 26.2

LO 1 LO 2 LO 3

The market value of a corporation as a whole can be estimated by multiplying the number of shares of common stock times the market value at any given time. The corporation's book value is simply the book value of its assets less the book value of its liabilities, or its recorded equity value. Discuss reasons why these two values might differ for the same firm and why the difference might be greater or less for different firms.

ETHICAL CHALLENGES

EC 26.1

LO 1 LO 2 LO 3

Assume that you work for a corporation and discover that the new product that it had developed, news of which had contributed greatly to the recent rise in its stock price, has been rendered obsolete by the new product of a competitor. You own a substantial number of shares of the corporation's stock. The news of the competitor's discovery has not been made public. Should you sell the stock? Why or why not?

EC 26.2

LO 1

The auditing profession relies on its reputation for integrity. If people do not trust the auditors to provide unbiased opinions about the presentation of financial information, demand for audit services will decline and so will audit fees. To avoid this, auditors must be independent of their clients. However, presently the auditor's fee is paid by the client. Does this keep the auditor from conducting an independent audit? What can auditors do to show that they are independent? Is there an alternative to the auditor's fee being paid by the client being audited?

COMPUTER APPLICATIONS

CA 26.1

LO 2

The following list of accounts was taken from the 1999 annual report of Brittain Industries:

Cash and cash equivalents	$21,989,062
Marketable securities	9,188,490
Notes receivable, current, net	3,560,747
Accounts receivable, net	23,247,355
Inventories	4,411,714
Prepaid expenses	1,086,561
Miscellaneous current assets	1,610,043
Notes receivable, long-term, net	21,406,772
Miscellaneous long-term assets	1,201,849
Franchise rights, net	83,770,710
Rental properties, net	3,451,108
Miscellaneous revenue-producing assets	39,036
Property, plant, and equipment, net	9,349,670
Drafts and accounts payable	16,901,824
Committed advertising	2,092,851
Other current liabilities	6,962,960
Income taxes payable	761,626
Current maturities of long-term debt	1,913,481
Deferred franchise income	278,917
Deferred income taxes	4,955,000
Long-term debt	23,901,770
Class A common stock	156,594
Class B common stock	90,291
Paid-in capital	3,340,075
Retained earnings	122,957,728
Net sales	241,625,862
Service fees	51,601,113
Franchise sales and other fees	7,611,539
Real estate finance and rental income	8,988,027
Other revenue	1,267,434
Cost of sales	217,441,994
Expenses applicable to real estate	8,159,375
Selling, general, and administrative expense	37,515,701
Interest income	1,425,788
Income taxes	19,520,000

Required   Use a computer spreadsheet program to determine each of the following ratios:
    a. Current ratio
    b. Quick ratio
    c. Accounts receivable turnover
    d. Collection period
    e. Inventory turnover
    f. Selling period
    g. Payables turnover
    h. Payment period

 CA 26.2 LO 2   Refer to the account information on Brittain Industries in CA 26.1.

Required   Use a computer spreadsheet program to determine each of the following ratios and comment on your results:
    a. Debt-to-equity
    b. Return on equity
    c. Return on sales
    d. Return on assets
    e. Asset turnover
    f. Du Pont formula for return on investment
    g. Long-term debt-to-equity

 CA 26.3   Using Quicken.com, or a similar online financial information service, find the PE ratios for the
    LO 3   most recent year for the eight firms compared in this chapter. Compare the PEs you find with the ones calculated from the data in this chapter. What trends appear?

Present and Future Value Tables

| TABLE | 1 | Future Value of the Amount of $1 |

Periods	1.0%	1.5%	2.0%	2.5%	3.0%	4.0%	5.0%	6.0%	7.0%	8.0%	9.0%
1	1.0100	1.0150	1.0200	1.0250	1.0300	1.0400	1.0500	1.0600	1.0700	1.0800	1.0900
2	1.0201	1.0302	1.0404	1.0506	1.0609	1.0816	1.1025	1.1236	1.1449	1.1664	1.1881
3	1.0303	1.0457	1.0612	1.0769	1.0927	1.1249	1.1576	1.1910	1.2250	1.2597	1.2950
4	1.0406	1.0614	1.0824	1.1038	1.1255	1.1699	1.2155	1.2625	1.3108	1.3605	1.4116
5	1.0510	1.0073	1.1041	1.1314	1.1593	1.2167	1.2763	1.3382	1.4026	1.4693	1.5386
6	1.0615	1.0934	1.1262	1.1597	1.1941	1.2653	1.3401	1.4185	1.5007	1.5869	1.6771
7	1.0721	1.1098	1.1487	1.1887	1.2299	1.3159	1.4071	1.5036	1.6058	1.7138	1.8280
8	1.0829	1.1265	1.1717	1.2184	1.2668	1.3686	1.4775	1.5938	1.7182	1.8509	1.9926
9	1.0937	1.1434	1.1951	1.2489	1.3048	1.4233	1.5513	1.6895	1.8385	1.9990	2.1719
10	1.1046	1.1605	1.2190	1.2801	1.3439	1.4802	1.6289	1.7908	1.9672	2.1589	2.3674
11	1.1157	1.1779	1.2434	1.3121	1.3842	1.5395	1.7103	1.8983	2.1049	2.3316	2.5804
12	1.1268	1.1956	1.2682	1.3449	1.4258	1.6010	1.7959	2.0122	2.2522	2.5182	2.8127
13	1.1381	1.2136	1.2936	1.3785	1.4685	1.6651	1.8856	2.1329	2.4098	2.7196	3.0658
14	1.1495	1.2318	1.3195	1.4130	1.5126	1.7317	1.9799	2.2609	2.5785	2.9372	3.3417
15	1.1610	1.2502	1.3459	1.4483	1.5580	1.8009	2.0789	2.3966	2.7590	3.1722	3.6425
16	1.1726	1.2690	1.3728	1.4845	1.6047	1.8730	2.1829	2.5404	2.9522	3.4259	3.9703
17	1.1843	1.2880	1.4002	1.5216	1.6528	1.9479	2.2920	2.6928	3.1588	3.7000	4.3276
18	1.1961	1.3073	1.4282	1.5597	1.7024	2.0258	2.4066	2.8543	3.3799	3.9960	4.7171
19	1.2081	1.3270	1.4568	1.5987	1.7535	2.1068	2.5270	3.0256	3.6165	4.3157	5.1417
20	1.2202	1.3469	1.4859	1.6386	1.8061	2.1911	2.6533	3.2071	3.8697	4.6610	5.6044
21	1.2324	1.3671	1.5157	1.6796	1.8603	2.2788	2.7860	3.3996	4.1406	5.0338	6.1088
22	1.2447	1.3876	1.5460	1.7216	1.9161	2.3699	2.9253	3.6035	4.4304	5.4365	6.6586
23	1.2572	1.4084	1.5769	1.7646	1.9736	2.4647	3.0715	3.8197	4.7405	5.8715	7.2579
24	1.2697	1.4295	1.6084	1.8087	2.0328	2.5633	3.2251	4.0489	5.0724	6.3412	7.9111
25	1.2824	1.4509	1.6406	1.8539	2.0938	2.6658	3.3864	4.2919	5.4274	6.8485	8.6231
26	1.2953	1.4727	1.6734	1.9003	2.1566	2.7725	3.5557	4.5494	5.8074	7.3964	9.3992
27	1.3082	1.4948	1.7069	1.9478	2.2213	2.8834	3.7335	4.8223	6.2139	7.9881	10.2451
28	1.3213	1.5172	1.7410	1.9965	2.2879	2.9987	3.9201	5.1117	6.6488	8.6271	11.1671
29	1.3345	1.5400	1.7758	2.0464	2.3566	3.1187	4.1161	5.4184	7.1143	9.3173	12.1722
30	1.3478	1.5631	1.8114	2.0976	2.4273	3.2434	4.3219	5.7435	7.6123	10.0627	13.2677
31	1.3613	1.5865	1.8476	2.1500	2.5001	3.3731	4.5380	6.0881	8.1451	10.8677	14.4618
32	1.3749	1.6103	1.8845	2.2038	2.5751	3.5081	4.7649	6.4534	8.7153	11.7371	15.7633
33	1.3887	1.6345	1.9222	2.2589	2.6523	3.6484	5.0032	6.8406	9.3253	12.6760	17.1820
34	1.4026	1.6590	1.9607	2.3153	2.7319	3.7943	5.2533	7.2510	9.9781	13.6901	18.7284
35	1.4166	1.6839	1.9999	2.3732	2.8139	3.9461	5.5160	7.6861	10.6766	14.7853	20.4140
36	1.4308	1.7091	2.0399	2.4325	2.8983	4.1039	5.7918	8.1473	11.4239	15.9682	22.2512
37	1.4451	1.7348	2.0807	2.4933	2.9852	4.2681	6.0814	8.6361	12.2236	17.2456	24.2538
38	1.4595	1.7608	2.1223	2.5557	3.0748	4.4388	6.3855	9.1543	13.0793	18.6253	26.4367
39	1.4741	1.7872	2.1647	2.6196	3.1670	4.6164	6.7048	9.7035	13.9948	20.1153	28.8160
40	1.4889	1.8140	2.2080	2.6851	3.2620	4.8010	7.0400	10.2857	14.9745	21.7245	31.4094
41	1.5038	1.8412	2.2522	2.7522	3.3599	4.9931	7.3920	10.9029	16.0227	23.4625	34.2363
42	1.5188	1.8688	2.2972	2.8210	3.4607	5.1928	7.7616	11.5570	17.1443	25.3395	37.3175
43	1.5340	1.8969	2.3432	2.8915	3.5645	5.4005	8.1497	12.2505	18.3444	27.3666	40.6761
44	1.5493	1.9253	2.3901	2.9638	3.6715	5.6165	8.5572	12.9855	19.6285	29.5560	44.3370
45	1.5648	1.9542	2.4379	3.0379	3.7816	5.8412	8.9850	13.7646	21.0025	31.9204	48.3273
46	1.5805	1.9835	2.4866	3.1139	3.8950	6.0748	9.4343	14.5905	22.4726	34.4741	52.6767
47	1.5963	2.0133	2.5363	3.1917	4.0119	6.3178	9.9060	15.4659	24.0457	37.2320	57.4176
48	1.6122	2.0435	2.5871	3.2715	4.1323	6.5705	10.4013	16.3939	25.7289	40.2106	62.5852
49	1.6283	2.0741	2.6388	3.3533	4.2562	6.8333	10.9213	17.3775	27.5299	43.4274	68.2179
50	1.6446	2.1052	2.6916	3.4371	4.3839	7.1067	11.4674	18.4202	29.4570	46.9016	74.3575

10.0%	11.0%	12.0%	13.0%	14.0%	15.0%	16.0%	17.0%	18.0%	19.0%	20.0%	Periods
1.1000	1.1100	1.1200	1.1300	1.1400	1.1500	1.1600	1.1700	1.1800	1.1900	1.2000	1
1.2100	1.2321	1.2544	1.2769	1.2996	1.3225	1.3456	1.3689	1.3924	1.4161	1.4400	2
1.3310	1.3676	1.4049	1.4429	1.4815	1.5209	1.5609	1.6016	1.6430	1.6852	1.7280	3
1.4641	1.5181	1.5735	1.6305	1.6890	1.7490	1.8106	1.8739	1.9388	2.0053	2.0736	4
1.6105	1.6851	1.7623	1.8424	1.9254	2.0114	2.1003	2.1924	2.2878	2.3864	2.4883	5
1.7716	1.8704	1.9738	2.0820	2.1950	2.3131	2.4364	2.5652	2.6996	2.8398	2.9860	6
1.9487	2.0762	2.2107	2.3526	2.5023	2.6600	2.8262	3.0012	3.1855	3.3793	3.5832	7
2.1436	2.3045	2.4760	2.6584	2.8526	3.0590	3.2784	3.5115	3.7589	4.0214	4.2998	8
2.3579	2.5580	2.7731	3.0040	3.2519	3.5179	3.8030	4.1084	4.4355	4.7854	5.1598	9
2.5937	2.8394	3.1058	3.3946	3.7072	4.0456	4.4114	4.8068	5.2338	5.6947	6.1917	10
2.8531	3.1518	3.4785	3.8359	4.2262	4.6524	5.1173	5.6240	6.1759	6.7767	7.4301	11
3.1384	3.4985	3.8960	4.3345	4.8179	5.3503	5.9360	6.5801	7.2876	8.0642	8.9161	12
3.4523	3.8833	4.3635	4.8980	5.4924	6.1528	6.8858	7.6987	8.5994	9.5964	10.6993	13
3.7975	4.3104	4.8871	5.5348	6.2613	7.0757	7.9875	9.0075	10.1472	11.4198	12.8392	14
4.1772	4.7846	5.4736	6.2543	7.1379	8.1371	9.2655	10.5387	11.9737	13.5895	15.4070	15
4.5950	5.3109	6.1304	7.0673	8.1372	9.3576	10.7480	12.3303	14.1290	16.1715	18.4884	16
5.0545	5.8951	6.8660	7.9861	9.2765	10.7613	12.4677	14.4265	16.6722	19.2441	22.1861	17
5.5599	6.5436	7.6900	9.0243	10.5752	12.3755	14.4625	16.8790	19.6733	22.9005	26.6233	18
6.1159	7.2633	8.6128	10.1974	12.0557	14.2318	16.7765	19.7484	23.2144	27.2516	31.9480	19
6.7275	8.0623	9.6463	11.5231	13.7435	16.3665	19.4608	23.1056	27.3930	32.4294	38.3376	20
7.4002	8.9492	10.8038	13.0211	15.6676	18.8215	22.5745	27.0336	32.3238	38.5910	46.0051	21
8.1403	9.9336	12.1003	14.7138	17.8610	21.6447	26.1864	31.6293	38.1421	45.9233	55.2061	22
8.9543	11.0263	13.5523	16.6266	20.3616	24.8915	30.3762	37.0062	45.0076	54.6487	66.2474	23
9.8497	12.2392	15.1786	18.7881	23.2122	28.6252	35.2364	43.2973	53.1090	65.0320	79.4968	24
10.8347	13.5855	17.0001	21.2305	26.4619	32.9190	40.8742	50.6578	62.6686	77.3881	95.3962	25
11.9182	15.0799	19.0401	23.9905	30.1666	37.8568	47.4141	59.2697	73.9490	92.0918	114.4755	26
13.1100	16.7386	21.3249	27.1093	34.3899	43.5353	55.0004	69.3455	87.2598	109.5893	137.3706	27
14.4210	18.5799	23.8839	30.6335	39.2045	50.0656	63.8004	81.1342	102.9666	130.4112	164.8447	28
15.8631	20.6237	26.7499	34.6158	44.6931	57.5755	74.0085	94.9271	121.5005	155.1893	197.8136	29
17.4494	22.8923	29.9599	39.1159	50.9502	66.2118	85.8499	111.0647	143.3706	184.6753	237.3763	30
19.1943	25.4104	33.5551	44.2010	58.0832	76.1435	99.5859	129.9456	169.1774	219.7636	284.8516	31
21.1138	28.2056	37.5817	49.9471	66.2148	87.5651	115.5196	152.0364	199.6293	261.5187	341.8219	32
23.2252	31.3082	42.0915	56.4402	75.4849	100.6998	134.0027	177.8826	235.5625	311.2073	410.1863	33
25.5477	34.7521	47.1425	63.7774	86.0528	115.8048	155.4432	208.1226	277.9638	370.3366	492.2235	34
28.1024	38.5749	52.7996	72.0685	98.1002	133.1755	180.3141	243.5035	327.9973	440.7006	590.6682	35
30.9127	42.8181	59.1356	81.4374	111.8342	153.1519	209.1643	284.8991	387.0368	524.4337	708.8019	36
34.0039	47.5281	66.2318	92.0243	127.4910	176.1246	242.6306	333.3319	456.7034	624.0761	850.5622	37
37.4043	52.7562	74.1797	103.9874	145.3397	202.5433	281.4515	389.9983	538.9100	742.6506	1020.6747	38
41.1448	58.5593	83.0812	117.5058	165.6873	232.9248	326.4838	456.2980	635.9139	883.7542	1224.8096	39
45.2593	65.0009	93.0510	132.7816	188.8835	267.8635	378.7212	533.8687	750.3783	1051.6675	1469.7716	40
49.7852	72.1510	104.2171	150.0432	215.3272	308.0431	439.3165	624.6264	885.4464	1251.4843	1763.7259	41
54.7637	80.0876	116.7231	169.5488	245.4730	354.2495	509.6072	730.8129	1044.8268	1489.2664	2116.4711	42
60.2401	88.8972	130.7299	191.5901	279.8392	407.3870	591.1443	855.0511	1232.8956	1772.2270	2539.7653	43
66.2641	98.6759	146.4175	216.4968	319.0167	468.4950	685.7274	1000.4098	1454.8168	2108.9501	3047.7183	44
72.8905	109.5302	163.9876	244.6414	363.6791	538.7693	795.4438	1170.4794	1716.6839	2509.6506	3657.2620	45
80.1795	121.5786	183.6661	276.4448	414.5941	619.5847	922.7148	1369.4609	2025.6870	2986.4842	4388.7144	46
88.1975	134.9522	205.7061	312.3826	472.6373	712.5224	1070.3492	1602.2693	2390.3106	3553.9162	5266.4573	47
97.0172	149.7970	230.3908	352.9923	538.8065	819.4007	1241.6051	1874.6550	2820.5665	4229.1603	6319.7487	48
106.7190	166.2746	258.0377	398.8813	614.2395	942.3108	1440.2619	2193.3464	3328.2685	5032.7008	7583.6985	49
117.3909	184.5648	289.0022	450.7359	700.2330	1083.6574	1670.7038	2566.2153	3927.3569	5988.9139	9100.4382	50

TABLE 2 Present Value of the Amount of $1

Periods	1.0%	1.5%	2.0%	2.5%	3.0%	4.0%	5.0%	6.0%	7.0%	8.0%	9.0%
1	0.9901	0.9852	0.9804	0.9756	0.9709	0.9615	0.9524	0.9434	0.9346	0.9259	0.9174
2	0.9803	0.9707	0.9612	0.9518	0.9426	0.9246	0.9070	0.8900	0.8734	0.8573	0.8417
3	0.9706	0.9563	0.9423	0.9286	0.9151	0.8890	0.8638	0.8396	0.8163	0.7938	0.7722
4	0.9610	0.9422	0.9238	0.9060	0.8885	0.8548	0.8227	0.7921	0.7629	0.7350	0.7084
5	0.9515	0.9283	0.9057	0.8839	0.8626	0.8219	0.7835	0.7473	0.7130	0.6806	0.6499
6	0.9420	0.9145	0.8880	0.8623	0.8375	0.7903	0.7462	0.7050	0.6663	0.6302	0.5963
7	0.9327	0.9010	0.8706	0.8413	0.8131	0.7599	0.7107	0.6651	0.6227	0.5835	0.5470
8	0.9235	0.8877	0.8535	0.8207	0.7894	0.7307	0.6768	0.6274	0.5820	0.5403	0.5019
9	0.9143	0.8746	0.8368	0.8007	0.7664	0.7026	0.6446	0.5919	0.5439	0.5002	0.4604
10	0.9053	0.8617	0.8203	0.7812	0.7441	0.6756	0.6139	0.5584	0.5083	0.4632	0.4224
11	0.8963	0.8489	0.8043	0.7621	0.7224	0.6496	0.5847	0.5268	0.4751	0.4289	0.3875
12	0.8874	0.8364	0.7885	0.7436	0.7014	0.6246	0.5568	0.4970	0.4440	0.3971	0.3555
13	0.8787	0.8240	0.7730	0.7254	0.6810	0.6006	0.5303	0.4688	0.4150	0.3677	0.3262
14	0.8700	0.8118	0.7579	0.7077	0.6611	0.5775	0.5051	0.4423	0.3878	0.3405	0.2992
15	0.8613	0.7999	0.7430	0.6905	0.6419	0.5553	0.4810	0.4173	0.3624	0.3152	0.2745
16	0.8528	0.7880	0.7284	0.6736	0.6232	0.5339	0.4581	0.3936	0.3387	0.2919	0.2519
17	0.8444	0.7764	0.7142	0.6572	0.6050	0.5134	0.4363	0.3714	0.3166	0.2703	0.2311
18	0.8360	0.7649	0.7002	0.6412	0.5874	0.4936	0.4155	0.3503	0.2959	0.2502	0.2120
19	0.8277	0.7536	0.6864	0.6255	0.5703	0.4746	0.3957	0.3305	0.2765	0.2317	0.1945
20	0.8195	0.7425	0.6730	0.6103	0.5537	0.4564	0.3769	0.3118	0.2584	0.2145	0.1784
21	0.8114	0.7315	0.6598	0.5954	0.5375	0.4388	0.3589	0.2942	0.2415	0.1987	0.1637
22	0.8034	0.7207	0.6468	0.5809	0.5219	0.4220	0.3418	0.2775	0.2257	0.1839	0.1502
23	0.7954	0.7100	0.6342	0.5667	0.5067	0.4057	0.3256	0.2618	0.2109	0.1703	0.1378
24	0.7876	0.6995	0.6217	0.5529	0.4919	0.3901	0.3101	0.2470	0.1971	0.1577	0.1264
25	0.7798	0.6892	0.6095	0.5394	0.4776	0.3751	0.2953	0.2330	0.1842	0.1460	0.1160
26	0.7720	0.6790	0.5976	0.5262	0.4637	0.3607	0.2812	0.2198	0.1722	0.1352	0.1064
27	0.7644	0.6690	0.5859	0.5134	0.4502	0.3468	0.2678	0.2074	0.1609	0.1252	0.0976
28	0.7568	0.6591	0.5744	0.5009	0.4371	0.3335	0.2551	0.1956	0.1504	0.1159	0.0895
29	0.7493	0.6494	0.5631	0.4887	0.4243	0.3207	0.2429	0.1846	0.1406	0.1073	0.0822
30	0.7419	0.6398	0.5521	0.4767	0.4120	0.3083	0.2314	0.1741	0.1314	0.0994	0.0754
31	0.7346	0.6303	0.5412	0.4651	0.4000	0.2965	0.2204	0.1643	0.1228	0.0920	0.0691
32	0.7273	0.6210	0.5306	0.4538	0.3883	0.2851	0.2099	0.1550	0.1147	0.0852	0.0634
33	0.7201	0.6118	0.5202	0.4427	0.3770	0.2741	0.1999	0.1462	0.1072	0.0789	0.0582
34	0.7130	0.6028	0.5100	0.4319	0.3660	0.2636	0.1904	0.1379	0.1002	0.0730	0.0534
35	0.7059	0.5939	0.5000	0.4214	0.3554	0.2534	0.1813	0.1301	0.0937	0.0676	0.0490
36	0.6989	0.5851	0.4902	0.4111	0.3450	0.2437	0.1727	0.1227	0.0875	0.0626	0.0449
37	0.6920	0.5764	0.4806	0.4011	0.3350	0.2343	0.1644	0.1158	0.0818	0.0580	0.0412
38	0.6852	0.5679	0.4712	0.3913	0.3252	0.2253	0.1566	0.1092	0.0765	0.0537	0.0378
39	0.6784	0.5595	0.4619	0.3817	0.3158	0.2166	0.1491	0.1031	0.0715	0.0497	0.0347
40	0.6717	0.5513	0.4529	0.3724	0.3066	0.2083	0.1420	0.0972	0.0668	0.0460	0.0318
41	0.6650	0.5431	0.4440	0.3633	0.2976	0.2003	0.1353	0.0917	0.0624	0.0426	0.0292
42	0.6584	0.5351	0.4353	0.3545	0.2890	0.1926	0.1288	0.0865	0.0583	0.0395	0.0268
43	0.6519	0.5272	0.4268	0.3458	0.2805	0.1852	0.1227	0.0816	0.0545	0.0365	0.0246
44	0.6454	0.5194	0.4184	0.3374	0.2724	0.1780	0.1169	0.0770	0.0509	0.0338	0.0226
45	0.6391	0.5117	0.4102	0.3292	0.2644	0.1712	0.1113	0.0727	0.0476	0.0313	0.0207
46	0.6327	0.5042	0.4022	0.3211	0.2567	0.1646	0.1060	0.0685	0.0445	0.0290	0.0190
47	0.6265	0.4967	0.3943	0.3133	0.2493	0.1583	0.1009	0.0647	0.0416	0.0269	0.0174
48	0.6203	0.4894	0.3865	0.3057	0.2420	0.1522	0.0961	0.0610	0.0389	0.0249	0.0160
49	0.6141	0.4821	0.3790	0.2982	0.2350	0.1463	0.0916	0.0575	0.0363	0.0230	0.0147
50	0.6080	0.4750	0.3715	0.2909	0.2281	0.1407	0.0872	0.0543	0.0339	0.0213	0.0134

10.0%	11.0%	12.0%	13.0%	14.0%	15.0%	16.0%	17.0%	18.0%	19.0%	20.0%	Periods
0.9091	0.9009	0.8929	0.8850	0.8772	0.8696	0.8621	0.8547	0.8475	0.8403	0.8333	1
0.8264	0.8116	0.7972	0.7831	0.7695	0.7561	0.7432	0.7305	0.7182	0.7062	0.6944	2
0.7513	0.7312	0.7118	0.6931	0.6750	0.6575	0.6407	0.6244	0.6086	0.5934	0.5787	3
0.6830	0.6587	0.6355	0.6133	0.5921	0.5718	0.5523	0.5337	0.5158	0.4987	0.4823	4
0.6209	0.5935	0.5674	0.5428	0.5194	0.4972	0.4761	0.4561	0.4371	0.4190	0.4019	5
0.5645	0.5346	0.5066	0.4803	0.4556	0.4323	0.4104	0.3898	0.3704	0.3521	0.3349	6
0.5132	0.4817	0.4523	0.4251	0.3996	0.3759	0.3538	0.3332	0.3139	0.2959	0.2791	7
0.4665	0.4339	0.4039	0.3762	0.3506	0.3269	0.3050	0.2848	0.2660	0.2487	0.2326	8
0.4241	0.3909	0.3606	0.3329	0.3075	0.2843	0.2630	0.2434	0.2255	0.2090	0.1938	9
0.3855	0.3522	0.3220	0.2946	0.2697	0.2472	0.2267	0.2080	0.1911	0.1756	0.1615	10
0.3505	0.3173	0.2875	0.2607	0.2366	0.2149	0.1954	0.1778	0.1619	0.1476	0.1346	11
0.3186	0.2858	0.2567	0.2307	0.2076	0.1869	0.1685	0.1520	0.1372	0.1240	0.1122	12
0.2897	0.2575	0.2292	0.2042	0.1821	0.1625	0.1452	0.1299	0.1163	0.1042	0.0935	13
0.2633	0.2320	0.2046	0.1807	0.1597	0.1413	0.1252	0.1110	0.0985	0.0876	0.0779	14
0.2394	0.2090	0.1827	0.1599	0.1401	0.1229	0.1079	0.0949	0.0835	0.0736	0.0649	15
0.2176	0.1883	0.1631	0.1415	0.1229	0.1069	0.0930	0.0811	0.0708	0.0618	0.0541	16
0.1978	0.1696	0.1456	0.1252	0.1078	0.0929	0.0802	0.0693	0.0600	0.0520	0.0451	17
0.1799	0.1528	0.1300	0.1108	0.0946	0.0808	0.0691	0.0592	0.0508	0.0437	0.0376	18
0.1635	0.1377	0.1161	0.0981	0.0829	0.0703	0.0596	0.0506	0.0431	0.0367	0.0313	19
0.1486	0.1240	0.1037	0.0868	0.0728	0.0611	0.0514	0.0433	0.0365	0.0308	0.0261	20
0.1351	0.1117	0.0926	0.0768	0.0638	0.0531	0.0443	0.0370	0.0309	0.0259	0.0217	21
0.1228	0.1007	0.0826	0.0680	0.0560	0.0462	0.0382	0.0316	0.0262	0.0218	0.0181	22
0.1117	0.0907	0.0738	0.0601	0.0491	0.0402	0.0329	0.0270	0.0222	0.0183	0.0151	23
0.1015	0.0817	0.0659	0.0532	0.0431	0.0349	0.0284	0.0231	0.0188	0.0154	0.0126	24
0.0923	0.0736	0.0588	0.0471	0.0378	0.0304	0.0245	0.0197	0.0160	0.0129	0.0105	25
0.0839	0.0663	0.0525	0.0417	0.0331	0.0264	0.0211	0.0169	0.0135	0.0109	0.0087	26
0.0763	0.0597	0.0469	0.0369	0.0291	0.0230	0.0182	0.0144	0.0115	0.0091	0.0073	27
0.0693	0.0538	0.0419	0.0326	0.0255	0.0200	0.0157	0.0123	0.0097	0.0077	0.0061	28
0.0630	0.0485	0.0374	0.0289	0.0224	0.0174	0.0135	0.0105	0.0082	0.0064	0.0051	29
0.0573	0.0437	0.0334	0.0256	0.0196	0.0151	0.0116	0.0090	0.0070	0.0054	0.0042	30
0.0521	0.0394	0.0298	0.0226	0.0172	0.0131	0.0100	0.0077	0.0059	0.0046	0.0035	31
0.0474	0.0355	0.0266	0.0200	0.0151	0.0114	0.0087	0.0066	0.0050	0.0038	0.0029	32
0.0431	0.0319	0.0238	0.0177	0.0132	0.0099	0.0075	0.0056	0.0042	0.0032	0.0024	33
0.0391	0.0288	0.0212	0.0157	0.0116	0.0086	0.0064	0.0048	0.0036	0.0027	0.0020	34
0.0356	0.0259	0.0189	0.0139	0.0102	0.0075	0.0055	0.0041	0.0030	0.0023	0.0017	35
0.0323	0.0234	0.0169	0.0123	0.0089	0.0065	0.0048	0.0035	0.0026	0.0019	0.0014	36
0.0294	0.0210	0.0151	0.0109	0.0078	0.0057	0.0041	0.0030	0.0022	0.0016	0.0012	37
0.0267	0.0190	0.0135	0.0096	0.0069	0.0049	0.0036	0.0026	0.0019	0.0013	0.0010	38
0.0243	0.0171	0.0120	0.0085	0.0060	0.0043	0.0031	0.0022	0.0016	0.0011	0.0008	39
0.0221	0.0154	0.0107	0.0075	0.0053	0.0037	0.0026	0.0019	0.0013	0.0010	0.0007	40
0.0201	0.0139	0.0096	0.0067	0.0046	0.0032	0.0023	0.0016	0.0011	0.0008	0.0006	41
0.0183	0.0125	0.0086	0.0059	0.0041	0.0028	0.0020	0.0014	0.0010	0.0007	0.0005	42
0.0166	0.0112	0.0076	0.0052	0.0036	0.0025	0.0017	0.0012	0.0008	0.0006	0.0004	43
0.0151	0.0101	0.0068	0.0046	0.0031	0.0021	0.0015	0.0010	0.0007	0.0005	0.0003	44
0.0137	0.0091	0.0061	0.0041	0.0027	0.0019	0.0013	0.0009	0.0006	0.0004	0.0003	45
0.0125	0.0082	0.0054	0.0036	0.0024	0.0016	0.0011	0.0007	0.0005	0.0003	0.0002	46
0.0113	0.0074	0.0049	0.0032	0.0021	0.0014	0.0009	0.0006	0.0004	0.0003	0.0002	47
0.0103	0.0067	0.0043	0.0028	0.0019	0.0012	0.0008	0.0005	0.0004	0.0002	0.0002	48
0.0094	0.0060	0.0039	0.0025	0.0016	0.0011	0.0007	0.0005	0.0003	0.0002	0.0001	49
0.0085	0.0054	0.0035	0.0022	0.0014	0.0009	0.0006	0.0004	0.0003	0.0002	0.0001	50

TABLE 3 **Future Amount of an Annuity of $1**

Payments	1.0%	1.5%	2.0%	2.5%	3.0%	4.0%	5.0%	6.0%	7.0%	8.0%	9.0%
1	1.0000	1.0000	1.0000	1.0000	1.0000	1.0000	1.0000	1.0000	1.0000	1.0000	1.0000
2	2.0100	2.0150	2.0200	2.0250	2.0300	2.0400	2.0500	2.0600	2.0700	2.0800	2.0900
3	3.0301	3.0452	3.0604	3.0756	3.0909	3.1216	3.1525	3.1836	3.2149	3.2464	3.2781
4	4.0604	4.0909	4.1216	4.1525	4.1836	4.2465	4.3101	4.3746	4.4399	4.5061	4.5731
5	5.1010	5.1523	5.2040	5.2563	5.3091	5.4163	5.5256	5.6371	5.7507	5.8666	5.9847
6	6.1520	6.2296	6.3081	6.3877	6.4684	6.6330	6.8019	6.9753	7.1533	7.3359	7.5233
7	7.2135	7.3230	7.4343	7.5474	7.6625	7.8983	8.1420	8.3938	8.6540	8.9228	9.2004
8	8.2857	8.4328	8.5830	8.7361	8.8923	9.2142	9.5491	9.8975	10.2598	10.6366	11.0285
9	9.3685	9.5593	9.7546	9.9545	10.1591	10.5828	11.0266	11.4913	11.9780	12.4876	13.0210
10	10.4622	10.7027	10.9497	11.2034	11.4639	12.0061	12.5779	13.1808	13.8164	14.4866	15.1929
11	11.5668	11.8633	12.1687	12.4835	12.8078	13.4864	14.2068	14.9716	15.7836	16.6455	17.5603
12	12.6825	13.0412	13.4121	13.7956	14.1920	15.0258	15.9171	16.8699	17.8885	18.9771	20.1407
13	13.8093	14.2368	14.6803	15.1404	15.6178	16.6268	17.7130	18.8821	20.1406	21.4953	22.9534
14	14.9474	15.4504	15.9739	16.5190	17.0863	18.2919	19.5986	21.0151	22.5505	24.2149	26.0192
15	16.0969	16.6821	17.2934	17.9319	18.5989	20.0236	21.5786	23.2760	25.1290	27.1521	29.3609
16	17.2579	17.9324	18.6393	19.3802	20.1569	21.8245	23.6575	25.6725	27.8881	30.3243	33.0034
17	18.4304	19.2014	20.0121	20.8647	21.7616	23.6975	25.8404	28.2129	30.8402	33.7502	36.9737
18	19.6147	20.4894	21.4123	22.3863	23.4144	25.6454	28.1324	30.9057	33.9990	37.4502	41.3013
19	20.8109	21.7967	22.8406	23.9460	25.1169	27.6712	30.5390	33.7600	37.3790	41.4463	46.0185
20	22.0190	23.1237	24.2974	25.5447	26.8704	29.7781	33.0660	36.7856	40.9955	45.7620	51.1601
21	23.2392	24.4705	25.7833	27.1833	28.6765	31.9692	35.7193	39.9927	44.8652	50.4229	56.7645
22	24.4716	25.8376	27.2990	28.8629	30.5368	34.2480	38.5052	43.3923	49.0057	55.4568	62.8733
23	25.7163	27.2251	28.8450	30.5844	32.4529	36.6179	41.4305	46.9958	53.4361	60.8933	69.5319
24	26.9735	28.6335	30.4219	32.3490	34.4265	39.0826	44.5020	50.8156	58.1767	66.7648	76.7898
25	28.2432	30.0630	32.0303	34.1578	36.4593	41.6459	47.7271	54.8645	63.2490	73.1059	84.7009
26	29.5256	31.5140	33.6709	36.0117	38.5530	44.3117	51.1135	59.1564	68.6765	79.9544	93.3240
27	30.8209	32.9867	35.3443	37.9120	40.7096	47.0842	54.6691	63.7058	74.4838	87.3508	102.7231
28	32.1291	34.4815	37.0512	39.8598	42.9309	49.9676	58.4026	68.5281	80.6977	95.3388	112.9682
29	33.4504	35.9987	38.7922	41.8563	45.2189	52.9663	62.3227	73.6398	87.3465	103.9659	124.1354
30	34.7849	37.5387	40.5681	43.9027	47.5754	56.0849	66.4388	79.0582	94.4608	113.2832	136.3075
31	36.1327	39.1018	42.3794	46.0003	50.0027	59.3283	70.7608	84.8017	102.0730	123.3459	149.5752
32	37.4941	40.6883	44.2270	48.1503	52.5028	62.7015	75.2988	90.8898	110.2182	134.2135	164.0370
33	38.8690	42.2986	46.1116	50.3540	55.0778	66.2095	80.0638	97.3432	118.9334	145.9506	179.8003
34	40.2577	43.9331	48.0338	52.6129	57.7302	69.8579	85.0670	104.1838	128.2588	158.6267	196.9823
35	41.6603	45.5921	49.9945	54.9282	60.4621	73.6522	90.3203	111.4348	138.2369	172.3168	215.7108
36	43.0769	47.2760	51.9944	57.3014	63.2759	77.5983	95.8363	119.1209	148.9135	187.1021	236.1247
37	44.5076	48.9851	54.0343	59.7339	66.1742	81.7022	101.6281	127.2681	160.3374	203.0703	258.3759
38	45.9527	50.7199	56.1149	62.2273	69.1594	85.9703	107.7095	135.9042	172.5610	220.3159	282.6298
39	47.4123	52.4807	58.2372	64.7830	72.2342	90.4091	114.0950	145.0585	185.6403	238.9412	309.0665
40	48.8864	54.2679	60.4020	67.4026	75.4013	95.0255	120.7998	154.7620	199.6351	259.0565	337.8824
41	50.3752	56.0819	62.6100	70.0876	78.6633	99.8265	127.8398	165.0477	214.6096	280.7810	369.2919
42	51.8790	57.9231	64.8622	72.8398	82.0232	104.8196	135.2318	175.9505	230.6322	304.2435	403.5281
43	53.3978	59.7920	67.1595	75.6608	85.4839	110.0124	142.9933	187.5076	247.7765	329.5830	440.8457
44	54.9318	61.6889	69.5027	78.5523	89.0484	115.4129	151.1430	199.7580	266.1209	356.9496	481.5218
45	56.4811	63.6142	71.8927	81.5161	92.7199	121.0294	159.7002	212.7435	285.7493	386.5056	525.8587
46	58.0459	65.5684	74.3306	84.5540	96.5015	126.8706	168.6852	226.5081	306.7518	418.4261	574.1860
47	59.6263	67.5519	76.8172	87.6679	100.3965	132.9454	178.1194	241.0986	329.2244	452.9002	626.8628
48	61.2226	69.5652	79.3535	90.8596	104.4084	139.2632	188.0254	256.5645	353.2701	490.1322	684.2804
49	62.8348	71.6087	81.9406	94.1311	108.5406	145.8337	198.4267	272.9584	378.9990	530.3427	746.8656
50	64.4632	73.6828	84.5794	97.4843	112.7969	152.6671	209.3480	290.3359	406.5289	573.7702	815.0836

10.0%	11.0%	12.0%	13.0%	14.0%	15.0%	16.0%	17.0%	18.0%	19.0%	20.0%	Payments
1.0000	1.0000	1.0000	1.0000	1.0000	1.0000	1.0000	1.0000	1.0000	1.0000	1.0000	1
2.1000	2.1100	2.1200	2.1300	2.1400	2.1500	2.1600	2.1700	2.1800	2.1900	2.2000	2
3.3100	3.3421	3.3744	3.4069	3.4396	3.4725	3.5056	3.5389	3.5724	3.6061	3.6400	3
4.6410	4.7097	4.7793	4.8498	4.9211	4.9934	5.0665	5.1405	5.2154	5.2913	5.3680	4
6.1051	6.2278	6.3528	6.4803	6.6101	6.7424	6.8771	7.0144	7.1542	7.2966	7.4416	5
7.7156	7.9129	8.1152	8.3227	8.5355	8.7537	8.9775	9.2068	9.4420	9.6830	9.9299	6
9.4872	9.7833	10.0890	10.4047	10.7305	11.0668	11.4139	11.7720	12.1415	12.5227	12.9159	7
11.4359	11.8594	12.2997	12.7573	13.2328	13.7268	14.2401	14.7733	15.3270	15.9020	16.4991	8
13.5795	14.1640	14.7757	15.4157	16.0853	16.7858	17.5185	18.2847	19.0859	19.9234	20.7989	9
15.9374	16.7220	17.5487	18.4197	19.3373	20.3037	21.3215	22.3931	23.5213	24.7089	25.9587	10
18.5312	19.5614	20.6546	21.8143	23.0445	24.3493	25.7329	27.1999	28.7551	30.4035	32.1504	11
21.3843	22.7132	24.1331	25.6502	27.2707	29.0017	30.8502	32.8239	34.9311	37.1802	39.5805	12
24.5227	26.2116	28.0291	29.9847	32.0887	34.3519	36.7862	39.4040	42.2187	45.2445	48.4966	13
27.9750	30.0949	32.3926	34.8827	37.5811	40.5047	43.6720	47.1027	50.8180	54.8409	59.1959	14
31.7725	34.4054	37.2797	40.4175	43.8424	47.5804	51.6595	56.1101	60.9653	66.2607	72.0351	15
35.9497	39.1899	42.7533	46.6717	50.9804	55.7175	60.9250	66.6488	72.9390	79.8502	87.4421	16
40.5447	44.5008	48.8837	53.7391	59.1176	65.0751	71.6730	78.9792	87.0680	96.0218	105.9306	17
45.5992	50.3959	55.7497	61.7251	68.3941	75.8364	84.1407	93.4056	103.7403	115.2659	128.1167	18
51.1591	56.9395	63.4397	70.7494	78.9692	88.2118	98.6032	110.2846	123.4135	138.1664	154.7400	19
57.2750	64.2028	72.0524	80.9468	91.0249	102.4436	115.3797	130.0329	146.6280	165.4180	186.6880	20
64.0025	72.2651	81.6987	92.4699	104.7684	118.8101	134.8405	153.1385	174.0210	197.8474	225.0256	21
71.4027	81.2143	92.5026	105.4910	120.4360	137.6316	157.4150	180.1721	206.3448	236.4385	271.0307	22
79.5430	91.1479	104.6029	120.2048	138.2970	159.2764	183.6014	211.8013	244.4868	282.3618	326.2369	23
88.4973	102.1742	118.1552	136.8315	158.6586	184.1678	213.9776	248.8076	289.4945	337.0105	392.4842	24
98.3471	114.4133	133.3339	155.6196	181.8708	212.7930	249.2140	292.1049	342.6035	402.0425	471.9811	25
109.1818	127.9988	150.3339	176.8501	208.3327	245.7120	290.0883	342.7627	405.2721	479.4306	567.3773	26
121.0999	143.0786	169.3740	200.8406	238.4993	283.5688	337.5024	402.0323	479.2211	571.5224	681.8528	27
134.2099	159.8173	190.6989	227.9499	272.8892	327.1041	392.5028	471.3778	566.4809	681.1116	819.2233	28
148.6309	178.3972	214.5828	258.5834	312.0937	377.1697	456.3032	552.5121	669.4475	811.5228	984.0680	29
164.4940	199.0209	241.3327	293.1992	356.7868	434.7451	530.3117	647.4391	790.9480	966.7122	1181.8816	30
181.9434	221.9132	271.2926	332.3151	407.7370	500.9569	616.1616	758.5038	934.3186	1151.3875	1419.2579	31
201.1378	247.3236	304.8477	376.5161	465.8202	577.1005	715.7475	888.4494	1103.4960	1371.1511	1704.1095	32
222.2515	275.5292	342.4294	426.4632	532.0350	664.6655	831.2671	1040.4858	1303.1253	1632.6698	2045.9314	33
245.4767	306.8374	384.5210	482.9034	607.5199	765.3654	965.2698	1218.3684	1538.6878	1943.8771	2456.1176	34
271.0244	341.5896	431.6635	546.6808	693.5727	881.1702	1120.7130	1426.4910	1816.6516	2314.2137	2948.3411	35
299.1268	380.1644	484.4631	618.7493	791.6729	1014.3457	1301.0270	1669.9945	2144.6489	2754.9143	3539.0094	36
330.0395	422.9825	543.5987	700.1867	903.5071	1167.4975	1510.1914	1954.8936	2531.6857	3279.3481	4247.8112	37
364.0434	470.5106	609.8305	792.2110	1030.9981	1343.6222	1752.8220	2288.2255	2988.3891	3903.4242	5098.3735	38
401.4478	523.2667	684.0102	896.1984	1176.3378	1546.1655	2034.2735	2678.2238	3527.2992	4646.0748	6119.0482	39
442.5926	581.8261	767.0914	1013.7042	1342.0251	1779.0903	2360.7572	3134.5218	4163.2130	5529.8290	7343.8578	40
487.8518	646.8269	860.1424	1146.4858	1530.9086	2046.9539	2739.4784	3668.3906	4913.5914	6581.4965	8813.6294	41
537.6370	718.9779	964.3595	1296.5289	1746.2358	2354.9969	3178.7949	4293.0169	5799.0378	7832.9808	10577.3553	42
592.4007	799.0655	1081.0826	1466.0777	1991.7088	2709.2465	3688.4021	5023.8298	6843.8646	9322.2472	12693.8263	43
652.6408	887.9627	1211.8125	1657.6678	2271.5481	3116.6334	4279.5465	5878.8809	8076.7603	11094.4741	15233.5916	44
718.9048	986.6386	1358.2300	1874.1646	2590.5648	3585.1285	4965.2739	6879.2907	9531.5771	13203.4242	18281.3099	45
791.7953	1096.1688	1522.2176	2118.8060	2954.2439	4123.8977	5760.7177	8049.7701	11248.2610	15713.0748	21938.5719	46
871.9749	1217.7474	1705.8838	2395.2508	3368.8380	4743.4824	6683.4326	9419.2310	13273.9480	18699.5590	26327.2863	47
960.1723	1352.6996	1911.5898	2707.6334	3841.4753	5456.0047	7753.7818	11021.5002	15664.2586	22253.4753	31593.7436	48
1057.1896	1502.4965	2141.9806	3060.6258	4380.2819	6275.4055	8995.3869	12896.1553	18484.8251	26482.6356	37913.4923	49
1163.9085	1668.7712	2400.0182	3459.5071	4994.5213	7217.7163	10435.6488	15089.5017	21813.0937	31515.3363	45497.1908	50

TABLE 4   Present Value of an Annuity of $1

Payments	1.0%	1.5%	2.0%	2.5%	3.0%	4.0%	5.0%	6.0%	7.0%	8.0%	9.0%
1	0.9901	0.9852	0.9804	0.9756	0.9709	0.9615	0.9524	0.9434	0.9346	0.9259	0.9174
2	1.9704	1.9559	1.9416	1.9274	1.9135	1.8861	1.8594	1.8334	1.8080	1.7833	1.7591
3	2.9410	2.9122	2.8839	2.8560	2.8586	2.7751	2.7232	2.6730	2.6243	2.5771	2.5313
4	3.9020	3.8544	3.8077	3.7620	3.7171	3.6299	3.5460	3.4651	3.3872	3.3121	3.2397
5	4.8534	4.7826	4.7135	4.6458	4.5797	4.4518	4.3295	4.2124	4.1002	3.9927	3.8897
6	5.7955	5.6972	5.6014	5.5081	5.4172	5.2421	5.0757	4.9173	4.7665	4.6229	4.4859
7	6.7282	6.5982	6.4720	6.3494	6.2303	6.0021	5.7864	5.5824	5.3893	5.2064	5.0330
8	7.6517	7.4859	7.3255	7.1701	7.0197	6.7327	6.4632	6.2098	5.9713	5.7466	5.5348
9	8.5660	8.3605	8.1622	7.9709	7.7861	7.4353	7.1078	6.8017	6.5152	6.2469	5.9952
10	9.4713	9.2222	8.9826	8.7521	8.5302	8.1109	7.7217	7.3601	7.0236	6.7101	6.4177
11	10.3676	10.0711	9.7868	9.5142	9.2526	8.7605	8.3064	7.8869	7.4987	7.1390	6.8052
12	11.2551	10.9075	10.5753	10.2578	9.9540	9.3851	8.8633	8.3838	7.9427	7.5361	7.1607
13	12.1337	11.7315	11.3484	10.9832	10.6350	9.9856	9.3936	8.8527	8.3577	7.9038	7.4869
14	13.0037	12.5434	12.1062	11.6909	11.2961	10.5631	9.8986	9.2950	8.7455	8.2442	7.7862
15	13.8651	13.3432	12.8493	12.3814	11.9379	11.1184	10.3797	9.7122	9.1079	8.5595	8.0607
16	14.7179	14.1313	13.5777	13.0550	12.5611	11.6523	10.8378	10.1059	9.4466	8.8514	8.3126
17	15.5623	14.9076	14.2919	13.7122	13.1661	12.1657	11.2741	10.4773	9.7632	9.1216	8.5436
18	16.3983	15.6726	14.9920	14.3534	13.7535	12.6593	11.6896	10.8276	10.0591	9.3719	8.7556
19	17.2260	16.4262	15.6785	14.9789	14.3238	13.1339	12.0853	11.1581	10.3356	9.6036	8.9501
20	18.0456	17.1686	16.3514	15.5892	14.8775	13.5903	12.4622	11.4699	10.5940	9.8181	9.1285
21	18.8570	17.9001	17.0112	16.1845	15.4150	14.0292	12.8212	11.7641	10.8355	10.0168	9.2922
22	19.6604	18.6208	17.6580	16.7654	15.9369	14.4511	13.1630	12.0416	11.0612	10.2007	9.4424
23	20.4558	19.3309	18.2922	17.3321	16.4436	14.8568	13.4886	12.3034	11.2722	10.3711	9.5802
24	21.2434	20.0304	18.9139	17.8850	16.9355	15.2470	13.7986	12.5504	11.4693	10.5288	9.7066
25	22.0232	20.7196	19.5235	18.4244	17.4131	15.6221	14.0939	12.7834	11.6536	10.6748	9.8226
26	22.7952	21.3986	20.1210	18.9506	17.8768	15.9828	14.3752	13.0032	11.8258	10.8100	9.9290
27	23.5596	22.0676	20.7069	19.4640	18.3270	16.3296	14.6430	13.2105	11.9867	10.9352	10.0266
28	24.3164	22.7267	21.2813	19.9649	18.7641	16.6631	14.8981	13.4062	12.1371	11.0511	10.1161
29	25.0658	23.3761	21.8444	20.4535	19.1885	16.9837	15.1411	13.5907	12.2777	11.1584	10.1983
30	25.8077	24.0158	22.3965	20.9303	19.6004	17.2920	15.3725	13.7648	12.4090	11.2578	10.2737
31	26.5423	24.6461	22.9377	21.3954	20.0004	17.5885	15.5928	13.9291	12.5318	11.3498	10.3428
32	27.2696	25.2671	23.4683	21.8492	20.3888	17.8736	15.8027	14.0840	12.6466	11.4350	10.4062
33	27.9897	25.8790	23.9886	22.2919	20.7658	18.1476	16.0025	14.2302	12.7538	11.5139	10.4644
34	28.7027	26.4817	24.4986	22.7238	21.1318	18.4112	16.1929	14.3681	12.8540	11.5869	10.5178
35	29.4086	27.0756	24.9986	23.1452	21.4872	18.6646	16.3742	14.4982	12.9477	11.6546	10.5668
36	30.1075	27.6607	25.4888	23.5563	21.8323	18.9083	16.5469	14.6210	13.0352	11.7172	10.6118
37	30.7995	28.2371	25.9695	23.9573	22.1672	19.1426	16.7113	14.7368	13.1170	11.7752	10.6530
38	31.4847	28.8051	26.4406	24.3486	22.4925	19.3679	16.8679	14.8460	13.1935	11.8289	10.6908
39	32.1630	29.3646	26.9026	24.7303	22.8082	19.5845	17.0170	14.9491	13.2649	11.8786	10.7255
40	32.8347	29.9158	27.3555	25.1028	23.1148	19.7928	17.1591	15.0463	13.3317	11.9246	10.7574
41	33.4997	30.4590	27.7995	25.4661	23.4124	19.9931	17.2994	15.1380	13.3941	11.9672	10.7866
42	34.1581	30.9941	28.2348	25.8206	23.7014	20.1856	17.4232	15.2245	13.4524	12.0067	10.8134
43	34.8100	31.5212	28.6616	26.1664	23.9819	20.3708	17.5459	15.3062	13.5070	12.0432	10.8380
44	35.4555	32.0406	29.0800	26.5038	24.2543	20.5488	17.6628	15.3832	13.5579	12.0771	10.8605
45	36.0945	32.5523	29.4902	26.8330	24.5187	20.7200	17.7741	15.4558	13.6055	12.1084	10.8812
46	36.7272	33.0565	29.8923	27.1542	24.7754	20.8847	17.8801	15.5244	13.6500	12.1374	10.9002
47	37.3537	33.5532	30.2866	27.4675	25.0247	21.0429	17.9810	15.5890	13.6916	12.1643	10.9176
48	37.9740	34.0426	30.6731	27.7732	25.2667	21.1951	18.0772	15.6500	13.7305	12.1891	10.9336
49	38.5881	34.5247	31.0521	28.0714	25.5017	21.3415	18.1687	15.7076	13.7668	12.2122	10.9482
50	39.1961	34.9997	31.4236	28.3623	25.7298	21.4822	18.2559	15.7619	13.8007	12.2335	10.9617

10.0%	11.0%	12.0%	13.0%	14.0%	15.0%	16.0%	17.0%	18.0%	19.0%	20.0%	Payments
0.9091	0.9009	0.8929	0.8850	0.8772	0.8696	0.8621	0.8547	0.8475	0.8403	0.8333	1
1.7355	1.7125	1.6901	1.6681	1.6467	1.6257	1.6052	1.5852	1.5656	1.5465	1.5278	2
2.4869	2.4437	2.4018	2.3612	2.3216	2.2832	2.2459	2.2096	2.1743	2.1399	2.1065	3
3.1699	3.1024	3.0373	2.9745	2.9137	2.8550	2.7982	2.7432	2.6901	2.6386	2.5887	4
3.7908	3.6959	3.6048	3.5172	3.4331	3.3522	3.2743	3.1993	3.1272	3.0576	2.9906	5
4.3553	4.2305	4.1114	3.9975	3.8887	3.7845	3.6847	3.5892	3.4976	3.4098	3.3255	6
4.8684	4.7122	4.5638	4.4226	4.2883	4.1604	4.0386	3.9224	3.8115	3.7057	3.6046	7
5.3349	5.1461	4.9676	4.7988	4.6389	4.4873	4.3436	4.2072	4.0776	3.9544	3.8372	8
5.7590	5.5370	5.3282	5.1317	4.9464	4.7716	4.6065	4.4506	4.3030	4.1633	4.0310	9
6.1446	5.8892	5.6502	5.4262	5.2161	5.0188	4.8332	4.6586	4.4941	4.3389	4.1925	10
6.4951	6.2065	5.9377	5.6869	5.4527	5.2337	5.0286	4.8364	4.6560	4.4865	4.3271	11
6.8137	6.4924	6.1944	5.9176	5.6603	5.4206	5.1971	4.9884	4.7932	4.6105	4.4392	12
7.1034	6.7499	6.4235	6.1218	5.8424	5.5831	5.3423	5.1183	4.9095	4.7147	4.5327	13
7.3667	6.9819	6.6282	6.3025	6.0021	5.7245	5.4675	5.2293	5.0081	4.8023	4.6106	14
7.6061	7.1909	6.8109	6.4624	6.1422	5.8474	5.5755	5.3242	5.0916	4.8759	4.6755	15
7.8237	7.3792	6.9740	6.6039	6.2651	5.9542	5.6685	5.4053	5.1624	4.9377	4.7296	16
8.0216	7.5488	7.1196	6.7291	6.3729	6.0472	5.7487	5.4746	5.2223	4.9897	4.7746	17
8.2014	7.7016	7.2497	6.8399	6.4674	6.1280	5.8178	5.5339	5.2732	5.0333	4.8122	18
8.3649	7.8393	7.3658	6.9380	6.5504	6.1982	5.8775	5.5845	5.3162	5.0700	4.8435	19
8.5136	7.9633	7.4694	7.0248	6.6231	6.2593	5.9288	5.6278	5.3527	5.1009	4.8696	20
8.6487	8.0751	7.5620	7.1016	6.6870	6.3125	5.9731	5.6648	5.3837	5.1268	4.8913	21
8.7715	8.1757	7.6446	7.1695	6.7429	6.3587	6.0113	5.6964	5.4099	5.1486	4.9094	22
8.8832	8.2664	7.7184	7.2297	6.7921	6.3988	6.0442	5.7234	5.4321	5.1668	4.9245	23
8.9847	8.3481	7.7843	7.2829	6.8351	6.4338	6.0726	5.7465	5.4509	5.1822	4.9371	24
9.0770	8.4217	7.8431	7.3300	6.8729	6.4641	6.0971	5.7662	5.4669	5.1951	4.9476	25
9.1609	8.4881	7.8957	7.3717	6.9061	6.4906	6.1182	5.7831	5.4804	5.2060	4.9563	26
9.2372	8.5478	7.9426	7.4086	6.9352	6.5135	6.1364	5.7975	5.4919	5.2151	4.9636	27
9.3066	8.6016	7.9844	7.4412	6.9607	6.5335	6.1520	5.8099	5.5016	5.2228	4.9697	28
9.3696	8.6501	8.0218	7.4701	6.9830	6.5509	6.1656	5.8204	5.5098	5.2292	4.9747	29
9.4269	8.6938	8.0552	7.4957	7.0027	6.5660	6.1772	5.8294	5.5168	5.2347	4.9789	30
9.4790	8.7331	8.0850	7.5183	7.0199	6.5791	6.1872	5.8371	5.5227	5.2392	4.9824	31
9.5264	8.7686	8.1116	7.5383	7.0350	6.5905	6.1959	5.8437	5.5277	5.2430	4.9854	32
9.5694	8.8005	8.1354	7.5560	7.0482	6.6005	6.2034	5.8493	5.5320	5.2462	4.9878	33
9.6086	8.8293	8.1566	7.5717	7.0599	6.6091	6.2098	5.8541	5.5356	5.2489	4.9898	34
9.6442	8.8552	8.1755	7.5856	7.0700	6.6166	6.2153	5.8582	5.5386	5.2512	4.9915	35
9.6765	8.8786	8.1924	7.5979	7.0790	6.6231	6.2201	5.8617	5.5412	5.2531	4.9929	36
9.7059	8.8996	8.2075	7.6087	7.0868	6.6288	6.2242	5.8647	5.5434	5.2547	4.9941	37
9.7327	8.9186	8.2210	7.6183	7.0937	6.6338	6.2278	5.8673	5.5452	5.2561	4.9951	38
9.7570	8.9357	8.2330	7.6268	7.0997	6.6380	6.2309	5.8695	5.5468	5.2572	4.9959	39
9.7791	8.9511	8.2438	7.6344	7.1050	6.6418	6.2335	5.8713	5.5482	5.2582	4.9966	40
9.7991	8.9649	8.2534	7.6410	7.1097	6.6450	6.2358	5.8729	5.5493	5.2590	4.9972	41
9.8174	8.9774	8.2619	7.6469	7.1138	6.6478	6.2377	5.8743	5.5502	5.2596	4.9976	42
9.8340	8.9886	8.2696	7.6522	7.1173	6.6503	6.2394	5.8755	5.5510	5.2602	4.9980	43
9.8491	8.9988	8.2764	7.6568	7.1205	6.6524	6.2409	5.8765	5.5517	5.2607	4.9984	44
9.8628	9.0079	8.2825	7.6609	7.1232	6.6543	6.2421	5.8773	5.5523	5.2611	4.9986	45
9.8753	9.0161	8.2880	7.6645	7.1256	6.6559	6.2432	5.8781	5.5528	5.2614	4.9989	46
9.8866	9.0235	8.2928	7.6677	7.1277	6.6573	6.2442	5.8787	5.5532	5.2617	4.9991	47
9.8969	9.0302	8.2972	7.6705	7.1296	6.6585	6.2450	5.8792	5.5536	5.2619	4.9992	48
9.9063	9.0362	8.3010	7.6730	7.1312	6.6596	6.2457	5.8797	5.5539	5.2621	4.9993	49
9.9148	9.0417	8.3045	7.6752	7.1327	6.6605	6.2463	5.8801	5.5541	5.2623	4.9995	50

Credits

© Amy C Etra/PhotoEdit, p. 445

© Steve Niedorf/3M Corporate Marketing and Public Affairs, p. 445

© Courtesy of 3M/3M Corporate Marketing and Public Affairs, p. 446

© Frank Siteman/Image Quest, p. 451

© Amy C Etra/PhotoEdit, p. 453

© Courtesy of PaineWebber Incorporated, p. 483

© Ed Lallo/Gamma Liaison International, p. 483

© Myrleen Ferguson/PhotoEdit, p. 485

© Andrew Olney/Tony Stone Images, p. 497

© Adamsmith Productions/Corbis, p. 506

© Tony Freeman/PhotoEdit, p. 517

© George Hall/Corbis, p. 517

© Ted Kawalerski/The Image Bank, p. 521

© Paula Lerner/Woodfin Camp & Associates, p. 539

© Elena Rooraid/PhotoEdit, p. 539

© Judy Griesedieck/Corbis, p. 553

© Gamma Liaison International, p. 553

© DILBERT reprinted by permission of United Feature Syndicate, Inc./United Media, p. 557

© Universal Press Syndicate, p. 550

© Terry Vine/Tony Stone Images, p. 566

© Michael Newman/PhotoEdit, p. 567

© Amy C Etra/PhotoEdit, p. 581

© Christine Boyd/FSP/Gamma Liaison International, p. 581

© Bruce Ayres/Tony Stone Images, p. 586

© Steve Benbow/Woodfin Camp & Associates, p. 594

© Porter Gifford/Gamma Liaison International, p. 596

© Churchill & Klehr/Gamma Liaison International, p. 611

© Evan Kafka/Gamma Liaison International, p. 611

© Jeff Greenberg/PhotoEdit, p. 616

© Michael Newman/PhotoEdit, p. 623

© Kaluzny/Thatcher/Tony Stone Images, p. 638

© Tom Tracy/Courtesy of Smurfit-Stone, p. 649

© Courtesy of Smurfit-Stone, p. 649

© AP/Wide World Photos, p. 653

© Matthew McVay/Tony Stone Images, p. 656

© Marty Heitner/Impact Visuals, p. 663

© Paul S Howell/Gamma Liaison International, p. 679

© Jeffry Scott/Impact Visuals, p. 679

© David Hanover/Tony Stone Images, p. 680

© Stephen Ferry/Gamma Liaison International, p. 685

© Marc Muench/Tony Stone Images, p. 709

© Adam Woolfitt/Corbis, p. 709

© SuperStock International, p. 712

© Bill Aron/PhotoEdit, p. 717

© Gamma Liaison International, p. 729

© 1997 Paramount Pictures/20th Century Fox/Kobal Collection, p. 729

© Corbis, p. 747

© Corbis, p. 747

© Michael Newman/PhotoEdit, p. 750

© Rob Brown/The Samuel Goldwyn Company/Kobal Collection, p. 765

© Felicia Martinez/PhotoEdit, p. 779

© John Neubauer/PhotoEdit, p. 779

© Bill Aron/PhotoEdit, p. 784

© Dan Bunik/Woodfin Camp & Associates, p. 789

© Tony Freeman/PhotoEdit, p. 801

© Bonnie Kamin/PhotoEdit, p. 813

© Bonnie Kamin/PhotoEdit, p. 813

© Tony Freeman/PhotoEdit, p. 819

© Tom Keck/Gamma Liaison International, p. 830

© Ann Summa/Gamma Liaison International, p. 832

© Rudi Von Briel/PhotoEdit, p. 847

© David Young-Wolff/PhotoEdit, p. 847

© Michael Newman/PhotoEdit, p. 858

© Alex S. MacLean/Landslides, p. 868

© Courtesy of Dell Computers, p. 887

© David Young Wolff/PhotoEdit, p. 887

© David Young Wolff/PhotoEdit, p. 894

© R Ramirez/PhotoEdit, p. 903

© David Young Wolff/PhotoEdit, p. 905

© Michael Newman/PhotoEdit, p. 905

Index

A

AB (Anheuser-Busch Companies, Inc.), 867
Accelerated cost recovery system (ACRS), 720
Accelerated depreciation, 717–718
　declining-balance, 717
　double-declining balance, 717–718
　modified accelerated cost recovery system
　　and, 720–722, 733
Accounting software. *See* Spreadsheets
Accounts. *See also specific account names*
　contra-equity, 651–652
Accounts receivable, as current asset, 819
Accounts receivable turnover, 900
Accrual accounting, discounted cash flow
　analysis versus, 537–538
Acquisition phase of capital expenditure
　evaluation, 522
ACRS (accelerated cost recovery system), 720
Activity ratios, 900–902
Adams, J. S., 572
Adverse opinion, 833
AFS. *See* Available-for-sale (AFS) securities
After-tax cash flows, 529–531
Albertsons, 911
American Skiing Company, 709–712, 719n,
　724–727, 732, 733
Amortization
　cash flow statement adjustment for, 861
　of intangible assets, 731
　setting up tables for, 617
Amortized discount, 620
Amortized premiums, 622
Anheuser-Busch Companies, Inc. (AB), 867
Annual rate of return, 487
Annual reports, components of, 829–835
Annuities, 498–505
　compound interest and, 501
　future value of, 498–500
　present value of, 500–501
　problems involving, solving, 501–503
Arthur Andersen, LLP, 557
Asset turnover ratio, 900, 906–907
Asset valuation
　before admission of new partner, 590, 656
　time value of money and, 505–506
Assets
　on balance sheet, 818–823
　current. *See* Current assets
　depreciation of. *See* Depreciation
　intangible, 728–731, 822–823
　noncapitalized. *See* Human resources (HR)
　　management; Noncapitalized assets
　plant. *See* Depreciation; Plant assets
　revaluation before admission of new
　　partner, 590, 656
Attitudes, leadership and, 573
Auditors, 892
Auditor's report, 833–835
Authorized shares, 594

B

Available-for-sale (AFS) securities, 752–753,
　755–758, 761–762
　adjusting to market value, 755–756
　trading securities versus, 756–758

Balance sheet, 814–829
　assets on, 816–823
　classifications used for, 818
　equity investments on, 763–764
　information provided by, 814–816
　for internal reporting, 835–836
　liabilities on, 816–818, 823–828
　operational investments on, 733
　stockholders' equity on, 828–829
Balanced scorecard approach, 564–568
　customer perspective and, 566–567
　financial perspective and, 565
　internal process perspective and, 566
　learning and growth perspective and,
　　567–568
　reward systems and, 568
Balances, compensating, 819
Bank of America, 618–622
Bearer bonds, 628
Beatty, Robert Cord, 765
Ben & Jerry's, 581–583, 591–595, 662, 867
Bergen, Candice, 611
Berkshire Hathaway, 599
Betterments, 722–723
Boeing Company, 867
Bond certificates, 626
Bond indentures, 626
Bond market, 626–627, 692–693
Bond registers, 628
Bonds, 626–630
　callable, 628, 693–694
　convertible, 628–629, 694
　early retirement of, 692–694
　ownership provisions of, 628
　ratings of, 627
　repayment provisions of, 628–629
　security provisions of, 629
　spreadsheets for payments and, 690
Bonus base, 560
Bonus rate, 560
Bonuses
　as employee benefits, 559–561
　to partners, 589–590, 655
Book value, 618, 713
Borrowing. *See also* Debt *entries;* Loans
　reasons for, 612–615
　risk and reward of, 612–615
Boston Celtics, 725
Budgeting, capital. *See* Capital budgeting
Budgets
　capital expenditure, 522
　financing, 522, 638
Burger King, 730

C

Calculators, for solving time value of money
　problems, 504–505
Callable bonds, 628, 693–694
Callable preferred stock, 593
Capital
　contributed (paid-in), 828
　cost of, selecting long-term investments
　　and, 520–521
　donated, 658, 828
　legal, 595
　valuation, 828–829
Capital account, interest allowance on balances
　of, for distribution of partnership income,
　　587–588
Capital account balances ratio, for distribution
　of partnership income, 586
Capital budgeting, 518–539
　accrual accounting for, 537–538
　discounted cash flow analysis for. *See*
　　Discounted cash flow analysis
　evaluating investments using, 522
　financing selected investments and,
　　521–522
　identifying long-term investment
　　opportunities for, 518–519
　illustration of, 534–537
　informed speculation in, 538–539
　selecting investments using, 519–521
　spreadsheets for, 540
Capital expenditure budget, 522
Capital expenditures, 710, 711
　analysis and evaluation of. *See* Capital
　　budgeting
Capital leases, 624–625, 694–696
　on balance sheet, 826
Capital markets, 888
　information for, 890–891
　societal role of, 889–890
　trading in, 890
Capital stock. *See* Stock
Capitalization, 710
Carnicle, Michael, 765
Carrying value, 713
　of notes, 618
Carslaw, Charles A., 902
Cash, as current asset, 818–819
Cash compensation, deferred, 561–562
Cash current debt coverage debt ratio, 903
Cash dividends, 597
Cash flow analysis, selecting long-term
　investments and, 521
Cash flow per share, 900, 902

Cash flows. *See also* Discounted cash flow analysis; Financing cash flows; Investing cash flows; Operating cash flows
  internal reporting of, 871–872
  net income versus, 867
  sources of, 528–529
  statement of. *See* Statement of cash flows
  uneven, effects on net present value, 526
Cessna Corporation, 658
Chariot Entertainment, 765
Citibank, 616
Closing entries, for partnerships, 653
Coercive power, 573
Cohen, Ben, 581
Collateral, 624
Commission pay, 558
Common stock, 591
Compensating balances, 819
Compensation plans, 558–559
Compound interest, 494–495
  annuities and, 501
Compounding, 494
Comprehensive income, 780–781
  other, 786
  reporting, 787
Computerized accounting software. *See* Spreadsheets
Conservatism, income statement and, 794
Consol Limited, 518
Consolidated financial statements, 749–750
Contingent liabilities, 831–832
Continuing operations, income from, 782
Contra-equity accounts, 651–652
Contributed capital, 828
Contributed capital in excess of par, 595
Contributory plans, 564
Convertible bonds, 628–629
Convertible preferred stock, 593
Copyrights, 729
Corporations, 656–666
  another company's investment in, 749–753
  capital contributed to, 656–658
  equity financing of, 583–584, 591–601. *See also* Stock
  financial statements of. *See* Financial statement *entries; specific financial statements*
  reporting of equity events of, 663–666
  retained earnings of, 658–660, 664, 829
  stock of. *See* Stock
  stockholders' equity of, 663–665
  subchapter S, 585
Cost allocations, income statement and, 794
Cost center, 796–797
Costing, full-absorption, 794–796
Costs
  of capital, selecting long-term investments and, 520–521
  of debt securities, determining, 759–760
  depreciable, 714–715
  historical, 794
  of recruitment and selection, 556–557
  of training and development, 557–558
Coupon bonds, 628
Covenants, 615
Creditors, perception of risk and return, 495
Cumulative accounting adjustments, 785–786
Cumulative preferred stock, 592
Current assets, 816–821
  cash inflows and, 855–856
  cash outflows and, 857, 859–860
  noncash, cash flow statement adjustments for, 861–862

Current liabilities, 816–818, 824
  cash inflows and, 856–857
  cash outflows and, 857–860
  changes in, cash flow statement adjustments for, 862–864
  operating, cash flow statement adjustments for, 862–864
Current ratio, 900
Customer perspective, balanced scorecard approach and, 566–567

D

Date of declaration, 598, 659
Date of payment, 598, 659
Date of record, 598, 659
DDB (double-declining balance depreciation), 717–718
Debenture bonds, 629
Debt financing, 582, 611–639. *See also* Borrowing
  choosing between equity financing and, 631–636
  financing budget and, 638
  long-term debt for. *See* Bonds; Long-term debt; Notes payable
  nonpublic sources of, 623–625
  public sources of, 626–630
  reasons for using, 612–615
  risk of, 612–615
  selecting instruments for, 636–638
  uses of, 612
Debt securities
  available-for-sale securities. *See* Available-for-sale (AFS) securities
  determining cost of, 759–760
  held-to-maturity securities, 759, 762–763
  as investments, 758–763
  trading securities. *See* Trading securities
Debt-to-equity ratio, 614, 900, 903–904
  long-term, 904
Decision making
  by external stakeholders about investing, 888–892
  about long-term debt, information for, 696–697
  ratio analysis for. *See* Ratio analysis
Declining-balance depreciation, 717
Deferrals, on balance sheet, 826
Deferred charges, on balance sheet, 823
Deferred compensation, 561–562
  cash, 561–562
  stock options, 562
Deficit in retained earnings, 658
Defined benefit plans, 563–564
Defined contribution plans, 563–564
Dell Computer, 867, 887–888, 892–899, 901–909, 911
Depletion, 728
  cash flow statement adjustment for, 861
Depreciable cost, 714–715
Depreciation, 713–722
  accelerated. *See* Accelerated depreciation
  business benefits from, 720–722
  cash flow statement adjustment for, 861
  continued use of fully depreciated assets and, 722
  partial-year, 718–719
  revision of estimates and, 722
  salvage value and, 714–715
  selecting method for, 719–722
  spreadsheets for, 719
  straight-line, 715
  for tax purposes, 719–720
  tax shield of, 532

Depreciation—*Continued*
  units-of-production, 715–717
  useful life and, 714
Development, costs of, 557–558
Diamond Entertainment Inc., 765
Diluted earnings per share, 788
Direct format for statement of cash flows, 851, 854–860, 865–866
Direct investment in partnerships, 589, 654–655
Direct placement of bond issues, 626
Disclaimer of opinion, 833
Discontinued operations, 782–784
Discount on Bonds Payable account, 689
Discount on Notes Payable account, 683
Discounted cash flow analysis, 522–534
  accrual accounting versus, 537–538
  advantages and disadvantages of, 527
  assumptions underlying, 527–528
  gains and losses on disposal and, 533–534
  income taxes and cash flows and, 529–531
  net present value method for, 523–525
  noncash expenses and, 531–533
  sources of cash flows and, 528–529
  time-adjusted rate of return method for, 525–527
  uneven cash flows' effects on net present value and, 526
Discounts
  amortized, 620
  on notes, 618
Disposal
  gains and losses on, 533–534
  of plant assets, 723–727, 734
Dissatisfiers, 571
Dividend payment ratio, 908
Dividend payout ratio, 900
Dividend reinvestment programs (DRIPs), 597
Dividend yield, 900
Dividend yield ratio, 910–911
Dividends, 597–598
  in arrears, 592
  dates affecting, 598, 659
  ratio analysis of, 908–909
  retained earnings and, 659–660
  stock, 597, 660–661
Divisional income reports, 799–801
Donated capital, 658, 828
Donated Capital account, 658
Double-declining balance depreciation (DDB), 717–718
Dow Corning, 905, 907
Drawing account, for sole proprietorships, 651–652
DRIPs (dividend reinvestment programs), 597
Du Pont Company, 905, 907, 911
Du Pont ROI (ROA), 900, 907

E

Eagle Automotive Inc., 765
Earnings, 781–782
  reporting of, 782
  retained, 658–660, 664, 829
Earnings multiple, 910
Earnings per share (EPS), 787–789, 900, 908
  calculating, 787–788
  diluted, 788
  disclosures related to, 788–789
Effective interest rate. *See* Market interest rate
Efficiency strategy, 554–555
Electronic spreadsheets. *See* Spreadsheets
Employee benefits, 558–561
  bonuses, 559–561